CIVIL COSTS

AUSTRALIA
Law Book Co.
Sydney

CANADA and USA
Carswell
Toronto

HONG KONG
Sweet & Maxwell Asia

NEW ZEALAND
Brookers
Wellington

SINGAPORE and MALAYSIA
Sweet & Maxwell Asia
Singapore and Kuala Lumpur

CIVIL COSTS
Third Edition

By

Peter T. Hurst, LL.B.
Senior Costs Judge
of the Supreme Court Costs Office

LONDON
SWEET & MAXWELL
2004

First Edition 1995
Second Edition 2000
Third Edition 2004

Published in 2004 by
Sweet & Maxwell Ltd of
100 Avenue Road, Swiss Cottage, London NW3 3PF
(http:www.sweetandmaxwell.co.uk)
Phototypeset by Interactive Sciences Ltd, Gloucester
Printed and bound in Great Britain by
William Clowes, Beccles, Suffolk

No natural forests were destroyed to make this product;
only natural timber was used and replanted

A CIP catalogue record for this book is available from the British Library

ISBN 0421 880201

100473708°

For DDH, EAH, CEH and CPBH.

FOREWORD

There used to be a tradition whereby the judges of the Commercial Court were always entrusted with appeals in what used to be called taxation of costs. For some reason or other, that tradition was broken one day, and I found myself, a novice in the mystique of costs, sitting with the new senior costs judge (whom I understandably held in awe) on my right, and an experienced solicitor who later became the President of the Law Society on my left. There came a time, after we retired, when I remarked that an arcane corner of costs practice was completely mad. My solicitor assessor agreed, and, greatly daring I put the point to the fountain of all knowledge about costs. "I agree, too", said Peter Hurst, and we were able with a stroke to tear away some of the undergrowth which was impeding the development of transparent and sensible modern costs practice.

And Peter Hurst has been illuminating the way ever since. We have been very fortunate to have had him in post as the senior costs judge in the last few difficult years when CPR costs practice, coupled with the horrendous difficulties created by new methods of litigation funding, have called for a light to shine in dark places as never before. Fortunately, too, the wisest of assessors has been frequently at hand to save the judges of the Court of Appeal from error as we have struggled with one virtually insoluble costs conundrum after another.

I therefore welcome unreservedly the third edition of this book. The reader is transported through difficult terrain by a latterday husky who apparently sees no difficulty anywhere but is very anxious to help those who do. I know how much value judges and practitioners will derive from having this book at hand in time of trouble. And I suspect that litigants in person, too, will find solace in it here and there: see, for instance, the happy fate that befell Mr Wulfshon in the Court of Appeal which does not go unremembered towards the end of Chapter 8.

Henry Brooke
Royal Courts of Justice
October 7, 2004

PREFACE

When I wrote the Preface to the Second Edition of Civil Costs I commented upon the speed and volume of the changes affecting the Law of Costs. Those changes have continued unabated. Positive progress has however been made both by amendments to the CPR and its Practice Directions and to Regulations, particularly with regard to CFAs.

I have been privileged to be invited to sit with the Court of Appeal on a number of important costs cases, including *Hollins v Russell*, where the Court dealt with a substantial number of compliance issues and laid down guidelines as to the correct approach to be taken by Judges in deciding such issues. More recently the Court has considered the complex topic of set off in *R (Burkett) v LB Hammersmith and Fulham*.

The attention of the Liability insurers (the most frequent paying parties in personal injury litigation) has switched from CFA compliance issues to ATE premium issues. The Claims Direct and Accident Group (TAG) litigation revealed numerous problems many of which remain to be resolved.

As a result of remarkable co-operation between Claimant and Defendant Lawyers and the Insurance Industry a large measure of agreement has been reached in relation to costs in RTA cases up to £10,000; and in relation to success fees in PI cases. Further progress along these lines is expected. CPR Part 45 although entitled Fixed Costs now deals with what are called predictable costs.

In light of all this activity it has been necessary to revise and update the book. The section dealing with Part 36 has been rewritten and a new section on the House of Lords added. I am very grateful for all the help I have received from the Costs Judges and other judges at every level. Once again I thank my PA Lisa Sanchez for typing and retyping my words. Finally, although I have attempted to show the law as at October 1, 2004, any mistakes and/or omissions are entirely my responsibility. I should however be glad if any mistakes could be pointed out.

Peter Hurst
Senior Costs Judge
October 7, 2004
Melbourne Australia.

TABLE OF CONTENTS

Chapter 3: The relationship with the client

PART IV: PRACTICE AND PROCEDURE

Chapter 8: Application for and Attendance Upon Detailed Assessment

PART V: APPEAL

Chapter 9: Review and Appeal

PART VI: PENALTIES AND SANCTIONS

Chapter 10: Wasted Costs Sanctions and the Court's Inherent Jurisdiction

PART VII: PARTICULAR MATTERS

Chapter 11: Court of Protection, Arbitration and Other Tribunals

TABLE OF CASES

TABLE OF STATUTES

TABLE OF STATUTORY INSTRUMENTS

TABLE OF CIVIL PROCEDURE RULES

PART I

Preliminary

CHAPTER 1

Introduction

A. COSTS

To those (particularly accountants) who are not lawyers, the word "costs" 1–001
means expenditure as opposed to income; to the lawyer however "costs"
means the income derived from the practice of law. Since that income is
obtained as a result of bills delivered to the solicitor's client, there is no
doubt that the money which the client pays is "costs" in the generally
accepted meaning of the word. It is partly as a result of this apparent conflict
in the meaning of "costs" that the term has been variously defined. Costs
include:

"fees, charges, disbursements, expenses and remuneration"[1]

In non-contentious business and common form probate business, "costs"
means the amount charged in a solicitor's bill, exclusive of disbursements
and value added tax.[2]

The Civil Procedure Rules 1998 apply to all proceedings in county courts,
the High Court and the Civil Division of the Court of Appeal.[3] They also
apply by analogy in detailed assessment proceedings in the House of Lords.[4]
In such proceedings "costs" include: fees, charges, disbursements, expenses,
remuneration, reimbursement allowed to a litigant in person,[5] any additional liability incurred under a funding arrangement and any fee or reward
charged by a lay representative for acting on behalf of a party in proceedings

---

[1] Solicitors Act 1974, s.87(1). There is a similar, but lengthier, definition in CPR r.43.2.
[2] Solicitors' (Non-contentious business) Remuneration Order 1994 (SI 1994/2616), art.2.
[3] CPR r.2.1(1).
[4] *Kuwait Airways Corp v Iraqi Airways Co*, unreported February 27, 2002, HL.
[5] Under CPR r.48.6.

allocated to the small claims track.[6] The CPR do not apply to certain types of proceedings in respect of which specific rules may be made.[7]

B. CONTENTIOUS AND NON-CONTENTIOUS BUSINESS

1–002   The way in which costs are dealt with by the courts varies depending upon whether the costs arise out of contentious or non-contentious business. The way in which costs are dealt with by the courts varies depending upon which category the costs fall into. It is usually necessary to decide whether the costs arise out of contentious or non contentious business. If a bill is delivered to a client who is happy to pay it without question, the type of business concerned is of no more than academic interest. Where, however, a dispute develops and an appropriate figure has to be arrived at (usually by detailed assessment), it is necessary to have regard to that distinction. The Solicitors Act 1974 defines "contentious business" and "non-contentious business" as follows:

> " 'Contentious business' means business done, whether as solicitor or advocate, in or for the purposes of proceedings begun before a court or before an arbitrator, not being business that falls within the definition of non-contentious or common form probate business contained in section 128 of the Supreme Court Act 1981"[8]

> " 'non-contentious business' means any business done as a solicitor which is not contentious business as defined by [the 1974 Act]."[9]

> "Non-contentious or common form probate business means the business of obtaining probate and administration where there is no contention as to the right thereto . . . "[10]

These definitions can give rise to somewhat nonsensical results in that proceedings before a tribunal are not before "a court or before an arbitrator" and are therefore non-contentious; and a dispute which is

---

[6] CPR r.43.2(1).
[7] The CPR do not apply to insolvency proceedings (Insolvency Act 1986, ss.411, 412); non-contentious or common form probate proceedings (Supreme Court Act 1981, s.127); proceedings in the High Court when acting as a Prize Court (Prize Courts Act 1994, s.3); proceedings before the Judge within the meaning of Pt VII of the Mental Health Act 1983 (Mental Health Act 1983, s.106); family proceedings (Matrimonial and Family Proceedings Act 1984, s.40); and adoption proceedings (Adoption Act 1976, s.66) CPR r.2.1(2).
[8] Solicitors Act 1974, s.87(1).
[9] Solicitors Act 1974, s.87(1).
[10] Supreme Court Act 1981, s.128.

4

bitterly fought but in respect of which no proceedings were ever commenced is also non-contentious business.

CPR Parts 44–48 apply to the costs of proceedings before an arbitrator or an umpire; costs of proceedings before a tribunal or other statutory body; and costs payable by a client to his solicitor. Costs which are payable by one party to another under the terms of a contract where the court makes an order for the assessment of those costs are also covered.[11]

C. SOLICITORS NON-CONTENTIOUS BUSINESS REMUNERATION ORDER

Types of costs

A committee (consisting of the Lord Chancellor, the Lord Chief Justice, the Master of the Rolls and certain others) set up under section 56 of the Solicitors Act 1974 is empowered to make general orders prescribing and regulating the remuneration of solicitors in respect of non-contentious business. The current order is the Solicitors (Non-Contentious Business) Remuneration Order 1994. So long as such an order is in operation, the detailed assessment of bills of costs of solicitors in respect of non-contentious business is regulated by that Order. Where the amount of a solicitor's remuneration in respect of non-contentious business is so regulated, the amount of the costs which will be allowed on detailed assessment will be decided in accordance with the Remuneration Order rather than the CPR.[12]

1–003

D. TYPES OF COSTS

Costs may be classified according to the following types:

1–004

    (a) solicitor and client;

    (b) between the parties;

    (c) public funded/legal aid; and

    (d) Central Funds

The basis of assessment

Where the court assesses costs, whether by summary or detailed assessment, it will (subject to any statutory provisions relating to, *e.g.* legal aid costs)

1–005

---

[11] CPR r.43.2(2).
[12] CPR r.44.4(5).

assess those costs on either the standard basis or the indemnity basis. In either case the court will not allow costs which have been unreasonably incurred or which are unreasonable in amount. Where the court is assessing costs on the standard basis it will in addition only allow costs which are proportionate to the matters in issue and will resolve any doubt which it may have as to whether costs were reasonably incurred or reasonable and proportionate in amount in favour of the paying party. Where the amount of costs is to be assessed on the indemnity basis there is no proportionality requirement but the court will resolve any doubt which it may have as to whether the costs were reasonably incurred or were reasonable in amount in favour of the receiving party.[13]

Where the court makes an order about costs without indicating the basis upon which costs are to be assessed or purports to make an order on a basis other than the standard or indemnity basis the costs will be assessed on the standard basis.[14]

Solicitor and client costs

1–006 Solicitor and client costs are those payable in respect of a bill delivered by a solicitor to the client. The bill may be composed of fees, charges, disbursements, expenses and remuneration.[15] The delivered bill shows separately the amount charged by way of profit costs and the amount claimed in respect of disbursements including counsel's fees. The bill may be in respect of contentious or non-contentious business. If the bill is in respect of non-contentious business the solicitor's remuneration will be such sum as may be fair and reasonable to both solicitor and the client (the entitled person) having regard to all the circumstances of the case.[16]

In the case of costs arising out of contentious business (except where the bill is to be paid out of the Community Legal Service Fund under the Legal Aid Act 1988 or the Access to Justice Act 1999) the costs as between solicitor and client are assessed on the indemnity basis.[17]

On the detailed assessment of a bill delivered by a solicitor to his client costs are presumed:

(a) to have been reasonably incurred if they were incurred with the express or implied approval of the client;

(b) to be reasonable in amount if their amount was expressly or impliedly approved by the client;

---

[13] CPR r.44.4(1)(2)(3).
[14] CPR r.44.4(4).
[15] Solicitors Act 1974, s.87(1).
[16] Solicitors (Non-Contentious Business) Remuneration Order 1994, art.3.
[17] CPR r.48.8(1) and (2).

    (c) to have been unreasonably incurred if:

        (i) they are of an unusual nature or amount; and

        (ii) the solicitor did not tell his client that as a result he might not recover all of them from the other party.[18]

A client and his solicitor may agree whatever terms they consider appropriate about the solicitor's charges for his services. If the costs are of an unusual nature, either in amount or in the type of costs incurred, the presumption of unreasonableness will arise unless the solicitor satisfies the court that the client was informed that the costs were unusual and, where the costs relate to litigation, that the client was informed that those costs might not be allowed on an assessment between the parties. That information must have been given to the client before the costs were incurred.[19]

Costs between the parties

Background

Costs between the parties are the costs payable by one party to another in litigation. The Civil Procedure Rules 1998 state that they are "a new procedural code". When the rules were introduced the Lord Chancellor Lord Irvine of Lairg argued that the correct approach was that adopted by the House of Lords and by Lord Herschell in particular, in Bank of *England v Vagliana Brothers*[20]   1–007

> " . . . the proper course is in the first instance to examine the language of the statute and to ask what is its natural meaning, uninfluenced by any consideration derived from the previous state of the law, and not to start with enquiring how the law previously stood, and then, assuming that it was probably intended to leave it unaltered, to see if the words of the enactment will bear an interpretation in conformity with this view . . .
>
> If a statute, intended to embody in a code a particular branch of the law, is to be treated in this fashion, it appears to me that its utility will be almost entirely destroyed, and the very object with which it was enacted will be frustrated. The purpose of such a statute surely was that on any point specifically dealt with by it, the law should be ascertained by interpreting the language used instead of, as before, roaming over a vast number of authorities in order to discover what the

---

[18] CPR r.48.8(2).
[19] Costs Practice Direction, para.54.1.
[20] [1891] A.C. 107 at 144–145.

law was, extracting it by a minute critical examination of the prior decisions . . . "

Lord Herschell accepted that there were circumstances where it would be legitimate to look back, but he returned to his emphatic point that the starting place was the legislation itself. He concluded that:

"An appeal to earlier decisions can only be justified on some special ground."

The Lord Chancellor envisaged limited circumstances where it would be appropriate to look back at earlier authority but in the overwhelming majority of cases thought that the proper meaning of the rule should be determined by looking only at the rules themselves. In considering what order to make about costs the old authorities are now of limited use and the court has a discretion to reconsider costs particularly in a situation where a successful litigant in a cost free jurisdiction (*i.e.* a tribunal) was unwillingly drawn into an appeal. The court was entitled notwithstanding that the appeal succeeded to express its disapproval of the way in which the appellant had conducted the litigation by refusing to award the costs of the appeal against the respondent.[21]

Having said that it is necessary to repeat the following statements of principle relating to costs generally.

Bramwell *B.* in *Harold v Smith* stated:

" 'Costs' as between party and party are given by the law as an indemnity to the person entitled to them; they are not imposed as a punishment on the party who pays them, nor given as a bonus to the party who receives them. Therefore, if the extent of the damnification can be found out, the extent to which costs ought to be allowed is also ascertained."[22]

Sir Richard Malins V.C. in *Smith v Buller* said:

"It is of great importance to litigants who are unsuccessful that they should not be oppressed by having to pay an excessive amount of costs . . . I adhere to the rule that has already been laid down that the costs chargeable under a taxation as between party and party are all that are necessary to enable the adverse party to conduct the litigation and no more. Any charges merely for conducting litigation more conveniently

---

[21] *Cerberus Software Ltd v Rowley (Costs)* [2001] EWCA Civ 497; [2001] C.P. Rep. 114, CA and see *Biguzzi v Rank Leisure Plc* [1999] 1 W.L.R. 1926, CA.
[22] (1860) 5 H. & N. 381 at 385.

may be called luxuries and must be paid by the party incurring them."[23]

Although tests of reasonableness and proportionality have been substituted for the test of necessity the principles set out above still hold good.

Parts 43–48 of the Civil Procedure Rules deal with the main provisions relating to costs and the way in which the court will award and assess costs. Other parts of the rules contain specific provisions about costs.

The Practice Direction Supplementing Parts 43–48 (the Costs Practice Direction) is itself divided into sections relating to each part. The introduction to the Practice Direction defines both "counsel" and "solicitor" which for the purposes of the Practice Direction have to have specific meanings.[24]

The standard and indemnity bases

The most common order for costs between the parties is on the standard basis but the court has power, in an appropriate case, to award costs on the indemnity basis. The Court of Appeal declined to give any definition of the exact circumstances in which indemnity costs might be ordered, stating that it was a matter in each case of the Judge exercising his discretion on the facts before him.[25] An order for costs on the indemnity basis will be made, for example where the defendant has attempted to mislead the court on an issue which was central to the case and on issues which were collateral to the central issues[26]; or where there has been serious unexcused and inexcusable dilatoriness, falling much closer to the role of misconduct than of mere failure.[27]

1–008.1

Where the court found it wholly unreasonable and unnecessary for the claimant to commence proceedings, where the claimant's conduct had been in breach of the general protocol practice direction and the claimant had also refused to enter into alternative dispute resolution, the court awarded the defendant its costs on the indemnity basis.[28]

Public funded/legal aid costs

Costs out of the Community Legal Service Fund   The Access to Justice Act 1999 introduced the Community Legal Service Fund as a replacement for legal aid under the Legal Aid Act 1988. Although this work does not concern itself with legal aid or CLS funding, it is necessary to understand the effect of certificates issued under the funding code and under the Legal Aid

1–008.2

---

[23] (1875) L.R. 19 Eq. 473.
[24] Costs Practice Direction, para.1.4.
[25] *Munkenbeck & Marshall v McAlpine* [1995] E.G.C.S. 24; 44 Con. L.R. 30, CA.
[26] *Johnson Matthey Plc v Eros Castings Ltd*, *The Times*, December 7, 1993 QBD.
[27] *Burgess v South Manchester HA*, unreported, October 4, 1994, Sedley J.
[28] *Paul Thomas Construction Ltd v Hyland* [2002] 18 Const L.J. 345 H.H. Judge Wilcox, TCC.

Act. Legal aid certificates issued under the Legal Aid Act will continue to be dealt with under the Civil Legal Aid (General) Regulations 1989 as amended. The Legal Services Commission will issue certificates under the funding code certifying the decision to fund services for the client. The Civil Legal Aid (General) Regulations 1989 as amended also apply to those certificates. Where a contract entered into by the Commission before April 1, 2003, provides that the procedures for assessing remuneration payable by the Commission will be the same as those set out in the above General Regulations, the Legal Aid in Civil Proceedings (Remuneration) Regulations 1994, or the Legal Aid in Family Proceedings (Remuneration) Regulations 1991, the court will assess the remuneration. (Community Legal Service (Funding) Order 2000, article 6). The Legal Aid Board ceased to exist on April 2, 2001.[29]

Where a legal representative has represented an assisted person or a "client" *i.e.* an individual who has received funded services,[30] the legal representative has a statutory right to the costs of representation and they can only be claimed and paid for out of the Community Legal Service Fund. Under the Civil Legal Aid (General) Regulations 1989, as amended, it is possible to recover from an opposing party more than the amount recoverable out of the CLS Fund, by virtue of the Legal Aid in Civil Proceedings (Remuneration) Regulations 1994 and the Legal Aid in Family Proceedings (Remuneration) Regulations 1991. The assisted person's/client's legal representatives are not prevented from recovering from the paying party the full amount of costs and interest awarded, by any rule of law which limits the costs recoverable by a party to proceedings to the amount which he is liable to pay his legal representatives (the indemnity principle). Subject to reimbursement of the CLS Fund in respect of any costs and interest which it has paid out, any costs recovered from the paying party in addition, belong to the solicitor.[31]

1–009   Although it is possible to recover from an opposing party costs of an amount more than that prescribed under the Regulations, the Court of Appeal decided (under an earlier version of the Regulations), that an unsuccessful defendant could not be ordered to pay costs on the indemnity basis to a legally aided claimant since the Regulations specified that costs were to be paid by the Legal Aid Board on the standard basis. Accordingly, it was a wrong exercise of discretion to direct the paying party to pay costs on the indemnity basis to a claimant who had been legally aided throughout the proceedings.[32] More recently, the Court of Appeal has decided that, following the introduction of the 1994 Regulations, it is clearly within a judge's discretion to award costs on the indemnity basis. The rationale for the award of indemnity costs is not merely to avoid a situation arising

---

[29] The Legal Aid Board (Abolition) Order 2001, SI 2001/779.
[30] Article 2, Community Legal Service (Funding) Order 2000.
[31] Civil Legal Aid (General) Regulations 1989, regulation 107B(3).
[32] *Willis v Redbridge HA* [1996] 1 W.L.R. 1228; [1996] 3 All E.R. 114, CA.

whereby a successful litigant was out of pocket, but also to penalise litigants who had behaved unreasonably. Section 31 of the Legal Aid Act 1988 provided that the rights of legally aided litigants should not affect the rights of other parties nor the manner in which the court exercised its discretion. The rationale for making an order for costs on the indemnity basis where a party was legally aided was as strong as where he was not. It was not desirable that litigation taking place at public expense should be conducted unreasonably. Where a litigant had behaved unreasonably the other parties lawyers often deserved to receive an increased fee.[33]

Costs of representation at public inquiries   In recent years there have been a number of ad hoc public inquiries and tribunals set up to investigate the circumstances surrounding various disasters and accidents, *e.g.* the Kings Cross fire, the Hillsborough disaster and the Clapham rail disaster. In a parliamentary answer[34] the Attorney General stated: 1–010

> "Tribunals and public inquiries can be set up in a variety of ways. So far as ad hoc tribunals and inquiries are concerned (for example, into major accidents) the Government already pays the administrative costs. So far as the costs of legal representation of parties to any inquiry are concerned, where the Government have a discretion they always take careful account of the recommendations on costs of the tribunal or inquiry concerned. In general, the Government accept the need to pay out of public funds the reasonable costs of any necessary party to the inquiry who would be prejudiced in seeking representation were he in any doubt about funds becoming available. The Government do not accept that the costs of substantial bodies should be met from public funds unless there are special circumstances."

Those guidelines are generally followed today. The Treasury Solicitor has issued Guidance on Payment of Legal Costs to Parties Represented at Public Expense in Public Inquiries.[35]

Costs out of central funds

Following the decision of the Court of Appeal in *Holden & Co. v Crown Prosecution Service*[36] it was generally assumed that there was an inherent power in the court to award costs out of central funds in an appropriate civil case. However, the House of Lords held that *Holden* had been wrongly   1–011

---

[33] *Brawley v Marczynski (No.2)* [2002] EWCA Civ 1453; [2003] 1 W.L.R. 813, CA.
[34] January 29, 1990 *Hansard* Com 25.
[35] See Appendix Y (Y–018–026).
[36] *Holden & Co. v Crown Prosecution Service (No.2)* [1992] 1 W.L.R. 407, CA.

decided and that there was no power to make such an order at all.[37] Unless, therefore, legislation is introduced enabling costs out of central funds to be awarded in civil cases the issue may be regarded as closed.

Notwithstanding the decision of the House of Lords, a trade association, having successfully applied for the Restricted Practices Court to recuse itself as a consequence of the apparent bias of one of its members, calculated that about £1 million worth of costs had been thrown away because the proceedings had had to begin again. The Association sought its costs relying on the Human Rights Act 1998 and alleging breach of their rights under Article 6(1) of the European Convention on Human Rights. The Court of Appeal found that the Trade Association was not a victim within Article 3(4) of the ECHR and since there was no breach of Article 6(1) there could be no entitlement to wasted costs as part of the compensation. Had the court decided otherwise it is not clear whether an order for costs out of Central Funds would have been made or whether the order would have been made against the Lord Chancellor. (*Director General of Fair Trading v Proprietary Association of Great Britain* [2001] EWCA Civ 1217; [2002] 1 All E.R. 853, CA).

Where a legal representative has represented an assisted person or a "client" (a "client" means an individual who has received funded services), (article 2, Community Legal Service (Funding) Order 2000) the legal representative has a statutory right to the costs of representation and they can only be claimed and paid for out of the Community Legal Service Fund. Under the Civil Legal Aid (General) Regulations 1989, as amended, it is possible to recover from an opposing party more than the amount recoverable out of the CLS Fund, by virtue of the Legal Aid in Civil Proceedings (Remuneration) Regulations 1994 and the Legal Aid in Family Proceedings (Remuneration) Regulations 1991. The assisted person's/client's legal representatives are not prevented from recovering from the paying party the full amount of costs and interest awarded, by any rule of law which limits the costs recoverable by a party to proceedings to the amount which he is liable to pay his legal representatives (the indemnity principle). Subject to reimbursement of the CLS Fund in respect of any costs and interest which it has paid out, any costs recovered from the paying party in addition, belong to the solicitor (Civil Legal Aid (General) Regulations 1989, regulation 107B(3)).

It has been held that in circumstances where an order for costs out of central funds might otherwise have been made, the public ought to pay via the pocket of the public body responsible for the proceedings.[38]

---

[37] [1993] 2 W.L.R. 934, HL.
[38] *Re W. (Drugs Trafficking Restraint Order: Costs)*, The Times, October 13, 1994, Schiemann J.

CHAPTER 2

The Civil Procedure Rules 1998

This Chapter contains a brief explanation of those parts of the Rules which 2–001
have a direct bearing on costs.

The court's powers in respect of costs

Parts 43–48 of the CPR deal with the main provisions relating to costs and 2–002
the way in which the court will award and assess costs. Other parts of the
rules contain specific provisions about costs (*e.g.* Part 36: Offers and
Payments) and those provisions are dealt with elsewhere in this Chapter
3.

A. THE OVERRIDING OBJECTIVE

The overriding objective of the rules is to enable the court to deal with cases 2–003
justly. This includes:

    (a) ensuring the parties are on an equal footing;

    (b) saving expense;

    (c) dealing with cases in ways which are proportionate:

        (i) to the amount of money involved;
        (ii) to the importance of the case;
        (iii) to the complexity of the issues; and
        (iv) to the financial position of each party;

(d) ensuring that it is dealt with expeditiously and fairly; and

(e) allotting to it an appropriate share of the court's resources, while taking into account the need to allot resources to other cases.[1]

Parties to litigation are required to help the court to further the overriding objective[2] and the court is required to further the objective by actively managing cases. Active case management includes:

(a) encouraging the parties to co-operate with each other in the conduct of the proceedings;

(b) identifying the issues at an early stage;

(c) deciding promptly which issues need full investigation and trial and accordingly disposing summarily of the others;

(d) deciding the order in which issues are to be resolved;

(e) encouraging the parties to use an alternative dispute resolution procedure if the court considers that appropriate and facilitating the use of such procedure;

(f) helping the parties to settle the whole or part of the case;

(g) fixing timetables or otherwise controlling the progress of the case;

(h) considering whether the likely benefits of taking a particular step justify the cost of taking it;

(i) dealing with as many aspects of the case as it can on the same occasion;

(j) dealing with the case without the parties needing to attend at court;

(k) making use of technology; and

(l) giving directions to ensure that the trial of a case proceeds quickly and efficiently.[3]

Modern litigation culture requires parties to litigation to co-operate with the court to ensure that litigation is conducted fairly and economically. The court must, as far as practicable, allot an appropriate share of the court's resources to each case. Thus, where a matter came before the court in complete disarray and the time of the court had been wasted, it was held

---

[1] CPR r.1.1(1) and (2).
[2] CPR r.1.3
[3] CPR r.1.4(1) and (2).

neither appropriate nor just that any further share of the court's resources should be allocated to a case conducted in that way.[4]

Proportionality has always been a target which the courts should aim at, it is now part of the overriding objective. The Court of Appeal has expressed the view that case management powers will allow a Judge to exercise the power of limiting costs either indirectly or even directly so that they are proportionate to the amount involved.[5]

It is a lawyer's duty to further the overriding objective. If parties turn down alternative dispute resolution out of hand they will suffer the consequences when costs come to be decided. Where a successful defendant refused ADR because it had been confident of winning, no order for costs was made.[6] Where the Government had pledged that Government Departments would use ADR in all suitable cases to settle disputes whenever the other party accepted it, the court made no order as to costs even though the Department was successful and the Department had not abided by the pledge which had been given.[7]

The Court of Appeal has addressed the question of ADR in greater detail.[7a] The court indicated that the burden was on the unsuccessful party to show why there should be a departure from the general rule on costs, in the form of an order to deprive the successful party of some or all of his costs on the grounds that he refused to agree to ADR. A fundamental principle was that such a departure was not justified unless it had been shown that the successful party had acted unreasonably in refusing to agree to ADR. In deciding whether a party had acted unreasonably the court should bear in mind the advantages of ADR over the court process and have regard to all the circumstances of the particular case. The factors that could be relevant included:

(i) the nature of the dispute;
(ii) the merits of the case;
(iii) the extent to which other settlement methods had been attempted;
(iv) whether the costs of ADR were disproportionately high:
(v) whether any delay in setting up and attending the ADR would have been prejudicial;
(vi) whether the ADR had a reasonable prospect of success.

---

[4] *Adoko v Jemal, The Times,* July 8, 1999, CA.
[5] *Solutia (U.K.) Ltd v Griffiths* [2001] EWCA Civ 736. As to the correct approach to proportionality, see para.4–022.
[6] *Dunnett v Railtrack Plc* [2002] EWCA Civ 302; [2002] 2 All E.R. 850, CA.
[7] *Royal Bank of Canada v Secretary of State for Defence* [2003] EWHC 1841 (Ch), Lewison J.
[7a] *Halsey v Milton Keynes General NHS Trust* [2004] EWCA Civ 576.

Where a successful party had refused to agree to ADR, despite the court's encouragement, that was a fact that the court would take into account when deciding whether his refusal was unreasonable. The court went on to decide that there was no basis for the court to discriminate against successful public bodies when deciding whether a refusal to agree to ADR should result in a cost penalty. The "ADR" pledge announced in March 2001 by the Lord Chancellor was no more than an undertaking that ADR would be considered and used whenever the other party accepts it in all suitable cases by all Government departments and agencies. It was difficult to see in what circumstances it would be right to give great weight to the pledge. The court's role was to encourage not compel ADR. It was likely that compulsion of ADR would be regarded by the European Court of Human Rights as an unacceptable constraint on the right of access to court and therefore a violation of Article 6 ECHR (White Book 44.3.8).

In a case in which a defendant barrister refused to proceed to mediation in a professional negligence case the court found that this was justified on the facts of the case because of the character and attitude of the claimant. The defendant was therefore not penalised or deprived of his entitlement to costs.[8] A willingness to mediate is something which is significant in deciding where costs are to lie. The Government having given a formal pledge committing government departments and agencies to settle cases by ADR techniques whenever the other side agreed, where the defendant department did not abide by that pledge and did not succeed on all issues the court declined to make an order in favour of the defendant.[9]

Where a defendant brought a Part 20 claim against a third party and the third party refused on three occasions to enter into mediation, the court refused to disallow the successful third party's costs on the basis that the refusal to mediate was reasonable in all the circumstances, including in respect of the third mediation, that the request was made too close to trial for a mediation to be realistic.[10] Where respondents put before the court an extensive bundle of correspondence, from which it was apparent that they had made real efforts to settle the dispute, by making offers which were reasonable and generous, and had sought a round the table meeting, the court held that the respondents had not acted unreasonably in refusing the claimant's offer of mediation after he had refused the offers and sought instead a payment of a large sum by the respondents.[11]

---

[8] *Hurst v Leeming* [2002] EWHC 1051 (Ch), Lightman J.
[9] *Royal Bank of Canada v Secretary of State for Defence* unreported, [2003] EWHC (Ch) May 14, Lewison J.
[10] *Société Internationale de Telecommunications Aeronautiques v Wyatt* [2002] EWHC 2401 (Ch), Park J.
[11] *Valentine v Allen* unreported, [2003] EWCA Civ July 29.

B. APPLICATION OF THE RULES

2–004

Specialist proceedings

When the CPR were originally published there were no rules in respect of 2–005
certain specialist proceedings. The rules provide that, subject to any
provision made in relevant practice directions the CPR apply to the specified
proceedings. As further parts have been added to the rules so the number of
specialist proceedings covered by this provision has dwindled. It now refers
only to proceedings under the Companies Act 1985 and the Companies Act
1989.[12] Of the proceedings previously listed as specialist proceedings they
are now dealt with as follows:

(a) Admiralty proceedings

Admiralty proceedings are now dealt with at CPR Part 61. At the request of 2–006
the Admiralty Registrar all costs, other than those summarily assessed in
Admiralty matters, will be assessed in the Supreme Court Costs Office.[13]

(b) Arbitration proceedings

Dealt with at CPR Part 62.[14]   2–007

(c) Commercial and mercantile actions

Dealt with at CPR Parts 58 and 59.   2–008

(d) Patent Court business

Dealt with under the heading IP proceedings at CPR Part 63.   2–009

(e) Technology and Construction Court business

Dealt with at CPR Part 60.   2–010

(f) Contentious Probate proceedings

Dealt with at CPR Part 57.   2–011

Family proceedings

Parts 43, 44 (except rules 44.9 to 44.12), 47 and 48 of the CPR apply to the 2–012
assessment of costs in family proceedings and proceedings in the Family

---

[12] CPR r.49(1)(2)(f) and see Practice Direction Supplementing Part 49—applications under the
Companies Act 1985; Part VII of the Financial Services and Markets Act 2000; and the
Insurance Companies Act 1982.
[13] Practice Direction (Admiralty—Taxation of Costs) [1986] 1 W.L.R. 1310.
[14] See Ch. 11.

Division. Rule 44.3(2), to the effect that costs usually follow the event, does not apply. By a practice direction, the President has applied the Practice Direction Supplementing Parts 43 to 48 to these proceedings.

Insolvency proceedings

2–013   The Insolvency Rules 1986 have been amended so that the costs provisions are compatible with and parallel to the Civil Procedure Rules.

Court of Protection

2–014   The Court of Protection Rules 2001 apply CPR Parts 43, 44, 47 and 48, with certain modifications contained in the Rules and such other modifications as may be necessary, to costs incurred in relation to proceedings under the Court of Protection Rules as they apply to costs incurred in relation to proceedings in the High Court.

The House of Lords

2–015   In *Kuwait Airways Corporation v Iraqi Airways Co Body Corporate*,[15] the Appellate Committee of the House of Lords stated:

> "16. The legal principles to be applied [in the taxation of costs in the House of Lords] are those also applicable to an inter partes taxation in the High Court and Court of Appeal. The order for the payment of costs is paramount and governs the taxation. If a party wishes to dispute the order for costs which has been made, he must exercise any rights of appeal or challenge which may be open to him outside the taxation. In the taxation the order for costs is decisive. If the order is expressly or by implication for the payment of costs taxed on the standard basis . . . that means costs reasonably incurred and reasonably proportionate in amount. What was reasonable and proportionate is a matter for the Taxing Officer to consider and assess."

The Appeal Committee of the House of Lords has recommended that certain rules should apply to costs including conditional fee agreements.[16] The rules are:

---

[15] February 27, 2002.
[16] *Designers Guild Ltd v Russell Williams (Textiles) Ltd trading as Washington DC*, February 11, 2002, [2003] 2 Costs L.R. 128, HL.

"(i) that conditional fee arrangements may properly be made by such parties to appeals before the Appellate Committee of the House of Lords. Such agreements are sanctioned by the Courts and Legal Services Act 1990 as amended by the Access to Justice Act 1999. They do not derive their validity from the Civil Procedure Rules, although those Rules govern the procedure relating to conditional fee arrangements in proceedings to which they apply . . . ;

(ii) that it is open to the Taxing Officer to reduce the percentage uplift recoverable under a conditional fee agreement if he considers it to be excessive. The approach followed under the Civil Procedure Rules should generally be followed by analogy;

(iii) that if a party appearing before the Appellate Committee seeks a ruling that the percentage uplift provided for in a conditional fee agreement should be wholly disallowed on legal grounds, such a ruling should (unless otherwise ordered) be expressly sought from the Committee before the end of the hearing."

C. TRANSITIONAL ARRANGEMENTS

The Practice Direction supplementing Part 51 deals with the extent to which   **2–016**
the CPR apply to proceedings issued before April 26, 1999.[17] It was recognised that litigation might well have been in progress for some considerable time before April 26, 1999 without the parties or their lawyers being aware that the new rules might alter the way in which the steps which they were undertaking would be viewed by the court at the time of assessment of costs. The Vice-Chancellor, as Head of Civil Justice, decided that when the court was assessing the costs of work done prior to April 26, 1999 the new rules would generally apply but there would be a general presumption that the judge dealing with the costs (whether by summary or detailed assessment), would not disallow anything in respect of that work which would not have been disallowed under the rules in force prior to April 26, 1999.[18]

Under the transitional arrangements the court cannot ignore that the parties have been acting under the old regime, but it is not constrained to reach the same decision as would have been made previously. The position under the CPR is fundamentally different; namely: a new procedural code with the overriding objective of enabling the court to deal with cases justly.[19]

---

[17] Practice Direction Supplementing Part 51, para.18.
[18] *ibid.*, para.18 and see also Costs Practice Direction, s.57.
[19] *Biguzzi v Rank Leisure PLC*, unreported, July 26, 1999, CA.

Where a bill was taxed before April 26, 1999 but the review took place after that date, the court held that paragraphs 57.6 and 57.7 of the Costs Practice Direction were intended to keep the application of the two sets of rules separate. Accordingly the review was conducted under the earlier rules.[20]

D. THE COURT'S CASE MANAGEMENT POWERS

2–017   The court is given wide general powers of management as to the way in which the case is to be conducted. When the court makes an order it may make it subject to conditions and specify the consequence of failure to comply with the order.[21] The court may also take into account whether or not a party has complied with any relevant pre-action protocol and may order a party to pay money into court if that party has, without good reason, failed to comply with the rule, practice direction or relevant pre-action protocol.[22] When exercising its powers of case management the court is required to have regard to the amount in dispute and the costs which the parties have incurred or which they may incur.[23] Where a party pays money into court, either in compliance with a condition attached to a case management order or as a result of an order made for failure to comply with a rule, practice direction or pre-action protocol, the money becomes security for any sum payable by that party to any other party in the proceedings. This is subject to the right of a defendant to treat all or part of any money paid into court as a Part 36 payment (see below). In order to do this the defendant must file a Part 36 payment notice.[24]

Estimates of costs

2–018   The court may, at any stage in a case, order any party to file an estimate of costs and serve copies of the estimate on all other parties. An estimate of costs is an estimate of those costs already incurred and to be incurred by the party who gives it, which it is intended to seek to recover from another party under an order for costs in the event of success. The estimate of costs should be in the form of the statement of costs annexed to the Practice Direction Supplementing Parts 43–48 of the Civil Procedure Rules.[25] A party who files an allocation questionnaire in relation to a claim which is outside the financial scope of the small claims track, must also file an estimate of costs

---

[20] *Morris v Wiltshire* [2001] EWHC QBD, November 30, Roderick Evans J.
[21] CPR r.3.1(3).
[22] CPR r.3.1(4) and (5).
[23] CPR r.3.1(6).
[24] CPR r.3.1(6A) and 37.2(2).
[25] CPR r.1.1(1) and (2).

and serve a copy of it on every other party unless the court directs otherwise. When a party to a claim on the multi track (or on the fast track or in proceedings under Part 8) files a listing questionnaire, the party must also file an estimate of costs and serve a copy of it as above.

The court's case management powers

Estimates need to be prepared with care and precision since the estimates of opposing parties will be compared one with another. An over-generous estimate may result in an opponent receiving a similar amount, while an under-generous estimate may result in a recovery on behalf of a client which does not reflect the actual costs involved.   **2–019**

The Court of Appeal has expressed the hope that Judges conducting cases will make full use of their powers under Costs Practice Direction, section 6 to obtain estimates of costs and to exercise their powers in respect of costs and case management to keep costs within the bounds of the proportionate in accordance with the overriding objective. Section 6.1 of the Costs Practice Direction expressly indicates that the amount of costs should play an important part both in the court's orders about costs and in its orders about case management.[25a]

Dealing with power to make a costs capping order the court (Gage J.) stated:

> "18. Having referred to section 51 of the 1981 Act, to the various Parts of the CPR which deal with costs, and giving full effect to the overriding objective of the CPR, in my judgment, the court has power to make a costs cap order. In my opinion the general powers of case management and in particular CPR 3.1(2)(m) and 44.3 are sufficiently wide to encompass the making of such an order in both GLOs and other actions. In addition, the provision for Estimates of Costs in the Practice Direction about Costs is, in my view, in keeping with such a power. Further, I am fortified by the encouragement provided by the Court of Appeal in *Solutia UK Limited v Griffiths* to conclude that in appropriate cases, of which GLOs are prime examples . . . the court should do so."[26]

The Court of Appeal subsequently expressed the view that Gage J. was correct to consider that the court possessed the power to make a costs capping order in an appropriate case:

[25a] *Solutia (U.K.) Ltd v Griffiths* [2001] EWCA Civ 736.
[26] *AB v Leeds Teaching Hospitals NHS Trust (Nationwide Organ Group Litigation (NOGL))* [2003] EWHC 1034 (QB), Gage J. This reasoning was followed in the Ledward Group Litigation [2003] EWHC 2551 (QB), Hallett J.

"The language of Section 51 of the Supreme Court Act 1981 is very wide and CPR 3.2(m) confers the requisite power. Needless to say, in deciding what order to make the court should take the principles set out in CPR 44.3 (which govern the retrospective assessment of costs) as an important point of reference."[26a]

Although the court does have jurisdiction to make cost cap orders, where the claimant solicitors were experienced in the field and there was not a real and substantial risk that costs would be disproportionately or unreasonably incurred, a post trial detailed assessment was sufficient to ensure that costs did not become disproportionate. The risk could be managed by conventional case management and detailed assessment after trial. It was very unlikely that it would be appropriate for the court to adopt a practice of capping costs in the majority of clinical negligence cases other than where group litigation was involved. When such an application was made it should be supported by evidence showing a *prima facie* case that the conditions could be satisfied. The allocation and pre trial questionnaire should have attached, estimates of the likely overall costs which should give a good guide; the court should be able to deal with an application at a comparatively short hearing; and the benefit of the doubt in respect of reasonableness of prospective costs should be resolved in favour of the party being capped.[27]

2–020   The Court of Appeal has held that the Costs Practice Direction relating to costs estimates[28] is expressed in clear mandatory terms: costs estimates must be provided. The court set out a non exhaustive guide as to the circumstances in which a costs estimate might be taken into account in determining the reasonableness of costs claimed, intended to assist judges in the application of the direction. First, estimates made by solicitors of the overall likely costs of litigation should usually provide a useful yardstick by which the reasonableness of the costs finally claimed may be measured. If there is a substantial difference between the estimated costs and the costs claimed that difference calls for an explanation. In the absence of a satisfactory explanation the court may conclude that the difference itself is evidence from which it can conclude that the costs claimed are unreasonable. Secondly the court may take the estimated costs into account if the other party shows that it relied on the estimate in a certain way. Thirdly the court may take the estimate into account in cases where it decides that it would probably have given different case management directions if a realistic

---

[26a] *King v Telegraph Group Ltd* [1004] EWCA Civ 613, para. 85. The court also referred to the judgment of Dyson L.J. in *Leigh v Michelin Tyre Plc* [2003] EWCA Civ 1766; [2004] 2 All E.R. 175 where he expressed the view that the prospective fixing of costs budgets was likely to achieve the objective of controlling the costs of litigation more effectively than estimates.

[27] *Smart v East Cheshire NHS Trust* [2003] EWHC 2806 (QB), Gage J.

[28] Costs Practice Direction Section 6.

estimate had been given. The court did not consider that it would be a correct use of the power conferred by the Costs Practice Direction to hold a party to his estimates simply in order to penalise him for providing an inadequate estimate. Thus, if the estimate had not been relied on by the paying party; the court concludes that even if the estimate had been close to the figure ultimately claimed its case management directions would not have been affected; and, the costs claimed were otherwise reasonable and proportionate, then it would be wrong to reduce the costs claimed simply because they exceed the amount of the estimate. The court considered that the Costs Judge should determine how, if at all, to reflect the costs estimates in the assessment before going on to decide whether, for reasons unrelated to the estimate, there are elements of the costs claimed which were unreasonably incurred or unreasonable in amount. This will avoid the danger of "double jeopardy" referred to by Lord Woolf C.J. in *Lownds*.[29]

Power to strike out a statement of case

Where the court strikes out a statement of case it may make any consequential order it considers appropriate. A claimant whose case has been struck out and who has been ordered to pay costs to the defendant may not start another claim against the same defendant arising out of the same or similar facts before the costs are paid. The court may, on the defendant's application, stay the other claim until the costs of the first claim have been paid.[30]   2–021

Judgment without trial after striking out

Where the court makes an order on terms that a case shall be struck out if the order is not complied with, and that party fails to comply with it, a party may obtain judgment with costs by filing a request for judgment.[31]   2–022

---

[29] See *Lownds v Home Office* [2002] EWCA Civ 365 at para.30; [2002] 1 W.L.R. 2450, CA; *Leigh v Michelin Tyres Plc* [2003] EWCA Civ 1766.
[30] CPR r.3.4(3) and (4) and the Practice Supplementing Part 3.
[31] CPR r.3.5(1) and (2). The order to strike out must relate to the whole of a statement of case and must be for:

    (i) a specified amount of money;
    (ii) an amount to be decided by the court;
    (iii) delivery of goods where the defendant is given the alternative of paying their value; or
    (iv) any combination of the above.

If those provisions do not apply a party must make an application in accordance with Part 23 in order to obtain judgment; CPR r.3.5(4).

Admissions

2–023   A party may make admissions as to the whole or any part of another party's case.[32] Where the only remedy which the claimant is seeking is the payment of a specified amount of money and the defendant admits the whole of the claim or part of it then, subject to the specific provisions of the rules, the claimant may obtain judgment for the amount admitted (less any payments made) and costs, to be paid by the date or at the rate specified in the request for judgment, or, if none is specified, immediately.[33]

Where the only remedy sought by a claimant is payment of money, the amount of which is not specified, and the defendant admits liability but does not offer to pay a specified amount, or alternatively does offer to pay a specified amount in satisfaction of the claim, the claimant may obtain judgment subject to the specific rules by filing a request. The judgment will be for an amount to be decided by the court and costs, or, if the claimant accepts the amount offered by the defendant, judgment will be for the amount offered (less any payment made) and costs, to be paid on the date or at a rate specified in the request for judgment, or, if none is specified, immediately.[34]

Where a defendant makes an admission of the whole or part of a specified amount of money or offers to pay a specified amount, the defendant may request time to pay. If the claimant accepts the defendant's request the judgment will in each case include costs and will be for payment at the time and rate specified in the defendant's request for time to pay.[35]

Interest

2–024   Where the defendant admits the whole of a claim for a specified amount of money, the judgment will include the amount of interest claimed at the date of judgment subject to certain conditions.[36] If the necessary conditions are not met, the judgment will be for an amount of interest to be decided by the court.[37]

---

[32] CPR r.14.1(1) and Part 14 PD.
[33] CPR r.14.4 and 14.5.
[34] CPR r.14.6 and 14.7.
[35] CPR r.14.9. For the procedure to be followed if the claimant does not accept the defendant's request for time see CPR r.14.10.
[36] The conditions are: the particulars of claim must include particulars as to interest in accordance with CPR r.16.4; where interest is claimed under s.35A of the Supreme Court Act 1981 or s.69 of the County Courts Act 1984 the rate must be no higher than the rate payable on judgment debts at the date when the claim form was issued; and the request for judgment must include a calculation of the interest claimed for the period after the date of judgment: CPR r.14.14(1).
[37] CPR r.14.14(2) and (3).

Default judgment

A default judgment is a judgment without trial where a defendant has failed   **2–025.1**
to file an acknowledgment of service or failed to file a defence.[38]

The claimant may not obtain a default judgment if the defendant has
applied to have the claimant's statement of case struck out under rule 3.4 or
for summary judgment under Part 24 and in either case the application has
not been disposed of.[39]

A claimant may not obtain a default judgment on a claim for delivery of
goods subject to an agreement under the Consumer Credit Act 1974; where
he uses the alternative procedure for claims (CPR, Pt 8); or in any other case
where a Practice Direction so provides.[40] If the defendant has satisfied the
whole claim including costs; or has filed or served an admission[41] together
with a request for time to pay, the claimant may not obtain a default
judgment.[42]

Where a claimant wishes to obtain a default judgment for costs only:

    (a) if the claim is for fixed costs he may obtain it by filing a request;

    (b) if the claim is for any other type of costs he must make an
        application in accordance with Part 23.

Where an application is made for a default judgment for costs only the
judgment will be for an amount to be decided by the court.[43]

Summary judgment

Summary judgment[44] is an extension of the court's case management   **2–025.2**
powers. The court is given the power to give summary judgment against a
claimant or a defendant, either on the whole of the claim or a particular
issue or of successfully defending, as the case may be.[45] When the court
determines the summary judgment application it may give directions as to
the filing and service of a defence; and give further directions about the
management of the case.[46] These powers enable the court to make an order
dealing with costs. The Practice Direction draws attention to the fact that if

---

[38] CPR r.12.1 and the Practice Direction Supplementing Pt 12.
[39] CPR r.12.3(3).
[40] CPR r.12.2.
[41] Under CPR r.14.4 or 14.7 (admission of liability to pay all of the money claimed).
[42] CPR r.12.3.
[43] CPR r.12.9(1) and (2), see CPR Pt 45 as to fixed costs.
[44] Under CPR Pt 24.
[45] CPR r.24.2.
[46] CPR r.24.6.

an order does not mention costs no party is entitled to costs relating to that order.[47]

Costs only proceedings

2–026 If the parties to a dispute reach an agreement on all the issues (including which party is to pay the costs) and confirm it in writing, but fail to agree the amount of the costs, an application for assessment may be made in costs only proceedings.[48] The procedure may be followed if no proceedings have been started or if the only proceedings which have been started are under CPR 21.10 or any other proceedings necessitated solely by reason of one or more of the parties being a child or patient.[49]

Costs only proceedings may be commenced by either party to the agreement by filing a claim form in accordance with CPR Part 8. The claim form must contain or be accompanied by the agreement or confirmation.[50]

When such an application is made the court may make an order for costs to be determined by detailed assessment or dismiss the claim and it must dismiss the claim if it is opposed. The claim is treated as opposed if the defendant files an acknowledgment of service stating that he intends to contest the making of an order for costs seeking a different remedy. A claim is not treated as opposed if the defendant files an acknowledgment of service saying that he disputes the amount of the claim for costs.[51]

In costs only proceedings to which CPR 45 Section 2 applies (road traffic accidents fixed recovery costs) (see below) the court will assess the costs as set out in that section.[52]

CPR r.44.12A provides a method of resolving disputes about costs, but nothing in the rule prevents a person from issuing a claim form under Part 7 or Part 8 to sue on an agreement made in settlement of a dispute where that agreement makes provision for costs, nor from claiming in that case an order for costs or a specified sum in respect of costs.[53]

E. FIXED COSTS

2–027 Part 45 of the Civil Procedure Rules deals with fixed costs and is divided into two sections. Section I deals with fixed costs in the normally accepted

---

[47] CPR r.44.13.
[48] CPR r.44.12A(1).
[49] CPR r.4.12A(1A) CPR 21.10 makes provision for compromise, etc, by or on behalf of a child or patient.
[50] CPR r.44.12A(2)&(3) Costs Practice Direction, s.17.
[51] CPR r.44.12A(4) Costs Practice Direction, para.17.9.
[52] CPR r.44.12A(4A).
[53] Costs Practice Direction, para.17.11.

sense, ie costs which are payable in a given set of circumstances; Section II deals with fixed recoverable costs in costs only proceedings arising out of road traffic accidents. Section III deals with fixed success fees in road traffic accident cases.

Section I—Fixed costs

Section I of Part 45 sets out the amounts which were to be allowed in respect of solicitors charges in cases to which it applies unless the court otherwise orders.[54] The fixed costs provisions apply where the only claim is a claim for a specified sum of money and certain circumstances apply[55]; or the only claim is one where the court gives a fixed date for a hearing when it issues a claim[56] and judgment is given for the delivery of goods and in either case the value of the claim exceeds £25.36.

The fixed costs provisions also apply where a judgment creditor has taken steps to enforce a judgment or order under CPR Parts 70–73.[57] Section I of Part 45 also sets out fixed enforcement costs. The additional fixed costs relating to service are also recoverable if appropriate.[58] The fixed enforcement costs apply to an application to enforce an award of a body other than the High Court or County Court[59]; on attendance to question the judgment debtor or officer of a company who has been ordered to attend court[60]; on the making of a final third party debt order or an order for the payment to the judgment creditor of money in court.[61] The court may also allow reasonable disbursements in respect of search fees and the registration of the order.

Any appropriate court fee will be allowed in addition to the fixed costs.[62]

2–028

---

[54] CPR r.45.1(1) and see Costs Practice Direction, s.24.
[55] The provisions apply where:

  (i) judgment in default is obtained under CPR r.12.4(1);
  (ii) judgment on admission is obtained under CPR r.14.4(3);
  (iii) judgment on admission on part of the claim is obtained under CPR r.14.5(6);
  (iv) summary judgment is given under Part 24;
  (v) the court makes an order to strike out a defence as disclosing no reasonable grounds for defending the claim and judgment without trial is obtained under CPR r.3.4(2)(a); or
  (vi) CPR r.45.3 applies (defendant only liable for fixed commencement costs).

[56] Pursuant to CPR r.7.9.
[57] CPR r.45.1(2).
[58] CPR r.45.6 and Table 4.
[59] Under CPR r.70.5(4).
[60] Under CPR r.71.2.
[61] Under CPR r.72.8(6)(a) and CPR r.72.10(1)(b).
[62] CPR r.45.1(3).

On the small claims track the court may not order a party to pay a sum to another party in respect of that other party's costs except the fixed costs under Part 45 attributable to issuing the claim.[63]

Fixed commencement costs may be claimed depending on the value of the claim, whether the claim form is served by the court or personally by the claimant and whether there is more than one defendant. The amount claimed or the value of any goods claimed, if specified in the claim form, is used to determine the band that applies to the claim.[64]

Where the only claim is for a specified sum of money and the defendant pays the money claimed, together with the fixed costs, within 14 days after service of the particulars of claim upon him, the defendant is not liable for any further costs unless the court orders otherwise. Fixed costs are payable on the issue of a default costs certificate under CPR, rule 47.11.[65]

Where the claimant gives notice of acceptance of a payment into court in satisfaction of the whole claim, the only claim is for a specified sum of money and the defendant made the payment into court within 14 days after service of the particulars of claim on him together with the fixed costs, the defendant is not liable for any further costs unless the court orders otherwise.[66]

Where the claimant claims fixed commencement costs[67] and judgment is entered (in certain specified circumstances[68]), the amount to be included in the judgment in respect of the claimant solicitor's charges is the aggregate of the fixed commencement costs and the relevant amount set out in the table depending on the particular type of judgment.[69]

Further fixed costs may be allowed in respect of solicitors' charges for personal service by a party of any document[70]; where the court makes an

---

[63] CPR r.27.14(2)(a). The rule provides other instances where the court may order costs in relation to injunctions, specific performance, appeals and where a party has behaved unreasonably.

[64] CPR r.45.2(1)(2)(3) and Table 1. Additional costs may also be claimed for service of any document required to be served personally; where service by an alternative method is permitted by an order under CPR r.6.8; and where a document is served out of the jurisdiction, CPR r.45.5 and Table 3.

[65] CPR r.45.3(1) and see Costs Practice Direction, s.25.

[66] CPR r.45.3(2).

[67] Under CPR r.45.2.

[68] The circumstances are:

> judgment in default of acknowledgment of service under CPR r.12.4(1);
> judgment in default of a defence under CPR r.12.4(1);
> judgment on an admission under CPR r.14.4 or 14.5 and the claimant accepts the defendant's proposals for payment;
> similarly where the court decides the date or times of payment;
> summary judgment under Part 24, or where the court strikes out a defence under CPR r.3.4(2)(a); and
> where judgment is given on a claim for delivery of goods under the Consumer Credit Act 1974 and no other entry in the table applies: CPR r.45.4 and Table 2.

[69] CPR r.45.4 and Table 2.

[70] Including preparing and copying a certificate of service for each individual served.

order for service by an alternative method[71]; and where a document is served out of jurisdiction. The amounts payable are as set out in the Table.[72]

Section II—Road traffic accidents fixed recovery costs in costs only proceedings

This section of Part 45 sets out the costs allowable in costs only proceedings in the particular circumstances governed by the section.[73] The provisions apply to road traffic accident disputes,[74] where the accident giving rise to the dispute occurred on or after October 6, 2003. The fixed costs provisions are intended to meet the case where the parties have been able to agree damages within certain limits but have been unable to agree the amount of costs. The agreed damages, include damages in respect of personal injury, damage to property or both. The total value of the agreed damages must not exceed £10,000 or be within the small claims limit.[75] The provisions of this section do not apply where the claimant is a litigant in person.[76]   2–029

Unless the court makes an order allowing costs in excess of the fixed recoverable costs,[77] the only costs allowable under these provisions are: the fixed recoverable costs calculated in accordance with the given formula[78]; disbursements[79]; and a success fee.[80]

The amount of fixed costs recoverable is calculated by totalling:

(a) the sum of £800;

(b) 20 per cent of the agreed damages up to £5,000; and

(c) 15 per cent of the agreed damages between £5,000 and £10,000.[81]

In calculating the amount of the agreed damages, account has to be taken of general damages, special damages and interest. Any interim payments made must be included. Where the parties have agreed an element of contributory negligence the amount of damages attributed to that negligence must be deducted. Any amount required by statute to be paid by the

---

[71] Under CPR r.6.8.
[72] CPR r.45.5 and Table 3.
[73] Under CPR r.72.8(6)(a) and CPR r.72.10(1)(b).
[74] "road traffic accident", "motor vehicle" and "road" are defined in r.45.7(4).
[75] CPR r.45.7(2), CPR r.26.8(2) sets out how the financial value of a claim is assessed for the purposes of allocation to track.
[76] CPR r.45.7(3).
[77] Under CPR r.45.12.
[78] See CPR r.45.9.
[79] In accordance with CPR r.45.10.
[80] In accordance with CPR r.45.11: CPR r.45.8.
[81] CPR r.45.9(1) Costs Practice Direction para.25A(5).

compensating party directly to a third party (such as sums paid by way of compensation recovery payments and National Health Service expenses) are not included.[82]

Where the claimant lives or works in certain specified areas (in or around London) and instructs a solicitor practising in that area, the fixed recoverable costs include an additional 12.5 per cent of the costs otherwise allowable.[83]

Where there is more than one potential claimant and two or more claimants instruct the same solicitor the provisions of the section apply in respect of each claimant separately.[84]

VAT

2–030   VAT may be recovered in addition to the amount of fixed recoverable costs. The figures set out in the Rule and Practice Direction are net of VAT.[85]

Disbursements

2–031   The court may allow a claim for a disbursement falling within the permitted types but may not allow a claim for any other type of disbursement. The permitted disbursements are:

>   (a) the cost of obtaining—
>
>   >   (i) medical records;
>   >   (ii) a medical report;
>   >   (iii) a police report;
>   >   (iv) an engineers report; or
>   >   (v) a search of the records of the driver, vehicle, licensing authority;
>
>   (b) the amount of an insurance premium[86]; or, where a prescribed body[87] undertakes to meet liabilities incurred to pay the costs of other parties to proceedings, a sum not exceeding such an insurance premium;

---

[82] Costs Practice Direction para.25A.3. The section applies to cases which fall within the scope of the uninsured drivers agreement dated August 13, 1999. It does not apply to cases falling within the scope of the untraced drivers agreement dated February 14, 2003, Costs Practice Direction para.25A.4.

[83] The areas referred to are (within London) the County Court Districts of Barnet, Bow, Brentford, Central London, Clerkenwell, Edmonton, Ilford, Lambeth, Mayors & City of London, Romford, Shoreditch, Wandsworth, West London, Willesden and Woolwich and (outside London) the County Court Districts of Bromley, Croydon, Dartford, Gravesend and Uxbridge. CPR r.45.9(2) and Costs Practice Direction para.25A.6.

[84] Costs Practice Direction para.25A.7.

[85] CPR r.45.9(3).

[86] "insurance premium" means an ATE insurance premium as defined in CPR 43.2.

[87] Within the meaning of s.30(1) Access to Justice Act 1994.

(c) fees necessarily incurred because one or more of the claimants is a child or patient, namely:

   (i) fees payable for instructing counsel; or
   (ii) court fees payable on an application to the court;

(d) any other disbursement that has arisen due to a particular feature of the dispute.[88]

Success fee

A claimant who has entered into a conditional fee agreement or a collective conditional fee agreement which provides for a success fee,[89] may recover a success fee. The amount of the success fee will be 12.5 per cent of the fixed recoverable costs.[90]   **2–032**

Where the only dispute between the parties is as to the payment of or amount of a disbursement or the amount of a success fee, the costs only proceedings will be under Rule 44.12A and will not be governed by Section II of Part 45.[91]

Claims for costs exceeding the fixed recoverable costs

If the court considers that there are exceptional circumstances making it appropriate to do so, it will entertain a claim for costs greater than the fixed recoverable costs (excluding any success fee or disbursements). If the court considers such a claim appropriate it may assess the costs or make an order for the costs to be assessed. If the court does not consider the claim appropriate it will make an order for fixed recoverable costs only.[92]   **2–033**

Where the court has allowed a claim for additional costs to proceed and assesses the costs at an amount which is less than 20 per cent greater than the amount of the fixed recoverable costs, the court will order the paying party to pay the lesser of the fixed recoverable costs, and the assessed costs.

Costs of costs only proceedings

Where the court makes an order for fixed recoverable costs only, or the claimant has failed to obtain an allowance of at least 20 per cent greater than the amount of the fixed recoverable costs, the court will make no award for the payment of the claimants' costs in bringing the proceedings   **2–034**

---

[88] CPR r.45.10 "insurance premium" means an ATE insurance premium as defined in CPR r.43.2.
[89] Within the meaning of s.58(2) of the Courts and Legal Services Act 1990, see CPR r.43.2(k)(i); or s.30(1) of the Access to Justice Act 1999.
[90] CPR r.45.11.
[91] Costs Practice Direction para.25A.10.
[92] CPR r.45.12.

under Rule 44.12A and will order the claimant to pay the defendant's costs of defending those proceedings.[93]

Section III—Fixed percentage increase in road traffic accident claims

2–035   The third section of Part 45 (fixed costs) lays down the success (percentage increase) which will be allowed to a successful claimant in a road traffic accident case conducted under a CFA with a success fee.[94] The provisions apply only where the road traffic accident giving rise to the dispute occurred on or after October 6, 2003. The provisions do not apply to a small claim, *i.e.* a claim on the small claims track or a claim for which that track is the normal track. If Section II of Part 45 is applicable Section III does not apply.[95]

Different provisions are made in respect of the fees of solicitors and counsel. In respect of solicitors the percentage increase which is to be allowed is 100 per cent where the claim concludes at trial, or 12.5 per cent where the claim concludes before a trial has commenced or the dispute is settled before a claim is issued.[96] "Trial" is a reference to the final contested hearing or to the contested hearing of any issue ordered to be tried separately. A case which "concludes at trial" includes both a claim which settles after the trial has commenced or one which is decided by judgment.[97]

In respect of counsels' fees the success fee is 100 per cent where the claim concludes at trial; if the claim is on the fast track 50 per cent, if the claim concludes 14 days or less before the date fixed for the commencement of the trial, or 12.5 per cent if it concludes more than 14 days before that date or before any such date has been fixed. On the multi track the success fee which will be allowed is 70 per cent, if the claim concludes 21 days or less before the date fixed for the commencement of the trial, or 12.5 per cent if it concludes more than 21 days before that date or before any such date has been fixed. Where a claim has been issued but concludes before it has been allocated to a track, or, in relation to costs only proceedings, the dispute is settled before a claim is issued, the success fee will be allowed at 12.5 per cent.[98]

In order to cope with the different methods of listing on the fast track, the multi track and at the Royal Courts of Justice the Section lays down

---

[93] CPR r.45.14.
[94] As specified in CPR r.43.2(k)(i).
[95] CPR r.45.15(2)–(4).
[96] CPR r.45.16.
[97] CPR r.45.15(6).
[98] CPR r.45.17(1).

provisions for establishing "the date fixed for the commencement of the trial".[99]

Application for an alternative percentage increase

Where the success fee which will be allowed either in respect of solicitors' fees or counsels' fees is 12.5 per cent, a party may, in certain circumstances, apply for a greater or lesser percentage. This may be done where the parties agree damages at an amount greater than £500,000 or the court makes an award greater than that figure; the court awards £500,000 or less but would have awarded more than £500,000 if it had not made a finding of contributory negligence; or the parties agree damages of £500,000 or less and "it is reasonable to expect" that, but for any finding of contributory negligence, the court would have awarded damages greater than £500,000.[1]

2–036

If the court is satisfied that the case falls within the relevant criteria it will assess the percentage increase or make an order for it to be assessed (by a costs judge or district judge). If the percentage increase allowed is greater than 20 per cent or less than 7.5 per cent the percentage allowed will be that assessed by the court. If the percentage increase is assessed at no greater than 20 per cent and no less than 7.5 per cent the increase allowed will remain at 12.5 per cent and the costs of the application and assessment will be paid by the applicant.[2]

F. SANCTION FOR NON-PAYMENT OF FEES

Where the claimant, having been required to do so, fails to pay the requisite fee on an allocation questionnaire or pre trial checklist or fails to pay the requisite fee, even though not required to file an allocation or pre trial checklist or the court has given permission to proceed with a claim for judicial review, and the party does not either pay the fee or make an application for exemption from or remission of the fee, the claim will be struck out and the claimant will be liable for the costs which the defendant has incurred, unless the court orders otherwise.[3]

2–037

Where an application for exemption from or remission of a fee is refused and the claimant does not pay the fee by the date specified by the court, the claim will be struck out and the claimant will be liable for the costs which the defendant has incurred unless the court orders otherwise.[4]

---

[99] See CPR r.45.17(2)–(5).
[1] CPR r.45.18(1) and (2).
[2] CPR r.45.18(4) and 45.19.
[3] CPR r.3.7(1)–(4). In such circumstances a costs order will be deemed to have been made on the standard basis in the defendant's favour: CPR r.44.12(1)(a).
[4] CPR r.3.7(5)–(6).

G. CASE ALLOCATION

2-038   There are three tracks: small claims, fast track and multi track.[5] The small claims track is the normal track for any claim which has a financial value of not more than £5,000 (not more than £1,000 in the case of damages for personal injury and certain housing claims).[6]

The fast track is the normal track for any case not on the small claims track which has a financial value of not more than £15,000. The case will only be retained on the fast track if the court considers that the trial is likely to last no longer than one day and the oral expert evidence at trial will be limited to one expert per party in relation to any expert field and to expert evidence in two expert fields.[7]

The multi track is the normal track for any claim for which the small claims track or fast track is not appropriate.[8]

In assessing the financial value of a claim the court will disregard any amount not in dispute, any claim for interest, costs and contributory negligence.[9]

In addition to the above, only money claims in excess of £15,000 may be issued in the High Court; below that figure the county court must be used. In the case of personal injury claims, other than clinical negligence, the claim may not be brought in the High Court unless the claim is for £50,000 or more.[10]

The omission to allocate a case to the small track does not preclude the court from considering whether it is reasonable to make an assessment in accordance with the costs regime for that track. In the absence of a practice suggesting otherwise where, if an allocation had been sought a case would have been allocated to the small claims track, the small claims costs regime should apply.[11]

Once a claim is allocated to a particular track special rules relating to costs on that track apply to the period before as well as after allocation unless the court or a practice direction provides otherwise.[12] Any costs orders made before a claim is allocated will not be affected by allocation.[13] Where a claim is allocated to a track and the court subsequently re-allocates it to a different track any special rules about costs applying to the first track

---

[5] CPR r.26.1(2) and the Practice Direction Supplementing Part 26 and particularly para.12.5.
[6] CPR r.26.6(1)(2) and (3).
[7] CPR r.26.6(4) and (5).
[8] CPR r.26.6(6).
[9] CPR r.26.8(2), CPR r.44.9 and Costs Practice Direction, s.15.
[10] The High Court and County Courts Jurisdiction (Amendment) Order 1999 (SI 1999/1014).
[11] *Boyce & Script International v Alghafar* [2003] EWCA Civ, May 8.
[12] CPR r.44.9(2).
[13] CPR r.44.11(1).

will apply up to the date of re-allocation and to the second track from the date of re-allocation unless the court makes a different order.[14]

H. THE SMALL CLAIMS TRACK

Part 27 of the CPR sets out the small claims track procedure. With regard to costs the court may not order a party to pay a sum to another party except: **2–039**

(a) the fixed costs attributable to issuing the claim which are payable under Part 45 (Section I), or which would be payable if that Part applied to the claim[15];

(b) a sum[16] for legal advice and assistance in proceedings which include a claim for an injunction or an order for specific performance;

(c) where there is an appeal, costs assessed summarily; and

(d) such further costs as the court may summarily assess and order to be paid by a party who has behaved unreasonably.[17]

The court may, in addition, order a party to pay all or part of any court fees paid by another party; expenses which a party or a witness has reasonably incurred in travelling or staying away from home for the purpose of attending a hearing; loss of earnings[18] suffered by a party or a witness due to attending the hearing or staying away from home; and, a sum[19] for expert's fees.[20]

The limits on costs imposed in relation to the small claims track also apply to any fee or award for acting on behalf of a party to the proceedings charged by a lay representative exercising a right of audience.[21]

Where the parties consent to a claim being allocated to the small claims track[22] and the financial limit of the claim exceeds the limit for small claims track, the claim will be treated, for the purposes of costs, as if it were

---

[14] CPR r.44.11(1)(2). Costs Practice Direction, s.16.
[15] See above para.2–027. Fixed costs.
[16] Not exceeding £260 as specified in the Practice Direction Supplementing Part 27, para.7.2.
[17] CPR r.17.14(2) and see Practice Direction Supplementing Part 27, paras 7.1–7.3.
[18] Not exceeding £50 per day specified in the Practice Direction Supplementing Pt 27, para.7.3.
[19] Not exceeding £200 specified in the Practice Direction Supplementing Pt 27, para.7.3.
[20] CPR r.27.14(3).
[21] CPR r.27.14(4) *i.e.* by virtue of an order under s.11 of the Courts and Legal Services Act 1990.
[22] In accordance with CPR r.26.7(3).

proceeding on the fast track. Trial costs are in the discretion of the court and may not exceed the appropriate amount of fast track trial costs.[23]

Any costs orders made before a claim is allocated to the small claims track will not be affected by the allocation.[24] Where a claim is allocated to the small claims track and subsequently re-allocated to another track the provisions relating to costs on the small claims track[25] cease to apply after re-allocation and fast track or multi track costs rules apply from that date.[26]

I. THE FAST TRACK

2–040   When the Court allocates a case to the fast track it will give directions for the management of the case and set up a timetable for the steps to be taken between the giving of the directions and the trial.[27] The court will either fix the trial date or fix a period within which the trial is to take place which will normally be not more than 30 weeks after the directions. The court's power to award trial costs is limited in accordance with Part 46.[28]

Fast track trial costs

2–041   Part 46 governs the amount of fast track trial costs and their application. "Fast track trial costs" means the cost of a party's advocate[29] for preparing for and appearing at the trial. It does not include any other disbursements; or any VAT payable on the advocate's fees. The "trial" includes a hearing where the court decides an amount of money or the value of goods.[30] "Trial" does not include the hearing of an application for summary judgment[31]; or the court's approval of a settlement or other compromise by or on behalf of a child or patient.[32]

The amount of fast track trial costs is set out in the table in Part 46 and ranges from £350 for cases up to £3,000 to £750 for cases exceeding £10,000.[33] The court may not award more or less than the amount shown in the table except where it decides not to award any fast track trial costs,

---

[23] CPR r.27.14(5).
[24] CPR r.44.11(1).
[25] CPR r.27.14.
[26] CPR r.27.15 and 44.11(2).
[27] CPR r.28.2(1).
[28] CPR r.28.2(3)–5.
[29] *i.e.* A person exercising a right of audience as a representative of or on behalf of a party.
[30] Following a judgment under Part 12 (default judgment) or Part 15 (admission).
[31] Under Part 24.
[32] Under CPR r.21.10: CPR r.46.1(1) and (2) and Costs Practice Direction, s.26.
[33] CPR r.46.2(1). The figures apply whether the court proceeds by way of summary or detailed assessment. See paras below.

or the circumstances described below arise.[34] The court may apportion the amount awarded between the parties to reflect their respective degrees of success on the issues at trial.[35]

The court may award an additional amount to that prescribed for fast track trial costs or may award less than those amounts in any of the following circumstances:

Additional legal representative

If, in addition to the advocate, the party's legal representative[36] attends the trial; the court considers that it was necessary for the legal representative to attend to assist the advocate; and, the court awards fast track trial costs to that party, the court may award an additional £250 in respect of the legal representative's attendance at the trial.[37]   2–042

Additional liability

The court may in addition award a sum representing an additional liability.[38] The requirements to provide information about a funding arrangement where a party wishes to recover any additional liability are set out in the Costs Practice Direction.[39]   2–043

Separate trials

If the court considers that it is necessary to direct a separate trial of an issue, then the court may award an additional amount in respect of the separate trial, but that amount is limited and must not exceed two-thirds of the amount payable for that claim subject to a minimum award of £350.[40]   2–044

Litigant in person

Where fast track trial costs are awarded to a litigant in person, if the litigant in person can prove financial loss, the court will award two-thirds of the   2–045

---

[34] *i.e.* CPR r.46.3 applies and see Costs Practice Direction, s.27.

[35] CPR r.46.2(2).

[36] "Legal representative" means a barrister or a solicitor, solicitor's employee or other authorised litigator (as defined by the Courts and Legal Services Act 1990) who has been instructed to act for a party in relation to a claim. CPR r.2.3(1).

[37] CPR r.46.3(2).

[38] "Additional liability" means the percentage increase, the insurance premium or the additional amount in respect of provision made by a membership organisation CPR r.43.2(1)(o), CPR r.46.3(2A).

[39] "Funding arrangement" means an arrangement where a person has: (i) entered into a conditional fee agreement or a collective conditional fee agreement which provides for a success fee within the meaning of s.58(2) of the Courts and Legal Services Act 1990; (ii) taken out an insurance policy to which s.29 of the Access to Justice Act 1999 (recovery of insurance premiums by way of costs) applies; or (iii) made an agreement with a membership organisation to meet his legal costs CPR r.43.2(1)(k).

[40] CPR r.46.3(3) and (4).

amount that would otherwise be awarded. If the litigant in person fails to prove financial loss, the amount allowed will be at the rate specified in the Costs Practice Direction[41] in respect of the time reasonably spent doing the work.[42]

Counterclaim

2–046 Where a defendant has made a counterclaim which is higher than the value of the claim and the claimant succeeds at trial both on the claim and the counterclaim, for the purpose of quantifying a fast track trial costs award to the claimant, the value of the defendant's counterclaim is taken for the purpose of calculating the value of the claim.[43]

Where a defendant has made a counterclaim and the claimant has succeeded on his claim and the defendant has succeeded on his counterclaim, the court will quantify the amount of the award of fast track trial costs to which, but for the counterclaim, the claimant would be entitled for succeeding on his claim; and, but for the claim, the defendant would be entitled for succeeding on his counterclaim; and will make one award of the difference to the party entitled to the higher award. This is an attempt to get away from difficulties caused by dealing with costs in such circumstances, in accordance with the decision of the House of Lords in *Medway Oil*.[44]

Unreasonable and improper behaviour

2–047.1 Where the court considers that the party to whom fast track trial costs are to be awarded, has behaved unreasonably or improperly during the trial, it may award an amount less than would otherwise be payable, as it considers appropriate. If the court feels that the paying party has behaved improperly during the trial, it may award such additional amount to the other party as it considers appropriate. This last provision appears to be entirely unlimited in amount.[45]

Quantifying fast track trial costs

2–047.2 The amount of fast track trial costs is arrived at by ascertaining the value of the claim. Where the only claim is for the payment of money, and the fast track trial costs are awarded to a claimant, the value of the claim is the total amount of the judgment, excluding interest and costs; and any reduction made for contributory negligence.[46] Where the defendant is successful, the value of the claim is the amount specified in the claim form (excluding

---

[41] £9.25 per hour at the time of writing. See Costs Practice Direction, s.52.
[42] CPR r.46.3(5).
[43] CPR r.46.2(6).
[44] CPR r.46.3(6): *Medway Oil and Storage Co v Continental Contractors* [1929] A.C. 88, HL.
[45] CPR r.46.3(7)(8).
[46] CPR r.46.2(3)(a).

interest and costs); or, if no amount is specified, the maximum amount which the claimant reasonably expected to recover[47]; or, more than £10,000 if the claim form states that the claimant cannot reasonably say how much he expects to recover.[48]

If the claim is only for a remedy other than payment of money the claim is deemed to be more than £3,000 and not more than £10,000 unless the court orders otherwise.[49]

Where the claim includes both a money claim and a claim for another remedy, the value is deemed to be the higher of the value of the money claimed; or the deemed value of the other remedy, decided in accordance with the preceding paragraph. The court may make a different order.[50]

More than one claimant or defendant

There will be only one award in respect of fast track trial costs for an advocate acting for more than one party. The parties represented by the advocate are jointly entitled to any fast track trial costs awarded by the court.[51]

2–048

In a case with more than one claimant, each of whom has a separate claim against the defendant, and in which the same advocate is acting, the value of the claim, for the purpose of quantifying the award of fast track trial costs, is ascertained in the following way: if the only claim of each claimant is for the payment of money, the award, if in favour of the claimants, will be based on the total amount of the judgment made in favour of all the claimants jointly represented. If the award is in favour of the defendant, it will be based on the total amount claimed by the claimants. The actual method of quantification of the value of the claim is as set out above (para. 2–047.2).[52] If the claims are for a remedy other than payment of money, the value is deemed to be more than £3,000 but not more than £10,000, and where the claims are mixed, including both a claim for payment of money and for a remedy other than payment of money, the value is deemed to be either, more than £3,000 but not more than £10,000, or if the value of the money claims is greater, their value.[53]

In the case of multiple defendants all or any of them, who are separately represented, may be awarded fast track trial costs.[54]

Whilst separately represented defendants may each receive an award of fast track trial costs, where there is more than one claimant and a single defendant, the court may only make one award in favour of the defendant,

---

[47] According to the statement of value included in the claim form under CPR r.16.3.
[48] CPR r.46.2(3)(b).
[49] CPR r.46.2(4).
[50] CPR r.46.2(5).
[51] CPR r.46.4(1).
[52] CPR r.46.4(2)(3)(a).
[53] CPR r.46.4(3)(b) and (c).
[54] CPR r.46.4(4).

for which the claimants are jointly and severally liable. The claim is calculated in the way described above (para.2–047.2).[55]

Where a fast track claim settles before trial

2–049 When a fast track claim settles before the start of a trial, and the court is considering the amount of costs to be allowed in respect of the advocate for preparing for the trial, it may not allow, in respect of the advocate's costs, more than the amount of fast track trial costs which would have been payable had the trial taken place.[56] The court is required to have regard to when the claim was settled and when the court was notified of the settlement.[57]

J. THE MULTI TRACK

2–050 When a case is allocated to the multi track the court will give directions and set a timetable for the steps to be taken between directions and trial. The trial date or period will be fixed as soon as practicable. The court will also specify the date by which the parties must file a pre-trial check list. In appropriate cases the court may fix a case management conference or a pre-trial review, or both.[58]

Group litigation

2–051 CPR Part 19 deals with Group Litigation Orders (GLO). Where a judgment is given in a claim on the group register, in relation to a (GLO) issue, that judgment is binding on all the parties to all other claims that are on the group register at the time the judgment is given, unless the court orders otherwise.[59] Unless the court orders otherwise, any order for common costs against group litigants imposes on each group litigant several liability for an equal proportion of those common costs. Normally where a group litigant is ordered to pay costs he will, in addition to any costs which he is liable to pay to the receiving party, be liable for the individual costs of his claim and an equal proportion (together with all the other group litigants) of the common costs. When making an order about costs, the court will direct the proportion of the costs that is to relate to the common costs and the

---

[55] CPR r.46.4(5) and (6).
[56] CPR r.44.10(1).
[57] CPR r.44.10(2).
[58] CPR r.29.2(1)(2) and (3) and see Practice Direction Supplementing Part 29.
[59] CPR r.19.12.

proportion that is to relate to the individual costs. If the court fails to do so the Costs Judge will make the apportionment.[60]

There should be no need for any detailed assessment of costs until the conclusion of group litigation. The solicitors for claimants in group litigation are entitled to an adequate cash flow from defendants once the general issue of liability has been admitted or determined in the claimants' favour. Similarly on determination of generic issues in the claimants' favour and on the assessment or settlement of awards of damages to individuals or batches of claimants. The court expressed the hope that defendants' solicitors would agree to pay, at various stages in group litigation, a realistic interim amount on account of a final detailed assessment of costs if necessary. If such an agreement cannot be reached it should be dealt with cheaply and shortly by the nominated trial judge under CPR r.44.3(8). If on such an application the judge is provided with a written summarised schedule of costs to date, together with a succinct skeleton of the issues and the rival contentions of the parties he may be able to make or refuse an interim award without the necessity for an oral hearing. Save in exceptional cases it is not appropriate to have detailed assessment costs by tranches in group litigation.[61]

It is sensible and consonant with justice that both the recoverability of common costs and the liability, if any, of discontinuing claimants for costs should be determined at the same time as orders for common costs were made in respect of those common issues. There is an inherent injustice to claimants and an inappropriate advantage to defendants if an order making a discontinuing claimant liable for his individual costs, together with his share of the common costs incurred by the defendants up to the last day of the quarter in which he discontinued, was allowed to remain the norm. To have a rule that any discontinuing claimant should have a crystallised inability to recover common costs and a potential liability for the common costs of the defendants at the end of the quarter in which he discontinued was too blunt an instrument and was necessarily favourable to the defendants when it was as yet unknown whether the claimants as a whole would be successful in the common issues which were to be tried.[62]

K. PART 36 OFFERS TO SETTLE AND PAYMENTS INTO COURT

Part 36 of the CPR deals with offers to settle and payments into court. The rules provide certain costs consequences where offers and payments in are   **2–052**

---

[60] CPR r.48.6A.

[61] *per* Moreland J., *Giambrone v JMC Holidays Ltd* [2002] EWHC QB 2932; [2003] 1 All E.R. 982.

[62] *Sayers v Smithkline Beecham PLC*; *XYZ v Schering Health Care Ltd*; *Afrika v Cape Plc* [2001] EWCA Civ 2017; [2002] 1 W.L.R. 2274 CA; [2003] 3 All E.R. 631, CA.

made in accordance with the rule, but parties are not prevented from making an offer to settle in whatever way they choose. The consequences of such an offer are however in the discretion of the court.[63] In deciding what order to make about costs the court is required to have regard to all the circumstances, including any payment into court or admissible offer to settle made by a party which is drawn to the court's attention whether or not it has been made in accordance with Part 36.[64]

The terms of CPR r.36.19 admit only one construction, namely that payments in can only be used on arguments as to costs.[65]

Where a Part 36 offer is made, the rules lay down certain provisions as to the form and content of the offer. Such an offer must be in writing and state whether it relates to the whole of the claim or to part of it or to an issue which arises in it; state whether it takes into account any counterclaim; and, if it is expressed not to be inclusive of interest, state whether interest is offered and if so the amount offered,[66] the rate or rates offered and the period or periods for which it is offered. Unless a claimant's Part 36 offer or a Part 36 payment notice indicates to the contrary it will be treated as inclusive of all interest until the last day upon which it could be accepted without needing the permission of the court.[67] A defendant may make a Part 36 offer limited to accepting liability up to a specified proportion.[68]

A defendant's offer to settle a money claim must be made by way of a Part 36 payment if it is to have the consequences set out in the rule.[69] Where the claim includes both a money claim and a non money claim and a defendant wishes to make an offer to settle the whole claim, the defendant is required to make a Part 36 payment in relation to the money claim and the Part 36 offer in relation to the non money claim. The payment notice must identify the document which sets out the terms of the offer and state that, if the claimant gives notice of acceptance of the Part 36 payment, he will be treated as also accepting the Part 36 offer.[70] If a Part 36 offer is withdrawn it does not have the consequences set out in Part 36.[71] A Part 36 payment may be withdrawn or reduced only with the permission of the court.[72]

An offer made not less than 21 days before the start of the trial must be expressed to remain open for acceptance for 21 days from the date it was made. It must also provide that after the 21 days the offeree may only accept it if the parties agree the liability for costs or the court gives permission. Where an offer is made less than 21 days before the start of the trial it must

---

[63] CPR r.36.1.
[64] CPR r.44.3(4)(c).
[65] *Johnson v Gore Wood & Co* [2004] EWCA Civ 14.
[66] CPR r.36.5(1)(2)(3), 36.22(2).
[67] CPR r.36.22(1).
[68] CPR r.36.5(4).
[69] CPR r.36.3(1).
[70] CPR r.36.4.
[71] CPR r.36.5(8).
[72] CPR r.36.6(5).

state that the offeree may only accept it if the parties agree the liability for costs or the court gives permission.[73]

Offers to settle before proceedings

If a person makes an offer to settle before proceedings are begun which complies with Part 36, the court will take that offer into account when making any order as to costs.[74] The rules lay down the time within which a party may accept a Part 36 offer or Part 36 payment. This is normally within 21 days after the offer or payment was made, unless the parties agree the liability for costs. If the parties do not agree the liability for costs the offer or payment may only be accepted with the permission of the court. Where the permission of the court is needed the court will, if it gives permission, make an order as to costs.[75]

2–053

Defendant's Part 36 offer or Part 36 payment

Where a defendant's Part 36 offer or Part 36 payment is accepted without needing the permission of the court, the claimant is entitled to the costs of the proceedings up to the date of serving notice of acceptance. If the claimant, in accepting an offer or payment relating to any part of the claim, abandons the balance of the claim, the claimant is entitled to the costs of the proceedings unless the court orders otherwise. The claimant's costs include any costs attributable to the defendant's counterclaim, if the Part 36 offer or Part 36 payment states that it takes into account the counterclaim. The costs will be on the standard basis unless they are agreed.[76]

2–054

Claimant's Part 36 offer

Where a claimant's Part 36 offer is accepted without needing the permission of the court, the claimant is entitled to the costs of the proceedings up to the date upon which the defendant serves notice of acceptance.[77] If a Part 36 offer or payment relating to the whole claim and is accepted the whole claim is stayed. The stay is upon the terms of the offer and either party may apply to enforce the terms without the need to commence a new claim. If approval of the court is required before a settlement can be binding, any stay which

2–055

---

[73] CPR r.36.5(6) and (7).
[74] CPR r.36.10(1).
[75] CPR r.36.11 and 36.12.
[76] CPR r.36.13.
[77] CPR r.36.14.

might otherwise arise takes effect only when that approval has been given.[78]

Part 36 offer or payment relating to part only of a claim

2–056   Where a Part 36 offer or payment which relates to part only of a claim is accepted, the claim will be stayed as to that part, and, unless the parties have agreed the costs, the liability for costs will be decided by the court.[79] Any stay of proceedings does not affect the power of the court to deal with any question of costs (including interest on costs) relating to the proceedings.[80]

Where a Part 36 payment relating only to part of a claim is accepted, Rule 36.15(3) makes it clear that unless the parties agree the costs, liability for costs will be decided by the court. The overall intention of the Rules is unmistakably clear, that the court should have a discretion except where the Part 36 payment covers the whole of the proceedings and brings the proceedings to an end.[81]

Costs consequences where claimant fails to do better than Part 36 offer or payment

2–057   Where a claimant fails to do better than a defendant's Part 36 offer or a Part 36 payment the court will, unless it considers it unjust to do so, order the claimant to pay any costs incurred by the defendant after the latest date on which the payment or offer could have been accepted without needing the permission of the court.[82]

The purpose of CPR r.36.20 is to encourage settlements in litigation and to require the offerree to pay the costs of the other side if it failed to accept an offer and it did not beat the offer made unless injustice would result from such an order. In a patent case the judge had erred in principle by treating the prior use defence and the absence of documentary evidence as establishing an unjust result. In the same case the Judge had made an error in principle in respect of the period prior to the Part 36 offer. The Court of Appeal held that it was appropriate for that period to have looked at the issues raised in the case and to regard them as distinct from each other. In

---

[78] CPR r.36.15(1)(2) and (4).

[79] CPR r.36.15(3).

[80] CPR r.36.15(5).

[81] *Clark Goldring & Page Ltd v ANC Ltd, The Times*, March 27, 2001, Mr John Martin Q.C.

[82] CPR r.36.20. See *Jones (Marilyn) v Jones (Margaret), The Times*, November 11, 1999, CA, and *Burgess v British Steel, The Times*, February 29, 2000.

respect of that period the Court of Appeal ordered the offerree to pay 75 per cent of the defendant's costs rather than each side pay its own costs.[83]

Costs consequences where claimant does better than his proposed Part 36 offer—CPR r.36.21.

Where a claimant does better than was proposed in the claimant's Part 36   2–058
offer the court may order interest on the whole or part of any sum of money (excluding interest) awarded to the claimant at a rate not exceeding 10 per cent above base rate for some or all of the periods, starting with the latest date on which the defendant could have accepted the offer without needing the permission of the court.[84] In addition, the court may order that the claimant is entitled to costs on the indemnity basis from the same date and interest on those costs at a rate not exceeding 10 per cent above base rate. The rule provides that the court will make orders in these terms unless it considers it unjust to do so.[85] In deciding whether or not it would be unjust to make such an order the court will take into account all the circumstances including the terms of the Part 36 offer, the stage in the proceedings when the offer was made, the information available to the parties at the time when the offer was made and the conduct of the parties with regard to the giving or refusing to give information for the purpose of enabling the offer or payment in to be made or evaluated.[86]

Where the court awards interest under CPR r.36.21 and also awards interest on the same sum and for the same period under any other power, the total rate of interest may not exceed 10 per cent above base rate.[87] A defendant was ordered to pay the claimant's costs of action on the indemnity basis together with interest which was awarded, to mark the view of the court that the case should have been settled before the action was started. The defendant had been unreasonable in refusing claimant's offers including an offer under CPR Part 36.[88]

Part 36 offers and payments do not have the consequences set out in the rules while the claim is being dealt with on the small claims track, unless the court makes a different order.[88a]

Rule 36.21 applies to costs and other consequences where a claimant does better than proposed in the claimant's Part 36 offer. There is no equivalent to a successful defendant's Part 36 offer. In considering what costs are payable there is a need to review CPR Part 44 including the conduct of the

---

[83] *Kavanagh Balloons Propriety Ltd v Cameron Balloons Ltd* [2003] EWCA Civ.
[84] CPR r.36.21(1), (2).
[85] CPR r.36.21(3), (4).
[86] CPR r.36.21(5).
[87] CPR r.36.21(6).
[88] *Padgham v Rochelle (Costs)* [2002] EWHC 2747 (Ch), [2003] W.T.L.R. 71, L. Henderson Q.C.
[88a] CPR r.36.2(5).

parties, whether a party has succeeded in part of its claim and whether a payment into court was made. It is incorrect for the judge to be guided by the pre CPR cases. In a case other than one covered by Part 36, the award of costs on the indemnity basis was normally reserved to cases where the court wished to indicate its disapproval of the conduct of the party against whom costs are awarded.[89]

The underlying rationale of Rule 36.21 to encourage claimants to make offers has simply no counterpart with regard to defendants. Conduct, albeit falling short of misconduct deserving of moral condemnation can be so unreasonable as to justify an order for indemnity costs. Such conduct would need to be unreasonable to a high degree; unreasonable in this context does not mean merely wrong or misguided in hindsight. An indemnity costs order made under Rule 44 (unlike one made under Rule 36) does carry at least some stigma. It is of its nature penal rather than exhortatory.[90] CPR r.36.21(4) is not an "all or nothing" provision requiring the court to make either all of the orders envisaged by rule 36.21(2) and (3) or none of them. Rather the rules provide the judge with a range of possible ways of marking a failure to meet a Part 36 offer.[91]

The conventional rate of interest in commercial cases to which CPR 36.21 applies is 1 per cent over base rate.[92]

The court has held that the penal provisions of CPR r.36.21 should apply unless it is unjust to order the offeree to pay costs on the indemnity basis or to pay higher interest. It would be unjust to so order where the offeree has a good reason for rejecting the offer, for example where he:

(1) had a reasonable belief in his own prospects of success on the law as it stood at the time; or

(2) by reason of the other party's conduct, *e.g.* inadequate disclosure, he was unable to asses the validity of the offer.[93]

CPR 36.21 does not apply where claims are settled, as opposed to determined by the court. Where the quantum of major claims was agreed during the quantum hearings and it was agreed that the defendants should pay the claimants' costs, the parties were unable to agree the basis upon which the costs should be paid and the claimants applied for costs on the indemnity basis to the court. The court exercised its discretion on principles similar to those set out in CPR 36.21.[94]

---

[89] *Reid Minty v Gordon Taylor* [2001] EWCA Civ, October 29.
[90] *Kiam v MGN Ltd* [2002] EWCA Civ, February 6.
[91] *The Maersk Co Ltd v Wilson* [2004] EWCA Civ, March 25.
[92] *Amstrad v Seegate Technology Inc* [1997] 86 B.L.R. 34.
[93] *Mamidoil Jetoil Greek Petroleum Co SA v Okta Crude Oil Refinery AD* [2002] EWHC 2462 (Comm), [2003] 1 Lloyd's Rep. 42, Aikens J.
[94] *Craig v Railtrack Plc* [2002] EWHC 168 (QB); [2002] All E.R. (D) 212, MacKay J.

In a claim where the claimant sought the actual total loss of a ship instead of confining the claim to a constructive total loss the court held that it was appropriate to order the defendant to pay 15 per cent of the claimant's costs and to order the claimant to pay 85 per cent of the defendant's costs even though the claimant had bettered its own Part 36 offer. Rule 36.21(4) applied and it would be unjust to award the claimant the costs. The words "his costs" meant those costs that would ordinarily be awarded to a claimant applying the principle set out in rule 44.3 without having regard to the impact of Part 36.[95] Both parties appealed. The Court of Appeal found that the claimant had lost on one major issue but recovered the full amount they had claimed and in doing so beat a Part 36 offer. The court confirmed the meaning of the words "his costs" and held that the Judge was entitled to adopt an issue by issue approach but erred in principle by simply visiting on the claimant the mathematical outcome of the issue by issue approach because that took no account of other relevant factors. The correct order was for there to be no order for costs either way.[96]

Decided cases on Part 36

The Court of Appeal has stated that a judge, in deciding what order for costs to make after a Part 36 payment, is required to take into account all relevant aspects of the litigation including late disclosure, late service of evidence or the development of unanticipated contentions. The judge should consider whether or not the parties had conducted the litigation in accordance with the system of litigation which had been designed to enable the parties to know where they stood at the earliest possible stage and at the lowest practicable cost so that they might make informed decisions about their prospects and the sensible conduct of their cases. In personal injury litigation where a defendant was asserting that the claimant was a malingerer or was exaggerating the symptoms, fairness demanded that the claimant should be given a reasonable opportunity to deal with those allegations.[97]

A claimant's Part 36 offer to accept a split of 95:5 on liability prior to proceedings being issued was held to have presented the defendant with a real opportunity of settlement. Once the claimant had bettered his own offer CPR r.36.21 applied regardless of the narrowness of any margin. The decision to award indemnity costs and interest at an enhanced rate is a discretionary one and it is permissible to ignore offers that are purely tactical.[98]

2–059

---

[95] *Kastor Navigation Co Ltd v AGF Mat (the Kastor Too) (Costs)* [2003] EWHC 472 (comm), *The Times* March 29, 2003, Tomlinson J.
[96] *Kastor Navigation Co Ltd v Axa Global Risks (UK) Ltd* [2004] EWCA Civ, March 10.
[97] *Ford v G.K.R. Construction Ltd* [2000] 1 All E.R. 802, CA.
[98] *Huck v Robson* [2002] EWCA Civ 398; [2002] 3 All E.R. 263 CA.

Claimants who, without making a formal Part 36 offer, made it clear to the defendants that they were prepared to accept 100 per cent of their claim, failed in their application for costs on the indemnity basis and enhanced interest pursuant to CPR 36.21 because they did not succeed in recovering more than the amount claimed in the letter of claim or amended particulars and the matter did not fall within Rule 36.21.

There are are compelling reasons of principle and policy why those prepared to make genuine offers of monetary settlement should do so by way of Part 36 payments rather than written offers. Part 36 payments offer greater clarity and certainty about genuineness, ability to pay, whether the offer is open or without prejudice and the terms on which the dispute could be settled. In a case where the defendant wrote offering settlement plus costs, and stating that it would be paid into court if the offer was not accepted, the offer was rejected. It was not until some 10 months later that the defendant made a Part 36 payment, and then only for half the original offer. A further payment in was made subsequently. At trial, the defendant's counterclaim was dismissed and the claimant was awarded less than the payment in. At first instance, the judge ordered the claimant to pay the defendant's costs from the date of the original written offer. On appeal it was held that the judge had erred in law in making the same costs order as he would have done if the defendant had made the payment in at the start of the period and succeeded on all issues at trial. Given the judge's conclusions as to the unreasonableness of the claimant's conduct in relation to the proceedings an order that the claimant pay half of the defendant's costs from the date of the written offer to the date of the Part 36 payment was appropriate.[99]

Where a defendant made two Part 36 payments and a written offer to settle and the award of damages exceeded the total paid in, the claimant was entitled to all its costs up to the date of the second payment in and to 70 per cent thereafter because of the way it had conducted the litigation.[1]

A Part 36 payment or offer should be regarded as the best to which a party is prepared to go and if the claimant recovers more than the payment in he is entitled to his costs and should not be deprived of them by reason of a comparison with his Part 36 offer. The costs order should reflect the fact that the claimant had not been frank about material matters but where the claimant has not exaggerated its claim, which was not unreasonable or too large, it being put forward in good faith and where there were reasonable grounds for advancing it, the court would not reduce the claimant's ordinary entitlement to costs on the basis that it had not been successful.[2]

A Part 36 offer terminates on its rejection and can no longer be accepted unless the party making the offer makes it clear that the offer remains open

---

[99] *Amber v Stacey* [2001] 2 All E.R. 88, CA.
[1] *Firle Investments Ltd v Datapoint International Ltd* [2001] EWCA Civ 1106.
[2] *Quorum A-S v Schramm* [2001] EWHC Comm, November 21, Thomas J.

notwithstanding its rejection. Even if an offer is not terminated by rejection it lapses after a reasonable period of time. In the particular case the court held that that period expired when the parties received the draft judgment.[3] In complex litigation where a detailed Part 36 offer or payment is made in the course of intensive preparation for trial, a period longer than 21 days may be required to consider whether or not to accept the offer or payment. The Court of Appeal held that the presumption that a claimant who fails to better a payment in should be treated as the unsuccessful party from the date fixed for acceptance can be dislodged in special circumstances, for example where the defendant has withheld material and has not allowed the claimant to make a proper appraisal of the defendant's case. There is no principle that a defendant at fault for failing to amend his case timeously should in fact provide the claimant with additional time for accepting payment in.[4]

Where a Part 36 payment is not accepted by a claimant he should not automatically be liable for costs on the indemnity basis. The question will always be: is there something in the conduct of the action or the circumstances of the case which takes the case out of the norm in a way which justifies an order for indemnity costs? Where a judge makes an order for costs other than the normal order he should explain the basis for it.[5]

In lengthy and complex litigation involving a mother and son the court at first instance decided that the general rule that the unsuccessful party should pay the costs should be set aside and each side should pay its own costs. The Court of Appeal held that the judge's exercise of discretion was flawed because he had failed to address the question whether the outcome had been more advantageous to the claimant than her Part 36 offer and if so whether he should make a costs order in her favour under CPR r.36.21. The judge was not entitled to disregard the specific provisions of CPR r.36.21 on the basis that he had taken the offers into account under CPR r.44.3(4)(c). It was not unjust to make the order for which CPR r.36.21 provided. The claimant was entitled to costs on the indemnity basis from the latest date on which the defendant could have accepted the Part 36 offer without needed the permission of the court together with interest on those costs of 4 per cent over base rate.[6]

Where a claimant had beaten an initial payment into court but had not beaten a subsequent payment in, the initial payment in was irrelevant when exercising the discretion as to costs. The claimant was awarded its costs up to the date of the second payment in.[7] The court indicated that the sanctions

---

[3] *Pitchmastic Plc v Burse Construction Ltd (No.2)* [2000] EW HC TCC, May 19, Dyson J.
[4] *Factortame Ltd v Secretary of State for Transport* [2002] EWCA Civ 22.
[5] *Excelsior Commercial and Industrial Holdings Ltd v Salisbury Hammer Aspden & Johnson* [2002] EWCA Civ 879 and see *Royal Mail Group Plc v I-CD Publishing (UK) Ltd* [2004] EWHC (Ch) February 13, Lloyd J.
[6] *Neave v Neave* EWCA Civ February 6, 2003.
[7] *Johnsey Estates 1990 Ltd v Secretary of State for the Environment, Transport and the Regions* [2001] EWCA Civ 535; [2001] L. & T.R. 32, CA.

of Rule 36.21 relate only to failure to accept a genuine offer to settle and not some tactical ploy (*e.g.* an offer to accept 99 per cent of the claim) for the purpose of advancing a claim under Rule 36.21.[8] The defendants appealed unsuccessfully and the claimants sought their costs of the appeal on the indemnity basis. In dismissing that application the Court of Appeal held that a claimant may make a Part 36 offer for the purpose of protecting himself against (a) the costs of the first instance proceedings; or (b) the costs of an appeal, but an offer made for the first purpose does not provide protection for the second. If the claimants had wished to obtain protection for the second purpose they should have made a made a further offer in the appeal proceedings.[9]

Once a claimant has accepted a payment into court the court has no discretion as to the basis of costs and CPR 36.21 has no application. Where quantum has not been assessed by the court, costs are payable on the standard basis by virtue of CPR r.36.13(4).[10]

Service of a Part 36 offer is effected when the offer is received by the offeree without the need to comply with the formal rules as to service in Part 6. The fact that solicitors had indicated that they were unwilling to receive service by fax was insufficient to prevent time, in respect of the offer, from running from the date of the fax.[11]

Group litigation

2–060   In group litigation arising out of child abuse eight of the claimants made Part 36 offers. In the case of four of the claimants the award of damages exceeded the offers made. The judge awarded interest under CPR r.36.21(2) and indemnity costs but no interest on those costs. On appeal, the Court of Appeal increased the general damages in all cases where Part 36 offers had been made with the result that the award of damages of all eight claimants exceeded the Part 36 offers. The Court of Appeal held that the order awarding Part 36 interest should run from the date of the Judge's original judgment and not from the date of the Court of Appeal judgment and that the Judge should have awarded interest on the indemnity costs. With regard to those claimants who were not party to the appeal the court joined them to the appeal. The sealed order on the main appeal was not final in the sense of precluding the court from considering the position under Part 36.[12]

---

[8] *P & O Nedlloyd BV v Utanko Ltd*—reported as: *East West Corporation v DKBS 1912* [2002] EWHC 83 (comm); [2002] 2 Lloyd's Rep. 182, Thomas J.

[9] *East West Corporation v DKBS 1912 (Costs)* [2003] EWCA Civ 174, *The Times*, February, 21, 2003 CA and see—*CEL Group Ltd v Nedlloyd Lines UK Ltd* [2003] EWCA Civ 1871.

[10] *Dyson Ltd v Hoover Ltd (No.2)*, unreported October 21, 2002, Jacob J.

[11] *Charles v NTL Group* [2002] EWCA Civ, December 13.

[12] *R v Bryn Alyn Community (Holdings)* [2003] EWCA Civ 784.

Claim and counterclaim

In a case where both claim and counterclaim failed, rendering the claimant   2–061
the effective winner, an offer by the defendant was found to be insufficiently
clear when it purported to settle the claim for a specified sum plus a
contribution to the claimant's costs. The Court of Appeal held that the offer
letter was an offer to enter into serious negotiations rather than a finalised
and clear offer. The question of legal costs was not defined or limited by "a
contribution to [the claimants] legal costs". There was no offer in a
particular sum or any agreement to pay a proportion of that sum.[13]

Deduction of benefits

The Court of Appeal has given guidance on the application of CPR r.36.23.   2–062
There is no machinery in the Social Security (Recovery of Benefits) Act 1997
for taking into account a finding of contributory negligence. The party liable
was required to pay the full amount of the certificate and there is no appeal
available either to the claimant or to the compensator. Where the certificate
was for a sum which exceeded any realistic quantification of the relevant
head of damage this would inevitably impinge on the general damages if the
certificate was taken into account in full for the purposes of a Part 36
payment. That result could not have been intended by Parliament since the
purpose of Section 8 was clearly to ring fence the general damages. CPR
r.36.23(3)(b) required the payment notice to state the name and the amount
of any benefit by which the gross amount was reduced in accordance with
the Act in the particular case. The defendant had not carried out this
calculation and the court found that the offer was not a proper and effective
Part 36 payment. The touchstone was that the claimant was entitled to the
full value of his general damages claim. If for instance a miscalculation by
the compensator as to the relevant amount of recoverable damages
impinged on the general damages figure but the Part 36 payment had been
properly made, justice required the court to exercise its discretion under
CPR 36.20.[14]

Interest and costs on the indemnity basis

While the provisions of Part 36 contemplate that a Part 36 offer might   2–063
include an offer as to interest, the draftsman of the rule could not have
contemplated that uplift interest should be any part of the offer to be taken

---

[13] *Perry Press T/A Pereds v Chipperfield* [2003] EWCA Civ, March 25.
[14] *Williams v Devon CC* [2003] EWCA Civ 365.

into account in determining the applicability of the rule.[15] Where defendants had not acted unreasonably in resisting an appeal and their conduct of the appeal was not in any way improper, the court had a wide discretion under CPR rule 44.3, to hold that this was not the rare case in which indemnity costs were appropriate.[16]

The power to award enhanced interest is designed to make a material difference to the final award and to force the parties to concentrate on the likely outcome of their dispute.[17]

The entitlement to enhanced interest does not apply where a defendant is found liable for a figure greater than that contained in the claimant's Part 36 offer, where summary judgment is obtained against the defendant.[18] In *Petrotrade Inc v Texaco Ltd*, the Court of Appeal explained why an order for the payment of indemnity costs made under Rule 36.21 should not be regarded as penal. "It would be wrong to regard the rule as producing penal consequences. An order for indemnity costs does not enable a claimant to receive more costs than he has incurred. Its practical effect is to avoid his costs being assessed at a lesser figure" (*per* Lord Woolf M.R.)

In a libel trial where the claimant's Part 36 offer was successful the Judge refused to order interest on damages or to make an order for indemnity costs. That was a question for the judge to determine in the exercise of his discretion and the Court of Appeal could only interfere if satisfied that the decision was so perverse that the judge must have fallen into error. In his judgment the Judge referred to "the modern presumption in favour of indemnity costs which still carries something of a stigma and is bound to be interpreted as a indication of the court's disapproval of the defendant's conduct". The decision in *Petrotrade* quoted above was not available to the judge. The court allowed the appeal and awarded the claimant costs on the indemnity basis with interest at rate of 4 per cent above base rate from the date upon which the work was done or liability for a disbursement was incurred. Interest was to run until the date of judgment, and thereafter interest on damages and costs would be payable at the judgment rate under section 17 of the Judgments Act 1838.[19]

The fact that a judge has been misled about the effectiveness of a Part 36 offer entitles the Court of Appeal to interfere with the judge's discretion when determining whether costs should have been assessed on the standard or the indemnity basis.[20]

---

[15] See *Mitchell v James* [2002] EWCA Civ 997.

[16] *Ali Reza-Delta Transport Co Ltd v United Arab Shipping Co SAG* [2003] EWCA Civ 811; [2003] 3 All E.R. 1297, CA.

[17] *Little v George Little Sebire & Co* (enhanced interest), *The Times*, November 17, 1999, David Foskett Q.C.

[18] *Petrotrade Inc v Texaco Ltd* [2002] 1 W.L.R. 947; [2001] 4 All E.R. 853, CA.

[19] *McPhilemy v Times Newspapers Ltd (No.2)* [2001] EWCA Civ 933; [2001] 4 All E.R. 861.

[20] *Nash v Daniel* [2002] EWCA Civ, July 9.

A term as to costs is not within the scope of a Part 36 offer. Although an offer may contain terms as to costs, to which the court should have regard in exercising its discretion at the end of the trial, such terms cannot be used to obtain an order for costs on the indemnity basis. The question of whether a judgment was more advantageous than a Part 36 offer was intended to refer to the substantive issues in the judgment rather than the ancillary issues of costs.[21]

L. DISCONTINUANCE

A claimant may discontinue all or part of a claim at any time but must, in certain circumstances, obtain the permission of the court.[22] Where a claimant discontinues without the permission of the court the defendant may apply to have the notice of discontinuance set aside.[23] Discontinuance against any defendant takes place on the date when notice of discontinuance is served upon him, the proceedings being brought to an end as against the defendant on that date: this does not affect proceedings to deal with any question of costs.[24]

    2–064

A claimant who discontinues is liable for costs incurred by a defendant on or before the date on which the notice of discontinuance was served. The court may order otherwise.[25] If proceedings are only partly discontinued the claimant's liability is limited to the costs relating to the part of the proceedings which are discontinued, and unless the court orders otherwise the costs which the claimant is liable to pay must not be assessed until the conclusion of the rest of the proceedings.[26] These provisions do not apply to claims allocated to the small claims track.

Where proceedings are partly discontinued and the court has ordered the claimant to pay costs, which the claimant fails to pay within 21 days of those costs either being agreed or assessed by the court, the court may stay the remainder of the proceedings until the claimant pays the whole of the costs which he is liable to pay.[27]

Claimants who discontinued an action were ordered to pay the defendant's costs on the indemnity basis for the period during which they acted unreasonably in trying to delay the trial of the action.[28]

---

[21] *Mitchell v James* [2002] EWCA Civ 997.
[22] CPR r.38.2.
[23] CPR r.38.4.
[24] CPR r.38.5.
[25] See *Camiller v Commissioner of Police for the Metropolis, The Times*, June 8, 1999, CA (discontinuance after jury failed to reach a verdict).
[26] CPR r.38.6.
[27] CPR r.38.8.
[28] *Naskaris v ANS Plc* [2002] EWHC 1782 (Ch), Blackburne J.

Where a claimant discontinued judicial review proceedings with permission of the court and the respondent was ordered to pay the claimant's costs, on assessment, the claimant's costs were limited to one only of several issue raised in the claim. On appeal, it was held that assessment is a different procedure from the decision whether a party was to be awarded all its costs or only part. The judge's order could only mean that the claimants had been awarded all their costs.[29]

In a libel action the claimant discontinued where his claim became worthless, not through any fault of his own but due to the defendant's supervening bankruptcy. The court held that the discontinuance could not be equated with defeat or an acknowledgement of likely defeat; permission was granted to discontinue with no order as to costs.[30]

M. APPLICATIONS, JUDGMENTS, ORDERS

Applications (Part 23)

2–065   Once a claim has started, an application must be made to the court by means of an application notice in which the applicant states the intention to seek a court order. An applicant may make an application without filing an application notice if this is permitted by a rule or practice direction or the court dispenses with the requirement for an application notice.[31]

The court may deal with an application without a hearing if the parties agree the terms of the order sought, or that the court should dispose of the application without a hearing, or the court does not consider that a hearing would be appropriate.[32]

Judgments and orders (Part 40)

2–066   A judgment or order takes effect from the date when it is given or made, or such later date as the court may specify.[33] A court officer may enter and seal certain agreed judgments or orders, (including a judgment or order for the payment, assessment or waiver of costs, or such other provision for costs as may be agreed), if none of the parties is a litigant in person; and the approval of the court is not required before an agreed order can be made.[34]

---

[29] R (Chorion Plc) v Westminster City Council [2002] EWCA Civ 1126; The Times, October 21, 2002, CA.
[30] Etherton v WPBSA (Promotions) Ltd EWHC QBD [2001], December 12, Gray J.
[31] CPR r.23.1, 23.2 and 23.3.
[32] CPR r.23.8.
[33] CPR r.40.7(1).
[34] CPR r.40.6(2) and (3)(b)(vii).

Where interest is payable on a judgment[35] interest begins to run from the date that judgment is given, unless the rules or practice direction make a different provision or the court orders otherwise. The court may order that interest shall begin to run from a date before the date that judgment is given.[36] The court may make an order that a party must pay interest on costs from or until a certain date including a date before judgment.[37]

The court has a discretion under CPR r.44.3(6)(g) to make a decision on interest on costs which accords with the justice of the circumstances of the case.[38]

A party must comply with a judgment or order for the payment of an amount of money (including costs) within 14 days of the judgment or order unless a different date is specified; the rules make a different provision; or the court has stayed the proceedings or judgment.[39]

Where the court gives judgment on both a claim and a counterclaim, if there is a balance in favour of one of the party it may order the parties whose judgment is for the lesser amount to pay the balance. The court may make a separate order as to costs against each party.[40]

The court may correct any accidental slip or omission in a judgment or order at any time and a party may apply for such a correction without notice.[41]

---

[35] Under s.17 of the Judgments Act 1838 or s.74 of the County Courts Act 1984.
[36] CPR r.40.8.
[37] CPR r.44.3(6)(g).
[38] *Powell v Herefordshire HA* [2002] EWCA Civ 1786; [2003] 3 All E.R. 253.
[39] CPR r.40.11.
[40] CPR r.40.13.
[41] CPR r.40.12.

CHAPTER 3

The relationship with the client

A. SOLICITORS

Information on costs to be provided to the client

3–001 In 1986, the Council of the Law Society issued a set written professional standards concerning responsibility for clients' matters, communication with clients and information on costs. This gave rise to the so-called "client care letter" which gave the client the relevant information. As a result of Rule 15 of the Solicitors' Practice Rules 1990 and the Solicitors' Costs Information and Client Care Code 1999.[1] Clients must be given the best information possible in relation to a number of matters including the likely overall costs of the work being undertaken.

In litigation where the court makes a costs order against a legally represented party and that party is not present when the order is made, it is the duty of the solicitor to notify the client in writing of the costs order made no later than seven days after the solicitor receives notice of the order.[2] There is similar provision where the court makes an order in the exercise of its powers in relation to misconduct.[3] When the solicitor gives an estimate to the court in accordance with section 6 of the Costs Practice Direction a copy of the estimate (which sets out the amount of costs incurred to date and an estimate of future costs) must be sent to the client. The purpose of all these measures is to keep the client as fully informed as possible in relation to the costs which are being incurred.

---

[1] See para.16–002.
[2] CPR r.44.2.
[3] CPR r.44.14(3).

Retainer

Retainer is the name given to the contract which exists between a solicitor   **3–002**
and the client. Where there is no retainer the relationship of solicitor and
client does not exist and the solicitor is not entitled to render a bill.[4]

The contract between the solicitor and the client may be on any terms
which are mutually agreeable provided that the terms do not infringe the
restrictions laid down in Part III of the Solicitors Act 1974 or the statutory
requirements relating to conditional fee agreements. Specific types of
retainer agreement include: contentious business agreements, non contentious business agreements and conditional fee agreements.[5]

If a solicitor has acquired relevant knowledge concerning a former client
during the course of acting for him he must not accept instructions to act
against him.[6] If grounds exist for fearing that a solicitor has a conflict of
interest in litigation it is not a point for the judge to take of his own motion,
it is for the opponent to do so. Even if there is quite modest material to
found the complaint it is clear from the decision of the House of Lords in
Bolkiah v KPMG[7] that caution has to be exercised and that if the solicitor
does not stand down he may be restrained by injunction from acting. The
essential starting point is the objection by the opposing party whose
interests and confidentiality the doctrine is there to protect.[8] It is for the
client to establish that the solicitor is in possession of potentially relevant
information and for the solicitor to establish the heavy burden of showing
that there is no risk of inadvertent disclosure.[9]

Written retainer

A retainer may arise by implication or orally but it is most satisfactory if the   **3–003**
retainer is in writing. In some cases absence of writing may render the
retainer unenforceable, *e.g.* where statute or rule requires the retainer to be
evidenced in writing, as in the case of liquidators and trustees in bankruptcy
and where there is a conditional fee agreement. In contentious business it is
the duty of the solicitor to obtain written instructions from his client before
commencing proceedings. In an emergency the proceedings may be commenced provided that written instructions are obtained as soon as possible
afterwards. What is required is "a note or memorandum signed by the party
to be charged therewith or some other person by him lawfully authorised"
which clearly identifies the nature and extent of the retainer.[10] The insertion

---

[4] *J.H. Milner & Son v Percy Bilton Ltd* [1966] 1 W.L.R. 1582. See also *Oswald Hickson Collier & Co v Carter-Ruck* [1984] A.C. 720.
[5] See Chapter 5.
[6] *Re A Firm of Solicitors* [1992] 1 KB 959.
[7] [1999] 2 W.L.R. 215.
[8] *Hood Sale Makers v Berthon Boat Co Ltd* [1999] EWCA Civ 1079.
[9] *Re a Firm of Solicitors* [2000] 1 Lloyd's Rep. 31, Timothy Walker J.
[10] *Allen v Bone* (1841) 4 Beav. 493. See also *R.E. Gray v Coles* (1891) 65 L.T. 743.

by solicitors of a "one-sided", provision into a contract between them and a client justified the construction of ambiguous provisions in that contract *contra proferentem*, that is in the client's favour.[11]

Oral retainer

3–004   Where a solicitor accepts an oral retainer there is a risk that if there is a subsequent dispute as to the existence of the retainer and there is no evidence other than the conflicting statements of the solicitor and the client, the presumption will be raised in favour of the client that there was no retainer and the solicitor will be treated as having acted without authority.[12] Where affidavits (witness statements) are filed more weight is given to the statement of the client than to that of the solicitor since the onus of proof of retainer is on the solicitor.[13]

> "On this question of retainer, I would observe that where there is a difference between a solicitor and his client on it, the courts have said for the last 100 years or more that the word of the client is to be preferred to the word of the solicitor, or, at any rate more weight is to be given to it, see *Crossley v Crowther* per Sir George J Turner V.–C.; *re Paine* per Warrington J. The reason is plain. It is because the client is ignorant and the solicitor is, or should be, learned. If the solicitor does not take the precaution of getting a written retainer, he has only himself to thank for being at variance with his client over it and must take the consequences."[14]

Implied retainer

3–005   The existence of a retainer may be implied from the conduct of the client, *i.e.* he may be estopped from denying that the solicitor is entitled to act on his behalf.[15] Where a solicitor commences proceedings without instructions it is open to the client to ratify what has been done and to instruct the solicitor to continue.[16] The application by a client for an order for detailed assessment of the solicitor's bill acts as an estoppel preventing the client from denying the existence of the retainer.[17] There is of course no estoppel where the solicitor seeks an order for a detailed assessment of his own bill; however, once the order for detailed assessment has been made, it is arguable that it is no longer open to the client to allege that there is no retainer.

---

[11] *Re a Debtor* (No.1594 of 1992), *The Times*, December 8, 1992, Knox J.
[12] *Allen v Bone*, above; *Morgan v Blyth* [1891] 1 Ch. 337 at 355.
[13] *Re Paine* [1912] 28 T.L.R. 201 and *Griffiths v Evans* [1953] 1 W.L.R. 1424 at 1428, CA.
[14] *per* Denning L.J. *Griffiths v Evans* [1953] 2 All E.R. 1364 at 1369.
[15] *Blyth v Fladgate* [1891] 1 Ch. 337.
[16] *Danish Mercantile Co. Ltd v Beaumont* [1951] Ch. 680, CA.
[17] *Re Jones* (1887) 36 Ch. D. 105.

The leaving of papers, including the claim in an action, with a solicitor has been held to be conduct sufficient to establish a retainer.[18] Similarly, where a client consents to a consolidation order. In a case where there are several defendants who have separately instructed the same solicitors, the order to consolidate will operate as a joint retainer by the defendants and they are liable accordingly.[19] On the other hand, failure by a client who has been joined as a claimant in a suit without his authority, to take steps to have his name removed from the record, will not of itself be sufficient to imply a retainer but the client will of course be unable to take the benefit from a successful action without having to bear the solicitor's costs.[20]

Retainer for an entire contract

As a general rule when a client retains a solicitor for a particular purpose there is an entire contract, *i.e.* the solicitor contracts to finish the business for which he was retained.[21] This rule applies both to contentious business and non-contentious business. The rule is variable and regard has to be had to the particular circumstances of each case,[22] including arbitrations.[23]   3–006.1

Termination of retainer

When considering termination it is necessary to decide whether the retainer is an "entire contract" or not. An entire contract is one to complete the work for which the retainer was given. This is most easily demonstrated by instructions to conduct a particular piece of litigation, or the conveyance of a particular property. The basic common law rule is that where an entire contract exists, a solicitor cannot discharge himself until the completion of the business unless there is good reason for doing so and the client has been given reasonable notice.[24] In contentious business if a solicitor requests the client to pay a reasonable sum on account of costs incurred or to be incurred and the client refuses or fails to do so, the refusal or failure is deemed to be good cause enabling the solicitor, on giving reasonable notice to the client, to withdraw from the retainer.[25] Since solicitors are entitled to deliver interim bills at any natural break which occurs in the course of proceedings, termination of an entire contract is possible from time to time.[26]   3–006.2

---

[18] *Parrott v Echells* (1839) 3 J.P. 771.
[19] *Anderson v Boynton* (1849) 13 Q.B. 308.
[20] *Re Becket, Purnell v Paine* [1918] 2 Ch. 72, CA.
[21] *Re Romer and Haslam* [1893] 2 Q.B. 286 at 298.
[22] *Underwood Son & Piper v Lewis* [1894] 2 Q.B. 306, CA.
[23] *Warmingtons v McMurray* [1937] 1 All E.R. 562, CA.
[24] *Re Hall and Barker* [1878] 9 Ch. D. 538.
[25] Solicitors Act 1974, s.65(2).
[26] *Re Hall and Barker*, above; *Davidson v Jones-Fenleigh* (1980) 124 S.J. 204, CA.

Where the retainer is not an entire contract, such as where the solicitor is employed to do non-contentious work over a period, on the basis that bills will be rendered and paid as the matters proceed, termination may occur for a number of reasons. In such a case the retainer may be terminated at the end of a particular period if it was for a fixed time.[27] If the client fails to provide sufficient funds to cover counsel's fees and disbursements when reasonably requested to do so, the solicitor is entitled to withdraw.[28]

The death, insanity or bankruptcy of either solicitor or the client will also terminate the retainer.[29] The retainer is ended immediately upon a client's death unless the personal representatives ratify the retainer and so make themselves liable.[30] The financial embarrassment of the solicitor, short of bankruptcy, is insufficient of itself to terminate the retainer,[31] but where a retainer has been given to a firm and the partnership is subsequently dissolved the retainer is effectively terminated.[32]

If a solicitor is imprisoned or disqualified from practice or assigns his business to another, the retainer will in each case be treated as terminated.[33]

If the solicitor has good cause to terminate the retainer, this may be done by giving reasonable notice setting out the reasons.[34] Good cause includes: failure to provide funds for disbursements; the discovery that an action which has been properly commenced cannot be maintained; where the solicitor has been asked to do something dishonourable; and where the solicitor is hindered or prevented from conducting the action properly by the client. Whatever the cause it should be set out in precise terms.[35] If the solicitor terminates the retainer without good cause he is not entitled to recover any remuneration on a quantum meruit basis.[36]

In contentious business so long as the solicitor's name remains on the record he is deemed by the court still to be acting for the client and is under a duty both to the court and to the client to act accordingly while his name remains on the record. The solicitor is entitled to charge the client for any

---

[27] *J.H. Milner and Son v Percy Bilton Ltd* [1966] 1 W.L.R. 1582.
[28] *Warmingtons v McMurray* [1936] 1 All E.R. 562, CA.
[29] *Pool v Pool* (1889) 58 L.J.P. 67; *Re Bentinck v Bentinck* (1893) 37 S.J. 233; *Whitehead v Lord* (1852) 7 Ex. Ch. 691; *Harris v Osbourn* (1934) 2 Cr. and M. 629; *Underwood Son & Piper v Lewis* [1894] 2 Q.B. 306; *Young v Toynbee* [1910] 1 K.B. 215; *Re Moss* (1866) L.R. 2 Eq. 345.
[30] *Re Bentinck v Bentinck*, above.
[31] *Re Smith* (1841) 4 Beav. 309.
[32] *Rawlinson v Moss* (1861) 30 L.J. Ch. 797.
[33] *Scott v Fenning* (1845) 15 L.J. Ch. 88; *Colgrave v Manley* (1823) turn. and R. 400.
[34] *Robins v Goldingham* (1872) L.R. 13 Eq. 440; *Lawrence v Potts* (1834) 6 C. and P. 428; *Underwood Son & Piper v Lewis* [1894] 2 Q.B. 306; *Forney v Bushe* (1954) 104 L.Jo. 604.
[35] *Re Wingfield v Blew* [1904] 2 Ch. 655 at 684, *per* Cozens-Hardy L.J.
[36] *Wild v Simpson* [1919] 2 K.B. 544.

work necessarily done between termination of the retainer and removal from the record.[37]

Where the retainer has been terminated by the death of the client, the solicitor is entitled to sue the personal representatives of the client in respect of the costs of work done while the retainer was in existence during the client's lifetime.[38]

In the case of the death of a solicitor, there may be a difficulty in the personal representatives recovering the costs of work done prior to the solicitor's death since the retainer is a contract for personal services. This difficulty does not arise in the event of a retainer to a firm.[39]

Where a retainer is terminated without breach or frustration or is repudiated by the client, the solicitor is entitled to recover costs for work done up to the date of termination.[40] Conversely, where a retainer relating to an entire contract is repudiated by the client following the unjustified withdrawal by the solicitor or some other breach, the client is not liable to pay for any costs for work done under the retainer.[41]

In respect of a retainer which is not an entire contract whether terminated by the solicitor justifiably or not, the solicitor can be compelled to deliver up the papers "subject to the lien", on the new solicitor undertaking to return them when no longer required, and to allow the original solicitor access to them in the meantime.[42] Where the client discharges the solicitor without just cause, the solicitor is entitled to refuse to hand over the papers until his lien is satisfied.[43] A solicitor is under no obligation to deliver up or produce or to allow inspection of the papers for the benefit of the client.[44]

Conflict of interest

There is no general rule of law to the effect that a solicitor should never act 3–007 for both parties in a transaction where their interests might conflict. The position is that a solicitor might act provided that the informed consent of both clients has been obtained. Informed consent means consent given in the knowledge that there is a conflict between the parties and that as a result the solicitor might be disabled from disclosing to each party the full knowledge which he possessed as to the transaction or might be disabled from giving advice to one party which conflicted with the interests of the other. If the

---

[37] *Lady De La Pole v Dick* (1885) 29 Ch. D 351.
[38] *Whitehead v Lord* (1852) 7 Ex. Ch. 691.
[39] *Underwood Son & Piper v Lewis* [1894] 2 Q.B. 306.
[40] *Re Lane Joynt* [1920] I.R. 228; *Colgrave v Manley* [1823] Turn. & R. 400.
[41] *Re Lane Joynt* above; *Colgrave v Manley*, above.
[42] *Gamlen Chemical Co. (U.K.) Ltd v Rochem Ltd* [1980] 1 W.L.R. 614, CA; as to lien generally see Chapter 13.
[43] *Hannaford v Hannaford* (1871) 24 L.T. 86.
[44] *Re Rapid Road Transit Co.* [1990] 1 Ch. 96.

parties are content to proceed upon that basis the solicitor might properly act.[45]

Lord Donaldson M.R. in *Saminadhen v Chan* stated:

> "I can conceive of no circumstances in which it would be proper for a solicitor who has acted for a defendant in criminal proceedings, the retainer having been terminated, to then act for a co-defendant where there is a cut-throat defence between the two defendants."[46]

If a solicitor has acquired relevant knowledge concerning a former client during the course of acting for him he must not accept instructions to act against him.[47] If grounds exist for fearing that a solicitor has a conflict of interest in litigation it is not a point for the judge to take of his own motion, it is for the opponent to do so. Even if there is quite modest material to found the complaint it is clear from the decision of the House of Lords in *Bolkiah v KPMG*[48] that caution has to be exercised and that if the solicitor does not stand down he may be restrained by injunction from acting. The essential starting point is the objection by the opposing party whose interests and confidentiality the doctrine is there to protect.[49] It is for the client to establish that the solicitor is in possession of potentially relevant information and for the solicitor to establish the heavy burden of showing that there is no risk of inadvertent disclosure.[50]

Security for costs and termination of retainer

Contentious business

3–008 Under the Solicitors Act 1974 it is open to a solicitor to take security from his client for his costs whether ascertained by detailed assessment or otherwise in respect of any contentious business to be done by him.[51] If a solicitor asks his client to make a payment of a reasonable sum on account of costs incurred or to be incurred in the conduct of contentious business and the client refuses or fails within a reasonable time to make the payment, the refusal or failure is deemed to be good cause whereby the solicitor may, upon giving reasonable notice to the client, withdraw from the retainer.[52]

---

[45] *Clarke Boyce v Mouat* [1993] 3 W.L.R. 1021, see also *Bolkiah v KPMG* [1999] 2 W.L.R. 215 and *Hood Sailmakers Ltd v Berthon Boat Co. Ltd* [1999] EWCA Civ 1079.
[46] [1992] 1 All E.R. 963, CA at 963.
[47] *Re A Firm of Solicitors* [1992] 1 K.B. 959.
[48] [1999] 2 W.L.R. 215.
[49] *Hood Sale Makers v Berthon Boat Co Ltd* [1999] EWCA Civ 1079.
[50] *Re a Firm of Solicitors* [2000] 1 Lloyd's Rep. 31, Timothy Walker J.
[51] Solicitors Act 1974, s.65(1).
[52] Solicitors Act 1974, s.65(2).

What amounts to a "reasonable time" depends upon the particular facts of each case.[53] At common law a solicitor can take security from his client for costs already due and the security is good for the amount justly due with interest.[54] No security may be taken in respect of future costs.[55]

An agreement to give security for costs to be ascertained by detailed assessment need not be in writing. But if the agreement contains terms, *e.g.* as to interest which might amount to a contentious business agreement, such an agreement would be invalid if not in writing in accordance with section 59 of the 1974 Act.[56]

The court will reopen a transaction and may set aside the security where it has been given in circumstances which amount to fraud or undue influence[57] or where there has been no proper settlement of accounts which could amount to a binding repayment and agreement of the amount.[58] Unless the matter is governed by a written agreement under section 57 or section 59 of the 1974 Act, the mere giving of security by a client does not relieve the solicitor from the obligation to deliver a bill of costs and to have that bill assessed if the client so desires.[59]

If the security takes the form of a mortgage it would seem that the client must be separately advised otherwise the court may well be persuaded to set aside the transaction and only enforce the security for such sum as it is equitable that the client should pay, bearing in mind all the circumstances of the case. This could well be less than the amount ascertained on detailed assessment.[60]

Non-contentious business

Where the business is non-contentious the solicitor may take from his client security for the payment of any costs, including the amount of any interest to which the solicitor may become entitled under Article 14 of the Solicitors' (Non-Contentious Business) Remuneration Order 1994.[61]   3–009

---

[53] *Burton v Griffiths* (1843) 11 M. & W. 817, 1 L.T.O.S. 289; *Poole v Smith Car Sales (Balham) Ltd* [1962] 1 W.L.R. 744, CA.

[54] *Williams v Piggott* (1825) Jac. 598; *Cheslyn v Dalby* (1836) 2 Y. & C. Ex. 170; *Nelson v Booth* (1857) 27 L.J. Ch. 110; *Radcliffe & Walker v Anderson* (1860) E.B. & E. 819; *Saunderson v Glass* (1742) 2 Atk. 296; *Morgan v Higgins* (1859) 1 Giff 270.

[55] *Pitcher v Rigby* (1821) 9 Price 79; *Jones v Tripp* (1821) Jac. 322; *Booth v Creswicke* (1844) 13 L.J. Ch. 217; *Williams v Piggott* above; *Shaw v Neale and Remnant* (1858) 6 H.L. Cas. 581.

[56] *Jonesco v Evening Standard Co.* (1932) 2 K.B. 340, CA.

[57] *Ward v Sharp* (1884) 53 L.J. Ch. 313; *Walmesley v Booth* (1741) 2 Atk. 275; *Watson v Rodwell* (1879) 11 Ch. D. 150, CA; *Eyre v Hughes* (1876) 2 Ch. D. 148.

[58] *David v Parry* (1859) 1 Giff. 174; *Morgan v Higgins* (1859) 1 Giff. 270.

[59] *Brown v Pring* (1750) 1 Ves. Sen. 407; *Morgan v Higgins*, above.

[60] *Cowdry v Day* (1859) 1 Giff. 316; *Cockburn v Edwards* (1881) 18 Ch. D. 449, CA; *Craddock v Roger* (1884) 53 L.J. Ch. 968.

[61] Solicitors' (Non-Contentious Business) Remuneration Order 1994, art.12(3).

B. COUNSEL

Direct access by certain clients

3–010   The BarDirect allow an authorised BarDirect client other than a solicitor to instruct a barrister. A barrister must not accept any instructions from a BarDirect client if he considers it in the interests of the client that a solicitor should be instructed and a barrister must decline to act further in such a matter if he considers it in the interests of the client that a solicitor should be instructed at that point.[62]

BarDirect Recognition Regulations

3–011   Barristers may accept instructions from clients who have been approved by the BarDirect Committee. The Committee will issue a licence to the client in such form as it may decide. The Code of Conduct of the Bar (including the requirements as to insurance) applies to BarDirect work as it applies to other work undertaken by a barrister in independent practice.[63] The Schedules to the BarDirect Recognition Regulations set out those who are deemed to be authorised BarDirect clients.[64]

Records

3–012   A barrister who accepts instructions from a BarDirect client must keep a case record which sets out:

(a) the date of receipt of the instructions, the name of the BarDirect client, the name of the case and any requirements of the professional client as to time-limits;

(b) the date on which the brief or instructions were accepted;

(c) the dates of subsequent instructions of the dispatch of advices and other written work, of conferences and of telephone conversations;

(d) when agreed, the fee.

The barrister must also retain:

(a) copies of instructions;

(b) copies of all advices given and documents drafted or approved;

(c) a list of all documents enclosed with any instructions;

(d) notes of all conferences and of all advice given on the telephone.

---

[62] BarDirect Rules.
[63] Code of Conduct of the Bar, Part IV.
[64] BarDirect Recognition Regulations Schs 1 and 2.

PART II

Entitlement to Costs

CHAPTER 4

General Principles Of Entitlement To Costs

A. SOLICITORS

Solicitor and client costs

A solicitor becomes entitled to charge the client in accordance with the terms of the retainer between them. In order to establish entitlement to the costs the solicitor must deliver a bill to the client which complies with the statutory requirements.[1]

4–001

Costs information for clients

The Law Society has set out in Practice Rule 15 and the Solicitors' Costs Information and Client Care Code what is expected of practitioners in relation to the giving of information on costs. Practice Rule 15 is designed to ensure that clients know the name and status of the person or persons responsible for the day to day conduct and overall supervision of their matters; and the clients, at all relevant times, should be given appropriate information as to the issues raised and the progress of those matters. The solicitor is also required to give to the client the best information possible as to the likely costs.[2]

4–002.1

Non-contentious business In respect of costs arising out of non-contentious business the Solicitors (Non-Contentious Business) Remuneration Order 1994 provides that a solicitor's costs will be such sum as may be

4–002.2

---

[1] See Solicitors Act 1974, s.69 and para.8–1, *et seq*.
[2] See para.16–002.

fair and reasonable to both the solicitor and entitled person[3] (client) having regard to all circumstances of the case and in particular to the nine factors set out in the Remuneration Order.[4] Donaldson J. stated that the proper approach was "to start by taking a broad look at all the circumstances of the case", and in particular the general nature of the business. This should be followed by systematic consideration of the factors specified in the paragraphs of Article 3 of the Order. In the end it is a value judgment based on "discretion and experience". Donaldson J. conceded that the figure finally reached by the court might not be the right figure and suggested that such a figure probably did not exist: he hoped that it would be a right figure, *i.e.* one which was reasonable in all the circumstances.[5]

Where detailed assessment takes place, if the costs officer allows less than one half of the costs, he is under a duty to bring the facts of the case to the attention of the Law Society.[6] It is not for the costs officer to make a complaint but merely to report the facts to the Law Society. The Law Society will arrange for the matter to be investigated and disciplinary proceedings may then follow. The provisions of the Remuneration Order are without prejudice to the general powers of the Council under the Solicitors Act 1974.[7]

The nine factors to be taken into account are:

(1) the complexity of the matter or the difficulty or novelty of the questions raised;

(2) the skill, labour, specialised knowledge and responsibility involved;

(3) the time spent on the business;

(4) the number and importance of the documents prepared or perused, without regard to length;

(5) the place where and the circumstances in which the business or any part thereof is transacted;

(6) the amount or value of any money or property involved;

(7) whether any land involved is registered land;

---

[3] *i.e.* a client or an entitled third party. An entitled third party means a residuary beneficiary absolutely and immediately (and not contingently) entitled to an inheritance, where a solicitor has charged the estate for his professional costs for acting in the administration of the estate, and either (a) the only personal representatives are solicitors (whether or not acting in a professional capacity); or (b) the only personal representatives are solicitors acting jointly with partners or employees in a professional capacity. Solicitors (Non-Contentious Business) Remuneration Order 1994, art.2.

[4] Solicitors (Non-Contentious Business) Remuneration Order 1994, art.3.

[5] *Property and Reversionary Investment Corp. Ltd v The Secretary of State for the Environment* (1975) 1 W.L.R. 1504; [1975] 2 All E.R. 436.

[6] Solicitors (Non-Contentious Business) Remuneration Order 1994, art.5(1).

[7] *ibid.*, art.5(2).

(8) the importance of the matter to the client;

(9) the approval (express or implied) of the entitled person or the express approval of the testator to

    (i) the solicitor undertaking all or any part of the work giving rise to the costs; or

    (ii) the amount of the costs.[8]

Contentious business On every detailed assessment of costs in respect of any contentious business the costs officer may, in determining the remuneration of the solicitor, have regard to the skill, labour and responsibility involved in the business done by him.[9] In fact on such a detailed assessment, the costs officer would have regard to the factors set out in CPR r.44.5.[10]

    4–003

A client consulting a firm of solicitors must be told if the work will not be undertaken by a qualified solicitor. Where the client is not told, the firm is not entitled to recover its costs if it provided an adviser who was not a solicitor, since this amounts to non-performance of a contract to provide legal services by a solicitor.[11]

Similarly, where a struck off solicitor fraudulently deceives a client into believing that he was a qualified solicitor.[12]

Special provisions as to contentious business done in the county court The remuneration of a solicitor in respect of contentious business carried on in a county court is regulated by sections 59–73 of the Solicitors Act 1974, subject to certain provisions.[13] The amount which may be allowed on the assessment of any costs or bill of costs in respect of any item relating to proceedings in a county court may not exceed the amount which could have been allowed in respect of that item between the parties in those proceedings having regard to the nature of the proceedings and the amount of the claim and of any counterclaim.[14]

    4–004

Unless the solicitor and client have entered into a written agreement which expressly permits payment to the solicitor of an amount of costs greater than that which the client could have recovered from another party to the proceedings, section 74(3) of the 1974 Act applies.[15]

Section 74(3) applies a cap where there are limits under the rules to the level of costs recoverable between the parties. Under the CPR the section still bites where there are fixed costs. Section 74(3) does not have the effect

---

[8] Solicitors (Non-Contentious Business) Remuneration Order 1994, art.3.
[9] Solicitors Act 1974, s.66(b).
[10] See para.7–002 below.
[11] *Pilbrow v Pearless de Rougemont & Co.* [1999] 3 All E.R. 355, CA.
[12] *Adriane Allen Ltd v Fuglers* [2002] EWCA Civ 1655.
[13] Solicitors Act 1974, s.74(1).
[14] Solicitors Act 1974, s.74(3).
[15] CPR r.48.8(1A), s.74(3) Solicitors Act 1974.

of making the assessment between the parties into a cap on the costs as between solicitor and client.[16]

4–005   **Costs of trustees and personal representatives**   Where a person is a party to proceedings in a capacity of trustee or personal representative and it is not a case where costs are payable pursuant to a contract, the general rule is that that person is entitled to be paid his costs of the proceedings insofar as they are not recovered from or paid by any other person, out of any fund held by him as a trustee or personal representative. The costs will be assessed on the indemnity basis.[17]

Community Legal Service funded costs

4–006   Costs payable out of the Community Legal Service (CLS) Fund are payable to the legal representative who has earned them and not to the client. To the extent that there is a shortfall between the amount payable by the CLS Fund to the legal representative and the amount recovered from an opposing party, the client may, by virtue of the statutory charge, have to pay some or all of that shortfall (section 10(7) Access to Justice Act 1999). The statutory charge operates on any contribution paid by the client and also on any property which is recovered or preserved for the client in the proceedings. Although a party to proceedings may have been funded by the CLS Fund it is still possible for the court to make an order for costs against that person with respect to those proceedings, but the liability of the funded client will not exceed the amount, if any, which is a reasonable one for him to pay having regard to all the circumstances, including the financial resources of all the parties and their conduct in connection with the dispute.[18]

While section 11(1) of the Access to Justice Act 1999 provides that costs ordered against an assisted party should not exceed a reasonable amount that protection does not apply to those whose conduct amounts to serious crime. A claimant who obtained legal aid and brought a claim against insurers founded upon fraudulent claims was ordered to pay the defendant's costs on the indemnity basis.[19]

An appellant who was granted a funding certificate which referred only to representation as an appellant was not covered in respect of the costs of a cross appeal. Costs protection under the CLS (Cost Protection) Regulations applies only to costs incurred after the issue of the certificate. The LSC had the power to amend a certificate retrospectively, but unless and until it did so, the appellant was only entitled to costs protection in respect of her own

---

[16] *Lynch v Taylor* [2004] EWHC 89 (QB), Hughes J.
[17] CPR r.48.4.
[18] Access to Justice Act 1999, s.11.
[19] *Jones v Congregational & General Insurance Plc* [2003] EWHC 1027 QB; [2003] 1 W.L.R. 3001, H.H. Judge Chambers Q.C.

appeal. There was a powerful argument for saying that the LSC should not effect such an amendment without giving the other party an opportunity to object. In those circumstances it was insufficient for the other party to say she would be prejudiced by the amendment, in the sense that she would be worse off. It would be necessary to demonstrate that she might have acted in a significantly different way had the original certificate reflected the LSC's intention.[20]

In certain circumstances, in proceedings to which a funded client is a party, and which are finally decided in favour of an unassisted party, the court may make an order for the payment out of the CLS Fund to the unassisted party of the whole or any part of the costs incurred by him in the proceedings.[21] Any application to the Costs Judge under regulation 10(2) of the CLS (Costs) Regulations 2000 following an order under section 11(1) of the Access to Justice Act 1999 has to be made within three months. A successful defendant argued that the Court of Appeal's costs order or the Costs Judge's determination should be postponed until after the underlying action had been resolved, because otherwise the requirement of regulation 5(2) of the Costs Protection Regulations, that the proceedings should have been finally decided in favour of the unassisted party, would mean that the Costs Judge would have no power to make an order against the LSC. The Court of Appeal held that the costs of the appeal should not be adjourned for a lengthy and indefinite period while the proceedings worked their way through to final disposal. An order should be made for the determination of the appellant's liability to pay costs and for any application by the respondent for an order for payment of such costs by the LSC to be referred to the Costs Judge in accordance with regulation 10 of the Costs Regulations. If the Commission took the point that the application was premature the Costs Judge would have power to adjourn until final resolution of the proceedings but that should not be necessary.[22] In the particular case the proceedings in the Court of Appeal had been finally determined and there was no difficulty in the exercise by a Costs Judge of his jurisdiction in relation to the costs of those proceedings.[23]

Transitional provisions preserve the position with regard to existing legal aid certificates. The earlier Regulations and the authorities relating to them are therefore to that extent still relevant.[24]

---

[20] *Hinde v Harbourne* [2003] EWHC 3109 (Ch), Neuberger J. See also *R & T Thew Ltd v Reeves (No.1)* [1982] Q.B. 172 and *R. v Legal Aid Board Ex p. Edwin Coe (A Firm)* [2000] 1 W.L.R. 1909.

[21] Access to Justice Act 1999, s.11.

[22] See *General Accident Fire & Life Assurance Corporation Ltd v Foster* [1972] 3 All E.R. 877, CA where it was held that the relevant proceedings referred to in comparable provisions in the Legal Aid Act 1964 were the proceedings in the Court of Appeal.

[23] *Masterman-Lister v Brutton & Co* [2003] EWCA Civ 70.

[24] Access to Justice Act 1999 (Commencement No.3, Transitional Proceedings and Savings) Order 2000, SI 2000/774.

Where the solicitor nominated in the legal aid certificate ceases to act for an assisted person, even though the certificate has not been discharged, the Court of Appeal has held that the legally assisted person ceases to be such for the purposes of sections 17 and 18 of the Legal Aid Act 1988 since the person is no longer receiving advice, assistance, mediation or representation under the Act. In consequence the former legally assisted person loses the protection provided by section 17 in respect of his own liability for costs and the Legal Aid Board ceases to be liable for him under section 18.[25] The same principle would appear to apply under the Access to Justice Act 1999.

B. COUNSEL

4–007 A barrister in independent practice may charge for any work undertaken by him (whether or not it involves an appearance in court) on any basis or by any method he thinks fit, provided that it is permitted by law and does not involve the payment of a wage or salary.[26] This applies also to BarDirect work.

The terms of work on which barristers offer their services to solicitors and the withdrawal of credit scheme 1988

4–008 A barrister looks for payment of his fee to the solicitor who instructs him and, save in the case of a BarDirect client, not to his client. Except in LSC funded cases, a solicitor is personally liable as a matter of professional conduct, for the payment of a barrister's proper fees, whether or not he has been placed in funds by his client. Where instructions have been given in the name of the firm all partners at that date incur personal liability and remain liable for the payment of counsel's fees incurred on behalf of the firm by a deceased, bankrupt, or otherwise defaulting former partner of the firm, and the liability of a sole practitioner and of partners for liabilities of their co-partners is a continuing one and is not cancelled or suspended by any transfer of the practice or dissolution of the partnership. The terms of work as to payment of fees and otherwise are the only terms on which barristers offer their services to solicitors. A solicitor who sends a brief or instructions to a barrister will, in the absence of any contrary stipulation made at the time in writing, be taken to be instructing the barrister on the basis of those terms.[27]

---

[25] *Burridge v Stafford*; *Khan v Ali* [1999] 4 All E.R. 660, CA.
[26] Code of Conduct of the Bar, para.405.
[27] Code of Conduct of the Bar Annexe B; Terms of Work (1)–(6).

Community Legal Service funded costs

Where counsel has undertaken work in respect of which he is entitled to be   4–009
paid out of the Community Legal Service Fund, it is the duty of the solicitor
to prepare and submit a bill for detailed assessment in the normal way.[28]
Where no application for detailed assessment has been made, or the client's
certificate is discharged before assessment, the Legal Services Commission
may authorise the making of an application for detailed assessment on his
behalf and the costs of the application and of the assessment will be deemed
to be costs in the proceedings to which the certificate related.[29] The Civil
Procedure Rules enable the Commission to put pressure on a solicitor who
has delayed in putting in his bill for assessment, by applying to the court for
an order that detailed assessment proceedings be commenced within a
certain time.[30] The funded client's solicitor must, within seven days after the
detailed assessment, notify counsel in writing where the fees claimed on his
behalf have been reduced or disallowed and must endorse the bill of costs
with the date on which the notice was given, or that no such notice was
necessary.[31] Once the bill is endorsed that no notice is necessary, the costs
officer may issue the certificate; where a notice has been given, the costs
officer may not issue the certificate until 14 days have elapsed from the date
when the notice was endorsed, in order to give counsel the opportunity to
question the disallowance.[32]

C. COSTS BETWEEN PARTIES

The court's discretion and circumstances to be taken into account when   4–010
exercising its discretion as to costs

The general rule is that the unsuccessful party will be ordered to pay the
costs of the successful party but the court may make a different order.[33] The
court has discretion as to whether the costs are payable by one party to
another, the amount of those costs and when they are to be paid.[34] The
normal time for payment is within 14 days of the order stating the amount
of the costs.[35]

The Rules and Costs Practice Direction provide that the general rule does
not apply:

---

[28] Civil Legal Aid (General) Regulations 1989, reg.107. Civil Legal Aid (General) Regulations
   1989, reg.107.
[29] Civil Legal Aid (General) Regulations 1989, reg.108.
[30] CPR r.47.8(4).
[31] *ibid.*, reg.112(1).
[32] *ibid.*, reg.112(2).
[33] CPR r.44.3(2).
[34] CPR r.44.3(1) and Supreme Court Act 1981, s.5.
[35] see CPR r.44.8.

(i) to proceedings in the Court of Appeal on an application or appeal made in connection with proceedings in the Family Division[36];

(ii) to proceedings in the Court of Appeal relating to a judgment, direction or order given or made in probate proceedings or family proceedings;

(iii) in a probate claim where a defendant has in his defence given notice that he requires the will to be proved in solemn form. The court will not make an order for costs against the defendant unless it appears that there was no reasonable ground for opposing the will.[37]

In deciding what order to make about costs the court is required to have regard to all the circumstances including the conduct of all the parties, the extent to which a party has succeeded on his case and any payment into court or admissible offer to settle which is drawn to the court's attention, whether or not such an offer is made in accordance with Part 36.[38] An award of costs that simply looked at the number of issues won and lost would not fairly reflect the realities of the case. Whilst claimants lost a good many issues which they had raised the court found that it was not unreasonable, in particular in the light of the first three defendants misleading conduct, for the claimants to have raised the issues that they did. The claimants were awarded 75 per cent of their costs.[39]

A solicitor, successfully sued for negligence by a former client, joined counsel instructed in the original action as a third party to the negligence claim. On appeal the solicitor was found to be liable as to 80 per cent and counsel as to 20 per cent of the damages awarded. The solicitor argued that the costs should be apportioned in the same way. The Court of Appeal held that the costs order should reflect that the matter should not have been defended by the solicitor and that the solicitor and counsel had entered into an unnecessary and costly mud slinging contest. The original order that the solicitor should pay all the costs was upheld. The counsel was ordered to pay 20 per cent of the solicitor's costs of the Part 20 proceedings. The solicitor was ordered to pay one third of its costs of the appeal, the balance to be paid by counsel.[40]

It is open to a judge where a split trial has been ordered to reserve the question of costs of the trial on liability until after the determination of the remaining issues. The Court of Appeal stated that there was much to be said

---

[36] Family proceedings: where the costs arise out of family proceedings, the provisions of CPR Pts 43, 44 (except pp.44.9–44.12), 47 and 48 apply. Rule 44.3(2) (the general rule that the unsuccessful party will be ordered to pay the costs) does not apply. Family Proceedings (Miscellaneous Amendments) Rules 1999.

[37] CPR r.44.3(3), Costs Practice Direction, section 8

[38] CPR r.44.3(4), Costs Practice Direction, para.8.2.

[39] *Douglas v Hello Ltd* [2004] EWHC 63 (Ch), Lindsay J.

[40] *Moy v Pettman Smith (A Firm) (Costs)* [2003] EWCA Civ 467; [2003] PNLR 31, CA.

for the view that the incidence of costs should be the same whether or not there has been an order for a split trial. Where there is a split trial and it remains uncertain whether the claimant will recover more than nominal damages it may be proper for the trial judge to defer making any order for the costs of the liability trial until the final outcome is known.[41]

The grounds upon which the court may depart from the usual order (that the successful party is to be awarded its costs) are set out in Rule 44.3(4) and (5). That list is not exhaustive and the Court of Appeal has held that it is wrong for the court to deprive a successful defendant of part of its costs on the grounds that the judgment might be of assistance to it in the future because it was a test case. Where litigation had been conducted at arms length the only appropriate order was for the successful defendant to have its costs.[42]

In a case where the claimant won on the single most important issue but failed on the facts, justice required that the second defendant should pay 35 per cent of her costs. The court held that the claimant had undoubtedly won a very real victory the fruits of which she would not have herself enjoyed but which would benefit those who came after her.[43]

In a test case on a point of construction of the Principal Civil Service Pension Scheme, the court held it was wrong to leave the defendant, a man of insubstantial means, to bear his own costs and the Minister for the Civil Service was ordered to pay the defendant's costs of and incidental to the appeal.[44]

A party who meets with "substantial" success is not necessarily entitled to all his costs. The situation has changed with the coming into force of the CPR. The new rules enable the court to do greater justice in cases where a successful party has caused an unsuccessful party to incur costs on an issue which later fails. In that the claimant was ordered to pay the defendant's costs of an issue which failed, to be set off against the claimant's costs of the issue which succeeded.[45] Where a claimant brought a money claim against the defendant in respect of which there were four principal issues the defendants were successful on a single determinative issue but lost on the other three issues. The court held that the award of costs to the defendant should be reduced by one quarter. The judge found that the unsuccessful points that were argued were not unreasonable and were inter-related with the determinative issue. If the points had not been taken the number of witnesses would not have been reduced, although the amount of evidence would have been. In deciding to reduce the award of costs the judge applied the following criteria:

---

[41] *Weill v Mean Fidler* [2003] EWCA Civ 1058.
[42] *Pexton v The Wellcome Trust* [2000] EWCA Civ, unreported, October 10.
[43] *R. (Watts) v Bedford Primary Care Trust* [2003] EWHC 2401 (Admin), Mumby J.
[44] *Minister for the Civil Service v Oakes (No.2)* [2003] EWHC (Ch), December 12, Lindsey J.
[45] *Winter v Winter* [2000] EW CA Civ, unreported, November 10.

(a) the reasonableness of taking the point;

(b) the extra time taken up prior to trial in preparing to argue the point;

(c) the extra time taken in court to argue the point;

(d) the extent to which it was just in all the circumstances to deprive the successful party of its costs; and

(e) the extent to which the unsuccessful point was related to any successful point.[46]

It is no longer necessary to establish that a successful party acted unreasonably or improperly in raising an issue to be deprived of its costs and to be ordered to pay the unsuccessful party's costs of that particular issue. The issue based approach requires the court to consider issue by issue where costs in each discrete issue fall.[47] Where a claimant had fundamentally altered its particulars of claim shortly before trial, resulting in the costs of the case substantially exceeding the original amount claimed in the case, the award of two thirds of the costs against the unsuccessful party was upheld.[48]

The Court of Appeal refused to alter a judge's rejection of a defendants' argument that an issue based order should be made reflecting the success of the defendant on a number of issues. The Judge refused this because matters in the claim and counterclaim were inextricably intertwined and because of the defendants' conduct contesting various items, in particular a claim for VAT in respect of which the Judge found that one of the defendants had lied.[49]

In all but straightforward cases a judge is entitled to say to the parties that if they have not reached an agreement on costs they have not settled their dispute. Where the substantive issues have been compromised in a case the judge should be slow to embark on determination of disputed facts solely in order to put himself in a position to make a decision about costs. Unless manifest injustice could be shown the Court of Appeal will not disturb a costs order made by the judge at the invitation of the parties after they have settled their action save for costs.[50]

At the end of a trial, the judge will normally do no more than direct who is to pay the costs and upon what basis. It is generally in the interests of justice that a judge should be free to dispose of applications as to costs in a speedy and uncomplicated way. However, the CPR sometimes require a

---

[46] *Antonelli v Alan* [2000] EWHC Ch.D., unreported, November 29, Neuberger J.

[47] *Summit Property Ltd v Pitmans* [2001] EWCA Civ 2020; [2002] C.P.L.R. 97.

[48] *Professional Information Technology Consultants Ltd v Jones* [2001] EWCA Civ, unreported, December 7.

[49] *Boynton v Willers* [2003] EWCA Civ 904.

[50] *BCT Software Solutions Ltd v C Brewer & Sons Ltd* [2003] EWCA Civ 939.

more complex approach as to costs, and judgments dealing with costs will more often need to identify the provisions of the rules which have been in play and why these have led to the order made. Where no express explanation is given for a costs order an appellate court will approach the material facts on the assumption that the judge will have had a good reason for the award made. Where it is apparent that there is a perfectly rational explanation for the order made the court is likely to draw the inference that this is what motivated the judge in making the order. In practice, it is only in those cases where an order for costs is made with neither reasons nor any obvious explanation for the order, that it is likely to be appropriate to give permission to appeal on the ground of lack of reasons against an order that relates only to costs. In general the question of what order for costs is appropriate is one for the discretion of the judge and an appellate court will be slow to interfere in its exercise.[51]

There have been a number of decisions concerning the way in which the court should exercise its discretion as to costs. Where the ordinary costs order is departed from it is incumbent upon the judge to give reasons, albeit short, for that departure.[52] The task for the judge is to take an overview of the case as a whole and reach a conclusion based on two questions:

(1) who has succeeded in the action?; and

(2) what order for costs does justice require?

Where the honours are even it is appropriate for there to be no order for costs.[53] Lord Woolf M.R. explained the most significant change of emphasis of the new rules is to require courts to be more ready to make separate orders which reflect the outcome of different issues. In doing this the new rules are reflecting a change in practice which has already started before the coming into force of the CPR. It is now clear that a too robust application of the "follow the event principle" encourages litigants to increase the cost of litigation since it discourages litigants from being selective as to the points they take. A litigant who will recover all his costs so long as he wins will leave no stone unturned in an effort to do so.[54] Lord Woolf M.R. has emphasised that costs could be awarded on the basis of the issues actually involved[55] so as to encourage good litigation practice, but such an approach could go too far.[56]

---

[51] *English v Emery Reimbold; Verrechia v Commissioner of Police for the Metropolis* [2002] EWCA Civ 605; [2002] 3 All E.R. 385, CA.
[52] *Brent LBC v Anienobe*, unreported, November 24, 1999, CA.
[53] *BCCI SA v Ali (No.4)* [1999] 149 N.L.J. 1734, Lightman J.
[54] *AEI Rediffusion Music Ltd v Phonographic Performance Ltd* [1999] 1 W.L.R. 1507, CA.
[55] See CPR r.44.3(4).
[56] *Universal Cycles Plc v Grangebriar Ltd*, unreported, February 8, 2000, CA.

There is no tradition that when a dispute is not judicially resolved the correct order is no order as to costs. The Court of Appeal gave the following guidance:

(1) the court has power to make a costs order when the substantive proceedings have been resolved without a trial but the parties have not agreed about costs.

(2) It is ordinarily irrelevant that the claimant is legally aided. The overriding objective is to do justice between the parties without incurring unnecessary court time and consequently additional costs.

(3) At each end of the spectrum there were cases where it was obvious that the other side would have won had the substantive issues been fought to a conclusion. In between the position was less clear. How far the court would be prepared to look into the previous unresolved substantive issues would depend on the circumstances of the particular case not least the amount at stake and the conduct of the parties.

(4) In the absence of a good reason to make any other order the fallback was to make no order as to costs.[57]

In a case where at first instance, the judge held that the defendant had unreasonably pursued two discrete issues in its counterclaim which it lost, although it was successful on the remainder of the counterclaim, the judge ordered the defendant to pay 10 per cent of its costs and those of the claimant. The Court of Appeal held that although the defendant had not succeeded on the two issues it had not acted unreasonably in pursuing them. Exercising the judge's discretion anew the Court of Appeal was satisfied there was nothing in the facts of the case which justified departure from the general rule that a successful party should be awarded the whole of its costs.[58]

Where the defendant succeeded on its counterclaim, which was the major monetary issue in the proceedings, and also enjoyed significant success in relation to its defence of the claimant's claim, and taking into account the defendants open offer of settlement which had been made, the Court of Appeal ordered that the claimant should have two thirds of its costs of the issue of repudiation of contract but that the defendant should have the balance of the costs of the proceedings.[59]

---

[57] *Brawley v Marczynski (No.1)* [2002] EWCA Civ 756; [2002] 4 All E.R. 1067, CA; [2002] 1 W.L.R. 813, CA.

[58] *Spice Girls Ltd v Aprilia World Service BV* [2002] EWCA Civ 15.

[59] *Dick Van Dijk v Wilkinson* [2002] EWCA Civ 1780.

Where claimants were granted an order but in an amended form from that originally sought, the Court of Appeal amended the original order that there be no order as to costs to reflect the claimant's degree of success on the application.[60]

A judge's order that a defendant should pay the claimant's costs was set aside on the basis that the judgment sum was an award of relative insignificance compared to the sum claimed. The Court of Appeal held that the judge had failed to have due regard to the fact that the defendant had won in principle given the large sums claimed, the eventual award made and the wide issues between the parties which were ultimately decided in the defendant's favour. The judge's costs order was set aside and "no order as to costs" substituted.[61]

Where the Government had pledged that government departments would use ADR in all suitable cases to settle disputes whenever the other party accepted it, the court made no order as to costs even though the Department was successful and the Department had not abided by the pledge which had been given.[62]

The conduct of the parties

This includes: 4–011

(a) conduct before as well as during the proceedings and in particular the extent to which the parties followed any relevant pre-action protocol;

(b) whether it was reasonable for a party to raise, pursue or contest a particular allegation or issue;

(c) the manner in which a party has pursued or defended his case or a particular allegation or issue; and

(d) whether a claimant who has succeeded in his claim in whole or in part exaggerated his claim.[63]

In proceedings against multiple defendants, three of the defendants were successful, the court made reduced orders for costs because of their conduct. The fourth defendant was involved in deliberately backdating relevant documentation (awarded 50 per cent costs); the sixth defendant's conduct as finance manager and director was unsatisfactory and improper in a

---

[60] *Jim Ennis Construction Ltd v Thewlis* [2003] EWCA Civ, unreported, July 29.
[61] *Islam v Ali* [2003] EWCA Civ 612.
[62] *Royal Bank of Canada v Secretary of State for Defence* [2003] EWHC 1841 (Ch), Lewison J., but see now *Halsey v Milton Keynes NHS Trust* [2004] EWCA Civ 576.
[63] CPR r.44.3(5).

number of respects, he also deliberately deceived the auditors and gave untrue answers in evidence (one-third costs); the tenth defendant gave untruthful evidence at the trial (one-third costs).[64]

In deciding how to apportion costs to reflect the conduct of the parties in proceedings the judge should structure the judgment on costs around the provisions of CPR r.44.3 which require the court to take into account "the conduct of the parties". The introduction of the CPR does not affect the pre-existing law which entitles a judge to consider any relevant aspect of the conduct of the parties including their conduct in relation to the matters which gave rise to the litigation.[65] Although the practice of the Commercial Court[66] is not to disallow a successful party its costs simply because of anterior dishonest conduct which "while it was part of the transaction which gave rise to the proceedings, could not be characterised as misconduct in relation to the proceedings themselves", that was no more than a matter of practice. On their proper construction CPR r.44.3(4)(a) and (5)(a) do not contain any limitation such as would shut out reliance, in an appropriate case, on misconduct in and about the matters which triggered the litigation.[67]

In an action where the defendant had succeeded but both parties had behaved unattractively, the Commercial Court declined to make any order as to costs. There needed to be encouragement to litigants to be selective as to the points they took and an incentive for responsible behaviour.[68]

A public body (the CPS) is not insulated from the normal costs rules simply because it is a public body. In confiscation proceedings, where the CPS was held to have acted unreasonably in ignoring documentary evidence, the intervener was awarded her costs. The Court of Appeal stated that there was no need for a judge to refer to CPR r.44.3 provided that he followed the philosophy of it which required him to start with the proposition that the general rule was that the unsuccessful party should pay the costs of the successful party and then to consider whether any of the specific matters in r.44.3(4) took the case out of the ordinary rule and then to consider all the circumstances.[69]

Where a claimant obtained interim relief in the form of an injunction, which was extended until trial of the preliminary issue between the parties, the court found that the judge's decision, to order the defendant to pay the costs of the application which had been summarily assessed, was inherently unjust since the judge had decided the issue on the balance of convenience until the dispute could be properly decided at a full hearing. It was

---

[64] *Grupo Torras SA v Al-Sabah*, July 5, 1999, Mance J. (unreported).
[65] See *Donald Campbell & Co Ltd v Pollak* [1927] A.C. 732.
[66] See *Hall v Rover Financial Services (GB) Ltd* [2002] EWCA Civ 1514.
[67] *Groupama Insurance Co Ltd v Overseas Partners Re Ltd* [2003] EWCA Civ 1846.
[68] See *Kastor Navigation Ltd* [2003] EWHC 472 (Comm); *Base Metal Trading Ltd v Ruslan Brisovich Shamurin* [2003] EWHC 2606 (Comm), Tomlinson J.
[69] *Crown Prosecution Service v Grimes* [2003] EWCA Civ, unreported, November 27.

inconsistent with such a basis that there could be any successful or unsuccessful parties. The proper exercise of the discretion would have been to reserve the costs of the application to the trial judge.[70] It was subsequently held that it could be right to depart from that general approach if, on the balance of convenience, it was so clearly a case in favour of the claimant that the defendant should have a costs order against them for wasting time and money in fighting the issues.[71] The Court of Appeal in allowing a defendants' appeal from a case management decision nonetheless ordered the defendants to pay the costs in any event because of the way the matter had been conducted in the court below.[72]

Claimants who pursued an appeal with no real prospect of success but as a device to park the proceedings whilst attempting to achieve a negotiated settlement with other defendants were ordered to pay costs on the indemnity basis because of the abuse of process.[73]

In proceedings to prove a will the unsuccessful defendant alleged undue influence but because there were reasonable grounds for suspecting undue influence the court ordered the defendant to pay half only of the claimants costs.[74]

Where proceedings had been commenced in the face of an offer, which clearly amounted to an admission of liability, and an invitation to the claimant to provide particulars (referable to a claim for specific performance), at trial the parties agreed that the defendant should pay the claimant a sum of money in full and final settlement of the claim. The court allowed the defendant its costs in relation to the steps taken referable to the issue of specific performance and the claimant was granted half its costs referable exclusively to the other parts of the claim.[75]

Where claimants claimed in excess of £1 million plus interest and judgment was finally entered for the claimants and damages of £190,000 awarded, the defendants argued that they should not have to pay all the costs because the claim had been substantially exaggerated. The court found that the claim had not been exaggerated. In the particular case the claimants recovered 25 per cent of the figure claimed but there was no evidence to show that the level of the claim had added to the cost or length of the case. Any suggestion that the decision in *Elgindata*[76] was still good practice needed to be approached with great caution.[77] In deciding what order to make about costs where a party had succeeded on part of the case, even though not wholly successful, the other party's reasonableness in raising,

[70] *Richardson v Desquenne et Giral UK Ltd*, unreported, November 23, 1999, CA.
[71] *Picnic at Ascot Inc v Derigs*, unreported, February 9, 2000, Neuberger J.
[72] *Daniels v Walker*, unreported, May 3, 2000, CA.
[73] *Sodeca SA v NE Investments Inc* [2002] EWHC 1700 (QB), Toulson J.
[74] In *Re Good, Carapeto v Good, The Times*, May 22, 2002, Rimer J.
[75] *Coakley v Lambeth LBC* [2001] EWHC Ch, unreported, October 12, Hart J.
[76] *Re Elgindata (No.2)* [1992] 1 W.L.R. 1207, CA.
[77] *Harrison v Bloom Camillin* [2001] EWHC Ch.D., March 13, Neuberger J.

pursuing or contesting a particular allegation was not necessarily relevant or a pre-condition to taking that factor into account.[78]

The Court of Appeal held that rule 44.3 did not apply where a claimant applied to discover the identity of a person posting information on the defendant's internet discussion board (a Norwich Pharmacal application). Such applications are not really *inter partes* disputes. The defendant had not resisted the court making the order, its attitude was neutral. Such applications are akin to proceedings for pre-action disclosure under rule 48.3. In general the costs incurred should be recovered from the wrongdoer, not from the party from whom disclosure was sought. In a normal case the applicant should be ordered to pay the costs of the party making disclosure, including the costs of disclosure.[79]

Exaggerated claims

4–012   A counterclaiming defendant was found to have exaggerated its counterclaim (claiming £33 million in what the judge found to be a £1–£5 million claim). The judge, having found that the counterclaim had been exaggerated, also found that there had been unnecessary complexity in dealing with the core matters introduced by the defendant's allegations. Thirdly, the defendant pursued issues in relation to bad faith which warranted the making of a discount in the order for costs. Fourthly there was a failure by the defendant to grasp the opportunity to resolve the dispute by ADR. The court found that these different aspects were not cumulative although they did overlap. The judge found that, although the defendant was *de facto* the winner, there were very many issues which were pursued which resulted in a waste of time and cost to all parties. On the facts of the case the defendant was awarded 50 per cent of its costs of both the claim and the counterclaim but the claimant was awarded its costs in respect of the issue of the taking of an account.[80]

The court ordered an unsuccessful claimant to pay costs on the indemnity basis and to pay interest on the costs from one year before the commencement date of the trial because of the claimants' unreasonable conduct in that the case had changed constantly throughout the course of the proceedings and the claimant had produced wholly unacceptable volumes of documentation.[81]

A claim issued for damages totalling £9,000 was eventually determined at a figure below the small claims track limit without the case ever having been allocated to track. The district judge summarily assessed the costs on the basis that the claim was not a small claim. The Court of Appeal held that

---

[78] *Stocznia Gdanskasa v Latvian Shipping Co., The Times*, May 8, 2001, Thomas J.
[79] *Totalise Plc v Motley Fool Ltd* [2001] EWCA Civ 1897; [2002] 1 W.L.R. 1233, CA.
[80] *Dunkin Donuts Inc v DD UK Ltd* [2002], unreported, July 24, H.H. Judge Alton.
[81] *ABCI v BFT* [2002] EWHC 567 Comm, H.H. Judge Chambers Q.C.

this was incorrect. Non-allocation to a track did not preclude the court from considering whether it would be reasonable to make an assessment consistent with the small claims costs regime or to apply the regime to a claim which should never have exceeded and never was anything more than a small claim. In the absence of any specific factor suggesting otherwise, in a case where, if sought, an allocation to the small claims track would have been made, the normal rule should be that the small claims costs regime should apply.[82]

Orders which the court may make

Section 51 of the Supreme Court Act 1981 gives the court full power to determine by whom and to what extent costs are to be paid. The CPR sets out a list of orders which the court may make but it is not an exhaustive list. The orders include:

4–013

(a) a proportion of another party's costs;

(b) a stated amount in respect of another party's costs;

(c) costs from or until a certain date only;

(d) costs incurred before proceedings had begun;

(e) costs relating to particular steps taken in the proceedings;

(f) costs relating only to a distinct part of the proceedings; and

(g) interests on costs from or until a certain date including a date before judgment.[83]

These orders are set out in descending order of desirability and the rule provides that where the court is considering making an order relating only to a distinct part of the proceedings it must, instead, if practicable, make an order for a proportion of the costs or an order for costs from or until a certain date.[84]

The list of possible orders which the court may make in CPR r.44.3(6) is not exhaustive. The court has a discretion to make an order subject to a cap but it is wrong to impose a cap for reasons of proportionality since proportionality applies to orders made on the standard basis.[85]

The Court of Appeal has emphasised that the CPR requires that an order which allows or disallows costs by reference to certain issues should be made only if other forms of order cannot be made which sufficiently reflect

---

[82] *Voice and Script International v Algafar* [2003] EWCA Civ 736.
[83] CPR r.44.3(6).
[84] CPR r.44.3(7).
[85] *SCT Finance Ltd v Bolton* [2002] EWCA Civ 56; [2003] 3 All E.R. 434, CA.

the justice of the case. The Court of Appeal pointed out the reasons for this rule: an order which allows or disallows costs of certain issues creates difficulties at the stage of the assessment of costs because the Costs Judge has to master the issue in detail to understand what costs were properly incurred in dealing with it and then analyse the work done by the receiving party's legal advisers to determine whether or not it was attributable to the issue the costs of which have been disallowed. In all the circumstances a percentage order made by the Judge who heard the application will often produce a fairer result than an issues based order. Such an order is consistent with the overriding objective of the CPR.[86]

CPR r.44.3(6)(g) gives the court the power to order the period during which interest on costs should run. The court may therefore look at the date when the costs were incurred in order to reach a conclusion as to interest suiting the particular circumstances.[87]

The courts should be ready, post-CPR, to make costs orders which reflect not merely the overall outcome of the proceedings but also the loss of particular issues. The court should not be forced into making an issue based order rather than a percentage order by the failure of the parties to provide sufficient information about costs to achieve the correct percentage.[88]

Where the court orders a party to pay costs it may make an order for an amount to be paid on account before the costs are assessed.[89] This is likely to happen where the court decides not to carry out a summary assessment of the costs. It may be inappropriate to make such an order where the paying party is a funded client because there will not have been a determination of that person's liability to pay those costs under section 11 of the Access to Justice Act 1999.[90] Where there is a conditional fee agreement in existence it is important that the judge is made aware of the existence of the agreement, although not of its terms. An order for payment on account or summary assessment might have unintended consequences in such a case.

There is no guidance in the CPR as to when a payment on account should be ordered but, in general, an interim order should be made of an amount which the successful party would almost certainly collect on detailed assessment.[91]

Where a losing claimant's resources were very limited the court held it should not force the receiving party to engage in a detailed assessment before receiving any money at all because that would simply be an

---

[86] *English v Emery Reimbold; Verrechia v Commissioner of Police for the Metropolis* [2002] EWCA Civ 605; [2002] 3 All E.R. 385, CA.

[87] *Powell v Herefordshire Health Authority* [2002] EWCA Civ 1786; [2003] 3 All E.R. 253.

[88] *Budgen v Andrew Gardiner Partnership* [2002] EWCA Civ 1125; *The Times*, September 9, 2002, CA.

[89] CPR r.44.3(8).

[90] As to summary assessment in such a case see Costs Practice Direction, ss.13 and 14.

[91] *Mars U.K. Ltd v Teknowledge Ltd (No.2), The Times*, July 8, 1999, Jacob J.

expenditure of further money on a process which would give no return. The appropriate order was an interim payment which would have the effect of rendering redundant the time, effort and cost which would subsequently need to be spent on a detailed assessment.[92]

If a claimant sues two defendants in the alternative and succeeds against only one, the court has a discretion to order the unsuccessful defendant to pay the successful defendant's costs. This may be done by an order that the unsuccessful defendant pay the successful defendant's costs directly to him (a Sanderson Order[93]) or by an order that the claimant pay the successful defendant's costs to him and recover them from the unsuccessful defendant as part of the claimant's costs of the action (a Bullock Order).[94] A defendant who was sued by an impecunious claimant joined another party as a Part 20 defendant in order to protect its position. The claim against the defendant was dismissed and the Part 20 claim also had to be dismissed. The defendant complained that if it were ordered to pay the Part 20 defendants' costs it would be doubly out of pocket since there was no prospect of recovery from the claimant. The court held that it was difficult to see why the apparent injustice to the defendant should ordinarily be spread to a third party who had been sued involuntarily by a sufficient resourced defendant. It would only be in exceptional circumstances that a successful third party would be deprived of its costs. There was no costs sharing agreement between the successful defendants upon which the court could retrospectively impose a sharing arrangement. The costs had to lie where they fell.[95]

Although CPR r.3.1(7) states that the court has power to vary or revoke its order, it has been held that a court cannot act as an appellate court in respect of its own order except where fraud has been shown in the original application for the order. The court could not therefore amend an order for costs made under r.44.3.42.

In a case where the claimant succeeded on some issues, failed on others and abandoned still others the Court of Appeal held that it was open to the judge to award the claimant a proportion of the costs in respect of those issues on which it had succeeded, but in respect of the abandoned issues, these should have been left to the costs judge. Those costs should be disallowed on detailed assessment as costs unreasonably incurred in the litigation.[96]

Where a claimant sued for delivery up of a vehicle which had been repaired and claimed damages for conversion and interest and the defendant counterclaimed for the unpaid repair costs, the claimant abandoned various issues including damages for misrepresentation, conversion and breach of contract. Judgment was subsequently entered by consent for the defendant

---

[92] *Allason v Random House UK Ltd* [2002] EWHC Ch, February 27, Laddie J.
[93] *Sanderson v Blyth Theatre Company* [1903] 2 K.B. 533, CA.
[94] *Bullock v London General Omnibus Co.* [1907] 1 K.B. 264, CA.
[95] *Arkin v Borchard Lines Ltd* [2003] EWHC 3088 (Comm), Colman J.
[96] *Shirley v Caswell*, The Independent, July 24, 2000, CA, [2000] Lloyd's Rep. P.N. 955.

on the counterclaim. At first instance the defendant was ordered to pay the claimant's costs in full up to the date of the return of the motor vehicle and one third of the claimant's costs thereafter. On appeal, the Court of Appeal held that given the nature of the misrepresentation allegations there must have been a notional increase in the cost to both parties. The Court of Appeal ordered the claimant to pay one half of the defendant's costs after the date of the return of the vehicle.[97]

What Chadwick L.J. was saying in *Shirley v Caswell* was that an order for costs should not penalise a party twice over. If a court made an order giving only a proportion of costs on the basis that the receiving party had failed on certain issues that would be evident to the costs judge from the judgment and the costs judge should take great care to see that a double penalty was not imposed.[98]

In the majority of cases the court will make an order that the claimant will pay the defendant's costs of a case which is struck out, usually because the whole claim is struck out not just some part of it, but where the order is for the claimants to have their costs of the action up to a certain date, *Shirley v Caswell* requires that unless the judge has some specific reason for interfering or intervening he can make an order leaving the question of assessment to the costs judge. On an assessment, the costs judge will in any event disallow the costs of any claims which were positively struck out as well as disallowing costs in respect of issues abandoned or not pursued.[99]

On an appeal the Court of Appeal ordered the claimants to pay the first, second and fourth defendant's costs "of the trial commencing on 6 October 1998". The court also ordered "that there be no order as to costs for the period of 23 August 1998 to start of trial". The question arose whether the brief fees of three counsel were recoverable under the terms of the order. The fees had been staged and paid in full during September 1998. On the hearing of the costs appeal, the judge decided that the words "commencing on 6 October" were not the most obvious words of limitation but were more descriptive of the trial (*i.e.*, when it commenced) and neither added to nor subtracted from the phrase "costs of the trial". In the circumstances it was held that the brief fees were recoverable.[1]

Where a claimant obtained without notice a freezing order in an excessive amount which was the subject both of an application to discharge by the defendant and an application to vary by the claimant which failed, the claimant being ultimately successful in the smaller sum at the trial, the court ordered that there should be no order as to costs in respect of the initial

[97] *Darougar v Belcher* [2002] EWCA Civ 1262 (this decision was given very shortly after the decision in *Shirley v Caswell*—the two decisions do not appear to sit together comfortably).
[98] *Dooley v Parker* [2002] EWCA Civ 1188.
[99] *Nugent v Michael Goss Aviation* [2002] EWHC Q.B. 1281, [2001] 3 Costs L.R. 359, Burton J.
[1] *Cantor Fitzgerald International v Tradition (UK) Ltd* [2003] EWHC 1907 Ch, Patten J.

application of the freezing order, that the claimant should pay the defendant's costs of the application to discharge the order, that there be no order as to the costs in respect of the claimant's unsuccessful application to vary and that the defendant should pay the claimant two thirds of its costs of the trial.[2]

A claimant who exaggerated his symptoms so that the claim proceeded on the fast track rather than the small claims track was restricted, when damages of £500 were awarded, to the fixed costs on the small claims track. CPR r.27.14 entitles the court to award further costs where a party has behaved unreasonably. The court ordered the defendant to pay a further £1,000 because of the way that he had driven his vehicle prior to the accident. There must be some doubt as to whether the rule is not intended to be confined to conduct in the course of proceedings rather than in the course of the matter giving rise to the cause of action.[3]

Common orders for costs and their general effect

The Costs Practice Direction contains a non-exhaustive list of orders which the court may make and their meanings.[4]   **4–014**

Counsel's fees

There is no requirement to obtain a certificate for the attendance of counsel but the court may express an opinion as to whether or not the hearing was fit for the attendance of one or more counsel. If such an opinion is expressed the costs officer conducting a detailed assessment in relation to that particular hearing must have regard to the opinion stated.[5]   **4–015**

Set-off

Where the court makes orders resulting in a party being entitled to costs and also liable to pay costs, the court may assess the costs which that party is liable to pay, and, either set off the amount assessed against the amount the party is entitled to be paid and direct him to pay the balance, or delay the issue of a certificate for the costs to which the party is entitled until he has paid the amount which he is liable to pay.[6]   **4–016**

---

[2] *Mr Biss v Sox Ltd* [2001] EWHC QBD, unreported, May 3, Holland J.
[3] *Devine v Franklin* [2002] EWHC 1846 (QB), Gray J.
[4] Costs Practice Direction, s.8.
[5] Costs Practice Direction, para.8.7.
[6] CPR r.44.3(9).

The Court of Appeal explained the operation of set off with particular reference to legal aid costs as follows:

" . . . the importance of the distinction between set off and other cross claims is that set off operates, . . . to reduce or extinguish the other party's claim. It operates as a defence. A mere cross claim does not . . .

The operation of a set off does not place the person whose chose in action is thereby reduced or extinguished under any obligation to pay. It simply reduces or extinguishes the amount that the other party has to pay. The operation of a set off, in respect of the liability of a legally assisted person under an order for costs does not require the legally aided person to pay anything. It does not lead to any costs being recoverable against the legally aided person accordingly . . . there is nothing [in the legal aid legislation] to prevent set off . . .

. . . the following propositions can be stated:

(1) a direction for the set off of costs against damages or costs of which a legally aided person has become or becomes entitled in the action may be permissible.

(2) The set off is no different from and no more extensive than the set off available to or against parties who are not legally aided.

(3) The broad criterion for the application of set off is that the plaintiff's claim and the defendant's claim are so closely connected that it would be inequitable to allow the plaintiff's claim without taking into account the defendant's claim. As it has sometimes been put, the defendant's claim must in equity impeach the plaintiff's claim.

(4) Set off of costs or damages to which one party is entitled against costs or damages to which another party is entitled depends upon the application of the equitable criterion I have endeavoured to express . . . but I would not have thought that a set off of damages against damages could properly be described as a discretionary matter nor that set off of costs against damages could be so described.

(5) If and to the extent that a set off of costs awarded against a legally aided party against costs or damages to which the legally aided party is entitled cannot be justified as a set off:

(i) the liability of the legally aided party to pay costs awarded against him will be subject to Section 17(1) of the Legal Aid Act 1988 [now Section 11 of the Access to Justice Act 1999] and Regulation 124(1) of the Civil Legal Aid (General) Regulations 1989 [now Regulation 9 of the Community Legal Service (Costs) Reglations 2000]; and

(ii) the Section 16(6) of the 1988 Act charge [now Section 10(7) of the 1999 Act] will apply to the costs or damages to which the legally aided party is entitled."

Although the Court of Appeal was dealing with the situation under the Legal Aid Act 1988 the broad principles laid down remain the same.[7] The court has confirmed that the position with regard to set off remains the same as it was before the introduction of the CPR. Whilst an assisted person remains protected against the making of enforceable orders for payment of costs, that protection is not available in respect of orders for costs to be used as a shield or set off.[8]

Where a claimant entered into a conditional fee agreement with his solicitors, and the solicitors entered into a conditional retainer agreement with counsel, and where in the course of the proceedings the claimant obtained certain pre-trial costs orders in his favour, and the defendants obtained an order in their favour, the claimant sought to set-off the opposing orders so as to extinguish any liability. The defendants argued that because of the CFA no costs had become due and therefore nothing was recoverable by the claimant. The court held that this argument was wrong. The word "recover" was used in the agreement to mean: obtain an order for payment as distinct from actually obtaining payment. The same applied to counsel's fees. "Winning" under the CFA included the client recovering costs during the litigation. Thus counsel and solicitors were entitled to their costs when the client obtained a pre-trial order for costs.[9]

Family proceedings

The court allowed a successful petitioning wife costs on the indemnity basis, **4–017.1** stating that the test of reasonableness or otherwise of the husband's conduct had to be given its natural meaning without any extra gloss. The husband had sent a calderbank letter to the wife shortly before the trial conceding that he saw no future in the marriage. From that point on it was wrong of him to continue to defend the petition on the basis that the marriage had not irretrievably broken down. The court found that the husband's conduct of the case was unreasonable and bordering on being dishonest.[10]

---

[7] *Lockley v National Blood Transfusion Service* [1992] 1 W.L.R. 492, CA.
[8] *Hill v Bailey* [2003] EWHC 2835 (Ch), Lightman J.
[9] *Arkin v Brochard Lines Ltd* [2001] EWHC QBD, June 19, Colman J.
[10] *Hadjimilitis v Tsavliris (Costs)* [2003] 1 F.L.R. 81, Alison Bull Q.C.

Solicitor's duty to notify client

4–017.2 If the court makes an order against a party who is legally represented but that party is not present when the order is made, it is the duty of that party's solicitor to notify the client in writing of the order which has been made no later than seven days after the solicitor receives notice of the order (this will usually be on the day of the hearing).[11] "Client" includes not only a person for whom a solicitor is acting but any other person, *e.g.* an insurer or trade union who has instructed the solicitor to act or who is liable to pay the solicitor's fees.[12]

The solicitor, as an officer of the court, owes a duty to the court to comply with this rule; failure to do so may also amount to professional misconduct. When the solicitor notifies a client of what has happened the explanation must state why the order came to be made. The court, in order to ensure that the rule is complied with, may require the solicitor to produce evidence showing that reasonable steps have been taken to notify the client.[13]

Cost orders deemed to have been made

4–018.1 Where costs orders are deemed to have been made a party acquires a right to costs in certain circumstances and in those circumstances the costs order is deemed to have been made on the standard basis.[14] Interest[15] on the costs deemed to have been ordered, begins to run from the date on which the event which gave rise to the entitlement to costs occurred.[16]

Special situations

4–018.2 If the court states that there will be no order as to costs, each party bears its own costs to which that order relates, whatever order the court makes at the end of the proceedings. Where the court makes an order which does not mention costs, no party is entitled to costs in relation to that order. It is not treated as being part of costs in the case.[17]

---

[11] CPR r.44.2.

[12] Direction relating to Part 44, para.1.1.

[13] Costs Practice Direction, paras 7.2 and 7.3.

[14] CPR r.44.12(1). The circumstances are under: r.3.7 (defendant's right to costs where claim struck out for non payment of fees); r.36.13(1) (claimant's right to costs where he accepts defendant's Part 36 offer or Part 36 payment); r.36.14 (claimant's right to costs where defendant accepts the claimant's Part 36 offer); or r.38.6 (defendant's right to costs where claimant discontinues).

[15] Pursuant to s.17 of the Judgments Act 1838 or s.74 of the County Courts Act 1984.

[16] CPR r.44.12(2).

[17] CPR r.44.13(1).

In such a case this does not affect any entitlement of a party to recover costs out of a fund held by him as trustee or personal representative or pursuant to any lease, mortgage or other security.[18]

Unless the appeal is dismissed, the court hearing an appeal may make orders about the costs of proceedings giving rise to the appeal as well as to the costs of the appeal itself.[19] Where proceedings are transferred from one court to another, the court to which they are transferred may, subject to any order of the transferring court, deal with all the costs including the costs before transfer.[20]

Where an action had been automatically struck out due to the claimant's delay and the claimant successfully applied for it to be reinstated the order made on that application was silent as to costs between the parties. The question of wasted costs was reserved to the trial judge. When, at the trial, the claimant was successful the trial judge had no jurisdiction to vary the earlier order to make the defendant pay the costs arising out of the strike out and reinstatement application.[21]

The Administrative Court is entitled to order a coroner to pay costs when ordering a coroner to hold an inquest. Such an order was held to be consistent with the power in section 13(2)(b) of the Coroner's Act 1988.[22]

Remuneration of receivers

A receiver may only charge for his services if the court so directs and **4-019** specifies the basis on which the receiver is to be remunerated.[23] The court may specify who is to be responsible for paying the receiver and the fund or property from which the receiver is to recover his remuneration.[24] If the court directs that the receivers remuneration is to be determined by the court no remuneration is recoverable by the receiver without such determination and the receiver or any party may apply at any time for the determination to take place.[25]

In determining the remuneration of a receiver the court will award such sum as is reasonable and proportionate in all the circumstances. The sum awarded will take into account:

---

[18] CPR r.44.13(1).
[19] CPR r.44.13(2).
[20] CPR r.44.13(3), (4).
[21] *Griffiths v Commissioner of Police* [2003] EWCA Civ 313.
[22] *R. v H.M. Coroner for Inner London North, Ex p. Touche* [2001] EWCA Civ, March 23.
[23] CPR r.69.7(1).
[24] CPR r.69.7(2).
[25] CPR r.69.7(3).

(a) the time properly given by the receiver and his staff to the receivership;

(b) the complexity of the receivership;

(c) any responsibility of an exceptional kind or degree which falls on the receiver in consequence of the receivership;

(d) the effectiveness with which the receiver appears to be carrying out or to have carried out his duties; and

(e) the value and nature of the subject matter of the receivership.

The court may refer the determination of the remuneration to a costs judge. The court may also make a different order in relation to the determination of the remuneration.[26]

The court will normally determine the amount of the receiver's remuneration on the basis of the above criteria CPR Parts 43–48 do not apply to the determination of the remuneration of receivers.[27] An application by a receiver for the amount of his remuneration to be determined must be supported by written evidence showing the basis on which the remuneration is claimed and that it is justified in accordance with the rule. The receiver must also supply a signed certificate that he considers that the remuneration claimed is reasonable and proportionate. Before the determining the amount of the remuneration the court may require the receiver to provide further information in support of the claim and appoint an assessor[28] to assist the court.[29] Expenses incurred by a receiver in carrying out his functions are accounted for as part of his account for the assets he has recovered and are not dealt with as part of the determination of his remuneration.[30]

Basis of assessment

4-020   There are two bases of assessment, the standard basis and the indemnity basis. The court may not in either case allow costs which have been unreasonably incurred or are unreasonable in amount. On the standard basis the court will only allow costs which are proportionate to the matters in issue and will resolve any doubt which it may have as to whether the costs were reasonably incurred or reasonable and proportionate in amount in favour of the paying party.[31]

---

[26] CPR r.69.7(4) and (5).
[27] Practice Direction Supplementing Part 69, paras 9.1–9.3.
[28] Under CPR r.35.15.
[29] Practice Direction Supplementing Pt 69, paras 9.4 and 9.5.
[30] Practice Direction Supplementing Pt 69, para.9.6.
[31] CPR r.44.4(1) and (2).

In applying the test of proportionality the court will have regard to the overriding objective[32] and in particular to the amount of money involved; the importance to the client; the complexity of the issues and the financial position of each party. The Costs Practice Direction points out that the relationship between the total of the costs incurred and the financial value of the claim may not be a reliable guide. In any proceedings there will be costs which will inevitably be incurred and which are necessary for the successful conduct of the case Where a trial takes place, the time taken by the court in dealing with a particular issue may not be an accurate guide to the amount of time properly spent by the legal or other representatives in preparation for the trial of that issue.[33]

Where costs are to be assessed on the indemnity basis the court will resolve any doubt which it may have as to whether costs were reasonably incurred, or were reasonable in amount, in favour of the receiving party. There is no requirement for the costs to be proportionate on the indemnity basis.[34]

If the court makes an order which is not for costs to be assessed on the standard basis or the indemnity basis, or does not indicate on which basis the costs are to be assessed, the costs will be assessed on the standard basis.[35]

In applying the test of proportionality the court will have regard to the overriding objective[36] and in particular the amount of money involved; the importance to the client; the complexity of the issues and the financial position of each party. The Practice Direction points out that the relationship between the total of the costs incurred and the financial value of the claim may not be a reliable guide. In any proceedings, there will be costs which will inevitably be incurred and which are necessary for the successful conduct of the case. Where a trial takes place, the time taken by the court in dealing with a particular issue may not be an accurate guide to the amount of time properly spent by the legal or other representatives in preparation for the trial of that issue.[37]

When new legislation during the course of proceedings renders them abortive, it is inappropriate to make defendants who have instigated the legislation pay indemnity costs.[38]

An order for costs on the indemnity basis is not justified merely because the costs of defending the action would have been recoverable as damages had separate proceedings been brought.[39] Where the conduct of the

---

[32] CPR r.1.1(2)(c).

[33] Costs Practice Direction, s.11.

[34] CPR r.44.4(3).

[35] CPR r.44.4(4).

[36] CPR r.1.1(2)(C).

[37] Direction relating to Part 44, paras 3.1–3.3.

[38] *R. v IRC, Ex p. Leeds Permanent Building Society*; *R. v Same, Ex p. National and Provincial Building Society, The Times*, May 28, 1993, DC.

[39] *Penn v Bristol & West Building Society* [1997] 1 W.L.R. 1356.

litigation is deserving of moral condemnation (such as pursuing allegations without a proper investigation of the facts), an order for costs on the indemnity basis is justified.[40]

An order for costs to be paid on the indemnity basis may be made on the application of judicial principles in situations where a party to litigation has acted in a way that could be described as disgraceful or deserving moral condemnation.[41]

A judge was wrong to award costs on the indemnity basis against a claimant who had not acted improperly in availing himself of the opportunity presented by statute to apply to the court. The claimant had made an application under the provisions of section 263 of the Insolvency Act 1986. The application had failed on the basis that the claimant had no sufficient interest to make the application. The Court of Appeal found the claimant had not acted improperly and that the costs should be on the standard basis.[42]

Rule 44.4(4)

4–021   The court has held that Rule 44.4(3) merely provides what is to be the legal consequence of an unqualified order for indemnity costs:

> " . . . it in no way forecloses the court from making a qualified order for indemnity costs, that is to say, an order where the ordering provision is qualified by the imposition of the burden of proof of reasonableness on the third party entitled to the costs."

The court ordered that accountants should receive all their costs reasonably incurred in complying with an order for disclosure, but the burden of justifying and explaining the reasonableness of those costs should lie on them.[43] The terms of this order appear to cut directly across the provisions of Rule 44.4(4)(b) and may well result in the costs being assessed on the standard basis.

A party who presented a petition to wind up a company without first presenting a statutory demand in circumstances where the petitioner knew there was a serious dispute over the quality of the goods supplied was ordered to pay the costs on the indemnity basis. The presentation of a petition in those circumstances was an abuse of process.[44]

---

[40] *Glyne Investments Ltd v Hill Samuel Life Assurance Ltd* (1997) Moses J., CA (unreported), and see *Cooper v P & O European Ferries (Dover) Ltd*, October 30, 1998, Miss B. Bucknall Q.C. (unreported).

[41] *Wailes v Stapleton Construction & Commercial Services Ltd*; *Wailes v Unum Ltd* [1997] 2 Lloyd's Rep. 112, Newman J.

[42] *Raja v Rubin, The Times*, April 14, 1999, CA.

[43] *Westminster City Council v Porter* [2003] EWHC 2373 (Ch), Lightman J.

[44] *Re: a Company (No.2507 of 2003)* [2003] EWHC 1484 (Ch); [2003] B.C.L.C. 346, Rimer J.

Where in group litigation the defendants mounted an attack on expert medical evidence underpinning a field research programme which they had themselves helped to set up, the court held that the defendants expert evidence lost intellectual and professional credibility and that the defendants' conduct was unreasonable; therefore on the generic medical issues it was directed that the defendants should pay costs on the indemnity basis, whereas in respect of all other issues where the plaintiffs succeeded, costs were awarded on the standard basis.[45]

Cross-examination of a claimant in a libel action amounting to a totally uncalled for personal attack resulted in the court making an order for costs on the indemnity basis in favour of the claimant for that portion of the trial when the claimant was being cross-examined.[46]

Proportionality

The Court of Appeal has given guidance on the correct approach to proportionality. The court stated that the requirement of proportionality now applies to decisions as to whether an order for costs should be made and to the assessment of costs which should be paid when an order has been made. The court suggested that the considerations to be taken into account by the court when making an order for costs under Rule 44.3 are "redolent of proportionality".   4–022

Because of the central role that proportionality should have in the resolution of civil litigation, it is essential that courts attach the appropriate significance to the requirement of proportionality when making orders for costs and when assessing the amount of costs.

> " . . . what is required is a two stage approach. There has to be a global approach and an item by item approach. The global approach will indicate whether the total sum claimed is or appears to be disproportionate having particular regard to the considerations which Part 44.5(3) states are relevant. If the costs as a whole are not disproportionate according to that test then all that is normally required is that each item should have been reasonably incurred and the costs for that item should be reasonable. If on the other hand the costs as a whole appear disproportionate then the court will want to be satisfied that the work in relation to each item was necessary and, if necessary, that the cost of the item was reasonable. If, because of lack of planning or due to other causes, the global costs are disproportionately high, then the requirement that the costs should be proportionate means that no more

---

[45] *The British Coal Respiratory Disease Litigation*, January 23, 1998, Turner J. (unreported).
[46] *Clark v Associated Newspapers Ltd, The Times*, January 28, 1998, Lightman J.

should be payable than would have been payable if the litigation had been conducted in a proportionate manner. This in turn means that reasonable costs will only be recovered for the items which were necessary if the litigation had been conducted in a proportionate manner."

The court expressed the view that costs judges are well equipped to assess which approach a particular case requires. In a case where proportionality is likely to be an issue a preliminary judgment as to the proportionality of the costs as a whole must be made at the outset. This will ensure that the costs judge applies the correct approach to the detailed assessment.

"In considering that question the Costs Judges will have regard to whether the appropriate level of fee earner or counsel has been deployed, whether offers to settle have been made, whether unnecessary experts had been instructed and the other matters set out in Part 44.5(3). Once the decision is reached as to proportionality of costs as a whole, the Judge will be able to proceed to consider the costs, item by item, applying the appropriate test to each item."

In considering what was necessary a sensible standard of necessity has to be adopted. This is a standard which takes fully into account the need to make allowances for the different judgments which those responsible for litigation can sensibly come to as to what is required. The danger of setting too high a standard with the benefit of hindsight has to be avoided. The threshold required to meet "necessity" is higher than that of "reasonable" but it is still a standard that a competent practitioner should be able to achieve without undue difficulty. When a practitioner incurs expenses which are reasonable but not necessary he may be able to recover his fees and disbursements from his client but the extra expense which results from conducting litigation in a disproportionate matter cannot be recovered from the other party.

In deciding what is necessary, the conduct of the other party is highly relevant. A party who is unco-operative may render necessary, costs which would otherwise be unnecessary and it is acceptable that he should pay the costs for the expense which he has made necessary.

Dealing with the situation where a claimant recovers significantly less than he has claimed the court stated that the following approach should be followed:

"Whether the costs incurred were proportionate should be decided having regard to what it was reasonable for the party in question to believe might be recovered, thus:

(i) the proportionality of the costs incurred by the claimant should be determined having regard to the sum that it was

reasonable for him to believe that he might recover at the time he made his claim;
(ii) the proportionality of the costs incurred by the defendant should be determined having regard to the sum it was reasonable for him to believe that the claimant might recover should his claim succeed.

This is likely to be the amount that the claimant has claimed, for a defendant will normally be entitled to take a claim at its face value.

The rationale for this approach is that a claimant should be allowed to incur the cost necessary to pursue a reasonable claim but not allowed to recover costs increased or incurred by putting forward an exaggerated claim and a defendant should not be prejudiced if he assumes the claim which was made was one which was reasonable and incurs costs in contesting the claim on this assumption."[47]

The application of the decision in *Home Office v Lownds* (above) has been considered by Morland J.:

"28. ... I do not accept that if a Costs Judge has ruled at the outset of a detailed assessment that the bill as a whole is not disproportionate he is precluded from deciding that an item or a number of items are or appear disproportionate having regard to the 'matters in issue'.

[...]

30. ... The effect of a preliminary finding of disproportionality is like unto traffic lights at red. The receiving party will then face a stringent test to justify with regard to each item that it has been 'proportionately and by a sensible standard necessarily incurred' and 'proportionate and reasonable in amount'.

[...]

32. A preliminary finding of disproportionality must not be regarded as penalising the receiving party in terms of the amount ultimately awarded because the overriding objective requires that a case is dealt with justly and fairly.
33. The preliminary judgment of proportionality determines the manner of the detailed assessment. It does not determine the final sum payable to the receiving party but a finding of disproportionality does entail the receiving party being put to a stringent test the dual test of sensible necessity and reasonableness of amount for each item ... In

---

[47] *Home Office v Lownds* [2002] EWCA Civ 365, [2002] 4 All E.R. 775, CA; see also *Jefferson v National Freight Carriers Plc* [2001] EWCA Civ 2082; [2001] 2 Costs L.R. 313, CA.

the unlikely event that a Costs Judge at the initial stage is unable to say whether the bill viewed as a whole is proportionate or disproportionate he will be obliged to carry out a detailed assessment applying the dual test.

[...]

37. .... The Court of Appeal never envisaged that a costs judge before giving a preliminary judgment on proportionality of the costs as a whole would plough through in detail this gargantuan mass of material.
38. In my judgment even in very complex group litigation an experienced Costs Judge if provided with succinct skeletons of the parties contentions beforehand should be able to determine overall proportionality within an hour or less ... "

The court went on to state that in considering whether the costs claimed were proportionate it would be wrong to leave out of account pre-CPR costs since they must form part of the global view. The judge concluded:

"54. .... If certain facets of the bill of costs strike the judge as being disproportionate he is entitled ... to rule that the bills as a whole fail the proportionality test and carry out the detailed assessment on the basis of the dual test. Even if the costs judge has reached the preliminary view that the bill as a whole is proportionate, in my judgment that preliminary view does not disentitle the costs judge from concluding that certain items appear disproportionate and applying the dual test of sensible necessity and reasonableness to that item."[48]

In assessing costs, a costs judge should assess whether the costs overall are proportionate and then proceed to assess proportionality and reasonableness on an item by item basis. When giving a ruling it is not imperative for a Costs Judge to go through the items in CPR r.44.5 as a checklist.[49]

Costs payable by or to particular persons

Pre-commencement disclosure and orders for disclosure against a non-party

4–023   Where an order for pre-commencement disclosure is made,[50] the court will generally award the costs of the application, and of complying with any

---

[48] *Giambrone v JMC Holidays Ltd* [2002] EWHC 2932 (QB); [2003] 1 All E.R. 982, Morland J.
[49] *Rugby Mansions Ltd v Ortwein* [2003] EWHC (Ch) July 28, Lloyd J.
[50] Under s.34 of the Supreme Court Act 1981 or s.53 of the County Courts Act 1984.

order made, to the person against whom the order is sought, but the court may make a different order having regard to all the circumstances. These circumstances include the extent to which it was reasonable for the application to be opposed and whether the parties complied with any relevant pre-action protocol.[51]

There is a presumption under CPR r.48.1 that the court will award costs to the person against whom the order for production of documents is sought. The court is entitled as a matter of discretion to deprive that party of its costs on the basis that the application has been unreasonably and unsuccessfully resisted.[52]

The court allowed an application by a bank, whose employee had been served with a witness summons, to produce certain relevant documents held by the bank, which the claimant then decided were no longer required and refused to contribute to the costs incurred by the bank. The bank's application to be joined as a party and for an order for costs in its favour was allowed, the court holding that to deprive the bank of costs to which it would have been entitled, if the application had been correctly made under section 34 of the Supreme Court Act 1981, would be unjust.[53]

Costs order in favour of or against non-parties

Section 51 of the Supreme Court Act 1981 gives the court full power to determine by whom and to what extent costs are to be paid. This means that the court may make an order in favour of or against a person who was not previously a party to the proceedings. If the court decides to make such an order, the person in favour of whom, or against whom, the order is contemplated must be added as a party to the proceedings, for the purposes of costs only, and must be given a reasonable opportunity to attend a hearing at which the court will consider the matter further.[54]

4–024

The Court of Appeal has laid down guidelines for the exercise of this power.[55]

The following are material considerations:

    (a) An order for the payment of costs by a non-party is always exceptional[56]; the judge should treat any application for such an order with considerable caution.

---

[51] CPR r.48.1.

[52] *Bermuda International Securities Ltd v KPMG* [2001] EWCA Civ 26.

[53] *Individual Homes Ltd v MacBream Investments Ltd*, *The Times*, November 14, 2002, Alan Steinfeld Q.C.

[54] CPR r.48.2(1). This rule does not apply where the court is considering whether to make an order against the Legal Services Commission; to make a wasted costs order; or in proceedings for pre-commencement disclosure under CPR r.48.1: CPR r.48.2(2).

[55] See *Symphony Group Plc v Hodgson* [1993] 4 All E.R. 143, CA.

[56] *per* Lord Goff, *Aiden Shipping Co. Ltd v Inter Bulk Ltd* [1986] A.C. 965 at 980F.

(b) It is even more exceptional for an order for the payment of costs to be paid against a non-party where the applicant has a cause of action against the non-party and could have joined him as a party to the original proceedings. Joinder as a party to the proceedings gives the persons concerned all the protection conferred by the rules.

(c) [No longer relevant].

(d) An application for payment of costs by a non-party will normally be determined by the trial judge.[57]

(e) The fact that the trial judge in the course of his judgment has expressed views on the conduct of the non-party neither constitutes bias nor the appearance of bias.[58]

(f) The procedure for the determination of costs is a summary procedure not necessarily subject to all the rules which would apply in an action. Thus, subject to any relevant statutory exceptions, judicial findings are inadmissible as evidence of the facts upon which they are based in proceedings between one of the parties to the original proceedings and the stranger.[59] Yet in the summary procedure for the determination of the liability of a solicitor to pay the costs of an action to which he was not a party, the judge's findings of fact may be admissible.[60] This departure from basic principles can only be justified if the connection of the non-party with the original proceedings was so close that he will not suffer any injustice by allowing the exception to the general rule.

(g) The normal rule is that witnesses in either civil or criminal proceedings enjoy immunity from any form of civil action in respect of evidence given during those proceedings. One reason for that immunity is so that witnesses might give their evidence fearlessly.[61] In so far as the evidence of a witness in proceedings might lead to an application for the costs of those proceedings against him or his company, it introduces another exception to the general principle.

---

[57] *Bahai v Rashidian* [1985] 1 W.L.R. 1337.
[58] *Bahai v Rashidian*, above at 1342H–1346F.
[59] *Hollington v Hewthorn & Co. Ltd* [1943] K.B. 587. See also, *National Justice Compania Naviera SA v Prudential Assurance Co. Ltd ("The Ikarian Reefer" No.2)* [2000] 1 All E.R. 3, CA; and *Robertson Research International Ltd v ABG Exploration BV, The Times*, November 3, 1999, Laddie J.
[60] *Brendon v Spiro* [1938] K.B. 176 at 192 *per* Scott L.J.; *Bahai v Rashidian*, above at 1343D, 1345H.
[61] *Palmer v Durnford Ford* [1992] Q.B. 483 at 487.

(h) The fact that an employee, or even a director of a company gives evidence in an action does not normally mean that the company is taking part in that action in so far as that is an allegation relied upon by the party who applies for an order for costs against a non-party.[62]

(i) The judge should be alert to the possibility that an application for costs against a non-party is motivated by resentment or an inability to obtain an effective order for costs against a legally aided litigant. The courts are well aware of the financial difficulties faced by parties who are facing legally aided litigants at first instance where the opportunity of a claim against the Legal Aid Board (under section 18 of the Legal Aid Act 1988) is very limited. Nevertheless, the Civil Legal Aid (General) Regulations (particularly regs 67, 69 and 70) lay down conditions designed to ensure that there is no abuse of legal aid by a legally assisted person and are designed to protect the other party to the litigation as well as the legal aid fund. The court will be very reluctant to infer that solicitors to a legally aided party have failed to discharge their duty under the regulations.[63] The principle extends to a reluctance to infer that any maintenance by a non-party has occurred.[64] Exceptional circumstances are not a pre-condition to the power. Ultimately, the test is whether in all the circumstances it is just to exercise the power.[65]

Section 51 of the Supreme Court Act 1981 empowers the courts to determine by whom costs are paid, including by persons not party to the proceedings. The court necessarily has the ancillary power to order a party to proceedings, or solicitors who have been on the record for him, to disclose to the other party the names of those who have financed the litigation. Where a power exists to grant a remedy there must be, inherent in that power, the power to make ancillary orders to make the remedy effective.[66]

A Director and owner of a company in winding up proceedings could be ordered to pay the costs personally where he was the only person behind the company. He had not co-operated with the Secretary of State, the scheme run by his company was a swindle and he was responsible for the proceedings being contested.[67]

---

[62] *Gleeson v J. Wippel & Co.* [1977] 1 W.L.R. 510 at 513.
[63] *Orchard v South Eastern Electricity Board* [1987] Q.B. 565.
[64] *per* Balcombe L.J. in *Symphony Group Plc v Hodgson* [1993] 4 All E.R. 143.
[65] *Globe Equities Ltd v Globe Legal Services Ltd* [1999] B.L.R. 232, CA.
[66] See *Abraham v Thompson* [1997] 4 All E.R. 326; *Raiffeisenzentral Bank Osterreich AG v Crossseas Shipping Ltd* [2003] EWHC 1381 (Comm), Morrison J.
[67] *Secretary of State for Trade and Industry v Aurum Marketing Ltd*, *The Times*, August 10, 2000, CA.

A similar order was made against the owner of 75 per cent of the shares of a company which had been operating a swindle and was wound up. Although the shareholder was not a director he was the moving force behind the company and its opposition to the winding-up order. The court held that as the shareholder was operating the swindle he could not be heard to say that he was resisting the winding-up order in the public interest or that of the creditors or the company. Although there was cash in hand it could not be assumed that the company was solvent. The shareholder was ordered to pay the costs of the Secretary of State and of the company. The company's costs were not to be paid out of the assets of the company until all the unsecured creditors had been paid in full. If the shareholder paid the costs of the Secretary of State and if all the other creditors were paid he would be entitled to seek recovery of the company's costs from the company.[68]

Failure by a judge to consider the moral blameworthiness of the defendants does not amount to an error of law. The judge's discretion to award costs would not be interfered with by the Court of Appeal unless there had been some error of law in the exercise of that discretion.[69]

The court is only entitled to award the costs in respect of proceedings which are before the court: section 51 of the 1981 Act does not confer jurisdiction on the court to award costs other than those incurred in the proceedings before it.[70]

The jurisdiction given by section 51 of the Supreme Court Act was not limited so as to exclude an order in contribution proceedings in respect of a sum of costs paid to the claimant in the main proceedings. Accordingly a contribution could be ordered in respect of the costs of the main proceedings which had been settled.[71]

Where successful defendants sought an order for costs against the claimants' solicitors on the basis that they had acted as the true funders of the litigation the court held that deferring or limiting the claimants' costs until the outcome of the case does not make the solicitor a funder, maintainer or financier. Even though the solicitors might have acted rashly or over generously they did not act outside their role of solicitors when they made these decisions. Hale L.J. stated:

> "[the solicitors] did not engage in an improper no win/no fee agreement. They simply took a risk and extended credit to their client. It would be a sad day if solicitors could not extend credit even to their

---

[68] *Secretary of State for Trade v Liquid Acquisitions Ltd* [2003] EWHC 180 (Ch) Lloyd J.; [2003] 1 B.C.L.C. 375.
[69] *Arab Monetary Fund v Hashim (No.12)* Q.B. CMF 92/1618/B, March 12, 1996, CA.
[70] *Zanussi v Anglo Venezuelan Real Estate and Agricultural Development Ltd, The Times,* April 18, 1996, CA.
[71] *BICC v Cumbrian Industrial* [2001] EWCA Civ 1621; [2002] Lloyd's Rep. P.N. 526.

litigation clients, without fear of vulnerability to a Section 51 order."[72]

When considering whether a non-party insurer should be ordered to pay costs it does not necessarily always have to be shown that the insurer has acted out of self interest unless there is sufficient conflict of interest.[73]

In a case where the defendant was uninsured by a P. & I. Club, which supported the defence for a period and subsequently withdrew, the court refused the claimant's application that the insurers should pay the costs on the indemnity basis, the defendant having persisted with its defence and lost after a lengthy trial.[74]

In a case where insurers decided on behalf of the defendant that the claim would be fought, and funded the defence of the claim and had conduct of it, in circumstances where the claim had been fought exclusively to defend the insurers' interests and the defence had failed in its entirety, the court held that the insurers were liable to indemnify the defendant to the limit of the insurance policy but also liable to pay the successful claimant's costs of the action without limit. The insurers who took over the defence of an action and conducted themselves for their own benefit, even though not a party to the action, could expect to pay the costs of the claimant if the defence was unsuccessful.[75]

The mere existence of legal expenses insurance does not make it reasonable or just to order the insurer to pay the costs of the adverse successful party.[76] Similarly, the court refused to make an order against a liquidator personally in the absence of any impropriety.[77] On the other hand, the court did make an order against a non-party who was a director of an insolvent company and who had the management of the action and where that person had financed the proceedings and had improperly caused the company to defend the claim and to pursue a concocted counterclaim. In the judge's view the director's connection with the proceedings was so close that it was inconceivable that he would suffer any injustice.[78]

In the case of a trustee in bankruptcy who had taken steps to revive a moribund action, the court found that it would have been unjust had he

---

[72] *Floods of Queensferry v Shand* [2002] EWCA Civ 918; [2003] Lloyd's Rep. I.R. 181, CA.

[73] *Cormack v Excess Insurance Co Ltd, The Times,* March 30, 2000, CA.

[74] *Tharros Shipping Co. Ltd v Bias Shipping Ltd (No.3)* [1995] 1 Lloyd's Rep. 541, Rix J.

[75] *T.G.A. Chapman Ltd v Christopher* [1998] 1 W.L.R. 12, CA; *Cormack v Washbourne* [2000] Lloyd's Rep P.N. 459; *Pendennis Ship Yard Ltd v Margrathea (Pendennis) Ltd (in liquidation), The Times,* August 27, 1997, H.H. Judge Jack Q.C., Bristol Mercantile Court.

[76] *Murphy v Young & Co.'s Brewery plc* [1997] 1 W.L.R. 1591, CA; and see *Fulton Motors Ltd v Toyota (GB) Ltd,* unreported, July 23, 1999, CA.

[77] *Metalloy Supplies Ltd (in liquidation) v M.A. (U.K.) Ltd* [1997] 1 All E.R. 418, CA.

[78] *H. Leverton Ltd v Crawford Offshore (Excavation) Services Ltd (in liquidation), The Times,* November 22, 1996, Garland J. and see *Quadrant Holdings (Cambridge) Ltd v Quadrant Research Foundation (Costs)* [1999] F.S.R. 918, Pumfrey J.

been immune from liability for costs. By electing to adopt the claimant's action he ran the risk of obtaining a costs order against him if unsuccessful. The court compared the position of a liquidator of a company[79] and found that the position of a liquidator could not be equated with that of a trustee in bankruptcy since the liquidator, unlike the trustee, was not a person in whom the case vested.[80]

It is clear from the authorities that the court is to draw a clear distinction between (commercially) disinterested funders on the one hand and those whose interests stand to be advanced by a successful outcome of litigation on the other. It is a pre-condition for the making of an order that the funder was responsible for the litigation, in the sense that without the funding the litigation would not have taken place. If the funder was a pure disinterested funder the order would not be made. If that condition was not satisfied the question was whether, in all the circumstances, justice required that the order be made. Where the funding provided was causative of the defence to the action, which would not have been defended but for the funding, causing the claimants to run up costs unnecessarily, and the funding was for the funder's own commercial benefit, the funder was ordered to pay the costs.[81]

Three defendants to a commercial action were separately funded by two non-parties. The court found that they were not "pure" funders and that an order for costs could be made against them. In the absence of evidence that they had acted in collusion they were severally liable for costs in equal amounts rather than jointly and severally liable for the full amount.[82] On appeal by one of the funders the court found that it could not be criticised for assisting the first defendant financially in instructing solicitors of high standing and for assisting him in attempting to discharge his costs liability, particularly given the effect of a freezing order on that defendant's access to his own funds. The court found there was no logical basis for finding that the actions of the funder which had the desired consequence of ensuring that the first defendant's case did not go by default so transformed the nature of the funder's involvement as to justify a costs order against him. There was no suggestion that he had been personally interested in the outcome of the litigation.[83]

The Commercial Court has held that there are three principles of public policy material to determining how to exercise the discretion as to costs:

(i) discouraging ill founded claims or defences and compensating those obliged to protect their rights;

---

[79] See *Metalloy Supplies Ltd (in liquidation) v M.A. (U.K.) Ltd* above at 77.
[80] *Trustee of the property of Christopher Vickery (in bankruptcy) v Modern Security Systems Ltd* [1998] B.C.L.C. 428, CA.
[81] *Phillips v Princo* [2003] EWHC (Ch), unreported, September 16, Pumfrey J.
[82] *Gulf Azov v Idisi* [2003] EWHC (Comm), July 21, Arthur Marriott Q.C.
[83] *Gulf Azov Shipping v Idsi* [2004] EWCA Civ 292.

(ii) facilitating access to justice for impecunious claimants in the absence of public funding—insurance or trade union membership needed to be supported; and

(iii) the purpose of protecting administration of justice which required that the court should discourage interference by funders in the proper and responsible management and conduct of litigation in any manner adverse to that purpose.

Whether an order for third party costs against a professional funder should be made depended primarily on whether the court was satisfied that such an order was appropriate to reflect the defendant's success and the risk of prejudice to the objective of protecting the due administration of justice. The mere fact of a contract for a share in the proceeds of the litigation did not necessarily involve such material prejudice. This depended on the legal and practical relationship between the professional funder and the claimant. The interposition of independent and objective legal advice was a key consideration in deciding whether the funder's relationship with the prosecution of a claim justified a costs order against the funder. The fact that a professional funder failed to agree with an impecunious claimant to pay the defendant's costs if the claim failed, should not necessarily lead to a costs order being made against it. In the particular case, the court found that the funder's relationship with the claimant was not adverse to public policy considerations. The funder did not attempt to control or influence the conduct of the proceedings. If the claimant had not entered into the funding agreement, the claim would have had to have been abandoned or fought without expert evidence and therefore without equality of arms. ATE cover would have been so expensive as to render it impossible to bear the premium. The funder could not commercially undertake responsibility for the defendant's potentially huge costs as part of the funding agreement. The public policy objectives of the deterrence of weak claims and the protection of the due administration of justice from interference by non-party funders had to yield to the objective of making access to the courts available to impecunious claimants with claims of sufficient substance. The court declined to make an order for payment of the successful claimant's costs against the non-party funder.[84]

In relation to defamation cases the court has to have particular regard to the Convention right of freedom of expression. In a case where a unsuccessful claimant had been supported by others the court refused to make an order against the non parties in favour of the defendant stating that none of the respondents had played any active part in the litigation. Donations towards the claimant's funds were not made as a result of any obligation but as an act of charity through sympathy with his predicament and in some

---

[84] *Arkin v Borchard Lines Ltd* [2003] EWHC 2844 (Comm), Colman J.

cases affinity to the Conservative Party. Until the last minute emergence of certain evidence the claimant had had some realistic prospect of success; it was in the public interest and in the interests of justice that a litigant of limited means could assert a right against a rich opponent. A rich philanthropist who wished to act as a charity to achieve effective access and a measure of equality of arms should not be discouraged and it was in the public interest that these matters be decided by a jury.[85] The Court of Appeal upheld this decision, adding that the interests of justice did not generally require such a funder to contribute to the costs which the defendant was unable to recover from the claimant alone.[86]

A party, believing the constitution of the Restrictive Practices Court was biased, appealed to the Court of Appeal from the refusal of the lower court to recuse itself. The appellant submitted that their right to a fair trial under Article 6(1) the ECHR had been infringed and that they were entitled to be compensated for the wasted costs by the Lord Chancellor who was the emanation of the State responsible for providing impartial tribunals to conduct trials of civil litigation. The court held that the appellant could not properly be regarded as a victim for the purpose of making a claim and since the court had remedied the situation by providing an impartial tribunal to determine the party's civil rights and obligations there had been no violation of the party's right to a fair trial. The application was refused.[87]

The court made an order in favour of a non party where a defendant unsuccessfully pursued an inquiry into the damages sustained by him as a result of a mareva injunction granted (incorrectly as it turned out) in favour of the claimant and a wasted costs application against the claimants solicitors. The Solicitors Indemnity Fund (SIF) as the insurers of the claimant's solicitors gave the claimant an indemnity in respect of any claim that the defendant might have against the claimant arising out of the proceedings. Having lost his application the defendant accepted that he was liable to pay both the costs of the claimant and of the solicitors on the standard basis but objected to paying the costs of the inquiry incurred by SIF and argued that since the claimant had an indemnity she had incurred no liability for costs. It was held that it would be a grotesque injustice if the defendant were to escape liability for payment of the costs of the inquiry. Had the defendant won he would have sought his costs from SIF. The circumstances amounted to exceptional circumstances which permitted the court to make an order in its discretion under section 51 of the Supreme Court Act 1981 in favour of the SIF. The interests of the SIF could be taken into account in considering whether exceptional circumstances existed notwithstanding that they were external to the litigation itself. The SIF had acted in the public interest to reduce costs and not to award it its costs

---

[85] *Hamilton v Al-Fayed* [2001], *The Times*, July 25, Morland J.
[86] *Hamilton v Al Fayed (No.2)* [2003] 2 W.L.R. 128; [2002] 3 All E.R. 641, CA.
[87] *Director General of Fair Trading v Proprietary Association of Great Britain* [2001] EWCA Civ 1217; [2002] 1 All E.R. 853, CA.

would send out the message that it had acted wrongly in so doing. The SIF had in fact acted perfectly properly.[88]

Judicial review

The Administrative Court has considered what costs orders should be made where judicial review proceedings are concluded without a full hearing. The following principles were identified:

4-025.1

(i) the court has power to make a costs order where the substantive proceedings have been resolved without a trial but the parties have not agreed about costs;

(ii) it will normally be irrelevant that the claimant is LSC funded;

(iii) the overriding objective is to do justice between the parties without incurring unnecessary court time and consequently additional costs;

(iv) at each end of the spectrum there will be cases where it is obvious which side would have won had the substantive issues been fought to a conclusion. In between the position will, in differing degrees, be less clear. How far the court will be prepared to look into the previously unresolved substantive issues which depend on the circumstances of the particular case, not least the amount of costs at that stage and the conduct of the parties;

(v) in the absence of a good reason to make any other order the fallback is to make no order as to costs;

(vi) the court should take care to ensure that it does not discourage parties from settling judicial review proceedings, for example by a local authority making a concession at an early stage.[89]

In an appropriate case the court may reserve the costs of the application to be determined by the Immigration Appeal Tribunal.[90]

Since it is now open to a defendant in judicial review proceedings to resist the application for permission the court has held that if a defendant incurs costs in submitting an acknowledgment of service as required by the new rules, and in putting forward objections to the claim, the defendant ought to be able, if he succeeded, to recover his costs of so doing.[91]

---

[88] *Holden v Oysten* [2002] EWHC 819 (QB), McKinnon J.
[89] *Boxall v Waltham Forest LBC* [2000] EWHC Admin., December 21, Scott-Baker J.
[90] CPR r.54.27.
[91] *R. (Leach) v Commissioner for Local Administration, The Times*, August 2, 2001, Collins J.

In a case where the claimant sought judicial review of a local authority's failure to provide housing the case was adjourned for eight weeks to enable the defendant to identify suitable housing. The principal claimant died during that period, the Judge made no order as to costs among other things because each side was supported by public funds. The Court of Appeal approved the principles in *Boxall v Waltham Forest*, above and held that the judge ought not to have been influenced by the fact that the claimant had been legally aided.[92] In a case where the borough council had refused to supply relevant particulars which, when eventually supplied, rendered the judicial review application academic, the court ordered the council to pay the applicant's costs.[93]

There may be judicial review cases where public interest or analogous considerations make it inappropriate in all the circumstances to require an unsuccessful claimant to pay a defendant's costs. The presence or absence of any private interest is not a determining factor with regard to costs. The statutory duty of the court is to have regard to all the circumstances.[94]

The court has power to award costs against magistrates in judicial review proceedings where the magistrates have behaved unreasonably in all the circumstances. That includes the nature of the flaw in the original decision, the attitude of the applicant or appellant, the information provided to the magistrates and the type of consideration needed.[95]

In judicial review proceedings the applicant solicitors had written a well-argued letter before action to the Council, which continued to decline the applicant's request for accommodation. Application for judicial review was made but before the matter came before the single judge, the respondent conceded the claim. The Divisional Court, allowing the application for costs against the respondent stated that it was only in a very clear case that the court should exercise the power under the Supreme Court Act 1981, s.51 to order costs against respondents in such circumstances.[96]

The failure by a local authority to process a housing benefit claim expeditiously resulting in the tenant having to commence proceedings for judicial review resulted in the court making an order for costs on the indemnity basis against the local authority since the application was one to which the authority could have no answer.[97]

The Court of Appeal has given guidance on the proper approach to the award of costs against an unsuccessful claimant on an oral application for

---

[92] *R. (on the application of Kuzeva) v Southwark LBC* [2002] EWCA Civ 781; [2002] All E.R. (D) 488, CA.

[93] *Bernard v Dudley MBC* [2003] EWHC 147 (Admin), Henriques J.

[94] *Smeaton v Secretary of State for Health* [2002] EWHC 866 (Admin), Munby J.

[95] *R. v Newcastle-under-Lyme Magistrates, Ex p. Massey*; *R. v Stoke on Trent Magistrates' Court, Ex p. Knight* [1994] 1 W.L.R. 1684. *R. v Stoke on Trent Justices, Ex p. Booth, The Independent*, February 9, 1996, Owen J.

[96] *R. v Kensington & Chelsea RLBC, Ex p: Ghebregiogis* [1994] C.O.D. 502, DC.

[97] *R. (on the application of Taha) v Lambeth LBC* [2002] EWHC Admin February 7, Munby J.

permission to apply for judicial review. The effect of CPR Practice Direction 54 (judicial review paragraph 8.6) is that a defendant who attends and successfully resists the grant of permission at a renewal hearing should not generally recover from the claimant his costs of and occasioned by doing so. The court in considering an award against an unsuccessful claimant of the defendant's and/or any other interested party's costs at a permission hearing should only depart from the general guidance in the Practice Direction if it considers that there are exceptional circumstances for doing so. Exceptional circumstances may include:

(a) the hopelessness of the claim;

(b) the persistence in it by the claimant after its hopelessness has been demonstrated;

(c) the extent to which the court considers that the claimant has sought to abuse the process of judicial review; and

(d) whether the unsuccessful claimant has had in effect the advantage of an early substantive hearing of the claim.

A relevant factor for the court may be the extent to which the unsuccessful claimant has substantial resources which it has used to pursue the unfounded claim and which are available to meet an order for costs.[98]

Public Funding/Legal Aid

Under section 51(1) of the Supreme Court Act 1981 the court has jurisdiction to make an order for costs even against the Legal Services Commission provided that, exceptionally, the circumstances are such as to make it appropriate.   **4–025.2**

"The role of the Board in litigation in which it is assisting one of the parties is an essential one. The Board's efficient performance of its statutory duties is crucial to the proper and expeditious conduct of such litigation and the courts have an essential interest in seeing that those functions are performed in such a way that litigation is efficiently progressed . . . the relationship of the Board to litigation in which it is assisting a party is so close, its role in its financing is such and the effect of its actions upon the efficiency and speed of litigation are such that in the appropriate case,[99] which clearly will be the exceptional one, the

---

[98] R. (Mount Cook Land Ltd) v Westminster City Council [2003] EWCA Civ 1346; R. v (Clive Payne) v Caerphilly County BC [2004] EWCA Civ, March 17.

[99] Bearing in mind the factors set out in Symphony Group Plc v Hodgson [1994] Q.B. 179, CA, see para.4–024 above.

court has jurisdiction over the Board to make an order under Section 51(1)."[1]

Although the above decision referred to the Legal Aid Board there appears to be no reason why the principle should not apply in respect of the Legal Services Commission. In ordinary circumstances, an application for payment of costs by the Legal Services Commission would be made under the procedure laid down with regard to orders made under section 11 of the Access to Justice Act 1999.[2]

Orders for costs against solicitors

4–025.3   In *Tolstoy v Aldington*,[3] the solicitors acted without fee for the claimant who did not have the means to pay any damages or costs. The judge found the claim was "utterly hopeless" and struck it out as an abuse of process. The defendant sought an order that the claimant's solicitor should pay his costs either on the basis of maintenance or wasted costs. The judge at first instance accepted the maintenance argument and ordered the solicitors to pay 60 per cent of the defendant's costs. The Court of Appeal dismissed the solicitor's appeal but disagreed with the judge at first instance preferring to proceed on the wasted costs basis. The court held that where legal representatives act pro bono it cannot be said that they are liable for costs on a "non-party" basis. The court accepted the submission that there are only three categories of conduct which can give rise to an order for costs against a solicitor, namely:

(a) if it is within the wasted costs jurisdiction;

(b) if it is otherwise a breach of duty to the court;

(c) if the solicitor acts outside the role of a solicitor, *e.g.*, in a private capacity or as a true third party funder for someone else.

Other parties

4–025.4   The Division Court held[4] that it was *prima facie* right that third parties who have been supporting litigation should be ordered to meet costs orders. It is reasonable to infer that third parties who supported a previous application for habeas corpus would know that the applicant had exhausted his

---

[1] *Kelly v South Manchester Health Authority* [1997] 3 All E.R. 274, Thomas J.
[2] See para.4–006.
[3] *Tolstoy-Miloslavsky v Aldington* [1996] 1 W.L.R. 736; [1996] 2 All E.R. 556, CA.
[4] *R. v Secretary of State for the Home Department, Ex p. Osman (No.2)* [1993] C.O.D. 204, DC.

resources, had outstanding orders for costs which could not be met and had no immediate prospect of paying. The court was therefore able to order the applicant and his solicitors to disclose the identity of third parties so that they could make representations and be ordered to the costs if appropriate.

The court has no power to make an order for costs against individual officers of a respondent local authority who were not parties to the proceedings. The Court of Appeal set aside such an order because it had been made to punish the officers for the way in which they had handled (or failed to handle) a homeless person case.[5]

Where a claimant exercised its right to a statutory appeal under the Charities Act 1993 and applied for the Commissioners to be joined as defendants, the Court of Appeal held that it had a discretion to decide whether the Commissioners were proper defendants to the proceedings. The court decided it was neither necessary nor desirable for the Commissioners to be joined and, in relation to the question of costs, the claimant would be able to recover any costs against the Commissioners, even if not originally a party to the action under the principle in *Aiden Shipping*.[6]

In the case of a director of an insolvent company an order that that director should pay the costs personally would not normally be made unless it could be shown that the director had caused the company to bring or defend the proceedings improperly. The fact that the director might have benefited personally if the litigation had been successful is not enough by itself to justify an order under section 51 of the Supreme Court Act 1981. Something more is required such as deliberately misleading evidence, even if that evidence is not ultimately relied upon in court.[7]

Following a complaint by a member of a pension scheme to the Pensions Ombudsman, the Ombudsman required the trustee and employer of the complainant to secure the provision of additional benefits for him. The employer appealed to the High Court, as did the scheme's insurer. Both were separately represented on appeal. The complainant took no part in the appeals because of lack of means. The Ombudsman appeared by solicitors and counsel and the two appeals were successful. The court held that since the Ombudsman had made himself a party to the proceedings he put himself at risk as to an order for costs. In the case of appeals from tribunals other than the Pensions Ombudsman there was a settled practice that if the tribunal took no part in the appeal an order for costs would not be made against it, but if it did appear and make representations it made itself at least potentially liable for costs in the event that its decision was reversed. The court held that there was no reason to distinguish the position of the Ombudsman from that of other tribunals. There was no reason to depart

---

[5] *R. v Lambeth BC, Ex p. Wilson* [1998] 30 H.L.R. 64, CA.
[6] *Weth v H.M. Attorney General*, [1999] 1 W.L.R. 686, CA. *Aiden Shipping Co. Ltd v Inter Bulk Ltd (The Vimeria)* [1986] A.C. 965.
[7] *Gardiner v F.X. Music Ltd* [2000] All E.R. (D) 144, Geoffrey Vos Q.C.

from the general rule that the unsuccessful party should be ordered to pay the costs of the successful party, but on the facts of the case there was no justification for ordering the Ombudsman to pay two sets of costs. The Ombudsman was ordered to pay the employers' costs of the appeal.[8]

Maintenance and champerty

4–026.1   One of the recurring themes which the courts have had to deal with over the years is that of actions being supported by non-parties and the extent to which such parties can and should be made liable to pay the opposing party's costs in the event of failure.

Lord Mustill succinctly described the history of maintenance and champerty in a judgment in 1993[9]:

> " . . . the crimes of maintenance and champerty are so old that their origins can no longer be traced, but their importance in medieval times is quite clear. The mechanisms of justice lacked the internal strength to resist the oppression of private individuals through suits fomented and sustained by unscrupulous men of power. Champerty was particularly vicious since the purchase of a share in litigation presented an obvious temptation to the suborning of justices and witnesses and the exploitation of worthless claims which the defendant lacked the resources and influence to withstand. The fact that such conduct was treated as both criminal and tortious provided an invaluable external discipline to which, as the records show, recourse was often required. As the centuries passed the courts became stronger, their mechanisms more consistent and their participants more self reliant. Abuses could be more easily determined in accordance with the demands of justice, without recourse to separate proceedings against those who trafficked in litigation. In the most recent decades of the present century maintenance and champerty have become almost invisible in both their criminal and tortious manifestations. In practice, they have maintained a living presence in only two respects. First, as the source of the rule, now in the course of attenuation,[10] which forbids a solicitor from accepting payment for professional services on behalf of a plaintiff calculated as a proportion of the sum recovered from the defendant. Secondly, as the ground for denying recognition to the assignment of a "bare right of action". The former survives nowadays, so far as it survives at all (that is, champerty), largely as a rule of professional conduct, and the latter (that is, assignment), is in my opinion best

---

[8] *Moore's (Wallisdown) Ltd v Pensions Ombudsman* [2002] 1 W.L.R. 1649; [2002] 1 All E.R. 737, Ferris J.
[9] *Giles v Thompson* [1994] 1 A.C. 142 at 153.
[10] *i.e.* by the introduction of conditional fees.

treated as having achieved an independent life of its own. It therefore came as no surprise when Parliament, acting on the recommendation of the Law Commission,[11] abolished the crimes and torts of maintenance and champerty."[12]

The abolition of the crimes and torts does not affect any rule of that law where a contract is to be treated as contrary to public policy or otherwise illegal.[13]

Maintenance

The Law Commission defined maintenance as "the procurement, by direct or indirect financial assistance, of another person to institute, or carry on or defend civil proceedings without lawful justification".[14] The Commission went on to discuss what might constitute "lawful justification" and noted that the trend of judicial authorities was towards an increase in the number of interests which the courts are prepared to accept.[15]

Lord Denning M.R. commented on the developing law on a number of occasions, first in 1968:

> "A person is still guilty of maintenance if he supports litigation in which he has no legitimate concern without just cause or excuse. But the bounds of 'legitimate concern' have been widened: and 'just cause or excuse' has readily been found. . . .
>
> Much maintenance is considered justifiable today which would in 1914[16] have been considered obnoxious. Most of the actions in our courts are supported by some association or other, or by the State itself. Comparatively few litigants bring suits, or defend them, at their own expense. Most claims by workmen against their employers are paid for by a trade union. Most defences of motorists are paid for by insurance companies. This is perfectly justifiable and is accepted by everyone as lawful, provided always that the one who supports the litigation, if it fails, pays the costs of the other side."[17]

Lord Justice Scarman confirmed the continuing erosion of illegality in 1975:

4–026.2

---

[11] Proposals for the Reform of the Law relating to Maintenance and Champerty, 1966, Law Com. No. 7.
[12] s.14 of the Criminal Law Act 1967.
[13] s.14(2) the Criminal Law Act 1967.
[14] Para.9, Proposals for the Reform of the Law relating to Maintenance and Champerty, 1966, Law Com. No.7.
[15] Report, para.10.
[16] *i.e.* at the time of the judgment in *Oram v Hutt* [1914] 1 Ch. 98, CA.
[17] *Hill v Archbold* [1968] 1 Q.B. 686, CA.

"The maintenance of other people's litigation is no longer regarded as a mischief: trade unions, trade protection societies, insurance companies and the State do it regularly and frequently. The law has always recognised that there can be lawful justification for maintaining somebody else's litigation; today, with the emergence of legal aid, trade unions and insurance companies, a great volume of litigation is maintained by persons who are not parties to it . . . the law, therefore, may recognise exceptions to its illegality."[18]

Lord Denning expressed the view in a later judgment that although the abolition of the crimes and torts of maintenance and champerty struck down earlier authorities based on outdated public policy:

"it did not strike down our modern cases in so far as they carry out the public policy of today."[19]

He concluded:

"It is perfectly legitimate today for one person to support another in bringing or resisting an action—as by paying the costs of it—provided that he has a legitimate and genuine interest in the result of it and the circumstances are such as reasonably to warrant his giving his support."[20]

In *Trendtex Trading Corporation v Credit Suisse*,[21] the case which the court had to consider was the assignment of a bare right to litigate.[22] Both the House of Lords and the Court of Appeal were unanimous in holding that if no parties had been involved in the assignment other than Trendtex and Credit Suisse then the assignment would have been valid. The only point of difference was the effect of the onward sale to any anonymous third party.[23] The House of Lords considered the onward assignment to be objectionable on the ground of champerty. Lord Justice Lloyd went on to summarise the principles established by the House of Lords.[24]

---

[18] *Wallersteiner v Moir (No.2)* [1975] 1 All E.R. 849, CA. See also *Norglen Ltd (in liquidation) v Reeds Rains Prudential Ltd; Circuit Systems Ltd (in liquidation) v Zukeh-Redac (U.K.) Ltd* [1998] 1 All E.R. 218, HL.

[19] *Trendtex Trading Corp. v Credit Suisse* [1980] Q.B. 629, CA.

[20] [1980] Q.B. 629 at 653.

[21] [1980] Q.B. 629, CA; [1982] A.C. 692, HL.

[22] "The question was whether the subject matter of the assignment was in the view of the court property with an incidental remedy for its recovery, or was a bare right to bring an action either at law or in equity." *Glegg v Bromley* [1912] K.B. 474, Parker J.

[23] See *Brownton Ltd v Edward Moore Inbucon Ltd* [1985] 3 All E.R. 499 at 507, Lloyd L.J., CA.

[24] [1985] 3 All E.R. 499 at 509.

"i.   Maintenance is justified, *inter alia*, if the maintainer has a genuine commercial interest in the result of the litigation.

ii. There is no difference between the interest required to justify maintenance of an action and the interest required to justify the taking of a share in the proceeds or the interest required to support an out and out assignment.

iii. A bare right to litigate, the assignment of which is still prohibited, is a cause of action, whether in tort or contract, in the outcome of which the assignee has no genuine commercial interest.

iv. In judging whether the assignee has a genuine commercial interest for the purpose of (i) to (iii) above one must look at the transaction as a whole.

v.   If an assignee has a genuine commercial interest in enforcing the cause of action it is not fatal that the assignee may make a profit out of the assignment.

vi. It is an open question whether if the assignee does make such a profit, he is answerable to the assignor for the difference."

On the facts of *Trendtex* the House of Lords held that the contemplated assignment to the anonymous third party was objectionable, not because the third party was likely to make a profit out of the assignment, but because he had no genuine pre-existing commercial interest in the outcome of the cause of action. In the language of Fletcher Moulton L.J. in *British Cash and Parcels Conveyors Ltd v Lamson Store Service Co. Ltd* [1908] 1 K.B. 1006 at 1014 it was a case of "wanton and vicious inter-meddling with the disputes of others in which the defendant has no interest whatever"[25]

There is no doubt that the court may order a non-party to pay the costs of an unsuccessful plaintiff, whom he has supported, if the circumstances warrant it, by virtue of the power conferred by section 51 of the Supreme Court Act 1981.[26] There does not ever seem to have been a time when the court has regarded the support of a near relative of comparatively modest means as being contrary to public policy,[27] but the situation is otherwise in relation to commercial organisations:

"It may well be that it is not necessary to every case of lawful maintenance that the maintainer should accept a liability for a successful adverse party's costs; for example, a member of a family or a religious fraternity may well have a sufficient interest in maintaining an action to save such maintenance from contractual illegality, even

---

[25] *per* Lloyd L.J. at 509.
[26] *Aiden Shipping Co. Ltd v Inter Bulk Ltd* [1986] A.C. 965.
[27] See *Condliffe v Hislop* [1996] 1 W.L.R. 753, CA. In *Thistleton v Hendricks*, 32 Con. L.R. 123, the court held that a mother who had funded her son's unsuccessful litigation, knowing that he was unlikely to be able to pay his opponent's costs, should pay costs (limited to £7000) to the defendant.

without any acceptance of liability for such costs. But, in what one may call a business context (*e.g.* insurance, trade union activity or commercial litigation support for remuneration) the acceptance of such liability will always, in my view, be a highly relevant consideration."[28]

Where a claims consultant maintained the action of an unsuccessful claimant, the court was able to order the maintainer to pay the costs of the successful defendant. The fact that the maintainer had not accepted liability for the successful adverse party's costs tainted the contract with the claimant with illegality, quite apart from the additional illegality which arose from the champertous nature of the agreement.[28a]

Champerty

4–027　The Law Commission commented in 1966 that there was a substantial body of case law to the effect that champertous agreements (including contingency fee agreements), were unlawful as contrary to public policy. The Report continued:

> "This rule of public policy has many implications for solicitors. The following are important:
>
> i) Contingency fee agreements are unlawful ...
> ii) A solicitor cannot recover from professional indemnity insurers loss arising from his having entered into an agreement in fact champertous ...
> iii) A solicitor who has made, or knowingly participates in the furtherance of, a champertous agreement is not entitled to enforce a claim for costs ...
> iv) A solicitor who is conducting his client's litigation on a champertous basis may find himself ordered by the court to pay the other side's costs."[29]

Lord Denning M.R. explained in 1962:

> "The reason why the common law condemns champerty is because of the abuses to which it may give rise. The common law fears that the champertous maintainer might be tempted, for his own personal gain, to inflame the damages, to suppress evidence or even to suborn witnesses. These fears may be exaggerated; but, be that so or not, the

---

[28] *McFarlane v E.E. Caledonia Ltd (No.2)* [1995] 1 W.L.R. 366, Longmore J. and see *Nordstern Allgemeine Versicherungs AG v Internav Ltd* [1999] 2 Lloyd's Rep. 139, CA.
[28a] *McFarlane v E.E. Caledonia Ltd* (1995) 1 W.L.R. 366.
[29] Proposals for Reform of the Law relating to Maintenance and Champerty (Law Com. No.7 (1966)) paras 16 and 17.

law for centuries has declared champerty to be unlawful, and we cannot do otherwise than enforce the law ... "[30]

By section 58 of the Courts and Legal Services Act 1990 legal representatives are permitted to enter into conditional fee agreements in certain circumstances entitling the solicitor, in the event of a successful outcome, to a percentage uplift or success fee. Lord Justice Steyn was of the view that this:

"represents at least a concession to the view that the abuses associated with champerty are not the inevitable result of all variants of contingency fee agreements. And there is of course, no more cogent evidence of a change of public policy than the expression of the will of Parliament."[31]

Funding by non-parties

The Master of the Rolls has explained the up-to-date position with regard to maintenance and champerty: 4–028

"31. Champerty is a variety of maintenance. Maintenance and champerty used to be both crimes and torts. A champertous agreement was illegal and void, involving as it did criminal conduct. *Sections 13(1) and 14(1)* of the Criminal Law Act 1967 abolished both the crimes and the torts of maintenance and champerty. Section 14(2) provided, however:

'The abolition of criminal and civil liability under the law of England and Wales for maintenance and champerty shall not affect any rule of that law as to the cases in which a contract is to be treated as contrary to public policy or otherwise illegal.'

Thus, champerty survives as a rule of public policy capable of rendering a contract unenforceable.
32. A person is guilty of maintenance if he supports litigation in which he has no legitimate concern without just cause or excuse': see *Chitty on Contracts*, 28th ed (1999), vol 1, para 17–050. Champerty 'occurs when the person maintaining another stipulates for a share of the proceeds of the action or suit': *Chitty*, para 17–054. Because the question of whether maintenance and champerty can be justified is one of public policy, the law must be kept under review as public policy changes. As Danckwerts LJ observed in *Hill v Archbold*[32]:

---

[30] *Re Trepca Mines Ltd* [1963] Ch. 199 at 219.
[31] *Giles v Thompson* [1994] 1 A.C. 142 [1993] 3 All E.R. 321 at 331, CA.
[32] [1968] 1 Q.B. 686, 697.

'the law of maintenance depends upon the question of public policy, and public policy . . . is not a fixed and immutable matter. It is a conception which, if it has any sense at all, must be alterable by the passage of time.'

33. In *Trendtex Trading Corpn v Credit Suisse*[33] Oliver LJ remarked:

'There is, I think, a clear requirement of public policy that officers of the court should be inhibited from putting themselves in a position where their own interests may conflict with their duties to the court by agreement, for instance, of so-called "contingency fees" . . . '

34. The introduction of conditional fees shows that even this requirement of public policy is no longer absolute . . .

35. In *In re Trepca Mines Ltd (No 2)*[34] Lord Denning M.R. observed:

'The reason why the common law condemns champerty is because of the abuses to which it may give rise. The common law fears that the champertous maintainer might be tempted, for his own personal gain, to inflame the damages, to suppress evidence, or even to suborn witnesses. These fears may be exaggerated; but, be that so or not, the law for centuries has declared champerty to be unlawful, and we cannot do otherwise than enforce the law; and I may observe that it has received statutory support, in the case of solicitors, in section 65 of the Solicitors Act 1957.'

36. Where the law expressly restricts the circumstances in which agreements in support of litigation are lawful, this provides a powerful indication of the limits of public policy in analogous situations. Where this is not the case, then we believe one must today look at the facts of the particular case and consider whether those facts suggest that the agreement in question might tempt the allegedly champertous maintainer for his personal gain to inflame the damages, to suppress evidence, to suborn witnesses or otherwise to undermine the ends of justice.

37. In reaching this conclusion we have been particularly influenced by the approach of the Court of Appeal and the House of Lords in *Giles v Thompson*.[35] The issue in that case was whether the plaintiffs in two conjoined appeals could recover as damages the costs of hiring cars to replace those put out of commission by the defendants' negligence. The cars had been provided by hire companies under agreements which gave the hire companies the right to pursue actions against the

---

[33] [1980] Q.B. 629, 663.
[34] [1963] Ch. 199, 219–220.
[35] [1994] 1 A.C. 142; [1993] 3 All E.R. 321.

defendants in the plaintiffs' names to recover those damages. In one case the hire agreement gave the plaintiff credit in respect of payment of the hire charges until 'such time as the claim for damages has been concluded'. In the other case the credit was given 'until such time as damages, and statutory interest, have been recovered'. Thus, in the latter case, the hire company's right to payment of the hire was conditional upon the success of the action. The defendants objected to paying the hire charges in each case on the ground, among others, that the hire agreements were unenforceable as constituting maintenance or champerty.

38. In the leading judgment in the Court of Appeal[36] Steyn L.J.,[37] identified the public policy which renders champertous agreements illegal as resting on the perceived need to protect the integrity of public justice. Later,[38] he added that the policy focused on the protection of the party confronted with the maintained litigation, it did not exist to protect the plaintiff. He gave a valuable exposition,[39] of the history of this area of the law, culminating in the enactment of *section 58* of the Courts and Legal Services Act 1990, which we shall have to consider in more detail in due course. As to this, he remarked.[40]

> 'The relevance of section 58 is that Parliament has, subject to the requirements of the section, empowered the Lord Chancellor to validate by order agreements for a percentage uplift in the costs in the event of success. The ability to recover fees beyond what was otherwise reasonable was intended to be "an incentive to lawyers to undertake speculative actions". Such agreements were, and in the absence of an order still are, unlawful as being contrary to public policy. The rationale of the common law rule is that such agreements allowed the duty and interest of solicitors to conflict with a resultant risk of abuse of legal procedure. Section 58 evidences a proposed modification in relation to an important species of champerty. It represents at least a concession to the view that the abuses associated with champerty are not the inevitable result of all variants of contingency fee agreements. And there is, of course, no more cogent evidence of a change of public policy than the expression of the will of Parliament.'

Subsequently, he observed[41]:

---

[36] [1993] 3 All E.R. 321.
[37] At p.328.
[38] At p.336.
[39] At pp.328–329.
[40] At p.331.
[41] At p.332.

'Contingency fee agreements are nowadays perhaps the most important species of champerty. Such agreements are still unlawful. Yet an English solicitor may share in a contingency fee earned in foreign litigation: see rule 8 (contingency fees) of the Solicitors' Practice Rules 1990. This reinforces the point that the doctrine of champerty serves to protect only the integrity of English public justice. It is based not on grounds of morality but on a concern to protect the administration of civil justice in this country.'

He continued[42]:

'Ultimately, it is necessary to consider the questions posed in this case in the light of contemporary public policy. The correct approach is not to ask whether, in accordance with contemporary public policy, the agreement has in fact caused the corruption of public justice. The court must consider the tendency of the agreement. The question is whether the agreement has the tendency to corrupt public justice. And this question requires the closest attention to the nature and surrounding circumstances of a particular agreement. That is illustrated by the well known decision of the House of Lords in *Trendtex Trading Corpn v Credit Suisse* [1982] AC 679.'

39. Applying that approach, he held that neither agreement was contrary to public policy. The other members of the court concurred. 40. In the House of Lords[43] Lord Mustill gave the leading speech, in which the other members of the House concurred. After a brief reference to their history, he observed[44]:

'In the most recent decades of the present century maintenance and champerty have become almost invisible in both their criminal and their tortious manifestations. In practice, they have maintained a living presence in only two respects. First, as the source of the rule, now in the course of attenuation, which forbids a solicitor from accepting payment for professional services on behalf of a plaintiff calculated as a proportion of the sum recovered from the defendant. Secondly, as the ground for denying recognition to the assignment of a "bare right of action". The former survives nowadays, so far as it survives at all, largely as a rule of professional conduct, and the latter is in my opinion best treated as having achieved an independent life of its own.'

41. Lord Mustill then proceeded to analyse the facts of each case . . .

---

[42] At p.333.
[43] [1994] 1 A.C. 142.
[44] At p.153.

42. On these facts Lord Mustill held that it was appropriate to consider whether the mischief was established against which the public policy was directed. As to this, he observed[45]:

> 'It is sufficient to adopt the description of the policy underlying the former criminal and civil sanctions expressed by Fletcher Moulton LJ in *British Cash and Parcel Conveyors Ltd v Lamson Store Service Co Ltd* [1908] 1 KB 1006, 1014: "It is directed against wanton and officious intermeddling with the disputes of others in which the [maintainer] has no interest whatever, and where the assistance he renders to the one or the other party is without justification or excuse." This was a description of maintenance. For champerty there must be added the notion of a division of the spoils.'

43. Lord Mustill held that in neither case was this mischief established. Summarising the position, he said[46]:

> 'Returning to the company, is it wantonly or officiously interfering in the litigation; is it doing so in order to share in the profits? I think not. The company makes its profits from the hiring, not from the litigation. It does not divide the spoils, but relies upon the fruits of the litigation as a source from which the motorist can satisfy his or her liability for the provision of a genuine service, external to the litigation. I can see no convincing reason for saying that, as between the parties to the hiring agreement, the whole transaction is so unbalanced, or so fraught with risk, that it ought to be stamped out. The agreement is one which in my opinion the law should recognise and enforce ... '[47]

44. This decision abundantly supports the proposition that, in any individual case, it is necessary to look at the agreement under attack in order to see whether it tends to conflict with existing public policy that is directed to protecting the due administration of justice with particular regard to the interests of the defendant. This is a question that we have to address. In so doing we revert to the statement of Lord Mustill that 'the rule, now in the course of attenuation, which forbids a solicitor from accepting payment for professional services calculated as a proportion of the sum recovered from the defendant ... survives nowadays, so far as it survives at all, largely as a rule of professional conduct'. With respect, this statement is not correct. The basis of the rule is statutory ... "

---

[45] At p.161.
[46] At p.165.
[47] *R (Factortame Ltd) v Secretary of State for Transport* [2002] EWCA Civ 932; [2002] 2 W.L.R. 1104; [2002] 4 All E.R. 97, CA.

It is not an abuse of process for an impecunious claimant to bring proceedings for a proper purpose and in good faith while being unable to pay the defendant's costs if the proceedings fail. It may be unjust to a successful defendant to be left with unrecovered costs but the claimant's freedom of access to the courts has priority.[48] Even where maintenance was tortious and criminal (pre-1967) it was not an abuse of process for a claimant without means to bring proceedings with financial assistance provided by a third party and the court would not stay proceedings on this ground.[49] Similarly even today the presence of unlawful maintenance is not by itself an abuse.[50]

In 1993,[51] the Court of Appeal took the opportunity to review the decisions since 1986:

> "These decisions may be conveniently summarised under the following heads.
>
> (1) Where a person had some management of the action, *e.g.* a director of an insolvent company who causes the company improperly to prosecute or defend proceedings ... [52]
>
> (2) Where a person has maintained or financed the action. This was undoubtedly considered to be a proper case for the exercise of the discretion by Macpherson J. in *Singh v Observer Ltd*.[53]
>
> (3) In *Gupta v Comer*[54] this court approached the power of the court to order a solicitor to pay costs under RSC, Order 62, r.11 (now revoked) as an example of the exercise of the discretion under section 51 of the 1981 Act.
>
> (4) Where the person has caused the action. In *Pritchard v J.H. Cobden Ltd*[55] the [claimant] had suffered brain damage

---

[48] *per* Millett L.J. *Abraham v Thompson* [1997] 4 All E.R. 363, CA.

[49] See *Martell v Consett Iron Co. Ltd* [1995] Ch. 363.

[50] *Abraham v Thompson* above.

[51] *Symphony Group plc v Hodgson* [1993] 4 All E.R. 143, CA.

[52] "See *Re Land and Property Trust Co. plc* [1991] 1 W.L.R. 601, *Re Land and Property Trust Co. plc (No.2)*, *The Times*, February 16, 1999; *Re Land and Property Trust Co. plc (No.3)*, [1991] B.C.L.C. 856, *Taylor v Pace Developments Ltd* [1991] B.C.C. 406, *Re A Company (No.004055 of 1991), Ex p. Doe Sport Ltd* [1991] B.C.L.C. 865 and *Framework Exhibitions Ltd v Matchroom Boxing Ltd* (1992) CA, Transcript 873. It is of interest to note that, while it was not suggested in any of these cases that it would never be a proper exercise of the jurisdiction to order the director to pay the costs, in none of them was it the ultimate result that the director was so ordered."

[53] [1989] 2 All E.R. 777. An arrangement by a wife in divorce proceedings to pay her solicitors out of the money she expected to receive under the order of the court was not necessarily champertous or invalid. In the particular case it was held to be a valid contract for valuable consideration to assign a future chose in action. *Sears Tooth v Payne Hicks Beach, The Times*, January 24, 1997, Wilson J.

[54] [1991] 1 Q.B. 629.

[55] [1988] Fam. 22.

through the defendant's negligence. That resulted in a personality change which precipitated a divorce. This court held that the defendant's agreement to pay the costs of the divorce proceedings could be justified as an application of the Aiden Shipping principle.[56]

(5) Where the person is a party to a closely related action which has been heard at the same time but not consolidated—as was the case in Aiden Shipping itself.

(6) Group litigation where one or two actions are selected as test actions.[57]

In proceedings where there were related actions, the claimant was being funded by a third party in relation to the litigation and the defendant in separate winding-up proceedings was also being funded by a third party, the Court of Appeal held that there were two questions for decision:

(1) whether the agreements were unlawful and contrary to public policy on the ground of champerty;

(2) if so whether further proceedings should be stayed on that ground.

If the court decided that the proceedings should not be stayed, even if the agreements were champertous, it was unnecessary to resolve the first question. The question of whether the court's process was affected or threatened by an agreement for the division of spoils was one to be considered in the light of the facts of each case. In coming to its conclusion the court stressed that where a subsidiary company involved in litigation is funded by its parent company, the nature of the parent company's interest in the proceedings is the key to the question whether the company may be made liable in costs as a non-party.[58]

Orders for costs against non-parties—summary of principles

In November 1996, Lord Justice Phillips sitting with Sir John Balcombe, who had given the leading judgment in *Symphony Group Plc v Hodgson*,[59] reviewed the decisions relating to payment of costs by a non-party and formulated a number of principles in the light of those decisions[60]:

4–029

---

[56] See [1988] Fam. 22 at 51.
[57] See *Davies (Joseph Owen) v Eli Lilly & Co.* [1987] 1 W.L.R. 1136.
[58] *Stocznia Gdanska SA v Latreefers Inc*, unreported, February 9, 2000, CA. The court confirmed that *Globe Equities Ltd v Globe Legal Services Ltd* [1999] B.L.R. 232, CA, was the leading authority on non-party costs.
[59] (1994) Q.B. 179, CA.
[60] *Murphy v Young & Co.'s Brewery Plc* [1997] 1 W.L.R. 159 [1997] 1 All E.R. 518 at 528, CA.

"1. In *Giles v Thompson*[61] Lord Mustill suggested that the current test of maintenance should ask the question whether—

> 'there is wanton and vicious inter-meddling with the disputes of others in (which) the meddler has no interest whatever, and where the assistance he renders to one or other party is without justification or excuse.'

Where such a test is satisfied I would expect the court to be receptive to an application under section 51 (of the Supreme Court Act 1981) that the meddler pay any costs attributable to his inter-meddling.

2. Where a non-party has supported an unsuccessful party on terms that place the non-party under a clear contractual obligation to indemnify the unsuccessful party against his liability to pay the costs of the successful party, it may well be appropriate to make an order under section 51 that the non-party pay those costs directly to the successful party. *Bourne v Colodense*[62] is a case where the court might well have thought fit to make such an order had it appreciated that it had jurisdiction to do so.

3. Where a trade union funds unsuccessful litigation on behalf of a member, the following factors, in addition to the funding itself, are likely to be present and, where they are, to make it appropriate to order the union to pay the successful party's costs should such an order be necessary:

    (a) an implied obligation owed by the union to its member to do so—see 2 above;
    (b) an interest on the part of the union in supporting and being seen to support the member's claim;
    (c) responsibility both for the decision whether the litigation is to be pursued and for the conduct of the litigation; and
    (d) expectation based on convention that the union will bear the costs of the successful party should the member lose.

4. Where an unsuccessful defendant's costs are funded by insurers who have provided cover against liability, which is not subject to any special limit, the same considerations that I have set out under 3 are likely to apply.

5. The position is more complex where a defendant's costs have been funded by insurers at risk under a policy under which their liability is limited to a sum which is insufficient to cover both liability and costs.[63]

---

[61] [1994] 1 A.C. 142 at 164.

[62] [1985] I.C.R. 291.

[63] Phillips L.J. went on to consider the judgment in *T.G.A. Chapman Ltd v Christopher, The Times*, July 21, 1997, CA.

[. . .]

I am not persuaded that it will always be appropriate to order liability insurers to pay the [claimants'] costs where they have unsuccessfully defended a claim made against their insured, if the result of such an order will be to render them liable beyond their contractual limit of cover. It seems to me that the appropriate order may well turn on the facts of the particular case.

[. . .]

I accept the submission that legal expense insurance is in the public interest . . . Such insurance not only provides desirable protection to the insured it is of benefit to the adverse party in that;

i.   it is likely to ensure that careful consideration is given to the merits of the litigation at an early stage, and
ii. it provides a potential source of funding of the adverse party's costs should the assured be unsuccessful."

Group actions

An order for common costs against group litigants imposes on each group   **4–030** litigant several liability for an equal proportion of the common costs. The general rule is that where a group litigant is the paying party, he will, in addition to any costs he is liable to pay to the receiving party, be liable for the individual costs of his claim and an equal proportion together with all the other group litigants of the common costs.[64] Where the court makes an order about costs in relation to any application or hearing which involved one or more of the group litigation issues and issues relevant only to individual claims the court will direct the proportion of the costs that is to relate to the common costs and the proportion that is to relate to the individual costs.[65] Where common costs have been incurred before a claim is entered on the group register the court may order the group litigant to be liable for a proportion of those costs. Where a claim is removed from the group register the court may make an order for costs in that claim which includes a proportion of the common costs incurred up to the date on which the claim is removed from the register.[66]

Taking the indemnity principle as a starting point, where several clients instruct the same solicitor in a group action, the liability of each is for the

---

[64] CPR r.48.6A(1)–(4).
[65] CPR r.48.6A(5).
[66] CPR r.48.6A(5)–(7).

entirety of the individual costs of his claim and a per capita share of the common costs unless there were good evidential grounds for the court ordering otherwise.[67]

If the court does not direct the proportion of costs relating to common costs and to individual costs the costs judge will decide as to the relevant proportions at or before the commencement of the detailed assessment.[68]

In group litigation a costs order in favour of the successful party is generally to be adopted as being calculated to achieve the end of justice. The overriding objective of the court is to make the order which justice requires, but the court in a particular case may make a different order if on the facts of the case justice required, and the court should have regard to the success of the parties on parts only of their cases. It is no longer necessarily the case that a party who establishes, for example a breach of contract but is unable to prove loss, would be held to have lost and be subject to an adverse order for costs.[69] At a subsequent hearing it was decided that the costs of five test cases should be borne by all the employees of the bank who were affected rather than the five individuals whose cases had been litigated.[70]

In *Davies (Joseph Owen) v Eli Lilly & Co.*[71] the judge nominated to take charge of all the applications in a group action made an order to the effect that where particular claimants incurred costs either personally or through the legal aid fund pursuing lead actions, every other claimant should contribute rateably. The Court of Appeal in dismissing an appeal, held that the rules dealt with the manner in which not the time at which the court's discretion to order costs was to be exercised. Since there was nothing to prohibit the exercise of the discretion before the conclusion of the proceedings the judge had jurisdiction to make an order in advance of the apportionment of costs.

In *Nash v Eli Lilly & Co. Berger v Eli Lilly & Co.*[72] the judge had ordered the defendants to pay the costs of one of the successful claimants but only to the extent of 1/337 of the costs incurred. The successful claimant appealed contending that the order for costs did not reflect that he had succeeded on the limitation issue which was before the court and costs should follow the event. The Court of Appeal decided that the costs order made by the judge in respect of the successful claimant was unjust in its effect and could not be justified by reference to any relevant principle which could be derived from the nature of the litigation or from the original order

---

[67] *A B v Liverpool City Council* [2003] EWHC 1539 (QB), Holland J.
[68] Practice Direction Supplementing Pt 19, para.16.2.
[69] *Bank of Credit & Commerce International SA (in liquidation) v Ali (No.4)*, *The Times*, March 2, 2000, Lightman J.
[70] *BCCI v Ali*, unreported, April 13, 2000, Park J.; and see *Re Elgindata (No.2)* [1992] 1 W.L.R. 1207.
[71] [1987] 1 W.L.R. 1136, CA. See also *Aiden Shipping Co. Ltd v Inter Bulk Ltd* above.
[72] [1993] 4 All E.R. 383, CA. See also *AllTrans Express Ltd v CVA Holding Ltd* [1984] 1 All E.R. 685, CA; *Aiden Shipping Co. Ltd v Inter Bulk*, above; *Davies (Joseph Owen) v Eli Lilly & Co.*, above.

for costs sharing and contribution. Group action orders were not intended to modify the principle whereby in the absence of some reason to order otherwise the party who caused costs to be incurred on a separately disputed issue would, if he lost be ordered to pay the costs of the other side on that issue. This decision was reached under the previous rules and must now be read in the light of the CPR.

The court refused to make an order to the effect that if the claim was ultimately successful only those claimants still involved in the litigation should be entitled to their costs and if it failed all the claimants who had been involved at any stage should be liable to pay any costs order on a pro rata basis. The court held that the proposal was not suitable as it encouraged claimants with weaker cases to continue at all costs. The order should provide that both liability for and the benefit of costs in relation to the issues common to all claimants should be several rather than joint. It was not yet clear what would happen to an unsuccessful claimant at the end of group litigation conducted under a conditional fee agreement.[73]

The Court of Appeal has stated that both the recoverability of common costs and the liability, if any, of discontinuing claimants for costs should be determined at the same time as orders for common costs were made in respect of those common issues. The court would then have a full picture and could make whatever order was just in all the circumstances. A rule that any discontinuing claimant should have a crystallised inability to recover common costs and a potential liability for the common costs of the defendants at the end of a quarter in which he discontinued was too blunt an instrument and unnecessarily favourable to defendants, when it was as yet unknown whether the claimants as a whole were to be successful in the common issues which were to be tried.[74]

Where in a group action, lead cases were selected, it was open to the court to make anticipatory orders, since, the selection of lead cases should not depend on the means and willingness of claimants to accept a high degree of risk as to costs, the court accordingly made an order for the costs liability of the individual claimants in the lead cases to be several and not joint, and to be limited to their proportionate share of the overall costs, whether incurred by them or payable by them to the defendant.[75]

Group actions have thrown up increasingly complex problems in the field of costs. The court has had to be "flexible" and "inventive"[76] in dealing with them. Different considerations apply in group litigation where lead actions are fought and lost the defendants are not necessarily entitled to all of their costs against the losing claimant and it may therefore be proper for the court to reflect the situation in the order for costs. The purpose of a common costs

---

[73] *Hodgson v Imperial Tobacco Ltd (No.2)* [1998] 2 Costs L.R. 27, Wright J.
[74] *Sayers v Smith Kline Beecham Plc*; *XYZ v Schering Health Care Ltd*; *Afrika v Cape Plc* [2001] EWCA Civ 2017; [2002] 1 W.L.R. 2274; [2003] 3 All E.R. 631, CA.
[75] *Ward v Guiness Mahon & Co. Limited* [1996] 1 W.L.R. 894, CA.
[76] See *Davies v Eli Lilly* [1987] 3 All E.R. 94, CA.

order is to permit a group of claimants whose individual means and probable damages are modest to spread the cost risk amongst all of them in the event of the lead claimants losing, otherwise the burden on the lead claimants would be intolerable and no claimant would be prepared to lead. Where common issues are tried on a preliminary basis a costs sharing scheme may sensibly be limited to those issues, but if the litigation proceeds by lead actions it must be contemplated that the group will stand behind the lead claimants for the whole of their costs.[77]

Refusal to carry out an order

4–031 Neither a costs officer nor the Court on an appeal against a detailed assessment can properly refuse to carry out an order for detailed assessment because it is considered to be wrong or *ultra vires*; the only remedy if the order is wrong is by way of appeal against that order.[78]

Costs payable pursuant to a contract

4–032 In a case where liability for costs is provided for by a contract, the costs will be presumed to be costs which have been reasonably incurred and are reasonable in amount and the court must assess them accordingly. The court may make an order that all or part of the costs payable under the contract should be disallowed if it is satisfied that the costs have been unreasonably incurred or are unreasonable in amount.[79]

The claimant and defendant entered into a series of contracts which contained an English jurisdiction clause. The claimant commenced proceedings in England against the defendant for sums due under the contracts. The defendant issued its own proceedings in New York. The claimant successfully applied in New York for those proceedings to be struck out as being in breach of the jurisdiction clause. No application was made to the New York court for costs since costs are not recoverable in New York in such circumstances. The claimant subsequently added a further claim to the English proceedings seeking to recover the costs of the New York proceedings as damages for breach of contract. The Court of Appeal held that absent a separate cause of action the costs of foreign proceedings could not be recovered in separate proceedings in England. In this case the claimant had a separate cause of action and there were no policy reasons why it should not be entitled to pursue that cause of action. In particular:

---

[77] *Ochwat v Watson Burton*, unreported, December 10, 1999, CA.
[78] *Cope v United Dairies (London) Ltd* [1963] 2 Q.B. 33, Megaw J.
[79] CPR r.48.3 and Costs Practice Direction, s.60. See also *Gomba Holdings UK Ltd v Minories Finance Ltd (No.2)* [1992] 3 W.L.R. 723 and *Mortgage Funding Corp. Plc v Kashef-Hamadani*, unreported, April 26, 1993, CA and *Fairview Investments Ltd v Sharman*, unreported, October 14, 1999, CA.

(i) international comity would not be breached by permitting such recovery;

(ii) there was no issue of *res judicata* because there was an independent cause of action and there had been no adjudication by the New York court;

(iii) the principle in *Henderson v Henderson*[80] (issue estoppel) was manifestly inapplicable to the facts of the present case; and

(iv) the mere fact that the English courts had for many years proceeded on the presumption that such costs were not recoverable was no reason for permitting one party to a contract to escape liability for damages that he had caused by attempting to sue in a country where a different costs regime prevailed.[81]

Costs payable by or to a child or patient

In general the court must order a detailed assessment of the costs payable by any party who is a child or patient to his solicitor. On the assessment of those costs, the court must also assess any costs payable to that party in the proceedings unless the court has issued a default costs certificate.[82]   **4–033.1**

The court does not need to order detailed assessment of costs payable by any party who is a child or patient where there is no need to do so to protect the interests of the child or patient or his estate. Detailed assessment need not be ordered where another party has agreed to pay a specified sum of money in respect of the costs and the solicitor acting for the child or patient has waived the right to claim any further costs. The same applies where the court has decided the costs payable to the child or patient by summary assessment and the solicitor has waived the right to further costs. If an insurer or other person is liable to discharge the costs which the child or patient would otherwise be liable to pay, and the court is satisfied that the insurer or other person is financially able to discharge those costs, detailed assessment need not be ordered.[83]

Where the appointment of a litigation friend ceases, the liability of the litigation friend for costs continues until the person for whom he was acting serves notice on the other parties stating that the appointment of the litigation friend has ceased, giving his address for service and stating whether or not he intends to carry on the proceedings; or the litigation friend serves notice on the parties that his appointment to act has ceased.[84]

---

[80] [1843] 3 Hare 100.
[81] *Union Discount Co Ltd v Robert Zoller* [2001] EWCA Civ, November 21; [2002] 1 All E.R. 693, CA.
[82] *i.e.* under CPR r.47.11: CPR r.48.5(1) and (2).
[83] Costs Practice Direction, s.51.
[84] CPR r.21.9(4) and (6).

Misconduct

4–033.2 In assessment proceedings the court has power to disallow all or part of the costs which are being assessed, or to order a party at fault, or his legal representative, to pay the costs which he has caused any other party to incur where there has been misconduct.[85] This power is in addition to the Wasted Costs jurisdiction under CPR r.48.7. Misconduct may arise where a party or his legal representative fails to conduct the detailed assessment proceeding sin accordance with Part 47, or any direction of the court, or it appears to the court that the conduct of the party or the legal representative before or during the proceedings which gave rise to the assessment proceedings was unreasonable or improper.[86] The court is given power to penalise either the party or the legal representative depending upon the circumstances of the case. In this context it is suggested that behaving unreasonably or improperly means failing to comply with the overriding objective or failing to assist the court to further the overriding objective. Unreasonable or improper behaviour includes steps which are calculated to prevent or inhibit the court from furthering the overriding objective.[87] Where the court makes an order under this rule against a legally represented party and that party is not present when the order is made, the party's solicitor must notify the client in writing of the order no later than seven days after the solicitor received notice of the order (this will usually be at the time of the hearing). The court may require the solicitor to produce evidence that reasonable steps have been taken to notify the client.[88]

Before making an order under this rule the court must give the party or the legal representative a reasonable opportunity to attend the hearing to explain why such an order should not be made.

The Justices and Justices Clerks' (Costs) Regulations 2001 and the General Commissioners of Income Tax (Costs) Regulations 2001

4–034 The above Regulations give the court power to make an order that the Lord Chancellor should pay the costs of proceedings.[89] The amount of costs payable is determined in accordance with the Regulations and is a separate procedure to that laid down under the CPR. When making the order for costs the court will normally determine the amount it considers sufficient reasonably to compensate the receiving party for any costs properly incurred by him in the proceedings and specify that amount in the order; but the court may direct the amount of costs to be determined by a costs judge

---

[85] CPR r.44.14(2).

[86] CPR r.44.14(1). The intention of the Rule committee was that this provision should apply to both summary and detailed assessment. It is however, arguable that the wording of the rule does not achieve this.

[87] Costs Practice Direction, s.18.

[88] CPR r.44.14(3).

[89] Under s.53A of the Justices of the Peace Act 1997 or under s.2A of the Taxes Management Act 1970.

where the hearing has lasted more than one day or there is insufficient time for the court to determine the costs on the day of the hearing, or the court considers that there is other good reason for the costs judge to determine the amount of the costs.

The Regulations (Appendix V) set out the procedure to be followed. The time for filing a claim for costs in the Supreme Court Costs Office is three months from the date on which the order was made. The costs judge has the power in exceptional circumstances to extend that period. The claim must be made on Form N258D which must be filed at the Supreme Court Costs Office accompanied by copies of: the order of the court giving the right to costs; the bill of costs; a copy of all the orders made by the court relating to the costs of the proceedings which are to be determined; any fee notes of counsel, receipts or accounts or other disbursements relating to items claimed; and, the relevant papers in support of the bill. No fee is prescribed in respect of determinations under these Regulations.

In determining the claim for costs the costs judge is required to take into account all the relevant circumstances of the case, including the nature, importance, complexity or difficulty of the work and the time involved. The costs judge will allow such costs in respect of:

(a) such work as appears to him to have been actually and reasonably done; and

(b) such disbursements as appear to him to have been actually and reasonably incurred,

as he considers sufficient reasonably to compensate the receiving party for any expenses properly incurred by him in the proceedings.

Any doubt which the costs judge may have as to whether the costs were reasonably incurred or were reasonable in amount must be resolved against the receiving party. When the costs judge carries out a determination of the claim for costs he will also determine any claim for the costs of drawing the bill and attending upon the determination.

There is no power[90] to enable the costs judge to order that the costs of the proceedings before the Costs Judge should be paid by the receiving party. The costs judge does however have the power where a receiving party has behaved unreasonably to disallow some or all of the costs of the proceedings before the costs judge. The provisions of CPR Part 52 (Appeals) apply in respect of the proceedings before a costs judge under these Regulations.

Admiralty

The Secretary of State ordered a rehearing of the formal investigation under section 269 of the Merchant Shipping Act 1995 into the loss of the *MV*   4–035.1

---

[90] Under s.53A(3) of the Justices of the Peace Act 1997 or s.2A(3) of the Taxes Management Act 1970.

Derbyshire. The ship builder, ship owner and classification society each claimed their costs of attending and assisting the investigation. The court found that the ship owner was not involved in any continuing litigation arising out of the casualty and was exposed to the risk of adverse criticism. The owners were found to be free of fault, their evidence did make a contribution to the investigation and report. They played an important part in the meeting of experts. They were awarded 30 per cent of the aggregate of their solicitors' overall profit costs and disbursements, including counsel's fees from public funds. The ship builders had been made a party to the investigation by the court's order. They were exposed to the risk of criticism. They provided important evidence to the investigation. They played an important part in the meetings of experts. They were awarded 75 per cent of their costs. The classification society occupied a unique position in the Inquiry since its existence was directed to the objective of ship safety which underlay the investigation. It contributed substantially to the investigation and report but the time and money involved had been in the course of performing its function as a classification society. The society was awarded 15 per cent of its costs.[91]

Family proceedings

4–035.2 CPR, Parts 43, 44 (except rr.44.9–44.12), 47 and 48 apply. Rule 44.3(2) (the general rule is that the unsuccessful party will be ordered to pay the costs) does not apply.[92]

The Court of Appeal has stated that in ancillary relief proceedings the correct approach to costs must as a matter of principle be governed by CPR r.44.3 together with the Family Proceedings Rules 1991. The harmonious integration of the separate codes is best to be achieved by treating CPR 44.3 as covering all cases. Under the Family Proceedings Rules the court has to consider a number of factors including the respective means of the parties, thus enabling the court to look at the whole position of the parties after the order has been made and to see whether costs might fall disproportionately on one party rather than the other. That rule gives the court a greater latitude in making costs orders than might so far have been recognised.[93]

D. LITIGANTS IN PERSON

4–036 In certain specified proceedings, where any costs of a litigant in person are ordered to be paid by another party to the proceedings or in any other way,

---

[91] Re-hearing of formal investigation into the loss of NV Derbyshire [2001] EWHC (Admiralty) October 22, Colman J.

[92] Family Proceedings (Miscellaneous Amendments) Rules 1999, SI 1999/1012. The Family Proceedings (Costs) Rules 1991 are revoked.

[93] *Norris v Norris: Haskins v Haskins* [2003] EWCA Civ, July 28.

there may be allowed on the assessment or other determination of the costs, sums in respect of any work done and any expenses and losses incurred by the litigant in or in connection with the proceedings to which the order relates.[94] This provision applies to civil proceedings as follows:

(a) in a county court, in the Supreme Court or in the House of Lords on appeal from the High Court or the Court of Appeal;

(b) before the Lands Tribunal or the Lands Tribunal for Northern Ireland;

(c) in or before any other court or tribunal specified in an order made under section 1 of the Litigants in Person (Costs and Expenses) Act 1975 by the Lord Chancellor.[95]

A litigant in person who does not fall within the provisions of the 1975 Act can claim only out of pocket expenses, although these may include fees and expenses charged by a solicitor to a litigant to equip him to argue a case in person.[96] There is no provision for the costs of litigants in person in criminal proceedings. Proceedings before the VAT Tribunal are also excluded. The Court of Appeal has held that the power to award costs for tribunal hearings is confined to sums recoverable at common law.[97]

The official receiver, acting without a solicitor in disqualification proceedings, is a litigant in person, and is not limited to disbursements merely because he is salaried. Where costs over and above disbursements have been incurred these are pecuniary in nature and amount to pecuniary loss. The costs will be assessed in accordance with CPR r.48.6.[98]

The court has no power to award costs to a litigant in person in respect of assistance given by a non legally qualified acquaintance. "Legal services" refer to services that are legal and provided by or under the supervision of a lawyer. Any payment made by the litigant to the assistant is not recoverable because it is not a disbursement which would have been made by a legal representative. The assistance being given was not expert assistance within CPR r.48.6(3)(c).[99]

---

[94] Litigants in Person (Costs and Expenses) Act 1975, s.1(1).

[95] The scope of the Act has been extended to the Employment Appeal Tribunal by the Litigants in Person (Costs and Expenses) Order 1980, (SI 1980/1159) and to Magistrates' Courts in England and Wales in relation to civil proceedings before these courts by the litigants in person (Magistrates' Courts) Order 2000 (SI 2001/3438).

[96] *Buckland v Watts* [1970] 1 Q.B. 27; *Mulloch v Aberdeen Corp.* [1973] 1 W.L.R. 71. See also *Commissioners of Customs and Excise v Ross* [1992] All E.R. 65.

[97] *Nader (t/a Tryus) v Customs and Excise Commissioners* [1998] S.T.C. 806, CA, and see *Customs and Excise Commissioners v Ross* (1990) 2 All E.R. 65, Simon Brown J.

[98] *Re Minotaur Data Systems Ltd: Official Receiver v Brunt* [1999] 3 All E.R. 122, CA. (Magistrates' Courts) Order 200 (SI 2001/3438)

[99] *Uhbi (t/a United Building and Plumbing Contractors) v Kajla* [2002] All E.R. (D) 265, CA.

It is a question of fact whether a solicitor in sole practice is acting for himself as a true litigant in person or, instead, represented by himself in the firm name. It was relevant that the underlying litigation concerned a claim for professional fees with allegations of negligence and breach of duty since those were matters arising out of the solicitor's practice as a solicitor and not out of the course of his private life.[1]

In proceedings where the claimant was a solicitor who had at the same time practised as a costs draftsman until July 1999, the court had to decide whether or not she was a litigant in person before April 26, 1999 and also whether she was a litigant in person after that date under the CPR. The question depended upon the criteria used to define the term "practising solicitor". Prior to April 26, 1999 the court found that the claimant was undoubtedly a practising solicitor from a regulatory point of view under the Solicitors Act and the Rules of Practice, but she was not a practising solicitor who was able to charge for her time for the purposes of RSC Order 62 r.18(6) and the rule in the *London Scottish Benefits Society v Chorley*.[2] The court therefore held that she was only entitled to recover costs for that period as a litigant in person. With regard to the period after April 26, 1999 it was accepted by the claimant that if a court found that she was not a practising solicitor for the purposes of RSC Order 62 r.18 then she was unable to take advantage of section 52.5 of the Costs Practice Direction. The court held that this provision was designed to do no more than preserve the rule in *London Scottish Benefits Society*. The criteria remained the same.[3]

---

[1] *Hatton v Kendrick* [2002] EWCA Civ 1783; [2003] C.P. Rep. 32, CA.
[2] [1884] 13 Q.B.D. 872.
[3] *Boyd & Hutchinson v Joseph* [2003] EWHC 413 Ch., Patten J.

CHAPTER 5

Agreements as to Costs

A. NON-CONTENTIOUS BUSINESS AGREEMENTS UNDER SECTIONS 57 AND 58 OF THE SOLICITORS ACT

A solicitor and client may make an agreement as to the solicitor's remuneration in respect of non-contentious business before, after or in the course of the transaction of the business.[1] The agreement may provide for remuneration by a gross sum or by reference to an hourly rate, a commission, percentage, a salary or otherwise. The agreement may also include or exclude all or any disbursements made by the solicitor.[2]

The agreement must be in writing and signed by the person to be bound by it or his agent. The agreement may be sued and recovered on, or set aside, in the same way and on the same grounds as any other agreement.[3] All the terms of the agreement must be contained within the document itself.[4] Neither party can rely on an agreement which is not in writing, although the agreement must be signed only by the person against whom it is sought to enforce it (whether solicitor or a client).[5]

Where a detailed assessment of the solicitor's bill has been ordered and the solicitor seeks to rely on a non-contentious business agreement, the costs judge may, if the client objects to the agreement as being unfair and unreasonable, inquire into the facts and certify that the agreement should be set aside or the amount payable under it reduced and may order accordingly.[6] Where solicitors enter into a written agreement signed by the client

5–001

---

[1] Solicitors Act 1974, s.57(1).
[2] *ibid.*, s.57(2).
[3] *ibid.*, 57(3), (4).
[4] *Re Frappe* [1893] 2 Ch. 284.
[5] *Re West King & Adams* [1892] 2 Q.B. 102; *Re A Solicitor (No.2)* [1956] 1 Q.B. 155. See also *J.J. Milner & Son v Percy Bilton Ltd* [1966] 1 W.L.R. 1582.
[6] Solicitors Act 1974, s.57(5).

concerning their costs or remuneration (including hourly rates) in accordance with section 57 of the Solicitors Act 1974 the Law Society's remuneration certificate procedure does not apply and, if there is a binding agreement, the right to detailed assessment is severely limited. For a section 57 agreement to be valid the terms must be precise and unambiguous.[7] A properly worded client care letter signed by the client as well as the solicitor could constitute a non-contentious business agreement.

Where the agreement provides for remuneration by reference to an hourly rate, and on detailed assessment the solicitor seeks to rely on the agreement and the client objects to the amount of costs (but not that the agreement is unfair or unreasonable) the costs judge may enquire into the number of hours worked by the solicitors and whether the number of hours worked was excessive.[8] The insertion by solicitors of a one-sided provision into a contract with a client justifies the construction of any ambiguous provisions in the contract in the client's favour.[9]

Where an agent entered into an unauthorised agreement in relation to legal fees on behalf of his principals, but had passed a copy of the solicitor's letter to the principals, the court held that whilst it would be slow to conclude that an unauthorised act by an agent had been ratified by the principal when the only evidence of ratification was silence and/or inactivity of the principal. To any objective observer the principal's conduct could only be rationally explained by their acceptance of the unauthorised agreement made by the agent on their behalf. The solicitor's fees having been agreed by the agent there was no obligation upon them to prove or justify the amount of their fees and they were entitled to sue for the balance on the basis of the agreement reached and without recourse to section 57 of the 1974 Act.[10]

B. REMUNERATION OF A SOLICITOR WHO IS A MORTGAGEE

5–002   Where a solicitor is a mortgagee, either alone, or jointly with any other person, he or the firm of which he is a member, is entitled to recover from the mortgagor all such usual costs for any work done by him in connection with the mortgage as he would have been entitled to receive if the mortgage had been made to a person who was not a solicitor and who had retained him, or the firm, to transact the business.[11] Similarly, where a mortgage has

---

[7] *Chamberlain v Boodle and King*, [1982] 1 W.L.R. 1443; [1982] 3 All E.R. 188.

[8] *ibid.*, s.57(6), (7).

[9] *Re a Debtor* (No.1594 of 1992), *The Times*, December 8, 1992. See also *Rutter v Sheridan-Young* [1958] 1 W.L.R. 444, CA.

[10] *Lass Salt Garvin v Pommeroy* [2003] EWHC, March 27 (QBD), Richard Fernyhough Q.C.

[11] Solicitors Act 1974, s.58(1).

been made to, or had become vested in, a solicitor alone or jointly with any other person, the solicitor is entitled to recover the usual costs of any business transacted or acts done in relation to the transaction from the person on whose behalf the business was transacted or the acts were done in the same way as if the mortgage had remained vested in a person who was not a solicitor.[12]

An agreement by a mortgagor to pay the mortgagee's solicitor (acting for both parties) a lump sum is within the ambit of the 1974 Act.[13] Where there is an agreement between a mortgagee or a lessor and his solicitors in respect of costs ultimately payable by the mortgagor or lessee, the mortgagor/lessee is not prevented from objecting to items in the bill on the grounds that they have been unreasonably incurred or were of an unreasonable amount.[14]

The court has no power to require, against the wishes of the claimant mortgagees, that the costs be assessed if not agreed or to direct that the claimants recover no other costs by other means.[15]

C. CONTENTIOUS BUSINESS AGREEMENTS UNDER THE SOLICITORS ACT 1974, SS.59–63

In respect of any contentious business done or to be done by a solicitor a written agreement may be reached with the client providing that the solicitor is to be remunerated by a gross sum, or by reference to an hourly rate, a salary or otherwise at a higher or lower rate than that at which he would otherwise have been entitled to be remunerated.[16] A solicitor is not permitted to purchase any interest which the client may have in any action, nor may the agreement be based on the success of the action.[17]   5–003

Such an agreement must be in writing, must show all the terms of the bargain between the parties and the agreement of both parties to the terms. Where those three conditions are not met, there is no contentious business agreement within the Act and the matter must proceed to detailed assessment. The Act simply refers to the solicitor making the agreement in writing and it may therefore be that a client is entitled to rely on an oral agreement. There appears to be no authority on the point at the moment.[18] The client's rights under the Act are not defeated where the solicitors sue on a dishonoured cheque received in payment of their account.[19] An agreement

---

[12] *ibid.*, s.58(4).
[13] *Re Palmer* [1890] 45 Ch.D. 291, CA.
[14] *Gomba Holdings UK Ltd v Minories Finance Ltd (No.2)* [1992] 3 W.L.R. 723, CA and see para.12–006.
[15] *Mortgage Funding Corp. Plc v Kashef-Hamdani*, April 26, 1993, CA (unreported).
[16] Solicitors Act 1974, s.59(1).
[17] *ibid.*, s.59(2). But see CFAs para.5–008ff.
[18] *Electrical Trades Union v Tarlo* [1964] Ch. 720.
[19] *Martin Boston & Co. v Levy* [1982] 1 W.L.R. 1434.

in writing can be contained in letters, but the letters ought at least to be signed by the client if he is to be deprived by the agreement of his right to detailed assessment.[20]

Effect of contentious business agreements

5–004 Where a contentious business agreement is in existence the costs of the solicitor will not be assessed (except in the case of an agreement which provides for remuneration at an hourly rate), nor do the restrictions concerning action to recover costs imposed by section 69 of the 1974 Act apply.[21]

A client is not entitled to recover from any other person, under an order for payment of costs to which a contentious business agreement relates, more than the amount payable by him to his solicitor under the agreement.[22] This provision is the indemnity principle, which underlies all costs, given statutory force.[23] A claimant who has an oral agreement with his solicitor to pay no costs cannot recover anything from the defendant.[24]

A contentious business agreement does not affect the amount of, or any rights or remedies for the recovery of, any costs payable by or to the client by a person other than the solicitor, and that person may require the costs to be assessed.[25] As a result of this, a paying party may claim the benefit of a contentious business agreement as limiting the amount of the liability for costs.[26]

Where a public authority employs a solicitor at a fixed annual salary and obtains an order for costs on the indemnity basis, costs will be assessed and allowed in the normal way unless the paying party can show that the amount allowed would exceed the amount of the salary.[27]

Russell L.J. in *Re Lloyd's Bank Ltd v Eastwood*[28] stated:

"But it would be impracticable and wrong in all cases for an employed solicitor to require a total exposition and breakdown of the activities and expenses of the department (in which he worked) with a view to ensuring that the (indemnity) principle is not infringed and it is

---

[20] *per* Lord Denning M.R. in *Chamberlain v Boodle & King* [1982] 1 W.L.R. 1443; 3 All E.R. 188, CA.
[21] Solicitors Act 1974, s.60(1).
[22] *ibid.*, s.60(3) and see *Geraghty v Awwad* [2000] 1 All E.R. 608, CA.
[23] *Harold v Smith* [1860] 5 H. & N. 381; *Gundry v Sainsbury* [1910] 1 K.B. 645, CA.
[24] *Gundry v Sainsbury* [1910] 1 K.B. 645, CA.
[25] Solicitors Act 1974, s.60(2).
[26] See also *General of Berne Insurance Co. v Jardine Reinsurance Management Ltd* [1998] 2 All E.R. 301, CA.
[27] *Henderson v Merthyr Tydfil UDC* [1900] 1 Q.B. 434.
[28] [1975] Ch. 112 at 132, CA.

doubtful to say the least whether by any method, certainty on the point can be reached." (at 132E).

Provided the client is ultimately responsible to the solicitor for the costs it does not affect the indemnity principle that the client is being indemnified by another,[29] or is a member of a trade union,[30] or where an employer is indemnified by an insurance company.[31] A similar principle applies in criminal cases.[32]

A solicitor may not claim, in respect of the business to which contentious business agreements relate, anything other than the agreed costs or such costs as are expressly excepted from the agreement.[33] A provision that the solicitor shall not be liable for negligence and that he shall be relieved from any responsibility to which he would otherwise be subject as a solicitor is void.[34]

Enforcement of contentious business agreements

Any person (or his representative) who is a party to a contentious business agreement or is liable to pay, or is entitled to be paid, the costs due in respect of the business to which the agreement relates, may apply to the court to enforce or set aside the agreement and determine every question as to its validity or effect. Otherwise no action may be brought on any contentious business agreement.[35] In spite of the wording of section 61(1) of the Solicitors Act 1974 an action for damages for breach of a contentious business agreement does not appear to be precluded.[36]

Where an application is made to the court, if the court is of the opinion that the agreement is in all respects fair and reasonable it may enforce it. If it is of the opinion that it is in any respect unfair or unreasonable it may set it aside and order the costs covered by it to be assessed as if it had never been made. It may in any case make such order as to the costs of the applications as it thinks fit.[37] The question of whether an agreement is fair and reasonable is for the court to determine in its unfettered discretion. The agreement must not only be fair as between the parties but must also be reasonable. Where a costs judge has already pronounced an agreement to be

5–005

---

[29] *Baillie v Neville* [1920] 149 L.J.T. 300.
[30] *Adams v London Improved Motor Coach Builders* [1921] 1 K.B. 495.
[31] *Cornish v Lynch* [1910] 3 B.W.C.C. 343, CA.
[32] *R. v Miller & Glennie* [1983] 1 W.L.R. 1056.
[33] Solicitors Act 1974, s.60(4).
[34] *ibid.*, s.60(5).
[35] Solicitors Act 1974, s.61(1).
[36] *Rees v Williams* [1875] L.R. 10 Ex. 200.
[37] Solicitors Act 1974, s.61(2).

fair and reasonable the court would require a very strong case to act after the jurisdiction of the costs judge has already been exercised.[38]

Save in the case of a contentious business agreement made by a client as a representative of a person whose property would be chargeable with the whole or part of the amount payable under the agreement,[39] if the business covered by a contentious business agreement is done or to be done in any action, a client who is a party to the agreement may apply to a costs judge for the agreement to be examined.[40] The costs judge may either allow the agreement or if he is of the opinion that it is unfair or unreasonable may allow the agreement or reduce the amount payable under it or set it aside and order the costs covered by it to be assessed as if it had never been made.[41] The allowance of the agreement by the costs judge does not preclude an independent application to set it aside or to reopen it.[42]

Where a contentious business agreement provides for the remuneration of the solicitor to be by reference to an hourly rate and the agreement is relied on by the solicitor on detailed assessment, if the client objects to the amount of costs but does not allege that the agreement is unfair or unreasonable, the costs judge may inquire into the number of hours worked by the solicitor and whether the hours worked are excessive.[43]

Where the amount agreed under a contentious business agreement is paid by or on behalf of the client, the person making the payment may, at any time within 12 months from the date of payment, apply to the court and, if it appears to the court that the special circumstances of the case require it to be reopened, the court may, on such terms as may be just, reopen it and order the costs covered by the agreement to be assessed and the whole or any part of the amount received by the solicitor to be repaid.[44] The payment referred to above must be made under such circumstances as to show that the client understands that in making the payment he is carrying out the terms of the agreement and ratifying it.[45]

Contentious business agreements by certain representatives

5–006   Where the client who makes a contentious business agreement makes it as a representative of a person whose property will be charged with the whole

---

[38] *Re Stuart, ex p. Cathcart* [1893] 2 Q.B. 201, CA. See also *Re Hoggart's Settlement* [1912] 56 S.J. 415.

[39] Solicitors Act 1974, s.62.

[40] *ibid.*, s.61(3).

[41] *ibid.*, s.61(4). The subsection refers to the costs judge requiring the opinion of the court to be taken on the agreement, but by virtue of CPR, Sched. 1, RSC, Ord. 106(2), the costs judge may exercise the jurisdiction of the court.

[42] *Re Stuart, ex p. Cathcart* [1893] 2 Q.B. 201; *Re Simmons & Politzer* [1954] 1 Q.B. 296.

[43] Solicitors Act 1974, s.61(4A), (4B).

[44] *ibid.*, s.61(5).

[45] *Re Jackson* [1915] 1 K.B. 371.

or part of the amount payable under the agreement, the agreement must be laid before a costs judge before payment.[46] The costs judge is required to examine the agreement and may either allow it or if he is of the opinion that it is unfair or unreasonable reduce the amount payable under it or set it aside and order the costs covered by it to be assessed as if it had never been made.[47]

A client who makes a contentious business agreement and pays money in accordance with it, without it having been allowed by a costs judge under the above provisions, is liable at any time to account to the person whose property is charged and the solicitor who accepts the payment may be ordered by the court to refund the amount received by him.[48]

A client makes a contentious business agreement as the representative of another if he makes it:

(a) as his guardian;

(b) as a trustee for him under a deed or will;

(c) as his receiver appointed under Part VII of the Mental Health Act 1983; or

(d) as a person other than a receiver authorised under Part VII of the 1983 Act to act on his behalf.[49]

Effect on contentious business agreement of death, incapability or change of solicitor

If a solicitor dies, or becomes incapable of acting, or the client changes his solicitor after some business has been done under a contentious business agreement but before the solicitor has wholly performed it, any party (or his representative) may apply to the court, and the court has the same jurisdiction as to enforcing the agreement or setting it aside as it would have had if one of those events had not occurred.[50] A client is entitled to change solicitor notwithstanding the existence of a contentious business agreement.[51]

5–007

Even though the agreement is in all respects fair and reasonable, the court may order the amount due in respect of business under it to be ascertained by detailed assessment. In that case the costs judge is required to have

---

[46] Solicitors Act 1974, s.62(1).
[47] *ibid.*, s.62(2). The subsection refers to the costs judge requiring the opinion of the court to be taken, however by reason of CPR, Sch.1, RSC, Ord.106(2) the jurisdiction of the High Court is vested in the costs judge.
[48] *ibid.*, s.62(3).
[49] *ibid.*, s.63(1).
[50] *ibid.*, s.63(1).
[51] *ibid.*, s.63(1)(b).

regard, as far as possible, to the terms of the agreement and the amount found due on detailed assessment may be enforced in the same way as if the agreement had been completely performed.[52]

If an order for detailed assessment is made on a change of solicitor, the costs judge will have regard to the circumstances under which the change of solicitor has taken place and the costs judge will not allow to the solicitor the full amount of the remuneration agreed to be paid by him unless he is of the opinion that there has been no default, negligence, improper delay or other conduct on the part of the solicitor affording the client reasonable ground for challenging the solicitor.[53]

D. LITIGATION FUNDING

5-008   In 1995, the Government, realising that many potential litigants were not eligible for legal aid and not wealthy enough to contemplate undertaking litigation at their own expense and risk, introduced Conditional Fee Agreements (CFAs), with a view to taking a large portion of the risk away from the client and transferring it to the legal representatives. The statutory provisions enabled the legal representative to reflect the risk being taken by charging a success fee by way of an uplift on the fees charged to the client. Originally the success fee was borne by the successful client and not by the other party to the litigation. The maximum uplift was set at 100 per cent which was intended to enable lawyers to take cases with a risk up to 50 per cent. Lord MacKay of Clashfern, the Lord Chancellor, made it clear that he did not intend 100 per cent to become the standard uplift, stating:

> " . . . the availability of detailed assessment will help to ensure that uplifts reflect the true risks in individual cases."

The Court of Appeal in 1998 came to the view that there was nothing unlawful in a solicitor acting for a party to litigation agreeing to forego all or part of his fee if he lost, provided that he did not seek to recover more than his ordinary profit costs and disbursements if he won.[54] That judgment fundamentally altered the perception of what was and what was not lawful in relation to contingent fees, maintenance and champerty.[55]

The Divisional Court in a subsequent case disagreed with the Court of Appeal decision and did not follow it.[56] That court held that the Solicitors Practice Rules 1990 (r.8(1)) imposed a mandatory prohibition on entering

---

[52] *ibid.*, s.63(2).
[53] *ibid.*, s.63(3).
[54] *per* Millett L.J. *Thai Trading Co v Taylor* [1998] 3 All E.R. 65, CA.
[55] ss.27–31 Access to Justice Act 1999 gives statutory effect to the judgment.
[56] *Hughes v Kingston upon Hull City Council* [1999] 2 All E.R. 49, DC.

into any arrangement to receive a contingency fee in respect of proceedings, and that provision had the force of statute.[57] Following this the Law Society altered its Practice Rules to permit any agreement between solicitor and client which was not contrary to the law. A differently constituted Court of Appeal, considering itself bound by the House of Lords decision in *Swain v The Law Society*, found that an oral arrangement, partly reflected in writing, entered into in 1993 was unenforceable as being both contrary to legislation and common law.[58]

The Access to Justice Act 1999 provides that CFAs, including *Thai Trading* type agreements, are enforceable provided they comply with the Regulations. There remains some uncertainty for agreements signed between January 1, 1999 (when the Law Society's Practice Rules were altered) and April 1, 2000 (when the Access to Justice Act came into force).

The 1999 Act permits the recovery of costs under a CFA, including one which provides for a success fee.[59] The Act also provides for recovery of insurance premiums by way of costs and recovery of an additional amount where a membership organisation undertakes to meet liabilities which members of the organisation, or other persons who are party to the proceedings, may incur to pay the costs of other parties to the proceedings.[60]

The development of CFA jurisprudence

The introduction of recoverable success fees and insurance premiums as part of the costs between the parties gave rise to considerable problems. The issue came before the Court of Appeal which considered four main questions: 5–009

  (i) the time at which it is appropriate to enter into a CFA and take out an ATE policy;

  (ii) the reasonableness of the success fee when a claim is quickly resolved without the need for court proceedings;

  (iii) whether the claimants are entitled to recover an ATE premium where there has been no need to commence proceedings;

  (iv) the reasonableness of ATE premiums.

---

[57] *Swain v The Law Society* [1982] 2 All E.R. 827, HL.
[58] *Geraghty v Awwad* [2000] 1 All E.R. 608, CA.
[59] Access to Justice Act 1999, s.27.
[60] *ibid.*, s.29 and 30.

After a hearing at which representatives of interested bodies were also allowed to make representations the court found:

(i) it is in principle permissible for a claimant to enter into a CFA with a success fee and to take out ATE insurance when he first consults his solicitor and before the solicitor writes a letter of claim and receives the prospective defendant's response;

(ii) in relation to modest and straightforward claims for compensation resulting from road traffic accident cases where a CFA is agreed at the outset, 20 per cent is the maximum uplift that can reasonably be agreed in such a case[61];

(iii) ATE premiums are in principle recoverable as part of a claimant's costs even though his claim is quickly resolved without the need for proceedings;

(iv) the court requested a costs judge to investigate and report on the reasonableness of ATE premiums.

The court also considered that it is open to a solicitor and to a client to agree a two stage success fee at the outset of proceedings. It gave an example of an uplift agreed at 100 per cent subject to a reduction to a maximum of 5 per cent should the claim settle before the end of the period fixed by a pre-action protocol. Such an uplift would normally reflect the risks of the individual case. The court suggested that once the necessary data became available, consideration would need to be given to the question whether the requirement to act reasonably mandates the agreement of a two stage success fee in a case where a CFA with a success fee is agreed at the outset.[62]

The Court of Appeal subsequently held that the words "insurance against the risk of incurring a costs liability" in section 29 of the Access to Justice Act 1999 mean "insurance against the risk of incurring a costs liability that cannot be passed on to the opposite party". In the particular case, a small element of cover for "own costs insurance" could be regarded as falling within the description of insurance against the risk of liability within section 29 and the premium of £350 in the particular case was held to be reasonable.

The circumstances in which and the terms upon which "own costs" cover would be reasonable in relation to other policies, so that the whole premium could be recovered as costs, would have to be determined by the courts when dealing with individual cases. Other issues mentioned in the Costs Judge's report would fall to be judicially determined as and when they arose in individual cases. A copy of the report was annexed to the Court of Appeal

---

[61] And see now the Fixed Costs provisions in CPR Pt 45, s.2.
[62] *Callery v Gray* [2001] EWCA Civ, 1117; [2001] 1 W.L.R. 2112, CA.

judgment with the warning that views expressed might be helpful but were not definitive.[63]

The Court of Appeal again considered the question of success fees in simple claims which settle without the need for court proceedings. The court stated:

"34. . . . it is now time to re-appraise the appropriate level of success fee which should be recoverable on these simple claims when they are settled without the need for court proceedings . . .

. . .

36. . . . we consider that Judges concerned with questions relating to the recoverability of a success fee in claims as simple as this which are settled without the need to commence proceedings should now ordinarily decide to allow an uplift of 5 per cent on the claimant's lawyers costs (including the costs of any costs only proceedings which are awarded to them) pursuant to their powers contained in CPD 11.8(2) unless persuaded that a higher uplift is appropriate in the particular circumstances of the case. This policy should be adopted in relation to all CFAs, however they are structured, which are entered into on and after 1 August 2001 when both *Callery* judgments had been published and the main uncertainties about costs recovery had been removed."[64]

The Court of Appeal (Brooke L.J.) subsequently stated:

"101. Subsequent events have shown that I should have expressed myself with greater clarity [in paragraphs 34 to 36 of the *Halloran* judgment]. The type of case to which I was referring was a case similar to *Callery v Gray* and *Halloran v Delaney* in which . . . the prospects of success are virtually 100 per cent. The two step fee advocated by the court in *Callery v Gray (No.1)* is apt to allow a solicitor in such a case to cater for the wholly unexpected risk lurking below the limped waters of the simplest of claims. It did not require any research evidence or submissions from other parties in the industry to persuade the court that in this type of extremely simple claim a success fee of over 5 per cent was no longer tenable in all the circumstance. The guidance given in that judgment was not intended to have any wider application."[65]

In a simple clinical negligence case where the claimant undergoing dental treatment swallowed a reamer, which was passed naturally during the

---

[63] *Callery v Gray (No.2)* [2001] E.R. CA Civ, 1246; [2001] 1 W.L.R. 2142, CA; and see *Callery v Gray (Nos 1 & 2)* [2002] UKHL 28; [2002] 1 W.L.R. 2000, [2002] 3 All E.R. 417, HL.

[64] *Halloran v Delaney* [2002] EWCA Civ 1258; [2003] 1 W.L.R. 28, CA; [2003] 1 All E.R. 775, CA.

[65] *In the matter of Claims Direct Test Cases* [2003] EWCA Civ 136.

course of the next few days, the claimant suffering no injury other than shock and upset, the claim settled before proceedings and in the costs only proceeding the court allowed a success fee of 20 per cent as against the 50 per cent claimed.[66]

Before the event insurance

5-010   The Court of Appeal dealt with a case of a passenger who suffered injury in a road traffic accident for which the driver of the car in which he was travelling was responsible. He took out after the event (ATE) insurance and the claim settled for a comparatively small sum without proceedings having been commenced. During the course of the subsequent costs only proceedings the defendant's insurers disclosed that the defendant's policy contained a provision for legal expenses insurance which covered a claim made by a passenger in the car against the insured driver. The Court of Appeal stated:

> "45. In our judgment proper modern practice dictates that a solicitor should normally invite a client to bring to the first interview any relevant motor insurance policy, any household insurance policy and any stand alone BTE insurance policy belonging to the client and/or any spouse or partner living in same household of the client"

The court went on to say that if the claim was likely to be less than about £5,000 and there were no features of the cover which made it inappropriate, the solicitor should refer the client to the BTE insurer without further ado. A solicitor is not obliged to embark on a treasure hunt in case by chance an insurance policy belonging to a member of the client's family contains relevant BTE cover. The Court of Appeal held that on the facts of the case the BTE policy did not provide the claimant with appropriate cover in the circumstances of the case. Representation arranged by the insurer of the opposing party, to which the claimant had never been a party, and of which he had no knowledge at the time it was entered into and where the opposing insurer through its chosen representative reserved to itself the full conduct and control of the claim, was not a reasonable alternative to representation by a lawyer of the claimant's own choice backed by an ATE policy.[67]

After the event insurance

5-011   Section 29 of the Access to Justice Act 1999 came into force in April 2000. In May 2000 defendants to proceedings took out ATE insurance and in July

---

[66] *Bensusan v Freedman* [2001] September 20, Senior Costs Judge.
[67] *Sarwar v Alam* [2001] EWCA Civ 1401; [2002] 1 W.L.R. 125, CA.

obtained judgment in their favour, the claimant being ordered to pay their costs. On July 3, 2000 before judgment, transitional provisions were introduced as to the giving of notice of funding. The court held that CPR r.44.15 and its related practice direction were not retrospective in their effect, there were therefore no rules of court requiring notice to be given between April 1 and July 2, 2000. The premium was therefore recoverable.[68]

In relation to the existsence of ATE insurance the Court of Appeal accepted the reasoning of the Senior Costs Judge in *Tilby v Perfect Pizza Ltd.*[69]

"17. In deciding that the policy remained in force until the conclusion of costs only proceedings Master Hurst was influenced by the language of the Law Society model CFA which was also used in that case. This agreement expressly covered the claim and also covered any proceedings taken to enforce a judgment, order, or agreement . . . in these circumstances Master Hurst accepted an argument by counsel for the claimant in these terms:

'[counsel for the claimant], in support of his argument that costs only proceedings precede the conclusion [of the case], relies upon the duration of the conditional fee agreement which he submits covers enforcement proceedings. The assessment of costs is not an enforcement proceeding but, until costs are assessed, the agreement to pay costs cannot be enforced. By commencing costs only proceedings the claimant will obtain a detailed assessment of her costs which will result in a final certificate and that certificate will be enforceable in the same way as any other judgment for a civil debt.'

18. Master Hurst went on to say:

' . . . taken together, the insurance policy and the CFA made it clear that the insurance cover extended to all necessary steps in relation to resolving the claimant's claim, including her claim to be paid her reasonable costs.'

He therefore found that the ATE insurance policy was still in force, the case not having yet concluded. The case would be concluded when the costs were finally assessed.

19. We accept Master Hurst's conclusion and the reasons he gave."[70]

---

[68] *Inline Logistics Ltd v UCI Logistics Ltd* [2002] EWHC Ch 519, *The Times*, May 2, 2002, Ferris J.
[69] Unreported February 28, 2002.
[70] *Halloran v Delaney* [2002] EWCA Civ 1258; [2003] 1 W.L.R. 28; [2003] 1 All E.R. 775, CA.

In relation to recoverable premium the Court of Appeal has stated:

> "88. It was not in my judgment the intention of Parliament when it enacted Section 29 of the 1999 Act to overload the recoverable premium by adding to costs customarily embraced by such a premium the costs which a company . . . had to incur if insurers were to accept the risk at all. I would look equally askance at the recoverability, in similar circumstances, of a premium for a fire policy which included the cost the insured had to incur in installing and maintaining a sprinkler system as a condition of his insurance cover or a premium for a household insurance policy which included the cost of installing and maintaining a burglar alarm.
>
> 89. The obligation which the insurer undertook under his contract of insurance with the claimant was to provide an indemnity in the event that the claimants compensation claim was dismissed or was discontinued. It was not an obligation to provide 'the continuing insurance services' described in the 26 August agreement. The claimant would be provided with these services in any event, where or not the claim was unsuccessful. If and in so far as the work done by a claims manager represented an appropriate disbursement for work the solicitor would otherwise have to perform himself then the cost of that work would be properly recoverable as part of the solicitor's bill."

The Court of Appeal confirmed the allowance of recoverable premium of £621.13 including IPT to be reasonable and proportionate.[71]

In libel proceedings the defendants argued that the availability of CFAs in defamation actions had a potentially chilling effect on the activities of journalists incompatible with the right to freedom of speech under ECHR since the potential costs liability (including a 100 per cent success fee) was enormous. The court would not be drawn into an assessment of the merits of the case beyond deciding whether the summary judgment test was met. There was nothing inconsistent with the intention of the legislature in lawyers agreeing to support a claim by means of a CFA even where a cold dispassionate assessment of the likely outcome would lead them to the conclusion that the claim was unlikely to succeed.[72] In another libel case the claimants funded their action with a CFA but without ATE cover so that even if the defendant succeeded it would be unable to recover its costs. The defendant argued that this infringed the right to freedom of expression in Article 10 ECHR. The court held that the ability of the claimants to pursue

---

[71] *In the matter of Claims Direct Test Cases* [2003] EWCA Civ 136.
[72] *King v Telegraph* [2003] EWHC 1312 (QB), Eady J.

their claim at no cost risk to themselves and the exposure of the defendant to a considerable cost burden would have a stifling effect on the newspaper's freedom of expression. If the action were to proceed the features of the particular case gave rise to real unfairness to the newspaper.[73]

E. CONDITIONAL FEE AGREEMENTS

The Access to Justice Act 1999 makes provision for CFAs by substituting new sections 58 and 58A in the Courts and Legal Services Act 1990. A CFA is defined as an agreement with a person providing advocacy or litigation services, which provides for his fees and expenses, or any part of them, to be payable only in specified circumstances. A CFA provides for a success fee if it provides for the amount of any fees to which it applies to be increased in specified circumstances (usually success in the action), above the amount which would otherwise be payable.[74] All proceedings may be the subject of an enforceable CFA except specified family proceedings and criminal proceedings.[75] A CFA must relate to proceedings of a description specified by order made by the Lord Chancellor. The Lord Chancellor has specified all proceedings, except proceedings under section 82 of the Environmental Protection Act 1990.[76] The maximum percentage success fee specified by the Lord Chancellor is 100 per cent.[77]

5–012

A CFA must be in writing, it must not relate to proceedings which cannot be the subject of an enforceable CFA; and it must comply with any requirements prescribed by the Lord Chancellor.[78] If the CFA provides for a success fee it must relate to proceedings of a description specified by order made by the Lord Chancellor; it must state the percentage increase of the success fee; and that percentage must not exceed the maximum prescribed by the Lord Chancellor.[79] If the CFA is a non contentious business agreement within section 57 of the Solicitors Act 1974 it is not unenforceable.[80]

A costs order made in any proceedings may, subject to Rules of Court, include provision requiring the payment of any fees payable under a CFA which provides for a success fee (*ibid.*, section 58A(6)).

---

[73] *Pedder v Newsgroup Newspapers Ltd* [2003] EWHC 2442 (QB), Gray J.
[74] Courts and Legal Services Act 1990 s.58(2).
[75] Other than those under s.82 of the Environmental Protection Act 1990.
[76] Conditional Fee Agreements Order 2000, art.3.
[77] *ibid.*, art.4.
[78] Courts and Legal Services Act 1990, s.58(3).
[79] *ibid.*, s.58(4).
[80] *ibid.* s.58(5).

Requirements of a CFA

5–013   The agreement must specify:

(a) the particular proceedings or parts of them to which it relates;

(b) the circumstances in which the legal representative's fees and expenses are payable;

(c) what payment, if any, is due:

(i) if those circumstances only partly occur;
(ii) irrespective of whether those circumstances occur; and
(iii) on the termination of the agreement for any reason; and

(d) the amounts which are payable in all the circumstances and cases specified, or the method to be used to calculate them, and in particular whether the amounts are limited by reference to the damages which may be recovered on behalf of the client.[81]

If the CFA provides for a success fee, it must briefly specify the reasons for setting the percentage increase at the level stated in the agreement and must specify how much of the percentage increase, if any, relates to the cost to the legal representative of the postponement of the payment of his fees and expenses.[82] Any percentage which relates to the cost of postponement of payment is not recoverable from a paying party but is recoverable from the client. The reason for this is that the cost of funding litigation has never been a recoverable item between the parties.[83]

If the CFA relates to court proceedings, it must provide that where the percentage increase becomes payable as a result of those proceedings, then: if any fees subject to the increase are assessed and the legal representative or the client is required by the court to disclose the reasons for setting the percentage increase at the level stated in the agreement, he may do so; if any such fees are assessed and any amount in respect of the percentage increase is disallowed on the assessment on the ground that the level at which the increase was set was unreasonable, in view of the facts which were or should have been known to the legal representative at the time it was set, that amount ceases to be payable under the agreement, unless the court is satisfied that it should continue to be so payable. If the legal representative agrees with the paying party that a lower success fee than the amount payable in accordance with the CFA is to be paid, the amount payable under the agreement in respect of those fees will be reduced accordingly, unless the

---

[81] Conditional Fee Agreements Regulations 2000, reg.2.
[82] *ibid.*, reg.3(1).
[83] *Hunt v R M Douglas (Roofing) Ltd* [1987] EWCA Civ, unreported, November 18.

court is satisfied that the full amount should continue to be payable under it.[84]

Information to be given before CFA is made

Before the CFA is made the legal representative must inform the client about certain matters and provide such further explanation, advice or other information about those matters as the client reasonably requires.[85] The matters to be explained are:

    (a) the circumstances in which the client may be liable to pay the costs of the legal representative in accordance with the agreement;

    (b) the circumstances in which the client may seek assessment of the fees and expenses of the legal representative and the procedure for doing so;

    (c) whether the legal representative considers that the client's risk of incurring liability for costs in respect of the proceedings to which the agreement relates is insured against under an existing contract of insurance;

    (d) whether other methods of financing those costs are available and if so how they apply to the client and the proceedings in question;

    (e) whether the legal representative considers that any particular method or methods of financing those costs is appropriate, and, if he considers that a contract of insurance is appropriate or recommends a particular insurance policy, his reasons for doing so and whether he has an interest in doing so.[86]

5–014

Before a CFA is made the legal representative must explain its effect to the client. Information given to the client must be given orally whether or not it is also given in writing, but information required to be given in connection with any particular method or methods of financing the costs and whether or not he considers the contract of insurance as appropriate must be given both orally and in writing to the client, as must the explanation of the effect of the agreement.[87] These requirements do not apply in the case of an agreement between a legal representative and an additional legal representative.[88] A CFA must be signed by the client and the legal representative,

---

[84] *ibid.*, reg.3(2)(c).
[85] *ibid.*, reg.4(1).
[86] *ibid.*, reg.4(2).
[87] *ibid.*, reg.4(3) and (5).
[88] *ibid.*, reg.4(6).

although this requirement does not apply to an agreement between a legal representative and an additional legal representative.[89]

Unenforceability

5-015 The provision in Section 58 of the Courts and Legal Services Act 1990, that any conditional fee agreement which did not satisfy all of the conditions applicable to it should be unenforceable, led to paying parties taking every possible point on detailed assessment in an effort to demonstrate that the underlying CFA was unenforceable and that therefore by operation of the indemnity principle, no costs should be payable. Against this background six appeals came before the Court of Appeal (see *Hollins v Russell*, below), and at the same time the Lord Chancellor introduced amendments to the Conditional Fee Agreement Regulations, making it possible for legal representatives to enter into conditional fee agreements with their clients under which the client is liable to pay the legal representatives fees and expenses, only to the extent that sums are recovered in respect of the relevant proceedings, whether by way of costs or otherwise. In respect of such agreements Regulations 2, 3 and 4 of the CFA Regulations are disapplied. Corresponding amendments were made to CPR r.43.2, similar provisions were inserted into the Collective Conditional Fee Agreements Regulations 2000 and section 31 of the Access to Justice Act 1999 amending Section 51 of the Supreme Court Act 1981 was brought into force.

In *Hollins v Russell* (and five other appeals)[90] the Court of Appeal dealt with a number of CFA compliance issues:

(i) The circumstances in which the court should put a receiving party in detailed assessment proceedings to its election so that it must choose whether to disclose its CFA to the paying party or to prove its claim by other means.

(ii) The proper construction of the words "satisfies all of the conditions applicable to it" in section 58(1) of the 1990 Act and whether any costs or disbursements are recoverable from a paying party in the event of non compliance with the CFA Regulations.

(iii) Whether on the particular facts the requirements contained in one or other of regulations 2, 3 and 4 of the CFA Regulations were not complied with.

---

[89] *ibid.*, reg.5.
[90] [2003] EWCA Civ 718.

(i) Disclosure

The court referred to the decision in *Bailey v IBC Vehicles Ltd*[91] stating: 5–016

> "68 . . . In our judgment the solicitor's certificate as to accuracy, important though it is may not be sufficient where the quality and quantity of the information served on the paying party about the success fee is less than would be made available in respect of the other aspects of the bill in the case on an assessment where there is no additional liability claimed."

The court declined to extend the decision in *Bailey* beyond the facts with which it was dealing continuing:

> "71 . . . where there is a CFA a Costs Judge should normally exercise his discretion under the Costs Practice Direction and the Pamplin procedure[92] so as to require the receiving parties (subject to their right of election preserved by paragraph 40.14 of the Costs Practice Direction and the *Goldman* case[93]) to produce a copy of their CFAs to the paying parties in order that they can see whether or not the Regulations were complied with and (where a CFA provides for a success fee) whether the liability of the receiving party to pay that success fee is indeed enforceable.
> . . .
> 72 If the CFA contains confidential information which is not required to be disclosed for the purposes of fairly determining the receiving party's claim to costs . . . the Costs Judge may permit that material to be redacted before service."

The court declined to decide whether or not a CFA is of itself privileged. The court approved the decision of Pumfrey J. in *South Coast Shipping Co Ltd v Havant Borough Council*[94] when he found that there was no incompatibility of the European Convention on Human Rights.

(ii) Satisfying the conditions in section 58

Under this head, having rehearsed the arguments, the court stated: 5–017

> "107 . . . The key question therefore is whether the conditions applicable to the CFA by virtue of Section 58 of the 1990 Act have been sufficiently complied with in the light of their purposes. Costs Judges should accordingly ask themselves the following question: 'Has the

---

[91] [1998] 3 All E.R. 570, CA.
[92] *Pamlin v Express Newspapers Ltd* [1985] 1 W.L.R. 689.
[93] *Goldman v Hesper* [1988] 1 W.L.R. 1238.
[94] [2002] 3 All E.R. 779.

particular departure from a Regulation pursuant to Section 58(3)(c) of the 1990 Act or a requirement in Section 58, either on its own or in conjunction with any other such departure in this case, had a materially adverse effect either upon the protection afforded to the client or upon the proper administration of justice?' If the answer is 'yes' the conditions have not been satisfied. If the answer is 'no' then the departure is immaterial and (assuming that there is no other reason to conclude otherwise) the conditions have been satisfied.

108. We would not draw any formal distinction between the conditions contained in the section itself and those contained in the Regulations. The meaning of 'satisfies' must be the same in each case. However, it is more difficult to envisage questions of degree coming into the question whether the conditions in the section have been sufficiently met. Either the CFA relates to permissible proceedings or it does not. But one example might be that in section 58(4)(b) which requires that a CFA providing for a success fee 'must state the percentage by which the amount of the fees which would be payable if it were not a conditional fee agreement is to be increased'. Was that condition sufficiently met by agreement . . . which left blank the percentage in the clause where it should have been filled in but stated it clearly in the risk assessment . . .? The answer to that question is obviously 'yes'.

109. . . . . Sufficiency or materiality will depend upon the circumstances of each case. This is not to encourage paying parties to trawl through the facts of each case in order to try to discover a material breach. Quite the reverse. At the stage when the agreement has been made, acted upon, and success for the client has been achieved, it is most unlikely that any minor shortcoming which the paying party might discover in the agreement or the procedures leading up to its making will amount to a material breach of the requirements or mean that the applicable conditions have not been sufficiently met."

The court dealt with two other points under the heading of compliance which they felt could be of considerable importance in practice. First the recoverability of the ATE premium:

"114. . . . . ATE insurance premiums are recoverable as costs in any proceedings, irrespective of whether or not there is a CFA between the receiving party and her legal representatives. The clients liability to pay the insurance premium arises from the contract of insurance, not from her contract with the legal representative. It arises whether or not there is a CFA and whether or not the CFA is enforceable. . . . It would appear therefore that there is no bar to the recovery of the ATE insurance premium as costs whatever may be the bar to the recovery of the lawyers charges and success fee."

The second point which the court dealt with related to disbursements which the client has in fact paid to the solicitor either personally or by taking out a loan to do so:

"115. . . . The solicitor is required to retain this money on client's account until it is expended in accordance with the client's instructions. If the CFA fails, and the money has not been paid out, the solicitor would be required to pay it back to the client. If the money has been paid out, then this is money actually paid by the client. . . . This should be recoverable by the client as costs. The costs claim is that of the client not of the solicitor. If the client has actually paid a debt to a third party, properly incurred in the conduct of the litigation, there seems no reason why this should not be recoverable from the paying party, insofar as it is reasonable and proportionate . . . This is irrespective of whether the solicitor can enforce the CFA for his charges and success fee."

(iii) Particular allegations of breach

Regulation 2(1)(d)   Dealing with Regulation 2(1)(d) the court stated: 5–018

"118 . . . No difficulty will arise under Regulation 2(i)(d) for solicitors who use the Law Society's model CFA which came into use in July 2000 . . . "

On the facts of the particular appeals the court took the view that the effect of the CFA read as a whole was sufficiently clear and that the failure to specify the position accurately did not affect the protection given to the client or the administration of justice to any material degree. The result would have been different if the CFA was less clear as to its effect that is, if it would not have been reasonably comprehensible to the lay person.

Regulation 3(1)(b)   In respect of Regulation 3(1)(b) the point had been   5–019
taken that the CFA did not specify how much of the percentage increase related to the cost to the legal representative of the postponement of the payment of fees and expenses. The court found this submission unattractive and unmeritorious. It found that the language of the CFA made the position clear. The reality being that, despite what was said in the risk assessment calculation, none of the recoverable success fee was attributable to the postponement in payment of the solicitor's fees. The court found that taken together the clauses in the CFA prevailed over the risk assessment schedule and thus, on its true construction, the CFA complied with the Regulations.

Regulation 4(2)(c)   Under Regulation 4(2)(c) the paying parties argued   5–020
that there was a breach because the client had not been informed that the risk of incurring a liability for costs in respect of proceedings to which the

agreement related was insured against under an existing contract of insurance. The court found that attendance notes dealing with this issue should not ordinarily be disclosed. It was sufficient to satisfy Section 58 that the solicitor had discussed the matter with the client and had formed a view on the funding options. The court pointed out that the recovery of the insurance premium is an entirely separate matter from the enforceability of the CFA.

5–021   **Regulation 4(2)(e)(ii)**   The argument under Regulation 4(2)(e)(ii) was as to the meaning of "whether" and "whether or not". The court held:

> "144 . . . In this context there is no reason to construe 'whether' as meaning anything other than 'if'. The language of the Regulation . . . mirrored the language of the Government's February 2000 paper. . . The mischief which this Regulation was introduced to remedy was the risk that the client's legal representative might induce the client to enter into insurance arrangements in which he had an interest. If he had no interest, then there was no identified mischief . . . "

5–022   **Regulation 4(5)**   Regulation 4(5) requires the legal representative to explain the effect of the CFA in writing to the client before she enters into it and in addition to explain it orally. In the particular case the client had received an oral explanation and a copy of the CFA, which itself had attached to it an explanation of its clauses. The court stated:

> "153. All these cases turn on their own facts. The regulatory intention is that the client should not be left in . . . confusion . . . If these documents had been in small print and as far removed from winning a prize for plain English as many documents of their type, then it is obvious that Regulation 4(5) would have been breached . . .
> 154. We therefore agree with the approach adopted by the Judge and also with his preference for a free standing explanatory letter, which may of course cross refer to any part of the Law Society conditions which sets out the effect of the CFA with clarity."

5–023   **Regulation 4—Delegation**   In the Accident Group (TAG) Test Cases, the issue was whether the Regulation 4 information was given to the claimants by someone who qualified as "the legal representative" for the purposes of that Regulation. The court, having extensively reviewed the argument, felt that it was not driven to the conclusion that the person who actually gave the Regulation 4 advice must inevitably be someone who was himself qualified to conduct litigation services. Parliament had not made this requirement and, in the context of the liberalising effect of Part 2 of the 1990 Act, it would be wrong for the court to do so. The question therefore arose: if a wider degree of delegation is legally possible, can a solicitor lawfully delegate his responsibility to an organisation like TAG, and can TAG sub-delegate it to one of their representatives? The court concluded:

"216 . . . For the purposes [of this appeal], it is sufficient if we make it clear that it will be in theory permissible for a solicitors firm to delegate the performance of his Regulation 4 duties to an organisation like TAG, and for TAG to sub-delegate to it representatives, provided that in so doing the solicitor is not abandoning the supervisory responsibilities required of him by Practice Rule 3.07 and the Guide to Professional Conduct. Whether the TAG scheme can and does provide properly for this is a matter for the fact finding trial.

217. Part 2 of the 1990 Act is concerned with the search for new or better ways of providing litigation services. A national organisation like TAG may be able to achieve economies of scale and standards of client service which simply are not available to an ordinary solicitor's firm. Quality control, however, is all important, and if a solicitor abjurs his duty to maintain supervisory responsibility, through an established framework for reporting and accountability, over the TAG representatives when they visit his client's home on his behalf, it is likely that it would be found that it was not he who gave the information he was required by Regulation 4 to give and that the Regulation has therefore been broken."

The court concluded by saying:

"226. In future district judges and costs judges must be equally astute to prevent satellite litigation about costs from being protracted by allegations about breaches of the CFA Regulations where the breaches do not matter. They should remember that the law does not care about very little things, and that they should only declare a CFA unenforceable if the breach does matter and if the client could have relied on it successfully against his solicitor."[95]

Where a CFA made no mention of the fee deferral element in its schedule, although the body of the agreement stated that this was set out in the schedule, the solicitors argued that section 58(1) of the Courts and Legal Services Act 1990 should be interpreted by inserting words such as: "to the extent that it does not satisfy all requirements" so that the court could assess the effect of a particular breach. If the consequences were comparativelyivial this would penalise the solicitor far less than rendering the whole agreement unenforceable. The Court of Appeal rejected that argument

---

[95] *Hollins v Russell* and other appeals [2003] EWCA Civ 718; [2003] 1 W.L.R. 2487, CA, *sub nom. Sharratt v London Central Bus Co Ltd* [2003] 4 All E.R. 590, CA. See Also *Myler & Mirror Group Newspapers v Williams* [2003] EWHC 1387 QB, Crane J.

pointing out that in *Hollins v Russell*[96] the court had found "there is no graduated response to different types of breach: it is all or nothing". The words "shall be unenforceable" mean what they say. The court held that Parliament had decided that unless a CFA satisfied all the conditions applicable to it by virtue of section 58(1) it would not be exempt from the general rules as to the unenforceability of CFAs at common law.[97]

5–024 **Collective conditional fee agreements** The Conditional Fee Agreements Regulations and the Collective Conditional Fee Agreement Regulations established two mutually exclusive sets of requirements for CFAs and CCFAs, respectively. The Regulations governing CCFAs are less exacting than those governing CCFAs since CCFAs involve bulk users of legal services who are less vulnerable than a lay client who may need protection when contemplating entering into a CFA. Often, bulk users such as trade unions will contract to purchase, at their own expense, legal services to be provided to litigants. In those circumstances the litigants will not be exposed to significant risk of liability to pay for the legal services provided to them. Sections 58 and 58A of the Courts and Legal Services Act 1990 and the Regulations made under them are intended to give effect to fundamental changes to the manner in which litigation is funded.[98]

The position of legal representatives acting under CFAS

5–025 The Court of Appeal has considered the position of solicitors acting on behalf of claimants under CFAs. The court held that:

> "The existence of a CFA does not alter the relationship between the legal adviser and his client. The solicitor or counsel still owes to the client exactly the same duties that would be owed if there were no CFA. A solicitor or client acting under a CFA remains under the same duty to the client to disregard his own interests in giving advice to the client and in performing his other responsibilities on behalf of the client. This extends to advising the client of what are the consequences to the client of the client entering into the CFA. The lawyer also still owes the same duties to the court.
>
> The fact that there is a CFA cannot justify the legal adviser coming to any additional or collateral arrangement which would not be permissible if there were no CFA.
>
> The lawyer, as long as he puts aside any consideration of his own interests, is entitled to advise the client about commencing, continuing

---

[96] [2003] EWCA Civ 718.
[97] *Spencer v Wood* [2004] EWCA Civ 352.
[98] *Thornley v Lang* [2003] EWCA Civ 1484; [2004] 1 W.L.R. 378, CA.

or compromising proceedings but the decision must be that of the client and not of the lawyer. The lawyer has however, the right, if the need should arise, to cease to act for the client under a CFA in the same way as a lawyer can cease to act in the event of there being a conventional retainer.

There is no reason why the circumstances in which a lawyer acting under a CFA can be made personally liable for the costs of a party other than his client should differ from those in which a lawyer who is not acting under a CFA would be so liable.

The existence of a CFA should make the legal adviser's position as a matter of law no worse, so far as being ordered to pay costs is concerned, than it would be if there were no CFAs. This is unless the CFA is outside the statutory protection.

- The [claimant's] lawyers are in no different position because they are acting under a CFA than they would be acting for a legally aided client with a nil contribution.
- The court has a limited additional jurisdiction to make an order for costs against legal advisers personally in circumstances in which it would be possible to make a wasted costs order.
- The limited additional jurisdiction can arise under two heads. First there is the court's inherent jurisdiction to make such an order at least against solicitors.
- The second area of additional jurisdiction is that which arises under the general jurisdiction of the court as to costs contained in Section 51(1) and (3) of the Supreme Court Act 1981. This is a jurisdiction which cannot arise where a legal representative is acting only in that capacity in the context of legal proceedings.

What we intend to make clear is that lawyers acting under CFAs are at no more risk of paying costs personally than they would be if they were not so acting. In addition whether or not CFAs are properly the subject of professional privilege they are not normally required to be disclosed."[99]

Recovery of insurance premiums

Where an order for costs is made in favour of a party who has taken out an   5–026
insurance policy against the risk of incurring a liability in proceedings, the costs payable to him may, subject to Rules of Court, include costs in respect of the premium of the policy.[1]

---

[99] *per* Lord Woolf M.R., *Hodgson v Imperial Tobacco Ltd* [1988] 1 W.L.R. 1056, CA.
[1] Access to Justice Act 1999, s.29.

It was not the intention of Parliament when it enacted section 29 of the Access to Justice Act 1999 to overload the recoverable premium by adding to the costs customarily embraced by such a premium, the costs which a company providing personal injury claims handling services (including a costs indemnity in the event that a claimants compensation claim was dismissed or discontinued), had to incur if insurers were to accept the risk at all.[2]

Recovery of additional amount by membership organisation

5–027   Where a prescribed body or membership organisation undertakes to meet liabilities which its members, or other persons who are parties to proceedings, may incur to pay the costs of other parties to the proceedings, if the court makes a costs order in favour of the member or other person the costs may, subject to Rules of Court, include an additional amount in respect of any provision made by or on behalf of the body in connection with the proceedings against the risk of having to meet those liabilities.[3]

Recovery of additional amount for insurance costs

5–028   Where an additional amount is included in costs in respect of any provision made by or on behalf of the body in connection with the proceedings against the risk of having to meet the specified liabilities, the additional amount must not exceed the likely cost to the member or other person of the premium of any insurance policy against the risk of incurring a liability to pay the costs of other parties to the proceedings.[4]

Requirements for arrangements to meet costs liabilities

5–029   Where a membership organisation or body specified by the Lord Chancellor,[5] undertakes to meet liabilities which members of the body or other persons, who are party to the proceedings may incur, to pay the costs of other parties, the arrangements which are made must satisfy certain conditions. The arrangements must be in writing and must contain a statement specifying:

---

[2] *Re Claims Direct Test Cases* [2003] EWCA Civ 136; [2003] 4 All E.R. 508, CA.
[3] Access to Justice Act 1999, s.30.
[4] Access to Justice (Membership Organisations) Regulations 2000, reg.4.
[5] The Lord Chancellor has approved a number of organisations, including many Trade Unions, Police Federations and motoring organisations.

(a) the circumstances in which the member or other party may be liable to pay costs of the proceedings;

(b) whether such a liability arises if those circumstances only partly occur, irrespective of whether those circumstances occur, and, on the termination of the arrangement for any reason;

(c) the basis on which the amount of the liability is calculated; and

(d) the procedure for seeking assessment of costs.

A copy of that part of the arrangement containing the above statement must be given to the member or other party to the proceedings whose liabilities the body is undertaking to meet as soon as possible after the undertaking is given.[6]

F. LITIGATION FUNDING AGREEMENTS

The Access to Justice Act 1999 inserts a new section 58B into the Courts and Legal Services Act 1990. A litigation funding agreement is an agreement under which the funder agrees to fund, wholly or partly, the provision of advocacy or litigation services (by someone other than the funder) to the litigant and the litigant agrees to pay a sum to the funder in specified circumstances.[7]   5–030

Conditions applicable to a litigation funding agreement

The funder must be prescribed by the Lord Chancellor, the agreement must be in writing, and it must not relate to criminal proceedings[8] or family proceedings, or to such proceedings as may be prescribed by the Lord Chancellor. The agreement must comply with any requirements which may be prescribed. The sum to be paid by the litigant must consist of any costs payable to him in respect of the proceedings to which the agreement relates together with an amount calculated by reference to the funder's anticipated expenditure in funding the provision of the services, and that amount must not exceed the percentage of the anticipated expenditure prescribed by the Lord Chancellor in relation to proceedings of the description to which the agreement relates.[9]   5–031

---

[6] The Access to Justice (Membership Organisations) Regulations 2000, reg.3.
[7] Courts and Legal Services Act 1990 s.58B(2). At the time of writing the provisions of this section have not been brought into force.
[8] apart from proceedings under s.82 of the Environmental Protection Act 1990.
[9] Courts and Legal Services Act 1990 s.58B(3).

The Lord Chancellor may require the funder to have provided prescribed information to the litigant before the agreement is made and may impose different requirements for different descriptions of litigation funding agreements.[10]

A costs order made in any proceedings may, subject to Rules of Court, include provision requiring the payment of any amount payable under a litigation funding agreement, and Rules of Court may make provision with respect to the assessment of any costs which include fees payable under a litigation funding agreement.[11]

G. OTHER AGREEMENTS AS TO COSTS

Costs payable to a solicitor by his client: r.48.8

5–032   Where the relationship of solicitor and client exists, Part III of the Solicitors Act 1974 deals with the remuneration of solicitors. Where the court makes an order for the assessment of costs payable to a solicitor by his client the solicitor is required to serve a breakdown of costs within 28 days of an order for costs to be assessed. The client is required to serve points of dispute within 14 days thereafter, and if the solicitors wish to serve a reply that must be done within 14 days after that. Either party may request a hearing date after points of dispute have been served but a limit of three months after the date of the order to be assessed is imposed.[12]

Except where the bill is to be paid out of the CLS fund, or there is a CFA, costs will be assessed on the indemnity basis and are presumed to have been reasonably incurred if they were incurred with the express or implied approval of the client, and to be reasonable in amount if their amount was expressly or impliedly approved by the client. Costs will be presumed to have been unreasonably incurred if they are of unusual nature or amount and the solicitor did not tell the client that, as a result, they might not be fully recoverable from the other party.[13] That information must have been given to the client before the costs were incurred.[14] If a party fails to comply with the requirement to serve a breakdown of costs or points of dispute any other party may apply to the court for an order requiring it may make it subject to conditions, including the condition to pay a sum of money into court and specify the consequence of failure to comply with that order or condition.[15]

---

[10] *ibid.*, s.58(b)(5).
[11] *ibid.*, s.58B(8) and (9). At the time of writing these provisions are not in force.
[12] CPR r.48.10. the Direction Relating to Part 48 effectively repeats the rule. The Direction to Part 48, paras 2.18 to 2.36 give detailed guidance as to the procedure.
[13] CPR r.48.8.
[14] Direction relating to Part 48, para.2.9.
[15] Direction relating to Part 48, para.2.12.

Solicitors acting for a client, where there is no specific contract to pay the sums claimed as fees, are entitled to reasonable and fair remuneration for the work which they have done. In a case where the time for applying for detailed assessment of the solicitors' costs had passed, the Court of Appeal held that the solicitor (who had sued for their costs) could not simply ask the court, without any further investigation, to underwrite the amount which they had chosen to claim:

> "Where a *quantum meruit* for work done, the benefit of which has been obtained under a contract, but where the contract sum has not been agreed, is claimed, there may be an order for judgment to be entered for the [claimant] with the quantum to be assessed."

The court went on to state that the judicial assessment should be carried out by a costs judge since they have the requisite expertise for that purpose.[16]

Where a client had been provided by the solicitor with an estimate of costs on the basis of an hourly rate shortly prior to trial it was not open to the solicitor subsequently to charge him a higher rate than he was led to believe he should be charged. In the particular case the correspondence amounted to a clear and considered indication of the client's maximum liability to the solicitor upon which the client relied. Where an estimate is given, the final amount payable should not vary substantially from the estimate unless the client has been informed of the changed circumstances in writing.[17] The court reduced the amount allowed to the solicitors to the amount of the solicitor's estimate.[18]

The presumption of reasonableness which arises from the express or implied approval of the client cannot and does not arise unless the information given by the solicitors to the client was sufficient to enable the client to give "informed" approval or consent.[19]

Detailed assessment of CFA with a success fee

Where the solicitor and client have entered into a CFA the client may apply   5–033
for assessment of the base costs or of the percentage increase or both. The base costs will be assessed in the same way as any other bill from a solicitor to his client (in accordance with Rule 48.8(2)) as if the solicitor and client had not entered into a CFA. Where the court is considering a percentage increase (whether on the application of the legal representative under Rule 44.16 or on the application of the client) it will have regard to all the

---

[16] *Thomas Watts & Co. v Smith*, unreported, March 16, 1998, CA.
[17] See the Law Society's guide to the Professional Conduct of Solicitors 7th ed., para. 13.07.
[18] *Wong v Vizards* [1997] 2 Costs L.R. 46, Toulson J.
[19] *MacDougall v Boote Edgar Esterkin* [2002] EWHC QBD, October 12, Holland J.

relevant factors as they reasonably appeared to the solicitor or counsel when the CFA was entered into or varied.[20]

The Court of Appeal has allowed a claimant who had no prospect of funding the prosecution of his action in a foreign jurisdiction, which was the most natural forum for its trial, to proceed in England, which was not an inappropriate forum, by means of a CFA with his solicitors. The court held that the interests of justice weighed in favour of the English forum where he could assert his rights. The solicitor gave an undertaking in relation to legal aid (the previous legal aid certificate had been discharged and it was unlikely that a new certificate would be granted).[21]

Agreement of costs between parties

5–034   It is open to the parties to agree to a figure for costs, either in a lump sum settlement, or separately from the damages, or even after judgment has been given in favour of a party awarding costs. If the agreement is reached before a request for a detailed assessment hearing has been made, no fee is payable to the court. Once such a request is made and the fee is paid, it is not refundable.[22]

Where it appears to the Lord Chancellor that the payment of any fees specified in the Fees Order would, owing to the exceptional circumstances of the particular case, involve undue financial hardship hardship, the Lord Chancellor may reduce or remit the fee in that case. This power is delegated to the Court Managers of district registries and county courts and to the finance officer of the Royal Courts of Justice.[23]

Where a defendant consented to judgment in a personal injury action with costs, it was not then open to the defendant to apply for leave to appeal to set aside the costs order on the grounds of mistake as to the terms on which the claimant's solicitors have been retained. The order could be challenged by a fresh action, but not by appeal to the Court of Appeal.[24] Where the parties agreed the damages payable with "Costs to be paid in full" this was held to mean something more than costs assessed on the standard basis. In the circumstances the court found that there was no final agreement between the parties in relation to costs, and that the action had not therefore been settled.[25]

A judge is not bound to accede to a request by the parties to decide costs where the parties have settled the remainder of their dispute. It is open to the

---

[20] CPR r.48.8(3).
[21] *Connelly v RTZ Corp Plc, The Times*, July 12, 1996, CA.
[22] Supreme Court Fees4 Order, 1999, County Court Fees Order 1998, Family Proceedings Fees Order 1999.
[23] Supreme Court Fees Order 1999, art.6; County Court Fees Order 1999, art.6.
[24] *Skinner v The Thames Valley & Aldershot Co. Ltd*, unreported, July 7, 1995, CA.
[25] *Gannon v Chubb Fire Ltd* [1996] P.I.Q.R. P1808, CA.

judge to say: "If you have not reached an agreement on costs you have not settled your dispute. The action must go on unless your compromise covers costs as well." There is no hard and fast rule precluding an appeal against the decision of a Judge following a joint request that he decide the costs. However once the Judge has acceded to the request an appellate court would approach an appeal against the order with an even greater reluctance than is usually the case when it is asked to interfere with the discretion of a trial judge.[26]

Where there was an agreement between the parties for consideration, that an appeal would be dismissed, and the respondent on the face of the agreement had acted to his detriment, it was a bar to the exercise of the court's discretion as the the payment of the parties' litigation costs. The court was precluded from considering the orders it had made on the merits so as to redress the injustice.[27]

Where parties to litigation agreed orders as to costs between the claimant and the first and third defendants and the first defendant became unable to pay the claimant sought indemnity from the third defendant on the basis that it had discovered that the third defendant had funded the first defendant. The court held that it did not have jurisdiction to revisit the consent order. The contract between the parties had been embodied in a court order, which, in the absence of fraud, misrepresentation or mistake could only be set aside or amended in the most exceptional circumstances. In the instant case the litigation had been settled on contractual terms and a very good reason would be required to add to the liability of the third defendant. Secondly, it was right as a matter of principle that there was finality to the proceedings.[28]

CLS Funded

It is possible to agree costs between parties in a case funded out of the Community Legal Service Fund without having to have the whole bill assessed, provided that the agreed costs have been paid.[29]   5–035

Where proceedings (other than where the funded client is a child or patient),[30] are settled without any direction of the court as to costs on terms, including a provision for the payment of agreed costs in favour of the funded client, the provisions relating to assessment set out below will apply.[31] Similarly where proceedings have been brought to an end by judgment, decree or final order and there has been agreement as to the costs

---

[26] *BCT v Brewer* [2003] EWCA Civ 939.
[27] *Neville v Wilson (No.2), The Times,* July 28, 1997, CA.
[28] *Centerhigh Ltd v Amen* [2001] EWHC CHD, July 18, Neuberger J.
[29] Civil Legal Aid (General) Regulations 1989, reg.106A.
[30] CPR r.48.5.
[31] Civil Legal Aid (General) Regulations 1989 reg.106A(2)(a).

to be paid in favour of the funded client,[32] and in circumstances where the retainer of a funded client's solicitor or counsel is determined[33] before proceedings are actually begun and there is an agreement for the payment of agreed costs in favour of the funded client those provisions also apply.[34]

The provisions relating to assessment referred to above are:

(a) the funded client's solicitor may apply to the Area Director for an assessment limited to costs payable from the Community Legal Service Fund only, if of the opinion that the amount of the costs, including counsel's fees, will not be more than £2,500[35];

(b) the solicitor must apply for a detailed assessment[36] limited to costs payable from the Community Legal Service Fund only, if of the opinion that the amount of costs, including counsel's fees, would be more than £2,500[37];

(c) before any assessment, the solicitor must confirm in writing to the relevant authority that the agreed costs have been paid.[38]

The authority may require the production of any information which it considers relevant to the determination.[39]

Children and patients

5–036   In general the court must order a detailed assessment of the costs payable by any party who is a child or patient to his solicitor. On the assessment of those costs, the court must also assess any costs payable to that party in the proceedings unless the court has issued a default costs certificate.[40]

The court does not need to order detailed assessment of costs payable by any party who is a child or patient where there is no need to do so to protect the interests of the child or patient or his estate. Detailed assessment need not be ordered where another party has agreed to pay a specified sum of money in respect of the costs and the solicitor acting for the child or patient has waived the right to claim any further costs. The same applies where the court has decided the costs payable to the child or patient by summary assessment and the solicitor has waived the right to further costs. If an insurer or other person is liable to discharge the costs which the child or

---

[32] *ibid.*, reg.107A(2)(b).
[33] In circumstances to which Civil Legal Aid (General) Regulations 1989 reg.105(2) refer.
[34] *ibid.*, reg.106A(2)(c).
[35] *ibid.*, reg.106A(3).
[36] *ibid.*, reg.107A(2).
[37] *ibid.*, reg.106A(4).
[38] *ibid.*, reg.106A(6).
[39] *ibid.*, reg.106A(6).
[40] *i.e.*, under Rule 47.11 see para.7–009.1, R.48.5(1) and (2).

patient would otherwise be liable to pay, and the court is satisfied that the insurer or other person is financially able to discharge those costs, detailed assessment need not be ordered.[41]

Offers to settle without prejudice save as to costs of the detailed assessment proceedings

This is the old Calderbank procedure retained for use under the costs rules. Either party may make a written offer to settle the cost of the proceedings, which is expressed to be without prejudice, save as to the costs of the detailed assessment proceedings. There is no time-limit for making such an offer but the earlier it is made the more effective it is likely to be. The court will take the offer into account in deciding who should be liable to pay the costs of the assessment proceedings.[42] The prohibition against making such offers where the receiving party was an assisted person was deleted by the Rule Committee but the LSC and the LCD were not prepared to allow that situation to continue and the Practice Direction provides that r.47.19 does not apply where the receiving party is an assisted person unless the court so orders.

Where *Calderbank* offers are made in respect of detailed assessment proceedings only those offers which comply with CPR r.47.19 and section 46 of the Costs Practice Direction need to be considered by the Costs Judge.[43] Whenever there is a fund out of which costs are to be paid there is not an order which attracts interest. The reason for that is that there is not an order of the court in adversarial litigation.[44] Where proceedings are settled by a Tomlin order the reality is that the substantive costs provisions may be found in the schedule. Such provisions as to payment of costs in the schedule do not fall within the Judgments Act and accordingly the statutory provisions relating to interest do not apply. Where there is a contractual agreement between the parties such as a *Tomlin* order, if interest is to be payable it should be expressly included or excluded.[45]

Where costs only proceedings under CPR 44.12A are commenced, in order to obtain a court order for detailed assessment, the "costs of the proceedings" within the meaning of CPR r.47.19 still relate only to the costs leading up to the disposal (by agreement) of the substantive claim. They are "the proceedings which gave rise to the assessment proceedings", and the assessment proceedings cover the whole period of negotiations about the amount of costs payable through the Part 8 proceedings to the ultimate disposal of those proceedings whether by agreement or court order. If the

5–037

---

[41] Direction relating to Part 48, para.1.2.
[42] r.47.19(1) and (2). Direction relating to Part 47, paras 7.4–7.6.
[43] *Wills v The Crown Estate Commissioners* [2003] EWHC 1718 (Ch), Peter Smith J.
[44] See *AG v Nethercote* [1841] 11 Sim 529 and *Re: Marsdens Estate* [1889] 40 Ch.D. 475.
[45] *Wills v The Crown Estate Commissioners*, above.

Costs Judge considers that the receiving party ought to have accepted an offer made before the Part 8 proceedings commenced then he is likely to conclude that the paying party should receive his costs including any costs involved in the subsequent Part 8 proceedings pursuant to CPR r.47.18(2). The substantive proceedings and the assessment proceedings are quite different.[46]

---

[46] *per* Brooke L.J., *Crosbie v Munro* [2003] EWCA Civ 350, [2003] 1 W.L.R. 2033, CA.

PART III

Ascertainment of Costs

Apportionment of Costs

CHAPTER 6

Non-contentious Costs

A. SOLICITORS' (NON-CONTENTIOUS BUSINESS) REMUNERATION ORDER

The remuneration of solicitors in respect of non-contentious business is **6–001** governed by the Solicitors (Non-Contentious Business) Remuneration Order 1994.[1] "Costs" for the purpose of the Remuneration Order means the amount charged in a solicitor's bill exclusive of disbursements and value added tax in respect of non-contentious business or common form probate business.[2] This definition differs considerably from the definition of costs, in CPR r.43.2.[3]

In order to comply with the Remuneration Order a solicitor's costs must be such sum as may be fair and reasonable to both the solicitor and entitled person[4] having regard to all the circumstances of the case and in particular to:

(a) the complexity of the matter or the difficulty or novelty of the questions raised;

(b) the skill, labour, specialised knowledge and responsibility involved;

(c) the time spent on the business;

---

[1] SI 1994/2616, which applies to all non-contentious business for which bills are delivered on or after November 1, 1994.

[2] *ibid.*, art.2.

[3] See Appendix V.

[4] *i.e.* a client or an entitled third party. An entitled third party means a residuary beneficiary absolutely and immediately (and not contingently) entitled to an inheritance where a solicitor has charged the estate for his professional costs for acting in the administration of the estate and either (a) the only personal representatives are solicitors (whether or not acting in a professional capacity); or (b) the only personal representatives are solicitors acting jointly with partners or employees in a professional capacity: Solicitors (Non-Contentious Business) Remuneration Order 1994, art.2.

(d) the number and importance of the documents prepared or perused without regard to length;

(e) the place where and the circumstances in which, the business or any part thereof is transacted;

(f) the amount or value of any money or property involved;

(g) whether any land involved is registered land;

(h) the importance of the matter to the client;

(i) the approval (expressed or implied) of the entitled person or the express approval of the testator to;

(i) the solicitor undertaking all or any part of the work giving rise to the costs or
(ii) the amount of those costs.[5]

Non-contentious costs can be ascertained in the event of a dispute either by utilising the Law Society's Remuneration Certificate Scheme or by detailed assessment. A Remuneration Certificate is no bar to an application for detailed assessment[6] but no application for a Remuneration Certificate may be made in respect of a bill for more than £50,000.

Information to be given in writing to the entitled person

6–002 Before a solicitor brings proceedings to recover costs against a client on a bill for non-contentious business (except where the bill has been assessed)[7] or if a solicitor deducts his costs from moneys held for or on behalf of a client or of an estate in satisfaction of a bill and an entitled person objects in writing to the amount of the bill within the prescribed time,[8] the solicitor must inform the client in writing of certain specified matters, unless he has already done so.

The entitled person must be informed of the following matters:

(a) Where a bill has been delivered for costs of not more than £50,000[9]

(i) that the entitled person may within one month of receiving from the solicitor the specified information or (if later) of

---

[5] ibid., art.3.
[6] See further paras 8–001ff.
[7] Solicitors (Non-Contentious Business) Remuneration Order 1994, art.6.
[8] ibid., art.7(1). The prescribed time is three months after the delivery of the relevant bill or notification of the amount of costs or a lesser time (not less than one month) specified in writing at the time of delivery or notification; ibid., art.7(2) (a) and (b).
[9] i.e. where art.4(1) applies.

delivery of the bill or notification of the amount of costs, require the solicitor to obtain a remuneration certificate; and

(ii) that (unless the solicitor has agreed to do so) the Council may waive the requirements to pay money on account[10] if satisfied from the client's written application that exceptional circumstances exist to justify granting a waiver.[11]

(b) That sections 70, 71 and 72 of the Solicitors Act 1974 set out the entitled person's rights in relation to detailed assessment.[12]

(c) That (where the whole of the bill has not been paid by deduction or otherwise) the solicitor may charge interest on the outstanding amount of the bill.[13]

Estimates and quotations

The Costs Information and Client Care Code issued by the Law Society expects all indications as to costs to be confirmed in writing to the client. The final amount payable should not vary substantially from the relevant indication unless the client has been informed, in writing, at the time that there was a change of circumstances. Toulson J., having referred to the Law Society's Guide to Professional Conduct of Solicitors, gave judgment limiting the amount recoverable by the solicitors to: 6–003

" . . . the maximum shown in their fee proposal (excluding counsel's and expert fees). In arriving at that conclusion I have borne in mind two competing factors [a reduction] on the ground that the trial took two days less than the time allowed for in the fee proposal. On the other hand, I am also mindful that while the sum claimed by the solicitor ought not to vary "substantially" (as the Law Society's Guide says) from that previously estimated without prior warning to the client, more especially if that estimate was expressed to be on a worst case basis, Mr Ryan's fee proposal was a projectional estimate rather than a warranty . . . I have effectively allowed to the solicitor a margin of approximately 15% over the worst case estimate given. I consider that a greater divergence would be substantial and unreasonable."[14]

The same principles apply where the indication has been given to a third party who is liable to pay the solicitor's fees. In relation to remuneration

---

[10] Under *ibid.*, art.11(1).
[11] *ibid.*, art.8(a).
[12] *ibid.*, art.8(b) and see paras 8–001ff.
[13] *i.e.* in accordance with *ibid.*, art.1, see paras 16–005 *ibid.*, art.8(c).
[14] *Wong v Vizards* [1997] 2 Costs L.R. 46, Toulson J.

certificates, if the solicitor has given an indication of the likely cost of a matter, this is a material consideration to be taken into account in the granting of a certificate, if it appears that the indication was given as an incentive to the client to give instructions to that solicitor, or that the client relied on the indication.[15]

The Law Society's Remuneration Certificate

6–004 An entitled person may require a solicitor to obtain a remuneration certificate from the Law Society in respect of a bill which has been delivered where the costs are not more than £50,000. This right is without prejudice to the provisions of sections 70, 71 and 72 of the Solicitors Act 1974 relating to detailed assessment of costs.[16] The remuneration certificate will state what sum in the opinion of the Society would be a fair and reasonable charge for the business covered by the bill (whether it be the sum charged or a lesser sum). If there is no detailed assessment the sum payable in respect of the costs will be the sum stated in the remuneration certificate.

The Law Society is concerned that only genuine costs disputes are dealt with under the remuneration certification procedure and that client grievances which fall outside the scope of the procedure are resolved by other methods or in more appropriate forms. Thus, where the client's complaint includes allegations of negligence, a dispute over whether or not instructions were given and/or their extent, allegations of professional misconduct, investigation of any part of the billing, a dispute on a question of law, a dispute over disbursements or VAT, or a dispute over whether the whole or part of the fee is payable by another person, it may not be appropriate for the remuneration certificate procedure to be used.

Where the client requests a remuneration certificate, the solicitor must submit a completed application form for each disputed bill (if a bill includes more than one fee a separate form is required for each separate fee) in addition to the application form (with a copy for each party to the application). The solicitor must also forward to the Law Society a copy of each disputed bill, the original file of working papers, a copy of any correspondence exchanged in connection with any attempt to resolve the complaint, and a copy of the terms of business letter sent to the client or other evidence of compliance with the Costs Information and Client Care Code.[17]

When the application is received it will be vetted to assess its conciliation prospects and an attempt at conciliation will be made. If this is successful the application will be withdrawn. If conciliation is not successful or is

---

[15] See *Wong v Vizards* [1997] 2 Costs L.R. 46, QBD.
[16] See below paras 8–001 *et seq.*; Solicitor's (Non-Contentious Business) Remuneration Order 1994, art.4(1).
[17] *ibid.*, art.15.

inappropriate the application will be checked and verified as correct and any points arising, clarified with the solicitors or clients. Copies of the verified application form will be sent to the parties named in the application for their comments.

Copies of the relevant comments from the parties are sent to the applicant's solicitors for observations; both the Society's and the applicant's file are checked to establish whether all the necessary information has been obtained. Once all the relevant information is to hand the remuneration certificate assessor will prepare a detailed report and assessment of fees. A provisional assessment is issued to the parties indicating the fee proposed to be certified and the reasons for the decision. The parties then have 28 days to lodge grounds of appeal against the provisional assessment if it is not agreed. If the assessment is agreed the remuneration certificate will be issued. If not representations on the grounds of appeal are taken from the non-appealing party before final determination of the matter is made by the Remuneration Certification Sub-Committee of the Adjudication and Appeals Committee of the Law Society. Following the Committee's determination, the final certificate is issued.

Requirement to pay a sum towards the costs

When a client requires a solicitor to obtain a remuneration certificate, the client is required to pay the disbursements already paid by the solicitor and value added tax, together with 50 per cent of the costs unless the client has already paid the amount required by deduction from moneys held or otherwise; or the solicitor or (if the solicitor refuses) the Law Society has agreed in writing to waive all or part of this requirement.[18] The Law Society is under no obligation to provide a remuneration certificate and a solicitor may take steps to obtain payment of the bill if the client, having been informed of his right to seek a waiver of the above requirement, has not within one month of receipt of the information required to be given by the Remuneration Order[19] either paid as specified above or applied to the Law Society, in writing, for a waiver of the requirement to pay; or made payment in accordance with the requirements, within one month of written notification that he has been refused a waiver by the Law Society.[20]

6–005

Once an application has been made by a solicitor for a remuneration certificate, the client may pay the bill in full without invalidating the application.[21] A solicitor and entitled person may agree, in writing, to waive the provisions concerning loss of the right to certification, particularly the

---

[18] *ibid.*, art.11(1).
[19] *ibid.*, art.8.
[20] *ibid.*, art.11(2).
[21] *ibid.*, art.12(1).

provisions with regard to the bill having been paid by the client and the time within which the application must be made.[22]

Loss of right to certification

6–006   A client or an entitled third party may not require a solicitor to obtain a remuneration certificate in certain circumstances. In respect of a client those circumstances are:

(a)   after a bill has been delivered and paid by the client other than by deduction;

(b)   where a bill has been delivered, after expiry of one month from the date on which the client was given, in writing, the information required by the Remuneration Order[23] or from the delivery of the bill if later;

(c)   after the solicitor and client have entered into a non-contentious business agreement[24];

(d)   after a court has ordered detailed assessment of the bill;

(e)   if the client has not, within one month of receipt of the written information, either paid a sum towards the costs[25] or applied to the Law Society, in writing, for (i) waiver of that requirement or (ii) made payment in accordance with the requirement, within one month of written notification that he has been refused a waiver of those requirements by the Law Society.[26]

In the case of an entitled third party the circumstances are:

(a)   after the prescribed time[27] has elapsed without any objection being received to the amount of the costs;

(b)   after expiry of one month from the date on which the entitled third party was given, in writing, the information specified by the Remuneration Order[28] or from notification of the costs if later;

(c)   after a court has ordered detailed assessment of the bill.[29]

---

[22] *i.e.* the provisions of *ibid.*, art.9(a) or (b) and art.10(a) or (b): *ibid.*, art.12(2).
[23] *i.e.* by art.8.
[24] In accordance with s.57 of the Solicitors Act 1974.
[25] As required by *ibid.*, art.11(1).
[26] *i.e.* in accordance with *ibid.*, art.11(2); *ibid.*, art.9.
[27] Within the meaning of *ibid.*, art.7(2)(b), see para.6–002.
[28] *i.e.* by *ibid.*, art.8.
[29] *ibid.*, art.10.

Refunds by a solicitor

If a solicitor has received payment of all or part of the costs, and a 6–007
remuneration certificate is issued for less than the sum already paid, the
solicitor must immediately repay to the entitled person any refund which
may be due (after taking into account any other sums which may properly
be payable to the solicitor whether for costs, disbursements which have been
paid, value added tax or otherwise), unless the solicitor has applied for an
order for detailed assessment within one month of receipt of the remuneration certificate.[30]

Where a solicitor applies for detailed assessment, his liability to pay any
refund is suspended for so long as the detailed assessment is still pending.[31]
The obligation to repay is without prejudice to any liability of the solicitor
to pay interest on the repayment by virtue of any enactment, rule of law or
professional rule.[32]

High value conveyancing

In assessing a solicitor's bill for high value conveyancing: 6–008

"The proper approach is to start by taking a broad look at 'all the
circumstances of the case' and in particular the general nature of the
business. This should be followed by a systematic consideration of the
factors specified in the paragraphs of Article 3 of the Order. A client
does not consult a solicitor in order to obtain an indirect and possibly
incomplete indemnity against the consequences of negligent advice and
action. He consults him to get skilled and careful advice and that is
what he pays for. In taking account of high values, while it is right in
principle to apply a value factor, this factor will vary according to the
particular circumstances and it should be remembered that the burden
of responsibility on the solicitor does not increase in direct proportion
to the value. The effect of increased value is regressive and the rate of
regression increases with the value. Furthermore, it is a matter of broad
bands of value rather than precision. Finer tuning can be achieved by
considering whether the value is at the bottom, the middle or the top of
the relevant band and there can be even more refined categorisation if
it were thought appropriate, but the essence of the approach is that it
involves classification and not remuneration. With these factors well in
mind it is necessary to assess a sum which is fair and reasonable. Each
case will always have to be considered on its merits and be subject

---

[30] Solicitors (Non-Contentious Business) Remuneration Order 1994, art.13(1).
[31] *ibid.*, art.13(2).
[32] *ibid.*, art.13(3).

ultimately to the discretion of the [costs judge.] In the end it is a value judgment based on discretion and experience."[33]

The Law Society from time to time publishes suggested bands of value and suggested percentage value elements. In addition to the factors set out in the remuneration order, there may be a further factor or factors:

"We then looked at the eight factors and asked ourselves what was the factor or factors, if any, which distinguished this transaction from the general run of transactions. The answer is clearly the 'adrenalin' factor. By this we mean that the solicitor had not only to work fast, but had absolutely no margin for error. Our figure may not be the right figure and indeed such a figure probably does not exist, but we hope that it will be a right figure, one that is reasonable in all the circumstances and which is fair both to the client and to the solicitor."[34]

Non-contentious probate

6–009   The Supreme Court Act 1981 defines non-contentious probate as follows:

" 'non-contentious or common form probate business' means the business of obtaining probate and administration where there is no contention as to the right thereto, including:

(a) the passing of probates and administration through the High Court in contentious cases where the contest has been terminated;

(b) all business of a non-contentious nature in matters of testacy and intestacy not being proceedings in any action; and

(c) the business of lodging caveats against the grant of probate or administration."[35]

6–010   After the introduction of the CPR the Non-Contentious Probate Rules were amended to provide that RSC Order 62, as it was in force immediately before April 26, 1999, governed detailed assessment of any non-contentious probate costs. A subsequent amendment[36] provides that RSC Order 62 does not apply to costs in non contentious probate matters and that CPR Parts 43, 44,[37] 47 and 48 apply with certain modifications. Those modifications are to make clear the involvement of district judges of the Principal Registry and to enable the court to refer matters to the Principal Registry or such

---

[33] per Donaldson J. *Property and Reversionary Investment Corp. Ltd v Secretary of State for the Environment* [1975] 2 All E.R. 46.
[34] per Donaldson J. *Treasury Solicitor v Regester* [1978] 2 All E.R. 920.
[35] Supreme Court Act 1981, s.128.
[36] The Non-Contentious Probate (Amendment) Rules 2003 (SI 2003/185).
[37] except rules 44.9–44.12.

District Probate Registry as the court may specify.[38] CPR r.44.3(2) (costs follow the event) does not apply.[39]

Where detailed assessment of a bill of costs is ordered, the matter must be referred, where the order was made by a district judge (of the Principal Registry) to a district judge, a costs judge or an authorised court officer[40]; where the order was made by a registrar, to that registrar or, where this is not possible, in accordance with the above provisions.[41]

Appeals

Appeals from an authorised court officer are dealt with in accordance with CPR rr.47.20–47.23. Any other appeal, in assessment proceedings relating to costs in non-contentious probate matters, from the decision of a district judge, a costs judge or a registrar lies to the High Court. CPR Part 52 applies to all such appeals. The Non-Contentious Probate Rules make it clear that neither the Rules of the Supreme Court nor the County Court Rules apply to any such appeal.[42] **6–011**

In relation to high value probate the court (Walton J.) has stated:

"No professional man or senior employee of a professional man stops thinking about the day's problems the minute he lifts his coat and umbrella from the stand and sets out on the journey home. Ideas, often very valuable ideas occur to him in the train or car home or in the bath, or even whilst watching television. Yet nothing is ever put down on the timesheet, or can be put down on a timesheet adequately to reflect this out of hours devotion of time. Thus it will be a rare bill which can be simply compounded of time and value, there must always be a third element usually under the second head (the skill, labour, specialised knowledge and responsibility involved on the part of the solicitor).

The most important head in a large estate would, of course, always be the sixth 'the nature and value of the property involved' . . . No estate is typically concerned with just one single asset; there is usually a mixed bag of assets for consideration. Often there will be what might be described as a leading asset . . . in the ordinary case this would be a dwelling house. Any other assets will be of comparatively little value. In such simple cases it will be right to apply the traditional method of charging, namely by cumulative bands each attracting a diminishing rate of charge without modification."

---

[38] Non-Contentious Probate Rules 1987 r.60(1)(3)(4)(5) and (7).
[39] *ibid.*, r.60(6).
[40] Within CPR r.43.2(1)(d)(iii) or (iv).
[41] *ibid.*, r.60(2).
[42] *ibid.*, r.60(8) to (11).

Walton J. suggested bands of value to which a regressive percentage could be applied.

> "I must emphasise that these bands cannot be made to apply and are certainly not intended to apply to any other classes of work carried on by solicitors. They have no relevance whatsoever to ordinary straight-forward conveyancing, for example, where there is only one asset to deal with at a time. They are intended to be combined solely to the work involved with a large number of assets".[43]

The Court of Appeal gave further guidance in 2003. The court considered[44] whether solicitors, engaged in relation to the administration of an estate, are entitled, in the absence of agreement, to charge not only for the time they spend on the administration but also a fee based on the value of the estate. The court also considered how the value element should be calculated. The court saw no reason to say that it was no longer appropriate for solicitors to make a separate charge based on value provided that it was remembered that the solicitor was entitled only to what was fair and reasonable remuneration taking all relevant factors into account. It is not in any way decisive that, in an assessment of costs in contentious litigation, it is now usual to incorporate the value element of any money or property into the hourly rate. There are significant differences in the circumstances in which charges are made for contentious and non contentious business and the approach to such charges can properly differ, even though the same factors fall to be taken into account. The court was persuaded that it was right to make some increase in the bands to allow for inflation since 1978 when *Maltby* was decided. The court was of the view that the appropriate regressive scale should be 1.5 per cent up to £750,000, 0.5 per cent between £750,000 and £3 million, 0.1666 per cent £3 million to £6 million and 0.08333 per cent above £6 million. The court went on to emphasise the importance of looking at the final figure in the round in order to ensure that the appropriate factors were taken into account in every individual case to arrive at no more than fair and reasonable remuneration overall.

The court went on to give guidance suggesting that it would be appropriate for solicitors to adhere to the following principles:

> "(1) Much the best practice is for a solicitor to obtain prior agreement as to the basis of his charges not only from the executors but also, where appropriate, from any residuary beneficiary who is an entitled third party under the 1994 Order. This is encouraged in the 1994 booklet and letter 8 of Appendix 2 to the 1999 booklet provides a good working draft of such agreement. We support that encouragement;

---

[43] *Maltby v Freeman* [1978] 2 All E.R. 913 at 916, 917, Watton J.
[44] *Jemma Trust Co Ltd v Liptrott* [2003] EWCA Civ 1476; [2004] 1 W.L.R. 646, CA.

(2) in any complicated administration, it will be prudent for solicitors to provide in their terms of retainer for interim bills to be rendered for payment on account; this is, of course, subject to the solicitor's obligation to review the matter as a whole at the end of the business so as to ensure that he has claimed no more than is fair and reasonable, taking into account the factors set out in the 1994 Order;

(3) there should be no hard and fast rule that charges cannot be made separately by reference to the value of the estate; value can, by contrast, be taken into account as part of the hourly rate; value can also be taken into account partly in one way and partly in the other. What is important is that

(a) it should be transparent on the face of the bill how value is being taken into account; and
(b) in no case, should it be taken into account more than once;

(4) in many cases, if a charge is separately made by reference to the value of the estate, it should usually be on a regressive scale. The bands and percentages will be for the costs judge in each case; the suggestions to the costs judge set out in paragraph 30 may be thought by him to be appropriate for this case but different bands and percentages will be appropriate for other cases and the figures set out in paragraph 30 cannot be any more than a guideline;

(5) it may be helpful at the end of the business for the solicitor or, if there is an assessment, for the costs judge, when a separate element of the bill is based on the value of the estate, to calculate the number of hours that would notionally be taken to achieve the amount of the separate charge. That may help to determine whether overall the remuneration claimed or assessed is fair and reasonable within the terms of the 1994 Order.

(6) it may also be helpful to consider the Law Society's Guidance in cases where there is no relevant and ascertainable value factor which is given in the 1994 booklet at paragraph 13.4. If the time spent on the matter is costed out at the solicitors' expense rate (which should be readily ascertainable from the Solicitors' Expense of Time calculations) the difference between that sum (the cost to the solicitor of the time spent on the matter) and the final figure claimed will represent the mark-up. The mark-up (which should take into account the factors specified in the 1994 Order including value) when added to the cost of the time spent must then be judged by reference to the requirement that this total figure must represent "such sum as may be fair and reasonable to both solicitor and entitled person".

CHAPTER 7

Contentious Costs

A. SUMMARY AND DETAILED ASSESSMENT

The bases of assessments

7–001 The court must first decide whether the order is to be for costs on the standard basis or the indemnity basis. More often than not it will be on the standard basis, in which case the costs must be not only proportionate and reasonable in amount, but also proportionately and reasonably incurred. The test of proportionality does not apply to costs on the indemnity basis.[1]

Proportionality is not defined by the rules, but, in applying the test of proportionality, the court will have regard to the overriding objective[2] and in particular to:

(i) the amount of money involved;

(ii) the importance of the case;

(iii) the complexity of the issues; and

(iv) the financial position of each party.[3]

It is not correct to apply a fixed percentage to the value of the claim in order to ascertain whether or not the costs are proportionate. All litigation involves solicitors in certain minimum costs which will necessarily be incurred in the conduct of the case. Where a trial takes place, the time taken by the court in dealing with a particular issue is not necessarily an accurate guide to the amount of time spent by the legal representatives in preparing

---

[1] CPR r.44.5(1). Costs PD, s.1.
[2] CPR r.1.1.
[3] CPR r.1.1(2)c.

for the trial of that issue. The parties may very well have narrowed the issues between themselves, thereby reducing the length of the trial, but as a result of a great deal of preparatory work. A judge's refusal to permit counsel to address him in relation to the successful claimant's statement of costs could have caused substantial injustice.[4]

Factors to be taken into account in deciding the amount of costs

In dealing with costs the court must give effect to any orders which have   7–002
already been made and must have regard to the conduct of all the parties before as well as during the proceedings. This means, in particular, compliance with pre-action protocols. The court must also have regard to the efforts made, if any, before and during the proceedings to attempt settlement.[5]

The remaining factors to which the court must have regard are:

(a) the amount or value of any money or property involved;

(b) the importance of the matter to all the parties;

(c) the particular complexity of the matter, or the difficulty or novelty of the questions raised;

(d) the skill, effort, specialised knowledge and responsibility involved;

(e) the time spent on the case; and

(f) the place where and the circumstances in which work or any part of it was done.[6]

A successful party to litigation may only be deprived of his costs if the misconduct for which he is being penalised relates to the proceedings themselves. Conduct in the transaction, even misconduct in the transaction, is not enough on its own. In a case in which the business dealings of the claimant involved doing business in cash in an attempt to avoid the Inland Revenue and failing to keep proper accounts the court held that the conduct was outside the proceedings and the claimants costs should not have been disallowed simply because of anterior dishonest conduct which may have given rise to the transaction but was not part of the proceedings.[7]

---

[4] *Edwards v Devon and Cornwall Constabulary* [2001] EWCA Civ 388; [2001] C.P.L.R. 323, CA.
[5] CPR r.44.5(2) and (3)(a).
[6] CPR r.44.5(3)(b)–(d).
[7] *Hall v Rover Financial Services GB Ltd* [2002] EWCA Civ 1514; *The Times*, November 8, 2002, CA.

In deciding how to apportion costs to reflect the conduct of the parties in proceedings the judge should structure the judgment on costs around the provisions of CPR r.44.3 which require the court to take into account "the conduct of the parties". The introduction of the CPR does not affect the pre-existing law, which entitles a judge to consider any relevant aspect of the conduct of the parties including their conduct in relation to the matters which gave rise to the litigation.[8] Although the practice of the Commercial Court[9] is not to disallow a successful party its costs simply because of anterior dishonest conduct which "while it was part of the transaction which gave rise to the proceedings, could not be characterised as misconduct in relation to the proceedings themselves", that was no more than a matter of practice. On their proper construction CPR r.44.3(4)(a) and (5)(a) do not contain any limitation such as would shut out reliance, in an appropriate case, on misconduct in and about the matters which triggered the litigation.[10]

The court must take care, in calculating the amount of costs, to ensure that it does not penalise a party more than once, first by taking conduct into account as regards entitlement,[11] by deciding that the receiving party should recover only, say 75 per cent of the costs and then for the same reason by further reducing the amount allowed on assessment of costs.[12]

"Summary assessment is a relatively rough and ready process ... proportionality is a more complex exercise than simply comparing the amount of the cost with the amount that was recovered and scaling down the costs accordingly"). The Court of Appeal held that the Judge had given too much weight to the size of the claimant's bill in relation to the amount recovered and insufficient weight to the fact that a substantial proportion of the claimant's costs were incurred before CPR came into effect.[13]

"Every case and every consequential costs order depends upon the individual facts of the case".[14] A claimant who pursues an exaggerated and inflated claim for damages must expect to bear the consequences when his costs come to be assessed. In the absence of special circumstances, a claimant, who knows or must be taken to know that his claim for damages is unsustainable in whole or in part, cannot be heard to assert that a defendant, who has disclosed evidence (*e.g.* video evidence) which establishes the unsustainability of the claim, ought to have disclosed that evidence at an earlier stage in the proceedings. The defendants should not be required to bear any part of the costs expended in pursuit of the unsustainable claim.[15]

---

[8] See *Donald Campbell & Co Ltd v Pollak* [1927] A.C. 732.
[9] See *Hall v Rover Financial Services (GB) Ltd* [2002] EWCA Civ 1514.
[10] *Groupama Insurance Co Ltd v Overseas Partners Re Ltd* [2003] EWCA Civ 1846.
[11] Under CPR r.44.3(5).
[12] Under CPR r.44.5(3).
[13] *per* Arden L.J., *Contractreal Ltd v Davies* [2001] EWCA Civ 928.
[14] *per* Judge L.J., *Ford v GKR Construction* [2000] 1 W.L.R. 1397.
[15] *Booth v Britannia Hotels Ltd* [2002] EWCA Civ 579.

Where separate actions between several claimants against several defendants were tried together, even though the actions had not been consolidated, some costs incurred by the defendants were common to all four actions, others were specific to each claim. The actions were dismissed by the trial judge who decided to carry out a summary assessment. The court held that the unsuccessful claimants were jointly and severally liable for the common costs.[16]

In an action where four different commercial interests brought actions against the same defendant, the court, ordering detailed assessment, directed that the costs judge was free to consider the four actions as if they had been consolidated at the date of the order for mutuality of evidence and that regard should be had to the reasonableness of the claimants maintaining separate representation and separate expert witnesses during the period after that order. The ordinary rule was that the successful claimant was entitled to the reasonable costs of bringing and succeeding in the action. If the court took the step of depriving one or more of the successful claimants of costs there had to be some basis on which such order could be made. Given the factors surrounding the proceedings there was difficulty and potential injustice in depriving any one of the claimants of a fixed portion of costs they had incurred in successful proceedings. The fairest way was to direct that the costs judge consider the four actions as if they had been consolidated at the date of the evidence order.[17]

Except where the costs are fixed, the amount of costs payable must be assessed by the court, either by summary assessment by the judge at the time of the trial or hearing, or by detailed assessment[18] by a costs officer.[19] An order for costs will result in a detailed assessment unless the order otherwise provides.[20]

B. ASSESSMENT OF COSTS

Summary assessment

Rule 44.7 gives the court power to make a summary assessment of costs or order a detailed assessment.[21]   7–003

Summary assessment will take place at the conclusion of a trial on the fast track and at the conclusion of any other hearing which has lasted less than

---

[16] *Bairstow v Queens Moat Houses Plc* [2000] EW QBD, April 14, Nelson J.

[17] *Simpla Ltd v Glaxo Group Ltd; Generics UK Ltd v Glaxo Group Ltd; Ivaxx Pharmaceuticals UK Ltd v Glaxo Group Ltd; Arrows Generics Ltd v Glaxo Group Ltd* [2004] EWHC (Ch) April 5, Pumfrey J.

[18] In accordance with CPR, Pt. 47.

[19] CPR r.44.7.

[20] Costs PD, s.12.

[21] CPR r.44.7. Costs PD, s.12.

one day.[22] If the summary assessment takes place at the end of an interlocutory hearing it will deal with the costs of that application. If it takes place at the end of a hearing which disposes of the case it will deal with the costs of the whole claim, some of which may already have been summarily assessed.

There is no rebuttable presumption against summary assessment in relation to costs where hearings last longer than one day. The court held that the exercise of the power to make a summary assessment should be considered in every case. In family cases in particular, the aggravation of detailed assessment of costs could run counter to the design of reducing contention and achieving satisfactory resolution of disputes.[23]

Whenever a court makes an order about costs which does not provide for fixed costs to be paid it should consider making a summary assessment unless it is not practicable to do so. The court will not make a summary assessment of the costs where the receiving party is either an assisted person, a funded client or is a child or patient.

If there is to be a summary assessment the successful party needs to know as early as possible what he can recover. When the court makes a summary assessment it will specify the amount payable as a single figure, which will include all sums in respect of profit costs, disbursements and VAT, which it has allowed and (in the case of a fast track trial) the amount of fast track trial costs awarded under Part 46. A party must comply with an order for the payment of costs within 14 days of the order stating the amount of those costs.[24-25]

It is the duty of the parties and their legal representatives to prepare in advance to assist the judge in making a summary assessment. Each party who intends to claim costs (and this will usually mean all the parties who are attending) must prepare a written statement of the costs which he intends to claim showing separately in the form of a schedule:

(a) the number of hours to be claimed;

(b) the hourly rate to be claimed;

(c) the amount and nature of any disbursement to be claimed, other than counsel's fee for appearing at the hearing;

(d) the amount of solicitor's costs to be claimed for attending or appearing at the hearing;

(e) the fees of counsel to be claimed in respect of the hearing; and

(f) any value added tax to be claimed on these amounts.

---

[22] Costs PD, s.13.
[23] *Q v Q (Family proceedings: costs order)*, *The Times*, July 16, 2002, Wilson J.
[24-25] CPR, r.44.8.

The statement of costs should follow as closely as possible Precedent H in Schedule of Costs Precedents. The form must be signed by the party or his legal representative. That statement must be filed at court and copies of it must be served on any party against whom an order for costs is to be sought. This should be done as early as possible and in any event not less than 24 hours before the hearing. The failure by a party, without reasonable excuse, to comply with those requirements will be taken into account by the court in deciding what order to make about costs.

In general, no summary assessment costs will be made if the court has ordered that the costs in question will be costs in the case. If no summary assessment is made, the judge at the trial will have to deal with all the costs which have not so far been assessed and that will include the costs of the hearing where the order for costs in the case was made.

If the parties have agreed the amount of costs it is merely a matter of the court making the order in the agreed terms.

The court must decide whether or not it is impracticable to make a summary assessment. There will certainly be some cases which are so large and complex, or which throw up such difficult technical problems, that it would not be sensible to proceed otherwise than by detailed assessment, but it should be possible, in the vast majority of cases falling within the Practice Direction criteria, for summary assessment to be carried out. Inevitably the subject will arise at the end of a long day when there is little time to consider the subject of costs. The option of delegating this function to the costs judge or district judge is simply not available. If summary assessment is to be carried out it must be carried out by the judge dealing with the matter. It may be that the parties, for good reason, do not have the complete information to hand. In these circumstances it is appropriate to adjourn the matter for a few days and dispose of it at a short hearing when both the judge, and the parties are in a position to proceed. If summary assessment is not carried out, detailed assessment must be ordered.

The court will consider whether or not to order a payment on account in accordance with r.44.3(8). The question of whether an interim payment on account of costs prior to formal assessment should be ordered, is within the discretion of the court. If the issue is considered broadly as a matter of principle there is no good reason why a successful party should have to wait to receive their costs following judgment. Any delay is simply attributable to the assessment process itself. In the interests of justice it may therefore be right and proper to make an order for an interim payment of a sum approximating to an amount which the successful party was almost certain to recover on a detailed assessment. In deciding whether or not such an order should be made the court should have regard to all the circumstances of the case including the likelihood of an appeal, the parties' respective financial positions and the overall interests of justice.[26]

---

[26] *Mars UK Ltd v Teknowledge Ltd (No.2)* [1999] 2 Costs L.R. 44, Jacob J.

In a case where there had been a settlement of a dispute and the court had no detailed knowledge of the nature and strength of the arguments advanced at trial the court should take a number of factors into account: all the circumstances of the particular case; the likelihood of an appeal and prospects of success; the financial position of each party; the effect of the interest provisions in CPR Part 44; and, the ability of the receiving party to repay part of an interim payment if there had been an over-estimate. In the particular circumstances of the case the Judge knowing that a costs judge would be in a position to do a fairer job of ordering interim payment under CPR r.47.15 declined to make an order for interim payment and ordered detailed assessment instead.[27]

The failure of a party to file and serve a copy of the statement of costs not less than 24 hours before the date fixed for the hearing does not warrant the wholesale disallowance of costs. Where the only factor against awarding costs is merely the failure to serve a statement of costs without aggravating factors, a party should not be deprived of all his costs, the court will take the matter into account but its reaction should be proportionate. The court should ask itself what if any prejudice there had been to the paying party and how that prejudice should be dealt with, *e.g.* by allowing a short adjournment or adjourning the summary assessment to another date or directing detailed assessment.[28]

In carrying out a summary assessment the Judge is required to analyse the statement of costs and not to apply his own tariffs as to what costs were appropriate, *e.g.* for a one day paper only appeal, that approach is wrong in principle.[29]

Only the judge who has heard a case is in the position to make a summary assessment of the costs of that case, otherwise the issue of costs should be sent to a Costs Judge for consideration.[30]

In the county court an order for costs following a summary assessment (other than one made at a final hearing) is exempt from registration.[31]

Disbursements

7–004 When making a summary assessment the court will have to deal with disbursements which may include expert's fees. The court has power to restrict expert evidence[32] and to limit the amount of the expert's fees and expenses.[33]

---

[27] *Dyson Appliances Ltd v Hoover Ltd (No.4)* [2003] EWHC 624 (Ch); [2004] 1 W.L.R., Laddie J.
[28] *MacDonald v Taree Holdings Ltd, The Times,* December 28, 2000, Neuberger J.
[29] *One-800 Flowers Inc v Phonenames Ltd, The Times,* July 9, 2001 CA.
[30] *Mahmood v Penrose* [2002] EWCA Civ, March 15.
[31] Register of County Court Judgments (Amendment) Regulations 1999 (SI 1999/1845).
[32] See CPR r.35.4.
[33] CPR r.35.4(4).

Appeals

Decisions on summary assessment are appealable in accordance with the ordinary rules as to appeals. Permission is required.[34]

C. DETAILED ASSESSMENT

Costs will, in general, not be assessed by detailed assessment until the conclusion of the proceedings, but the court may make an order for immediate assessment.[35] The existence of an appeal does not stay detailed assessment unless the court makes an order to that effect.[36]   7–005

In a passing off action, which failed at the interim injunction stage, the court ordered that the defendant should have their costs in any event and that the costs should not be assessed and paid forthwith but should await the outcome of the proceedings. Since there was a real prospect that the proceedings would go no further the defendant was given liberty to apply to convert the order into an order that the costs be assessed forthwith.[37]

Detailed assessment will be carried out by a costs judge, a district judge, or an authorised court officer. Authorised court officers have all the powers of the court when making a detailed assessment except certain penal powers. Such officers do not have the power to carry out a detailed assessment of costs payable to a solicitor by a client.[38]

There will be many cases which come to an end without the court having had the opportunity to assess costs summarily, for example cases which are discontinued, or where a Part 36 offer or payment is accepted, and there will inevitably be cases where the court declines to carry out a summary assessment. In all those cases detailed assessment will have to take place. The procedure for detailed assessment of costs is set out at CPR Part 47.

In proceedings in which a discreet issue as to jurisdiction arose, the Court of Appeal decided to order assessment forthwith of those costs, but that the question of payment was to be deferred to await the outcome of an

---

[34] CPR Pt 52.
[35] CPR r.47.1. Costs PD, s.28.
[36] CPR r.47.2. Costs PD, s.29.
[37] *Local Sunday Newspapers Ltd v Johnston Press Ltd* unreported, June 19, 2001, Neuberger J.
[38] CPR, r.47.3, see Costs PD, s.30. The penal powers are the power to make a wasted costs order under r.48.7 and the power to make an order under r.44.14 (powers in relation to misconduct), r.47.8 (sanction for delay in commencing detailed assessment proceedings) or the power under r.47.3(2) to make an order on an objection to detailed assessment by an authorised court officer.

application for security for costs which was to be made against the claimants. The question of payment overall was referred to the Commercial Judge to decide whether it should be made on terms including terms as to security.[39] It is the practice in the Court of Appeal that, where the appeal is a discrete matter, the assessment of costs is ordered there and then and does not wait for the conclusion of the proceedings as a whole, that practice was said to precede the CPR.[40] The fact that claimants are legally aided is material in some ways. Summary assessment of costs is not permissible. In a case where the Court of Appeal found that the eventual outcome of the claimant's action was unpredictable, the court held that if it were to order immediate detailed assessment and payment of the claimant's costs and those costs were assessed and paid before trial, it might work a substantial injustice on the defendants. The court declined to order assessment and to defer payment since this was not an economic use of resources. The court accordingly followed the normal practice under CPR r.47.1 and ordered detailed assessment to take place at the conclusion of the substantive proceedings.[41]

Venue

7–006   Normally detailed assessment will take place at the court where the action proceeded. The court including a county court may direct where the assessment is to take place and may direct, in an appropriate case, that the assessment proceedings should be in the Supreme Court Costs Office.[42] At the request of the Admiralty Registrar all costs in Admiralty matters are dealt with in the Supreme Court Costs Office.[43]

Procedure

7–007   Once an order for the detailed assessment of costs has been made the receiving party has three months in which to commence the assessment proceedings.[44–45] This is done by serving on the paying party notice of commencement (Form N252), and a copy of the bill of costs[46] together with certain supporting documents. Copies are also served on all other relevant

---

[39] *Saab v Saudia American Bank*, unreported, July 2, 1999, CA.
[40] *Morris v Bank of America National Trust*, unreported, December 21, 1999, CA.
[41] *Hicks v Russell Jones & Walker*, unreported, October 27, 2000, CA.
[42] CPR r.47.4. Costs PD, s.31.
[43] Practice Note, Queen's Bench Division (Admiralty Court) [1996] 1 All E.R. 188, Clarke J.
[44–45] CPR r.47.7. Costs PD, s.33.
[46] As to the form of Bill, see Costs PD, s.4 and Appendix K and as to VAT, see s.5.

persons, *i.e.* those who may be affected by the outcome of the detailed assessment.[47]

If the receiving party fails to commence detailed assessment within the period specified by the rules or by any direction of the court, the paying party may apply for an order requiring the receiving party to commence detailed assessment proceedings within such time as the court may specify.[48] The court may direct that unless the receiving party commences detailed assessment proceedings within the time specified the costs will be disallowed.[49]

Where the receiving party commences detailed assessment proceedings out of time, but before the paying party has applied to the court, the only sanction which the court may then impose is to disallow interest[50] which would have been payable but for the period of delay. The Lord Chancellor exercised his powers to amend the Judgments Act to enable interest to be disallowed for a particular period. This power is in addition to the court's powers to make an order in relation to misconduct.[51]

In a case where the claimant did not apply for detailed assessment within the three month time limit and the claimant did not apply until two years later for an unless order the disallowance of £60,000 over and above that already paid was held to be too drastic a penalty for the delay on the part of the claimant where the cause of the delay was neglect rather than intention. The court also found that the defendants had failed to co-operate when they could easily have done so. The claimant was ordered to recover 80 per cent of the assessed costs which sufficiently met the seriousness of the delay and the failure to comply with the court order as well as the delay before seeking an extension of time.[52]

Once the paying party has received the bill and notice, that party may serve points of dispute on the receiving party and every other party to the assessment proceedings. The points of dispute must be served within 21 days after the service of the notice of commencement.[53]

Many claims are settled on terms which are confidential and the terms are contained in a schedule to the order concluding the proceedings (Tomlin Order) but, unless the order itself contains a provision for costs to be paid and assessed if not agreed, the right to detailed assessment does not arise. The fact that the terms of the schedule deal with the position with regard to costs is insufficient.

---

[47] CPR r.47.6. PD, s.42.
[48] CPR r.47.8(1).
[49] CPR r.47.8(2).
[50] Under s.17 of the Judgments Act 1838 or s.34 of the County Courts Act 1984.
[51] Under r.44.14, CPR r.47.8(3).
[52] *Q v J* [2003] EWHC Fam, March 3.
[53] CPR r.47.9 and Costs PD, s.35.

Rules applicable to funding arrangements

7–008　The court will not assess any additional liability until conclusion of the proceedings or the part of the proceedings to which the funding arrangement relates. At the conclusion of the proceedings, or the relevant part of the proceedings, the court may make a summary assessment of all the costs including any additional liability; make an order for detailed assessment of the additional liability but make a summary assessment of the other costs; or make an order for detailed assessment of all the costs.[54]

A party may not recover as an additional liability:

(a) any proportion of the percentage increase relating to the cost to the legal representative of a postponement of the payment of his fees and expenses;

(b) any provision made by a membership organisation which exceeds the likely costs of that party of the premium of an insurance policy against the risk of incurring a liability to pay the costs of other parties to the proceedings;

(c) any additional liability for any period in the proceedings during which he failed to provide information about a funding arrangement in accordance with a rule, practice direction or court order;

(d) any percentage increase where a party has failed to comply with a requirement in the Costs Practice Direction; or a court order to disclose in any assessment proceedings the reasons for setting the percentage increase at the level stated in the CFA.[55]

A party who seeks to recover an additional liability must provide information about the funding arrangement to the court and to the other parties. The information must be given in a notice of funding in Form N251. Unless the court orders otherwise a party who is required to supply information about a funding arrangement must state whether he has entered into a CFA which provides for a success fee; taken out an ATE insurance policy; made an arrangement with a prescribed organisation or more than one of these. Section 19 of the Costs Practice Direction sets out the information which must be given.[56]

If the funding arrangement changes and the information previously provided is no longer accurate the party providing the information must file

---

[54] CPR r.44.3A Costs PD, s.9.
[55] CPR r.44.3B(1) This rule does not apply in an assessment under CPR r.48.9 of a solicitor's bill to his client. Costs PD, s.10.
[56] CPR r.44.15(1) Costs PD, s.19.

a notice of the change and serve it on all other parties within seven days.[57]

If on assessment the court disallows any amount of a legal representatives' success fee the legal representative may apply for an order that the disallowed amount should continue to be payable by the client. In those circumstances the court may adjourn the hearing to allow the client to be notified of the order sought and to be separately represented. Section 20 of the Costs Practice Direction sets out the procedure to be followed.[58] If in detailed assessment proceedings the points of dispute disclose that a percentage increase claimed by counsel is challenged the solicitors must deliver a copy of the relevant points of dispute to counsel and the relevant part of the bill. Counsel then has the opportunity to inform the solicitor in writing whether or not the reduction is accepted or what reply he wishes to make.[59]

Default costs certificate

If the paying party does not serve points of dispute, the receiving party may obtain a default costs certificate.[60] The default costs certificate includes an order to pay the costs to which it relates.[61] Fixed costs for the commencement of the detailed assessment proceedings are recoverable in accordance with the Practice Direction.[62]

7–009.1

If a party serves points of dispute out of time, but before the issue of a default costs certificate, the court may not issue such a certificate.[63] In such a case however, the party who has served points of dispute late, may not be heard further in the detailed assessment proceedings unless the court gives permission.[64] The court must set aside a default costs certificate if the receiving party was not entitled to it, and may set aside or vary a certificate if it appears that there is some good reason why the detailed assessment proceedings should continue.[65]

Procedure where costs are agreed

The parties may agree some or all of the costs, and, if there is a partial agreement, the court may issue an interim costs certificate in relation to the agreed costs. If all the costs are agreed the court may issue a final certificate.[66]

7–009.2

---

[57] CPR r.44.15(2) Costs PD, para.19.3.
[58] CPR r.44.17 Costs PD, s.20.
[59] Costs PD, s.20.
[60] CPR r.47.11. Costs PD, s.37, and see Appendix K.
[61] CPR r.47.11(2). Costs PD, s.38.
[62] CPR r.47.11(3) and Costs PD, s.37 the amount recoverable is £80.
[63] CPR r.47.9(5).
[64] CPR r.47.9(3).
[65] CPR r.47.12. Costs PD, s.38.
[66] CPR r.47.10, 47.15 and 47.16. Costs PD, s.36 and see Appendix K.

Procedure where points of dispute are served

7–009.3   If the receiving party serves points of dispute it is open to the receiving party to serve a reply but this is not compulsory. The reply must be served within 21 days after service of the points of dispute.[67]

Where points of dispute are served, the receiving party may request a hearing within three months after the end of the period for commencing assessment proceedings under CPR r.47.7 or by any direction of the court.[68] If the receiving party does not file a request for a hearing date, the paying party may apply for an order requiring the receiving party to do so within a specified time. The court may direct that, unless the receiving party requests a hearing within the time specified, the costs will be disallowed.[69] There is a similar provision with regard to the disallowance of interest where the receiving party asks for a hearing date out of time but before the paying party makes an application in respect of that default.[70] At the hearing only the receiving party, the paying party and any other party who has served points of dispute may be heard, and only items specified in the points of dispute may be raised at the hearing, unless the court permits otherwise.[71] Article 6.1 of the European Convention on Human Rights confers a right to "a hearing within a reasonable time by a tribunal". This is wide enough to include the situation where the court fails to resolve a costs dispute within a reasonable time after judgment.[72]

Court fees

7–010   The first time the court will come into contact with the detailed assessment proceedings will be, either when the receiving party applies for a default costs certificate, or when that party applies for an assessment hearing, it is also at this point that any fee would be payable to the court in full in advance.

Costs payable out of a fund

7–011   CPR r.47.17 deals with detailed assessment procedure where costs are payable out of the CLS Fund. It is possible for LSC costs to be assessed separately from costs between the parties, although normally the two sets of costs will be looked at together.[73] CPR r.47.17A deals with costs payable out of a fund other than the CLS Fund. It is only in respect of costs payable

---

[67] CPR r.47.13. Costs PD, s.39.
[68] CPR r.47.14. Costs PD, s.40.
[69] CPR r.47.14(3) and (4).
[70] CPR r.47.14(5).
[71] CPR r.47.14(5) and (6).
[72] *Robins v United Kingdom, The Times,* October 24, 1997, ECHR. Delay of more than four years was held to be unreasonable and a breach of Article 6.1.
[73] CPR r.47.17. Costs PD, s.43.

out of the CLS Fund that provisional detailed assessment may take place.[74] There is a fee on the certificate of LSC costs. In an LSC case an interim order for LSC detailed assessment is not sufficient authority to assess the bill; there must be either a final order or a discharge of the certificate.[75] A cause or matter is concluded when the court in question has finally determined the matters in issue, whether or not there is an appeal from that determination.[76]

Privileged documents and disclosure

The costs officer may direct the disclosure of a privileged document to the court, if it is necessary to enable the paying party to raise a bona fide challenge to an item.[77] The disclosure is limited to the specific purpose of assessment.[78] An order for disclosure may include a requirement that the document be edited so as to remove irrelevant material. A draft edited bundle may be lodged for the judge or Costs officer to approve in order that justice may be done.[79] It is permissible to blank out parts of a document disclosed on discovery on the grounds of irrelevance to the matters in issue.[80]

7–012

When a party lodges a privileged document for detailed assessment in order to claim the costs of it, that party must elect either to rely on the document or withdraw it.[81] If the other party wishes to see the document to dispute the claim for costs the receiving party must be given the right to elect to withdraw it and not claim costs or he must disclose it.[82] Discovery of privileged documents should only be ordered in clear cases, and, where fraud is alleged, there must be strong evidence of fraud. A similar principle applies in the case of improper conduct.[83]

The views of Hobhouse J. in *Pamplin v Express Newspapers Ltd* are still valid. The court was not persuaded that the client care letter and payment calculations were privileged but if anything in them had been privileged the documents could have been redacted. The basic principle is that if a party wishes to prove his version of a disputed issue of fact by reference to certain

---

[74] CPR r.47.17(5).
[75] *R. v Shoreditch CC, Ex p. Daniel Davies and Co.*, unreported, September 22, 1994, Dyson J.
[76] *per* Saville J. in *Rafsanjan Pistachio Producers Corp. v Bank Leumi (U.K.) Ltd*, unreported, November 4, 1994.
[77] *Goldman v Hesper* [1988] 1 W.L.R. 1238, CA; *Pamplin v Express Newspapers Ltd* [1985] 2 All E.R. 185 and see *Bourns Inc v Raychem Corp. (No.3)*, *The Times*, May 12, 1999, CA.
[78] *British Coal Corp. v Rye (Dennis) (No.2)* [1988] 1 W.L.R. 1113.
[79] *Skuse v Granada Television* [1994] 1 W.L.R. 1156, Drake J.
[80] *G.E. Capital Corporate Finance Group v Bankers Trust Co.*, *The Times*, August 3, 1994, CA.
[81] *Pamplin v Express Newspapers Ltd* [1985] 1 W.L.R. 689, Hobhouse J; *Goldman v Hesper*, above no.77.
[82] See *Derby v Weldon (No.7)* [1990] 1 W.L.R. 652.
[83] *Skuse v Granada Television Ltd*, above n.73.

documents those documents must be disclosed to the opposing party.[84] The court did not suggest that the costs judge may potentially put the receiving party to its election in respect of every document relied on. It was expected that in the majority of cases the paying party would be content to agree that the Costs Judge alone should see the privileged documents. Only where it is necessary and proportionate should the receiving party be put to his election. The redaction and production of privileged documents or the adducing of further evidence would lead to additional delay and increase costs. Detailed assessment is litigation without discovery or disclosure. The rule that the other party is entitled to see the material even if the party which possesses it does not deploy it can have no application when the material is privileged. The principle is an absolute one, privilege will not be overridden by the court and must be waived by the party entitled to assert it. Paragraph 40.14 of the Costs Practice Direction is consistent with the requirements of ECHR. The protection which is afforded to the receiving party by the rule that the waiver is for the purpose of the assessment only, and that the document remains otherwise privileged, should play a much more significant role than it appears to in the decision whether or not to waive privilege in a proper case.[85] The court has indicated that it should be standard practice where a client care letter is affirmatively relied on that it should be produced to the paying party.[86]

In detailed assessment proceedings the paying party sought an order requiring the receiving party's solicitors to give full particulars of their dealings with their client both in relation to their original retention as his solicitors and in relation to a subsequent CFA. Information was sought by way of disclosure of documents and otherwise to support the contention that there had in truth been an agreement whereby the client was liable for the solicitors' costs prior to a particular date and as to the validity of the CFA. In the event full details of the CFA and files and attendance notes were disclosed. The paying party argued that a retainer is or becomes champertous and therefore unlawful and unenforceable if a solicitor is or becomes aware at any time that his client could not possibly have afforded to pay his costs whatever might have been the formal agreement between them and the solicitor continues to act. The court held that costs judges undoubtedly had jurisdiction to make the orders requested and if it had been necessary to make such an order to ensure fair determination of the issue, the application should have been acceded to. The mere fact that the issue has been raised is not of itself sufficient if there is no prospect that cross examination could either undermine or further elucidate the receiving party's case. To refuse to accede to the application will not be unfair and will not breach the requirement of the overriding objective that the parties are on an equal

---

[84] *Dickinson v Rushmer* [2001] EWHC (Ch). December 21, Rimer J.

[85] *South Coast Shipping Co Ltd v Havant BC* [2001] EWHC (Ch), December 21, [2002] 3 All E.R. 779, Pumphrey J.

[86] *Adams v MacInnes* [2001] EWHC QBD, November 8, *per* Gray J.

footing but would save expense and deal with the issues proportionately and expeditiously.[87] In detailed assessment proceedings a possible breach of the indemnity principle was raised. The costs judge in reading the papers which had been filed discovered letters which raised a concern as to whether the principle had been breached. There was ample material before the judge to give rise to such concern, the letters themselves were *prima facie* privileged and the privilege had not been waived either by the claimants including them in the filed bundle or by the claimant's counsel quoting from them. The correct procedure was as set out in *Dickinson v Rushmer*.[88]

In large multi handed commercial litigation the successful 53rd defendant sought costs under a CFA with a 100 per cent success fee. He declined to serve on the paying party a statement of the reasons for the success fee[89] and applied for an order restricting disclosure to solicitors, counsel and costs draftsman for the paying party. The defendant feared that that the information might be used for the purpose of criminal proceedings against him in Kuwait. On appeal from the costs judge's refusal to restrict disclosure, the court held that it had inherent jurisdiction to restrict disclosure in an appropriate case for which it was necessary to show a tangible risk of misuse of the information. On the facts the appeal was dismissed.[90]

Costs of detailed assessment proceedings

Once the detailed assessment hearing is over, the general rule is that the receiving party is entitled to his costs of those proceedings, except where the provisions of any Act or any of the Civil Procedure Rules provide otherwise, or the court makes some other order.[91] In deciding whether to make some other order the court must have regard to all the circumstances, including:

    7–013

(a) the conduct of all the parties;

(b) the amount, if any, by which the bill of costs has been reduced; and

(c) whether it was reasonable for a party to claim the costs of a particular item or to dispute that item.[92]

CPR r.47.18 raises a rebuttable presumption that the receiving party should have his costs of the detailed assessment, subject to the right of the costs judge to make some other order. Offers to settle have been held to be

---

[87] *Times Newspapers Ltd v Burstein* [2002] EWCA Civ 1739.
[88] *Giambrone v JMC Holidays Ltd* [2002] EWHC 495 (QB), Nelson J.
[89] In accordance with Costs PD, para.32.7.
[90] *Gruppo Torras v Al-Sabah* [2003] EWHC 262 (QB); [2003] 2 Costs L.R. 294, Treacy J.
[91] CPR r.47.18(1), Costs PD, s.45.
[92] CPR r.47.18(2).

irrelevant where an LSC funded party is involved. The fact that the claimant had delayed considerably before applying for detailed assessment did not engage CPR r.47.8 since the paying party had not made any application under that provision.[93]

Interim Certificates

7–014 The court may, at any time after the receiving party has filed a request for a detailed assessment hearing, issue an interim costs certificate for such sum as it considers appropriate; or amend or cancel an interim certificate. If the court issues an interim certificate it may order the costs certified in it to be paid into court.[94] The interim certificate will include an order to pay the costs to which it relates unless the court otherwise orders.[95]

Final certificates

7–015 Where a final costs certificate is issued, it will include an order to pay in the same way.[96]

Time for payment

7–016 Where the court makes an order to pay costs, or an order to pay costs is deemed to have been made by virtue of any of the CPR, the party must comply with the order within 14 days of the date of judgment or order if it states the amount of those costs, or, if the amount is decided later, in accordance with Part 47 the date of the certificate which states the amount.[97] The court may extend the time for payment under its case management powers.[98]

The court has a discretion under Rule 44.3 as to when costs are to be paid. Unless otherwise ordered however, the costs become payable within 14 days of the date of the order by virtue of Rule 44.8. If a party seeks an extension of time in which to pay costs, it is for that party to make such an application supported by evidence. In the absence of any alternative order costs are payable within 14 days.[99]

---

[93] *Bufton v Hill* [2002] EWHC 477 (QB); [2002] 3 Costs L.R. 381, Silber J.
[94] CPR r.47.15(1) and (3). Costs PD, s.42.
[95] CPR r.47.15(2).
[96] CPR r.47.16(5). Costs PD, s.42.
[97] CPR r.44.8.
[98] CPR r.3.1.
[99] *Pepin v Watts and The Chief Constable of Surrey Police* [2000] EWCA Civ, October 4.

PART IV

Practice and Procedure

CHAPTER 8

Application For and Attendance Upon Detailed Assessment

A. SOLICITOR AND CLIENT

Before either a solicitor can commence proceedings for recovery of costs, or 8–001
a party can apply for detailed assessment, a bill must have been delivered by
the solicitor to the client in accordance with the requirements of the
Solicitors Act 1974.

Statutory requirements of a delivered bill

The bill must be signed by the solicitor, or if the costs are due to a firm, one 8–002
of the partners of that firm, either in his own name, or in the name of the
firm, or the bill may be enclosed in, or accompanied by a letter, which is
signed and refers to the bill.[1] The bill must be delivered to the party to be
charged with the bill, either personally, or by being sent to him by post to,
or left for him at, his place of business, dwelling house, or last known place
of abode.[2] Where the solicitor can prove that the bill has been delivered in
compliance with those requirements it is not necessary, in the first instance,
for the solicitor to prove the contents of the bill and there is a rebuttable
presumption that the bill is *bona fide* and complies with the Act.[3]

The bill must be complete in itself and contain sufficient information to
enable the client to obtain advice as to its assessment and for the costs judge
to assess it.[4] If an order for costs between the parties has been made and that

---

[1] Solicitors Act 1974, s.69(2)(a).
[2] *ibid.*, s.69(2)(b).
[3] *ibid.*, s.69(2).
[4] *Haigh v Ousey* [1857] E. & B. 578; *Slingsby v Att-Gen* [1918] P. 236; *Waller v Lacey* [1840]
1 M. & Gr. 54; *Eversheds v Osman*, unreported, April 7, 1998, CA.

the bill has been assessed and paid by the opponent, or if disbursements have been paid by a client, they must still be included in the solicitor's bill to the client.[5] The question of the amount of information properly to be contained in a solicitors bill has been extensively examined by the Court of Appeal.[6] Ward L.J. stated:

> "63. I accept the principle . . . that the defendant who undertakes to prove that the bill is not a bona fide compliance with the Act cannot found an objection upon want of information in the bill if it appears that he is already in possession of that information . . .
> 64. Thus I will accept the proper principle to be that there must be something in the written bill to indicate the ambit of the work but that inadequacies of description of that work may be redressed by accompanying documents . . . or by other information already in possession of the client. That it seems to me would serve the purpose of the Act to give the client the knowledge he reasonably needs in order to decide whether to insist on taxation. If the solicitor satisfies that then the bill is one bona fide complying with the Act.
>
> . . .
>
> 70. This review of the legislation and the case law leads me to conclude that the burden on the client under Section 69(2) to establish that a bill for a gross sum in contentious business will not be a bill "bona fide complying with the Act" is satisfied if the client shows
>
> (i) that there is no sufficient narrative in the bill to identify what it is he is being charged for; and
> (ii) that he does not have sufficient knowledge from other documents in his possession or from what he has been told reasonably to take advice whether or not to apply for that bill to be taxed.
>
> The sufficiency of the narrative and the sufficiency of his knowledge will vary from case to case and the more he knows the less the bill may need to spell it out for him. The interests of justice require that the balance to be struck between protection of the client's right to seek taxation and the solicitor's right to recover not being defeated by opportunistic resorts to technicality."

Ward L.J. then went on to suggest that a copy of the solicitor's computer print-out containing a description of the fee earner, the rate of charging and some description of the work done adjusted to remove items recorded for administrative purposes but not chargeable to the client could easily be

---

[5] *Cobbet v Wood* [1908] 2 K.B. 420, CA; *Re Osborne & Osborne* [1913] 3 K.B. 862, CA; *Aaron v Okoye* [1998] 2 Costs L.R., CA.
[6] *Ralph Hulme Garry v Gwillim* [2002] EWCA Civ 1500; [2003] 1 W.L.R. 510, CA; [2003] 1 All E.R. 103 8, CA.

rendered to a client and thus avoid the problems which had arisen in the instant case:

> "In these days where there seems to be a need for transparency in all things, is a print-out not the least a client is entitled to expect?"

Signature

The signature on the bill must be that of the solicitor or a partner on behalf of the firm. The signature of a clerk is not enough.[7] The signature may be reproduced by a stamped impression, though this is not desirable.[8] The client may by his actions preclude himself from objecting that the bill was unsigned.[9] There is no requirement that the name of the firm be set out in full so long as there is no doubt that the bill is an authoritative document.[10] Where an unsigned bill has been delivered it may still be assessed,[11] as may a bill which has been paid.[12] A bill once delivered cannot be withdrawn without leave.[13]

Where the court is confronted with a defective bill it is entitled to look into all the circumstances and in appropriate cases to allow the solicitor to withdraw the bill and to deliver a fresh one; an action brought on the bill does not necessarily have to be dismissed without consideration of the merits.[14]

8–003

Disbursements

The solicitor's bill may include disbursements payable by the solicitor in discharge of a liability properly incurred by and on behalf of the party to be charged with the bill (including counsel's fee). This is so notwithstanding that those disbursements have not been paid before the delivery of the bill. Outstanding disbursements must be described in the bill as "unpaid" and if the bill is assessed the costs officer may not allow the disbursement unless it is paid before the detailed assessment is completed.[15] Section 67 of the 1974 Act imposes a dual requirement, namely that the disbursement be described as "unpaid" and that it be paid before the detailed assessment is completed. If the disbursement is not described as "unpaid", the situation cannot be remedied by paying it after delivery of the bill. If a bill has been delivered it cannot be withdrawn and a new bill substituted without the consent of the

8–004

---

[7] *Angell v Tratt* [1883] 1 Cab. & E1. 118.
[8] *Goodman v Eban Ltd* [1954] 1 Q.B. 550.
[9] *Re Pender* [1846] 2 P.H. 69; *Re Gedge* (1851) 14 Beav. 56; *Young v Walker* (1847) 16 M.N.W. 445.
[10] *Bartletts de Reya v Byrne* (1983) 127 S.J. 69, CA.
[11] *Ex p. D'Aragon* (1887) 3 T.L.R. 815.
[12] *Re Sutton* (1883) 11 Q.B.D. 377.
[13] *Re Jones* (1886) 54 L.T. 648.
[14] *Zuliani v Veira* [1994] 1 W.L.R. 1149, PC.
[15] Solicitors Act 1974, s.67.

parties or an order of the court.[16] There reposes in the court a wide discretion to deal with the circumstances which arise in any particular case.[17]

When the detailed assessment of a solicitor's bill is concluded, the solicitor's rights against the client are determined at the sum certified by the court. There is no further liability in respect of matters which have been included in the bill of costs. Therefore where unpaid disbursements have been struck out the solicitor cannot afterwards recover them from the client.[18]

In *Tearle & Co. v Sherring*,[19] Wright J. gave leave to a solicitor to amend his bill stating:

> "In *Re Grant Bulcraig & Co.*[20] Farwell J. . . . . held that a solicitor could add or strike out items or increase amounts by special application to the court. If that can be done I can see no reason why the omitted words in relating to unpaid disbursements cannot also be added to the bill. Farwell J. continued:
>
>> 'The solicitor is treated strictly because he is dealing with his client in a matter in which the solicitor is an expert and the client is not, but the reasoning has no application to details which are not the subject of [detailed assessment] and the accuracy of which the client is as well able to test as the solicitor; such matters become mere matters of evidence and the [costs judge] may allow the solicitor to correct blunders therein if, in his discretion, he thinks proper to do so. Thus in *Williams v Barber*[21] it was held that a mistake in the dates did not vitiate a bill . . . By parity of reasoning, I think that the [costs judge] might assess an item though the date was wrongly given and might allow the error to be corrected if he finds that he can do so without injustice to the client.'
>
> Against that background I conclude that I do have the power to permit the [claimants] to amend their original bill of costs to include the necessary words against these items of disbursement . . . "

Disbursements, which must be included in the bill, have been defined as:

---

[16] *Polak v Marchioness of Winchester* [1956] 1 W.L.R. 819, CA; *Chappel v Mehta* [1981] 1 All E.R. 349, CA.
[17] *per* Newman J., *Rezvi v Brown Cooper* (a firm) [1997] 1 Costs L.R. 109.
[18] *Sad v Griffin* [1908] 2 K.B. 510; *Elsworth v Fox*, unreported, November 27, 1909, Hamilton J.
[19] Unreported, October 29, 1991. Review of detailed assessment.
[20] [1906] 1 Ch. 124.
[21] (1813) 4 Taunt. 806.

"Such payments as the solicitor in the due discharge of his duties is bound to make (whether his client furnishes him with the money for the purpose or with money on account or not) as for example court fees, counsel's fees, expenses of witnesses, agents, stationers or printers are properly introduced into the bill; but payments which the solicitor is not bound either by law or custom to make, as for example purchase monies or interest paid into court, damages or costs paid to opponent parties, bills due to the solicitors of trustees, mortgagees or other parties, estate duties or other payments of a like description are properly charged on the cash account . . . The question is not affected by the state of the cash account between the solicitor and the client and that, *e.g.* counsel's fees would not the less properly be introduced into the bill of costs as a professional disbursement because the client may have given money expressly for paying them, and purchase money or damages would not be properly so introduced though the solicitor may have advanced the money out of his own funds."[22]

Petty disbursements

The practice of adding any disbursements such as postage, telephone calls and faxes to the final bill is regarded by the Law Society as unacceptable. On detailed assessment such disbursements are usually regarded as overheads and are not allowed.   8–005

Power of court to order a solicitor to deliver a bill

The High Court has inherent jurisdiction to make orders for the delivery by a solicitor of a bill of costs and for the delivery up or otherwise in relation to any documents in his possession, custody or power. The Solicitors Act 1974 specifically extends that power to cases in which no business has been done by the solicitor in the High Court.[23] A county court has the same jurisdiction as the High Court to make orders of this nature, in cases where the bill of costs or the documents relate wholly or partly to contentious business done by the solicitor in that county court.[24] It is a matter for the discretion of the court whether it will order the delivery of a bill in any particular circumstances.[25] Delivery of a bill can be waived by conduct or agreement.[26] If a third party has paid the costs the client is not entitled to an   8–006

---

[22] *Re Remnant* (1849) 11 Beav. 603 at 611 confirmed *Re Buckwell & Berkeley* [1902] 2 Ch. 596, CA; *Brown v Barber* [1913] 2 K.B. 553.
[23] Solicitors Act 1974, s.68(1).
[24] *ibid.,* s.68(2).
[25] *Re A Solicitor* [1953] Ch. 480.
[26] *Re Van Laun* [1907] 1 K.B. 155 affirmed [1907] 2 K.B. 23, CA; *Re Chapman* (1903) 20 T.L.R. 3, CA.

order for delivery.[27] Where a solicitor does not make any charge he will not be ordered to deliver a bill.[28] The solicitor may be ordered to deliver a cash account.[29]

Form of bill of costs for contentious business

8–007 In a case involving contentious business, where there is no contentious business agreement, the solicitor may deliver either a bill containing detailed items or a gross sum bill.[30] Where a gross sum bill is delivered the party chargeable may, at any time before he is served with a writ or other originating process for the recovery of the costs included in the bill, and before the expiration of three months from the date on which the bill was delivered to him, require the solicitor to deliver, in lieu of that bill, a bill containing detailed items, and on such a requirement being made the gross sum bill is of no effect.[31] The detailed bill which is subsequently delivered will frequently be for a larger amount than the gross sum bill, but since the gross sum bill has ceased to have effect it is the detailed bill which will be assessed and paid. Where a client seeks a detailed bill more than three months after delivery, it is a matter for the discretion of the court.[32]

Enforcement

8–008 Where an action is commenced on a gross sum bill the court must, if requested by the party chargeable with the bill before the expiration of one month from the service of the writ or originating process, order detailed assessment of the bill.[33] By this means a party chargeable can obtain detailed assessment of a solicitor's costs long after the time-limits laid down in sections 70 and 71 of the 1974 Act. This provision is mandatory.

Interim and final bills

8–009 Because of the time limits imposed by the Solicitors Act 1974 in respect of applications for detailed assessment, etc., it is important to distinguish between bills which are merely interim and those which are final. For example, where three out of a series of four bills have been paid more than

---

[27] *Re Chapman*, above.
[28] *Re Griffiths* (1891) 7 T.L.R. 268.
[29] *Re Landor* [1899] 1 Ch. 818.
[30] Solicitors Act 1974, s.64(1).
[31] *ibid.*, s.64(2).
[32] *Carlton v Theodore Goddard & Co.* [1973] 1 W.L.R. 623, Megarry J. (Solicitor's application for leave to substitute the larger detailed bill for the gross sum bill refused.)
[33] Solicitors Act 1974, s.64(3).

12 months prior to the application for detailed assessment it might be found that each was complete and final in its own right and that only the fourth bill should be assessed.[34] Alternatively, a series of bills rendered in succession on account might be treated as one bill all of which must be assessed.[35] It is a question of fact whether a bill delivered in such circumstances is an on account bill or a final bill.[36] Natural breaks may occur in the proceedings which permit the solicitor to deliver a bill for work done up to that time.[37] Where a retainer is an entire contract the solicitor is normally required to complete the business for which he was retained before submitting a bill.[38] That principle has been somewhat modified by the recognition of the natural break.

Roskill L.J. in *Davidsons v Jones-Fenleigh*[39] stated:

"There is now no doubt, I venture to think, what the law is . . . a solicitor is entitled to select a point of time which he regards as an appropriate point of time at which to send in a bill, but before he is entitled to require that bill to be treated as a complete self contained bill of costs to date he must make it plain to the client, either expressly or by necessary implication, that that is his purpose in sending in that bill for that amount at that time. Then of course one looks to see what the client's reaction is. If the client's reaction is to pay the bill in its entirety without demur it is not difficult to infer an agreement that the bill is to be treated as a complete self-contained bill of costs to date."

Lord Denning M.R. in *Chamberlain v Boodle & King*[40] stated:

"It is a question of fact whether there are natural breaks in the work done by a solicitor so that each portion of it can and should be treated as a separate and distinct part in itself capable of and rightly being charged separately and assessed separately."

A natural break cannot simply mean a date thought by the claimant solicitors to be a convenient date upon which to deliver a bill, since otherwise the concept of a natural break would be meaningless and section 65(2) of the Solicitors Act 1974 would be rendered largely redundant. The law does provide for the possibility of interim bills being payable by virtue of an inferred agreement, such an agreement can be inferred from the

---

[34] *Davidsons v Jones-Fenleigh* (1980) 124 S.J. 204, CA, and see *Winchester Commodities Group PLC v Re RD Black & Co.* unreported, July 16, 1999, Mr J. Martin Q.C.

[35] *Chamberlain v Boodle & King* [1982] 1 W.L.R. 1443, CA.

[36] *Re Hudson* [1904] W.N. 32.

[37] *Re Romer and Haslam* [1893] 2 Q.B. 286, CA; *Re Hall & Barker* (1878) 9 Ch. D. 538; *Harris v Osbourn* [1834] 2 C.R. & M. 629.

[38] *Re Romer & Haslam*, above.

[39] (1980) 124 S.J. 204, CA.

[40] [1982] 1 W.L.R. 1443, CA at 1446B.

conduct of the parties. (In the particular case the defendant had paid the first 26 of 42 bills rendered monthly.[41])

The cash account

8–010 Prior to the introduction of the Solicitors Accounts Rules 1991 various principles were laid down to ensure that clients knew and understood their financial situation as regards the solicitor. It is the duty of a solicitor delivering a bill of costs to deliver with it a cash account showing in detail the receipts and payments for and on behalf of the client.[42] The cash account should not contain disbursements which belong in the delivered bill. However where the solicitor has received or paid money for or on behalf of the client, that should be shown.

Where the relationship of solicitor and client exists or has existed, the court may make an order for the delivery by the solicitor of a cash account.[43] The court may also order the payment of delivery up by the solicitor of money or securities; the delivery to the claimant of a list of the moneys or securities which the solicitor has in his possession or control on behalf of the claimant; and the payment into or lodging in court of any such moneys or securities.[44] If the solicitor alleges that he has a claim for costs the court may make such order for detailed assessment and payment or securing the payment and protecting the solicitor's lien as it thinks fit.[45] The cash account may be amended or a fresh account delivered at any time prior to the completion of the detailed assessment. The cash account is settled by the costs officer when the bill itself is assessed.

In the High Court

8–011 Applications for the detailed assessment of a solicitor's bill of costs are made under Part III of the Solicitors Act 1974 and particularly under sections 70 and 71. The application must be made under CPR Part 8 or, in the course of proceedings, by an application under CPR Part 23.[46]

The jurisdiction of the High Court under Part III of the 1974 Act may be exercised by:

(a) a judge;

---

[41] *Penningtons (a firm) v Abedi*, unreported, March 23, 2000, CA.
[42] *Re Harman* (1915) 59 S.J. 351, CA.
[43] RSC, Ord.106, r.3(1)(a).
[44] *ibid.*, r.3(1)(b),(c),(d).
[45] *ibid.*, r.3(3).
[46] CPR, Sched.1; RSC, Ord.106, r.3(2).

(b) a master, a costs judge or a district judge of the Family Division; or

(c) a district judge if the costs are for contentious business done in a cause or matter which proceeded in the district registry of which he is the district judge, or for non-contentious business.[47]

Where a solicitor applies for an order under the 1974 Act for the detailed assessment of his own bill of costs, he must lodge with the application a certificate that all the relevant requirements of the Act have been satisfied.[48]

Detailed assessment on the application of the client or party chargeable

Where the client or party chargeable makes an application for detailed assessment of the solicitor's bill within one month from the delivery of the bill, the court must, without requiring any sum to be paid into court, order detailed assessment of the bill and that no action be commenced on it until the detailed assessment is completed.[49]

8–012

If the application is made after one month from delivery of the bill, the court may order, on such terms as it thinks fit (not being terms as to the costs of the detailed assessment), that the bill be assessed, and that no action be commenced on the bill and that any action already commenced be stayed until the detailed assessment is completed.[50]

Where the application is made after the expiration of 12 months from delivery of the bill, or after a judgment has been obtained for the recovery of the costs covered by the bill, or after the bill has been paid but before the expiration of 12 months from the payment of the bill, no order may be made except in special circumstances. If an order is made it may contain such terms as regards the costs of the detailed assessment as the court may think fit.[51]

Where a client was unhappy with the bill delivered by the solicitor and applied for a remuneration certificate from the Law Society which took more than 12 months to determine, the court found that this delay amounted to special circumstances and accordingly an order for detailed assessment of the solicitor's bill could be made.[52]

The court has no power to order detailed assessment of the bill on the application of the client or party chargeable after the expiration of 12 months from the payment of the bill.[53] Payment may be by transfer of funds

---

[47] *ibid.*, r.2(2).
[48] *ibid.*, r.5A.
[49] Solicitors Act 1974, s.70(1).
[50] *ibid.*, s.70(2).
[51] *ibid.*, s.70(3).
[52] *Riley v Dibb Lupton Alsop*, unreported, June 5, 1997, Sedley J.
[53] *ibid.*, s.70(4).

from the solicitor's client account to office account and the 12-month time-limit runs from the date of such payment, provided the party chargeable is in receipt of the relevant bill of costs.[54] The client or party chargeable may seek an order for detailed assessment of the profit costs covered by the bill,[55] and the court may order detailed assessment of all the costs or of the profit costs or of the costs other than profit costs. Where part of the costs is not to be assessed the court may allow an action to be commenced or to be continued for that part of the costs.[56]

The costs officer is required, not only to assess the bill but also the costs of the detailed assessment, and must certify what is due to or by the solicitor in respect of the bill and in respect of the costs of the detailed assessment.[57] If, after due notice of detailed assessment, either party fails to attend, the costs officer may proceed with the detailed assessment in his absence.[58]

In order to prevent an abuse of its order the court, in the exercise of its inherent powers, may direct that the order shall be discharged unless for example the client obtains an appointment within 14 days.[59]

Where the time for applying for detailed assessment of a solicitor's bill under section 70 of the Solicitors Act 1974 has expired, the solicitor is not entitled to summary judgment for the amount due if the client wishes to defend the action on the basis that the charges are unreasonably high. The 1974 Act does not exclude any other common law right to challenge the bill.[60] The burden of proving the reasonableness of the bill is on the solicitors.[61]

Where a solicitor was instructed to act in liquidation proceedings by the liquidator, the bills were delivered but remained unpaid. The solicitor sued for non payment of fees and the liquidator counterclaimed seeking an account and enquiry in respect of the bills as well as claiming damages for negligence in the course of the litigation. The court held that this was sufficient to enable it to order assessment under section 70(2) of the Solicitors Act 1974 even though no formal written application had been made. The order was made on the implicit application under section 70(2) and/or under the relevant inherent jurisdiction of the court.[62]

Application by the solicitor

8–013   Provided that the client or party chargeable has not made an application within one month from the delivery of the bill, a solicitor may apply and the

---

[54] *Gough v Chivers & Jordan, The Times*, July 15, 1996, CA.

[55] *ibid.*, s.70(5).

[56] *ibid.*, s.70(5),(6).

[57] *ibid.*, s.70(7).

[58] *ibid.*, s.70(8).

[59] *Re Plummer* [1917] 2 Ch. 432.

[60] See *Re Park* (1889) 41 Ch. D. 326; *Jones v Whitehouse* [1918] 2 K.B. 61; and *Thomas Watts & Co. v Smith* [1998] 2 Costs L.R. 59.

[61] *O. Paloma SA v Turner & Co.* [1999] 4 All E.R. 353, CA.

[62] *Connolly v Harrington* [2002] EWHC (QB) May 17, H.H. Judge Chapman.

court may, on such terms as it thinks fit (not being terms as to the costs of the detailed assessment), order that the bill be assessed, that no action be commenced on the bill and that any action already commenced be stayed until the detailed assessment is completed.[63]

Detailed assessment on the application of third parties

Where a person, other than the client or party chargeable with the bill, has paid or is liable to pay a bill, either to the solicitor or to the party chargeable with the bill, that person may apply for an order for the detailed assessment of the bill as if he were the party chargeable with it and the court may make the same order as it might have made in those circumstances.[64] If it is necessary for the court to consider whether or not there are special circumstances sufficient to justify the making of an order it may take into account circumstances which affect the application but do not affect the party chargeable with the bill.[65]

8–014

Except in special circumstances (discussed below) no order may be made on the application of a third party for the detailed assessment of the bill which has already been assessed.[66] If the court orders a bill to be assessed it may order the solicitor to deliver to the applicant a copy of it on payment of the cost of that copy.[67]

Where the Law Society intervened in a solicitors practice on the grounds of suspected dishonesty the solicitor nominated to intervene submitted five bills to the Society for the work done on its behalf. The Law Society paid the bills and sought reimbursement from the solicitor whose practice had been intervened. That solicitor applied for an order under section 71 of the 1974 Act for detailed assessment of the bills. The Society argued that the bills were not "solicitors bills" within the meaning of section 70 since that solicitor had not been retained to act as its solicitor, either to give advice or to conduct proceedings and in any event the provisions of section 71 were overriden by paragraph 13 of Part 2 of Schedule I to the 1974 Act. The court held that the bills were solicitor's bills within the meaning of section 70(1) of the Act. The court was required to consider whether the business was connected with the profession of a solicitor, whether the solicitor had been employed because he was a solicitor and whether the solicitor would not have been appointed if he had not been a solicitor or the relationship of solicitor and client had not existed between him and his employer. The court found the tests satisfied and that each of the bills was a solicitor's bill. The court also found that paragraph 13 of Schedule 1 did not override or exclude the right conferred by section 71 of the Act. That section recognised

---

[63] Solicitors Act 1974, s.70(2).
[64] *ibid.*, s.71(1).
[65] *ibid.*, s.71(2).
[66] *ibid.*, s.71(6).
[67] *ibid.*, s.71(7).

that the person chargeable with the bill might not be ultimately liable to pay the costs thereby claimed. Its evident purpose was to confer on one with a secondary liability for those costs a right comparable to that possessed by the person primarily liable. Given that the Law Society was entitled to have the bills taxed under section 70 of the Act it was unlikely that Parliament had intended that there should be degrees of secondary liability some of which were excluded from the ambit of section 71. The application was allowed.[68]

A solicitor whose practice was intervened by the Law Society sought to have the bills of the solicitors instructed by the Law Society assessed. He suggested that sections 70 and 71 of the Solicitors Act 1974 did not comply with the Human Rights Act. The court held that the correct "person chargeable with the bill" under section 70(1) of the Act could only be the Law Society. The costs judge at first instance had in fact ordered a detailed assessment but imposed a requirement for the payment of £50,000 as a pre-condition to the assessment taking place. Permission to appeal was refused.[69]

An application by a beneficiary for assessment of costs charged to an estate was allowed even though there had been a lapse of 12 months since the payment of those costs before the beneficiary's application. The court held that in considering the application under section 71(3) the court should have regard to the provisions of section 70 relating to applications by the party chargeable for assessment so far as they were capable of being applied to an application made under section 71(3). There was no doubt that the power to order assessment under section 70(2) would not be exercisable on the application of a party chargeable more than 12 months from the payment of the bill. This however was a different power to that in section 71(3) although it was a matter to be taken into account it was not determinative of the application. It was for the applicant who was interested in the bill to persuade the court that it should nonetheless order assessment at his request.[70]

Trustees, executors and administrators

8–015 Where a trustee, executor or administrator has become liable to pay the bill of a solicitor, then on the application of any person interested in any property out of which the bill is or is likely to be paid, the court may order detailed assessment of the bill on such terms as it thinks fit and that such payments in respect of the amount found to be due to or by a solicitor and in respect of the costs of the detailed assessment be made to or by the

---

[68] *Pine v The Law Society* [2002] EWCA Civ 175; [2002] 1 W.L.R. 2189; [2002] 2 All E.R. 658, CA.
[69] *MacPherson v Bevan Ashford* [2003] EWHC 636 (Ch), Patten J.
[70] *McIlwraith v McIlwraith* [2002] EWHC (Ch), July 24, H.H. Judge Rich Q.C.

applicant, the solicitor or the executor, administrator or trustee as it thinks fit.[71]

In considering applications under the previous paragraph the court must have regard to the provisions of the 1974 Act[72] as to applications by the client or party chargeable, so far as they are capable of being applied in respect of this type of application. The court must also have regard to the extent and nature of the interest of the applicant.[73] If such an applicant pays any money to the solicitor he has the same rights to be paid that money by the trustee, executor or administrator chargeable with the bill as had the solicitor.[74]

Supplementary provisions as to detailed assessments

Every application for an order for detailed assessment or for the delivery of a bill or delivery of documents must be made in the matter of that solicitor.[75] A costs officer may in the course of the detailed assessment request the costs officer of any other court to assist him in assessing any part of the bill and the costs officer so requested must assess that part of the bill and return it with his opinion on it to the original costs officer.[76] The costs officer who is requested to assess part of a bill in this way has such powers and may take such fees as he would have had had he been assessing the bill pursuant to an order in the normal way. The costs officer who makes the request may not take any fee in respect of that part of the bill assessed by the other costs officer.[77] Since only one fee payable in advance is now required, this provision is of little consequence.   8–016

The certificate of the costs officer is final as to the amount of costs covered by it, unless it is set aside or altered by the court. The court may make such order in relation to the certificate as it thinks fit, including, in a case where the retainer is not disputed, an order that judgment be entered for the sum certified to be due with costs.[78]

Special circumstances

Special circumstances are "those which appear to the judge exercising such discretion, so special and exceptional as to justify [detailed assessment] and are not confined to misconduct or fraud".[79] There are no hard and fast rules as to what are special circumstances. Each case must stand on its own. The Court of Appeal will not lightly interfere with the exercise of the judge's   8–017

---

[71] *ibid.*, s.71(3).
[72] *i.e.* s.70.
[73] Solicitors Act 1974, s.71(4).
[74] *ibid.*, s.71(5).
[75] *ibid.*, s.72(1).
[76] *ibid.*, s.72(2).
[77] *ibid.*, s.72(3).
[78] N.B. the final costs certificate is now an order to pay CPR, r.47.16.
[79] *Re Hirst & Capes* [1908] 1 K.B. 982, CA (affirmed [1908] A.C. 416).

discretion.[80] Special circumstances are not confined to pressure or gross overcharging amounting to fraud.[81]

The applicant should be in a position to identify specific items so the court may be in a position to exercise its judgment. The charges may be unreasonably large or there may be gross blunders in the bill.[82] The bill may also contain items which require explanation.[83]

Special circumstances have been held to exist in the situation where a bill is paid with a reservation of the right to assessment, the application is issued within a year and the bill contains items which ought to be disallowed.[84] Similarly, if the solicitor overcharges under a misapprehension as to the charges permitted by the current Remuneration Order, this will amount to a special circumstance.[85] Delivery of a bill with a right reserved to deliver further bills can itself be a special circumstance.[86]

Where a series of bills are delivered which are regarded as one bill, time runs from the date of delivery of the last bill.[87] Where a bill is paid with an express reservation of a right to detailed assessment, although this may not necessarily be conclusive in showing a special circumstance, it is a highly important factor to be weighed with others, so that when a reservation is made it is not necessary to achieve such an onerous standard of proof in relation to other matters.[88] There can be no payment of a bill before it is delivered. But if the solicitor deducts the amount of the costs even if by agreement "payment"; is not made until the bill itself is delivered.[89] Where a solicitor has told the client that, if he intends to have the bill assessed, payment may be postponed and the client in those circumstances gives the solicitor security, it has been held that the giving of such security amounts to payment.[90] Retention by the solicitor of the client's money with the client's express consent may amount to payment,[91] but mere acquiescence in the retention is not sufficient.[92]

---

[80] *Re Cheeseman* [1891] 2 Ch. 289, CA; *Re Ward Bowie & Co.* [1910] 102 L.T. 881, CA.

[81] *Re Srother* [1857] 3 K. & J. 518; *Re Pybus* [1887] 35 Ch. D. 568.

[82] *Re Boycott* [1885] 29 Ch. D 571, CA; *Re A Solicitor* [1961] Ch. 491; *Re Norman* [1886] 16 Q.B.D. 673.

[83] *Re Robinson* [1867] LR 3 Ex. 4.

[84] *Re Tweedie Solicitors* [1909] 53 S.J. 469.

[85] *Re A Solicitor* [1909] 53 S.J. 469.

[86] *Harris v Yarm* [1960] Ch. 256.

[87] *Davidsons v Jones-Fenleigh* [1980] 124 S.J. 204, CA; *Chamberlain v Boodle & King* [1982] 1 W.L.R. 1443, CA.

[88] *Sanders v Isaacs* [1971] 1 W.L.R. 240.

[89] *Re Foster* [1920] 3 K.B. 306; *Re Frape* [1895] 2 Ch. 284; *Re Foss Bilborough & Co.* [1912] 2 Ch. 161.

[90] *Re Boyle, ex p. Turner* [1854] 5 De. G.M. & G. 540; *Templeman v Day* (1881) 16 L.J.N.C. 91; *Re van Laun, ex p. Pattulo* [1907] 1 K.B. 155 (applied in *Re Exchange Securities & Commodities Ltd* (in liquidation) [1988] Ch. 46.

[91] *Re David* (1861) 30 Beav. 278; *Hitchcock v Stretton* [1892] 2 Ch. 343; *Re Thompson, Ex p. Bayliss* [1894] 1 Q.B. 462; *Re Bayliss* [1896] 2 Ch. 107.

[92] *Re Ingle* (1855) 21 Beav. 273; *Re West, King & Adams, Ex p. Clough* [1892] 2 Q.B. 102.

Where there was an agreement between solicitors and their client that there should be a detailed assessment of the solicitor's charges and that no point would be taken as to the lapse of time before applying for assessment, such agreement was sufficient to constitute a "special circumstance" under section 70(3) of the 1974 Act. The fact that there was an agreement between the solicitor and the client that the bills should be assessed was held by the court to be as powerful a special circumstances as it was possible to conceive for ordering detailed assessment, even though there had been unexplained delay by the client in making the application. Given that there was no evidence of significant prejudice to the solicitors as a result of the delay, detailed assessment was ordered.[93]

A costs judge held that certain bills sent by a solicitor to its client were interim bills not statute bills and that the client was entitled to detailed assessment. The costs judge further held that if the bills were not interim bills there were special circumstances[94] that justified assessment of the bills including that the letter of retainer between the parties failed to deal with the calculation of legal costs, the disparity between the estimated legal costs and the costs as billed. Permission to appeal was refused by the single judge and the application to rely on fresh evidence was refused since the evidence was available at the time of the hearing before the costs judge.[95]

Inherent jurisdiction

The Court of Appeal has held that the inherent jurisdiction of the court[96] **8–018** should only be invoked to avoid a clear injustice. The court has a threefold jurisdiction:

   (i) the statutory jurisdiction under the 1974 Act;

   (ii) the inherent jurisdiction to deal with solicitors' costs under the general jurisdiction over officers of the court; and

   (iii) the ordinary jurisdiction of the court in dealing with contested claims.[97]

The Court of Appeal has held, and the House of Lords has confirmed, that where the legislature has stepped in with legislation in a particular area then within that particular area the inherent jurisdiction is ousted or curtailed, at any rate insofar as it is negative in character. It follows

---

[93] *Arrowfield Services v BP Collins* [2003] EWHC 830 (Ch), Michael Briggs Q.C.
[94] Within the meaning of the Solicitors Act 1974, s.70(3).
[95] *Nigel Adams & Co. v Al Malick Carpets Ltd* [2003] EWHC (QB), December 4, Fulford J.
[96] *Symbol Park Lane Ltd v Steggles Palmer* [1985] 1 W.L.R. 668, CA.
[97] *Re Park Cole v Park* (1888) 41 Ch. D. 326.

therefore that the courts do not have inherent jurisdiction which can override the provisions of section 70 of the 1974 Act.[98]

The costs of detailed assessment

8–019 As a general rule the costs of detailed assessment are paid according to the event of the detailed assessment, *i.e.* if one-fifth of the amount of the bill is disallowed the solicitor must pay the costs but otherwise the party chargeable will pay the costs.[99] This rule operates unless the application for detailed assessment was made by the solicitor and the party chargeable does not attend upon the detailed assessment or the court orders otherwise.[1]

The costs officer may certify any special circumstances relating to a bill or to the detailed assessment and may make such order in respect of the detailed assessment as may be appropriate.[2] The reference to one-fifth of the bill being disallowed is taken, where the detailed assessment concerns only part of the costs covered by the bill, as a reference to one-fifth of those costs which are being assessed.[3] The amount on which the one-fifth is calculated includes disbursements,[4] and costs already assessed and paid by an opposing party.[5]

Where the order to assess relates to a number of bills, the one-fifth is calculated on the total of those bills. If each bill is assessed as a result of a separate order the one-fifth is calculated on each bill individually.[6] Items struck out of a bill on the grounds that the business referred to in those items was not covered by any retainers given by the client are not taken into account in estimating whether or not one-fifth has been disallowed.[7]

In calculating the one-fifth for the purpose of this rule, VAT is not taken into account. This is so even when a bill is delivered, *e.g.* for "£483 but say £475", the larger of the two figures is the amount upon which the calculation is made.[8]

The costs officer is bound to follow the statutory provisions unless special circumstances are certified relating to the bill or the detailed assessment. Once special circumstances have been certified the costs officer may make such order as to the costs of the detailed assessment as he thinks fit.[9]

---

[98] *Shiloh Spinners Ltd v Harding* [1973] A.C. 691; *Harrison v Tew* [1989] Q.B. 307, CA; [1990] 2 W.L.R. 210, HL, but see *Thomas Watts & Co. v Smith* [1998] 2 Costs L.R. 59, CA.

[99] Solicitors Act 1974, s.70(9).

[1] *ibid.*, r.70(9)(a),(b).

[2] *ibid.*, r.70(10).

[3] *ibid.*, r.70(12).

[4] *Re Haigh* (1849) 12 Beav. 308.

[5] *Re Osborn v Osborn* [1913] 3 K.B. 861, CA.

[6] *Devereaux v White* (1896) 13 T.L.R. 52.

[7] *Re A Solicitor* [1936] 1 K.B. 523.

[8] *Re Carthew, Re Paull* (1884) 27 Ch. D. 485; *Re Mackenzie, ex p. Short* (1893) 69 L.T. 751. These authorities appear somewhat narrow and restrictive and it may be that they would not be followed if the point were to arise today.

[9] *Re Elwes and Turner* (1888) 58 L.T. 580.

The application

The application is made using a Part 8 claim form or if made in the course 8–020
of proceedings, by an application in accordance with CPR, Part 23.[10] It is
always necessary for the original or a certified copy of the bill in question to
be lodged.

Where a solicitor sues for the amount of a bill of costs and the only
question in dispute is one of quantum the practice is to order detailed
assessment of the bill under section 70 of the 1974 Act and that judgment
be signed for the amount found to be due and for the costs of the action.[11]
The detailed assessment proceedings are treated as if the defendant had
made the application. Thus if the client fails to appear at the detailed
assessment the solicitors may still recover the costs.[12]

Assessment procedure under Part III of the Solicitors Act 1974

Where the court has made an order under Part III of the Solicitors Act 1974 8–021
the solicitor must serve a breakdown of costs within 28 days of that order.
The client must serve points of dispute within 14 days after service on him
of the breakdown of costs. Any reply must be served within 14 days after
service of the points of dispute. Either party may request a hearing date after
the points of dispute have been served but in any event not later than three
months after the date of the order for detailed assessment. The court may
vary these provisions.[13] The breakdown must contain details of the work
done under each of the bills sent for assessment and, if appropriate, a cash
account showing money received by the solicitor to the credit of the client
and sums paid out of that money on behalf of the client but not payments
out which were made in satisfaction of the bill or of any items which are
claimed in the bill.[14] It is not possible to obtain a default costs certificate in
assessment proceedings under Part III of the Solicitors Act 1974.[15]

If, during the course of a detailed assessment hearing of a solicitor's bill
to his client, it appears to the costs officer that the solicitor will, in any
event, be liable in connection with that bill to pay money to the client, the
costs officer may issue an interim certificate specifying an amount which is
payable by the solicitor to the client.[16]

In the County Court

Where a bill of costs relates wholly or partly to contentious business done 8–022
in the county court and the amount of the bill does not exceed £5,000 the

---

[10] CPR, Sched.1.; RSC, Ord.106, r.3(2).
[11] *Smith v Edwardes* (1888) 22 Q.B.D. 10; *Lumley v Brooks* (1889) 41 Ch.D. 323.
[12] *Smith v Howes* [1922] 1 K.B. 590.
[13] CPR r.48.10 and Costs Practice Direction, s.56.
[14] Costs Practice Direction para.56.5.
[15] Costs Practice Direction, para.56.7.
[16] Costs Practice Direction, para.56.17.

powers and duties of the High Court[17] in relation to that bill may be exercised and performed by any county court in which any part of the business was done.[18] The district judge of a county court is the costs officer of that court but any detailed assessment of costs by him may be reviewed by a judge assigned to the county court district, on the application of any party to the detailed assessment.[19]

Costs out of the Community Legal Service Fund

8–023   The detailed assessment of the costs of proceedings to which a funded client is a party, must be in accordance with any direction or order given or made in the proceedings, irrespective of the interest of the funded client in the detailed assessment.

Costs will be assessed on the standard basis subject to the Legal Aid in Civil Proceedings (Remuneration) Regulations 1994, the Legal Aid in Family Proceedings (Remuneration) Regulations 1991, the Community Legal Service (Funding) Order 2000 and the Community Legal Service (Funding) (Counsel in Family Proceedings) Order 2001.

Any certificate or notice of revocation or discharge must be made available on the detailed assessment.[20] In cases where a notice of discharge has been issued or the certificate has been revoked the costs of the funded client will be assessed on production of a copy of the notice of discharge or revocation at the appropriate office.[21]

Basis of detailed assessment

8–024.1   With the introduction of prescribed rates for work funded by the Community Legal Service Fund, the costs recoverable will be assessed on the standard basis subject to the appropriate remuneration regulations. Where the retainer of a funded client's solicitor or counsel is determined before proceedings have actually been commenced, and there is no subsequent change of solicitor or counsel under the certificate, the amount of costs is assessed by the Area Director. "Assessment" in this context means an assessment of costs with a view to ensuring that the amounts of costs to be allowed are those which would be allowed on a detailed assessment in accordance with the Regulations.[22]

Where proceedings have been commenced and the total claim for costs does not exceed £2,500, the solicitor must apply to the Area Director for the

---

[17] Under ss.69, 70 and 71 of the Solicitors Act 1974.
[18] Solicitors Act 1974, s.69(3). See also High Court and County Courts Jurisdiction Order 1991 (SI 1991/724).
[19] *ibid.*, s.74(2).
[20] Civil Legal Aid (General) Regulations 1989, reg.107(2).
[21] *ibid.*, reg.107(4).
[22] Civil Legal Aid (General) Regulations 1989, regs 105(1), (2) and 107A(2).

costs to be assessed, unless there is also to be a detailed assessment between the parties.[23] Where the total claim for costs exceeds £2500 the solicitor may apply to the Area Director for an assessment of those costs if there are special circumstances[24] where the detailed assessment would be against the interests of the funded client, or would increase the amount payable from the Fund, or the solicitor incurs costs after a direction that there should be a detailed assessment of costs in recovering monies payable to the CLS Fund, the solicitor may apply to the Area Director for an assessment.[25]

Where solicitors represent a number of clients, only some of whom are funded by the Legal Services Commission, when the bill of costs comes to be assessed the overriding principle for the court is that each client is to be charged only with the costs of his own case. The general costs which cannot be attributed to particular clients on the basis of separate claims/defences or distinct issues must be apportioned pro rata.[26]

Where judgment is signed in default, or the court gives final judgment, the judgment must include a direction for the costs of any funded client to be assessed on the standard basis.[27] The court must make a direction even though no other order for costs is made.[28] The direction is automatically included in any judgment or final order in family proceedings. This is also the usual practice in other Divisions. Such a direction extends to all the costs of action whether or not reserved between the parties.[29]

In *Storer v Wright*, Lord Denning M.R. said:

> "The legal aid [detailed assessment] is different from all others: in that there is no one to oppose it. It is not adversarial but inquisitorial. A [costs judge] is the inquisitor. The Legal Aid Act 1974 says . . . that 'a solicitor who has acted for a person receiving legal aid should be paid for so acting out of the legal aid fund', but who is to challenge his bill? There is no one to contest the amount at all. If the client has lost the case—and has a nil contribution—he is not concerned in the least with the amount the solicitor charges. If he has won the case—and (has been) awarded damages—he may be concerned—because a solicitor gets a charge—for his costs—on the amount of damages recovered. The higher the solicitor's bill the less his damages . . .
>
> Seeing that there is no one to oppose it it seems to me that on a legal aid [detailed assessment] it is the duty of the [costs officer] to bear in mind the public interest. He should himself disallow any item which is unreasonable in amount or which is unreasonably incurred. In short,

---

[23] *ibid.*, reg.105(2A) and (12).
[24] *ibid.*, reg.105(3).
[25] *ibid.*, reg.105(3).
[26] *Baylis v Kelly, The Times*, June 6, 1997, Chadwick J.
[27] Civil Legal Aid (General) Regulations 1989, reg.107(3).
[28] *Page v Page* [1953] Ch. 320, CA.
[29] *Pace v Pace* [1957] 1 W.L.R. 1011.

whenever it is too high he must reduce it. Otherwise the legal aid system could be much abused by solicitors and counsel."[30]

Although the client is now given notice of the bill and is entitled to be heard on any detailed assessment if he has a financial interest in it, the basic principles set out by Lord Denning above still apply.

It is the duty of a funded client's solicitor to safeguard the interests of the Community Legal Service Fund on any detailed assessment between the parties, pursuant to an order for costs made in favour of the funded client, where that person may himself have no interest in the result of the detailed assessment. The solicitor is required to take such steps as may appear to be necessary to appeal the detailed assessment.[31]

B. COUNSEL

8–024.2 There is no machinery for assessment of barrister's fees incurred in a direct charging situation.[32] Where counsel's fees have been incurred on the instructions of solicitors in the normal way, these fees may be the subject of detailed assessment, since they will form part of the solicitor's bill to the client, however, while detailed assessment will decide the client's liability to the solicitor for costs and disbursements, it does not necessarily affect the solicitor's liability to the barrister for the fees which may have been agreed. This may have to be resolved by referring the matter to a tribunal at the conclusion of the case.[33]

Privately funded fees

8–025.1 Where counsel is instructed by a solicitor or under the direct access provisions of the Code of Conduct of the Bar, the ascertainment and payment of fees is governed by the Bar's Terms of Work, or the BarDirect Terms of Engagement.[34] The non-payment of counsel's fees by a solicitor is likely to be a disciplinary matter.

---

[30] [1981] 1 Q.B. 336 at 347.
[31] Civil Legal Aid (General) Regulations 1989, reg.107(3).
[32] See para.3–010, above.
[33] See the Terms of Work on Which Barristers Offer Their Services to Solicitors: Code of Conduct of the Bar Annex B.
[34] Annex B.

Costs out of the Community Legal Service Fund

Assessment/Detailed Assessment

The onus is upon the solicitor to have the costs, including counsel's fees, assessed by the Legal Services Commission. The solicitor must, within seven days after an assessment notify counsel in writing where the fees claimed on his behalf have been reduced or disallowed.[35] There is a similar duty in respect of detailed assessment or provisional assessment.[36]

8–025.2

Counsel's fees will always be included in the solicitor's bill for detailed assessment in a case funded out of the Community Legal Service Fund. The solicitor must endorse the bill with the date on which notice was given to counsel of any reduction or disallowance, or a statement that no such notice was necessary.[37]

Where the bill of costs is endorsed to the effect that no notice was necessary the costs officer may issue the final certificate but where a notice has been given, the certificate may not be issued until 14 days have elapsed from the date of the endorsement.[38]

Standard fees for junior counsel in care proceedings and prescribed family proceedings are set out in Schedules 1A and 2A to the Legal Aid in Family Proceedings (Remuneration) Regulations 1991 and the Community Legal Service (Funding) (Counsel in Family Proceedings) Order 2001.

Where a standard fee is prescribed for work done by junior counsel that fee must be allowed unless the relevant authority considers that it would be unreasonable to do so, in which case, such lesser or greater fee as may be reasonable will be allowed.[39] The fee allowed must not exceed any maximum fee specified in the schedules, unless the relevant authority considers that, owing to the time and labour expended by counsel or to any other special circumstances of the case, the maximum fee specified would not provide reasonable remuneration for some or all of the work done, in which case the fee to be allowed is in the discretion of the relevant authority.[40]

C. COSTS BETWEEN PARTIES

For Summary and Detailed assessment and the Procedure see Chapter 7.

8–026

---

[35] Civil Legal Aid (General) Regulations 1989, reg.105(8).
[36] *ibid.*, reg.112(1).
[37] *ibid.*, reg.112(1).
[38] *ibid.*, reg.112(2).
[39] Legal Aid in Family Proceedings (Remuneration) Regulations 1991, reg.3(5).
[40] *ibid.*, reg.3(5).

Form and contents of bill of costs

The Practice Direction sets out some Model forms of bills of costs. The bill should include background information including a brief description of the proceedings up to the date of notice of commencement, the status of the person doing the work and the hourly rates claimed and an explanation of any agreement or arrangement between the receiving party and the solicitors which affects the costs claimed in the bill.[41] The bill should then set out as appropriate:

> costs between parties;
> attendances on the court and counsel;
> attendances on and communications with the receiving party, and with witnesses including expert witnesses;
> attendances to inspect any property or place for the purposes of the proceedings;
> searches and enquiries made, e.g. at the Companies Registry;
> attendances on and communications with other persons including the court and counsel;
> work done on documents: preparing and considering documentation which was of and incidental to the proceedings, including time spent on pre-action protocols and time spent collating documents;
> work done in connection with mediation, alternative dispute resolution and negotiations with a view to settlement;
> attendances on and communications with agents and other work done which was of and incidental to the proceedings and not previously covered.[42]

If the number of attendances and communications which are other than routine is twenty or more these must be set out in a separate schedule recording dates and details. In relation to work done by solicitors, routine letters and telephone calls will generally be allowed on a unit basis of six minutes each. No separate allowance is made for incoming letters. E-mails sent by solicitors may be reflected in a discretionary allowance of time spent in preparation of e-mails, and the court may also allow a sum in respect of e-mails sent where it is satisfied that had e-mails not been sent the number of communications which it would have been reasonable to allow would have been substantially greater than the number actually claimed. Local travelling expenses are not allowed, and "local" is generally taken to be within a radius of 10 miles of the court dealing with the case at the relevant time. The costs of postage, couriers, telephone calls, etc. are not generally allowed since they are overheads but the court has a discretion to allow such

---

[41] Costs Practice Direction, para.4.5.
[42] Costs Practice Direction, para.4.6.

expenses in unusual circumstances or where the cost is unusually heavy. Photocopying is not generally allowed but the court has a discretion to make an allowance for copying in unusual circumstances or where the documents copied are unusually numerous in relation to the nature of the case. Where agency charges have been incurred, the actual work done by the agent should be included in the bill, the agents charges should not be claimed as a disbursement. Finally a claim may be made for the reasonable cost of preparing and checking the bill of costs.[43]

Although the Costs Practice Direction enables a claim for the reasonable costs of preparing a bill to be allowed, where a claim is made subject to the Legal Aid in Family Proceedings (Remuneration) Regulations 1991 or similar provisions which do not allow for such an item, the statutory provision is not overridden by the Practice Direction. Accordingly the amount to be allowed is the figure specified in the Regulations. The costs of drawing up a bill may be distinguished from the costs of preparing for and attending the assessment hearing, and an additional figure may be allowed in respect of it.[44]

D. LITIGANTS IN PERSON

For Summary and Detailed assessment and the procedure see Chapter 7.   **8–027**

Form of bill

The information required from a litigant in person to be included in a bill of costs should, so far as possible, follow the requirements of the Rules and the Costs Practice Direction. The court will normally accept a bill in any form so long as it sets out clearly what is being claimed and details of the work done, set out in chronological order with details of the time, costs and disbursements claimed against each item. The court is usually prepared to recognise that the litigant in person may not have the necessary expertise and, provided that the bill lodged contains the relevant information to enable it to be assessed, will accept the bill. It is a matter for the discretion of the costs officer whether or not the bill is accepted.

A litigant in person includes a company or other corporation which is acting without a legal representative and a barrister, solicitor, solicitor's employee or other authorised litigator[45] who is acting for himself.[46] A

---

[43] Costs Practice Direction, para.4.18.
[44] *A Local Authority v A Mother and Child (Family Proceedings: Legal Aid Assessment)* 2000 EWCA Fam., December 20.
[45] As defined in the Courts and Legal Services Act 1990.
[46] CPR r.48.6(6).

solicitor who instead of acting for himself is represented in the proceedings by his firm, or by himself in his firm name, is not, for the purposes of the Civil Procedure Rules, a litigant in person.[47]

Where the costs of a litigant in person are to be paid by any other person the costs allowed are to be:

(a) costs for the same categories of work and disbursements which would have been allowed if the work had been done or the disbursements made by a legal representative on a litigant in person's behalf;

(b) the payments reasonably made by him for legal services relating to the conduct of the proceedings; and

(c) the costs of obtaining expert assistance in connection with assessing the claim for costs.[48]

This does mean that a litigant in person may recover the cost of obtaining legal advice in addition to the cost of doing the work on his or her own behalf.

Expert assistance in connection with assessing the claim for costs may be obtained from a barrister, solicitor, Fellow of the Institute of Legal Executives, Fellow of the Association of Law Costs Draftsmen, a law costs draftsman who is a member of the Academy of Experts or a law costs draftsman who is a member of the Expert Witness Institute.[49]

Except in the case of a disbursement, the costs allowable to a litigant in person may not exceed two-thirds of the amount which would have been allowed if the litigant in person had been represented by a legal representative. If the litigant in person fails to prove financial loss the amount to be allowed will be an amount in respect of the time reasonably spent doing the work at the rate specified in the Costs Practice Direction.[50] Where the litigant can prove financial loss, the amount of costs to be allowed will be the amount he can prove he has lost for time reasonably spent on doing the work.[51] It is necessary to distinguish between leisure time and financial loss time. Work done during leisure time will be remunerated only at the prescribed rate.[52]

8–028   This puts a cap upon any particular claimed item of two-thirds of what the notional solicitor would have charged, but it does not allow two-thirds

---

[47] Costs Practice Direction para.52.5. See also *London & Scottish Benefit Society v Chorley* [1884] 13 Q.B.D. 872 and *Stubblefield v Kemp* [1999] EWHC Ch.D, November 10, Arden J., [2001] 1 Costs L.R. 130.

[48] CPR r.48.6(3).

[49] Costs Practice Direction, para.52.1.

[50] CPR r.48.6(2) & (4). The rate specified is, at the time of writing, £9.25 per hour, Costs Practice Direction, para.52.4.

[51] CPR r.48.6(4).

[52] *McLeod-Johnstone-Hart v Aga Khan Foundation (UK)* [1984] 1 W.L.R. 994, CA.

of what a notional solicitor would have charged if the sum in fact payable is less than that two-thirds. The exercise is as follows: find out in respect of the item what, at the litigant in person charging rate, the total is. Compare that with two-thirds of the notional solicitor rate. Give the lower of the two items. That does mean that the bill of costs drawn by the litigant in person must be gone through in some detail item by item.[53] A costs judge should keep in mind that it is appropriate in a proper case to allow a litigant in person more time for a particular task than would be allowed to a solicitor. A solicitor's charging rate takes account of the fact that he has support staff, secretaries and messengers. "The time spent reasonably doing the work" permits a reasonable assessment of the time spent by the litigant in person and should reflect matters such as posting letters, taking files to court and photocopying documents.[54]

The onus of showing financial loss is upon the litigant in person who seeks to establish it.[55]

A litigant in person wishing to prove financial loss must produce to the court any written evidence to be relied on to support that claim and a copy of that evidence must be served on any party against whom costs are sought at least 24 hours before the hearing at which the question may be decided. Where the litigant in person commences detailed assessment proceedings the written evidence should be served with the notice of commencement.[56] A litigant who is allowed costs for attending at court to conduct his case is not entitled to a witness allowance in addition.[57]

Where a litigant in person succeeded in judicial review proceedings and was awarded costs, the court at first instance decided that he was not entitled to costs for research (1200 hours). The Court of Appeal decided that in principle the litigant in person was entitled to his time for researching his case at the rate fixed by statute subject to a cap of two-thirds of what he would have recovered if legally represented. The Court of Appeal found no reason to disbelieve the litigant's assertion that he had spent 1200 hours on the case and decided that he was entitled to be paid for it. The court held that the starting point was the cap of two-thirds and took the figure of £15,000 as a rough estimate (from information supplied by solicitors). The litigant was entitled to two-thirds of that figure plus expenses for photocopying and travel. He was accordingly awarded £10,460.[58]

Where an action is brought against a solicitor who defends it in person and obtains judgment, he is entitled, upon assessment, to the same costs as

---

[53] per Jacob J. *Morris v Wiltshire & Woodspring District Council*, January 16, 1998 (unreported).

[54] *Mealing-McLeod v Common Professional Examination Board*, unreported, March 30, 2000, Buckley J.

[55] *Mainwaring v Goldtech Investments Limited* [1997] 1 All E.R. 467, Robert Walker J.

[56] In accordance with Rule 47.6: Costs Practice Direction, para.52.4.

[57] CPR r.48.6(5).

[58] *R. v Legal Services Commission (formerly Legal Aid Board), Ex p. Wulfsohn* [2002] EWCA Civ, February 8.

if he had employed a solicitor, except in respect of items which the fact of his acting directly renders unnecessary.[59] The Court of Appeal has considered whether that principle has survived the introduction of the CPR. Chadwick L.J. stated:

> "20. . . . The position of a practising solicitor who chooses to represent himself in his firm name, or (where in partnership) to be represented by his firm, remains unaltered by the provisions of CPR 48.6. His costs are allowed (or not as the case may be) by virtue of, and in accordance with the principle established in the London Scottish Benefit Society case.
>
> . . .
>
> 24. . . . A partner who is represented in legal proceedings by his firm incurs no liability to the firm; but he suffers loss for which under the indemnity principle he ought to be compensated, because the firm of which he is a member expends time and resources which would otherwise be devoted to other clients. The only sensible way in which effect can be given to the indemnity principle is by allowing those costs. And, as I have sought to explain, that is the solution which for over 100 years the courts have adopted as a rule of practice."[60]

Disbursements

8–029   A payment made by a doctor litigant to a locum is not a disbursement for the purpose of costs.[61] A litigant in person is not entitled to a notional disbursement in respect of a brief fee in quantifying two-thirds of the daily attendance fee.[62] Although a notional disbursement cannot be recovered, a litigant in person is entitled to recover a disbursement actually incurred so as to avoid the necessity of employing, not only a solicitor, but also counsel. Thus, in *The Law Society v Persaud*[63] travelling expenses from South Africa were held to be recoverable.

Fast track trial costs

8–030   Where a litigant in person is awarded fast track trial costs if the litigant can prove financial loss the court will award two-thirds of the amount which would otherwise be awarded,[64] or if the litigant in person fails to prove

---

[59] *London Scottish Benefit Society v Chorley Crawford & Chester* [1884] 12 Q.B.D. 452; [1885] 13 Q.B.D. 872, CA.
[60] *Malkinson v Trim* [2002] EWCA Civ 1273; [2003] 1 W.L.R. 463, CA.
[61] *Parikh v Midland Bank Ltd*, unreported, 1982, CA.
[62] *McLeod-Johnstone-Hart v Aga Khan Foundation (U.K.)* [1984] 1 All E.R. 239, Lloyd J.
[63] *The Times*, May 10, 1990.
[64] In accordance with CPR r.46.2.

financial loss an amount in respect of the time reasonably spent doing the work at the rate specified in the Costs Practice Direction.[65]

McKenzie Friends

The Court of Appeal has summarised the way in which McKenzie Friends are to be treated as follows:

8–031

1. In relation to proceedings in public, a litigant in person should be allowed to have the assistance of a McKenzie Friend unless the judge is satisfied that fairness and the interests of justice do not require the litigant in person to have that assistance.

2. The position is the same where the proceedings are in chambers unless the proceedings are in private.

3. Where the proceedings are in private then the nature of the proceedings which makes it appropriate for them to be heard in private may make it undesirable in the interests of justice for a McKenzie Friend to assist.

4. A judge should give reasons for refusing to allow a litigant in person the assistance of a McKenzie Friend.

5. The assistance of a McKenzie Friend is available for the benefit of the litigant in person and whether or not a McKenzie Friend is paid or unpaid for his services he has no right to provide those services; the court is solely concerned with the interests of the litigant in person.[66]

---

[65] CPR r.46.3(5): Costs Practice Direction, para.52.4, the amount specified at the time of writing is £9.25 per hour.
[66] *R. v Bow County Court, Ex p. Pelling* [1999] 4 All E.R. 751, CA. As to granting permission for a litigant in person to have an advocate who has no right of audience, see *Clarkson v Gilbert, The Times*, July 4, 2000, CA.

PART V

Appeal

CHAPTER 9

Review and Appeal

APPEALS

Appeals generally

CPR Part 52 governs appeals from all decisions except appeals against an 9–001
authorised court officer in detailed assessment proceedings. Part 52 applies
in respect of appeals against summary assessment as well as against detailed
assessment. An appellant or respondent requires permission to appeal in
every case. The application for permission to appeal may be made to the
lower court at the hearing at which the decision to be appealed against was
made or to the appeal court in an appeal notice (CPR r.52.1 and r.52.3).

Appeal lies to the next level of judge in the court hierarchy. Thus in the
county court appeal lies from a district judge to a circuit judge and from a
circuit judge to a High Court judge; and in the High Court appeals lie from
a costs judge or district judge of the High Court to a High Court judge and
from a High Court judge to the Court of Appeal. The court hearing a first
appeal is described in Part 52 as the appeal court and the court from whose
decision an appeal is brought is described as the lower court.[1]

Brooke L.J. subsequently amended what he had said in *Tanfern* to read
(at paragraph 17):

> "A final decision includes the assessment of damages or any other final
> decision where it is 'made at the conclusion of part of a hearing or trial
> which has been split up into parts and would if made at the conclusion
> of that hearing or trial be a final decision': Article 1(3) of the
> [Destination of Appeals] Order of 2000; it does not include a decision
> only on the detailed assessment of costs."[2]

---

[1] *per* Brooke L.J. in *Tanfern Ltd v Cameron-MacDonald* [2000] 1 W.L.R. 1311; [2000] 2 All
E.R. 801, CA, Practice Direction and see PD 52, para.2A.
[2] *Dooley v Parker* [2002] EWCA Civ, February 7.

Where the court does not request submissions from or attendance by the respondent costs will not normally be allowed who volunteers submissions or attendance. If the court requests submissions from or attendance by the respondent, or attendance by the respondent with the appeal to follow if permission is granted the court will normally allow the respondent his costs if permission is refused.[3]

In granting permission to appeal it is open to a judge to impose a condition which provides the proposed respondent with an assurance that he will not be faced with a ruinous bill of costs in order that the motor insurance industry could resolve a troublesome issue of law in a claim for an amount which by itself could not possibly have justified the costs of an appeal. The judge's order that the appellant should pay all the claimant's costs in the Court of Appeal in any event was varied by the Court of Appeal to a condition under which no order for costs in the Court of Appeal or below would be enforced by the appellant against the respondent personally.[4]

The Court of Appeal did impose a condition that appellants should not be entitled to the costs of appeal even if successful, one of the reasons being that the appellant was a very large corporation which had spared no expense in prosecuting the relatively straightforward appeal, whereas the respondents were a group of individual objectors who had succeeded on a preliminary issue and still had to face the costs of the main trial. The court pointed out that CPR r.3.1(2)(a) gave the court power to make an order subject to conditions, in a matter that was out of the ordinary.[5]

Where appellants had failed to comply with orders to pay costs into court, the Court of Appeal ordered that unless the outstanding costs were paid within seven days the appeal would be dismissed. The court had jurisdiction to make such an order under CPR r.3.1(3). The appellants were being financed as to costs by a third party whose aim was to fund the litigation without incurring any liability for the other side's costs in the event that the appellants failed. There was no reason why the third party who had financed the trial and was financing the appeal should be allowed to conduct the litigation in such a way.[6]

The High Court has a jurisdiction to re-open an appeal that has already determined so as to avoid real injustice in exceptional circumstances. The power will only be exercised where it is clearly established that a significant injustice has occurred and that there is no alternative effective remedy.[7]

CPR 52.4(2) provides that the appellant must file the appellant's notice at the appeal court within such period as may be directed by the lower court,

---

[3] PD 52, paras 4.22–4.24.
[4] *King v Daltray* [2003] EWCA Civ 808.
[5] *Lloyd Jones v T Mobile (UK) Ltd* [2003] EWCA Civ 1162.
[6] *Contract Facilities v Rees* [2003] EWCA Civ 1105.
[7] *Seray-Wurie v Hackney LBC* [2002] EWCA Civ 909; [2002] 3 All E.R. 448 CA, and see *Taylor v Lawrence* [2002] EWCA Civ 90; [2002] 2 All ER 353, CA.

or, where that court makes no such direction, 14 days after the date of the decision of the lower court that the appellant wishes to appeal. In detailed assessment proceedings the 14 days starts from the date of the particular decision complained of, even if the detailed assessment hearing continues over a number of days. The time does not run from the conclusion of the detailed assessment hearing.[8]

The proper approach of the court on an appeal from a costs judge was considered by Buckley J.:

"Broadly speaking a judge will allow an appeal . . . if satisfied that the decision of the Costs Judge was wrong . . . that is easy to apply to matters of principle or construction. However where the appeal includes challenges to the details of the assessment, such as hours allowed in respect of a particular item, the task in hand is one of assessment or judgment, rather than principle. There is no absolute answer. Notwithstanding that the judge to whom the appeal is made may sit with assessors . . . the appeal is not a re-hearing and, given the nature of the Costs Judge's task and his expertise, I would usually regard it as undesirable for it to be so. . . .

. . .

[S]ince the appeal is not a re-hearing I would regard it as inappropriate for the judge on appeal to be drawn into an exercise calculated to add a little here or knock off a little there. If the judge's attention is drawn to items which, with the advice of his assessors, he feels should in fairness be altered, doubtless he will act. That is a matter for his good judgment. Permission to appeal should not be granted simply to allow yet another trawl through the bill, in the absence of some sensible and significant complaint. If an appeal turns out to be no more than such an exercise the sanction of costs may be used."[9]

The approach of the court was further clarified by the Court of Appeal in *Tanfern v Cameron-McDonald*[9a] as follows:

"The first ground of interference speaks for itself. The epithet 'wrong' is to be applied to the substance of the decision made by the lower court. If the appeal is against the exercise of a discretion by the lower court the decision of the House of Lords in *G v G* [(*Minors: Custody Appeal*) [1985] 1 W.L.R. 647] warrants attention. In that case Lord Fraser of Tullybelton said [at page 652] 'certainly it would not be useful to enquire whether different shades of meaning are intended to be conveyed by words such as 'blatant error' used by the President in the

[8] *Kasir v Darlington & Simpson Rolls Mills Ltd* [2001] 2 Costs L.R. 228, Popplewell J.
[9] *Mealing-McLeod v The Common Professional Examination Board*, unreported, March 30, 2000, Buckley J.
[9a] [2000] 1 W.L.R. 1311.

present case, and words such as 'clearly wrong', 'plainly wrong' or 'simply wrong' used by other Judges in other cases. All these various expressions were used in order to emphasise the point that the Appellate Court should only interfere when they consider that the Judge at first instance has not merely preferred an imperfect solution, which is different from an alternative imperfect solution which the Court of Appeal might or would have adopted, but has exceeded the generous ambit within which such a reasonable disagreement is possible."

Appeals from authorised court officers in detailed assessment proceedings

9–002   Any party to detailed assessment proceedings may appeal against a decision of an authorised court officer without having either to obtain permission or request reasons. The appeal is to a costs Judge or district judge of the High Court.[10] The appeal is a re-hearing of the proceedings which gave rise to the decision appealed against and the court may make any order and give any direction it considers appropriate.[11] Permission to appeal is required from a decision made by a Costs Judge or District Judge of the High Court in such proceedings because the exception to the requirement to obtain permission applies only to appeals in detailed assessment proceedings against the decision of an authorised court officer and not at this higher level of appeal in such proceedings. Such an appeal is not a "second appeal". Where costs are summarily assessed by a judge as part of a final decision in a multi track claim the principles relating to appeals against final decisions in multi track claims will be applied.[12]

Assessors

9–003   Previous rules made provision for the court to appoint assessors under section 70 of the Supreme Court Act 1981 or section 63 of the County Courts Act 1984. CPR Part 52, which now governs appeals, makes no separate provision for assessors, but rule 35.15 deals with the court's power to appoint assessors. As a matter of practice, on appeals from decisions in the Supreme Court Costs Office each appeal will be considered by the Senior Costs Judge or another Costs Judge appointed by him to decide whether assessors should be appointed, and if so how many, and whether a barrister

---

[10] CPR rr.47.20, 47.21 and see Costs PD, Sections 47 and 48.
[11] CPR r.47.23.
[12] *per* Brooke L.J. in *Tanfern Ltd v Cameron-MacDonald* [2000] 1 W.L.R. 131; [2000] 2 All E.R. 801, CA.

or a solicitor. The fees of assessors form part of the costs of the proceedings.[13] The court will give notice to the parties of the intention to appoint assessors giving the name of the proposed assessor, the matter in respect of which the assistance of the assessor will be sought and the qualifications of the assessor to give that assistance. Any party may object in writing to the proposed appointment within seven days of receipt of the notification. The objection will be taken into account by the court in deciding whether or not to make the appointment.[14] The court may order any party to deposit in the court office a specified sum in respect of the assessor's fees and where it does so the assessor will not be asked to act until the sum has been paid.[15]

Appeals relating to costs out of the community legal service fund

A funded client's solicitor may appeal against a decision in detailed **9–004** assessment proceedings in accordance with CPR Part 52 (or in the case of appeal from an authorised court officer)[16] and if counsel, acting for the funded client, notifies the solicitor that he is dissatisfied with the decision, the solicitor must appeal, but the costs of any such appeal are deemed to be costs to which the funded client's certificate relates only to the extent that the court hearing the appeal so orders.[17]

The funded client is not required to make any contribution to the fund on account of the costs of any appeal against a decision in detailed assessment proceedings and the charge created by section 10(7) of the Access to the Justice Act 1999 does not apply in relation to any increase in the net liability of the fund in consequence of any order made in such an appeal.

Where permission to appeal is obtained, the funded client's solicitor is required to give written notice to the Lord Chancellor and must send to the Lord Chancellor with that notice, copies of the bill of costs and the request for permission to appeal. When filing the notice of appeal the solicitor must file with the court a copy of the notice given to the Lord Chancellor. The notice of appeal must be sent without delay to the Lord Chancellor once it has been filed.[18]

In the Court of Appeal costs are likely to be summarily assessed at the following hearings:

(i) contested directions hearings;

---

[13] CPR r.35.15.
[14] PD 35 paras 6.1–6.4.
[15] CPR r.35.15.
[16] CPR rr.47.20–47.23.
[17] Civil Legal Aid (General) Regulations 1989, reg.113(2).
[18] *ibid.*, regs 113(4)–(7).

   (ii) applications for permission to appeal at which the respondent is present;

  (iii) dismissal list hearings in the Court of Appeal at which the respondent is present;

  (iv) appeals from case management decisions; and,

   (v) appeals listed for one day or less.[19]

---

[19] PD 52, paras 14.1 and 14.2.

PART VI

Penalties and Sanctions

CHAPTER 10

Wasted Costs Sanctions and the Court's Inherent Jurisdiction

A. PERSONAL LIABILITY OF LEGAL REPRESENTATIVES FOR WASTED COSTS

CPR 48.7 sets out the procedure when the Court is considering whether to make an order for wasted costs under Section 51(6) of the Supreme Court Act 1981 against a legal representative. The court cannot act as an appellate court in respect of its own order for costs except where fraud has been shown in the original application for the order.[1] This decision was distinguished in a case where the Defendant was successful and an order was made for costs as between the parties. Prior to the detailed assessment the defendant sought a wasted costs order against the claimants' legal representative. On appeal it was held that the court did have jurisdiction to make a wasted costs order. The case was not concerned with revisiting costs with a view to a wasted costs order under section 51(6) of the 1981 Act but with revisiting a decision on costs as between the parties under section 51(1). This involved the exercise of two separate discretions and the discretion in relation to a possible wasted costs order could be exercised at any time until detailed assessment.[2]

10–001

It is open to a litigant to seek a wasted costs order against the legal representatives of any party including his own representatives.[3]

The court does not have jurisdiction to make a wasted costs order against a legal representative who is not within the definition of "persons exercising

---

[1] *Commissioners for Customs and Excise v Anchor Foods* [1999] EWHC (CH), July 8, Neuberger J.
[2] *Melchior v Vettivel* [2002] C.P. Rep. 24, Patten J.
[3] *Brown v Bennett* EWHC (Ch), November 16, Neuberger J., *The Times*, November 21, 2001.

a right to conduct litigation" *e.g.*, because the representative has not issued proceedings.[4]

Delay in the conduct of proceedings can give rise to a wasted costs order. When considering making a wasted costs order the Judge is obliged to carry out some enquiry into the costs incurred, although not a detailed enquiry. Provided that a reasoned assessment of the costs wasted is made the judge may make an order in broad terms.[5]

Decided cases on wasted costs

10–002   The court has a general power to order costs, even against someone not representing a party to the proceedings (under section 51(3) of the Supreme Court Act 1981) thus where a solicitor did not draw attention to his client's bankruptcy in possession proceedings, the court was nonetheless able to make an order that the solicitor pay the costs of subsequent freezing injunction proceedings which would not have been brought had the bankruptcy been disclosed.[6]

The Code of Conduct of the Bar imposes a personal duty on counsel not to make allegations of fraud or other dishonest or dishonourable conduct without the evidence to make good the allegation. The House of Lords has confirmed that the court does have jurisdiction under section 51 of the 1981 Act to make a wasted costs order against the legal representative of any opposing party. A barrister may be liable for a wasted costs order in relation to conduct immediately relevant to the exercise of a right of audience although not involving advocacy in open court. When drafting pleadings alleging fraud counsel did not need to have admissible evidence of fraud but only material of such character as to lead responsible counsel to conclude that serious allegations could be based on it. A court considering making a wasted costs order had to make full allowance for the inability of the respondent lawyers to tell the full story because of the privilege of the client. The court should therefore not make an order against a lawyer precluded by professional privilege from advancing his full answer to the complaint against him without satisfying itself that it was in all the circumstances fair to do so.[7]

In order for a wasted costs order to be made against a legal representative any impropriety should be a very serious one and there had to be something more than negligence; there had to be something akin to abuse of process. The cases of *Ridehalgh v Horsefield* and *Medcalf v Weatherill* should now

---

[4] *Byrne v South Sefton Health Authority* [2001] EWCA Civ 1904.
[5] *Kilroy v Kilroy* [1997] P.N.L.R. 66, CA.
[6] *Kleinwort Benson v de Montenegro* [1994] N.P.C. 46, Aldous J.
[7] *Medcalf v Weatherill* [2002] UKHL 27; [2002] 3 W.L.R. 172, HL and see *Brown v Bennett* [2002] 1 W.L.R. 713; [2002] 2 All E.R. 273, Neuberger J.

be taken to state the law in relation to this area.[8] The Court of Appeal in *Persaud* stated that there had to be something more than mere negligence for the wasted costs jurisdiction to arise: there had to be something akin to abuse of process. Following a review of the authorities relied on in *Persaud* the Court of Appeal did not accept that the meaning of "negligent" had been modified as suggested. In cases where the allegation is that the legal representative has pursued a hopeless case, the question is whether no reasonably competent legal representative would have continued with the action. This question could not be answered affirmatively unless the representative also acted unreasonably which is akin to establishing abuse of process. Where privilege was not waived and the judge did not have the benefit of seeing counsel's advice in relation to the claim which had proceeded, the court could not infer simply from the extension of legal aid for the trial, that the solicitors had asserted that there were good prospects of success.[9]

It has more recently been held that unless an applicant for a wasted costs order can establish that the legal representative acted in a way that was not only "improper, unreasonable or negligent" but was also in some way in breach of any duty to the court, the court could not make a wasted costs order. In a case where it was found that the legal representative had been "negligent" the act occurred at a time when there were no legal proceedings on foot and therefore there could be no question of that negligence representing any sort of breach of any duty to the court.[10] The normal situation is that solicitors cannot be liable for wasted costs as a result of actions before litigation has started, especially where the actions were no more than negligent and the solicitors never acted in the litigation once it started.[11]

The Court of Appeal considered in detail the wasted costs jurisdiction introduced by the Courts and Legal Services Act 1990 in a judgment delivered on January 26, 1994.[12] The court held that while litigants should not be financially prejudiced by the unjustifiable conduct of litigation by their or their opponent's lawyers, the courts in the exercise of the wasted costs jurisdiction should be astute to control the threat of a new and costly form of satellite litigation. The Master of the Rolls reviewed the court's long standing jurisdiction against solicitors[13] and noted that the jurisdiction was for the first time extended to barristers. There could be no room for doubt about the mischief against which the new provisions were aimed: the

---

[8] *Persaud v Persaud* [2003] EWCA Civ 394.
[9] *Dempsey v Johnstone* [2003] EWCA Civ 1134.
[10] *Charles v Gillian Radford & Co* [2003] EWHC (Ch) 3180, Neuberger J.
[11] *Byrne v Sefton HA* [2002] EWCA Civ 1904.
[12] *Ridehalgh v Horsefield; Allen v Unigate Dairies Ltd; Roberts v Coverite (Asphalters) Ltd; Philex plc v Golban; Watson v Watson; Antonelli v Wade Gery Farr (A Firm)*; [1994] Ch. 205; [1994] 3 W.L.R. 462, CA.
[13] He referred to *Myers v Elman* [1940] A.C. 282; *Edwards v Edwards* [1958] p.235; *Wilkinson v Wilkinson* [1963] P. 1; *Maroux v Soc. Com. Abel Periera Da Fonseca SARL*

causing of loss and expense to litigants by the unjustifiable conduct of litigation by their or the other side's lawyers. Where such conduct was shown, Parliament clearly intended to arm the courts with an effective remedy for the protection of those injured. The Master of the Rolls affirmed the statement of principle in *Re A Barrister (Wasted Costs Order) (No.1 of 1999)*[14] that when a wasted costs order was contemplated a three stage test should be applied:

(a) Had the legal representative of whom complaint was made acted improperly, unreasonably or negligently?

(b) If so, did such conduct cause the applicant to incur unnecessary costs?

(c) If so, was it, in all the circumstances, just to order the legal representative to compensate the applicant for the whole or part of the relevant costs?

In the same judgment the court discussed various issues concerning the wasted costs jurisdiction. These are set out below.

Improper, unreasonable or negligent

10–003   The court considered the meaning of "improper, unreasonable or negligent". "Improper" covered, but was not confined to, conduct which would ordinarily be held to justify disbarment, striking off, suspension from practice or other serious professional penalty. While it covered any significant breach of a substantial duty imposed by the relevant code of professional conduct it was not limited to that. Conduct which would be regarded as improper according to the consensus of professional, including judicial, opinion could be fairly stigmatised as such whether it violated the letter of a professional code or not.

10–004   **"Unreasonable"**   aptly described conduct which was vexatious, designed to harass the other side rather than advance the resolution of the case, and it made no difference that the conduct was the product of excessive zeal and not improper motive. Conduct could not be described as unreasonable simply because it led, in the event, to an unsuccessful result or because other more cautious legal representatives would have acted differently. The acid test was whether the conduct permitted of a reasonable explanation. If so,

---

[1972] 1 W.L.R. 962; *Currie v Law Society* [1977] Q.B. 990; *R & T Thew Ltd v Reeves (No. 2) (Note)* [1982] Q.B. 1283; *Davy-Chiesman v Davy-Chiesman* [1984] Fam. 48; *Orchard v South Eastern Electricity Board* [1987] Q.B. 565; *Sinclair-Jones v Kay* [1989] 1 W.L.R. 114; *Holden v CPS* [1990] Q.B. 261 and *Gupta v Comer* [1991] 1 Q.B. 6290.
[14] [1993] Q.B. 293.

the course adopted might be regarded as optimistic and as reflecting on a practitioner's judgment, but could not be described as unreasonable.

"Negligence" Should be understood in an untechnical way to denote 10–005 failure to act with the competence reasonably expected of ordinary members of the profession. In adopting that approach the court firmly discountenanced any suggestion that an applicant for a wasted costs order needed to prove, under the negligence head, anything less than he would have to prove in an action for negligence.[15]

Pursuing a hopeless case: A person's legal representative, could not be said 10–006 to have acted improperly and unreasonably or negligently simply because he acted for a party who pursued a claim or defence which was plainly doomed to fail. Barristers in private practice cannot pick and choose their clients and although solicitors are not subject to an equivalent rule, many would and do respect the underlying public policy by affording representation to the unpopular and unmeritorious. Legal representatives will advise their clients of the perceived weakness of their case and the risk of failure but, in the final analysis, clients are free to reject advice and insist that cases be litigated.

The court went on to state it was rarely if ever safe for a court to assume that a hopeless case was being litigated on the advice of the lawyers involved. They were there to present the case, and it was for the judge and not the lawyers to judge it.

However, a legal representative could not lend his assistance to proceedings which were an abuse of the process and was not entitled to use litigious procedures for purposes for which they were not intended, as by issuing or pursuing proceedings for reasons unconnected with success in the litigation or pursuing a case known to be dishonest, nor was he entitled to evade rules intended to safeguard the interests of justice, as by knowingly failing to make full disclosure on an application without notice, or knowingly conniving at incomplete disclosure of documents.

In deciding whether or not to make a wasted costs order on the basis of negligent non-disclosure on an application without notice, the court held that section 51(7) of the Supreme Court Act 1981 did not require knowing complicity of a legal representative. A solicitor did not have to know he was failing to make a disclosure which he ought to make, it was sufficient if he knew of a material fact which was not disclosed but negligently or unreasonably believed it was not material or negligently failed to make inquiries which would have revealed material matter.

It is not entirely easy to distinguish by definition between the hopeless case and the case which amounts to an abuse of the process. However, in practice it is not hard to say which is which and if there is doubt the legal representative is entitled to the benefit of it.

---

[15] See *Saif Ali v Sydney Mitchell & Co.* [1980] A.C. 198 at 218.

Care must be exercised to avoid the fallacy that the proper inference from what proved to be a hopeless case is that the conduct of the legal representatives must have been improper or unreasonable.[16]

Lawyers in immigration cases should be aware of the sanction of the wasted costs order where a hopeless case is being pursued. Far too many hopeless immigration cases are pursued in the High Court. Practitioners should note that in such circumstances a wasted costs order was made against them, if appropriate. Solicitors would be protected in such circumstances, however, if they had been advised by counsel that there was merit in the case.[17]

10–007 **Legal aid/CLS funded work:** The Court of Appeal has set out the procedure to be adopted where a funded client has been unsuccessful and the unassisted party seeks to recover costs against the Legal Services Commission or under the wasted costs jurisdiction.[18] In relation to the issue of legal aid, it was held that the effect of section 31(1) of the Legal Aid Act 1988 was that the existence of legal aid did not affect the client/representative relationship nor the rights of other parties to the proceedings or the principles on which any discretion was exercised. It was incumbent on the courts to which wasted costs applications were made to bear prominently in mind the peculiar vulnerability of legal representatives acting for funded clients.[19] It would subvert the benevolent purposes of the legal aid legislation if such representatives were subject to any unusual personal risks. The court should also bear prominently in mind that the advice and conduct of legal representatives is not to be tempered by the knowledge that their client is not their paymaster and so not in all probability liable for the costs of the other side.

In considering whether or not to make a wasted costs order in a LSC funded case the court should be slow to supplement statutory or regulatory duties by placing a higher standard on the parties. Where the wasted costs would effectively be recovered by the Community Legal Service Fund, the consent of the Commission should be obtained before embarking on proceedings for a wasted costs order.[20]

10–008 **Immunity:** The court referred to cases[21] where the House of Lords had held that a barrister and a solicitor acting as advocate were immune from action for negligence at the suit of a client in respect of his conduct and management of a case in court and the pre-trial work immediately

---

[16] *Jones v Chief Constable of Bedfordshire*, unreported, July 30, 1999, CA.

[17] *R v Secretary of State for the Home Department Ex p. Singh (Atrvinder)* [1993] Imm. A.R. 450, McPherson J.

[18] *re O (a minor) (costs: liability as a Legal Aid Board)* [1977] 1 F.L.R. 465, CA.

[19] *Symphony Group Plc v Hodgson* [1993] 3 W.L.R. 830 at 842.

[20] *Tate v Hart, The Independent*, March 8, 1999, CA.

[21] *Rondel v Worsley* [1969] 1 A.C. 191; *Saif Ali v Sydney Mitchell*, above n.9.

connected with it. This, it was said, is based on public policy considerations including the requirement that advocates should be free to conduct cases in court fiercely and independently, the need for finality, the advocate's duty to the court and to the administration of justice, the barrister's duty to act for a client however unsavoury, the general immunity accorded to those taking part in court proceedings, the unique role of the advocate, and the subjection of advocates to the discipline of their professional bodies.

In the court's judgment, if an advocate's conduct in court is improper, unreasonable or negligent he is liable to a wasted costs order subject to the qualification that although the court was satisfied that the legislation intended to encroach on the traditional immunity of the advocate by subjecting him to the wasted costs jurisdiction, it did not follow that the public interest considerations on which the immunity was founded were to be regarded as irrelevant or lacking in weight.

Any judge invited to make or contemplating making such an order must make full allowance for the fact that an advocate in court often had to make decisions quickly and under pressure. Mistakes would inevitably be made, things done which the outcome showed to have been unwise. Advocacy was more an art than a science and it could not be conducted according to formulae.

It is only when, with all allowances made, an advocate's conduct of court proceedings is quite plainly unjustifiable that it would be appropriate to make a wasted costs order against him.

Immunity of counsel The immunity of counsel (and presumably other advocates) ought to be confined as closely as possible to those circumstances where public interest requires that immunity ought to be recognised. The claim to immunity for the conduct of an advocate can only arise if the case falls squarely within one or more of the following: **10–009**

  (i) participation in court proceedings;

 (ii) intimate connection with the conduct of the case; or

(iii) a collateral attack on a final decision.

Settlement of litigation is not normally encompassed within the principles on which the immunity of the advocate is based.[22]

Since the decision in *Ridehalgh v Horsefield* the House of Lords has again considered the immunity of advocates.[23] In each of the three cases the Judge at first instance had concluded that solicitors enjoyed an advocate's immunity and struck out the claims as an abuse of process. The Court of

---

[22] *Kelley v Corston*, unreported July 10, 1997, CA, and see *Rondel v Worsley* [1969] 1 A.C. 191 and *Saif Ali v Mitchell & Co.* [1980] A.C. 198.
[23] *Arthur J. S. Hall & Co v Simons; Barratt v Woolf Seddon; Harris v Schofield, Roberts & Hill* [2000] 3 W.L.R. 543, HL.

Appeal decided that in none of the cases were the solicitors immune and restored the client's claim. The House of Lords decided that it was appropriate to reconsider the issue of advocate's immunity and went on to find that none of the reasons said to justify immunity had sufficient weight to sustain immunity in relation to civil proceedings. The House of Lords found that the powers of the courts and the CPR were such as to restrict the ability of clients to bring unmeritorious and vexatious claims against advocates, and accordingly public interest in the administration of justice no longer required that advocates should enjoy immunity from suit for alleged negligence in the conduct of civil proceedings. There was a similar finding in respect of criminal proceedings.

10–010   **Privilege:**   The liability of a barrister for a wasted costs order is not limited to his conduct of the proceedings in court. A barrister is within the definition of a person "exercising a right of audience or a right to conduct litigation" under Section 51(13) of the Supreme Court Act 1981.[24]

Whilst a barrister cannot be asked to reveal the contents of his instructions or brief, or be asked to answer a question which would in practice reveal part of the contents of the brief, the barrister could be asked, in respect of non privileged documents, whether he saw or knew of the particular document, provided that the purpose of the question was merely to find out specifically whether counsel had seen or knew of those documents. If the purpose of the question was to find out if a particular document was in his instructions that question would be impermissible even if the document was not privileged.[25]

A material factor in deciding the culpability of legal representatives' conduct is whether the client has waived legal professional privilege. If not the court must make assumptions in favour of those legal representatives.[26]

In a case where it was alleged that the legal representatives had pursued a hopeless case the judge should have asked whether no reasonably competent legal adviser would have evaluated the chance of success as being such as to justify continuing with the proceedings. In determining that question the judge could only come to a conclusion adverse to the legal representatives if he had the opportunity of seeing counsel's advice which was privileged. In the absence of waiver of privilege it could not be inferred that the evaluation of the claim was negligent in the relevant sense within section 51 of the Supreme Court Act 1981.[27]

Before the court makes a wasted costs order more is required than an assertion that the claim was "doomed to fail". The same tests apply equally

---

[24] *Brown v Bennett* [2001] EWHC Ch.D, November 16, Neuberger J., *The Times*, November 21, 2001.
[25] *Brown v Bennett (No.3)* Neuberger J., [2002] 1 W.L.R. 713; [2002] 2 All E.R. 273.
[26] *Daly v Hubner* [2001] EWHC Ch.D, Etherton J.
[27] *Dempsey v Johnstone* [2003] EWCA Civ 1134.

to a legally aided claimant and the court "should be very slow to draw adverse inferences as to the quality of advice given by the legal representatives to the LSC.[28]

In a case where the allegation was that the legal representative had pursued a hopeless case on instructions, the court found that the legal representative had himself been negligent in failing to address the relevant test for the existence of a contract of employment to which the opponent's legal representatives had drawn its attention. The involvement of counsel did not absolve the solicitors. The judge was entitled to make a wasted costs order notwithstanding considerations arising from the fact that the client was publicly funded.[29]

The court noted that in circumstances where an applicant seeks a wasted costs order against his opponent's lawyers, legal professional privilege might be relevant, both as between the applicant and his lawyers and as between the respondent lawyers and their clients. In either case it is the client's privilege and only he can waive it.

If an applicant's privileged communications are germane to the application he can waive privilege. If he were to decline to do so it would be possible to draw adverse inferences. The respondent lawyers are in a different position in that privilege is not theirs to waive. Judges invited to make such orders should therefore make full allowance for the inability of the respondent lawyers to tell the whole story and where there is room for doubt the respondent lawyers are entitled to the benefit of it. It is only when, with all allowances made, a lawyer's conduct of proceedings is quite plainly unjustifiable that it could be appropriate to make an order for wasted costs.

Causation: Demonstration of the causal link between the improper, unreasonable, or negligent conduct and the waste of costs is essential. Where conduct is proved but no waste of costs shown to have resulted, the case might be referred to the appropriate disciplinary body or the legal aid authorities. It is not a matter for the exercise of the wasted costs jurisdiction. 10–011

Reliance on counsel: The court stated that a solicitor did not abdicate his professional responsibility when he sought the advice of counsel. He had to apply his mind to the advice received. The more specialist the nature of the advice, the more reasonable it was likely to be for him to accept it.[30] 10–012

---

[28] *Daly v Hubner (Wasted Costs)* [2002] Lloyd's Rep. PN 461 Etherton J. and see *Orchard v South Eastern Electricity Board* [1987] QB 565.

[29] *The Isaacs Partnership v Umm Al-Jawaby Oil Service Co Ltd* [2003] EWHC (QB) November 5, Gross J.

[30] *Lock v Camberwell HA* [1991] 2 Med. L.R. 249; also see *Davy-Chiesman v Davy-Chiesman* [1984] Fam. 48; [1984] 2 W.L.R. 291, CA.

The proposition that a solicitor who acted on counsel's advice had to bear responsibility for that advice in all circumstances could not be supported.[31]

A solicitor, representing litigants who gave evidence in other proceedings rendering their pleaded defence untenable, could not escape liability for wasted costs on the basis that the defence had been settled by counsel. The court found that the solicitor knew about his clients' evidence in the other proceedings and it was startlingly clear that the pleaded defence was not a true statement of the defence case. The court found the solicitor's conduct had been unreasonable and had caused the wasted costs.[32]

10–013 **Threats to apply for wasted costs orders:** Threats to apply for wasted costs orders should not be made as a means of intimidation. However, if one side considered that the conduct of the other was improper, unreasonable or negligent, and was likely to cause a waste of costs it was not objectionable to alert the other side to that view.

Timing of the application: The court expressed agreement with the view of *Aldous J. in Filmlab Systems International Ltd v Pennington*[33] that in general wasted costs applications are best left until after the end of the trial.

In family proceedings where the husband changed his legal advisers which required the wife's solicitors to seek discovery of documents held by his original solicitors, the trial being vacated without directions either being sought or given, it was appropriate to hear the wife's application for a wasted costs order against the husband's former legal team before the main trial began.[34]

10–014 **The applicant:** A court might itself initiate an inquiry into wasted costs but, save in the most obvious cases, the courts should be slow to do so. The courts would usually be well advised to leave an aggrieved party to make the application as then costs would in the ordinary way follow the event between the parties.

Procedure: Where counsel made a hopeless application to suspend a warrant and, with the senior partner of the solicitors sitting behind him, accepted that it was hopeless, resulting in the making of a wasted costs order against the solicitors, the absence of any explanation or any application for adjournment suggested that the solicitors had been playing for time and the low level of costs involved, together with the run of the mill nature

---

[31] *R. v Luton Family Proceedings Court Justices, ex p. R.* [1998] 4 C.L. 51; *Reaveley v Safeway Stores plc* [1998] P.N.L.R. 526, CA.
[32] *General Mediterranean Holdings SA v Patel*, unreported January 27, 2000, Curtis J.
[33] *Film Lab Systems International Ltd v Pennington*, *The Times*, July 2, 1993, Aldous J.
[34] *B v B (Wasted costs: abuse of process)* [2001] 1 F.L.R. 843, Wall J.

of the application, rendered it unnecessary for there to be a full investigation.[35]

The procedure to be followed in determining applications for wasted costs orders, was to be laid down by the courts so as to meet the requirements of the individual cases before them. The overriding requirements are that any procedure had to be fair and as simple and summary as fairness permitted. The respondent lawyer should be very clearly told what he is said to have done wrong and what is claimed. The requirements of simplicity and summariness mean that elaborate pleadings should in general be avoided. No formal process of discovery is appropriate. The court could not imagine any circumstances in which the applicant should be permitted to interrogate the respondent lawyer or vice versa. Hearings should be measured in hours not days or weeks. Judges must not reject the weapon which Parliament intended to be used for the protection of those injured by the unjustifiable conduct of the other side's lawyers, but they must be astute to control what threatens to become a new and costly form of satellite litigation.

CPR, Part 48.7(2) provides that no order shall be made without giving the legal representative the opportunity to give reasons why an order should not be made.[36] It not be understood to mean that the burden is on the legal representative to exculpate himself. An order should not be made unless the applicants have satisfied the court or the court itself is satisfied that an order should be made. The rule clearly envisages that the representative shall not be called upon to reply unless an apparently strong prima facie case has been made against him. The language of the rule recognises a shift in the evidential burden.

Discretion: The jurisdiction to make a wasted costs order depends, at two   **10–015** stages, on the court's discretion:

(1) At the stage of initial application when the court is invited to give the representative an opportunity to show cause. This is not something to be done automatically. The costs of the inquiries compared with the costs claimed are always a relevant consideration. The discretion, like any other, is to be exercised judicially. However, judges might not infrequently decide that further proceedings are not likely to be justified.

(2) At the final stage, because even if the court is satisfied that legal representatives have acted improperly, unreasonably or negligently so as to waste costs, it is not bound to make an order but

---

[35] *Woolwich Building Society v Fineberg* [1998] P.N.L.R. 216, CA.
[36] The Costs Practice Direction, s.53, relating to r.48.7, sets out the procedure and the approach which the court will adopt when considering such an application.

will have to give sustainable reasons for the exercise of its discretion in that way.

Crime: The court reiterated the undesirability of there being a divergence in the practice of the civil and criminal courts.[37] Parliament, it was said, had acted substantially to assimilate the practice in the two. The court fully appreciated that the conduct of criminal cases would often raise different questions and depend on different circumstances but expressed the hope that its judgment might give guidance which would be of value to both the civil and criminal courts.

Appeal from order for wasted costs

10–016   The normal Rules governing appeals under the CPR apply.

A judge is a competent witness, and although not compellable, would if required, wish to assist the court, however, the authorities show that judges should only be called to give evidence as a last resort. The exception to the principle of compellability was in connection with matters related to and resulting from the exercise of judicial function.[38]

Whether or not there should be a wasted costs hearing is a matter for the judge's discretion; unless the proceedings can take place in summary form, or very soon after judgment, they are unlikely to be appropriate. A wasted costs application which requires full scale re-litigation of the issues in the original trial should not proceed.[39]

> "The time has long since passed when the civil courts at appellate level or at first instance can afford litigants the luxury of unrestrained oral or written contention ... the proper conduct of litigation does not require every point to be taken and every stone to be turned. The proper, efficient and effective conduct of litigation requires all involved to concentrate on the real issues in the case.
>
> The legal profession in general and the Bar in particular must re-learn or at least re-apply, the skill, which historically has been the hallmark of the profession but which, in too many types of litigation, appears to be fast vanishing. I refer to the ability to identify and present to the court, in however complex a case, the few crucial determinative issues and to discard as irrelevant or immaterial dross, the minor points and excessive detail. This of course requires the exercise of discretion,

---

[37] *Holden v CPS* [1990] 2 Q.B. 261; *Gupta v Comer* [1991] Q.B. 629, CA.
[38] *Warren v Warren* [1996] 3 W.L.R. 1129 and see *Duke of Buccleuch v Metropolitan Board of Works*, [1872] L.R. 5 H.L. 418.
[39] *Re Freudiana Holdings Limited, The Times*, December 4, 1995, CA.

judgment and skill which are all qualities to be expected of those who practise in a learned profession."[40]

The Court of Appeal has again summarised the principles to be applied when making wasted costs orders.[41]

"Improper" conduct within the meaning of section 51 of the Supreme Court Act 1981 is conduct which would be so regarded "according to the consensus of professional (including judicial) opinion." "Unreasonable" conduct "aptly describes conduct which is vexatious, designed to harass the other side rather than advance the resolution of a case and it makes no difference that the conduct is the product of excessive zeal and not improper motive ... the acid test is whether the conduct permits of a reasonable explanation." "Negligent" conduct is to be understood "in an untechnical way to denote failure to act with the competence reasonably to be expected of ordinary members of the profession."[42]

"A solicitor does not abdicate his professional responsibility when he seeks the advice of counsel."[43] Where counsel have put their signatures to a statement of claim this "did not exonerate the solicitors from their obligation to exercise their own independent judgment to consider whether the claim could properly be pursued, they were not entitled to follow counsel blindly."[44]

"The jurisdiction to make a wasted costs order must be exercised with care and only in clear cases."[45] "It should not be used to create satellite litigation which is as expensive and as complicated as the original litigation. It must be used as a remedy in cases where the need for a wasted costs order is reasonably obvious. It is a summary remedy which is to be used in circumstances where there is a clear picture which indicates that a professional adviser has been negligent etc."[46] Where a wasted costs application has been settled, a short and succinct statement should be placed before the court without counsel or other lawyers having to attend. If it is not possible to agree the statement the position of the other parties can be protected by their also being allowed to submit a short statement in response.[47]

An application for a wasted costs order is inappropriate where complicated proceedings requiring detailed investigation into the facts would ensue. The procedure is a summary one to be applied in uninvolved and

---

[40] per Rose L.J. in *Re Freudiana Holdings Ltd, The Times*, December 4, 1995, CA.
[41] *Fletamentos Maritimos SA v Effjohn International BV*, December 10, 1997, CA (unreported). The principles are derived from *Ridehalgh v Horsefield* [1994] Ch. 205; *Tolstoy-Miloslavsky v Aldington* [1996] 1 W.L.R. 736 and *Wall v Lefever, The Times*, August 1, 1997.
[42] Derived from *Ridehalgh v Horsefield* above.
[43] See *Ridehalgh v Horsefield*, above.
[44] Derived from *Tolstoy-Miloslavsky v Aldington*, above.
[45] Derived from *Tolstoy-Miloslavsky v Aldington*, above.
[46] Derived from *Wall v Lefever*, above.
[47] *Manzanilla Ltd v Corton Property and Investments Ltd, The Times*, August 4, 1997, CA.

clear cases where unnecessary costs are incurred. The summary procedure might be inappropriate in circumstances where a solicitor is alleged to be in breach of his professional duty to his client.[48] The application should be made especially to the judge who heard the substantive proceedings, the principle of proportionality must also be borne in mind.[49]

Counsel who was over optimistic in failing to anticipate delays in a first trial when committed to appear in a second, was held not to have acted unreasonably, when the daily demands of practice were taken into account, and allowance made for difficulties with time estimates.[50] Where an action to set aside a libel judgment alleged to have been obtained by fraud, was struck out as an abuse of the process, it was held to be appropriate for a wasted costs order to be made against the claimant's solicitors, even though they had acted without fee.[51]

In winding-up proceedings, a solicitor who swore an affidavit in support of a petition asserting that the company was insolvent, acted improperly if he did not hold that belief and acted unreasonably if there were no grounds upon which a competent solicitor could have reached that view on the material available. In the particular circumstances of the case the solicitor was ordered to pay the whole of the wasted costs incurred by the company.[52]

The Divisional Court has held that the action of solicitors, in seeking committal to prison for contempt of court for breach of undertaking by local authority officials, without any communication with the council, was a drastic and unjustifiable measure warranting an order that they personally should pay the council's costs.[53]

A wasted costs order may be made against a patent agent in respect of costs incurred as a result of the agent continuing to act without actual authority.[54]

The failure by a solicitor to warn the court that an adjournment might be necessary due to difficulties with the Legal Aid Board was held not to warrant a wasted costs order by the Court of Appeal.[55]

Solicitors who failed adequately to instruct a junior clerk who appeared on an application for removal from the record, were held to have acted unreasonably and negligently and a wasted costs order was made against them.[56]

Where a wasted costs application was made against the legal representative fairness required that the respondent lawyer had to be told very clearly

---

[48] *Turner Page Music v Torres Design Associates Ltd, The Times* August 3, 1999, CA.
[49] *Re Merc Property Ltd, The Times*, May 19, 1999, Lindsay J.
[50] *Re a Barrister (Wasted Costs Order No. 4 of 1993, The Times*, April 21, 1995, CA.
[51] *Tolstoy-Miloslavsky v Aldington, The Times*, December 27, 1995, CA.
[52] *Re a Company (No. 006798 of 1995)* [1996] 2 All E.R. 417, Chadwick J.
[53] *R v Liverpool City Council, ex p. May* [1994] C.O.D. 144, DC.
[54] *Bellfruit Manufacturing Co. v Twin Falcon* [1995] F.S.R. 144, Ford J.
[55] *Re a Solicitor (Wasted Costs Order)* [1993] 2 F.L.R. 959, CA.
[56] *Shah v Singh* [1996] 1 P.N.L.R. 83, DC.

what he or she had done wrong and what was claimed. There should be no pleadings and discovery was not appropriate. The applicant should not be permitted to interrogate the respondent lawyer or vice versa. The court should not exercise its discretion to order a legal representative to show cause without careful appraisal of the relevant circumstances. A representative would not be called on to make a reply unless an apparently strong *prima facie* case had been made against him.[57] The claimant applied for a wasted costs order in the sum of £1,200 and appealed against the dismissal of that application. The Court of Appeal found that had it been trying the matter at first instance it would have found considerable difficulty in being satisfied that wasted costs proceedings were justified. The principle set out in *Ridehalgh v Horsefield* should have governed the judge's approach. The court was reluctant to interfere with the exercise of discretion, added to which, having regard to proportionality the appellant's case ought to be rejected. The court stated that this was just the type of satellite litigation that should be discouraged at the appeal stage.[58]

Other examples of wasted costs

A barrister practising from home without a clerk was under a duty to ascertain the date of trial of any case in which he was instructed: it was unreasonable to rely wholly on instructing solicitors to notify him. The barrister himself was responsible for keeping abreast of listing details and should have adopted some system that enabled him to do that.[59] Solicitors and counsel holding themselves out as competent to handle judicial review proceedings will be taken to be familiar with the warning that legal advisers should reconsider the merits of the application once they have received the respondent's evidence. They should also note:

10–017

(1) that it should not be regarded as unnecessary to write a letter before action merely because a denial of the client's claim was felt to be inevitable;

(2) judicial review proceedings are wholly inappropriate for the resolution of issues of disputed facts; and

(3) all material matters must be placed before the judge from whom leave is being sought.[60]

The Court of Appeal has indicated that in future any delay which occurs will be assessed not only from the point of view of the prejudice caused to

---

[57] *S. v M. (Wasted Costs Order)*, *The Times* (1998), March 26, Pumfrey J.
[58] *White v White* [2003] EWCA Civ 20 January.
[59] *Re a Barrister (Wasted Costs Order) (No.4 of 1992)*, *The Times*, March 15, 1994, CA.
[60] *R. v Horsham District Council, ex p. Newman* [1991] 1 All E.R. 681, Brooke J. and see *R. v Lambeth LBC Ex p. Wilson*, *The Times*, March 25, 1997, CA.

the particular litigants whose case it is but also in relation to other litigants and the prejudice which is caused to the due administration of justice. The change in culture which is already taking place will enable courts to recognise for the future more readily than before that a wholesale disregard of the rules is an abuse of process which is a ground for striking out or staying an action, which does not depend on the need to show prejudice to the defendant or that a fair trial is no longer possible.[61] "Unless" orders are to be treated as one step away from the dismissal of the action in order to ensure that court orders are obeyed. Where the solicitor's default prejudices the client the solicitor is under a duty to ensure that the client is advised by fresh solicitors at the earliest opportunity. The person who suffers because the action is dismissed is not the claimant's solicitor but the claimant personally, therefore it could be said that the judge is visiting the sins of the solicitor on the client and should not let the desire to discipline the solicitor injure the claimant personally.[62]

Where proceedings before the Restrictive Practices Court had to be abandoned by reason of the appearance of bias by a member of the court, an application was made for payment of the wasted costs by the Lord Chancellor who was the emanation of the State responsible for providing impartial tribunals to conduct trials of civil litigation and that there had been a breach of Article 6 of the European Convention on Human Rights. The Court of Appeal held there had been no breach of the article because the situation had been remedied by providing an impartial tribunal. The applicant was unable to show any authority for the contention that the Lord Chancellor should have to pay the wasted legal costs as compensation.[63]

Where proceedings are compromised and a Tomlin Order made, the proceedings remain in existence and the Judge has jurisdiction to make a wasted costs order. The provisions of section 51(6) of the Supreme Court Act 1981 do not require the application to be made during the currency of the proceedings since the words "in any proceedings" mean "in connection with" or "in relation to".[64]

Wasted costs in cases concerning children

10–018   The Court of Appeal has set out a recommended course to be adopted at the conclusion of appeals relating to children.

1.   The successful unassisted party should consider whether there were circumstances justifying seeking:

---

[61] *Arbuthnot Latham Bank Ltd v Trafalgar Holdings Ltd; Christity Coveney & Co. v Raja, The Times,* December 29, 1997, CA.
[62] *Lownes v Babcock Power Ltd, The Times,* February 19, 1998, CA.
[63] *Re Medicaments and Related Classes of Goods (No.4), The Times,* August 7, CA.
[64] *Wagstaff v Colls* [2003] EWCA Civ 469.

(a) an order for costs against the assisted party if that party was not legally aided; or

(b) a wasted costs order against the party's legal representatives.

If the circumstances did not exist no further action was required.

2. If circumstances could justify (a) above, such an application should be made.

3. If it were appropriate to apply for (b) above, that application should be made.

4. If the court considered either of its own motion or because of the application that it appeared to be so clear a case for making a wasted costs order, that it would not be just and equitable to make an order nisi against the LSC, the court should adjourn the application against the LSC and proceed to take the steps necessary to establish that a wasted costs order were necessary.

  If the court made that order in relation to all relevant costs, there should ordinarily be no reason to proceed further with the application against the LSC.

5. If the application against the LSC was not adjourned:

(a) The court should ascertain whether the requirements of section 18 of the Legal Aid Act 1988 (Now Section of the Access to Justice Act 1999) were met, and if so, make any order against the assisted party which was appropriate and, if justified, an order nisi against the LSC

  In addition, if the court considered that there was a real possibility that a wasted costs order would be made, it should direct that that should be drawn to the LSC's attention.

(b) The lawyers representing the funded litigant should regard it as their responsibility to draw to the court's attention any matters relevant in determining whether the requirements of section 18 (section 11) had been met.

(c) If the LSC decided to object to an order, it could raise, as part of the objection, any contention it wished to pursue, that a liability for costs, for which it might otherwise be responsible, should be met by a wasted costs order, and that could be considered as part of the objection to the order for costs against the LSC.

6. If an application against the LSC was adjourned pending investigation of an application for a wasted costs order, and no such order was made, the application against the LSC should be restored and determined.[65]

---

[65] *Re O. (A Minor) (Costs: Liability of Legal Aid Board, The Times,* November 25, 1996, CA.

Different considerations arise in non-adversarial care proceedings when contrasted with litigation, and the court has a special role in initiating wasted costs enquiries in such proceedings should this be necessary, *e.g.* where legal representatives failed to arrange for expert witnesses to have access to all relevant documents in breach of the guidance given by Family Division Practice Directions.[66]

B. SANCTIONS AND THE COURT'S CASE MANAGEMENT POWERS

10–019 The overriding objective requires the court to deal with cases justly in accordance with CPR Part 1, and the parties are required to help the court to further the objective.[67] The Rules set out some of the factors in active case management.[68] The court's general powers of management include the power to make an order subject to conditions, including a condition to pay a sum of money into court. The court may also specify the consequence of failure to comply with the order of condition.[69]

A number of rules impose requirements, breach of which may result in a sanction, or the court may impose a sanction (usually as to costs).[70]

Relief from sanctions

10–020 Any sanction for failure to comply with the rule, practice direction or court order will take effect unless the party in default applies for and obtains relief from the sanction.[71] Where the sanction is the payment of costs, relief may only be obtained by appealing the order for costs.[72] Where a rule, practice direction, or court order specifies a time within which a party must do something and also specifies the consequences of failure to comply, the parties may not by agreement between themselves extend the time for doing that act.[73] In deciding whether or not to grant relief from any sanction the court is required to consider all the circumstances including:

    (a) the interests of the administration of justice;

    (b) whether the application for relief has been made promptly;

---

[66] *(Children) (G Care Proceedings: Wasted Costs)* [2000] 2 W.L.R. 1007; [1999] 4 All E.R. 371, Wall J.
[67] CPR rr.1.1–1.3.
[68] CPR r.1.4.
[69] CPR r.3.1.
[70] *e.g.* CPR r.3.7, sanction for non-payment of fees.
[71] CPR r.3.8(1).
[72] CPR r.3.8(2).
[73] CPR r.3.8(3).

(c) whether the failure to comply was intentional;

(d) whether there is a good explanation for the failure;

(e) the extent to which the party in default has complied with other rules, practice directions and court orders and any relevant pre-action protocol;

(f) whether the failure to comply was caused by the party or his legal representative;

(g) whether the trial date or the likely trial date can still be met if relief is granted;

(h) the effect which the failure to comply had on each party; and

(i) the effect which the granting of relief would have on each party.[74]

The Court's power to rectify errors

Where there has been an error of procedure, such as a failure to comply with the rule or practice direction, the error will not invalidate any step taken in the proceedings unless the court so orders and the court may make an order to remedy the error.[75]

10–021

The court may at any time correct an accidental slip or omission in a judgment or order. A party may apply for a correction without notice. The court has inherent power to vary its own orders to make its meaning and intention clear.[76]

C. INHERENT JURISDICTION

The Court of Appeal has held that the inherent jurisdiction of the court should only be invoked to avoid a clear injustice.[77] But where the legislature has stepped in with particular legislation in a particular area, then within that particular area the existing (inherent) jurisdiction is ousted or curtailed, at any rate insofar as the particular legislation is negative in character.[78] Given the extent of the statutory wasted costs provisions, it is unlikely that

10–022

---

[74] CPR r.3.9(1) and see *Woodhouse v Consignia Plc* [2002] EWCA Civ 275; [2002] 1 W.L.R. 2558, CA; *R.C. Residuals v Linton Fuel Oils Ltd* [2002] EWCA Civ 911; 2002 1 W.L.R. 2782, CA.
[75] CPR r.3.10.
[76] CPR r.40.12(1) and (2) and the Practice Direction Supplementing Part 40 (Judgments and Orders) paras 4.1–4.5.
[77] *Symbol Park Lane Ltd v Steggles Palmer* [1985] 1 W.L.R. 668.
[78] *Shiloh Spinners Ltd v Harding* [1973] A.C. 691; *Harrison v Tew* [1989] Q.B. 307, HL.

the inherent jurisdiction of the court will be relied upon save in the rarest of circumstances.

Where the court was persuaded that a solicitor had not acted negligently in continuing to act for a company which had been struck off the register, nonetheless the court was able to make an award of costs against the solicitor under its inherent jurisdiction on the basis that the solicitor had been acting without authority. The award was however reduced on the basis that the defendants were clearly in a position to know the status of the company.[79]

D. LSC FUNDED CASES AND LEGAL AID

10–023   Without prejudice to the wasted costs jurisdiction under section 51(6) of the Supreme Court Act 1981, or to the powers under the CPR, on any assessment of an assisted person's costs in connection with proceedings,[80] any wasted costs must be disallowed or reduced, and where a solicitor has without good reason delayed putting in his bill for detailed assessment, the whole of the costs may be disallowed or reduced.[81] No reduction or disallowance of costs may be made until notice has been served by the costs officer on the solicitor whose name appears on the assisted person's certificate, and in a case where the wasted costs relate to counsel's fees, on the assisted person's counsel, requiring the solicitor or counsel to show cause orally, or in writing, why those costs should not be disallowed or reduced.[82]

The court has power, under its inherent jurisdiction, to order a solicitor to repay personally to the LSC fund costs which have been incurred by a funded client as the result of a serious dereliction of duty on the part of the solicitor, but the court will not exercise that power if the Legal Services Commission is dilatory in seeking an order that the solicitor pay the cost personally.[83]

Where an issue is to be taken as to the costs of any proceedings, it is essential that it should follow swiftly upon the event. Notice should be given of an application as soon as possible and in the normal course of events that should be at the conclusion of the substantive hearing or very shortly afterwards. There may be exceptional circumstances where for good reason notice of an application in relation to costs is not, or cannot be made at the end of a hearing and some delay is inevitable.[84]

---

[79] *Padhiar v Patel*, [2001] Lloyd's Rep. P.N. 328, Miss H. Heilbron Q.C.
[80] Other than authorised summary proceedings.
[81] Civil Legal Aid (General) Regulation 1989, reg.109(1).
[82] *ibid.*, reg.109(2).
[83] *Clark v Clark (No.2)* [1991] 1 F.L.R. 179.
[84] *Clark v Clark*, above.

Slow action by the LSC and delay in obtaining counsel's written opinion that contributed to the tardy prosecution of a case has been held to entitle solicitors to have set aside an order that they personally were liable for wasted costs.[85] It has also been held that a solicitor's failure to warn, either the court or his opponent, in sufficient time, that because of his difficulties with the LSC he might have to seek at a late stage an adjournment of the hearing, was an error of judgment on his part but did not warrant the making of a wasted costs order against him personally.[86]

E. THE LAW SOCIETY'S POWERS IN RESPECT OF INADEQUATE PROFESSIONAL SERVICES

Where it appears to the Council of the Law Society, that the professional services provided by a solicitor in connection with any matter in which he or his firm have been instructed by a client, have in any respect not been of the quality that it is reasonable to expect of him as a solicitor, the Council may take a number of steps if they are satisfied that in all the circumstances of the case it is appropriate to do so.[87]

10–024

In determining whether or not it is appropriate to take any such step, the Council may have regard to the existence of any remedy, which it is reasonable to expect to be available to the client in civil proceedings, and where such proceedings have not been begun by him, to have regard to whether it is reasonable to expect him to begin them.[88] The power of the Council to take steps is not confined to cases where the client may have a cause of action against the solicitor for negligence.[89]

The steps which may be taken are:

(a) determining that the cost to which the solicitor is entitled in respect of his services, is to be limited to such amount as may be specified in the determination and directing him to comply with any requirements imposed by the Council in order for effect to be given to their determination;

(b) directing him to secure the rectification, at his expense or that of his firm, of any error, omission or other deficiency arising in connection with the matter in question as they may specify;

---

[85] *Trill v Sacher (No.2), The Times,* November 14, 1992. See also *R & T Thew Ltd v Reeves (No.2)* [1981] 3 W.L.R. 190 (and in the Court of Appeal [1982] Q.B. 1283); *Davy-Chiesman v Davy-Chiesman* [1984] Fam. 48.
[86] *Re a Solicitor (Wasted Costs Order), The Times,* April 16, 1993, CA.
[87] Solicitors Act 1974, Sched.1A, paras. 1 and 2.
[88] *ibid.,* Sch.1A, para.1(3).
[89] *ibid.,* Sch.1A, para.2(3).

    (c) directing him to pay such compensation to the client as they see fit to specify;

    (d) directing him to take, at his expense or that of his firm, such other action in the interests of the client as they may specify.[90]

If the Council directs compensation to be paid by the solicitor the amount awarded may not exceed £5,000.[91]

The requirements which the Council may impose are:

    (a) that the whole or part of any amount already paid by or on behalf of the client in respect of the costs be refunded;

    (b) that the whole or part of the costs be remitted;

    (c) that the right to recover the costs be waived whether wholly or to any specified extent.[92]

Where the Council has given a direction limiting the amount of costs to which the solicitor is entitled in respect of his services then for the purposes of any detailed assessment of a bill covering the costs, the amount charged by the bill in respect of them is deemed to be limited to the amount specified in the determination. Where a bill covering the costs has not been assessed, the client is[93] deemed to be liable to pay only the amount specified in the determination. Where the bill covering the costs has been assessed the Council's direction, so far as it relates to the costs, ceases to have effect.[94]

Where the Council takes any of the steps described above they may also direct the solicitor to pay to the Council the amount of any fee repayable by the Council to the client and an amount calculated by the Council as the cost to them of dealing with the complaint or which, in their opinion, represents a reasonable contribution towards that cost.[95]

Restriction on requiring security for the costs

10–025   No person, other than an appellant who was the applicant in proceedings relating to solicitors, under the Solicitor's Act 1974 before the Solicitor's Disciplinary Tribunal, may be ordered to give security for the costs of an appeal to the Divisional Court.[96]

---

[90] *ibid.*, Sch.1A, para.2(1).
[91] Solicitors Act 1974, Sch.1A, para.3, as amended by the Solicitors (Compensation for Inadequate Professional Services) Order 2000 (SI 2000/644).
[92] *ibid.*, Sch.1A, para.2(2).
[93] *ibid.*, Sch.1A, para.4(1).
[94] *ibid.*, Sch.1A, para.4(2).
[95] *ibid.*, Sch.1A, para.7.
[96] CPR, Sch.1; RSC, Ord.106, rr.11 and 14.

PART VII

Particular Matters

CHAPTER 11

Court of Protection, Arbitration and Other Tribunals

A. COURT OF PROTECTION

Costs in relation to proceedings under the Court of Protection Rules 2002 **11–001**
(and not provided by way of remuneration[1]) are in the discretion of the
court which may order or direct them to be paid by the patient or charged
on or paid out of his estate by any other person attending or taking part in
the proceedings. Such an order or direction is enforceable in the same way
as an order as to costs made in the High Court. An order or direction that
costs incurred during the lifetime of a patient be paid out of or charged on
his estate may be made within six years after his death.[2]

CPR Parts 43, 44, 47 and 48 apply, with certain modifications, to costs
incurred in relation to proceedings under the Court of Protection Rules as
they apply to costs incurred in relation to proceedings in the high Court.
The modifications unable a Judge or the Master of the Court of Protection
to deal with relevant matters as to costs. CPR 4.3(2) (costs follow the event)
does not apply. The provisions of CPR 44.9–44.12 relating to costs on the
small claim and fast track and on track allocation or re-allocation do not
apply. Similarly CPR 48.1–48.3 (costs payable by or to particular persons)
and CPR 48.7–48.10 (costs relating to solicitors and other representatives)
do not apply. The provisions in CPR 44.7(a) relating to summary assessment do not apply where the patient is a paying party and the provisions of
CPR 47.9(4), 47.10 and 47.11 relating to default costs certificates do not

---

[1] Under r.43 of the Court Protection Rules 2001.
[2] Court Protection Rules 2001, r.84. In relation to applications under s.36(9) or s.54 of the
Trustee Act 1925 the court may make any such order as to costs as the High Court could
make under s.60 of the Trustee Act in relation to any matter referred to in that
section—*ibid.*, r.85.

apply where the patient is the paying party. Where the court orders costs to be assessed by detailed assessment, the detailed assessment proceedings must take place in the High Court.[3]

No receiver for a patient, other that the Official Solicitor, is entitled, at the expense of the patient's estate, to employ a solicitor or other professional person to do any work not usually requiring professional assistance unless authorised by the court. Where two or more persons, having the same interest in relation to the matter to be determined, attend any hearing by separate legal representatives, only one set of costs will be allowed for the hearing unless the court is satisfied that the circumstances justify separate representation.[4]

Any costs incurred by the Official Solicitor in relation to proceedings under the Court of Protection Rules or in carrying out any directions given by the court, not provided for by remuneration under CPR r.43, must be paid by such person on or out of such funds as the court may direct.[5] Where, in any proceedings relating to a patient, a claim is made against his estate in respect of any costs alleged to have been incurred by him, otherwise than in relation to proceedings, the court may refer the claim to a Costs Judge so that the amount due to the claimant may be ascertained.[6]

Remuneration of receiver

11–002   Where a receiver is appointed for a patient under the Court of Protection Rules or where the court directs and names a person to deal with a patient's property or affairs, the court may, during the receivership or the period for which the order remains in force, allow, the receiver or named person, remuneration for those services at such moment or at such rate as it considers reasonable and proper, and any such remuneration constitutes a debt due to the receiver or named person from the patient and his estate.[7] Unless the court has, during the receivership or the period of the order, directed that remuneration be allowed, no request by a receiver or named person to have the sum payable for this remuneration fixed after the death or recovery of the patient will be entertained. The request must in any event be made within the six years from the date of the receiver's discharge or the date on which the order ceases to have effect.[8]

---

[3] Court Protection Rules 2001, r.86.
[4] *ibid.*, r.87.
[5] *ibid.*, r.88.
[6] *ibid.*, r.89.
[7] Court of Protection Rules 2001, r.43(1).
[8] *ibid.*, r.43(2).

B. ARBITRATION ACT 1996

Unless the parties agree otherwise the tribunal will award costs on the **11–003** general principle that costs should follow the event except where it appears to the tribunal to be inappropriate in relation to all or part of the costs.[9]

The parties are free to agree what costs of the arbitration are recoverable.[10] The tribunal may make an award allocating the costs of the arbitration as between the parties, subject to any such agreement.[11] If there is no such agreement the tribunal may determine by award the recoverable costs of the arbitration on such basis as it thinks fit. If it does so it must specify, the basis on which it has acted and the items of recoverable costs and the amount referable to each.[12] The tribunal must award the costs on the general principle that costs should follow the event, except where it appears to the tribunal that in the circumstances this is not appropriate in relation to the whole or part of the costs.[13]

Unless the parties agree otherwise, any obligation under an agreement between them as to how the costs of the arbitration are to be borne, or under an award allocating the costs of the arbitration, extends only to such costs as are recoverable.[14] An agreement which has the effect that a party is to pay the whole or part of the costs of the arbitration in any event is only valid if made after the dispute in question has arisen.[15]

Where the tribunal does not determine the recoverable costs, any party to the arbitral proceedings may apply to the court, which may determine the costs on such basis as it thinks fit, or order that they shall be determined by such means and upon such terms as it may specify.[16] Unless the tribunal or the court determines otherwise the recoverable costs will be determined on the basis that there should be allowed a reasonable amount in respect of all costs reasonably incurred and any doubt as to whether costs were reasonably incurred or were reasonable in amount must be resolved in favour of the paying party.[17] This is the same as the standard basis under RSC, Ord. 62, r.12(1), but different from the standard basis under CPR, Part 44.4, *i.e.* there is no test of proportionality. Where an arbitrator employed a draftsman to help draft an arbitral award the legal fees incurred in drafting the award were reduced significantly on the grounds of proportionality where the services of a lay draftsman rather than a lawyer would have sufficed in what was a relatively straightforward dispute. In the particular

---

[9] Arbitration Act 1996, s.61(2).
[10] *ibid.*, s.63(1).
[11] *ibid.*, s.61(1).
[12] *ibid.*, s.63(2) and (3).
[13] *ibid.*, s.61(2).
[14] *ibid.*, s.62.
[15] *ibid.*, s.60.
[16] *ibid.*, s.63(4).
[17] *ibid.*, s.63(5).

case the draftsman had not been employed as a legal adviser, there was no reason for him to have attended the hearing and accordingly the time spent by him was grossly excessive and could not be justified given his limited function.[18]

Recoverable fees and expenses of arbitrators

11-004   The recoverable fees and expenses of arbitrators are only those which are reasonable and appropriate in the circumstances.[19] If a question arises as to what reasonable fees and expenses are appropriate in the circumstances, the court may, on application by any party, determine the matter, or order that it be determined by such means and upon such terms as it may specify.[20] These provisions apply subject to any order of the court in relation to entitlement to fees and expenses where the arbitrator has been removed or has resigned.[21]

Tribunal's power to limit recoverable costs

11-005   In dealing with an arbitration the tribunal is under a general duty to act fairly and impartially between the parties, giving each a reasonable opportunity of putting its case and dealing with that of the opponent. The tribunal is also under a duty to adopt procedures suitable to the circumstances of a particular case, avoiding unnecessary delay or expense so as to provide a fair means for the resolution of the matters falling to be decided.[22] Unless the parties agree otherwise the tribunal may direct that the recoverable costs of the arbitration, or any part of the proceedings, shall be limited to a specified amount.[23] Such a direction may be made or varied at any stage, but it must be done sufficiently in advance of the incurring of costs to which it relates, or the taking of any steps in the proceedings which might be affected by it, for the limit to be taken into account.[24]

Where an arbitrator made a final award in favour of the applicants on some issues and in favour of the respondent on others and ordered the applicants to pay the respondent's costs, and in giving reasons for his costs order, relied on two matters which had not been raised by the parties, it was held that the arbitrator's power to award costs[25] was subject to the general duty to act fairly and impartially. The court held that the arbitrator should

---

[18] *Agrimex Ltd v Tradigrain SA* [2003] EWHC (Com) July 9, Thomas J.
[19] Arbitration Act 1996, s.64(1).
[20] *ibid.*, s.64(2).
[21] See s.24(4) and 25(3)(b): *ibid.*, s.64(3).
[22] *ibid.*, s.33(1).
[23] *ibid.*, s.65(1).
[24] *ibid.*, s.65(2).
[25] Under s.61 of the Arbitration Act 1996.

have brought the matters upon which he relied to the attention of the parties to enable them to deal with them. Failure to do so amounted to a serious irregularity.[26]

An award of costs made by an arbitrator as a result of a mathematical error by the arbitrator in the calculation of the value of a previous calderbank offer was a "procedural mishap" and the court had power to remit the matter for correction by the arbitrator even though the arbitration agreement governing the conduct of the proceedings excluded all rights of appeal. Since "substantial injustice" was apparent the power to remit was exercised.[27]

Applications to the Court

The Act requires applications to be made in relation to legal proceedings "upon notice" to the other parties to the arbitral proceedings. This means that such notice of the originating process as is required by Rules of Court must be given, and where a particular period is specified, the Rules of Court relating to the reckoning of time will apply.[28]   **11–006**

The Act provides that provision may be made by Rules of Court amending Part 1 of the Act with respect to the time within which any application or appeal must be made; so as to keep any provision made by the Act, in relation to arbitral proceedings, in step with the corresponding provision of the Rules of Court applying in relation to proceedings in the Court; or so as to keep any provision made in relation to legal proceedings, in step with the corresponding provisions of Rules of Court applying generally in relation to proceedings in the court.[29]

Charging orders in respect of solicitors' costs

The powers of the court to make declarations and orders charging property recovered in proceedings with the payment of solicitors' costs[30] may be exercised in relation to arbitral proceedings as if those proceedings were proceedings in court.[31]   **11–007**

Security for costs in arbitration appeals

The Arbitration Act 1996 makes provision for a party to arbitral proceedings to challenge the award of the arbitral tribunal as to its substantive   **11–008**

---

[26] Within s.63(2)(a) of the 1996 Act: *Gbangbola v Smith & Sherriff* (1998) 3 All E.R. 730, H. H. Judge Humphrey Lloyd Q.C.
[27] *Danae Air Transport SA v Air Canada, The Times*, August 5, 1999, CA.
[28] Arbitration Act 1996, s.80(1)–(5) and see CPR Part 62.
[29] *ibid.*, s.80 sub-section 6.
[30] Under s.73 of the Solicitors Act 1974.
[31] Arbitration Act 1996, s.75.

jurisdiction or on the ground of serious irregularity affecting the tribunal, the proceedings or the award, or to appeal on a point of law.[32] The court dealing with the application or appeal may order the applicant or appellant to provide security for costs of the application or appeal and may direct that the application or appeal be dismissed if the order is not complied with. The power to order security for costs will not be exercised on the ground that the applicant or appellant is: an individual or ordinarily resident outside the United Kingdom; or a corporation or association incorporated or formed under the law of a country outside the United Kingdom or whose central management and control is exercised outside the United Kingdom.[33] The court may order that any money payable under the award shall be brought into court or otherwise secured pending the determination of the application or appeal and may direct that the application or appeal be dismissed if the order is not complied with.[34]

The object of arbitration is to obtain the fair resolution of disputes by an impartial tribunal without unnecessary delay or expense.[35] Bearing that in mind it would be a rare case in which a court would order security if an applicant had sufficient assets to meet any order for costs and those assets were available to satisfy any such order. Where the evidence showed that the assets were not sufficiently available for the purpose of enforcing an English costs order it was appropriate to make an order for security for costs.[36] The court has jurisdiction to grant an order for security for costs in favour of a party challenging the enforcement of a foreign arbitration award. The party seeking enforcement of the award was to be treated by the court as the applicant and accordingly liable to an order for security. The paying party was to be regarded as challenging the enforcement of the award rather than the award itself and so fell to be treated as a defendant with the consequence that the court had the jurisdiction to grant security.[37]

C. INSOLVENCY

11–009   Following the passing of the Civil Procedure Rules, the Insolvency Rules 1986 have been amended[38] to make them compatible. Chapter 6 of the 1986 Rules dealing with costs and detailed assessment has been entirely replaced. CPR, Parts 43 (Scope of Costs Rules and Definitions), 44 (General

---

[32] Arbitration Act 1996, ss.67, 68 and 69.
[33] Arbitration Act 1996, s.70(6).
[34] *ibid.*, s.70(7).
[35] Arbitration Act 1966, s.1(a).
[36] *Azov Shipping Co v Baltic Shipping Co. (No.2)* [1999] 1 All E.R. 716, Longmore J.
[37] *Dardana Ltd v Yukos Oil Co (No.2)* [2002] *The Times*, February 4, H.H. Judge Chambers Q.C.
[38] By the *Insolvency (Amendment) (No.2) Rules 1999.* (SI 1999 No. 1022).

Rules About Costs), 45 (Fixed Costs), 47 (Procedure for Detailed Assessment of Costs and Default Provisions) and 48 (Costs—Special Cases) are applied to insolvency proceedings with any necessary modifications.[39] All insolvency proceedings will be allocated to the multi track.[40]

The limitation period in respect of an order for costs begins to run when the order becomes enforceable by action which is at the date of certification, not on the date the costs order was made.[41]

Where it is sought to enforce an order for summarily assessed costs by invoking the bankruptcy regime the policy considerations of the CPR favouring summary assessment of costs and their early recovery has to be weighed against the operation of a bankruptcy regime including the fact the court could set aside a statutory demand whether the debtor appeared to have a counterclaim set off or cross demand. The court ordered the application to set aside would be adjourned until after judgment in the substantive proceedings and ordered that no bankruptcy proceedings should be commenced in the meantime.[42–43]

Winding-up petition

The general costs principle applicable when a creditor is entitled to more than the statutory minimum, the debt is due and it is decided to be so either by concession or by the court, is that the creditor is entitled to payment of his costs by the debtor. This applies also to costs of applications connected with the petition unless there are good reasons to the contrary.   **11–010**

Requirement for detailed assessment

Unless there is an agreement between the responsible insolvency practitioner and the person entitled to payment of costs, the amount of any costs payable out of the insolvent estate must be decided by detailed assessment. In such a case the responsible insolvency practitioner may serve notice on the receiving party requiring that person to commence detailed assessment proceedings in the court to which the insolvency proceedings are allocated,   **11–011**

---

[39] Insolvency Rules 1986, r.7.33.
[40] In accordance with CPR, Part 29: Insolvency Rules 1986, r.7.51(2). As to the principles to be considered when setting aside a statutory demand: *Bayoil SA* [1999] 1 W.L.R. 147. Provided the judge properly directs himself upon the matters to be considered costs are always discretionary: *Re: A Debtor (No.87 of 1999)*, January 17, 2000, Rimmer J. (unreported), as to setting aside statutory demands in relation to costs in family proceedings see *Levy v Legal Aid Board*, February 4, 2000, Evans-Lombe J. (unreported).
[41] (*Times Newspapers Ltd v Chohan* [2001] *The Times*, August 1.)
[42–43] *Cohen v TSB Bank Plc* [2001] EWHC, Ch D, November 29, Etherton J.

or in the case of a company where there is no such court, in the court having jurisdiction to wind up the company.[44]

If detailed assessment is required by a liquidation or creditors, committee in insolvency proceedings (except administrative receivership), the insolvency practitioner must require detailed assessment in accordance with CPR, Part 47.[45] The insolvency practitioner may make payments on account to any person employed in insolvency proceedings notwithstanding that the costs have to be decided by detailed assessment. In those circumstances the person to whom payment is made must give an undertaking to pay, immediately, any money which may prove to have been overpaid when detailed assessment takes place, together with interest at the rate specified in section 17 of the Judgments Act 1838 for the period from payment to repayment.[46]

The court may order costs to be decided by detailed assessment in any proceedings before the court including proceedings on a petition. Unless the court directs otherwise the costs of a trustee in bankruptcy or a liquidator are to be allowed on the standard basis and these provisions also apply to winding up and bankruptcy proceedings commenced before the coming into force of the Insolvency Rules 1986.[47]

Procedure

11–012 Before the costs officer makes a detailed assessment of the costs of any person employed in insolvency proceedings by a responsible insolvency practitioner, the officer will require a certificate of employment which must be endorsed on the bill and signed by the insolvency practitioner. The certificate must set out the name and address of the person employed, details of the functions to be carried out under the employment and the note of any special terms of remuneration which have been agreed.[48]

The detailed assessment proceedings are commenced in accordance with CPR, Part 47.[49] If proceedings for detailed assessment are not commenced within three months of the requirement, the insolvency practitioner may deal with the insolvent estate without regard to any claim by that person whose claim is forfeited by the failure to commence proceedings.[50]

---

[44] Insolvency Rules 1986, r.7.34(1).
[45] *ibid.*, r.7.34(2).
[46] *ibid.*, r.7.34(3).
[47] *ibid.*, r.7.34(4)(5) and (6).
[48] *ibid.*, r.7.35(1) and (2).
[49] See CPR 47.6.
[50] Insolvency Rules 1986, r.7.35(3), (4), (5).

Petitions presented by insolvents

Any solicitor acting for a company or individual who has presented a **11–013** petition against himself, must give credit in the bill of costs for any sum or security received from the insolvent as a deposit on account of the costs and expenses to be incurred in the petition. The deposit must be noted by the costs officer on the final costs certificate.[51]

Where a petition is presented by a person other than the insolvent to whom the petition relates, and before it is heard the insolvent presents a petition which results in an order, then, unless the court considers that the insolvent estate has benefited from the insolvent's conduct, or there are special circumstances, no costs will be allowed to the insolvent or his solicitor out of the insolvent estate.[52]

Costs paid otherwise than out of the insolvent estate

Where the court directs that costs are to be paid otherwise than out of the **11–014** insolvent estate, the costs officer must, after the detailed assessment, note on the final costs certificate by whom or the manner in which the costs are to be paid.[53] Where petitioning creditors agreed a compromise with the debtor after the appointment of the trustee in bankruptcy and agreed to the setting aside of the statutory demand and to the annulment of the bankruptcy, the court ordered both the creditors and the debtor to be jointly liable for the trustee's costs. This was on the basis that it was the least unjust way of dealing with the matter since both parties were legally aided.[54]

Award of costs against official receiver or responsible insolvency practitioner

Where the Official Receiver or responsible insolvency practitioner is made a **11–015** party to any proceedings on the application of another party, he will not be personally liable for costs unless the court otherwise directs.[55]

Applications for costs

Where a party to or person affected by proceedings in insolvency applies to **11–016** the court for an order for costs incidental to the proceedings, and the

---

[51] *ibid.*, r.3.37(1).
[52] *ibid.*, r.7.37(2) and (3).
[53] *ibid.*, 1986, r.7.38.
[54] *Butterworth v Soutter* February 8, 2000, Neuberger J. (unreported).
[55] Insolvency Rules 1986, r.7.39.

application is not made at the time of the proceedings, the applicant must serve a sealed copy of the application on the responsible insolvency practitioner, and, in winding-up by the court or bankruptcy, on the Official Receiver who may appear on the application. No costs of the application will be allowed to the applicant unless the court is satisfied that the application could not have been made at the time of the proceedings.[56]

Costs and expenses of witnesses

11–017   No allowance will be made to the bankrupt or an officer of the insolvent company for attending as a witness in any examination or proceedings before the court unless the court so directs. The person presenting a petition in insolvency proceedings is not regarded as a witness on the hearing of the petition but the costs officer may allow travelling expenses and subsistence.[57]

Final costs certificate

11–018   A final costs certificate is final and conclusive as to all matters which have not been objected to in the manner provided for under the rules of court. Where a final costs certificate has been lost or destroyed the costs officer may issue a duplicate.[58]

D. EMPLOYMENT APPEAL TRIBUNAL

11–019   Where it appears to the Appeal Tribunal that any proceedings were unnecessary, improper or vexatious or that there has been unreasonable delay or other unreasonable conduct in bringing or conducting proceedings, the Tribunal may order the party at fault to pay any other party, the whole or such part as it thinks fit of the costs or expenses incurred by that other party in connection with the proceedings. When such an order is made the Appeal Tribunal may assess the sum to be paid or may direct that it be assessed by the Costs Officer from whose decision an appeal lies to a Judge.[59]

The rules governing appeals from the Registrar apply to an appeal in respect of costs or expenses.[60]

---

[56] *ibid.*, r.7.40.
[57] *ibid.*, r.7.41.
[58] *ibid.*, r.7.42.
[59] Employment Appeals Tribunal Rules 1993, r.34(1) and (2). A "cost officer" means any officer of the Appeal Tribunal authorised by the President to assess costs or expenses.
[60] *ibid.*, r.34(3) and se *ibid.*, rr.21 and 22.

The costs of an assisted person will be taxed or assessed in accordance with Regulation 149(7) of the Civil Legal Aid (General) Regulations 1989.[61]

To order costs in the Tribunal is an exceptional course of action and the reason for, and the basis of an order should be specified clearly especially when a substantial sum is involved.[62]

On a complaint of racial discrimination the claimant was successful and the Tribunal rejected the respondent's claim for an award of costs based on the applicant's amended claim for compensation. The Employment Appeal Tribunal found that the decision not to award costs could not be said to be perverse and awarded the applicant the costs of the appeal. The court observed, in considering the award the applicant the costs of the appeal. The court observed, in considering the award of costs on appeal, that the fact that a case had been allowed through at a preliminary hearing was not a bar to arguing that the appeal was "unnecessary".[63]

E. COMPETITION APPEAL TRIBUNAL

The Tribunal may, at any stage of proceedings, make any order it thinks fit **11–020** in relation to payment of costs by one party to another in respect of the whole or part of the proceedings. In determining how much the party is required to pay, the Tribunal may take into account the conduct of all the parties in relation to the proceedings. In this context "costs" means costs and expenses recoverable before the Supreme Court of England and Wales, the Court of Session or the Supreme Court of Northern Ireland. The Tribunal may assess the sum to be paid or may direct that it be assessed by the President, a Chairman or the Registrar or dealt with by the detailed assessment of a Costs Officer of the Supreme Court or a Taxing Officer of the Supreme Court of Northern Ireland or by the Auditor of the Court of Session. The power to award costs includes the power to direct any party to pay the Tribunal, such sum as may be appropriate, in reimbursement of any costs incurred by the Tribunal in connection with the summoning or citation of witnesses or the instruction of experts on the Tribunal's behalf. Any sum due as a result of such a direction may be recovered by the Tribunal as a civil debt due to the Tribunal.[64] The rules as to funding arrangements, made under the Civil Procedure Rules 1998 as amended, apply to proceedings before the Tribunal.[65]

---

[61] *ibid.*, r.34(4).
[62] *Lodwock v Southwark LBC* [2004] *The Times*, April 9, CA.
[63] *Tesco Stores Ltd & Anor v Wilson*, January 12, 2000, H.H. Judge Peter Clark EAT.
[64] Competition Appeal Tribunal Rules 2003, SI 2003/1372, r.55.
[65] *ibid.*, r.65.

F. THE LANDS TRIBUNAL

Orders for costs

11–021   Costs of and incidental to any proceedings before the Lands Tribunal are in the discretion of the tribunal.[66]

Where the simplified procedure is utilised[67] no award may be made in relation to the costs of the proceedings.[68] The tribunal may make an award of costs in cases where an offer of settlement has been made by a party, and the tribunal considers it appropriate to have regard to the fact that the offer has been made; or in cases where the tribunal regards the circumstances as exceptional. Where an award of costs is made in such circumstances, the amount must not exceed that which would have been allowed if the proceedings had been heard in a county court.[69]

The registrar may make an order as to costs in respect of any application or proceedings heard by him.[70] In respect of any application relating to costs, the registrar may refer the application to the President for a decision, and must do so if requested by the applicant or a party objecting to the application.[71] A person dissatisfied with the order of the registrar may within 10 days of the order appeal to the President who may make such order as to the payment of costs, including the costs of the appeal, as he thinks fit.[72] An appeal to the President does not act as a stay of proceedings unless the President so orders.[73]

Interest on an award by the Lands Tribunal runs from the date of the award.[74] In deciding which is the correct date of the award it is necessary to ascertain the date of the final effective award.[75]

Fees

11–022   A solicitor who is on the record of the tribunal as acting for a party is responsible for the payment of all the fees of the tribunal, which are the responsibility of that party whilst he remains on the record.[76]

---

[66] Subject to the provisions of s.4 of the Land Compensation Act 1961: r.52(1), Lands Tribunal Rules 1996.
[67] Pursuant to r.28, Lands Tribunal Rules 1996.
[68] Save in cases to which s.4 of the Land Compensation Act 1961 applies.
[69] Rule 28(11), of the Lands Tribunal Rules 1996.
[70] *ibid.*, s.52(2).
[71] *ibid.*, r.38(8).
[72] *ibid.*, r.52(3).
[73] *ibid.*, r.38(10).
[74] S.20 of the Arbitration Act 1950 and Lands Tribunal Rules 1975, r.38.
[75] *Barclays Bank Plc v Kent CC* [1998] R.V.R. 74, CA.
[76] Lands Tribunal Rules 1996, r.53(5).

Review and appeal

Where a party is dissatisfied with a detailed assessment of costs, that party **11–023** may, within seven days of the assessment, serve on any other interested party and on the registrar, written objection specifying the items objected to and applying for the assessment to be reviewed in respect of those items.[77] The registrar will review the assessment of the items objected to and must state in writing the reasons for his decision.[78]

A person dissatisfied with the decision of the registrar on review, may within 10 days of that decision apply to the President to review the detailed assessment, and the President may then make such order as he thinks fit, including an order as to the payment of the costs of the review.[79]

G. THE COPYRIGHT TRIBUNAL

The Copyright Tribunal has a wide discretion as to costs and may at any **11–024** stage of the proceedings make any order it thinks fit in relation to the payment of costs by one party to another in respect of the whole or part of the proceedings.[80]

The tribunal may direct any party against whom an order for costs is made to pay to any other party a lump sum, or such a proportion of the costs that may be just and the tribunal may assess the sum to be paid, or may direct it to be assessed by the chairman or to be assessed by a Costs Officer of the Supreme Court.[81]

The Copyright Tribunal has power to make such order as it determines to be reasonable in all circumstances in relation to costs.[82] The determination of the Tribunal is far more likely than ordinary civil litigation to produce an outcome in which there is no clear winner and loser and the Tribunal's discretion is not fettered by any reference to the outcome of the application.[83]

H. SPECIAL EDUCATIONAL NEEDS TRIBUNAL

In deciding whether or not a child with special needs could go to a particular **11–025** school the Tribunal erred in preferring the effect of the Education (Special

---

[77] R.52(5), Lands Tribunal Rules 1996.

[78] *ibid.*, r.52(6).

[79] *ibid.*, r.52(7).

[80] Copyright Tribunal Rules 1989, r.48(1). Copyright, Designs and Patents Act 1988, s.151(1) and see *AEI Rediffusion Music Ltd v Phonographic Performance Ltd* (Costs) *The Times*, March 3, 1999, CA.

[81] Or the Supreme Court of Northern Ireland or by the Auditor of the Court of Session in Scotland. Copyright Tribunal Rules 1989, r.48(2).

[82] S.135D of the Copyright Designs & Patents Act 1988.

[83] *AEI Rediffusion Music Ltd v Photographic Performance Ltd* [1999] 1 W.L.R. 1507, CA.

Schools) Regulations 1994 over the provisions of section 9 of the Education Act 1996. On appeal the Education Authority did not contest the issue. The Treasury Solicitor wrote to the court stating that the Tribunal would not be represented and drew the court's attention to the fact that new Regulations had been made: Education (Maintained Special Schools) (England) Regulations 1999. The Tribunal did however seek to oppose the order to pay the costs of the appeal. The court found that the Tribunal should have consented to the appeal being allowed in conformity with the overriding objective of the CPR. Nevertheless the Tribunal's error fell well short of the perversity or flagrant disregard of the principles of justice which was the threshold for a costs order to be made against Justices or tribunals.[84] The Tribunal's conduct fell just short of the stringent criteria for a costs order.[85]

I. THE ADJUDICATOR TO HM LAND REGISTRY

11–026 Practice and procedure before the Adjudicator are laid down in rules. The provisions relating to costs are similar to but not identical with the CPR. The rules contain an overriding objective.[86] The Adjudicator may on the application of a party or of his own initiative make an order as to costs in deciding what order as to costs to make. The Adjudicator must have regard to all the circumstances. This means all the circumstances of the proceedings including the conduct of the parties during (but not prior to) the proceedings; whether a party has succeeded on part of his case, even if he has not been wholly successful; and any representations made to the Adjudicator by the parties. The conduct of the parties during the proceedings includes:

   (i) whether it was reasonable for a party to raise, pursue or contest a particular allegation or issue;

   (ii) the manner in which a party has pursued or defended his case or a particular allegation or issue; and

   (iii) whether a party who has succeeded in his case in whole or in part exaggerated his case.[87]

The order for costs may require a party to pay the whole or part of the costs of another party and specify a fixed sum or proportion to be paid; or specify that the costs are to be assessed by the Adjudicator if not agreed; and specify

---

[84] *R. v Lincoln Justices Ex p. Count* [1996] 8 Admin L.R. 233.
[85] *S. v Metropolitan Borough of Dudley* [1999] 149 N.L.J. 1904.
[86] The Adjudicator to Her Majesty's Land Registry (Practice and Procedure) Rules 2003, SI 2003/2171, r.13.
[87] *ibid.*, r.42(1)(2)(3).

the time within which the costs are to be paid. A costs order must be made in writing giving the date, setting out the order as to costs and be signed by the Adjudicator. It must be served by the Adjudicator on the parties.[88]

The Adjudicator may assess the costs on the standard or the indemnity basis. The parties must be informed of the basis upon which the assessment is to take place. The standard and indemnity basis provisions are contained in the rules but are identical with the provisions of CPR 44.4. In carrying out the assessment the Adjudicator is again required to: "have regard to all the circumstances". Once the costs have been assessed the Adjudicator must serve on the parties written notice of the amount which had to be paid, by whom and to whom and if appropriate the time by when the amount must be paid.[89]

Costs thrown away

The rules contain provisions similar to the wasted costs provisions. "Costs thrown away" means costs of the proceedings resulting from any neglect or delay of the legal representative during (but not prior to) the proceedings and which have been incurred by a party; or have been: **11–027**

(i) paid by a party to another party; or

(ii) awarded to a party under an order for costs.[90]

The adjudicator may make an order as to costs thrown away provided he is satisfied that a party has incurred costs in the proceedings unnecessarily as a result of the neglect or the delay of the legal representatives; and it is just in all the circumstances for the legal representative to compensate the party who has incurred or paid the costs thrown away for the whole or part of those costs. An order for costs thrown away may specify the amount of costs to be paid and, if appropriate, specify the time within which the costs are to be paid. Such an order must be recorded in a costs thrown away order, in writing, dated and signed by the Adjudicator. It must be served by the Adjudicator on the parties and the legal representative.[91] If the Adjudicator has received an application for, or proposes to make an order for costs thrown away, he may give directions to the parties and the legal representative about the procedure to be followed to ensure that the issues are dealt with in a way that is fair and as simple in summary as the circumstances permit.[92]

---

[88] *ibid.*, r.42(4)(5)(6).
[89] *ibid.*, r.42(7)–(13).
[90] *ibid.*, r.43(1).
[91] *ibid.*, r.43(2)(4)(5) & (6).
[92] *ibid.*, r.43(3).

CHAPTER 12

Costs of Trustees, Personal Representatives and Under Contract

A. GENERAL PRINCIPLES

12–001 Where a person is, or has been, a party to any proceedings in the capacity of trustee or personal representative and costs are not payable pursuant to a contract,[1] he is entitled to the costs he paid of those proceedings, insofar as they are not recovered from or paid by any other person, out of the relevant trust fund or estate.[2] Sir Andrew Morritt V.C. issued a Practice Statement (Trust Proceedings: Prospective Costs Orders) on May 1, 2002 dealing with the costs of proceedings brought by trustees or beneficiaries or other persons concerned in relation to the administration of a trust including questions of construction, questions relating to the exercise of powers conferred on the trust, or questions as to the validity of the trust.

The court has jurisdiction to make an order as to the ultimate incidence of costs in proceedings ahead of the trial of the action.[3] There is discretion to make an order in terms which ensure that win or lose the litigant would be entitled to costs out of the property in dispute before the facts have been fully explored and before the relevant law has been fully argued. This is known as a *Beddoe* order, and is normally made in favour of trustees and executors.[4] The discretion has also been exercised in favour of an executor who, on application to the court, has been authorised to bring or defend proceedings, so that even if unsuccessful, he would be entitled to be indemnified out of the estate for all the costs for which he might be liable.[5]

---

[1] Under CPR, r.48.3.
[2] CPR, r.48.4 and Costs PD Section 50A.
[3] *Re Wedstock Realisations Ltd* [1988] B.C.L.C. 354.
[4] *Re Beddoe* [1893] 1 Ch. 547 CA.
[5] *Re Dallaway (deceased)* [1982] 1 W.L.R. 756.

If a trustee defends proceedings without obtaining a *Beddoe* order he does so at his own risk as to costs.[6]

The court will only make a pre-emptive costs order in a "public interest challenge" case in the most exceptional circumstances. The necessary conditions for the making of such an order are that the court should be satisfied that the issues raised are truly ones of general public importance and that it has sufficient appreciation of the merits of the claim to conclude it was in the public interest to make the order. The court also has to have regard to the financial resources of the applicant and respondent and the amount of costs likely to be in issue. The court would be more likely to make the order where the respondent clearly had a superior capacity to bear the costs.[7]

In a case where the Campaign for Nuclear Disarmament sought permission to apply for a declaration that the UN Security Council Resolution 1441 did not authorise the sue of force in the event of there being a breach, the court was asked to make a pre-emptive costs order that, in the event of costs being awarded against it such costs be limited to £25,000. Agreeing to make the order, the court found that there were compelling reasons in that CND's resources were modest and without the order sought they would be unable to proceed with the challenge; there was obvious public importance in the issues raised by the case; there was an imminent hearing on the issue of justiciability and the sum of £25,000 ought to be sufficient to cover the defendant's entitlement to costs in any case. The court commented that it was wrong o say that such an order should not be made before permission had been granted although that might often be the case. A claimant should always give notice of an application of this type at an early stage. The court stated that this was the first time such a pre-emptive order had been made in public law proceedings.[8]

In *Holding Ltd v Property Trust Plc*[9] the claimant was the trustee of a maintenance fund in respect of a block of flats and was seeking, in a manner hostile to the tenants (to whom the claimant owed, together with the landlord, a fiduciary duty) to ratify proposed expenditure to which the tenants were opposed and which the landlord did not support. It was held that the claimant had acted unreasonably. The proceedings were not brought in the capacity of the trustee and the claimant did not come within the indemnity provisions of RSC Ord. 62, r.6(6) (which then applied, see now CPR, Part 48.4). Neither was the trustee entitled to reimbursement under section 30(2) of the Trustee Act 1925 as the cost had been improperly incurred.

---

[6] *Singh v Bhashin, The Times*, August 21, 1998, Mr Alan Boyle Q.C.
[7] *R. v The Lord Chancellor, Ex p. Child Poverty Action Group; R. v DPP Ex p Bull & Anor* (1998) 2 All E.R. 755, Dyson J.
[8] *R. (CND) v Prime Minister* [2002] EWHC 2712 (Admin); [2003] C.P.Rep. 28 Simon Browne L.J.
[9] [1989] 1 W.L.R. 1313.

The court is much influenced by the following: (1) that it is the duty of trustees and executors to protect the estate; (2) that they are entitled to be indemnified for costs properly incurred for the benefit of the state; and (3) that Order 62, r.6(2) (CPR, r.48.4) expressly provides that executors and trustees are entitled to their costs out of any fund held by them in that capacity.[10] Thus the court may make an order that the costs of liquidation should be paid from the fund held by a receiver,[11] or may decline to make an order ahead of the final hearing of liquidator's summons for directions.[12]

The court may make a pre-emptive costs order in the case of an action by a minority shareholder in a way similar to a *Beddoe* order.[13] The essence of the discretion depends on the facts of each case.[14] It is not necessarily limited to categories of case which have arisen to date, *e.g.* trustee, executor, liquidator, receiver, minority shareholder. It must be exercised judicially having regard only to the relevant factors.[15] Among the factors taken into account as relevant to the court's jurisdiction to make pre-emptive costs orders are:

    (a) the merits;

    (b) the likely order for costs of trials;

    (c) the justice of the case; and

    (d) special factors.

12–002   **(a) The merits**   The prospect of success of a claim, or a defence, is the most important question to be taken into account in considering whether the action or defence should be financed out of the estate or fund in dispute.[16] The fund in dispute should not be used to support contentions which were not made in good faith or on reasonable grounds.

12–003   **(b) The likely order for costs at trial**   Unless the court is satisfied that it is likely that an order would be made after trial that the costs in question should be paid out of the fund, it is not, in general, right to make such an order before trial.[17] In the case of a trustee, the court will in general give effect to the trustee's right to indemnity out of the trust fund if he has acted properly for the benefit of the fund and the pursuit or defence of

---

[10] *National Anti-Vivisection Society Ltd v Duddington, The Times*, November 23, 1989, Mummery J.
[11] *Re Wedstock Realisations Ltd*, above n.3.
[12] *Re Change Card Services Ltd* [1986] B.C.L.C. 136, Hoffman J.
[13] *Wallersteiner v Moir* [1975] Q.B. 373; *Smith v Croft* [1986] 1 W.L.R. 580.
[14] *Re Evans (deceased)* [1986] 1 W.L.R. 101.
[15] *National Anti-Vivisection Society Ltd v Duddington*, above n.10.
[16] *Re Evans (deceased)*, above n.14.
[17] *Re Wedstock Realisations Ltd*, above n.3.

proceedings, even if he is ultimately unsuccessful. The position is different in the case of hostile litigation with rival claims of entitlement to property. In such a case, the normal order is that costs should follow the event in accordance with CPR, Part 44.3.[18]

(c) The justice of the case A pre-emptive order should not be made if there is a real possibility of it acting unjustly. It might be unjust in a particular case for the successful claimant to the property in dispute to be placed in a position where, even if he wins property held to be his, he is burdened with payment of the unsuccessful party's costs. That is a powerful consideration where the persons who would benefit from the pre-emptive order are all adult and *sui juris*.[19]

12–004

(d) Special factors Other special factors which might make a pre-trial order appropriate include where it is essential for the due administration of justice for a liquidator or an administrator to obtain the court's decision because there are large classes of persons, *e.g.* creditors who might be affected by the decision.[20] The application might also be a test case in which a decision is necessary on a point in order to resolve a number of pending cases.[21]

12–005

In a case which depends on the resolution of the question whether the property is held in trust by the defendant or the claimant, the very existence of the trustee/beneficiary relationship is an issue in the action. Since that involves hostile litigation between two rival claimants, it is wrong for the court to fetter the discretion of the trial judge by making a pre-emptive, interim order for costs in favour of the defendants, to be paid out of the property in dispute, which might operate unjustly against the claimant.[22]

The court may make a pre-emptive costs order in favour of employees who are representative claimants in an action against their employers and the trustees of relevant pension funds where they do not have the resources to pursue major litigation and their claim is so strong that it is inconceivable that if an independent trustee were appointed he would not apply for and obtain such an order. It is open to the court before the hearing of the action to appoint judicial trustees in place of defendant trustees where the hearing is distant in time and the charges made are such as to justify the employees in losing confidence in them.[23]

---

[18] *National Anti-Vivisection Society Ltd v Duddington*, above n.10.
[19] *Re Evans (deceased)*, above n.14.
[20] *Re Exchange Securities Ltd (No.2)* [1985] B.C.L.C. 392.
[21] *Re Wedstock Realisations Ltd*, above n.3.
[22] *National Anti-Vivisection Society Ltd v Duddington*, above n.10.
[23] *Mcdonald & Ors. v Horn*, (1995) 1 All E.R. 961, Vinelott J.

B. COSTS PAYABLE PURSUANT TO A CONTRACT

12–006 Costs which are payable under a contract are payable in accordance with the terms of the contract unless the court orders otherwise. These provisions do not apply to a contract between a solicitor and his client.[24]

Where costs payable under a contract are assessed, the costs are presumed, unless the contract expressly provides otherwise, to have been reasonably incurred and to be reasonable in amount. The court may make an order that all or part of the costs payable shall be disallowed if it is satisfied by the paying party that the costs have been unreasonably incurred or are unreasonable in amount.[25] Where there is a contractual right to costs the discretion under section 51 of the Supreme Court Act 1981 should be exercised so as to reflect that right.[26]

It is a frequent occurrence that a mortgagor enters into an agreement to pay to the mortgagee "all cost charges and expenses which may be incurred, *e.g.* in enforcing or obtaining payment of the sums of money due from the principal . . . or attempting to do so". However, this does not oust the discretion of the court to grant costs on the indemnity or standard basis. Walton J. in *Bank of Baroda v Panessar* stated:

> "It seems to me that it is not possible for a person in the position of a bank to exclude the discretion of the court, but one nevertheless starts from the position that the contractual position between the parties is that the costs will be paid on an indemnity basis. I cannot think that the words 'all costs' mean anything other than that.
>
> So one starts from the position that this is the contractual position, but not . . . binding on the court. The court may very well take the view that in the circumstances of any particular case, that was a contractual provision which it ought to overlook and it ought not to give effect to."[27]

The costs of preparing a mortgage cannot be charged against the security.[28] A mortgagee is allowed to reimburse himself out of the mortgage property for all costs, charges and expenses reasonably and properly incurred in enforcing or preserving his security. Often the process of enforcement or preservation makes it necessary for him to take or defend

---

[24] CPR, Part 48.3.

[25] Costs PD Section 50.

[26] *Fairview investments Ltd v Sharma*, October 14, 1999, CA (unreported).

[27] [1986] 3 All E.R. 751 at 765. Walton J. was not referred to *Re Adelphi Hotel (Brighton) Ltd* [1953] 1 W.L.R. 955 where it was held that, in the absence of an express provision to the contrary, the cost for enforcement would be assessed on the standard basis only. Both these decisions pre-date the CPR.

[28] *Wales v Carr* [1902] 1 Ch. 860.

proceedings. In regard to such proceedings three propositions may be stated:

(i) the mortgagee's costs, reasonably and properly incurred, of proceedings between himself and the mortgagor as his surety are allowable;

(ii) the mortgagee's costs reasonably and properly incurred of proceedings between himself and a third party where what is impugned is the title to the estate are also allowable;

(iii) but where a third party impugns the title to a mortgage or the enforcement or exercise of some right or power accruing to the mortgagee thereunder, the mortgagee's costs of the proceedings, even though they may be reasonably and properly incurred, are not allowable.[29]

Under the terms of the mortgage deed, a mortgagee is entitled to recover the actual costs, charges and expenses incurred except for any costs that have not been reasonably incurred or were unreasonable in amount. Both litigation and non-litigation costs may be referred to a Costs Judge for quantification, and the mortgagee is contractually entitled to payment on an indemnity basis as defined by CPR 44.4. The court's discretion as to the basis of a mortgagee's costs will normally be exercised so as to correspond with the contractual entitlement. It follows that the Court has power to order that the contractual costs, charges and expenses, and the costs incurred in the litigation be assessed on the indemnity basis, including those costs ordered to be assessed on a standard basis.[30]

The Court of Appeal has set out a number of principles to be applied:

(i) an order for the payment of costs of proceedings by one party to another is always a discretionary order under section 51 of the Supreme Court Act 1981;

(ii) where there is a contractual right to the costs, the discretion should ordinarily be exercised so as to reflect that contractual right;

(iii) the power of the court to disallow a mortgagee's costs sought to be added to the mortgage security, is a power that does not derive from section 51 but from the power of the courts of equity to fix the terms on which redemption will be allowed.

---

[29] *per* Nourse L.J. in *Parker-Tweedale v Dunbar Bank Plc (No. 2)* [1990] 2 All E.R. 588 at 591. Proposition (i) and (ii) form the general rule (iii) is the exception to it. The general rule is to be found in *Detillin v Gale* (1802) 7 Vcs. 583; *Dryden v Frost* (1838) 3 My. & Cr. 670; *National Provincial Bank of England v Games* [1886] 31 Ch. D. 582. The exception is to be found in *Owen v Crouch* (1857) 5 W.R. 545; *Parker v Watkins* [1859] John 133; *Re Smith's Mortgage*; *Harrison v Edwards* [1931] 2 Ch. 168. The decision of the Court of Appeal in *Re Leighton's Conveyance* [1937] Ch. 149 supports both propositions.

[30] *Gomba Holdings (U.K.) Ltd v Minories Finance Ltd (No. 2)* [1992] 3 W.L.R. 723.

(iv) a decision by a court to refuse costs in whole, or in part, to a mortgage litigant may be a decision in the exercise of the section 51 discretion, or a decision in the exercise of the power to fix the terms on which redemption will be allowed, or a decision as to the extent of the mortgagee's contractual right to add his cost to the security, or a combination of two or more of these things. The pleadings in the case and the submissions made to the judge may indicate which of the decisions has been made;

(v) a mortgagee may not be deprived of a contractual or equitable right to add costs to the security merely by reason of an order for payment of costs made without reference to the mortgagee's contractual or equitable rights and without any adjudication as to whether or not the mortgagee should be deprived of those costs.

The court did not agree that a complaint about the fixing of the receiver's remuneration at an unreasonably high level could only be pursued by a separate action. The claimants were entitled to object to the remuneration on the grounds that it was "plainly excessive" or unreasonably high. The issue could be dealt with by the Chancery Master, who could, in relation to this and any other issue on the account, direct points of claim and points of defence, or could refer the issue to the costs judge. A separate action was not necessary.[31]

If mortgagees seek to deduct an excessive sum in respect of their costs the remedy of the defendant mortgagor is to ask for an account and to challenge the figure which the claimant mortgagees seek to charge for their costs. At this stage the court is not bound by the contractual provisions between mortgagor and mortgagee and will be entitled to say that the costs sought to be challenged were excessive and could make the appropriate order at that point. This would however depend on the mortgagees having behaved unreasonably.[32]

C. PRE-EMPTIVE COSTS ORDERS IN RESPECT OF TRUSTEES AND OTHER FIDUCIARIES, BENEFICIARIES, DERIVATIVE ACTIONS AND PENSION FUNDS

12–007   The Court of Appeal has reviewed the law relating to pre-emptive costs orders where costs are to be paid out of a fund.[33]

---

[31] *Gomba Holdings (U.K.) Ltd v Minories Finance Ltd (No. 2)*, above and see Costs PD section 50.
[32] *per* Balcombe L.J. *Mortgage Funding Corporation Plc v Kashef-Hamadani*, April 26, 1993, CA, (unreported).
[33] *McDonald v Horne* (1995) 1 All E.R. 961.

In a case where trustees of a charity applied to the court for directions in relation to an appeal against an order appointing a receiver and manager of the charity, and whether they might be indemnified out of the charity's property in respect of the costs incurred by them in prosecuting the appeal, the court allowed the Attorney-General to be heard and to submit evidence on the application. The court held that the practice in pre-emptive costs applications was that they should be between the parties.[34] Justice required that a party had a right to be heard before an order was made that the party would bear the whole costs of substantial litigation whether it won or lost. The Attorney-General was, for the purpose of the application, regarded as being in the same position as a beneficiary. There was strong public interest in the Attorney-General being present on an application which, if successful, would involve the expenditure of a large proportion of the charity's funds.[35] A policyholder objecting to a proposed scheme of re-organisation of an insurance company was entitled to a pre-emptive costs order in his favour because his position was closely analogous to that of a shareholder bringing a derivative action against the controllers of a company on behalf of the company as a whole, in that he had given consideration in exchange for his interest. The application also enabled the proposed reorganisation to be fully tested by the court.[36]

Statutory costs jurisdiction

The Court's jurisdiction to deal with litigation costs is based upon section 51 of the Supreme Court Act 1981; this discretion must be exercised in accordance with the Rules of Court and established principles.   **12–008**

The general principles

Costs follow the event (subject to CPR, r.44.3).   **12–009**

The special principle—costs out of a fund

(a) Costs of trustees and other fiduciaries: In the case of a fund held on   **12–010**
trust the trustee is entitled to his costs out of the fund on the indemnity basis provided only that he has not acted unreasonably or "in substance for his own benefit rather than that of the fund".[37]

---

[34] CPR 19.9 (derivative claims).
[35] *Weth & Ors v HM Attorney-General & Ors*, November 21, 1997, Mr L. Collins Q.C. (Deputy High Court Judge) (unreported).
[36] *Re Axa Sun Life Plc* [2000] EW Ch.D., November 1, Evans-Lombe J.
[37] CPR, r.48.4.

Trustees are able to protect themselves against the possibility that they may be held to have acted unreasonably or in their own interest by applying at an early stage for directions as to whether to bring or defend proceedings.[38]

(b) Extensions of special principle to beneficiaries: The Chancery Courts have been willing in certain circumstances to extend to other parties to trust litigation an entitlement to costs in any event by analogy with that accorded to trustees.[39] Kekewich J. said that trust litigation could be divided into three categories:

  (i) proceedings brought by trustees to have the guidance of the court as to the construction of the trust instrument or some question arising in the course of the administration: in such cases the costs of all parties are usually treated as necessarily incurred for the benefit of the estate and ordered to be paid out of the fund:

  (ii) cases in which the application is made by someone other than the trustees that raise the same kind of point as in (i) and would have justified an application by the trustees: this trust is treated in the same way as the first:

  (iii) cases in which a beneficiary is making a hostile claim against the trustees or another beneficiary. This is treated in the same way as ordinary common law litigation and costs usually follow the event. The court may sometimes feel sufficiently confident that the case is within (i) or (ii) to be able to make a prospective order that parties other than the trustees are to have their costs in any event.[40]

(c) Extension of principle to derivative action: In *Wallersteiner v Moir*,[41] the Court of Appeal said that a minority shareholder bringing a derivative action on behalf of a company could obtain the authority of the court to sue as if he were a trustee suing on behalf of a fund with the same entitlement to be indemnified out of the assets against his costs and any costs he may be ordered to pay to the other party. The Court said that the minority shareholder could make a *Beddoe* application in the same way as the trustee.

(d) Extension of *Wallersteiner* to Pension Funds: There is a compelling analogy between a minority shareholder's action for damages on behalf of a company and an action by a member of a pension fund to compel trustees or others to account to the fund. In both cases

---

[38] See *Re Beddoe* [1893] 1 Ch. 547, at 557.
[39] See *Re Buckton* [1907] 2 Ch. 406, Kekewich J.
[40] See *Re Exchange Securities Ltd (No.2)* (1985) B.C.L.C. 392, 395.
[41] [1975] Q.B. 373.

a person with a limited interest in a fund, whether the company's assets or a pension fund, is alleging injury to the fund as a whole and seeking restitution on behalf of the fund. What distinguishes the shareholder and pension fund member on the one hand from the ordinary trust beneficiary on the other is that the former have both given consideration for their interests, they are not just recipients of the settler's bounty. The relationship between the parties is a commercial one and the pension fund members are entitled to be satisfied that the fund is being properly administered. Even in a long contributory scheme the employer's payments are not bounty, they are part of the consideration for the services of the employee.

Pension funds are a special form of trust and the analogy between them and companies with shareholders is so much stronger than in the case of ordinary trusts that in a judgment of the court it would do no violence to established authority if the court were to apply to them the *Wallersteiner* procedure.[42]

Practice: The power to make a *Wallersteiner v Moir* order in a pension fund should be exercised with considerable care.[43]

The question is whether the claimants have shown a sufficient case for further investigation. Once the judge is satisfied that there are matters which need to be investigated, caution should take the form of choosing the most economical form of investigation. This will not necessarily involve authorising a full trial or even full pleadings and discovery. The court should not authorise any legal process until it has explored the possibility of independent investigation by a person or persons acceptable to both parties.

Even if further investigation is required it need not necessarily take the form of a full-scale trial, the court might in the first instance authorise only discovery (preferably limited) or appoint judicial trustees with power to take possession of the documents and investigate for themselves. The court may also think that if the action is to be pursued beyond the stage of investigation and discovery it should be put into the hands of independent judicial trustees in which case the pre-emptive costs order will expire when the handover has been completed.

In general the court should try to secure the fairest and most economical judicial or extra judicial resolution of the dispute.[44]

---

[42] The attention of the court was drawn to a decision of the House of Lords in *Chapman v Chapman* [1954] A.C. 429 but it was held that the jurisdiction has to be found in s.51 of the Supreme Court Act 1981 which is subject only to rules of court and established principles. The court was not persuaded that any such rule or principle would be violated.

[43] See *Smith v Croft* [1986] 1 W.L.R. 580, Walton J.

[44] *per* Hoffman L.J., *McDonald v Horn* [1995] 1 All E.R. 961, CA.

The application for a pre-emptive costs order should be heard by a judge of first instance in the Chancery Division, even if the case was to be heard by the Court of Appeal.[45]

Under the CPR the court may take a more robust view about costs to be paid out of the trust fund. Where trustees are able and willing to bring proceedings themselves a successful claimant who is a beneficiary will not necessarily be awarded costs out of the fund.[46]

The court should avoid the temptation to be swayed by a comparison between the costs of a potential appeal and the funds in a scheme so as to be generous with the money of another. Trusts did not exist to fund litigation by a minority group of members at the expense of its members as a whole but to use its assets for the benefit of all those members in accordance with the rules that defined its existence and purpose.[47]

Other orders for the costs of trustees

12–011 Whilst it is normal practice on an application to the court for directions by trustees for the costs to be paid out of the trust funds, the court has a discretion to diverge form that practice where appropriate. Such a course was held to be appropriate where the trustees had decided to adopt a partisan role, where they had argued positively for a specific outcome in the interests of one class of beneficiary against the interests of another class. In those circumstances the court held that the role adopted by the trustees was not neutral and the trustees had to accept that they might be subject to costs consequences. The existence of an exoneration clause within the trustees' terms of office was no protection against a court order, nor was it a factor which inclined the court to exercise its discretion in the trustees favour.[48]

Where the Charity Commission appointed a receiver and manager of the charity, and subsequently on his advice appointed new trustees and removed the former chairman of trustees, under section 18 of the Charities Act 1993, the former trustee appealed against the appointment of the receiver and applied for an order indemnifying him out of the charity's property in respect of the costs of the appeal. The trustees' application was dismissed and permission to appeal refused by the Court of Appeal on the basis that the trustee had not been acting for the benefit of the charity (by refusing to compromise an earlier action) and was therefore liable to pay the costs.[49]

---

[45] *Machin v National Power plc (No.1)*, May 18, 1998, Laddie J. (unreported). See also *Machin v National Power plc (No.2)*, July 31, 1998, Carnwath J. (unreported).
[46] *D'Abo v Paget (No.2)*, *The Times*, August 10, 2000, Lawrence Collins Q.C.
[47] *Chessels v British Telecommunications Plc* [2001] EWHC, Ch. D., December 20: [2002] PENS L.R. 141, Laddie J. (pre-emptive costs order refused).
[48] *Breadner v Granville and Grossman* [2000] EWHC, Ch. D., July 16, Park J.
[49] *Weth v H.M. Attorney General* [2001] EWHC, Ch. D., February 23.

Where the trustees of a pension scheme brought proceedings, and the beneficiary representative of the active members of the scheme was a defendant, the defendant's application for a pre-emptive costs order was granted taking into account the size of the fund and the fact that the trustees had named the particular beneficiary as a defendant. Even if it could be said that it had not been absolutely necessary for the beneficiary to be joined, the fact that he had been would normally entitle such a party to their costs.[50]

In a case where a company went into administration after a shareholder had brought a petition under section 459 of the Companies Act 1985 the administrator sought directions from the court in relation to possible appeals from orders made relating to the petition. The court gave directions relating to the appeals and made pre-emptive costs order in relation to those proceedings in favour of the administrators to the effect that the costs were to be paid out of the estate of the company, in any event in priority to the claims of the other creditors. On appeal it was held that the pre-emptive costs order should not have been made in circumstances where the litigation was hostile. The court was required to be particularly cautious in making a pre-emptive costs order. To make such an order the court needed complete confidence that the administrators would win and that all the costs would be properly incurred. A pre-emptive costs order could be made only on the strongest possible grounds once it was established that there was a more than negligible chance that the administrators might fail. It was potentially unjust to make a pre-emptive costs order.[51]

---

[50] *Stevens v Bell* (Costs) [2001] OP L.R. 123, Park J.
[51] *Ciro Citterio Menswear Plc* [2002] EWHC, Ch, May 3, Pumfrey J.

CHAPTER 13

Lien and Recovery of Costs

A. INTRODUCTION

13–001 The liens to which a solicitor is entitled to look for protection when his right to recover costs from his client is in question, are the two common law liens exercisable (a) by retention of documents and (b) on property recovered or preserved by his efforts.

B. THE RETAINING LIEN

13–002 The solicitor has a right of lien over the client's deeds, papers or other personal chattels which come into his possession in the course of his professional employment with the sanction of the client:

> "The solicitor's lien upon, or right to retain, his client's papers till the bill is paid is of a nature wholly different (from a fund realised in the cause). It applies to all his bills of costs; but he cannot actively enforce it. So long as the client leaves the papers in the solicitor's hands, the solicitor's lien is unavailing. It is merely a right to retain; and if the solicitor refuses to act for the client it is of little if any value, as he cannot in that case deprive the client of the full use of the papers ... But if the client discharges or ceases to employ the solicitor, the solicitor is not compellable to afford any facilities to the client by the use of the papers"[1]

The right of lien is a general right and does not merely extend to the costs of any specific document but to the whole of the costs which may be

---

[1] *Bozon v Bolland* (1839) 4 My. & CR. 354.

outstanding.[2] The general rule that a solicitor can retain any papers in his possession until his costs are paid was upheld by the Court of Appeal in a case[3] where the solicitor of a petitioning wife had an absolute lien over the papers for his costs, and would not therefore be ordered upon any undertaking to return them to the wife's new solicitors. The lien cannot however be asserted where the action is one in which third parties are interested.[4] A solicitor's lien only attaches to documents which are the client's property. It cannot attach to that which is the solicitor's own property,[5] e.g. a mortgage deed in respect of the costs for preparation of the deed. It applies to bills of exchange, letters patent, policies of assurance and letters of administration.[6]

A solicitor's lien over the documents in his custody is a right at common law depending upon an implied agreement. Lord Evershed M.R. in *Barratt v Gough-Thomas*[7] stated:

> "It has not the character of an incumbrance or equitable charge. It is merely passive and possessory, that is to say the solicitor has no right of actively enforcing his demand. It confers on him merely the right to withhold possession of the documents or other personal property of his client or former client—in the words of Sir E. Segden in *Blunden v Desart* [1842] 2 Dr. & War. 405:
>
> > ' . . . to lock them up in his box and to put the key into his pocket until his client satisfies the amount of the demand.'
>
> It is wholly derived from, and therefore co-extensive with, the right of the client to the documents or other property".

The lien extends only to a solicitor's assessable costs, charges and expenses incurred by virtue of acting as solicitor for the client, but should the solicitor take security for costs, either by way of charge or cash, then the solicitor forfeits his right of lien.[8] This proposition can be overcome by an express or implied intention to the contrary, depending upon the particular circumstances of the case. Prima facie where a solicitor whose duty is to advise his client as to his rights and liabilities does so without explaining that he intends to reserve his lien, that lien is abandoned. The lien does not extend to general debts, but only to that which is due to the solicitor when

---

[2] *Colmer v Ede* (1870) 40 L.J. Ch. 185.
[3] *Hughes v Hughes* [1958] 3 All. E.R. 179, CA.
[4] *Re Rapid Road Transit Co.* [1909] 1 Ch. 96.
[5] *Sheffield v Eden* (1878) 10 Ch. D. 291.
[6] *Gibson v May* [1853] 4 De G.M. & G.512; *Re Aubusson, Ex p. Solomon* [1821] 1 G1. & J. 25; *West of England Bank v Batchelor* (1882) 51 L.J. Ch. 199; *Barnes v Durham* [1869] L.R. 1 P. & D.728.
[7] [1951] Ch. 242 at 250.
[8] *Re Taylor Stileman & Underwood* [1891] 1 Ch. 590.

acting as a solicitor.[9] The court in its legitimate concern for the solicitor should not disregard the rights of the client. The court will intervene to the extent necessary to safeguard the lien.[10]

The Court of Appeal has held that where the lien was based on possession, a unilateral reservation by a solicitor not accepted by the recipient was a sufficient reservation.[11] The court's power to order that former solicitor's hand over papers relating to a case to new solicitors is not exercised automatically. It is a matter of discretion to be exercised judicially depending upon the circumstances of the case.[12] Regard must be had in exercising the power, as to what would best serve the interests of justice and the principle that a litigant should not be deprived of material relevant to the conduct of the case. To be weighed against those considerations is the principle that litigation should be conducted with due regard to the interests of the court's officers and that they should be remunerated for what they have done.

The court has a wide discretion to order delivery up of property in respect of which a lien is claimed. Under the common law a person claiming a lien must either claim it for a definite amount or give the owner particulars from which that amount may be calculated.[13] The solicitor has no better right to retain documents or property than the client would have if still in possession of them.[14] Therefore, the retaining lien cannot prevail against an order made upon the client to produce those documents.[15]

A company's solicitor cannot maintain a lien as against the liquidator of the company in respect of documents required by statute to be kept at a particular place,[16] or which have come into his possession after the commencement of winding up proceedings.[17] Similarly, a solicitor cannot maintain a lien as against the official receiver or trustee in bankruptcy over the debtor's books of account,[18] and production or delivery of the debtor's property may be ordered.[19]

A solicitor's lien will be allowed over documents such as debentures and land charges which confer title to property, despite the company from whom the documents have been received, being in liquidation. Section 246

---

[9] *Worral v Johnson* [1820] 2 Jac. & W. 214.

[10] *Re Fuld* [1967] 2 All E.R. 649.

[11] *Caldwell v Sumpters* [1972] Ch. 478.

[12] *A. v B.* [1983] Com. L.R. 226.

[13] *Singh v Thaper, The Times*, August 7, 1987, CA.

[14] *Furlong v Howard* [1804] 2 Sch. & Lef. 115; *Re Hawkes, Ackerman v Lockhart* [1898] 2 Ch. 1, CA.

[15] *Ex p. Shaw* [1821] Jac. 270; *Bell v Taylor* (1836) 8 Sim.216; *Ley v Barlow* [1848] 1 Ex. Ch. 800; *Vale v Oppert* (1875) 10 Ch. App.340; *Lewis v Powell* [1897] 1 Ch. 678.

[16] *Re Capital Fire Insurance Association* (1883) 24 Ch.D. 408, CA. *Re Anglo Maltese Hydraulic Dock Co. Ltd* (1885) 54 L.J. Ch. 730.

[17] *Re Capital Fire Insurance Association*, above; *Re Rapid Road Transit Co. Ltd* [1901] 1 Ch. 96.

[18] Insolvency Act 1986, s.349.

[19] *Re Toleman & England, Ex p. Bramble* (1880) 13 Ch. D. 885.

of the Insolvency Act 1986 which connotes a manner or capacity in which the documents are held so as to confer a lien, does not require that the documents should be held in a capacity which confers on the holder a proprietary interest in the underlying property.[20]

When seeking an order under section 236 of the Insolvency Act 1986 for production by a company's solicitors of documents relating to the company, a receiver is not acting on behalf of the company alone, but is in the same position as a third party entitled to production of documents as against the client company. Thus, since solicitors cannot assert a lien as against a third party, they cannot refuse to produce documents to a receiver on the ground that they have a lien over the document for the company's unpaid costs.[21] Where a solicitor holds title deeds on trust for a mortgagee, this is inconsistent with the existence of a lien over the deeds in respect of costs owed by the client.[22]

In bankruptcy the trustee in bankruptcy stands in no better position than the bankrupt himself as to the lien claimed by the bankrupt's solicitor.[23] After the commencement of his bankruptcy no lien can be given by the bankrupt.[24] A lien created before the date of the receiving order is protected if a solicitor had no notice of an available act of bankruptcy,[25] although the existence of the lien will not entitle a solicitor to refuse production of any documents of the bankrupt in his possession, for the inspection of the trustee. Monies paid by the debtor after an act of bankruptcy to oppose those proceedings cannot be claimed by the trustee.[26] Nevertheless such a lien is in respect of costs incurred solely in opposition and does not extend to costs incurred in endeavouring to avoid proceedings.[27]

Change of solicitor

The court will impose a restriction on a solicitor's exercise of his lien to avoid injustice, which the client might otherwise suffer if prevented from pursuing litigation. Where a solicitor terminated his retainer in relation to a live case, the problem of doing justice as between solicitor and client was not altered by the fact that the solicitor had previously been instructed on a matter which had by then become dead, and thereby had a concurrent lien

13–003

---

[20] *Brereton v Nicholls* [1993] B.C.L.C. 593, Morritt J.
[21] *Re Aveling Barford Ltd* [1989] 1 W.L.R. 360.
[22] *Re Galda Properties* [1988] 1 I.R. 213 (Irish Supreme Court).
[23] *Re Hemsworth Ex p. Underwood* [1845] De G. 190; *Re Messenger Ex p. Calvert* (1876) 3 Ch. D. 317.
[24] *Ex p. Lee* (1793) 2 Ves. 283.
[25] *Re Gershon & Levy* [1915] 2 K.B. 527.
[26] *Re Sinclair Ex p. Payne* (1885) 15 Q.B.D. 616.
[27] *Re Spackman Ex p. Foley* (1890) 24 Q.B.D. 728; 59 L.J. Q.B. 306, CA (distinguishing *Re Sinclair* above).

over the papers in the case which was still live. The principles that can be extracted from the authorities include the following:

(i) the solicitor is entitled to a general lien in respect of his costs on any property belonging to his client which came into his possession in his capacity as a solicitor;

(ii) however, a solicitor who has discharged himself is not allowed so to exert his lien as to interfere with the course of justice;

(iii) where a solicitor terminates his retainer his lien does not affect the client's entitlement to an order that papers required for the conduct of pending litigation be delivered to the new solicitor against tan undertaking to return them at the end of the litigation, although in exceptional cases the court could attach conditions to such an order;

(iv) the refusal by a solicitor to act unless he was put in funds is generally treated by the court as an effective discharge of his retainer.[28]

If a solicitor is discharged by his client otherwise than for misconduct, the solicitor is under no obligation to deliver, or to produce, or to allow inspection of, the papers until his bill of costs has been paid.[29] Where the solicitor has discharged himself he cannot retain any documents or papers essential to the litigation but may be ordered to hand over the papers to the new solicitor on the new solicitor undertaking to hold them without prejudice to his lien to return them intact after the action is over and to allow the former solicitor access to them in the meantime and, if necessary, to prosecute the proceedings in an active manner.[30] A solicitor who gives an undertaking to hold documents to the order of another firm of solicitors in the interest of preserving the retaining lien for unpaid fees, is in breach of the undertaking if the documents are photocopied and sent to the client.[31] Where other parties apart from the client are interested in the litigation,[32] and who would be prejudiced by the retention of the papers by the solicitor who discharges himself, it seems that the solicitor cannot maintain his lien.[33]

The jurisdiction of the court in respect of making orders for delivery up of papers is derived from the solicitor's duty towards the court and the

---

[28] *Ismail v Richards Butler* [1996] 2 All E.R. 506, Moore-Bick J.
[29] *Re Rapid Road Transit Co. Ltd* [1909] 1 Ch. 96; *Leo Abse & Cohen v Evan G. Jones (Builders) Ltd, The Times,* April 21, 1984, CA.
[30] *Hughes v Hughes* [1958] P. 228, CA.
[31] *Bentley & Another v Gaisford & Another* 1997 2 W.L.R. 401, CA.
[32] *Commerell v Poynton* [1818] 1 Swan. 1; *Moir v Mudie* [1823] 1 Sim. St. 282; *Gamlen Chemical Co. (U.K.) Ltd v Rochem Ltd* [1981] 1 W.L.R. 614, CA.
[33] *Re Boughton v Boughton* (1883) 23 Ch. D. 169.

nature of the proceedings are not relevant. The burden of proving the extent of the retainer is on the solicitor and the matter may be decided on the balance of hardship. An order for delivery up may be made on terms that the client should pay an amount into court to await the outcome of assessment.[34]

On the question of whether the court has power to override a solicitor's lien where the client has terminated the retainer, as opposed to the solicitor discharging himself, it appears that the jurisdiction does exist and that the court has discretion under CPR 25.1(1)(m). On the particular facts of the case an order was made for delivery up of documents notwithstanding the lien and the client was required to pay the amount in dispute into court.[35]

There is no reason in principle why, in appropriate circumstances, a court should not be able to interfere in the enforcement of a common law lien on equitable principles even where it was the client and not the solicitor who had terminated the retainer. The court must be satisfied that there were matters affecting the relationship between the solicitor and the client which, as a matter of conscience, make it inappropriate for the lien to continue and be enforced in particular circumstances.[36]

Priorities of successive solicitors

In proceedings in the Chancery Division the rule is that the solicitor who actually conducts the litigation to its conclusion has the first claim to payment, but subject to that, the court will grant to a solicitor employed at an earlier stage of the action, a charging order in respect of his costs.[37] If the first solicitor receives the whole of the costs he must pay over the second solicitor's share without deduction in respect of any set-off to which he may be entitled as between himself and the client.[38] In order to preserve a lien as a prior charge when handing over papers it is necessary to obtain an undertaking to that effect and to make delivery of papers subject to the lien and to give no priority.[39]

In a company's winding up or a debenture holder's action the rights of successive solicitors to payments rank *pari passu*.[40]

13–004

---

[34] *Sea Voyager Maritime Inc v Hughes Hooker*, June 30, 1997, Timothy Walker J. (unreported).

[35] *Paragon Finance Plc v Rosling King*, May 26, 2000 Hart J. (unreported).

[36] *Slater v Ronaldson* [2001] EWHC, Ch D, December 14, Patten J.

[37] *Cormack v Beisly* [1858] 3 De G. & J. 157; *Re Robsworth, Rhodes v Sugden* (1886) 34 Ch. D. 155; *Re Knight v Gardner* [1892] 2 Ch. 368; *Hyde v White* [1933] P. 105.

[38] *Re Barnard Ex p. Bailey & Hope* (1851) 14 Bevan 18; *Mornington v Wellsley* (1857) 4 Jur. N.S. 6.

[39] *Batten v Wedgwood Coal & Iron Co.* (1884) 28 Ch. D. 317; *Re Capital Fire Insurance Association* (1883) 24 Ch. D. 408, CA. *Re Gloucester Aberwystwythe & Central Wales Railway Co.* (1860) 8 W.R. 175; *Re Audley Hall Cotton Spinning Co.* [1868] L.R. 6 Eq. 245; *Gibbs v Tredwell, Re Armstrong* (1886) 30 S.J. 181, CA.

[40] *Batten v Wedgewood Coal & Iron Company*, above.

Discharge of lien

13–005 A retaining lien may be discharged in one of the following ways:

(1) By taking security on other property, which is inconsistent with the lien. The lien is not[41] lost if the lien and security are consistent with one another. There is a general presumption that the lien is abandoned if the solicitor takes a security for the costs secured by the lien without explaining that he is entitled to a lien which he is not abandoning, but there is no waiver if a solicitor expressly reserves his lien.[42]

(2) By proving in bankruptcy or in a winding up for the amount of the costs without valuing or mentioning the lien. If the omission to value is due to inadvertence the court may allow the proof to be withdrawn. Such leave will be given unless the omission was deliberate.[43]

(3) By the solicitor parting with possession of the documents over which the lien was claimed, but not if the possession is given to an agent or third party subject to the lien.[44]

(4) By the solicitor receiving payment of the costs in respect of which the lien arises. However, the lien is not discharged by the solicitor obtaining judgment or a charging order for his costs.[45]

C. LIEN ON PROPERTY RECOVERED OR PRESERVED

13–006 A solicitor has at common law a lien over property recovered or preserved or the proceeds of any judgment obtained[46] by his work on his client's behalf, in respect of which the solicitor may apply to the court for enforcement.[47] The property must have been recovered or preserved in the

---

[41] *Chase v Westmore* (1816) 5 M.S. 180; *Hewison v Guthrie* [1836] 2 Bing. N.C. 755; *Jones v Pappecorn* [1858] John 430.

[42] *Re Taylor Stileman & Underwood* [1891] 1 Ch. 590, CA; *Bissill v Bradford & District Tramways Co. Ltd* (1893) 9 T.L.R. 337, CA; *Re Douglas Norman & Co.* [1898] 1 Ch. 199; *Currey v Rea* [1937] N.I. 1; *Re Morris* [1908] 1 K.B. 473, CA.

[43] *Re Safety Explosive Ltd* [1904] 1 Ch. 226, CA; *Re Tulton Ex p. Hornby* [1819] Buck. 351; *Re Aubusson Ex p. Solomon* [1821] 1 G.L. & J. 25.

[44] *Clarke v Gilbert* [1835] 2 Bing. N.C. 343; *Jacobs v Latour* (1828) 5 Bing. 130; *Blunden v Dessart* [1842] 2 Dr. & War. 405; *Re Phoenix Life Assurance Co, Howard & Dollman's Case* [1863] 1 M. & N. 433; *Watson v Lyon* (1855) 7 De Gm. & G.288; *Bull v Faulkner* [1848] 2 De G. & Sm. 772; *Caldwell v Sumpters* [1972] Ch. 478.

[45] *Re Emma Silver Mining Co. v Turner* (1875) 24 W.R. 54; *Re Aikins Assignees Estate* [1894] 1 I.R. 225; *Hector v Jolliffe* (1846) 6 Jur. 120; *Re Lumley* (1892) 37 S.J. 83.

[46] *Sullivan, Re Pearson Ex p. Morrison* [1868] L.R. 4 Q.B. 153.

[47] *Bozon v Bolland* (1839) 4 My. & Cr. 354.

course of litigation or arbitration by the solicitor's exertions.[48] Property recovered as a result of negotiation without litigation cannot be made the subject of a lien.[49]

The lien is in fact a right to ask for the equitable interference of the court to have the judgment held as a security for costs when, having obtained judgment for the client, it appears probable that the client will not pay the solicitor's costs.[50]

It is a "particular lien" in that it is not available for any costs other than the costs properly incurred in the recovery or preservation of the property in question.[51] The lien may be asserted by the solicitor even though his right to recover the costs may be barred by lapse of time.[52]

The lien attaches to all property except real property,[53] although maintenance payments are usually excluded.[54] Property which will be covered includes money payable under a judgment or award,[55] the proceeds of execution,[56] or money paid under a compromise[57] or paid into court,[58] either by way of security for costs[59] or by way of defence.[60] The property recovered must be the result of the proceedings,[61] including arbitration in which the solicitor has acted[62] for the person against whom the lien is claimed.[63] A solicitor's lien entitles him at common law to retain property in his possession until he has been paid costs due to him in his professional capacity. "Property" in this context includes money held in a client account. It is wrong in principle for such monies to be included within the ambit of an injunction freezing the assets of the client. In these circumstances the money is not really client's money at all, but only held by the solicitors in that manner because of the mandatory requirements of the Solicitors' Accounts Rules.[64] When, as a condition imposed by the court, the defendant

---

[48] *Ex p. Price* [1751] 2 Ves. Sen. 407; *McBride's Executors v Clarke* (1839) 11 Eq. R. 203; *Re Wadsworth Rhodes v Sugden* (1886) 34 Ch. D. 155.
[49] *Meguerditchian v Lightbound* [1917] 2 K.B. 298, CA.
[50] *Puddephatt v Leith (No.2)* [1916] 2 Ch. 168; *Mason v Mason & Cotterell* [1933] P. 199, CA.; *Re Fuld's Estate (No.4)* [1968] P. 727.
[51] *MacKenzie v MacIntosh* (1891) 64 L.T. 706, CA; *Smith v Betty* [1903] 2 K.B. 317, CA; *Simpson v Protheroe* (1857) 26 L.J. Ch. 671; *Re Meter Cabs Ltd* [1911] 2 Ch. 557; *Re Hill* (1886) 33 Ch. D. 266.
[52] *Higgins v Scott* [1831] 2 B. & Ad. 413; *Re Born Curnock v Born* [1900] 2 Ch. 433.
[53] *Shaw v Neale & Remnant* (1858) 6 H.L. Cas. 581.
[54] *Cross v Cross* (1880) 43 L.T. 533; *Leete v Leete* (1879) 48 L.J.P. 61.
[55] *Jones v Turnball* [1837] 2 M. & W. 601; *Aspinall v Stamp* [1827] 3 B. & C. 108; *Campbell v Campbell and Lewis* [1941] 1 All E.R. 274, CA; *Re Fuld's Estate (No.4)* [1958] P.727.
[56] *Re Bank of Hindustan, China and Japan Ltd Ex p. Smith* [1867] 3 Ch. Apps. 125.
[57] *Ross v Buxton* (1889) 42 Ch. D. 190.
[58] *Hall v Hall & Kay* [1891] P. 302, CA.
[59] *Hall v Hall & Kay*, above.
[60] *Emden v Carte*, (1881) 19 Ch. D. 311.
[61] *Meguerditchian v Lightbound* [1917] 2 K.B. 298, CA; *Re Graydon, Ex p. Official Receiver* [1896] 1 Q.B. 417.
[62] *Hodgens v Kelly* [1826] 1 Hog. 388; *Townsend v Reade*; *Dooley v Reade* [1835] 4 L.J. Ch. 233; *Lord v Colvin (No.2)* [1862] Drew. & Sm. 82.
[63] *Re Clark Ex p. Newland* [1876] 4 Ch. D.515; *Chick v Nicholls* (1877) 266 W.R. 231.
[64] per Hirst J.: *Prekookeanska Plovidba v L.N.T. Lines S.R.L.* [1988] 3 All E.R. 897.

pays money into an account held by the claimant's and the defendant's solicitors, the claimant's solicitors do not have a lien over the account in respect of the unpaid fees. However, the solicitor has an equity in the fund and has a right to have his interest taken into account when any sum is paid out of the account to the claimant.[65]

Set-off

13–007   The court may, under CPR, Part 44.3, where a party entitled to be paid costs is also liable to pay costs, set off one against the other without regard to any lien of a solicitor. In other words, the lien only extends to the ultimate balance.[66] It is the general rule that a set-off should not be used on account of a solicitor's lien if, as between the parties themselves it would be just and there has been no fraud or collusion against the solicitor.[67] The Court of Appeal may allow the respondent's costs of an unsuccessful appeal to be set off against money paid into court in the action.[68] The House of Lords will not, after final judgment, set off costs due by an appellant in the House of Lords against costs due to the appellant in the Court of Appeal.[69]

The effect of compromise

13–008   If an action is compromised in good faith, the court will not interfere with the compromise for the purpose of preserving the solicitor's lien,[70] whether the damages sought are liquidated[71] or unliquidated.[72] If the compromise is dishonest and made with the intention of cheating the solicitor of his proper charges the court will interfere for the solicitor's protection.[73] In such circumstances the court may order payment of the solicitor's costs[74] or may impose conditions, if asked, to make an order staying proceedings.[75]

---

[65] *Halvanon Insurance Company Ltd v Central Reinsurance Corporation* [1988] 1 W.L.R. 1122.

[66] *Hedwards v Hope* (1885) 15 Q.B.D. 922, CA; *Goodfellow v Gray* [1899] 2 Q.B. 498; *Reid v Cupper* [1915] 2 K.B. 147, CA; *Puddephatt & Leith (No. 2)* [1916] 2 Ch. 168; *Young v Mead* [1917] 2 I.R. 258; *Mason v Mason & Cottrell* [1933] P. 199.

[67] *Young v Meade* above.

[68] *Knight v Knight* [1925] Ch. 835; *Hall v Hall & Kay* [1891] P.302, CA.

[69] *Russell v Russell* [1898] A.C. 307, HL.

[70] *Morse & Holder v Cooke & Morse* (1824) 13 Price 473; *McPherson v Allsop* (1839) 8 L.J. Ex. 262; *Quested v Callis* [1842] 1 Dowl. N.S. 888; *Brunsdon v Allard* [1859] 2 E. & E. 19; *Re Sullivan, Re Pearson Ex p. Morrison* [1868] L.R. 4 Q.B. 153.

[71] *Brunsdon v Allard*, above.

[72] *Tovery v Payne Ex p. Hart* [1830] 1 B. & Ad. 660.

[73] *Chapman v Haw* [1808] 1 Taunt. 341; *Jordon v Hunt* [1835] 3 Dowl. 666; *The Hope* (1833) 8 P.D. 144, CA; *Reynolds v Reynolds* (1809) 26 T.L.R. 104, CA; *Bovril v Podmore* (1829) 7 de Gm & G. 27.

[74] *Ex p. Games Williams v Lloyds* [1864] 3 H. & C. 294; *Sullivan v Pearson, Ex p. Morrison*, above n. 66; *Price v Crouch* (1891) 60 L.J. Q.B. 767; *Re Margetson & Jones* [1897] 2 Ch. 314.

[75] *Saunderson v Consolidated Credit & Mortgage Corporation Ltd* (1890) 6 T.L.R. 404.

Enforcement

The solicitor having a lien on property recovered or preserved may take active steps to enforce it.[76] The solicitor may either apply to the court for an injunction restraining the client from receiving payment without notice to himself,[77] or may apply at common law,[78] or under the Solicitor's Act 1974 for a charging order.[79] In addition, the solicitor may protect his lien by giving notice of it to the party liable to pay under an order to pay costs or a judgment or compromise.[80] Notice may also be given to that party's solicitors who, if payment is made without regard to the solicitor's claim,[81] will be liable to repay the sum to the solicitors claiming under the lien. Where a solicitor has money in hand in respect of which the lien is claimed he may retain his costs out of that money and pay the balance over to the client.[82]

13–009

D. LEGAL AID/CLS FUNDING

In a publicly funded case, as a matter of law, a solicitor's lien arises in respect of costs due for work done on the instructions of the client for which he has undertaken personal liability. Thus pre-certificate costs and disbursements fall within this category and the lien is protected by regulation 103 of the Civil Legal Aid (General) Regulations 1989. Once the certificate has been issued no lien can arise in respect of costs and disbursements payable under a certificate.

13–010

---

[76] *Wiedermann v Walpole (No.2)* (1891) 56 J.P. 5, CA.
[77] *Hobson v Shearwood* (1845) 8 Beav. 486; *Lloyd v Jones* (1879) 40 L.T. 514; *Lloyd v Mansell* (1853) 22 L.J. Q.B. 110.
[78] *Campbell v Campbell & Lewis* [1941] 1 All E.R. 274, CA.
[79] *Re Born, Curnock v Born* [1900] 2 Ch. 433.
[80] *Read v Dupper* (1795) 6 Term Rep. 361; *Ex p. Bryant* [1815] 1 Madd. 49; *Ormerod v Tate* [1801] 1 East. 464; *White v Pearce* (1849) 7 Hare. 276; *Ross v Buxton* (1889) 42 Ch. D. 190.
[81] *Welsh v Hole* [1779] 1 Doug. K.B. 238; *Read v Dupper*, above n. 7; *Ormerod v Tate*, above n.7; *Ross v Buxton*, above.
[82] *Watson v Maskell* [1834] 1 Bing N.C. 366; *Hanson v Reece* (1857) 27 L.J. Ch. 118; *Re Blake, Clutterbuck v Bradford* [1945] Ch. 61, CA.

CHAPTER 14

Charging Orders

A. UNDER THE SOLICITORS ACT 1974, S. 73

14–001 Any court in which a solicitor has been employed to prosecute or defend any proceedings may, at any time, declare the solicitor entitled to a charge on any property recovered or preserved through his instrumentality for his assessed costs in relation to those proceedings. It may make such orders for detailed assessment and for paying them out of that property as the court thinks fit and all conveyances and acts done to defeat that charge are (except in the case of a bona fide purchaser for value without notice) void as against the solicitor.[1] In the exercise of its discretion the court must also have regard to the client's rights[2] and no order may be made if the right to recover the costs is barred by any statute of limitations. However, the limitation periods do not run while the solicitor's name is on the record and a receiver is in possession.[3]

Under the 1974 Act, the power to make a charging order can only be exercised by a civil court.[4] In order to succeed under the 1974 Act, the solicitor must make out a prima facie case that he will not otherwise obtain his costs.[5] Provided that his conduct is not such as to justify his being deprived of costs, exceptional circumstances must be shown for depriving him of the opportunity of enforcing his lien.[6] The existence of the common law retaining lien may be important as it has been held that the application for a charging order is simply a cheap and speedy way of enforcing a right already possessed by the solicitor at common law.[7]

---

[1] Solicitor's Act 1974, s.73(1)(2).
[2] *Re Fuld's Estate (No.4)* [1968] P. 727.
[3] *Baile v Baile* [1872] L. R. 13 Eq. 497.
[4] *Humphreys Ex p. Lloyd George & George* [1898] 1 Q.B. 520, CA.
[5] *Harrison v Harrison* (1888) 13 P.D. 180, CA.
[6] *Re Blake, Clutterbuck, v Bradford* [1945] Ch. 61; *Dallow v Garrold Ex p. Adams* (1884) 13 Q.B.D. 543.
[7] *Re Born, Curnock v Born* [1900] 2 Ch. 433.

Where the solicitor has acted in bad faith the order will be refused. Similarly, where he has stood by while the property was dealt with in such a way that it would be unjust to third persons to make a charging order an order will not be made.[8] The right to a charging order may be lost if a solicitor acts in a manner inconsistent with its continuance, such as by proving in bankruptcy as an unsecured creditor[9] or accepting security for the costs.[10] The application for a charging order may be refused if the costs are recoverable from another person not interested in the property to be charged.[11] Where a claimant brought proceeding for infringement of two chemical processes and was unsuccessful in respect of one of the processes, the claimant was ordered to pay the defendant's costs. The defendant was ordered to take certain steps in relation to the other process which it failed to do. The defendant subsequently went into receivership and its assets were sold to another company. Its solicitors obtained a charging order under the 1974 Act to protect their fees. The claimant sought judgment in default in respect of the process in respect of which the defendant had failed to comply with the directions. The claimant also sought to set off its costs against the costs which it has been ordered to pay the defendant in respect of the other process. The court refused to order set off since, although there would be no prejudice to the defendant in allowing set off, the existence of the charging order meant that there would be prejudice to the defendant's solicitors. The protection afforded by the charging orders under section 73 of the 1974 Act should be upheld unless there were good reasons to come to a contrary decision.[12]

Arbitrations

The power of the court to charge property recovered or preserved in proceedings, with the payment of solicitors' costs, applies as if an arbitration were proceeding in the High Court and the High Court may make declarations and orders accordingly.[13]   14–002

Community Legal Service Fund

By virtue of section 10(7) of the Access to Justice Act 1999 there is a first charge for the benefit of the CLS Fund on any property, wherever situated, which is recovered or preserved on behalf of a funded client in the proceedings to which the funding relates.   14–003

---

[8] *Dallow v Garrold Ex p. Adams*, above.
[9] *Higgs v Higgs* [1934] P. 95.
[10] *Groome v Cheesewright* [1895] 1 Ch. 730.
[11] *Harrison v Harrison*, above; *Re Keane Lumley v Desborough* [1871] L.R. 12 Eq. 115.
[12] *Rohm & Hass Co v Collag Ltd* [2001] EWHC Ch. D., November 14, Pumfrey J.
[13] Arbitration Act 1996, s.75. This is a mandatory provision and is not affected by any agreement to the contrary ibid., s.4(1) and Sch. 1.

The application under the Solicitors Act 1974

14–004   The application is made using the procedure under CPR, Part 8 and it is not necessary to obtain permission to issue. The jurisdiction of the High Court under Part III of the 1974 Act may be exercised by a judge, a master, a costs judge, or a district judge of the Family Division, or a district judge for the costs of the contentious business done in a cause or matter which proceeds in the district registry of which he is district judge or for non-contentious business.[14]

In the Court of Appeal, where the judgment relied on is that of the Court of Appeal, any judge of the Division in which the action was brought may make a charging order.[15]

In bankruptcy the judge has no power, in the exercise of his bankruptcy jurisdiction, to make a charging order except perhaps where the property is recovered or preserved in bankruptcy proceedings.[16] But he may do so by virtue of his jurisdiction as a judge of the High Court and may direct the power to be exercised by a registrar.[17] The provisions of section 73(1) of the 1974 Act are plainly directed to cases in which the court has made an order for costs. Where the order for costs is dealt with in a compromise agreement there is therefore no power to continue a freezing order or make a declaration under section 73(1).[18]

The provisions of section 73 of the 1974 Act apply in respect of contentious business in the county court, subject to certain restrictions on the total amount allowable.[19] A solicitor seeking a charging order under Section 73 of the 1974 Act does not exempt himself from the limitations imposed by Section 69 of the 1974 Act (restriction on the right to recover costs by action). Sections 69–71 are stringent codes laid down to protect a client who could possibly be in a disadvantageous position. That legislation has not changed even with the advent of CPR and the transfer of more work to the County Court. The Court may exercise the power only where a bill of costs relates wholly or partly to contentious business done in a County Court and the amount of the bill does not exceed £5,000.[20]

Property subject to charge

14–005   The order may be made where "property" has been "recovered or preserved" through the instrumentality of the solicitor. "Property" is not defined in the 1974 Act and any property whether real or personal which

---

[14] CPR Sch. 1, RSC Ord. 106, r.2(2).
[15] *Re Deakin Ex p. Daniell* [1900] 2 Q.B. 489.
[16] *Re Deakin Ex p. Daniell*, above.
[17] *Re Wood Ex p. Farshawe* [1897] 1 Q.B. 314.
[18] *Al-Abbas v Al-Dabbagh* [2002] EWCA Civ, November 21.
[19] Solicitors Act 1974, s.74(1), (2), (3).
[20] Solicitors Act 1974, s.69(3). *Jones v Twinsectra Ltd* [2002] EWCA Civ, April 16.

can be brought within section 73 may be made the subject of a charge.[21] The court will not make a charging order on property which by statute or provision of the court is intended to be personal to the holder and is inalienable.

"Property" has been held to extend to all kinds of real and personal property.[22] Thus damage in respect of a collision[23]; or an unsatisfied judgment,[24] or costs payable to a client under a judgment,[25] even where the judgment is for costs alone,[26] or paid under a judgment of a court of first instance and ordered to be repaid on appeal,[27] may each be the subject of a charging order. A judgment debtor's beneficial interest in a house held under a trust for sale may also be the subject of a charging order.[28]

The court has jurisdiction to make a charging order over costs recoverable in an action by a client company where that company has become dormant and incapable of acting or unwilling to act further, even though the order for costs contains no direction that the costs be assessed and the costs have not been assessed. The court is not bound to make an order for detailed assessment of costs as between solicitor and client when making a charging order.[29]

B. UNDER THE CHARGING ORDERS ACT 1979

In addition to the rights conferred by the Solicitors Act 1974, the Charging Orders Act 1979 confers rights which may be relevant to the recovery of costs. Under the 1979 Act where a person is required to pay a sum of money to the solicitor under a judgment or order of the High Court or a county court for the purpose of enforcing that judgment or order, the appropriate court is empowered to impose a charge on any specified property of the judgment debtor, who by the judgment or order of the court is required to pay a sum of money to another person to secure the payment of such money due or to become due under the judgment or order.[30]

14–006

In deciding whether to make a charging order the court must consider all the circumstances of the case and in particular any evidence before it as to

---

[21] *Shaw v Neale & Remnant* (1856) 6 H.L. Cas. 581; *Redfern & Son v Rosenthall Bros.* (1902) 86 L.T. 855, CA.

[22] *Birchall v Pugin* [1875] L.R. 10 C.P. 397.

[23] *The Marie Gartz (No.2)* [1920] P. 460.

[24] *Farrant v Caley* (1924) 68 S.J. 898, CA; *Birchall v Pugin*, above.

[25] *Dallow v Garrold Ex p. Adams* (1884) 14 Q.B.D. 543; *Re Deakin Ex p. Daniell* [1900] 2 Q.B. 489, CA; *Johnston v McKenzie* [1911] 2 I.R. 118; *Campbell v Lewis* [1941] 1 All E.R. 274.

[26] *Re Blake, Clutterbuck v Bradford* [1945] 1 Ch. 61.

[27] *Guy v Churchill* [1887] 35 Ch. D. 489, CA.

[28] *National Westminster Bank Ltd. v Stockman* [1981] 1 W.L.R. 67.

[29] *Fairfold Properties Ltd v Exmouth Docks Co. Ltd (No.2)* [1993] 2 W.L.R. 241.

[30] Charging Orders Act 1979, s.1(1).

the personal circumstances of the debtor and whether any other creditor of the debtor would be likely to be unduly prejudiced by the making of the order.[31] It appears that the court has no power to impose a charge on property of a judgment debtor for an unascertained sum such as costs which have not been assessed.[32] However, interest runs on a judgment debt, including costs, which have yet to be ascertained.[33] Although a charging order may not be expressed to cover interest on the judgment debt or costs it does in fact cover both. Section 20(5) of the Limitation Act 1980 does not limit the right to interest on a charging order to six years.[34] A charging order takes effect and is enforceable as an equitable charge, so that the holder of a charging order is entitled to add to his security the costs of obtaining possession and sale against the mortgagor and any third party claiming an interest.[35] The argument that a charging order cannot be made for unassessed costs confuses the jurisdiction to make a charging order under section 1(1) of the 1979 Act, with the rights of the holder of a charging order to add further sums for interest and costs to the security as a result of the terms of section 3(4). In the particular case the court ordered the costs of the proceedings to be paid to the claimants out of the proceeds of sale of the property.[36]

The procedure relating to charging orders, stop orders and stop notices is now contained in CPR Part 73 and its related practice direction. The 1979 Act defines the property which may be charged under it. The list is exhaustive so far as applications under the Act are concerned. The charge may be imposed by a charging order under the 1979 Act on any interest held by the debtor beneficially in any asset (as defined), or under any trust, or any interest held by a person as trustee, if the interest is such an asset or is an asset under another trust and:

(a) the judgment or order in respect of which a charge is to be imposed was made against that person as trustee of the trusts;

(b) the whole beneficial interest under the trusts is held by the debtor unencumbered and for his own benefit; or

(c) in cases where there are two or more debtors all of whom are liable to the creditor for the same debt, they together hold the whole beneficial interest under the trust encumbered and for their own benefit.[37]

---

[31] *ibid.*, s.1(5).
[32] *A. & M. Records Inc. v Darakejian* [1975] 1 W.L.R. 1610.
[33] *Thomas v Bunn* [1991] 2 W.L.R. 27, HL. See also *Fairfold Properties Ltd v Exmouth Docks Co. Ltd (No.2)*, above.
[34] *Ezekiel v Orakpo* [1997] 1 W.L.R. 340; [1997] 1 W.L.R. 527, HL (Petition Dismissed).
[35] *Parker-Tweedale v Dunbar Bank Plc (No.2)* [1991] Ch. 26 and *Ezekiel v Orakpo* above.
[36] *Holder v Hupperstone* [2000] 1 All E.R. 473 Evans-Lombe J.
[37] Charging Orders Act 1979, s.2(1).

"Assets" are defined by the 1979 Act as land and securities of any of the following kinds: government stock; stock of any body (other than a building society) incorporated within England and Wales; stock of any body incorporated outside England and Wales or of any state or territory outside the United Kingdom, being stock registered in a register kept at any place within England and Wales; and units of any unit trusts in respect of which a register of the unit holders is kept in any place within England and Wales or funds in court.[38]

The High Court has[39] jurisdiction to make a charging order only:

(a) where the property to be charged is a fund in court which is lodged in the High Court;

(b) where the order to be enforced is a maintenance order of the High Court; or

(c) where the judgment or order to be enforced is a judgment or order of the High Court and exceeds £5,000.[40]

---

[38] *ibid.*, s.2(2).
[39] By virtue of s.1(2)(a), (b), (c) of the Charging Orders Act 1979.
[40] This amount is the county court limit for the purposes of the Charging Orders Act 1979 specified by the County Courts Jurisdiction Order 1981 (SI 1981/1123).

CHAPTER 15

Security for Costs in Litigation

15–001 In certain circumstances (Part 25, Part 2) a defendant (or a person who is in the position of a defendant in respect of a Part 20 claim) may apply to the court for security for his costs of the proceedings.[1] The application must be supported by written evidence and, where the court makes an order for security it will determine the amount and direct the manner in which and the time within which the security must be given.[2]

The court will make an order for security of it is satisfied, having regard to all the circumstances of the case, that it is just to do so, one or more of the conditions set out below applies or an enactment permits the court to require security for costs.[3] The conditions to be fulfilled before the court will make an order for security are:

(a) that the claimant is an individual who is ordinarily resident out of the jurisdiction (and is not a person against whom a claim can be enforced under the Brussels Convention or the Lugano Convention as defined by section 1(1) of the Civil Jurisdiction and Judgments Act 1982);

(b) the claimant is a company or other incorporated body which is ordinarily resident out of the jurisdiction (and is not a body against whom a claim can be enforced under the Brussels Convention or the Lugano Convention);

(c) the claimant is a company or other body (whether incorporated inside or outside Great Britain) and there is reason to believe that it will be unable to pay the defendant's costs if ordered to do so;

---

[1] CPR r.25.12(1).
[2] *ibid.*, r.25.12(2) and (3).
[3] *ibid.*, r.25.12 and 25.13(1).

(the fact that the claimant's poor financial situation may be due to the defendant's breach of contract may be reason for not ordering security[4];

(d) the claimant has changed his address since the claim was commenced with a view to evading the consequences of the litigation;

(e) the claimant failed to give his address in the claim form or gave an incorrect address in that form;

(f) the claimant is acting as a nominal claimant (other than as a representative claimant under Part 19) and there is reason to believe that he will be unable to pay the defendant's costs if ordered to do so;

(g) the claimant has taken steps in relation to his assets that would make it difficult to enforce an order for costs against him.[5]

Where the court makes an order for security it will determine the amount of the security and direct the manner in which and the time within which the security must be given.[6]

The court may make an order for security for costs against someone other than the claimant on the defendant's application if it is satisfied that it is just to make such an order an one or more of the following conditions applies. The conditions are: that the person assigned the right to the claim to the claimant with a view to avoiding the possibility of a costs order being made against him; or has contributed or agreed to contribute to the claimant's costs in return for a share of any money or property which the claimant may recover in the proceedings; and is a person against whom a costs order may be made.[7]

It is clear from CPR 24.2, 24.6 and Practice Direction 24 (summary disposal of claims) that there is now jurisdiction under the CPR to make orders which are tantamount to orders for security for costs outside the provisions of CPR Part 25. Relevant considerations besides the ability of the person concerned to pay would be: (a) his conduct of the proceedings; and (b) the apparent strength of his claim or defence. Whilst the court would not ordinarily penalise breaches of the rules by making orders for payment into court under CPR 3.1(5) such an order might be appropriate if there was a history of repeated breach of timetables or court orders, or if there was something in the conduct of the party that gave rise to suspicion that the party was not bona fide and the court was of the opinion that the other side

---

[4] *Fernhill Mining Ltd v Kier Construction Ltd* January 27, 2000 CA (unreported).
[5] CPR r.25.13(2); *Chandler v Brown* [2001] CP Rep. 103, Park J.
[6] CPR r.25.12(3).
[7] *ibid.*, r.25.14(1) and r.(2).

should have some financial security or protection.[8] The modern principles relating to security for costs were explained in *Olatawura v Aboilye* (above). The court should always be on its guard against exorbitant applications for summary judgment in a misguided attempt to obtain conditional orders for security for costs. The court should be reluctant to be drawn into an assessment of the merits beyond what was necessary to establish whether the Part 24 test had been fulfilled.[9]

The purpose of Rule 25.13 is to eliminate any covert discrimination against nationals of other convention states. In the context of the rule, "claim" is to be construed as including any claim whether or not a money claim and not limited to an order for costs. The conditions in the rule, (a) confine the jurisdiction to individuals who are not ordinarily residents either in the UK or another convention state. Such a claimant cannot deprive the court of jurisdiction by placing an asset in a convention state. The court has jurisdiction under Rule 25.13 to order security to be given by a claimant by reason of the fact that he was an individual claimant who was ordinarily resident out of the jurisdiction and not ordinarily resident in a convention state. On the particular facts of the case in which the claimant had assets in Switzerland, although there was in principle no reason to suppose an order for costs might not be fully enforceable in Switzerland, the court had to take into account the ease with which the assets held there could be moved, including the most valuable asset which was some shares in a US company. Bearing in mind the nature and potential size of the risk security was ordered to be given.[10]

The wording of Rule 25.13 was introduced in order to abolish the discriminatory effect under Community Law of the language of the old Rule.[11] Against that background the Rule is to be interpreted as being confined to persons who were nationals or residents of other convention countries. As a matter of discretion it was not just to make an order for security against a foreign company whose ships came so regularly to the ports of the UK and of other convention countries that the whereabouts of the vessels could easily be tracked and a judgment easily enforced in the UK or another convention country if a vessel owned by the claimant was there. In the circumstances no order for security was made.[12]

The discretion under CPR 25.13 and 25.15 to award security for costs against an individual not resident in a contracting state of the enforcement conventions is to be exercised only on objectively justified grounds relating to obstacles to or the burden of enforcement in the context of the particular

---

[8] *Olatawura v Abiloye* [2002] EWCA Civ 998; [2003] 1 W.L.R. 275, CA; [2002] 4 All E.R. 903 CA.

[9] *King v Telegraph Group Ltd* [2003] EWHC, QB, June 9, Eady J.

[10] *De Beer v Kanaar & Co* [2001] EWCA Civ 1318; [2003] 1 W.L.R. 38; [2002] 3 All E.R. 1020, CA.

[11] *Cheque Point SARL v McClelland* [1997] Q.B.D. 51.

[12] *White Sea & Omega Shipping v International Transport Workers Federation* [2001] EWCA Civ, March 7.

individual or country concerned. If there are likely to be no obstacles to or difficulty about enforcement but simply an extra burden in the form of costs or moderate delay the appropriate course is to limit the amount of the security ordered by reference to that potential burden. The mere absence of reciprocal arrangements or legislation providing for enforcement of foreign judgments cannot of itself justify an inference that enforcement would not be possible.[13]

Given the decision in *Nasser v United Bank of Kuwait* an order for security should only be made if there was evidence of difficulty of enforcement. The fact that the claimants' actions were suspicious was not a sufficient ground for seeking the fortification of an undertaking in damages. The application for security therefore failed.[14]

The test under CPR 25.13 is objective and the claimant's motivation in taking steps in relation to his assets which would make it difficult to enforce an order for costs against him was irrelevant as to whether the test was satisfied though it might be relevant to the exercise of the discretion to order security. In a case where the claimant was a Lebanese citizen in the UK and his only substantial asset was a house in Australia which he had recently sold, the court held there were solid grounds for thinking that if the claimant were unsuccessful it would be difficult to enforce an order for costs against him and security was ordered.[15] The decision at first instance was appealed, with permission, but the defendants sought an order setting aside the permission unless the claimant complied with the original order for security. The Court of Appeal held that the effect of the order to provide security was to stay the proceedings below unless security was provided. The claimant was not disregarding the order simply because he chose to submit to the stay rather than provide the security. In any event a stay in the High Court did not have the effect of staying proceedings in the Court of Appeal. On the facts there was no reason to place onerous conditions on the future of an appeal for which the Lord Justice had granted permission.[16]

There is no public policy rule which prevents security being provided by way of undertaking of the party's solicitors.[17]

Where it was alleged that a claimant was being maintained by his mother, the Court of Appeal took the view that provision of financial support for litigation by way of a close relative did not amount to maintenance, even if the maintainer was not prepared to undertake to pay between the parties

---

[13] *Nasser v United Bank of Kuwait* [2001] EWCA Civ 556; [2002] 1 W.L.R. 1868; [2002] 1 All E.R. 401, CA. As to ordering security against a claimant who has taken steps in relation to his assets that would make it difficult to enforce an order for costs against him, see *Chandler v Brown* [2001] C.P. Rep. 103, Park J.

[14] *Mattos Junior & 3 Others v MacDaniels Ltd & Ors* [2002] EWHC, CH, November 22, Peter Smith J.

[15] *Aoun v Bahri* [2002] EWHC 29 (Comm); [2002] 3 All E.R. 182, Moore-Bick J.

[16] *Aoun v Bahri* EWCA Civ 1141.

[17] *A Limited v B Limited* [1996] 1 W.L.R. 665, Sir John Vinelott.

costs in the event of failure. The application for the security for costs was refused.[18]

In divorce proceedings, where the former husband, who was liable to pay the costs of ancillary proceedings, removed virtually all his assets out of the country, and sought a downward variation of the periodical payments order, the Court of Appeal held that an application for security for costs, which was directed exclusively to past costs could not be made. Security applications were not intended as a remedy for enforcement of costs already incurred. The judge at first instance who had made an order for security lacked jurisdiction and the order was reversed.[19]

Where both parties were founding their claims on the same body of facts, the claimant was entitled to be secured to the full extent of the costs (as defendant to the counterclaim), and not merely for the amount by which the costs were increased in defending the counterclaim.[20]

Where an application for security is made against's a claimant ordinarily resident within the European Community, the court would not order security on the grounds of residence against a claimant who was a national of, and resident in, another state, which was a signatory to the Brussels Convention, in the absence of cogent evidence of substantial difficulty of enforcing a judgment in that state. Notwithstanding the decision in *Fitzgerald v Williams*[21] the court continues to have discretion to order security for costs, provided that it is necessary in the interests of justice and that discretion is not exercised in such a way as to offend against EC law principles. An English company in a similar position would be treated in the same way.

The amount of security is in the discretion of the court but it is normal to support an application with a draft bill showing the estimated costs likely to be incurred in the future together with details of the costs to date. Security for costs is not necessarily confined to future costs but can extend to costs already incurred, provided there is no delay in the application.[22]

A defendant may make subsequent applications for further security as the action proceeds and the court may increase the amount ordered.[23] The usual penalty for failure to give security is that the action be dismissed. The court has power under its inherent jurisdiction to dismiss an action where it is satisfied that the action is not being pursued with due diligence, there is no

---

[18] *Condliffe v Hislop* [1996] 1 All E.R. 431, CA.

[19] *Penny v Penny* [1996] 2 All E.R. 329, CA.

[20] *Pretomin v Secnaf Marine, The Times*, March 9, 1995, Colman J.

[21] [1996] 2 W.L.R. 447, CA.

[22] *Brocklebank v Kings Lynn Steamship Company* [1878] 3 C.P.D. 365; *Massey v Allen* (1879) 12 Ch. D. 807; *Procon (Great Britain) Ltd v Provincial Building Co. Ltd* [1984] 1 W.L.R. 557, CA.

[23] *Sturla v Freccia* [1877] W.N. 166 at 188; [1878] W.N. 161; *Republic of Costa Rica v Erlanger* (1876) 3 Ch. D. 62; *Northampton Coal Etc. Co. v Midland Wagon Co.* (1878) 7 Ch. D. 500; *Massey v Allen* above.

reasonable prospect that the security will be paid, and the time-limit prescribed by the court for giving the security has been disregarded.[24]

On an application for security for costs during bankruptcy proceedings an order will normally be made unless the bankrupt can show that it would amount to a denial of justice to him.[25]

There are no fixed rules which apply to the question of whether security for costs should be ordered to be given by a counterclaiming defendant, but generally, where a counterclaim is entered by way of defence to an action, the defendant should not be required to provide security.[26] The court has power under section 726 of the Companies Act 1985 to make an order for security for costs in proceedings commenced by petition under section 459 of the Act. The phrase "other legal proceedings" in section 726 refers to any matter in which the jurisdiction of the court is invoked by an originating process other than a writ. A "claimant" within the section covers any person who has invoked the court's jurisdiction in such a way.[27] The court has power to stay the payment out of security pending an appeal, it is a matter of discretion and balance.[28]

It is appropriate for a judge to have regard to the possibility that a claimant would recover a substantial sum in another action before the time for costs arose in the action in which the application for security is made. The court was right to consider the interrelationship between the two actions when deciding what order for security, if any, to make.[29] An order for security should normally, within its terms, deal with failure to pay and the consequence of that failure would result in a dismissal of the claim without further order of the court.[30]

Security for costs in the Court of Appeal

The court may order security for costs of an appeal on the same grounds as it may order security for costs against a claimant under Part 25. The order may be made against an appellant and/or a respondent who also appeals. Such an order may be made where the person against whom the order is sought is a limited company and there is reason to believe that it will be unable to pay the costs of the other parties to the appeal should its appeal be unsuccessful.[31] Where, on an appeal the court ordered the claimant to

15–002

---

[24] *Speed Up Holdings Ltd v Gough & Co. (Handley) Ltd* [1986] F.S.R. 330.

[25] *Hocking v Walker, The Times,* August 11, 1993, CA.

[26] *Lehrer McGovern International v Circol Partnership* [1992] E.G.C.S. 140, CA.

[27] *Unisoft Group (No.1) Re Saunderson Holdings v Unisoft Group* [1993] B.C.L.C. 1292, CA.

[28] *Stabilad Ltd v Stephens & Carter Ltd* [1999] 1 W.L.R. 1201, CA.

[29] *Crisps v Heritage Distribution Corporation, The Times,* November 10, 1999, CA.

[30] *Clive Brooks & Co Ltd v Baynard, The Times,* April 30, 1998, CA and *CTSS Management Services Ltd v Charisma Records,* January 18, 2000, Jacob, J. (unreported).

[31] CPR r.25.15(1) and r.2.

pay security for costs, and the claimant complied with the order by borrowing that amount from her bank by subsequently withdrew the appeal, the court found that the money was held on trust, that it would be returned to the bank if the appeal was successful·or even paid by the claimant under the terms of the loan agreement if the appeal was unsuccessful. The court allowed the money to be repaid to the bank. The court also held that the reasonable costs of complying with the order for security for costs included both the arrangement fee and the interest payable on the loan, because when the order for security was made it was obvious that the order could not be met out of the claimants own funds.[32]

An order by the Court of Appeal for security in respect of the costs of the proceedings below which would only be awarded to an appellant if successful on an appeal may be made "for the purposes of and incidental to" the hearing of the appeal within the jurisdiction inferred by section 15 of the Supreme Court Act 1981. Such an order would also be "in relation to" an appeal within CPR 52.10. There is no general rule that security for the costs below of a defendant against whom judgment is given, should be released immediately. The security may be preserved pending the outcome of an appeal. Questions of security should usually be resolved at the time when the court has some readily exercisable and appropriate control over the claimant who is being asked to provide security.[33]

The Court of Appeal has case management powers enabling it to order that unless an unsuccessful claimant satisfied outstanding costs orders the appeal be struck out.[34]

In order to obtain an order for security for costs it is necessary to show that a company, which was appealing, would be unable to pay the respondents' costs if the appeal was unsuccessful within CPR rule 25.13(2)(c). In a case where the appellant company was unwilling to pay but not unable to do so, the application for security failed.[35] The Court of Appeal held that it was appropriate to make an order for security for costs against an opponent although it had no information about the company given that the company had failed to pay the outstanding costs orders without providing any evidence or explanation for breaching the order and the court was therefore entitled to draw an inference that the company would be unable to pay further costs relating to the appeal.[36]

Liquidators sought an order for security for their costs in proceedings brought by the applicant for the removal of the liquidators. The court held that the proper approach to the use of the powers conferred by Rule

[32] R. v Common Professional Examination Board ex p. Mealing-McCleod, May 2, 2000, CA (unreported).

[33] DAR International FEF Co v Aon Ltd [2003] EWCA Civ, December 10.

[34] Contract Facilities Ltd v Rees [2003] EWCA Civ 1105.

[35] Bell Electric Ltd v Aweco Appliance Systems GmbH & Co KG [2002] EWHC Comm October 31, 2002.

[36] Societe Eram Shipping Co Ltd v Compagnie International de Navigation (security of costs) [2001] EWCA Civ 568; [2001] CP Rep. 113 CA.

4.120(3) of the Insolvency Rules 1986 was a merit based approach rather than a security based approach. If a security based approach were adopted the wide ambit of the power conferred by Rule 4.120(3) would be inconsistent with the conditions for ordering the giving of security for costs contained in CPR 25.13.[37] An order for security for costs that would stifle a claim or an appeal will not ordinarily be made unless the party concerned can be shown to have regularly flouted court procedures or otherwise demonstrated lack of good faith. The power to order security for costs which would have the effect of stifling a claim or an appeal has to be exercised with great caution.[38]

A. STATUTORY POWERS TO AWARD SECURITY FOR COSTS

Certain enactments empower the court to require security to be given for the costs of any proceedings. The relevant Acts are: The Companies Act 1985 section 726(1) and the Arbitration Act 1996 section 38(3). The court may make an order for security against someone other than the claimant if it is satisfied, having regard to all the circumstances of the case, that it is just to do so and one or more of the following conditions applies. Those conditions are that the person: 15–003

(a) has assigned the right to the claim to the claimant with a view to avoiding the possibility of a costs order being made against him; or

(b) has contributed or agreed to contribute to the claimant's costs in return for a share of any money or property which the claimant may recover in the proceedings; and is a person against whom a costs order may be made.[39]

The Companies Act 1985, s.726(1)

Section 726(1) of the Companies Act 1985 states: 15–004

"Where in England and Wales a limited company is claimant in an action or other legal proceedings, the court having jurisdiction in the matter may, if it appears by credible testimony that there is reason to believe that the company will be unable to pay the defendant's costs if

---

[37] In the matter of Buildhead Ltd (in creditors voluntary liquidation) Quicksons (*South & West Ltd v Katz*) [2003] EWHC, Ch, August 8, Evans-Lombe J.
[38] *Ali v Hudson* [2003] EWCA Civ 1793.
[39] CPR r.25.14.

successful in his defence, require sufficient security to be given for those costs, and may stay all proceedings until security is given."[40]

The fact that a company is in liquidation is prima facie evidence that it is unable to pay the costs unless evidence to the contrary is given.[41] Otherwise the application for security must be supported by evidence which credibly and reasonably shows the inability of the company to pay the costs of the successful defendant.[42]

There are well established principles, in the context of liquidators, to the effect that an adverse costs order made against a company being wound up would be paid in full and in priority to virtually every other claim against the insolvent's estate. These principles are based on fairness and justice which also apply to provisional liquidators. A provisional liquidator is expressly appointed by the court in order to produce a resolution of a company's financial problems and has the power to expend the assets of the company as seen fit without further order of the court. If a provisional liquidator in the pursuance of his powers as officer of the court embarks on litigation, justice requires that the costs should come out of the assets of the company.[43]

The new regime relating to appeals and the requirement to obtain permission does not alter the approach of the court to security for costs. Whether an appeal has much merit or not may be a relevant factor but it does not follow that because permission has been granted therefore security for costs should not be ordered. The real concern is whether it is appropriate for an appellant to be able to pursue an appeal without running a risk of actually having to pay the costs of the other side if unsuccessful.[44]

Where an impecunious defendant against whom the claimant had initially obtained a freezing injunction sought an inquiry as to damages, the claimant was held not to be entitled to security of the costs of the inquiry.[45]

The phrase "other legal proceedings" in section 726 of the 1985 Act refers to any matter in which the jurisdiction of the court is invoked by an originating process other than a claim form. It applies to a person who has invoked the jurisdiction by whatever originating process. The word "Plaintiff" (Claimant) in section 726 covers such a person. It follows that an application for security for costs can be made against a person who brings a petition under section 459 of the 1985 Act.[46]

---

[40] Companies Act 1985, s.726(1).

[41] *Northampton Coal Iron & Wagon Co. v Midland Wagon Co.* (1878) 7 Ch. D. 500, CA. *Pure Spirit Co. v Fowler* (1890) 25 Q.B.D. 235.

[42] *National Bank of Wales v Atkins* (1894) 38 S.J. 186; *Diamond Steel Manufacturing Co. v Harrison* (1910) 27 R.P.C. 451.

[43] *Smith v UIC Insurance Co Ltd*, January 19, 2000 Dean J. (unreported).

[44] *Federal Bank of the Middle East v Hadkinson, The Times*, December 7, 1997, CA.

[45] *C.T. Bowering & Co. (Insurers) v Corsi & Partners, The Times*, June 28, 1994, CA.

[46] *Unisoft Group (No.1)* [1993] B.C.L.C. 528, Morrit J. and on appeal *Unisoft Group, Re Saunderson Holdings v Unisoft Group* [1994] B.C.C. 11, CA.

The mere fact that a company has issued a debenture charging all its assets to secure repayment of all monies to a particular person has been considered not to be a sufficient reason for ordering security.[47] The court may not ignore the unchallenged evidence of an accountant as to a company's present ability to pay the costs of an action.[48]

"Sufficient Security" should be neither illusory nor oppressive.[49] It is not intended that it should be complete security although it should be for the probable amount of costs taking into account the circumstances of the case.[50]

Lord Denning M.R. laid down circumstances which the court might take into account in arriving at its decision. The list, which follows, is not exclusive:

(1) whether the claimant's claim is bona fide and not a sham;

(2) whether the claimant has a reasonably good prospect of success;

(3) whether there is an admission by the defendants on the pleadings or elsewhere that money is due;

(4) whether there is a substantial payment into court or an "open offer" of a substantial amount;

(5) whether the application for security was being used oppressively, *e.g.* so as to stifle a genuine claim;

(6) whether the claimant's want of means has been brought about by any conduct of the defendant's such as delay in payment or doing their part of the work;

(7) whether the application for security is made at a late stage in the proceedings.[51]

The court may order one of two claimants to give security.[52] It will not allow section 726(1) to be used as an instrument of oppression or allow an impecunious company to put unfair pressure on a prosperous company.[53] If an order for security against a claimant company might result in oppression, in that the company would be forced to abandon a claim which has a reasonable prospect of success, the court is entitled to refuse to make the

---

[47] *Universal Aircraft Ltd v Hickey*, May 4, 1943 (unreported), Morton J.
[48] *Kim Barker v Aegon Insurance Company (U.K.) Ltd, The Times*, October 9, 1989, CA.
[49] *Dominion Brewery v Foster* (1897) 77 L.T. 507; *Imperial Bank of China & Japan v Bank of Hindustan* [1866] L.R. 1 Ch. 437.
[50] *Innovaire Displays v Corporate Booking Services* [1991] B.C.C. 174, CA.
[51] *Sir Lindsay Parkinson & Co. Ltd v Triplan Ltd* [1973] Q.B. 609, CA.
[52] *John Bishop (Caterers) Ltd v National Union Bank Ltd* [1973] 1 All E.R. 707.
[53] *Pearson v Naydler* [1977] 1 W.L.R. 899.

order notwithstanding that the claimant company, if successful, would be unable to pay the defendant's costs.[54]

It is sufficient for the claimant to show that there is a probability rather than a certainty that he will be unable to pursue the action if the order for security is made. An application for security should not be made the occasion for a detailed examination of the merits of the case.[55] Parties should not attempt to go into the merits of the case unless it can be clearly established one way or another that there is a high degree of probability of success or failure.[56]

The question whether any order should be made pursuant to section 726 of the Companies Act 1985 is one of discretion. Where on the trial of a defendant's counterclaim the same matters would be canvassed as would be canvassed if the claimant were able to pursue the claim, and the stay of proceedings could be lifted if the claimant won on those issues, it has been held that there was no point in ordering security other than to give the defendant a tactical advantage in the litigation.[57]

An applicant for an order for security for costs under section 726 of the 1985 Act is required to show that the company will not (as opposed to may not) be able to meet its debts when an order for costs is made against it. The question is to be answered at the time of the application although the court has a discretion and the application does not have to be determined on an all or nothing basis. The court has power to order security in a sum less than the total potential order for costs. A balancing exercising is required.[58]

The Arbitration Act 1996, s.38(3)

15–005   Unless the parties to the arbitration agree otherwise, the tribunal has the power to order a claimant to provide security for the costs of the arbitration.[59]

The tribunal may not exercise the power on the ground that the claimant is an individual ordinarily resident outside the United Kingdom, or a corporation or association incorporated or formed under the law of a country outside the United Kingdom, or whose central management and control is exercised outside the United Kingdom.[60] Apart from the above there appears to be no restriction on the tribunal's power to order security.

---

[54] *Aquila Design (GRB) Products Ltd v Cornhill Insurance plc* [1988] B.C.L.C. 134, CA.
[55] *Trident International Freight Services Ltd v Manchester Ship Canal Company* [1990] B.C.L.C. 263, CA.
[56] *Porzelack K.G. v Porzelack (U.K.) Ltd* [1987] 1 All E.R. 1074.
[57] *B.J. Crabtree (Insulations v G.P.T. Communications Systems)* (1900) 59 B.L.R. 43, CA.
[58] *Unisoft Group (No.2)* [1993] B.C.L.C. 532, Sir Donald Nicholls V.C.
[59] Arbitration Act 1996, s.38(1), (2), (3).
[60] *ibid.*, s.38(3).

In unique arbitration between two parties having no connection with England, but who had chosen London as a convenient place in which to arbitrate, the question of whether or not an order for security for costs was appropriate, was determined by the parties' intention arising from the arbitration agreement itself. In the particular case the parties had expressly embraced the arbitration law of England, including the power to order security for costs, and an appropriate order was therefore made.[61]

B. INTERNATIONAL CONVENTIONS

A number of international conventions[62] expressly forbid any requirement **15–006** of security for costs particularly in relation to carriage of goods and passengers by road and rail. Security for costs may not be required from a person seeking to enforce a foreign judgment against an EC country.[63]

The Court of Appeal has held that there should be no presumption that members of the EC will not honour orders made by the courts of England notwithstanding that claimants (including United Kingdom citizens) resident outside the jurisdiction and with no assets inside the United Kingdom can be ordered to give security for costs.[64]

The Court of Appeal has held that CPR Sch.1; RSC, Ord. 23 (see now CPR Part 25 section II) does not offend against Art.7 of the EEC Treaty since residence abroad is not itself a ground for making an order under the rule. It is merely a pre-condition to the existence of the jurisdiction. The rules apply where the claimant resides outside the jurisdiction whether or not such residence is in a member state of the EC and it applies no matter what the nationality of the claimant. The discretion given to the court under the rules is exercised equally without regard to nationality.[65]

There is no inflexible assumption that a person not resident in a Brussels or Lugano state should provide security for costs. The question is whether security is objectively justified having regard to the difficulties of enforcement in relation to this particular foreign claimant and country concerned. Impecuniosity might be relevant to the issue of enforcement. The absence of reciprocal enforcement arrangements does not justify an inference that enforcement will not be possible.[66]

---

[61] *Regia Autonoma Electricitate Renel v Gulf Petroleum International Limited* [1996] 2 All E.R. 319, Rix J.

[62] Information regarding the nature and extent of international conventions relating to security can be obtained from the Queens Bench Masters' Secretary's Department, Royal Courts of Justice, Strand, London WC2A 2LL.

[63] Art.45 of the Civil Jurisdiction and Judgments Act 1982 bringing into force the 1968 Convention on the Enforcement of Foreign Judgments.

[64] *C. Van Der Lely N.V. v Watveare Overseas Ltd* [1982] F.S.R. 122; *De Bry v Fitzgerald* [1990] 1 All E.R. 560, CA.

[65] *Berkeley Administration Inc. v McClelland* [1990] 2 Q.B. 407, CA.

[66] *Nasser v United Bank of Kuwait* [2001] EWCA Civ, April 11.

Security in the form of a charge over property is in principle adequate to fulfill an order for security for costs. In the ordinary course of events however if a property were valuable enough there would be no difficulty in obtaining a secured bank guarantee. In a commercial case the court would wish to know why undertakings could not be given, or why no secured bank guarantee was possible.[67]

C. SECURITY BY UNDERTAKING

15-007 If the parties agree, a claimant or the claimant's solicitor may undertake to pay the whole or a specified proportion of the costs or a specified sum in lieu of security for costs, in which case there is no need for an application to the court. Where such an undertaking is given and is accepted in lieu of security, it lasts until there is a final judgment from which an appeal lies.[68]

It is permissible for a solicitor to meet an order for security by way of a personal undertaking before the client's liability to meet an order for costs, even if the solicitor knows that there is no real prospect of his being reimbursed by the client, save in the event of the litigation being successful.[69]

D. CLS FUNDING/LEGAL AID

15-008 The fact that the claimant is a legally assisted person is not a reason why security should not be ordered. It may of course affect the amount of security ordered as the amount depends upon the costs likely to be awarded to the defendant if successful at the end of the proceedings.[70]

Where a defendant was ordered to pay money into court as security for the claimant's costs and the defendant was subsequently granted legal aid, in order to apply to set aside the judgment which had been entered against him, and to defend (which application was successful), the money paid into court by the defendant was held not to be subject to the statutory legal aid charge, since it was not the subject matter of the proceedings and had not been recovered or preserved by the defendant's success.[71]

---

[67] *AP (U.K.) Ltd v West Midlands Fire & Civil Defence Authority* [2001] EWCA Civ, November 16.
[68] *Hawkins Hill Co. v Want* (1893) 69 L.T. 297.
[69] *A Limited v B Limited* 1996 1 W.L.R. 665, Vinelott J.
[70] *Jackson v John Dickinson & Co. (Bolton) Ltd* [1952] W.N. 9, CA.; *Friedmann v Austay (London) Ltd* [1954] 1 W.L.R. 466; *Williams v Williams* [1953] 1 W.L.R. 905.
[71] *McKay v The Legal Aid Board, The Times,* March 7, 1997.

E. SECURITY IN PROCEEDINGS FOR DETAILED ASSESSMENT OF A SOLICITOR AND CLIENT BILL

A party resident out of the jurisdiction who applies for detailed assessment of his solicitor's bill of costs may be ordered to give security, unless the solicitor already holds sufficient security for the costs which may be ordered to be paid on detailed assessment including the costs of the detailed assessment itself.[72]

15–009

F. SECURITY FOR COSTS ON ENFORCEMENT OF JUDGMENTS OF FOREIGN COURTS IN ENGLAND AND WALES

Subject to certain restrictions section II of CPR Part 25 applies to an application for security for the costs of: (a) the application for the registration of the foreign judgment; (b) any proceedings brought to set aside the registration; and, (c) any appeal against the granting of the registration, as if the judgment creditor were a claimant.[73] A judgment creditor making an application under the Civil Jurisdiction and Judgments Act 1982 or the Judgment Regulations[74] may not be required to give security solely on the ground that he is resident out of the jurisdiction.[75] CPR 74.5(1) does not apply to an application under the Foreign Judgments (Reciprocal Enforcement) Act 1933 where the relevant Order in Council otherwise provides.[76]

15–010

An order by the Court of Appeal for security in respect of the costs of the proceedings below which would only be awarded to an appellant if successful on an appeal may be made "for the purposes of and incidental to" the hearing of the appeal within the jurisdiction inferred by Section 15 of the Supreme Court Act 1981. Such an order would also be "in relation to" an appeal within CPR 52.10. There is no general rule that security for the costs below of a defendant against whom judgment is given, should be released immediately. The security may be preserved pending the outcome of an appeal. Questions of security should usually be resolved at the time when the court has some readily exercisable and appropriate control over the claimant who is being asked to provide security.[77]

---

[72] *Re Pasmore* [1839] 1 Beav. 94; *Anon.* [1841] 12 Sin. 262.
[73] CPR 74.5(1).
[74] Council Regulation (EC) No.44/2001 of December 22, 2000 on jurisdiction and the recognition and enforcement of judgments in civil and commercial matters.
[75] CPR 74.5(2).
[76] CPR 74.5(3).
[77] *DAR International FEF Co v Aon Ltd* [2003] EWCA Civ, December 10.

CHAPTER 16

Recovery, Interest and Reimbursement of Costs

A. RECOVERY OF COSTS

By proceedings

16–001 A solicitor may seek to recover his costs by proceedings which may be commenced at the expiration of one month from the delivery of the bill of costs of the client. If there is a probable case for believing that the party chargeable with the costs is about to leave England and Wales, to become bankrupt or to compound with his creditors or is about to do any other act which would tend to prevent or delay the solicitor obtaining payment, the court may order that the solicitor be at liberty to commence proceedings to recover his costs and may order that those costs be assessed notwithstanding that one month has not expired from the delivery of the bill.[1] The court may make an order restraining the solicitor from pursuing the action until after detailed assessment.[2] The prohibition of any action being brought before the expiration of a month from delivery of the bill applies equally to a counterclaim.[3]

Before a solicitor brings proceedings to recover costs, against a client on a bill for non-contentious business (except where the bill has been assessed)[4] or if a solicitor deducts his costs from moneys held for or on behalf of a client or of an estate in satisfaction of a bill and an entitled person objects in writing to the amount of the bill within the prescribed time[5] the solicitor

---

[1] Solicitor's Act 1974, s.69(1), (2).

[2] *Re Webster* [1891] 2 Ch. 102; *Slater v Cathcart* (1891) 8 T.L.R. 1992.

[3] *Spencer v Watts* [1889] W.N. 121.

[4] Solicitors (Non-Contentious Business) Remuneration Order 1994, Art.6.

[5] *ibid.*, Art.7(1). The prescribed time is three months after the delivery of the relevant bill or notification of the amount of costs or a lesser time (not less than one month) specified in writing at the time of delivery or notification. *ibid.*, Art.7(2)(a) and (b).

must inform the client in writing of certain specified matters unless he has already done so. The entitled person must be informed of the following matters:

(a) Where a bill has been delivered for costs of not more than £50,000[6]

    (i) that the entitled person may within one month of receiving from the solicitor the specified information or (if later) of delivery of the bill or notification of the amount of costs, require the solicitor to obtain a remuneration certificate and

    (ii) that (unless the solicitor has agreed to do so) the Law Society may waive the requirement to pay money on account[7] if satisfied from the client's written application that exceptional circumstances exist to justify granting a waiver[8]

(b) That sections 70, 71 and 72 of the Solicitors Act 1974 set out the entitled person's rights in relation to detailed assessment.[9]

(c) That (where the whole of the bill has not been paid by deduction or otherwise) the solicitor may charge interest on the outstanding amount of the bill.[10]

The solicitor may claim the full amount of his bill of costs and apply for summary judgment. Judgment may be entered for the full amount claimed without reference to detailed assessment. If however the client disputes the bill the claimant's solicitor may be given leave to sign judgment for the amount found due on detailed assessment together with the costs of the action.[11] It is not open to the court to refer a bill for detailed assessment under the inherent jurisdiction notwithstanding the time for making application for an order to tax has passed[12] but the 1974 Act does not exclude any other common law right to challenge the bill.[13] For the purpose of the limitation period, time begins to run from the date when the work to which the bill relates is completed, not from the date of delivery of the bill nor from the expiration of one month thereafter.[14] A claim by a solicitor for his

---

[6] *i.e.* where Art.4(1) applies.
[7] Under *ibid.*, Art.11(1).
[8] *ibid.*, Art.8(a).
[9] *ibid.*, Art.8(b) and *see* para.8–001 *et seq.*
[10] *i.e.* in accordance with *ibid.*, Art.14: *ibid.*, Art.8(c).
[11] *Smith v Edwardes* (1888) 22 Q.B.D. 10, CA; *Lagos v Grunwaldt* [1910] 1 K.B. 41, CA.
[12] *Harrison v Tew* [1990] 2 W.L.R. 210, HL.
[13] *Thomas Watts & Co v Smith* [1998] 2 Costs L.R.
[14] *Coburn v Colledge* [1897] 1 Q.B. 702, CA. It seems unlikely that this decision would be supportable today.

fees is a liquidated claim for the purposes of section 29(5) of the Limitation Act 1980.[15]

Costs information for clients in respect of legal services

16–002 The Law Society has set out in Practice Rule 15 (costs information and client care), what is expected of practitioners in relation to the giving of information on costs. Practice Rule 15 is designed to ensure that clients know what is happening generally and in particular in relation to the cost of legal services both at the outset and as the matter progresses, and the name and status of the person or persons responsible for the day to day conduct and overall supervision of their matters. A client consulting a firm of solicitors must be told if the work will not be undertaken by a qualified solicitor. Where the client is not told, the firm is not entitled to recover its costs if it provided an adviser who was not a solicitor, since this amounts to non-performance of a contract to provide legal services by a solicitor.[16] Similarly where a struck off solicitor fraudulently deceives a client into believing that he was a qualified solicitor.[17]

Solicitors are required to give clients clear information about costs at the outset of a matter and at appropriate stages throughout. Any information given orally should be confirmed in writing to the client as soon as possible.[18] The solicitor is required to give the client the best information possible about the likely overall costs including a breakdown between fees, VAT and disbursements. "The best information possible" includes agreeing a fixed fee or giving a realistic estimate or giving a forecast within a possible range of costs while explaining to the client the reasons why it is not possible to fix or give a realistic estimate or forecast of the overall costs and giving instead the best information possible about the costs of the next stage of the matter.[19] In an appropriate case the solicitor should explain to a privately paying client that the client may set an upper limit for which the client will be liable without further authority. If the basis of charge is an hourly rate this must be made clear and the client must be told if charging rates are to be increased. In addition the solicitor must inform the client what reasonably foreseeable payments the client may have to make either to the solicitor or to a third party and when those payments are likely to be needed and the solicitor should discuss with the client the client's ability to pay and the source of funding. The solicitor should discuss with the client whether the likely outcome of a matter will justify the expense of a risk

---

[15] *Byatt v Nash* [2002] 2 All E.R. (D) 254 Mr J. Crowley Q.C.
[16] *Pilbrow v Pearless de Rougemnont & Co* [1999] 3 All E.R. 355, CA.
[17] *Adriane Allen Ltd v Fuglers* [2002] EWCA Civ 1655.
[18] Solicitors Practice Rules 1990, r.15 and Solicitors Costs Information and Client Care Code 1999, para.3.
[19] *Wong v Vizards* [1997] 2 Costs LR 46 Toulson J.

involved, including, if relevant, the risk of having to bear an opponent's costs.[20]

In the case of a client who is legally aided the solicitor is required to explain to the client (i) the liability for the client's own costs and those of any other party including the effect of the statutory charge and its likely amount; (ii) the client's obligation to pay any contribution and the consequences of failure to pay the contribution; (iii) the fact that the client may still be ordered by the court to contribute to the opponent's costs if the case is lost, even though the client's own costs are covered by legal aid; and (iv) the fact that even if the client wins the opponent may not be ordered to pay, or be capable of paying, the full amount of the costs due.[21]

Privately paying clients should be told (i) their potential liability for their own costs and for those of any party, including the fact that the client will be responsible for paying the solicitor's bill in full regardless of any order for costs made against an opponent; (ii) the probability that the client will have to pay the opponent's costs as well as the client's own costs if the case is lost; (iii) the fact that even if the client wins the opponent may not be ordered to pay, or may not be capable of paying, the full amount of the client's costs; and (iv) the fact that if the opponent is legally aided the client may not recover the costs even if successful.[22]

In non-contentious matters if a client may be liable for the costs of a third party this must be explained by the solicitor and where appropriate the solicitor should obtain a firm figure for those costs or agree a cap.[23] The costs information must be regularly updated and unless the client agrees otherwise this should be done at least every six months at which point the client should be told how much the costs are. The solicitors should also explain any changed circumstances which are likely to affect the amount of costs, the degree of risk involved or the costs benefit to the client of continuing with the matter. The client must be told as soon as it appears that a costs estimate or limit will be exceeded. If there is a material change in the client's means the client's eligibility for legal aid must be considered.[24]

Proceedings in bankruptcy

A solicitor may present a petition in bankruptcy against a client in respect **16–003** of his costs even though he has not delivered his bill and could not therefore commence proceedings for recovery of the costs. Application may be made for the petition to be stayed until a bill has been delivered and the costs

---

[20] *ibid.*, para.4.
[21] *ibid.*, para.5(a).
[22] *ibid.*, para.5(b).
[23] *ibid.*, para.5(c).
[24] *ibid.*, para.6.

assessed.[25] The service of a statutory demand for payment of solicitors' costs does not constitute the bringing of an action, accordingly a statutory demand may be served before the expiration of a month from the date of delivery of the bill.[26] In the case of non-contentious costs the solicitor is under a duty to inform the client of his right to a remuneration certificate and must also inform the client of the detailed assessment provisions of the Solicitors Act 1974. The provision applies equally to a limited company.[27]

Where a solicitor's client is bankrupt the solicitor may prove in the bankruptcy for the amount of his costs notwithstanding that no bill has been delivered or that the costs have not been assessed.[28] The trustee in bankruptcy is entitled to full particulars of how the amount claimed is made up.[29]

A creditor who serves a statutory demand before obtaining judgment does so at his own risk as to costs. The service of a statutory demand is a step in bankruptcy proceedings and a cause of action in its own right.[30] Where an order for costs is made following service of the petition resulting in payment of the debt, the creditor would normally be entitled to costs and the dismissal of the petition but the order for costs must reflect the ultimate success of the creditor but also the avoidable defects in the creditor's proceedings which have given rise to adjournments. In a case where substantial additional costs have been incurred quite unnecessarily by the debtor, the proper order was that there should be no order as to costs.[31]

Where a party to litigation served a statutory demand on a debtor for payment of assessed costs the fact that there was a pending review in respect of the detailed assessment of costs was not sufficient ground to set aside the statutory demand.[32]

The costs certificate (default, interim and final)

16–004　Once a costs certificate has been obtained it is final and conclusive evidence as to the amount of costs covered by it[33] and it is an order to pay within 14 days.[34] The order for payment is enforceable by execution.[35] An order made

---

[25] *Re Symes Ex p. Prideaux* [1821] 1 GL. & J. 28.

[26] *Re A Debtor (No.88 of 1991)* [1992] 4 All E.R. 301.

[27] *Re Laceward Ltd* [1981] 1 W.L.R. 133.

[28] *Eicke v Noakes* [1829] Mood. & M. 303; *Re Woods Ex p. Ditton* (1880) 13 Ch. D. 318, CA.

[29] *Re Van Laun Ex p. Chatterton* [1907] 2 K.B. 23, CA.

[30] *In Re A Debtor (No.620 or 1997)*, *The Times*, June 18, 1998, Hart J.

[31] *In Re A Debtor (No.510 of 1997)*, *The Times*, June 18, 1998, Mr Stanley Burnton Q.C.

[32] *Cartwright v Staffordshire & Moorlands DC* 1998 B.P.I.R. 328, CA.

[33] Solicitors Act 1974, s.72(4).

[34] CPR, rr.47.11, 47.15, 47.16.

[35] *Deacon Ex p. Cathcart* [1900] 2 Q.B. 478, CA.

in proceedings brought by a solicitor for recovery of his costs will be for judgment for the amount found due upon detailed assessment.[36]

B. INTEREST ON COSTS AND DISBURSEMENTS

Non-contentious business

After the information specified in the remuneration order[37] has been given to an entitled person a solicitor may charge interest on the unpaid amount of the costs plus any disbursements which have been paid and value added tax.[38] The period for which interest may be charged may run from one month after the date of delivery of the bill unless the solicitor fails to lodge an application within one month of receipt of a request for a remuneration certificate in which case no interest is payable in respect of the period between one month after receiving the request and the actual date when the application is lodged.[39] The solicitor and client may agree different provisions both as to the length of time for which interest may be charged and as to the rate of interest. Subject to such an agreement the rate of interest must not exceed the rate for the time being payable on judgment debts.[40]

16–005

Interest has to be calculated by reference to the following:

(a) if a solicitor is required to obtain a remuneration certificate, the total amount of the costs certified by the Law Society to be fair and reasonable plus disbursements which have been paid and value added tax;

(b) if an application is made for the bill to be assessed, the amount ascertained on detailed assessment;

(c) if an application is made for the bill to be assessed, or a solicitor is required to obtain a remuneration certificate, and for any reason the detailed assessment or application for remuneration certificate does not proceed, the unpaid amount of the costs shown in the bill or such sum as may be agreed between the solicitor and the client plus disbursements which have been paid and value added tax.[41]

A costs certificate does not include any figure for interest. Interest is calculated in accordance with CPR 40.8.

---

[36] *Smith v Edwardes* (1888) 22 Q.B.D. 10, CA.
[37] Solicitors (Non-Contentious Business) Remuneration Order 1994, *i.e.* in *ibid.*, Art.8.
[38] *ibid.*, Art.14(1).
[39] *ibid.*, Art.14(2).
[40] *ibid.*, Art.14(3): the rate payable on judgment debts is 8 per cent (Judgment Debts (Rate of Interest) Order). 1993, SI 1993/564.
[41] *ibid.*, Art.14(4).

Contentious business

16–006   Both the High Court and the county court have the power to award interest wherever proceedings are brought for the recovery of debt or damages and this includes claims for the recovery of solicitors' costs.[42]

Interest may be awarded for all or any part of the period between the date when the cause of action arose and the date of payment or the date of judgment, whichever is earlier. No interest will be awarded for a period during which, for whatever reason, interest on the debt already runs.[43] The court has no power to award interest on a debt which is paid late but before recovery proceedings have commenced.[44] The appropriate rate of interest is the rate for judgment debts.[45]

On any detailed assessment of costs in respect of any contentious business, the costs officer may allow interest at such rate and from such time as he thinks just, on money disbursed by the solicitor for the client and on money of the client in the hands of and improperly retained by the solicitor.[46] There is no power to allow interest on profit costs nor is it open to the solicitor to appropriate payments received for profit costs so as to leave disbursements unpaid and earning interest.[47]

A contentious business agreement which includes a provision that the client should pay interest on costs appears to be binding if it is valid in all other respects.[48]

With regard to "money in the hands of and improperly retained by the solicitor", the mere receipt of client's money by the solicitor does not entitle the client to receive interest (save in accordance with the Solicitors' Accounts Rules relating to interest), but as soon as a demand is made by the client for payment which is not complied with within a reasonable time, interest will become payable.[49] Where, because of a reduction in the solicitor's bill on detailed assessment, a credit in favour of the client is produced, this does not of itself automatically carry interest.[50]

Interest on judgment debts

16–007   A litigant who has been awarded costs in a judgment is entitled to interest, under the Judgments Act 1838, ss.17 and 18, from the date upon which

---

[42] Supreme Court Act 1981, s.35A; County Courts Act 1984, s.69(1).
[43] Supreme Court Act 1981, s.35A(4); County Courts Act 1984, s.69(4).
[44] *President of India v Pintada Cia Navegacion S.A.* [1985] A.C. 104, HL.
[45] Currently 8 per cent: Judgment Debts (Rate of Interest) Order 1993; *Pinnock v Wilkins & Sons, The Times,* January 29, 1990.
[46] Solicitors Act 1974, s.66(a).
[47] *Hartland v Murrell* [1873] L.R. 16 Eq. 285.
[48] *Re Fanshawe* (1905) 49 S.J. 404.
[49] *Barclay v Harris & Cross* (1915) 85 L.J.K.B. 115.
[50] *Wright v Southwood* (1827) 1 Y. & J. 527.

judgment is pronounced.[51] Interest payable under section 17 of the Judgments Act or under section 74 of the County Court Act 1984 begins to run from the date that judgment is given, unless a rule of court or Practice Direction makes a different provision or the court orders otherwise. The court has the power to order that interest shall begin to run from a date before the date that judgment is given.[52] Where the court is exercising its discretion as to what if any order for costs to make, it may order that a party must pay interest on costs from or until a certain date including a date before judgment.[53] "In any event in principle there seems no reason why the court should not do so where a party has had to put up money paying its solicitors and been out of the use of that money in the meanwhile".[54] The court has expressed the view that the appropriate dates when one is seeking to measure the extent to which a party has been out of pocket will be the dates on which invoices were actually paid. The appropriate time for interest to stop is when interest on costs is replaced by judgment interest.[55]

Where an order is made by a county court requiring the payment of a sum of money, that judgment is registered in the Register of County Court Judgments. An order for a sum of money to be paid following a summary assessment, other than the final decision in the proceedings, is exempt from registration.[56]

Where the Court of Appeal made an order setting aside the costs order made in the lower court, and this had the effect of ordering that interest should run form the date of the Court of Appeal order, the Court of Appeal could not order that the interest should be recoverable on all costs from the date of the Judge's order because the slip rule could not enable the court to have second or additional thoughts. The slip rule did however enable the court to amend an order to give effect to the intention on costs which had already been ordered.[57]

Interest runs, on the costs, from the date of the order that costs be assessed.[58] Interest on the costs of the detailed assessment proceedings themselves runs from the date of the default, interim or final certificate.[59]

---

[51] *Hunt v R.M. Douglas (Roofing) Ltd.* [1991] A.C. 398, HL. The current rate of interest is 8 per cent: Judgment Debts (Rate of Interest) Order 1993 and the County Courts (Interest on Judgment Debts) Order 1991. The county court has power to order that judgment debts which have been expressed in currency other than sterling, should carry interest at such rate as the court thinks fit, instead of the prescribed rate of 8 per cent: County Courts (Interest on Judgment Debts) (Amendment) Order 1996.

[52] r.40.8(1) and r.(2).

[53] CPR 44.3(6)(g).

[54] *per* Waller L.J. in *Bim Kemie AB v Blackburn Chemicals Ltd* [2003] EWCA Civ 889.

[55] *Douglas v Hello Ltd* [2004] EWHC 63, Ch, Lindsay J.

[56] Register of County Court Judgments Regulations 1985.

[57] *British Myers Squibb Co v Baker Norton Pharmaceuticals Inc* [2001] EWCA Civ, March 28.

[58] *Ross v Owners of Marchioness & Bowbelle, The Times*, April 8, 1997, CA.

[59] Costs PD para.45.5.

Where a solicitor obtains judgment for the amount to be found due on detailed assessment (*i.e.* a *Smith v Edwardes* order) it is construed, for the purposes of section 17 of the Judgments Act 1838, as a judgment debt even though before detailed assessment has been completed there is no sum for which execution can be levied. The courts have accepted, since its enactment, that section 17 of the 1838 Act does apply to such an order and the balance of justice favours continuing to treat it in that way.[60]

Normally where a litigant is awarded costs under a consent order, interest on costs runs from the date when the proceedings are stayed. It is however open to the parties to modify that practice by agreement. In the absence of agreement, sections 17 and 18 of the Judgments Act 1838 apply.[61]

C. REIMBURSEMENT OF COSTS

Application

16–008   In proceedings in the Civil Division the Court of Appeal, civil proceedings in the High Court and proceedings in the county court, the Lord Chancellor is given the power,[62] if he thinks fit, to reimburse any party who has incurred any additional costs in consequence of a judge's incapacity or death. The amount to be reimbursed may not exceed £8,000.[63]

Section 53 of the Administration of Justice Act 1985 applies where the judge presiding over any of the proceedings already mentioned, including interlocutory proceedings, becomes temporarily or permanently incapacitated from presiding at the proceedings or dies at any time prior to the conclusion of the proceedings.[64] In order to claim, a party must be represented at the proceedings and incur additional costs in consequence of the incapacity or death. The incapacity or death of a presiding judge in the Civil Division of the Court of Appeal does not give rise to a claim, provided that the number of judges remaining is not less than two.[65]

"Judge" in relation to any proceedings includes a master, registrar or other person acting in a judicial capacity in the proceedings or a person assisting at the proceedings as an assessor or an adviser appointed by virtue of section 70(3) of the Supreme Court Act 1981.[66]

Where proceedings are due to be begun before a judge at a particular time but are not begun at that time by reason of the judge becoming temporarily or permanently incapacitated from presiding at the proceedings or by

---

[60] *Thomas v Bunn* [1991] 2 W.L.R. 27, HL.
[61] *Electricity Supply Nominees Ltd v Farrell* [1997] 2 All E.R. 498, CA.
[62] By the Administration of Justice Act 1985.
[63] Reimbursement of Costs (Monetary Limit) Order 1988 (SI 1988/1342).
[64] Administration of Justice Act 1985, s.53(1), (2).
[65] Administration of Justice Act 1985, s.53(3).
[66] *ibid.*, s.53(6).

reason of his death, the same provisions apply but claims are limited to those parties who would have been represented at the hearing but for the judge's incapacity or death.[67]

---

[67] *ibid.*, s.53(5).

PART VIII

General Principles of Assessment

CHAPTER 17

General Principles of Assessment

A. THE INDEMNITY PRINCIPLE

Bramwell B. in *Harold v Smith*[1] stated:

> "Costs as between party and party are given by the law as an indemnity   **17–001**
> to the person entitled to them; they are not imposed as a punishment on
> the party who pays them, nor given as a bonus to the party who
> receives them. Therefore, if the extent of the damnification can be
> found out, the extent to which costs ought to be allowed is also
> ascertained."

Sir Richard Malins V.C. in *Smith v Buller*[2] stated:

> "It is of great importance to litigants who are unsuccessful that they
> should not be oppressed into having to pay an excessive amount of
> costs ... I adhere to the rule which has already been laid down, that
> the costs chargeable under a taxation (detailed assessment) as between
> party and party are all that are necessary to enable the adverse party to
> conduct the litigation and no more. Any charges merely for conducting
> litigation more conveniently may be called luxuries and must be paid
> by the party incurring them".

Although a test of reasonableness and proportionality has been substituted for the test of necessity, the principles set out above remain unaltered.

The purpose of assessment pursuant to an order for costs between the parties is to ascertain the amount payable to the party recovering the costs.

---

[1] [1850] 5 H. & N. 381 at 385.
[2] [1875] L.R. 19 Eq. 473.

The intention is not to fix the remuneration of solicitors.[3] The award of costs may be no more than an indemnity, *i.e.* the amount which the successful party has to pay his own solicitor.[4] There is a presumption that if a party has a solicitor on the record that party is liable to pay the solicitor's costs.[5] The party seeking to recover costs does not have to adduce evidence to support the presumption. If the paying party puts the receiving party to proof of his entitlement to costs, the presumption could be relied upon, but where a genuine issue was raised as to whether or not the receiving party has incurred costs, the receiving party should be given notice of the issue and the court should decide whether it requires proof of the liability to pay or whether the paying party's case was insufficient to displace the presumption.[6]

A global cap or item by item?[7]

17–002 The Court of Appeal addressed this question on an appeal from a review of a detailed assessment. In the proceedings thirteen claimants had sued three defendants in separate related actions commencing in 1988. The claimants had participated in underwriting pools devised and run by the defendants. There was an allegation that the pools had been run in breach of duty which had caused loss to the claimants. The actions were settled in 1993 and 1994 when the claimants accepted payment into court or offers of settlement. The claimants became entitled to their costs on the standard basis.

The claimants' claim for costs was complicated because two firms of solicitors had acted: Firm A until 1990, and Firm B thereafter. Total costs of approximately £3.72 million were claimed, of that figure more than £3 million was solicitors' profit costs. During the litigation various costs orders were made in favour of the defendants for interlocutory matters. Costs were claimed in respect of these matters amounting to £73,610.

On detailed assessment the question of the indemnity principle was raised. The retainer of the claimants with Firm A did not stipulate any particular charging rates. However the agreement with Firm B, which was a contentious business agreement within the meaning of section 59 of the Solicitors Act 1974, provided for Firm B to charge their clients at various specific hourly rates for different classes of person working on the case.

Section 60(3) of the 1974 Act provides:

---

[3] *Gundry v Sainsbury* [1910] 1 K.B. 645.
[4] *ibid.*
[5] *R. v Miller; R. v Glennie* [1983] 1 W.L.R. 1056.
[6] *Hazlett v Sefton Metropolitan Borough Council* [1999] 149 N.L.J. 1869, DC.
[7] *The General of Berne Insurance Co. v Jardine Reinsurance Management Ltd* [1998] 1 W.L.R. 1231, CA.

"A client shall not be entitled to recover from any other person under an order for the payment of any costs to which a contentious business agreement relates more than <u>the amount payable by him</u> to his solicitor <u>in respect of those costs</u> under the agreement."

The costs judge was requested to decide, as a preliminary issue, whether the client was limited to recovering his costs on an item by item basis at the agreed hourly rates, or whether the limit only applied to the global amount payable under the contentious business agreement. The costs judge decided in favour of the global approach, as did Tuckey J. on review. When giving reasons for his decision Tuckey J. stated:

" . . . there are considerable practical difficulties in the item by item approach. [Detailed assessment] can of course be difficult and complicated and I have no doubt that if the item by item approach was right it could and would be done. However anything which makes things simpler in this field must be for the good."

The actual difference between the costs recoverable on the item by item basis and those recoverable on the global basis was said to exceed £700,000. The defendants accordingly appealed.

On appeal May L.J. gave the leading judgment. He found that *Gundry v Sainsbury* stated the general principle but did not address the question of whether the principle has to be applied to individual items or once only, by comparing the total amount of the assessed costs with the total amount which the solicitor is entitled to receive from his client.

The judgment turned next to *In Re Eastwood, Lloyds Bank Ltd v Eastwood.*[8] Again May L.J. found that the case in essence concerned the means whereby the court could be satisfied that the indemnity principle was not infringed, it did not address questions central to the present appeal —although in *Eastwood* the court was in fact considering an individual item in a larger bill.

May L.J. then considered *Universal Thermosensors v Hibben.*[9] In that case there was a contentious business agreement in which the solicitors agreed not to charge more than £80,000 plus VAT and disbursements. It was held that that figure was a ceiling to be imposed at the end of detailed assessment and not a ceiling which the bill lodged for assessment might not exceed. The Vice-Chancellor in *Hibben* went on to state that what the agreement did was to impose a cap on the total amount of the bill payable by the defendants to the solicitors (*i.e.* including disbursements). He concluded:

---

[8] [1975] Ch. 112.
[9] March 6, 1992 (unreported), Sir Donald Nichols V.C.

"So long as the total amount sought to be recovered by the defendants from the claimant does not exceed that sum, which having regard to this agreement that the solicitors can recover from their clients, then the cap does not preclude recovery."

The defendants submitted that *Hibben* was wrongly decided since not only would the client be able to recover sums by reference to a cap which included disbursements which had been allowed, the client would also have the benefit of a cap of the full total of his costs when the particular order in *Hibben* only entitled him to recover two-thirds of those costs. May L.J. ultimately disagreed with the decision of Nichols V.C. in *Hibben* in relation to disbursements in that case.

Before the costs judge there was argument as to whether or not it would in practice be difficult to apply a cap item by item. The costs judge found that this could lead to a complicated and painstaking task. May L.J. recognised that cases of this nature could arise. He did not think that difficulties of this kind were persuasive to any particular conclusion, detailed assessment "of costs can be a laborious procedure in any event and can be expensive in taxing fees".

May L.J. identified the various problems raised by the conflicting arguments. The problem with the gross sum approach was identified by Tuckey J.:

" . . . Section 60(3) does not . . . impose a single overall cap. It imposes a cap in respect of the cost to which the order relates. Where a party is awarded all his costs of the action the comparison will be simple. If the taxing officer is only concerned with a discrete interlocutory order or issues costs it will be necessary to isolate the costs payable under the CBA in respect of these [discrete costs orders] in order to make the comparison . . . it seems to me that the amounts payable by the plaintiffs under the CBA fall to be deducted from the total paid under the CBA in order to make a proper comparison since such costs simply do not come into the reckoning under Section 60(3)."

In respect of this difficulty May L.J. found:

"You would at least expect that the cap should be limited to that part of what they were obliged under the contentious business agreement to pay their own solicitors which was referrable to the part or parts of the litigation for which the paying party was obliged to pay them their costs. If this were not so the receiving party would either make a profit on the costs to which they were entitled or would be recovering part of the costs to which they were not entitled. That would offend the indemnity principle."

With the item by item approach the difficulty is that, if the cap is not applied once only, but to individual items, the paying party could get what might appear to be a windfall where some costs are reduced below an individual cap because, for instance, they are held to be unreasonable but other costs are capped at the agreed rate, although, but for the cap, they would have been allowed in a greater amount. An example of this was a single hourly rate agreed for partners which was higher than that which would be allowed for attendance at interlocutory hearings, but lower than that which would otherwise be allowed for preparation.

At the end of the day the judgment turned on the construction of section 60(3) of the 1974 Act. May L.J. agreed with the conclusion of Tuckey J. that costs referable to parts of the litigation for which the receiving party did not have the benefit of an order for costs had to be taken out of account in determining the application of section 60(3). Equally if the CBA encompassed more than one action it would be necessary to exclude costs payable by the client to his solicitor for any action in which the client had recovered no costs from another party. The same would apply where the order for costs is for part only of the total costs of a single action:

"A comparison is to be made between the costs to which the order relates and the amount payable by the receiving party to his solicitor 'in respect of those costs'."

May L.J. then continued:

"Once it is seen that the comparison is to be made between the costs to which the order relates and the amount payable by the receiving party to his solicitor 'in respect of those costs' it must follow that costs which are irrecoverable have to be left out of both sides of the comparison. 'Those costs' are the costs recoverable under the order after taxation but before consideration of the cap ... it also means that the comparison is not global and may require, in appropriate circumstances, an item by item comparison."

A little later he continued:

"There is no proper distinction to be made between costs disallowed by an order made in the proceedings and costs disallowed on taxation. A party will not be entitled to recover costs which are disallowed on taxation so that 'any costs' and 'those costs' must be taken to refer to costs which are allowable on taxation before consideration of the limitation imposed by Section 60(3). This construction of Section 60(3) does not in my view lead to the conclusion that paying parties may receive a windfall. The paying party receives nothing at all. It simply means that receiving parties will receive either what is reasonable or the relevant amount which they have agreed to pay their own solicitors whichever is the less. If it were otherwise they themselves would be receiving a windfall at least in the sense that they would be recovering costs which for one reason or another had been disallowed."

Sir Brian Neill also gave judgment in which he referred to the increasing frequency and importance of contentious business agreements in deciding the correct approach to the construction of section 60(3) of the 1974 Act. Sir Brian set out the practice and procedure governing the award and detailed assessment of costs, he included:

> "1. The principle that as between party and party an order for costs is not intended to provide more than an indemnity, the receiving party is not entitled to a bonus, see *Gundry v Sainsbury*.[10]
> 2. The rule that on a party and party taxation the recoverable costs are limited to those which were reasonably incurred and were reasonable in amount.
> 3. The practice whereby on a party and party taxation the profit costs in a bill of costs are taxed by reference to chargeable items. The taxing master's certificate sets out a final amount but this amount represents the aggregate of the sums allowed in respect of the items of costs which have been found to have been reasonably incurred. . . . "

In relation to section 60(3) Sir Brian found that:

> "The words 'any costs' in the phrase 'an order for the payment of any costs' in Section 60(3) appear to me in the context to relate not to costs at large, or to the costs payable by the receiving party to his own solicitor, but to the costs and items of costs to be identified on the party and party taxation as the proper and recoverable costs. The words 'those costs' clearly refer to the same costs.
> The operation of the cap then becomes readily intelligible, where applicable the figures in the contentious business agreement provide both a measure and a ceiling for each recoverable item of costs."

Bailey v IBC Vehicles Ltd[11]

17–003   The decisions of the Court of Appeal in *Bailey v IBC Vehicles Ltd*, and Tucker J. in a review of detailed assessment: *Nederlandse Reassurantie*

---

[10] [1910] 1 K.B. 645.
[11] [1998] 3 All E.R. 570, CA.

Groep Holding NV v Bacon & Woodrow[12] have extended and applied the decision of the Court of Appeal in *The General of Berne Insurance Company v Jardine Reinsurance Management Limited.*[13]

The position where there is no contentious business agreement

In the review before Tucker J. the court made a finding that no contentious   **17–004** business agreement was entered into. On detailed assessment the costs judge had made a finding (prior to the decision in *The General of Berne*) that the bill of the defendants did not breach the indemnity principle. The bill ran to several million pounds and the difference between the gross sum cap and the item by item approach would have been significant.

Although there was no contentious business agreement there was a long-standing relationship between the firm of solicitors and the defendants which the judge found might not exclude the possibility of the existence of some less formal arrangement as to remuneration.

On the review, counsel for the receiving party sought to distinguish *The General of Berne* on the basis that section 60(3) of the Solicitors Act 1974 did not necessarily enact the common law. Counsel also referred to the enormity of the task which would confront the defendants if they had to redraw their bill in accordance with *The General of Berne*. Counsel submitted that the correct approach to the indemnity principle in such a case was to apply a global cap and that this should be done at the end of the detailed assessment. Tucker J. found that this could give rise to problems if, for example, the final bill had not been rendered to the client, or, if rendered, had not been paid, or the solicitors' costs were, or could be, subject to detailed assessment. Furthermore a considerable time might elapse before the global sum cap could be identified. Tucker J. continued:

> "In my judgment there should be no distinction between those cases where a formal contentious business agreement is in place and which are governed by Section 60(3) of the 1974 Act and other cases where there is an agreement partly evidenced in writing, an unwritten agreement, or no agreement at all but merely an understanding arising perhaps from a long standing relationship as in the present case. It is desirable that there should be uniformity in approaches to taxation and highly undesirable and confusing for different approaches to be adopted according to whether any agreement can be brought within the statutory definition . . . I take the view that if in a contentious business

---

[12] *Nederlandse Reassurantie Groep Holding NV v Bacon & Woodrow (No.4)* [1998] 2 Costs L.R. Tucker J.
[13] *General of Berne Insurance Company v Jardine Reinsurance Management Limited* [1998] 1 W.L.R. 1231, CA.

agreement case an item by item approach should be adopted ... then there is no warrant for the adoption of any different approach in other cases."

Tucker J. declined to decide what constitutes an "item" for the purposes of detailed assessment.

Union backed litigation

17–005   The case of *Bailey v IBC Vehicles Ltd* involved a claimant employed by the defendants at their factory, where, in the course of his employment, he suffered personal injuries. The claimant consulted his union, who in turn instructed solicitors who commenced proceedings. The defendants agreed to pay damages to the claimant, together with costs to be assessed. When the bill was presented for detailed assessment the defendants objected to the hourly rate and mark-up and asked that the claimants should provide evidence to show that it was not in breach of the indemnity principle. Eventually a letter was produced to the district judge from the union representative which stated that the union's relationship with the solicitor was on the basis that the solicitors were entitled to make a full solicitor/client charge. The defendants were not satisfied with this response and the district judge supported the defendants' contention that they were entitled to discovery of the relevant material.

The Court of Appeal found that it was clearly established that the indemnity principle is not undermined merely because the successful litigant is a member of a trade union whose claim is being pursued with financial support from his union.[14] Although the claimant would not in practice have been called upon to pay the solicitors' fees if the action had failed, and the deliberate decision had been made not to inform him of the rate of fees less this caused him undue alarm, the appeal was not argued by the defendants on the basis that the solicitors had agreed that the claimant's primary liability for their charges should be extinguished. The argument was directed towards the figures actually agreed between the solicitors and the union.

Discovery and disclosures

17–006   During the hearing of the appeal it was accepted by the defendants that a costs officer was entitled, if he saw fit, to be provided with the information which he needed. The court stated:

---

[14] See *Adams v London Improved Motor Coach Builders Ltd* (1921) 1 K.B. 499 and *R. v Miller* [1993] 1 W.L.R. 1057 at 1061, Lloyd J.

"The [costs] officer is exercising a judicial function with substantial financial consequences for the parties. To perform them he is trusted properly to consider material which would normally be protected from disclosure under the rules of legal professional privilege. If, after reflecting on the material available to him, some feature of the case alerts him to the need to make further investigation or causes him to wonder if the information with which he is being provided is full and accurate, he may seek further information. No doubt he would begin by asking for a letter or some form of written confirmation or reassurance as appropriate. If this were to prove inadequate he might then make orders for discovery or require affidavit evidence ... It would theoretically be open to him to order interrogatories. However if the stage has been reached where interrogatories might reasonably be ordered the conclusion that the receiving party had not been able to satisfy the [costs] officer about the bill or some particular aspect of it would seem inevitable ... An emphatic warning must be added against the over enthusiastic deployment of these powers, particularly at the behest of the party against whom the order for costs has been made ... The danger of satellite litigation is acute. As far as possible, consistent with the need to arrive at a decision which does broad justice between the parties, it must be prevented or avoided and the additional effort required of the parties kept to the absolute minimum necessary for the [costs] officer properly to perform his function."[15]

The court also turned its attention to the client care letter and the signing of the bill of costs.

The client care letter and signing the bill

As officers of the court solicitors are trusted not to mislead or to allow the court to be misled. This elementary principle applies to the submission of a bill of costs. The court indicated that it would expect solicitors to have disclosed the existence of a cap or similar arrangement that applied in the case, and would have expected the solicitors to ensure that the information before the court represented a comprehensive, rather than a partial explanation of the facts, and, if it was not, to supplement it with information of their own.

17–007

"They would not have produced a signed bill of costs which included a claim for 'reasonable costs' which would have fallen foul of the indemnity principle."

---

[15] *per* Judge L.J., *Bailey v IBC Vehicles Ltd.*

Judge L.J. continued:

" . . . in the ordinary case in which a 'client care letter' has been provided the hourly rate claimed in the bill of costs should coincide with the terms of that letter. In *The General of Berne Insurance Co.* the same principle was applied to a contentious business agreement under Section 60(3) of the Solicitors Act 1974, Sir Brian Neill observing:

> 'Where applicable, the figures in the contentious business agreement provide both a measure and a ceiling for each recoverable item of costs.'

Moreover, in view of the increasing interest taken in this issue by unsuccessful parties to litigation, coupled with the developing practice in relation to conditional fees, the extension of the 'client care' letter and contentious business agreements under Section 60(3), in future copies of the relevant documents (where they exist) or a short written explanation . . . should normally be attached to the bill of costs. This will avoid skirmishes which add unnecessarily to the costs of litigation."[16]

Henry L.J. agreeing with the judgment of Judge L.J. stated:

"Order 62 rule 29(7)(c)(iii)[17] requires the solicitor who brings proceedings for taxation to sign the bill of costs. In so signing he certifies that the contents of the bill are correct. That signature is no empty formality. The bill specifies the hourly rates applied and the care and attention uplift claimed. If an agreement between the receiving solicitor and his client . . . restricted (say) the hourly rate payable by the client that hourly rate is the most that can be claimed or recovered on . . . The signature of the bill of costs under the rules is effectively the certificate of an officer of the Court that the receiving party's solicitors are not seeking to recover in relation to any item more than they have agreed to charge their client . . . "

Henry L.J. agreed that the client care letter, or any contentious business agreement, should be attached to the bill of costs. He concluded:

"For the avoidance of doubt I also agree that the [costs] officer may and should seek further information where some feature of the case raises suspicions that the whole truth may not have been told. On the other side of a presumption of trust afforded to the signature of an officer of

---

[16] *per* Judge L.J., *Bailey v IBC Vehicles Ltd.*
[17] See now Costs PD Section 4 and Precedent F.

the Court must be that breach of that trust should be treated as a most serious disciplinary offence."

B. THE BASIS OF CHARGE

Brightman J. in *Re Eastwood (deceased)*, *Lloyds Bank Ltd v Eastwood &* **17–008**
Ors.[18] outlined the following principles:

"At the present day, on the [detailed assessment] of a bill of costs of a firm of solicitors in private practice which has been engaged in litigation on behalf of a client (the expression 'firm of solicitors' being used to include a sole solicitor in private practice on his own account) the [detailed assessment] invariably proceeds on the following basis. The firm informs the [costs judge] of the period of time that has been spent by any partner or employee of the firm on any 'relevant' aspect of the case; (the word 'relevant' is intended to exclude time spent on a part of the case for which there is a fixed charge prescribed by statute or rule). The firm submits (A) what is the proper cost per hour of the time so spent having regard to a reasonable estimate of the overhead expenses of the solicitors' firm including (if the time spent is that of an employee) the reasonable salary of the employee or (if the time spent is that of a partner) a notional salary. The firm will also submit . . . what is a proper additional sum to be allowed over and above (A) by way of further profit costs."

On appeal to the Court of Appeal, Russell L.J. who was dealing specifically with the charges of an employed solicitor, stated:

"In our view, the system of direct application of the approach to [detailed assessment] of an independent solicitor's bill to a case such as this has relative simplicity greatly to recommend it, and it seems to have worked without it bring thought for many years to lead to significant injustice in the field of [detailed assessment] where justice is in any event rough justice, in the sense of being compound of much sensible approximation.
    In summary, therefore, in our opinion: (1) . . . (2) There is no reason to suppose that the conventional A plus B method is other than appropriate to the case of both independent and employed solicitors. (3) It is a sensible and reasonable presumption that the figure arrived at on this basis will not infringe the principle that the assessed costs

---

[18] [1973] 3 All E.R. 1079 at 1081–2.

should not be more than an indemnity to the party against the expense to which he has been put in the litigation. (4) ... "

It became normal practice on detailed assessment between parties, based on the above principles, to allow a solicitor an "A" figure, which reflected the broad average direct cost of doing the work for the particular grade of fee earner involved, plus a "B" figure for care and conduct which was arrived at after considering the factors set out in RSC, Ord. 62, Appendix 2, the A and B figures interrelate and cannot be considered wholly in isolation from each other but the starting point undoubtedly was the assessment of the actual rate that ought to be allowed as a cost rate.[19] The case of *Eastwood* quoted above established that the conventional method appropriate to assessing a bill of a solicitor in private practice was also appropriate for the bill of an in-house solicitor in all but special cases where it was reasonably plain that that method would infringe the indemnity principle. This had the merit of simplicity and of avoiding the burden of detailed enquiry. A special case could arise under the principles in *Eastwood* where a sum could be identified different from that produced by the conventional approach, which was adequate to cover the actual cost incurred in doing all the work done. Such a sum might be identified by concession or factual assessment of the assessing tribunal itself, but that possibility did not justify a detailed investigation in every case.[20]

Hirst J. in *Stubbs v Board of Governors of the Royal National Orthopaedic Hospital*[21] stated:

"The appropriateness of the total of 'A' and 'B' arrived at in this way is then considered against the background of the proceedings as a whole, and rounded off to a convenient sum which appears right in all the circumstances.

... At the end of the day the most important final exercise must be undertaken, namely: consideration of the appropriateness of the total of 'A' and 'B' against the background of the proceedings as a whole in order to arrive at a convenient sum which appears right in all the circumstances ... "

In June 1999 the Lord Chancellor published a consultation paper "Controlling Costs" which indicated that he wished to move away from the A + B method of charging, accordingly are now bills for assessment drawn

---

[19] *per* Hobhouse J. in *Finlay v Glaxo Laboratories Ltd* (October 9, 1989, QBD; unreported), cited in *Johnson v Reed Corrugated Cases Ltd* [1992] 1 All E.R. 169.

[20] *Cole v British Telecommunications Plc* [2000] EWCA Civ, 208; [2000] 2 Costs L.R. 310 CA.

[21] (December 21, 1989, unreported), cited in *Johnson v Reed Corrugated Cases Ltd* [1992] 1 All E.R. 169. Hirst J. referred to and quoted from the decision of Kerr J. in *Lazarus (Leopold) v Secretary of State for Trade and Industry, The Times*, April 8, 1976.

on the basis of a single charging rate without any additional uplift for care and conduct. There is nothing to prevent solicitors agreeing with their clients that they will charge a basic rate with an uplift, but the more sophisticated clients will want to know exactly what they are to be charged in advance.

The Guide to the Summary Assessment of Costs was held to be of only limited assistance to a Judge in a case, such as brain damage at birth, which is a particularly sensitive subject matter for litigation, and the specific demands placed on solicitors by clients and litigation friends vary from case to case. The guideline figures are not supposed to replace the experience or knowledge of those familiar with the local area and the field generally. The judgment was however not to be read as indicating that a particular hourly rate for partners or leading counsel were in any sense the norm. The conclusion was based on the particular factors that exceptionally resulted in those figures being appropriate in heavy and difficult negligence litigation involving an unusually intensive level of input from solicitors and counsel. In that case the court adopted the A plus B calculation as a cross check.[22]

C. THE STANDARD BASIS AND THE INDEMNITY BASIS

Costs between parties may be assessed either on the standard basis or on the indemnity basis in accordance with CPR, r.44.4.[23] A bill payable to a solicitor by his client is assessed on the indemnity basis in accordance with CPR, r.48.8.[24]   **17–009**

The test applied on both the standard and the indemnity basis of costs is a test of reasonableness, on the standard basis the additional test of proportionality applies.

D. HOURLY RATES

As a general rule, a litigant is expected to litigate as economically as possible   **17–010** (*i.e.* it would be unreasonable not to do so). Accordingly it is normal to instruct solicitors local to where the client lives, or the cause of action arose, as appropriate. However, where a claimant sought legal advice through his union, in relation to an accident in Sheffield, and where the union's London-based solicitors were instructed, it was held that it was reasonable in the circumstances for the London solicitors to be instructed; thus their (London) expense rate should be allowed. The court made reference to the fact

---

[22] *Higgs v Camden & Islington Health Authority* [2003] EWHC 15, QB, Fulford J.
[23] See para.4–020 above.
[24] See para.1–005 above.

that the union's solicitors had great expertise in the type of personal injury litigation concerned, and was persuaded that it was appropriate for the union's solicitors to be instructed.[25]

The Court of Appeal upheld the judge at first instance in principle but disagreed over the way in which the principle had been applied to the facts of the case since the trade union knew, or ought to have known, what sort of legal fees it would have to expend to obtain competent services for the claimant who lived in Sheffield and who had sustained an accident there.

> "It is the duty of unions and insurers in each individual case to keep down the costs of litigation this means that if they instruct London solicitors who charge London rates for a case which has no obvious connection with London and which does not require expertise only to be found there, they will, even if successful, recover less than the solicitors have charged."[26]

The Court of Appeal dealt with another case at the same time as *Wraith* in which solicitors acting for a wife in family proceedings had wrongly applied for a charging order. They persisted with this application even after having been told that it was incorrect. The husband became dissatisfied with his own local solicitors and transferred to a firm in London who were successful in having the order for sale struck out and in obtaining a wasted costs order against the wife's solicitors. It was argued that the husband should have obtained the services of solicitors local to where he lived (Brighton or Tunbridge Wells) and the court set out certain matters which were relevant when considering the reasonableness of instructing a distant (London) firm.

> "1. The importance of the matter to him. It was obviously of great importance, it threatened his home.
> 2. The legal and factual complexities in so far as he might reasonably be expected to understand them. Due to the incompetence of the wife's solicitors the matter had taken on an appearance of some complexity.
> 3. The location of his home, his place of work and the location of the court in which the relevant proceedings had been commenced.
> 4. The husband's, possibly well founded, dissatisfaction with the solicitors he had originally instructed, which may well have resulted in a natural desire to instruct solicitors further afield who would not be inhibited in representing his interests.

---

[25] *Wraith v Sheffield Forgemasters*, [1996] 1 W.L.R. 617, Potter J.
[26] *Wraith v Sheffield Forgemasters Ltd*; *Truscott v Truscott* [1998] 1 W.L.R. 132, CA.

5. The fact that he had sought advice as to who to consult and had been recommended to consult the London firm.

6. The location of the London firm including their accessibility to him and their readiness to attend at the relevant court.

7. What, if anything, he might reasonably be expected to know of the fees likely to be charged by the London firm, as compared with the fees of other solicitors whom he might reasonably be expected to have considered."

Having applied those considerations to the facts the court allowed the London rate for the husband's solicitors.[27]

In another union case, the claimant had instructed London solicitors, when the case was closely connected with Manchester. The Court of Appeal found that the case had no special feature or unusual implication, there was no obvious connection with London and there were many legal practitioners capable of handling the case in Manchester. The case did not require medical expertise to be found only in London. The court held that it was not objectively reasonable for the claimant to have instructed London solicitors.[28]

In a case where a claimant suffering from repetitive strain injury was represented first by solicitors in Liverpool and subsequently, when that fee earner left, by the Manchester office of the same firm, applying the principles set out in the authorities,[29] the court found that costs recoverable by the party in whose favour an order for costs had been made are recoverable only to the extent that they are reasonably incurred:

"if a party chooses a particular status or type of solicitor or counsel or one located in a particular area, then the costs will have been reasonably incurred if, having regard to the circumstances, a reasonable choice has been made."

These circumstances include the importance and complexity of the litigation and the value of the claim. The question to be asked is whether the solicitor chosen is the sort of solicitor that a person would have instructed with a view to the proper conduct of his case and minimising the cost of litigation.[30]

---

[27] *Truscott v Truscott* above.

[28] *Sullivan v Co-operative Insurance Society Ltd.* The Times, May 19, 1999, CA and see *Solutia (U.K.) Ltd v Griffiths* [2001] EWCA Civ 736.

[29] *i.e.* the judgments of Neill L.J. and Aldous L.J. in *L. v L. (legal aid taxation)* [1996] 1 F.S.R. 873 and the judgment of Potter J. in *Wraith v Sheffield Forgemasters Ltd* [1996] 2 All E.R. 527.

[30] *per* Hooper J., review of taxation, *A v F Co. Ltd* SCCO Digest No. 13 of 1996.

Expense rate surveys

In relation to the putting in of affidavits of accountancy evidence relating to expense rates, it has been held[31] that presenting such figures requiring non-expert analysis, *i.e.* by persons who are not accountants, is misconceived as a means of assisting the court in a particular case. Assessing costs is not an exact science, neither is accountancy. Treating the latter as if it were, so that the results of an accountancy exercise can be used as a basis for the former, achieved the worst of both worlds. The costs officer's general knowledge and experience of local conditions and circumstances remains the only firm basis for reliable and consistent assessment. The court did not support any idea that part of its function on a detailed assessment between parties was to discipline solicitors into charging less than they have done or to regulate the amount of their charges to their clients. The court is not concerned with charges, only with costs. It is not concerned with any market except indirectly and it is certainly not concerned to influence any market. Its function is to assess the reasonable amount of costs for work reasonably and proportionately done and nothing else.

17–011   Evans J. in *Johnson v Reed Corrugated Cases Ltd*[32] stated:

> "Does it follow then that the information contained in [the solicitors' accounts setting out their expense rate] must be disregarded and that the [costs officer] should remain in ignorance of it? In my judgment the answer to this is a vehement no. It is part of each [costs officer's] stock in trade that he has a general—again, I stress the word 'general' —knowledge of these matters and that if necessary he has some knowledge of the figures for local firms. It appears from the reasons given by [district judges] in other cities ... that there have been communications between local firms acting individually or collectively through local law societies and [costs officers] ... all with the aim of informing [costs officers] what the current level of overheads is and what the likely consequences of inflation are. I can see no objection to these consultations taking place and I for one would encourage them. They are the most practicable way of equipping the [costs officer] directly with the local knowledge which he needs for the discharge of his function and they are the only practicable way of informing him, not only of the figures for one or a small number of firms, but of a range of figures which enable him to form a view about the average.

---

[31] *per* Evans J. in *Johnson v Reed Corrugated Cases* [1992] 1 All E.R. 169. The following decisions were quoted with approval: *Re Eastwood (Deceased)* [1975] Ch. 112; *Lazarus (Leopold) v Secretary of State for Trade & Industry* [1976] S.J. 268; *Stubbs v The Royal National Orthopaedic Hospital* (December 21, 1988, QBD; unreported); *Finlay v Glaxo Laboratories Ltd* (October 9, 1989, QBD; unreported); and *R. v Wilkinson* [1980] 1 All E.R. 597.

[32] [1992] 1 All E.R. 169 at 183.

There remains, however, the fact that the [costs officer's] daily experience of the sums being claimed by local firms is an efficient way of giving him the same information though indirectly."

It is now common for designated civil judges, in consultation with district judges and local law societies, to publish the rates which they currently feel appropriate for run of the mill cases. In *Johnson v Reed Corrugated Cases Ltd*, Evans J. went on to state (at 183):

"If locally a certain figure becomes the going rate for routine cases *i.e.* ones of a particular kind with no unusual features, and that rate is unreaslistically low, then local solicitors are justified, in my view, in making approaches to [district judges] of the kind that already take place, these being for the purpose of providing general information and being unconnected with any particular case."[33]

In calculating the appropriate level of costs, the relevant time is the time at which the work was done, and no account is taken of inflation. The costs officer may take into account all relevant information, including his knowledge of the costs of other solicitors, the costs allowed to other solicitors, and the results of surveys.

"If it is reasonable for a party to instruct a solicitor in a particular location, then it is to the expense rates of the solicitors who practise in the field, in and around that location that the court must look for guidance".[34]

Overheads

If solicitors hold themselves out as competent and qualified to attract work **17–012** at particular levels, they have got to be equipped with appropriate overheads including appropriate indemnity and insurance in order to enable them to deal with it. This does not exclude the possibility that in a particular case the solicitor may come to an agreement with a private client who wishes to have his services to cover an extraordinary item, or the possibility that in an appropriate case the legal aid authorities might grant authority. In the absence of any special authority, claims in respect of overheads will be

---

[33] See also *Re A Company* [1995] 2 All E.R. 155, Lindsav J.; *KPMG Peat Marwick McLintoch v The HLT Group Limited* [1995] 2 All E.R. 180. Auld J.; *L. v L.* [1996] 1 F.S.R. 873, CA; *W. v G. (Costs: Taxation)* [1993] 2 F.L.R. 471, Eastham J. See also the guideline hourly rates contained in the *Guide to Summary Assessment.*
[34] *per* Aldous L.J. *L. v L.* [1996] 1 F.S.R. 873, CA.

disallowed.[35] Where a firm of solicitors acts in specialised proceedings and is clearly outside the range of local solicitors that go to make up the average rate, the court has power to allow a higher rate to reflect the higher overheads. Such a higher rate would not be appropriate if the firm had engaged in a case which could reasonably have been handled by other local firms, the costs would not then have been reasonably incurred, it must have been reasonable to instruct the particular firm for the particular case.[36]

Fee earners

17–013   It is normal to recover the cost of work done by a "fee earner". A fee earner is a person in respect of whom a charge is normally made to the client. This presupposes that the fee earner is undertaking fee earners' work. Thus if a solicitor spends time operating the photocopying machine, this is not regarded as fee earners' work and is not recoverable. Alternatively, if a non-fee earner such as a secretary attends court, that person is undertaking fee earners' work and the appropriate cost is recoverable. Brooke J. in *Brush v Bower Cotton & Bower*[37] stated:

> "To a large part, the work can properly be described as clerical work and, to that extent, I do not allow the claim. On the other hand there were features of the work which was done and which would be properly charged by a fee earner at an appropriate rate. To the extent that the work was fee earner's work in my judgment it ought to be allowed."

Advocates

17–014   Solicitors who hold current practising certificates may apply to the Law Society for an appropriate advocacy certificate. The certificates available are the Higher Courts (all proceedings) qualification; the Higher Courts (criminal proceedings) qualification; or the Higher Courts (civil proceedings) qualification. Rights of audience are exercisable by solicitors holding the appropriate qualification in the appropriate courts.[38]

Remuneration of solicitor advocates is based on the normal principles for remuneration of solicitors. It is not, therefore, appropriate to seek a brief fee and refreshers as if the advocate were a member of the bar. If the cost of

---

[35] *per* Brooke J. in *Brush & Anor. v Bower Cotton & Bower*, [1993] 1 W.L.R. 1328; [1993] 4 All E.R. 741.

[36] *Jones v Secretary of State for Wales and Glamorgan BC, The Times*, December 3, 1996, Buckley J.

[37] [1993] 4 All E.R. 741 at 766.

[38] See the Higher Courts Qualifications Regulations 2000.

using a solicitor advocate is more than the cost of instructing counsel, the higher cost is unlikely to be recovered. However, the figures properly recoverable by solicitor advocates should reflect the amount of preparation undertaken, the time spent in court and the weight and gravity of the case. In a heavy case the advocate may well have no prior knowledge of the litigation, particularly if the majority of the advocate's time is spent advocating in different cases on behalf of the particular firm. Furthermore, in a difficult case it may well be necessary for the fee earner having conduct of the litigation to be with the advocate in court for part or all of the hearing in the same way that counsel requires support in court, the level of this depends upon the difficulty of the case and the stage of the hearing.

Rights of audience on detailed assessment

In detailed assessment proceedings, rights of audience may be exercised by a litigant in person, an expert instructed by a litigant in person in accordance with CPR, r.48.6 (3)(c), a solicitor, any employee of a solicitor, and any counsel properly instructed by the solicitors. Costs consultants, costs draftsmen and the like, are heard on the basis that they are temporarily and for the purpose of those proceedings, employees of the solicitors. Solicitors are responsible for the conduct of detailed assessment proceedings and cannot avoid that responsibility merely by instructing a costs draftsman. Counsel clerks have no right of audience.

17–015

> "A costs draftsman can appear on behalf of a party, only as the duly authorised representative of the solicitor who has instructed him to be there. The scope of his apparent authority would be the same . . . as any costs draftsman employed by the firm".[39]

The existence or otherwise of a right of audience is determined exclusively by Part 2 of the Courts & Legal Services Act 1990. If the person attending is not a solicitor or barrister, or a member of any other authorised body and does not have rights granted by some statute, he may only have a right of audience in relation to proceedings if "granted by that court in relation to those proceedings". The grant of rights of audience is only to be exercised in exceptional circumstances. The courts should pause long before granting rights to individuals who make a practice of seeking to represent otherwise unrepresented litigants.

With regard to MacKenzie Friends the only right is that of the litigant to have reasonable assistance. A MacKenzie Friend has no right to act as such. A MacKenzie Friend is no entitled to address the court. If he does so he becomes an advocate and requires the grant of a right of audience. As a

---

[39] *per* Evans L.J. *Waterson Hicks v Eliopoulos*, November 14, 1995, CA (unreported).

general rule a litigant in person who wishes to have a MacKenzie Friend should be allowed to do so unless the Judge is satisfied that fairness and the interests of justice do not so require. The court can prevent a MacKenzie Friend from continuing to act in that capacity where the assistance he gives impedes the efficient administration of justice.[40]

In a case where costs negotiators were retained by liability insurers and in which the firm of costs negotiators purported to run the detailed assessment proceedings, it was held by the Senior Costs Judge that the representative of the costs negotiators did not have any right of audience and the terms of payment (a percentage of any reduction achieved in the claim for costs) were champertous. The decision was not appealed.[41]

E. CLAIM AND COUNTERCLAIM

17–016   Where there is a claim and a counterclaim and both are dismissed with costs, on detailed assessment the rule is that the claim is treated as if it stood alone, and the counterclaim bears only the amount by which the costs of the proceedings have been increased by it. In the absence of special directions by the court there should be no apportionment. The same principle applies where both the claim and the counterclaim have succeeded.[42] It is, however, within the judge's discretion to order the apportionment of the costs of a claim and counterclaim equally.[43] If there is likely to be a difficulty in relation to dividing the costs between the parties it seems that it is open to the court to state what the apportionment should be.

It is wrong in principle for a judge, having ordered part of a counterclaim to be struck out, to then order that any further proceedings on the counterclaim be stayed until the defendant has complied with an order to pay costs to the claimants. The error is in making an order which at one and the same time allows part of the counterclaim to proceed and then stays it until payment of costs which have only been ordered to be paid by the same order.[44] Whilst the Court of Appeal did not purport to comment on what should be the general approach to costs of claim and counterclaim, or even whether there should be such a general approach, it did express the view that the provisions of CPR rule 44.3(4) were inconsistent with any inflexible rule governing the costs of claims and counterclaims such as that in *Medway Oil v Continental Contractors.*[45]

---

[40] *Noueiri v Paragon Finance Ltd* [2001] EWCA Civ September 19.
[41] *Ahmed v Powell*, February 19, 2003, Senior Costs Judge, unreported.
[42] *Medway Oil & Storage Co. v Continental Contractors* [1929] A.C. 88, HL and see *Cartonneries De Thulin SA v CTP White Knight Ltd* (Costs) [1999] F.S.R. 922, Neuberger J.
[43] *Milican & Anor v Tucker* [1980] 1 W.L.R. 640, CA.
[44] *Theakston v Matthews*, *The Times*, April 13, 1998, CA.
[45] [1929] AC 88.

The Court of Appeal has given some general guidance as to the exercise of discretion in awarding costs arising out of difficulties which may arise when a split trial has taken place, the claimant being successful on liability, but largely unsuccessful on the questions of causation and *quantum*:

(a) On the trial of a preliminary issue, a court may ask itself "who essentially was the winner?" and make an order as to costs in the light of that; in which case it may be prudent to take much more care in formulating the preliminary issues to be tried in order to make it easier for a defendant to limit them by admissions.

(b) If for any reason a payment into court is not an available option in a personal injuries action, the defendant solicitors should bear in mind that a notice admitting facts may be a more effective device for limiting their clients liability for costs than a Part 36 offer.[46]

Where a claimant was unsuccessful on the claim and a defendant successful on a counterclaim it has been usual for the claimant and the defendant to be awarded the costs of their respective claims.[47] Costs could also be awarded on the basis of the issues actually involved in accordance with r.44.3(4) so as to encourage good litigation practice. It is one thing to award a successful claimant a proportion of the costs, it was quite another to order him to pay the defendant's costs. In deciding what order about costs to make it is relevant to good litigation practice to consider the ways in which both sides could have protected themselves as to costs.[48]

Fast track cases

The principle that where both claimant and defendant succeed, the costs recoverable on the counterclaim are only the increased costs[49] is done away with, and for the purpose of costs on the fast track, the values of the claim and counterclaim are looked at separately and the costs calculated accordingly.   **17–017**

Where a defendant has made a counterclaim which is higher than the value of the claim and the claimant succeeds at trial both on the claim and the counterclaim, for the purpose of quantifying the fast track trial costs awarded to the claimant, the value of the defendant's counterclaim is taken for the purpose of calculating the value of the claim.[50]

---

[46] *per* Brooke L.J. *Oksuzoglu v Kay* [1998] 2 All E.R. 361, CA.
[47] *Chell Engineering v Unit Tool & Engineering Co* [1950] 1 All E.R. 378.
[48] *Universal Cycles Plc v Grangebriar Ltd*, February 8, 2000, CA (unreported).
[49] *Medway Oil and Storage Co. v Continental Contractors* [1929] A.C. 88, HL.
[50] CPR, r.46.2(6).

Where a defendant has made a counterclaim and the claimant has succeeded on his claim and the defendant has succeeded on his counterclaim, the court will quantify the amount of the award of fast track trial costs to which, but for the counterclaim, the claimant would be entitled for succeeding on his claim; and but for the claim, the defendant would be entitled for succeeding on his counterclaim; and will make one award of the difference to the party entitled to the higher award. This is an attempt to get away from the difficulties caused by dealing with costs in such circumstances, in accordance with the decision of the House of Lords in *Medway Oil*.[51]

F. MISCELLANEOUS ITEMS

Amendment

17–018   Amendment to statements of case is governed by CPR, Part 17. There is no reason in principle why a person who has put forward a claim in a bill of costs should not amend it partially or indeed wholly. Whether that course should be permitted is a matter for the discretion of the court. The court will exercise that discretion on much the same basis as it exercises its general powers of amendment in relation to other aspects of litigation. The normal rule is that amendment will be allowed provided the opposite party is not prejudiced in some way other than as to costs. The courts have never said that a party cannot amend to increase the amount claimed because there might have been an offer on the basis of the original claim. Moreover even where that has happened, it is a matter which the court can, when it comes to consider the question of costs of the assessment or proceedings before it, take into account.[52]

Communication with the court

17–019   There is no reason in principle why solicitors should not be able to recover for time appropriately and reasonably spent in communicating with the court, on the same basis as they can recover for time appropriately and reasonably spent in other respects in furthering their client's interest.[53]

---

[51] CPR, r.46.3(6); *Medway Oil and Storage Co. v Continental Contractors* [1929] A.C. 88, HL.
[52] *per* Jacob J., *Morris v Wiltshire & Woodspring District Council* January 16, 1998, (unreported) and see Costs PD para.40.10.
[53] *Brush v Bower Cotton & Bower*, [1993] 4 All E.R. 741, Brooke J.

Time taken in preparing attendance

Brooke J. in *Brush v Bower Cotton & Bower stated:* **17–020**

" . . . work properly and reasonably done in furthering the client's interest may reasonably include the preparation of attendance and file notes recording what work has been done. The time spent in preparation of these notes should be recorded. The emphasis must always be on the question whether this work is 'reasonable'."[54]

Photocopying

Photocopying is not allowable unless it is reasonable and exceeds what one **17–021** would normally expect in a particular case. In other words, the solicitor is expected to bear the usual level of photocopying out of his overheads.[55] The amount allowed will normally be the equivalent commercial rate for copying the number of pages involved.

In litigation involving vast numbers of documents, it is common for one or other party to scan and organise the documents electronically on its information technology system. Where a dispute arose as to the appropriate form for inspection of documents relating to the appropriate charge for photostat copies or compact discs, the court held that it had power to give directions as to whether inspection should be by electronic means or hard copy.[56] On the particular facts of the case the court directed that inspection should be by means of compact disc which could be produced at a relatively modest cost as against production of photostat copies of the documents themselves which would have cost a very great deal of money. The actual work of assembling the database was a matter to be left to the outcome of the trial and subsequent detailed assessment.

G. COUNSEL'S FEES

Brief fee and refreshers

In assessing a brief fee it is always relevant to take into account what work **17–022** that fee together with the refreshers has to cover. The brief fee covers all the work done by way of preparation for representation at the trial, and attendance on the first day of trial, but in heavy litigation, particularly

---

[54] *Brush v Bower Cotton & Bower* above at 762.
[55] Evans J., *Johnson v Reed Corrugated Cases Ltd* [1992] 1 All E.R. 169.
[56] *Grupo Torras SA v Al Sabah; Jaffar v Grupo Torras SA, The Times,* October 13, 1997, Mance J.

where there is a team of barristers and experts, additional work is involved in ensuring that the client is properly represented and his case fully developed, beyond simply appearing in court. Counsel are only entitled to charge for work which they have been instructed to do and, where work is done with LSC funding and has been authorised by a certificate.[57]

Counsel is not normally entitled to be remunerated separately for necessary work which is an incident of the proper representation of the client. Rather, in a privately funded case a barrister must negotiate a brief fee sufficient to cover such work. In LSC cases the barrister may require that the brief fee and the refresher rate properly reflect the amount of work that actually had to be done.

In a LSC funded case the brief fee should be assessed and allowed having regard to the full history of the trial as known at the time of detailed assessment. It is proper to take into account the need for counsel to have meetings with each other and with experts out of court hours and to prepare final submissions. It is also necessary to take into account the fact that all heavy trials include such a need to a greater or lesser extent. The preparation by counsel of his examinations in chief and his cross-examinations, and of his final submissions are an ordinary part of his conduct of a trial on behalf of his client. It is all part of the work which he accepts an obligation to perform by accepting the brief, for which he is remunerated by the brief fee and the agreed refreshers. The daily refreshers are calculated by reference to time during which the trial is proceeding, and certainly cannot be charged for days when the court is not sitting.[58] This does not mean that counsel should not be paid for necessary work which is an incident of the proper representation of the client. It means that in a privately funded case a barrister must negotiate a brief fee that is sufficient to cover such work (or make other special arrangements for the delivery of supplementary instructions, and/or the agreement of an additional fee); and in legal aid work the barrister may on the legal aid detailed assessment require that the brief fee (and the refresher rates) properly reflect the amount of the work that actually had to be done for the client.[59]

Remuneration for taking a note of judgment is included in counsel's brief or refresher fees so that, save in exceptional circumstances there is no justification for charging an additional fee for that work. Counsel's usual entitlement to a further fee, when required to attend on a later date to take a note of a judgment which is not delivered at the end of the hearing, is not affected.[60] A publicly-funded claimant refused an increased Part 36 payment made after delivery of the brief to counsel. On the third day of the

---

[57] *Din v Wandsworth LBC* [1983] 1 W.L.R. 1171.
[58] *Lawson v Tiger* [1953] 1 W.L.R. 503.
[59] *per* Hobhouse J. in *Loveday v Renton (No.2)* [1992] 3 All E.R. 184. See also *A.T. & T. Istel Ltd v Tully (No.2)* [1994] 1 W.L.R. 279, HL.
[60] Practice Note (fee for note of judgment), *The Times*, December 30, 1993, Sir Thomas Bingham M.R.

assessment of damages hearing the claimant accepted the payment in. The defendant was ordered to pay the claimant's costs down to the date of payment in, and the claimant to pay the costs thereafter. In deciding how the brief fee should be apportioned the court decided that as at the date of payment in counsel was entitled to a commitment fee equivalent to half the brief fee. The court does not appear to have been persuaded by the argument that a brief fee is normally incurred in full on the day on which it is delivered.[61]

The court has indicated that the correct approach for assessing brief fees and skeleton argument fees for counsel in the Court of Appeal is in three stages. Stage 1—the fee for the skeleton argument should be assessed. This will be done largely by reference to the amount of time which counsel has reasonably and proportionately devoted to reading the documents, researching the law and drafting the skeleton argument. Stage 2—the brief fee should be assessed. This involves considering both the amount of time properly spent and many other factors (see r.44.5). The guidance given by Hobhouse J. in *Loveday v Renton (No.2)* [1992] 3 All E.R. 184 at 194 is still effective. In relation to a brief fee for the Court of Appeal it is important to avoid double payment. In so far as counsel has prepared whilst drafting the skeleton argument that preparation time should not be paid doe in the brief fee. Stage 3—having arrived at an appropriate skeleton argument fee and brief fee a cross check should then be done, the two figures should be aggregated to see whether the total is too large or too small for the overall conduct of the case in the Court of Appeal. If the total figure seems to be disproportionately large or disproportionately small then an appropriate adjustment should be made to the brief fee or the skeleton argument fee.[62]

Written closing submissions

Final submissions are an ordinary part of the conduct of a trial by a barrister on behalf of his client as part of the work which he accepts an obligation to perform by accepting the brief fee and for which he is remunerated by the brief fee and the agreed refreshers.[63] There may however be circumstances where the case is properly regarded as sufficiently complex or exceptional not to have been covered by the brief fee and hence for a separate brief fee to have been specifically agreed for the preparation of written submissions by counsel. Where such an agreement is made it may be perfectly proper for the costs judge to consider it allowable in principle subject to detailed assessment of the amount when assessing the bill of costs.[64]   **17–023**

---

[61] *Baucutt v Walding* [2003] October 14, Hallett J. unreported.

[62] *per* Jackson J. in *Hornsby v Clarke Kenneth Leventhal* [2000] EWHC, QBD, June 19.

[63] See *Loveday v Renton (No.2)* [1992] 3 All E.R. 184 at 191, Hobhouse J.

[64] *per* Nelson J., *Chohan v Times Newspapers Ltd*, September 7, 1998 (unreported).

Leading counsel and the two counsel rule

17–024 The most likely factors affecting the decision whether or not to instruct a leader include:

(a) the nature of the case, including in accident cases:

    (i) the nature and severity of the claimant's injury;

    (ii) the likely duration of the trial;

    (iii) difficult questions regarding the *quantum* of damages, including medical evidence and questions of law;

    (iv) difficult questions of fact, including expert engineering evidence, or issues as to causation;

(b) its importance for the client;

(c) the amount of damages likely to be recovered;

(d) the general importance of the case, *e.g.* as affecting other cases;

(e) any particular requirements of the case, *e.g.* the need for legal advice, or for special expertise, *e.g.* examining or cross-examining witnesses; and

(f) other reasons why an experienced and senior advocate may be required.[65]

The fact that the other party has instructed leading counsel or intends to do so cannot and should not be disregarded as a factor to be taken into account when deciding the question whether or not it is reasonable to have instructed leading counsel.[66]

The question of whether or not a junior should be instructed in addition to leading counsel or another advocate must be answered by reference to the test of reasonableness and proportionality. The test must be applied by the costs officer in the particular circumstances of each case. The correct approach is exemplified by The Code of Conduct (para.606.2) which states that reasonableness of the decision to instruct counsel in addition to another advocate must be judged by whether it is in the (lay) client's interests. These interests are paramount even on a detailed assessment when it is the losing party (or the legal aid fund) who is required to pay.

Some particular reasons why a junior may be necessary for the proper conduct of the case in the interests of the client include:

(a) to assist with the court proceedings either by taking an active part or by keeping a full note of the evidence, editing transcripts, etc.

---

[65] *Juby v London Fire & Civil Defence Authority; Saunders v Essex County Council* (April 24, 1990, (unreported). Evans J.

[66] See *British Metal Corp. Ltd v Ludlow Brothers (1913) Ltd* [1938] Ch. 987.

(b) dealing with documents generally, particularly when the same junior counsel has taken part in discovery;

(c) to carry out legal or other research, *e.g.* on matters on which expert evidence is given;

(d) to assist leading counsel in negotiations with the other party, particularly when, as in many accident cases, junior counsel has already advised the injured person and has become known to him. The lay client might well fail to understand why the junior who has dealt with his case up to trial should no longer be present when his claim is settled by negotiation or dealt with by judgment.

The fact that solicitors are experienced in a type of litigation and able to present comprehensive and competent instructions to counsel is not relevant to the question whether it is reasonable to instruct junior counsel. A balance has to be struck between the advantages of the more efficient presentation of the client's case and the extra expense involved in instructing leading counsel, or two counsel rather than one. The test laid down in *Francis v Francis & Dickerson*[67] has equal relevance to the assessment of costs today.[68]

With regard to the instruction of leading counsel the correct question is not whether the case was well within the capabilities of junior counsel but rather whether or not it was reasonable to instruct leading counsel.[69]

H. EXPERTS

The rules relating to the appointment of experts and assessors are contained in CPR Part 35.   **17–025**

No party may call an expert or put in evidence an expert's report without the court's permission. The court's permission will be in relation to a named expert or limited to the particular expert field. The court may limit the amount of the expert's fees and expenses that the party who wishes to rely on the expert may recover from any other party.[70] In a case on the small claims track the court may order a party to pay all or part of an expert's fee.[71]   **17–026**

The rules make provision for a party to put written questions to an expert instructed by another party or a single joint expert. Where a party puts a written question to an expert instructed by another party and the expert

---

[67] [1956] P. 87.
[68] *per* Evans J., *Juby v London Fire & Civil Defence Authority*, above n.55.
[69] *R. v Dudley Magistrates' Court Ex p. Power City Stores Ltd* (1990) 140 New L.J. 361.
[70] CPR, r.35.4.
[71] CPR, r.27.14(3)(d). The amount allowable is a sum not exceeding £200 for each expert. See Practice Direction Supplementing Part 27, para.7.3.

does not answer the question, the court may order that the party who instructed the expert may not rely on the evidence and/or may not recover the fees and expenses of that expert from any other party.[72]

Where a single joint expert is instructed the court may give directions about the payment of the expert's fees and expenses and may limit the amount that can be paid to the expert, it may also direct that the parties pay that amount into court. Unless the court makes a different order the instructing parties are jointly and severally liable for the payment of the expert's fees and expenses.[73]

The duties and responsibilities of expert witnesses in civil proceedings include:

(i) Expert evidence should be the independent product of the expert uninfluenced as to form or content by the exigencies of litigation.[74]

(ii) Independent assistance should be provided to the court by way of objective unbiased opinion regarding matters within the expertise of the expert witness.[75] An expert witness should never assume the role of advocate.

(iii) Facts or assumptions upon which the opinion is based should be stated together with material facts which could detract from the concluded opinion.

(iv) An expert witness should make it clear when a question or issue falls outside his expertise.

(v) If the opinion is not properly researched because insufficient data was available that must be stated with an indication that the opinion is provisional.[76] If the witness cannot assert that the report contains the truth, the whole truth and nothing but the truth that qualification must be stated on the report.[77]

(vi) If after exchange of reports, an expert changes his mind on a material matter then the change of view should be communicated to the other side through legal representatives without delay and, when appropriate, to the court.

---

[72] CPR, r.35.6.
[73] CPR, r.35.8.
[74] per Lord Wilberforce. *Whitehouse v Jordan* [1981] 1 All E.R. 267.
[75] See *Polivitte Ltd v Commercial Union Assurance Co. Plc* [1987] 1 Lloyd's Rep 379, 386 per Garland J. and *Re J.* [1990] F.C.R. 193, Cazalet J.
[76] See *Re J.* above.
[77] per Staughton L.J., *Derby & Co. Ltd v Weldon (No.9), The Times*, November 9, 1990.

(vii) Photographs, plans, survey reports and other documents referred to in the expert evidence must be provided to the other side at the same time as the exchange of reports.[78]

Lord Wilberforce in *Whitehouse v Jordan* stated:

"While some degree of consultation between experts and legal advisers is entirely proper, it is necessary that the expert evidence presented to the court should be seen to be independent product of the expert uninfluenced as to form or content by the exigencies of the litigation. To the extent that it is not, the evidence is likely to be not only incorrect, but self defeating."[79]

It is for the costs officer, whether or not an order is made under CPR, r.35.4 limiting the expert evidence, to determine whether the calling of any witness was reasonable. An order under the rule does not fetter the discretion of the costs officer, nor does it indicate that the view of the court was that the calling of the number of witnesses mentioned was necessarily to be regarded as reasonable.[80]

Solicitors acting for a LSC funded litigant may sometimes seek to engage an expert on terms that remuneration will be restricted to the amount allowed on detailed assessment. It has been held to be desirable in the interest of litigants that such an expert should receive remuneration on detailed assessment. It is the solicitor's duty to use his best endeavours to secure the allowance on detailed assessment of a proper fee for the expert. While the expert himself has no right to be heard on detailed assessment, in a heavy case, a costs officer would normally be expected both to permit the expert to give evidence in support of his charges and to receive evidence in respect of market rates of services as performed by the expert.[81]

In general the work of a party's employees in investigating, formulating and prosecuting a claim by legal proceedings does not qualify for an order for the payment of costs of and incidental to those proceedings. The exception to the general rule is in *Re: Nossen's Letter Patent* [1969] 1 W.L.R. 638 where the court held that the reasonable actual and direct costs of employed experts conducting experiments for the purpose of the proceedings were recoverable. More recently the court has found that the reasonable costs of claimant's expert employees in investigating, formulating and presenting claims against a defendant are potentially recoverable

---

[78] *National Justice Compania Naviera SA v Prudential Assurance Co. Ltd (Ikarian Reefer), The Times*, March 5, 1993, Cresswell J. and see now The Code of Guidance on Expert Evidence: A Guide for experts and those instructing them for the purpose of court proceedings (reproduced at 35.16 of Civil Procedure 2003 — the White Book).

[79] [1981] 1 All E.R. 267 at 276.

[80] *Atwell v Ministry of Public Buildings & Works* [1969] 1 W.L.R. 1074.

[81] *Cementation Construction Ltd v Keaveny, The Times*, July 21, 1989, Phillips J.

from the time that the claimant formed its suspicions that the defendant was committing the wrongs which were the subject of the claim. The costs could not include any element of overhead recovery or of profit. Whether the work of the claimant's employee's qualifies for inclusion in an order for costs depends on whether the employees are truly experts and on the nature of the work carried out.[82]

The Technology and Construction Court has held that it would be contrary to the overriding objective if necessary expenditure incurred by the claimants employees undertaking preparation of its claims for trial at a lower cost than that which solicitors would have charged was not recoverable in principle under an order for costs.[83]

An agreement between a claimant and a firm of accountants that they would undertake work relating to litigation on the basis that their charges would be 8 per cent of the damages recovered was held not to be champertous because the accountants were not conducting litigation and did not themselves act as the expert witnesses. They had specifically employed experts whose fees they paid. They advised on and co-ordinated the evidence of loss and provided back-up services for the expert witnesses. If the accountants had not performed those services they would have had to be carried out by the claimants solicitors at higher rates. The agreement was not a conditional fee agreement under section 58 of the Courts and Legal Services Act 1990 since that section applied only to agreements concluded by those conducting litigation or providing advocacy services. Section 58 does not apply to expert witnesses. For an expert to give evidence on a contingency fee basis would give the expert a significant financial interest in the outcome of the case which was highly undesirable and it would be very rare for the court to consent to an expert being instructed on that basis. The agreement was not contrary to public policy not champertous.[84]

Marine claims recovery agents agreed to act on behalf of cargo insurers following the loss of a vessel on the basis of a fee of 5 per cent of recovery on a "no cure no pay" basis. They carried out the initial work and then, when proceedings became necessary solicitors were instructed. The successful claimants sought the recovery agent's fees either as damages or costs. The court found that the fees were not claimable as damages only as costs. The arrangement was held not to be champertous (as asserted by the defendants) because:

> (i) the bills of lading had stipulated for foreign law and it was not until a late stage that the application of English law was agreed;

---

[82] *Admiral Management Services Ltd v Para Protect Europe Ltd* [2002] EWHC, Ch D, 233; [2002] 1 W.L.R. 2722, Stanley Burton J.

[83] *Amec Process and Energy Ltd v Stork Engineers and Contractors BV (No.3)*, March 15, 2002 H.H. Judge Thornton Q.C. TCC; [2002] All E.R. (D) 48.

[84] *R (on the application of Factortame) v The Secretary of State for Transport* [2002] EWCA Civ 932; [2002] 1 W.L.R. 2438 CA; [2002] 4 All E.R. 97 CA.

(ii) the paying party was protected by the fact that it would only have to pay standard basis costs and the 5 per cent operated as a cap;

(iii) there was little scope for the agents to influence the outcome as solicitors and counsel were acting;

(iv) the majority of claims of this sort were compromised without lawyers;

(v) the agents were already acting for other underwriters;

(vi) the agreement was not exclusively concerned with litigation.[85]

Other witnesses

CPR Part 34 deals with depositions and court attendances by witnesses and makes provision for the issue and service of witness summonses. At the time of service of the witness summons the witness must be offered or paid a sum sufficient reasonably to cover his expenses in travelling to and from the court and a sum by way of compensation for loss of time.[86] If the witness summons is to be served by the court, the party issuing the summons must deposit with the court the necessary amount to cover the travelling expenses and compensation for loss of time.[87]   **17–027**

Examiner

The court may order that a deponent be examined on oath before a judge and examiner of the court or such other person as the court appoints.[88] Where the deponent is outside the jurisdiction, the High Court may order the issue of a letter of request to the judicial authorities of the country in which the proposed deponent is; the request is that the judicial authority take the evidence of the deponent or arrange for it to be taken. If the Government of the country in which the letter is sent allows a person appointed by the High Court to examine a person in that country the High Court may make an order appointing a special examiner for that purpose.[89]   **17–028**

The examiner may charge a fee for the examination and need not send the deposition to the court until the fee is paid. The examiner's fees and

---

[85] *The Eurasian Dream (No.2)* [2002] Lloyd's Rep. [under appeal].

[86] CPR, r.34.7. The sum payable as compensation for lack of time is based on the sums payable to witnesses attending the Crown Court fixed pursuant to the Prosecution of Offences Act 1985 and the Costs in Criminal Cases (General) Regulations 1986.

[87] Practice Direction Supplementing Part 34 para.3.2.

[88] CPR, r.34.8.

[89] CPR, r.34.13.

expenses must be paid by the party who obtained the order for examination. If the fees are not paid within a reasonable time the examiner may report the fact to the court and the court may order the defaulting party to deposit in the court office a specified sum in respect of the examiner's fees and in such a case the examiner will not be asked to act until the sum has been deposited. The decision of the court as to which party should ultimately bear the cost of the examination is not affected by the above provisions.[90]

Planning cases

17–029   There is an evidential threshold which, if reached, is likely to put a planning authority beyond the risk of a finding that it has been guilty of unreasonable conduct, and thus liable to be ordered to pay the costs of an objection to a planning application. The threshold was whether there was "sufficient evidential basis", *i.e.* evidence not lacking real substance, capable of belief and which if accepted, would be capable of making good the claimant Authority's objection.[91]

The court has its own interest in preserving the high standards of civil administration and will mark its disapproval of a breach of an obligation by the Secretary of State to require an environmental plan by depriving the Secretary of State of a proportion of his costs.[92]

Where proceedings for statutory nuisance are brought, the Environmental Protection Act 1990 section 82(12) imposes a duty on the court to award costs incurred by a complainant in bringing the proceedings and that includes costs which the complainant incurred in establishing that the statutory nuisance existed prior to proceedings. The costs are limited to those considered necessary by the words "properly incurred", thus expenses which might have been avoided may be disregarded.[93]

The House of Lords has considered the position with regard to multiple representation in planning appeals.

> "As in all questions to do with costs, the fundamental rule is that there are no rules. Costs are always in the discretion of the court, and the practice, however widespread and longstanding, must never be allowed to harden into a rule"[94]

---

[90] CPR, r.34.14.

[91] *R. v Secretary of State for the Environment, Ex p. Wakefield Metropolitan Borough Council, The Times*, October 29, 1996, Jowitt J.

[92] *Berkeley v Secretary of State for the Environment (No.2), The Times*, April 7, 1998, CA. The court ordered the applicant to pay only two-thirds of the Secretary of State's costs.

[93] *Hollis v Dudley MBC; Probert v Dudley MBC, The Times*, December 12, 1997, Moses J.

[94] Lord Lloyd of Berwick in *Bolton MDC v Secretary of State for the Environment* [1995] 1 W.L.R. 1176, HL.

The court supported four propositions.

1. The Secretary of State, when successful in defending his decision, would normally be entitled to the whole of his costs, and would not be liable to share the award by apportionment, either by agreement by other parties or by further order of the court.

2. The developer would not normally be entitled to costs, unless it could be shown that there was likely to be a separate issue on which the developer was entitled to be heard, that is an issue not covered by counsel to the Secretary of State, or unless the developer had an interest which required separate representations.

3. A second set of costs was more likely to be awarded at first instance than in the Court of Appeal or House of Lords, since by that time the issues should have crystallised and the extent to which there were indeed separate interests should have been clarified.

4. An award of a third set of costs could rarely be justified, even if there were in theory, three or more separate interests.[95]

Where a citizens action group challenged the decision of the Secretary of State by way of judicial review and the Secretary of State and a developer shared the representation, the court held that, since the developer had incurred the costs of providing evidence for the Secretary of State in defence of the claim, and did not seek to incur any further or additional costs by way of obtaining separate legal representation at the hearing, it was convenient and sensible that the Secretary of State should be allowed to claim costs on behalf of himself and the developer. The developer was entitled to costs in providing the evidence, being costs which would have been recoverable by the Secretary of State had he obtained the evidence himself.[96]

Conditional fee agreements

The Conditional Fee Agreements Regulations and the Collective Conditional Fee Agreement Regulations established two mutually exclusive sets of requirements for conditional fee arrangements (CFAs) and collective conditional fee arrangement (CCFAs) respectively. The Regulations governing CCFAs are less exacting than those governing CCFAs since CCFAs involve bulk users of legal services who are less vulnerable than a lay client who may need protection when contemplating entering into a CFA. Often bulk users,   **17–030**

---

[95] per Lord Lloyd of Berwick in *Bolton MDC v Secretary of State for the Environment* above.

[96] *Issac v Secretary of State for the Environment Food and Rural Affairs* [2002] EWHC 1983 (ADMIN), Forbes J.

such as trade unions, will contract to purchase, at their own expense, legal services to be provided to litigants. In those circumstances the litigants will not be exposed to significant risk of liability to pay for the legal services provided to them. Sections 58 and 58A of the Courts and Legal Services Act 1990 and the Regulations made under them are intended to give effect to fundamental changes to the manner in which litigation is funded.[97]

[97] *Thornley v Lang* [2003] EWCA Civ 1484.

PART IX

House of Lords
European Court of Justice

CHAPTER 18

House of Lords

A. THE AWARD OF COSTS

The award and assessment of costs in the House of Lords (still referred to as taxation of costs) is governed by the Practice Directions and Standing Orders Applicable to Civil Appeals and the Practice Directions applicable to Judicial Taxations in the House of Lords.   **18–001**

Where a petition for leave to appeal is determined without an oral hearing the following awards of costs may be made: **18–002**

(a) to a publicly funded or legally aided petitioner: reasonable costs incurred in preparing papers for the Appeal Committee;

(b) to a publicly funded or legally aided respondent: only those costs necessarily incurred in attending the client, attending the petitioner's agents, perusing the petition, entering appearance and, where applicable, preparing the respondent's objections to the petition[1];

(c) to an unassisted respondent where the petitioner is publicly funded or legally aided: payment out of the CLS fund[2] of costs as in (b) above;

(d) to a respondent where neither party is publicly funded or legally aided: costs as set out at (b) above.

In respect of the last two heads, where costs are sought, application must be made in writing to the Judicial Office before the bill is lodged. Where a   **18–003**

---

[1] Also pursuant to reg.5(2) Community Legal Service (Cost Protection) Regulations 2000 and in accordance with the procedure requirements of rr.9 and 10 Community Legal Service (Costs) Regulations 2000.

[2] Pursuant to s.11 Access to Justice Act 1999 or s.18 Legal Aid Act 1988 or in Scotland pursuant to s.19 Legal Aid (Scotland) Act 1986 or in Northern Ireland pursuant to art.16 Legal Advice and Assistance (NI) Order 1981.

petition for leave to appeal is referred for an oral hearing and dismissed, application for costs must be made by the respondent at the end of the hearing. No order for costs will be made unless the request is made at that time. Where a petition for leave to appeal is allowed, the costs of the petition will be costs in the ensuing appeal.

18–004   Bills of costs for taxation must be lodged within three months from the date of the decision of the Appeal Committee or the date on which a petition for leave is withdrawn. If an extension of the three-month period is required, application must be made to the taxing officer in writing before the original time expires. If no application is made a bill lodged out of time will be accepted only in exceptional circumstances.[3]

Procedure on taxation

18–005   As a general rule CPR Parts 43–48 and the Costs Practice Direction are applied by analogy at the discretion of the taxing officers, with appropriate modifications for appeals from Scotland and Northern Ireland. The legal principles applied are those also applicable to taxations between the parties in the High Court and Court of Appeal in England and Wales.[4]

18–006   Taxations are conducted by taxing officers, namely the Clerk of the Judicial Office and the Senior Costs Judge of the Supreme Court of England and Wales or any Costs Judge nominated by him. The Taxing Officers normally sit together as a court of two.

18–007   Where a respondent is granted liberty to apply for his costs, where neither party is publicly funded or legally aided, the application may be made by letter addressed to the Judicial Office or may be included in a bill of costs lodged in the Judicial Office, conditional upon the application being granted. As a general rule the Judicial Office will not grant the application where the petition for leave was not served on the respondent making the application; where the respondent making application did not enter appearance to the petition for leave; where the application is made by one of two or more respondents and the Judicial Office is not satisfied that the applicant had an interest in the petition for leave that required separate representation.[5]

Orders under Section 11 of the Access to Justice Act 1999

18–008   In accordance with Section 11 of the Access to Justice Act 1999, any costs ordered to be paid by an LSC funded party must not exceed the amount

---

[3] Practice Directions applicable to Civil Appeals Direction 5.
[4] *Kuwait Airways Corporation v Iraqi Airways Co & Ors* Appeal Committee 102 Report (2001–02) para.16 HL paper 155.
[5] Practice Directions applicable to Judicial Taxations Direction 3.

which is a reasonable one for them to pay having regard to all the circumstances including the financial resources of all the parties to the proceedings and their conduct in connection with the dispute to which the proceedings relate. Costs which are not recoverable from an LSC funded party because of Section 11 of the 1999 Act may, in certain circumstances, be payable by the LSC itself.[6]

A party who seeks costs against the LSC must lodge with his bill of costs, copies of any documents (including a statement of resources and any notice served by him on the LSC), which he has served upon others in compliance with the Regulations. Within 21 days of being served with a bill of costs a party, who is or was LSC funded during a period covered by the bill, must respond by lodging in the Judicial Office a statement of resources and serving a copy of it on the receiving party and, where relevant, on the Regional Director of the LSC. The Regional Director may appear at any hearing at which a costs order may be made against the LSC.[7]   **18–009**

Time for lodging bills

Bills of costs for taxation must be lodged within three months of the date on which the final judgment in the appeal is delivered; or the date on which petition for leave to appeal is dismissed by an Appeal Committee; or the date on which petition for leave or a petition of appeal is withdrawn.[8] If an extension of time is required, application must be made in writing to the Taxing Officer before the end of that period. In deciding whether to grant an application the Taxing Officer will take into account all the circumstances including: **18–010**

  (a) the interests of the administration of justice;

  (b) whether the failure to lodge in time was intentional;

  (c) whether there is a good explanation for failure to lodge in time;

  (d) the effect which the delay has had on each party; and

  (e) the effect which granting of an extension of time would have on each party.[9]

When the bill is lodged it must be endorsed with a certificate of service on the parties entitled to be represented at the taxation. The bill when lodged must be accompanied by one further copy; counsel's fee note; and, written   **18–011**

---

[6] See Community Legal Service (Costs) Regulations 2000 and Community Legal Service (Cost Protection) Regulations 2000.
[7] Practice Directions applicable to Judicial Taxations Direction 4.
[8] *ibid.*, Direction 5.
[9] *ibid.*, Direction 6.

evidence of any other disbursement which is claimed which exceeds £250. The parties may lodge any other papers which they intend to rely on. Information about the date and time of the taxation will be sent to all the parties or their agents.[10]

Basis of taxation

18–012 Unless otherwise provided for by order or direction, the costs in the House of Lords will be ordered to be taxed on the standard basis or on the indemnity basis in accordance with CPR 44.4 or the equivalent bases applicable in Scotland and Northern Ireland.

Provisional taxation

18–013 Bills of costs involving public funding may be dealt with by provisional taxation. In such a case the provisional taxation will be conducted without the attendance of the parties and the Taxing Clerk will inform them in writing of the outcome. If this procedure proves unsatisfactory to the parties, or if points of disagreement cannot be resolved in correspondence, the Taxing Officer will appoint a date for hearing. Bills to be taxed between the parties in large or complex cases will not usually be dealt with by provisional taxation but by a hearing before the Taxing Officer. Any request for a hearing following a provisional taxation must be made within 14 days of the receipt of the letter from the Taxing Clerk.[11]

B. APPEALS AGAINST TAXATION IN THE HOUSE OF LORDS

18–014 Any party to a taxation who is dissatisfied with any decision of the Taxing Officer may seek leave to petition the House. Such an application may only be made on a question of principle and not in respect of the quantum allowed on any item. Such an application must be made within 14 days after the decision of the Taxing Officer or such longer period as may be fixed.[12] An application for leave to present a petition must be accompanied by written submissions setting out the items objected to and stating concisely the nature and ground of the objection. A copy of the grounds must be delivered to each party who attended the taxation, or to whom the Taxing Officer directs that a copy should be delivered. Any party to whom a copy

---

[10] *ibid.*, Directions 8 and 9.
[11] Practice Directions applicable to Judicial Taxations Direction 13.
[12] Practice Directions applicable to Judicial Taxations Directions 17.1–17.3.

of the grounds of appeal is delivered may, within 14 days after delivery, submit their answers in writing to the Taxing Officer. The answer should state concisely the reasons why they are opposed, and the party must at the same time deliver a copy of the answer to the party applying for review, and to each other party to whom grounds have been delivered or to whom the Taxing Officer directs that a copy of the answer should be delivered.[13]

When all the necessary documents have been received the Taxing Officer will refer the matter to a Lord of Appeal who will decide whether the matter should be referred to an Appeal Committee. If the Lord of Appeal is of the opinion that the matter should not be referred the decision of the Taxing Officer is affirmed.[14]   **18–015**

If the Lord of Appeal decides that the matter should be referred to an Appeal Committee, the party disputing the decision of the Taxing Officer may, within 14 days of that decision being communicated to the parties, present an incidental petition to the House.[15] The petition will be referred to an Appeal Committee which will consider whether it should be referred for hearing.[16]   **18–016**

Interest

Interest is chargeable on orders made in respect of costs between the parties and orders for costs in favour of successful unassisted parties, in accordance with the provisions of the Judgment Act 1838. Interest accrues from the day on which the order of the House is made. The Taxing Officer may vary the period for which interest is allowed, in any case where the circumstances make it appropriate to do so.[17]   **18–017**

---

[13] *ibid.*, Direction 17.4, 17.5.
[14] *ibid.*, Direction 17.6, 17.7.
[15] In accordance with Direction 39 of the Practice Directions applicable to Civil Appeals.
[16] Practice Direction applicable to Judicial Taxations 17.8, 17.9.
[17] Practice Directions applicable to Judicial Taxations Direction 24.

CHAPTER 19

European Court of Justice

A. THE RELEVANT COSTS

19–001   The European Court of Justice is not concerned with the question of costs between the legal representative and the client, such matters are essentially matters of contract and are dealt with under the jurisdiction of the national courts. Where cases are referred, in accordance with Part 68,[1] to the European Court of Justice, costs remain a matter for the national court.

In proceedings between the Communities and their servants the institutions must bear their own costs.[2] The court is therefore only concerned with costs between the parties and then only on certain occasions. If the institution is successful it will recover its costs, but these are normally minimal because the institutions only rarely employ outside lawyers. It is only where the institution is ordered to pay costs or where a losing private party is ordered to pay the costs of an intervener, that the issue of costs becomes relevant.

B. THE JUDGMENT

19–002   The court is required to adjudicate on costs in every case. Every judgment must contain a decision as to costs.[3] The judgment must contain a statement that it is the judgment of the particular court; the date of its delivery; the

---

[1] *i.e.* under E.C. Treaty, Art.234; Euratom Treaty, Art.150 or ECSC Treaty, Art.41. A preliminary ruling procedure is also provided for by the protocols to several conventions concluded by member States, in particular the Brussels Convention and the Enforcement of Judgments in Civil and Commercial Matters.

[2] Art.70, Rules of Procedure of the Court of Justice of the European Communities (June 19, 1991, as amended July 10, 2003) [CJRP]; Art.88, Rules of Procedure of the Court of First Instance of the European Communities (May 2, 1991) [CFIRP].

[3] E.C. Treaty, Art.35; Euratom Treaty, Art.36; ECSC Treaty, Art.32; and see, *e.g.* Case 204/85 *Stroghili v Court of Auditors* [1987] E.C.R. 389.

names of the President and of the judges taking part in it; the name of the Advocate General; the name of the registrar; the description of the parties; the names of the agents, advisers and lawyers of the parties; a statement of the forms of order sought by the parties; a statement that the Advocate General has been heard; a summary of the facts; the grounds for the decision; and the operative part of the judgment, including the decision as to costs.[4] The decision as to costs must be in either the final judgment or in the order which closes the proceedings.[5] If the court omits to give a decision on a specific head of claim, or on costs, any party, within a month after service of the judgment, may apply to the court to supplement its judgment. The application must be served on the opposite party and the President of the court must prescribe a period within which that party may lodge written observations. After observations have been lodged the court will, after hearing the Advocate General, decide both on the admissibility and on the substance of the application.[6] The judgment is binding from the date of its delivery.[7] Where the order or judgment is not final the decision on costs is reserved.[8]

If there is a dispute concerning the costs to be recovered, the chamber to which the case has been assigned will, on application by the party concerned and having heard the opposite party and the Advocate General, make an order from which there is no appeal.[9]

C. AWARDS OF COSTS

Preliminary rulings and other references for interpretation

Where a national court or tribunal refers a case for a preliminary ruling or interpretation[10] it is for that court to decide as to the costs of the reference.[11] If another member state or community institution has submitted observations but is not a party to the proceedings, the national court is only empowered to deal with the costs of the parties to the original action.[12]   19–003

Article 104(5) CJPR is to be interpreted as meaning that the costs of obtaining a preliminary ruling are governed by national law, as the rules of procedure do not lay down any specific costs rules for preliminary rulings, and reference proceedings are only a step in action pending before a

---

[4] Art.63, CJRP; Art.81, CFIRP.
[5] *ibid.*, Art.69(1); *ibid.*, Art.87(1).
[6] CJRP, Art.67; CFIRP, Art.85.
[7] *ibid.*, Arts 65 and 83.
[8] See Case 191/82 *Fediol v E.C. Commission* [1983] E.C.R. 2913 at 2936.
[9] CJRP Art.74(1) and CFIRP Art.92(1).
[10] Under *ibid.*, Art.103.
[11] *ibid.*, Art.104(6).
[12] Case 62/72 *Bollmann v Hauptzollamt Hamburg-Waltershof* [1973] E.C.R. 269.

national court.[13] The principle of equivalence requires that the rules on the costs of preliminary rulings should not be less favourable than those governing domestic actions, and the principle of effectiveness provides that the matter of costs should not render the exercise of community law excessively difficult.[14] It is for the national court, having direct knowledge of domestic law actions, to determine whether the principle of equivalence is satisfied.[15]

Intervention

19–004   Member States and institutions which intervene in the proceedings must bear their own costs.[16] When a party applies to intervene[17] the court will normally order the intervener to pay the costs. If the intervention is successful and the party being supported by the intervener is also successful, the court will normally award the intervener costs against the losing party.[18] On the other hand, if all the arguments put forward by the intervener fail, then notwithstanding that the party supported by the intervener is successful, the court may order the intervener to bear his own costs.[19]

If the party supported by the intervener is unsuccessful the intervener will be ordered to bear his own costs and also to pay the costs of the successful party attributable to the intervention.[20]

Principles of the award of costs

19–005   The unsuccessful party must be ordered to pay the costs if they have been asked for in that party's pleadings. Where there are several unsuccessful parties the court will decide how the costs are to be shared.[21] If there is no application for costs in the pleadings each party will bear its own costs.[22]

---

[13] See *Bollmann v Hauptozlooamt* above.

[14] See Case 279/96 *Ansoldo Energia SpA v Amministrazione delle Finanze dello Stato* [1998] E.C.R. 1–5025; Case 326/96 *Levez v TH Jennings (Harlow Pools) Ltd* [1999] All E.R. 1, EC.

[15] Case 472/99 *Clean Auto Service GmbH v Stadt Wien* [2003] 2 C.M.L.R. 40.

[16] CJRP, Art.69(4); CFIRP, Art.87(4).

[17] Under *ibid.*, Arts 93 and 115.

[18] Case 130/75 *Prais v E.C. Council* [1976] E.C.R. 1589.

[19] CJRP, Art.69(4); CFIRP, Art.87(4); and see Case 792/79R *Camera Care Ltd v E.C. Commission* [1980] E.C.R. 119.

[20] *e.g.* Case 118/77 *I.S.O. v E.C. Council* [1979] E.C.R. 1277; Case 119/77 *Nippon Seiko K.K. v E.C. Council and E.C. Commission* [1979] E.C.R. 1303; Case 120/77 *Koyo Seiko Ltd v E.C. Council and E.C. Commission* [1979] E.C.R. 1337; Case 121/77 *Nachi Fujikoshi Corporation v E.C. Council and E.C. Commission* [1979] E.C.R.; but see also Case 24/71 *Meinhardt v E.C. Commission* [1972] E.C.R. 269 and *Mrs P v E.C. Commission* [1981] E.C.R. 361.

[21] CJRP, Art.69(2); CFIRP, Art.87(2).

[22] *e.g.* Case 139/79 *Maizena GmbH v E.C. Council* [1980] E.C.R. 3393.

The court may be persuaded to award costs even if they had not been asked for in the proceedings if they are claimed at the hearing.[23]

In an action against a Member State for failure to fulfil its obligations, which was subsequently discontinued, it was open to the Court (under Article 69(5) of the Rules of Procedure) to order that the costs of the discontinued action be paid by that State.[24]

Where each party succeeds on some and fails on other heads or *where the circumstances are exceptional* the court may order that the costs be shared or that the parties bear their own costs. The court may order a party even if successful to pay costs which the court considers that party to have unreasonably or vexatiously caused the opposite party to incur.[25] Similarly, the costs of examining witnesses may fall to be paid by the party who loses on the issues in respect of which the witnesses were examined.[26]

Exceptional circumstances

It is a matter entirely for the court what circumstances it will regard as exceptional, but the circumstances may include the impossibility of apportioning costs equitably.[27] An order that each party bear their own costs may be made because of the complexity of the questions raised in the action.[28]

19–006

If the defendant's behaviour induces or encourages an applicant to bring an action this may amount to exceptional circumstances, so that if the applicant is unsuccessful the parties can properly be left to pay their own costs.[29] Each case must be decided on its own circumstances, but it does not appear that "where the circumstances are exceptional" requires the same quality of being out of the ordinary as is expected in relation to, for example, claims for enhancement in LSC funded cases in England and Wales. The provision appears rather, to be a device to enable the court to arrive at a just decision between the parties by dividing the liability for costs appropriately.

The provision that the court may order even a successful party to pay costs which the court considers that party to have unreasonably or

---

[23] Case 1137/77 *NTN Toyo Bearing Co. v E.C. Council* [1979] E.C.R. 1185.

[24] *E.C. Commission v Italian Republic*, Case 416/97, January 21, 1999, ECJ, unreported.

[25] CJRP, Art.69(3); CFIRP, Art.87(3); and see, *e.g.* Case 265/82 *Usinov v E.C. Commission* [1983] E.C.R. 3105 and Case 322/81 *Nederlandeche Banden-Industrie Michelin NV v E.C. Commission* [1983] E.C.R. 3461.

[26] *e.g.* Cases 40–48, 54–56, 111, 113 and 114/73 *Suiker Unieua v E.C. Commission* [1975] E.C.R. 1663.

[27] *e.g.* Cases 275/80 and 24/81 *Krupp v Stahl AG v E.C. Commission* [1981] E.C.R. 2489.

[28] *e.g.* Cases 2 and 3/60 *Niederrheinische Bergwerks AG v High Authority* [1961] E.C.R. 113; and on a question of "general interest" Case 175/73 *Union Syndicale, Massa and Kortner v E.C. Council* [1974] E.C.R. 917.

[29] Cases 783 and 786/79 *Venus and Obert v E.C. Commission and E.C. Council* [1981] E.C.R. 2445; Case 230/81 *Luxembourg v European Parliament* [1983] E.C.R. 255.

vexatiously caused the opposite party to incur,[30] is an extension of the discretion given to the court in respect of costs, thus the court may still award costs against a successful defendant if it was reasonable for the applicant to institute proceedings.[31] It has been argued[32] by the Advocate General that a test of reasonableness was appropriate but only if the commencement of proceedings was unreasonable should the party who brought them about (either claimant or defendant) be saddled with the costs. Where the applicant has been misled by the defendant or induced into commencing proceedings unnecessarily, the defendant may be ordered to pay all or part of the costs.[33]

This rule of procedure again appears to be designed to give the court a wide discretion as to costs and enables the court to deal with cases where costs have been unnecessarily incurred and where there has been an abuse of process or other behaviour meriting reproof. Given the wording of the rule the unreasonable or vexatious act of the successful party may have caused additional costs to be incurred.[34]

Discontinuance and failure to proceed to judgment

19–007 A party who discontinues or withdraws from proceedings will be ordered to pay the costs if they have been applied for in the other party's observations on discontinuance. However on application by the party who discontinues or withdraws from the proceedings, costs will be borne by the other party if this appears justified by the conduct of that party. If the costs are not claimed, each side bears their own costs.[35] There is an argument as to whether this particular rule refers to the discontinuance of the entire proceedings or merely the withdrawal of certain heads of claim. The English translation of the Rules of Procedure appears to favour the interpretation that the entire proceedings must have been terminated but that view is not confirmed by, for example the German translation. The situation is clearer where there are a number of joined cases, an order for costs can be made in respect of each case discontinued, even if all the cases are against the same defendant.[36] The parties may of course reach whatever agreement is appropriate in respect of costs.[37]

---

[30] *i.e.* under CJRP, Art.69(3); CFIRP, Art.87(3).
[31] Cases 53 and 54/63 *Lemmerz-Werke GmbH v High Authority* [1963] E.C.R. 239.
[32] In the *Lemmerz-Werke* case, above.
[33] *e.g.* Case 49/64 *Stripperger v High Authority* [1965] E.C.R. 521; Case 282/81 *Ragusa v E.C. Commission* [1983] E.C.R. 1245; Case 122/77 *Claes v E.C. Commission* [1978] E.C.R. 2085; and Case 40/71 *Richez-Parise v E.C. Commission* [1972] E.C.R. 73.
[34] Case 31/71 *Gigante v E.C. Commission* [1976] E.C.R. 1471.
[35] CJRP, Art.69(5); CFIRP, Art.87(5).
[36] Cases 39, 43, 85/81 *Halvvourgiki Inc. v E.C. Commission* [1982] E.C.R. 593.
[37] Case 16 18/59 *Geitling Ruhrkohlen-Verkaufsgesellschaft GmnH v High Authority* [1960] E.C.R. 17.

Where a case does not proceed to judgment the costs are in the discretion of the court.[38] The effect of this rule is intended to cover those cases where the proceedings are not discontinued or withdrawn. In such circumstances the court must terminate the proceedings, usually by finding that there are no grounds for proceeding to judgment.[39] Where the proceedings are terminated by the court, it has an unfettered discretion on the question of costs and will take into account the behaviour of the parties.

D. ENFORCEMENT

Costs necessarily incurred by a party in enforcing a judgment or order of the court will be refunded by the opposite party on the scale in force in the State where the enforcement takes place.[40]   19–008

The costs which are recoverable

Costs may be recovered both by the court in certain circumstances and by a party in whose favour an award of costs is made.   19–009

Proceedings before the court are free of charge except that:

(a) where a party has caused the court to incur avoidable costs, the court may, after hearing the Advocate General, order that party to refund them;

(b) where copying or translation work is carried out at the request of a party, the cost will, in so far as the registrar considers it excessive, be paid for by that party on the appropriate scale.[41]

Also regarded as recoverable costs are sums payable to witnesses and experts[42] and expenses necessarily incurred by the parties for the purpose of the proceedings, in particular travel and subsistence expenses and the remuneration of agents, advisers or lawyers.[43] Witnesses and experts are entitled to reimbursement of their travel and subsistence expenses which may be paid in advance by the court.[44] Witnesses are entitled to compensation for loss of earnings and experts to fees for their services. The

---

[38] CJRP, Art.69(6); CFIRP, Art.87(6).
[39] e.g. 256/81 Paul's Agriculture Ltd v E.C. Council and E.C. Commission [1983] 23 CMLR 176.
[40] CJRP, Art.71; CFIRP, Art.89.
[41] CJRP, Art.72(a),(b). The appropriate scale of charges is obtainable from the Registry pursuant to Art.16(5); CFIRP, Arts 90(a),(b) and 24(5).
[42] Under CJRP, Art.51; CFIRP, Art.74.
[43] CJRP, Art.73(a) and (b); CFIRP, Art.91(a),(b).
[44] ibid., Art.51(1); CFIRP, Art.74(1).

compensation or fees are paid by the court after they have carried out their respective duties or tasks.[45] Travel and subsistence expenses of the party personally are only recoverable if his presence at the hearing was necessary.[46]

E. LEGAL AID

19–010 A party who is wholly or in part unable to meet the costs of the proceedings may apply for legal aid at any time.[47] The question of legal aid is outside the scope of this work, but it may be noted that the application need not be made through a lawyer[48] and the decision as to whether or not legal aid shall be granted is reached after considering the written observations of the opposite party and after hearing the Advocate General. If legal aid is refused the chamber making the order will not give reasons and there is no appeal from a refusal.[49] Where legal aid is granted the cashier of the court will advance the funds necessary to meet the expenses.[50] The Court of First Instance is required to adjudicate on the lawyer's disbursements and fees. The President may, on application by the lawyer, order that he receive an advance.[51] In its decision as to costs the court may order the payment to the cashier of the court of the whole or any part of the amounts advanced as legal aid. The registrar will take steps to obtain the recovery of these sums from the party ordered to pay.[52] The chamber may at any time, of its own motion or on application withdraw legal aid if the circumstances which led to its being granted alter during the proceedings.[53]

F. WITNESSES

19–011 The court may make the summoning of a witness conditional upon the deposit, by the party summoning the witness, of a sum sufficient to cover the assessed costs. The court will fix the amount of the payment.[54]

The Rules of Procedure refer to "expenses necessarily incurred ... for the purpose of the proceedings".[55] The test of necessity would appear to be

---

[45] *ibid.*, Art.51(2); *ibid.*, Art.74(2).
[46] Case 24/79 *Oberthur v E.C. Commission* [1981] E.C.R. 2229.
[47] CJRP, Art.76(1); CFIRP, Art.94(1).
[48] *ibid.*, Arts 76(2), 94(2).
[49] *ibid.*, Arts 76(3), 94(2).
[50] *ibid.*, Arts 76(5), 97(1).
[51] CFIRP, Art.92(2).
[52] CFIRP, Arts 76(5), 97(3).
[53] *ibid.*, Arts 76(4), 96.
[54] *ibid.*, Arts 47(3), 68(3).
[55] CJRP, Art.73(b); CFIRP, Art.91(b).

stricter than that of reasonableness and proportionality used in the English courts and as a general rule costs are not recoverable for work done prior to the commencement of the proceedings.[56] It appears to be accepted, however, that work done by lawyers drafting the application commencing proceedings is recoverable.[57]

G. ASSESSMENT OF COSTS

If there is a dispute concerning costs to be recovered the chamber to which the case has been assigned will, on application by the party concerned and after hearing the requisite party and the Advocate General, make an order from which no appeal lies.[58] The Rules of Procedure do not lay down any particular requirements in relation to the claim for costs but the rules governing written procedure will apply.[59] There is no time-limit for the application to have the costs assessed, though the party entitled to costs should send details of the claim to the party liable to pay within a reasonable time.[60] Before an application for assessment can be made there must be a dispute between the parties, in other words attempts must have been made to agree the costs. If there is no dispute the court will dismiss the application as inadmissible.[61]

    19–012

The application for assessment may be made by either the paying or the receiving party although it will usually be the receiving party who makes the application. The party making the application will normally ask the court to fix the sum due in respect of costs as a specified amount. From the point of view of practitioners in England and Wales this is most easily done by drawing a bill in the same way as under CPR, Pt 47. This provides a narrative, details of the work done, the amount sought in respect of each item and the total amount sought in respect of the whole bill. The court will require evidence in support of the claim for costs and will also hear argument from the applicant, the opposing party and the Advocate General as to whether or not the costs have been "necessarily incurred".[62]

The court may permit the opposing party to make written submissions but there is no formal hearing as such. The Advocate General delivers his opinion direct to the chamber, it is not circulated to the parties and they do not have the opportunity to comment upon it. Once the chamber has

---

[56] Case 75/69 *Ernst Hake & Co. v E.C. Commission* [1970] E.C.R. 901.

[57] In this respect the judgment of Sir Robert Megarry V.C. in *Re Gibsons Settlement Trusts* [1981] Ch. 179 may be relevant.

[58] CJRP, Art.74(1); CFIRP, Art.92(1).

[59] See CJRP, Arts 37 and 38; CFIRP, Arts 43 and 44.

[60] See Case 126/76 *Gebrüder Deitz v E.C. Commission* [1979] E.C.R. 2131.

[61] See Case 25/65 *Simet v High Authority* [1967] E.C.R. 113; and Case 6/72 *Europea Europemballage Corp. and Continental Can Company Inc. v E.C. Commission (No.2)* [1975] E.C.R. 495.

[62] See Case 238/78 *Ireks-Arkady GmbH v E.E.C.* [1981] E.C.R. 1723.

considered the various submissions an order will be made, against which there is no appeal.[63] The parties may, for the purposes of enforcement, apply for an authenticated copy of the order.[64]

The amount allowed is entirely in the discretion of the court. There are no scales of costs relating to the court, nor does the court have to have regard to any scale in operation in a Member country.[65] Nor does it appear that the court has to reach its decision in accordance with any agreement between the party and its lawyers.[66] This is contrary to the normal indemnity principle observed by the English courts.

> " . . . the Court must undertake a free appreciation of the facts of the dispute having regard to its object and nature, its importance, from the point of Community law and the difficulties of the proceedings, the amount of work which the litigation may have caused the lawyers and what the dispute may have meant to the parties in financial terms."[67]

Where costs are awarded to a number of joint applicants or where cases have been joined the court may award a global figure to be divided between the parties in whose favour the order is made.[68]

H. INTEREST

19–013　Interest runs only when the order fixing the amount of costs is made. Interest on costs does not run from the date of judgment in the action.[69]

Enforcement

19–014　The procedure for enforcement is contained in the various treaties.[70] Costs necessarily incurred by a party in enforcing a judgment or order of the court must be refunded by the opposite party on the scale in force in the State where the enforcement takes place.[71] Any questions arising in relation to enforcement are dealt with by the national courts.

---

[63] CJRP, Art.74(1); CFIRP, Art.92(1).
[64] *ibid.*, Arts 74(2), 92(2).
[65] *Ireks Arkady GmbH v E.E.C.*, above n. 59.
[66] Case 4/73 *Nold Kohlen-Und Baustoffgrosshandlung v E.C. Commission* [1975] E.C.R. 1985.
[67] *Ireks Arkady GmbH v E.E.C.*, above.
[68] Cases 241, 242, 246–249/78 *DGV v E.E.C.* [1981] E.C.R. 1731.
[69] Case 6/72 *Europemballage Corp. and Continental Can Company Inc. v E.C. Commission (No.2)* [1975] E.C.R. 495.
[70] E.C. Treaty; Euratom Treaty; ECSC Treaty.
[71] CJRP, Art.71; CFIRP, Art.89.

SUPPLEMENTARY MATERIALS

APPENDIX A

Supreme Court Act 1981, s. 51

s. 51 Costs in civil division of Court of Appeal, High Court and county courts.

(1) Subject to the provisions of this or any other enactment and to rules of court, the costs of and incidental to all proceedings in—

(a) the civil division of the Court of Appeal;
(b) the High Court; and
(c) any county court,

shall be in the discretion of the court.

(2) Without prejudice to any general power to make rules of court, such rules may make provision for regulating matters relating to the costs of those proceedings including, in particular, prescribing scales of costs to be paid to legal or other representatives[or for securing that the amount awarded to a party in respect of the costs to be paid by him to such representatives is not limited to what would have been payable by him to them if he had not been awarded costs].

(3) The court shall have full power to determine by whom and to what extent the costs are to be paid.

(4) In subsections (1) and (2) "proceedings" includes the administration of estates and trusts.

(5) Nothing in subsection (1) shall alter the practice in any criminal cause, or in bankruptcy.

(6) In any proceedings mentioned in subsection (1), the court may disallow, or (as the case may be) order the legal or other representative concerned to meet, the whole of any wasted costs or such part of them as may be determined in accordance with rules of court.

(7) In subsection (6), "wasted costs" means any costs incurred by a party—

(a) as a result of any improper, unreasonable or negligent act or omission on the part of any legal or other representative or any employee of such a representative; or
(b) which, in the light of any such act or omission occurring after they were incurred, the court considers it is unreasonable to expect that party to pay.

(8) Where—

(a) a person has commenced proceedings in the High Court; but
(b) those proceedings should, in the opinion of the court, have been commenced in a county court in accordance with any provision made under section 1 of the Courts and Legal Services Act 1990 or by or under any other enactment, the person responsible for determining the amount which is to be awarded to that person by way of costs shall have regard to those circumstances.

(9) Where, in complying with subsection (8), the responsible person reduces the amount which would otherwise be awarded to the person in question

(a) the amount of that reduction shall not exceed 25 per cent; and
(b) on any taxation of the costs payable by that person to his legal representative, regard shall be had to the amount of the reduction.

(10) The Lord Chancellor may by order amend subsection (9)(a) by substituting, for the percentage for the time being mentioned there, a different percentage.

(11) Any such order shall be made by statutory instrument and may make such transitional or incidental provision as the Lord Chancellor considers expedient.

(12) No such statutory instrument shall be made unless a draft of the instrument has been approved by both Houses of Parliament.

(13) In this section "legal or other representative", in relation to a party to proceedings, means any person exercising a right of audience or right to conduct litigation on his behalf.

APPENDIX B

Courts and Legal Services Act 1990, s. 17 & s. 58, s. 58A, s. 58B

Introductory

The statutory objective and the general principle.

17.—(1) The general objective of this Part is the development of legal services in   **B–001** England and Wales (and in particular the development of advocacy, litigation, conveyancing and probate services) by making provision for new or better ways of providing such services and a wider choice of persons providing them, while maintaining the proper and efficient administration of justice.

(2) In this Act that objective is referred to as "the statutory objective".

(3) As a general principle the question whether a person should be granted a right of audience, or be granted a right to conduct litigation in relation to any court or proceedings, should be determined only by reference to—

(a) whether he is qualified in accordance with the educational and training requirements appropriate to the court or proceedings;

(b) whether he is a member of a professional or other body which—

  (i) has rules of conduct (however described) governing the conduct of its members;

  (ii) has an effective mechanism for enforcing the rules of conduct; and

  (iii) is likely to enforce them;

(c) whether, in the case of a body whose members are or will be providing advocacy services, the rules of conduct make satisfactory provision in relation to the court or proceedings in question requiring any such member not to withhold those services—

  (i) on the ground that the nature of the case is objectionable to him or to any section of the public;

  (ii) on the ground that the conduct, opinions or beliefs of the prospective client are unacceptable to him or to any section of the public;

  (iii) on any ground relating to the source of any financial support which may properly be given to the prospective client for the proceedings in question (for example, on the ground that such support will be available under the [1988 c. 34.] Legal Aid Act 1988); and

(d) whether the rules of conduct are, in relation to the court or proceedings, appropriate in the interests of the proper and efficient administration of justice.

(4) In this Act that principle is referred to as "the general principle".

(5) Rules of conduct which allow a member of the body in question to withhold his services if there are reasonable grounds for him to consider that, having regard to—

(a) the circumstances of the case;

(b) the nature of his practice; or

(c) his experience and standing,

he is not being offered a proper fee, are not on that account to be taken as being incompatible with the general principle.

Miscellaneous

Conditional fee agreements.

B–002   58.—(1) A conditional fee agreement which satisfies all of the conditions applicable to it by virtue of this section shall not be unenforceable by reason only of its being a conditional fee agreement; but (subject to subsection (5)) any other conditional fee agreement shall be unenforceable.

(2) For the purposes of this section and section 58A—

(a) a conditional fee agreement is an agreement with a person providing advocacy or litigation services which provides for his fees and expenses, or any part of them, to be payable only in specified circumstances; and

(b) a conditional fee agreement provides for a success fee if it provides for the amount of any fees to which it applies to be increased, in specified circumstances, above the amount which would be payable if it were not payable only in specified circumstances.

(3) The following conditions are applicable to every conditional fee agreement—

(a) it must be in writing;

(b) it must not relate to proceedings which cannot be the subject of an enforceable conditional fee agreement; and

(c) it must comply with such requirements (if any) as may be prescribed by the [Secretary of State].[1]

(4) The following further conditions are applicable to a conditional fee agreement which provides for a success fee—

(a) it must relate to proceedings of a description specified by order made by the [Secretary of State][2];

(b) it must state the percentage by which the amount of the fees which would be payable if it were not a conditional fee agreement is to be increased; and

(c) that percentage must not exceed the percentage specified in relation to the description of proceedings to which the agreement relates by order made by the [Secretary of State].[3]

(5) If a conditional fee agreement is an agreement to which section 57 of the Solicitors Act 1974 (non-contentious business agreements between solicitor and client) applies, subsection (1) shall not make it unenforceable.

---

[1] words substituted by SI 2003/1887 (Secretary of State for Constitutional Affairs Order), Sch. 2 Para.8 (1) (c).

[2] words substituted by SI 2003/1887 (Secretary of State for Constitutional Affairs Order), Sch 2 Para 8 (1) (c).

[3] words substituted by SI 2003/1887 (Secretary of State for Constitutional Affairs Order), Sch 2 Para 8 (1) (c).

Conditional fee agreements: supplementary

58A.—(1) The proceedings which cannot be the subject of an enforceable conditional fee agreement are— **B–003**

(a) criminal proceedings, apart from proceedings under section 82 of the Environmental Protection Act 1990; and

(b) family proceedings.

(2) In subsection (1) "family proceedings" means proceedings under any one or more of the following—

(a) the Matrimonial Causes Act 1973;

(b) the Adoption Act 1976;

(c) the Domestic Proceedings and Magistrates' Courts Act 1978;

(d) Part III of the Matrimonial and Family Proceedings Act 1984;

(e) Parts I, II and IV of the Children Act 1989;

(f) Part IV of the Family Law Act 1996; and

(g) the inherent jurisdiction of the High Court in relation to children.

(3) The requirements which the [Secretary of State][1] may prescribe under section 58(3)(c)—

(a) include requirements for the person providing advocacy or litigation services to have provided prescribed information before the agreement is made; and

(b) may be different for different descriptions of conditional fee agreements (and, in particular, may be different for those which provide for a success fee and those which do not).

(4) In section 58 and this section (and in the definitions of "advocacy services" and "litigation services" as they apply for their purposes) "proceedings" includes any sort of proceedings for resolving disputes (and not just proceedings in a court), whether commenced or contemplated.

(5) Before making an order under section 58(4), the [Secretary of State][2] shall consult—

(a) the designated judges;

(b) the General Council of the Bar;

(c) the Law Society; and

(d) such other bodies as he considers appropriate.

(6) A costs order made in any proceedings may, subject in the case of court proceedings to rules of court, include provision requiring the payment of any fees payable under a conditional fee agreement which provides for a success fee.

(7) Rules of court may make provision with respect to the assessment of any costs which include fees payable under a conditional fee agreement (including one which provides for a success fee)".

---

[1] words substituted by SI 2003/1887 (Secretary of State for Constitutional Affairs Order), Sch 2 Para 8 (1) (c).

[2] words substituted by SI 2003/1887 (Secretary of State for Constitutional Affairs Order), Sch 2 Para 8 (1) (c).

Litigation funding agreements

B–004   58B.—(1) A litigation funding agreement which satisfies all of the conditions applicable to it by virtue of this section shall not be unenforceable by reason only of its being a litigation funding agreement.

(2) For the purposes of this section a litigation funding agreement is an agreement under which—

(a) a person ("the funder") agrees to fund (in whole or in part) the provision of advocacy or litigation services (by someone other than the funder) to another person ("the litigant"); and

(b) the litigant agrees to pay a sum to the funder in specified circumstances.

(3) The following conditions are applicable to a litigation funding agreement-

(a) the funder must be a person, or person of a description, prescribed by the Lord Chancellor;

(b) the agreement must be in writing;

(c) the agreement must not relate to proceedings which by virtue of section 58A(1) and

(2) cannot be the subject of an enforceable conditional fee agreement or to proceedings of any such description as may be prescribed by the Lord Chancellor;

(d) the agreement must comply with such requirements (if any) as may be so prescribed;

(e) the sum to be paid by the litigant must consist of any costs payable to him in respect of the proceedings to which the agreement relates together with an amount calculated by reference to the funder's anticipated expenditure in funding the provision of the services; and

(f) that amount must not exceed such percentage of that anticipated expenditure as may be prescribed by the Lord Chancellor in relation to proceedings of the description to which the agreement relates.

(4) Regulations under subsection (3)(a) may require a person to be approved by the Lord Chancellor or by a prescribed person.

(5) The requirements which the Lord Chancellor may prescribe under subsection (3)(d)—

(a) include requirements for the funder to have provided prescribed information to the litigant before the agreement is made; and

(b) may be different for different descriptions of litigation funding agreements.

(6) In this section (and in the definitions of "advocacy services" and "litigation services" as they apply for its purposes) "proceedings" includes any sort of proceedings for resolving disputes (and not just proceedings in a court), whether commenced or contemplated.

(7) Before making regulations under this section, the Lord Chancellor shall consult—

(a) the designated judges;

(b) the General Council of the Bar;

(c) the Law Society; and

(d) such other bodies as he considers appropriate.

(8) A costs order made in any proceedings may, subject in the case of court proceedings to rules of court, include provision requiring the payment of any amount payable under a litigation funding agreement.

(9) Rules of court may make provision with respect to the assessment of any costs which include fees payable under a litigation funding agreement".

APPENDIX C

Access to Justice Act 1999, ss. 29–31

Costs

Recovery of insurance premiums by way of costs

29. Where in any proceedings a costs order is made in favour of any party who has taken out an insurance policy against the risk of incurring a liability in those proceedings, the costs payable to him may, subject in the case of court proceedings to rules of court, include costs in respect of the premium of the policy.

C–001

Recovery where body undertakes to meet costs liabilities

30.—(1) This section applies where a body of a prescribed description undertakes to meet (in accordance with arrangements satisfying prescribed conditions) liabilities which members of the body or other persons who are parties to proceedings may incur to pay the costs of other parties to the proceedings.

(2) If in any of the proceedings a costs order is made in favour of any of the members or other persons, the costs payable to him may, subject to subsection (3) and (in the case of court proceedings) to rules of court, include an additional amount in respect of any provision made by or on behalf of the body in connection with the proceedings against the risk of having to meet such liabilities.

(3) But the additional amount shall not exceed a sum determined in a prescribed manner; and there may, in particular, be prescribed as a manner of determination one which takes into account the likely cost to the member or other person of the premium of an insurance policy against the risk of incurring a liability to pay the costs of other parties to the proceedings.

(4) In this section "prescribed" means prescribed by regulations made by the Lord Chancellor by statutory instrument; and a statutory instrument containing such regulations shall be subject to annulment in pursuance of a resolution of either House of Parliament.

(5) Regulations under subsection (1) may, in particular, prescribe as a description of body one which is for the time being approved by the Lord Chancellor or by a prescribed person.

Rules as to costs

31. In section 51 of the Supreme Court Act 1981 (costs), in subsection (2) (rules regulating matters relating to costs), insert at the end "or for securing that the amount awarded to a party in respect of the costs to be paid by him to such representatives is not limited to what would have been payable by him to them if he had not been awarded costs."

C–002

APPENDIX D

Solicitors Act 1974, ss. 56–75, 87(1)

Orders as to remuneration for non-contentious business

56.—(1) For the purposes of this section there shall be a committee consisting of **D–001**
the following persons—

   (a) the Lord Chancellor;
   (b) the Lord Chief Justice;
   (c) the Master of the Rolls;
   (d) the President of the Society;
   (e) a solicitor, being the president of a local law society, nominated by the Lord Chancellor to serve on the committee during his tenure of office as president; and
   (f) for the purpose only of prescribing and regulating the remuneration of solicitors in respect of business done under the Land Registration Act 1925, the Chief Land Registrar appointed under that Act.

(2) The committee, or any three members of the committee (the Lord Chancellor being one) may make general orders prescribing and regulating in such manner as they think fit the remuneration of solicitors in respect of non-contentious business.

(3) The Lord Chancellor, before any order under this section is made, shall cause a draft of the order to be sent to the Council: and the committee shall consider any observations of the Council submitted to them in writing within one month of the sending of the draft, and may then make the order, either in the form of the draft or with such alterations or additions as they may think fit.

(4) An order under this section may prescribe the mode of remuneration of solicitors in respect of non-contentious business by providing that they shall be remunerated—

   (a) according to a scale of rates of commission or a scale of percentages, varying or not in different classes of business; or
   (b) by a gross sum; or
   (c) by a fixed sum for each document prepared or perused, without regard to length; or
   (d) in any other mode; or
   (e) partly in one mode and partly in another.

(5) An order under this section may regulate the amount of such remuneration with reference to all or any of the following, among other, considerations, that is to say—

   (a) the position of the party for whom the solicitor is concerned in the business, that is, whether he is vendor or purchaser, lessor or lessee, mortgagor or mortgagee, or the like;
   (b) the place where, and the circumstances in which, the business or any part of it is transacted;
   (c) the amount of the capital money or rent to which the business relates;
   (d) the skill, labour and responsibility on the part of the solicitor which the business involves;
   (e) the number and importance of the documents prepared or perused without regard to length.

(6) An order under this section may authorise and regulate—

(a) the taking by a solicitor from his client of security for payment of any remuneration, to be ascertained by taxation or otherwise, which may become due to him under any such order; and

(b) the allowance of interest.

(7) So long as an order made under this section is in operation the taxation of bills of costs of solicitors in respect of non-contentious business shall, subject to the provisions of section 57, be regulated by that order.

(8) Any order made under this section may be varied or revoked by a subsequent order so made.

(9) The power to make orders under this section shall be exercisable by statutory instrument which shall be subject to annulment in pursuance of a resolution of either House of Parliament; and the Statutory Instruments Act 1946 shall apply to a statutory instrument containing such an order in like manner as if the order had been made by a Minister of the Crown.

Non-contentious business agreements

D–002   57.—(1) Whether or not any order is in force under section 56, a solicitor and his client may, before or after or in the course of the transaction of any non-contentious business by the solicitor make an agreement as to his remuneration in respect of that business.

(2) The agreement may provide for the remuneration of the solicitor by a gross sum, or by reference to an hourly rate, or by a commission or percentage, or by a salary, or otherwise, and it may be made on the terms that the amount of the remuneration stipulated for shall or shall not include all or any disbursements made by the solicitor in respect of searches, plans, travelling, stamps, fees or other matters.

(3) The agreement shall be in writing and signed by the person to be bound by it or his agent in that behalf.

(4) Subject to subsections (5) and (7) the agreement may be sued and recovered on or set aside in the like manner and on the like grounds as an agreement not relating to the remuneration of a solicitor.

(5) If on any taxation of costs the agreement is relied on by the solicitor and objected to by the client as unfair or unreasonable, the taxing officer may enquire into the facts and certify them to the court, and if from that certificate it appears just to the court that the agreement should be set aside, or the amount payable under it reduced, the court may so order and may give such consequential directions as it thinks fit.

(6) Subsection (7) applies where the agreement provides for the remuneration of the solicitors to be by reference to an hourly rate.

(7) If, on the taxation of any costs, the agreement is relied on by the solicitor and the client objects to the amount of the costs (but is not alleging that the agreement is unfair or unreasonable), the taxing officer may enquire into—

(a) the number of hours worked by the solicitor; and

(b) whether the number of hours worked by him was excessive.

Remuneration of a solicitor who is a mortgagee

D–003   58.—(1) Where a mortgage is made to a solicitor, either alone or jointly with any person, he or the firm of which he is a member shall be entitled to recover from the mortgagor in respect of all business transacted and acts done by him or them in negotiating the loan, deducing and investigating the title to the property, and preparing and completing the mortgage had been made to a person who was not a solicitor and that person had retained and employed him or them to transact that business and do those acts.

(2) Where a mortgage has been made to, or has become vested by transfer or transmission in, a solicitor, either alone or jointly with any other person, and any business is transacted or acts are done by that solicitor or by the firm of which he is a member in relation to that mortgage or the security thereby created or the property thereby charged, he or they shall be entitled to recover from the person on whose behalf the business was transacted or the acts were done, and to charge against the security, such usual costs as he or they would have been entitled to receive if the mortgage had been made to and had remained vested in a person who was not a solicitor and that person had retained and employed him or them to transact that business and do those acts.

(3) In this section "mortgage" includes any charge on any property for securing money or money's worth.

Contentious business agreements

59.—(1) Subject to subsection (2) a solicitor may make an agreement in writing with his client as to his remuneration in respect of any contentious business done, or to be done, by him (in this Act referred to as a "contentious business agreement") providing that he shall be remunerated by a gross sum, or by reference to an hourly rate, or by a salary, or otherwise, and whether at a higher or lower rate than that at which he would otherwise have been entitled to be remunerated.   **D–004**

(2) Nothing in this section or in section 60 to 63 shall give validity to—

(a) any purchase by a solicitor of the interest, or any part of the interest, of his client in any action, suit or other contentious proceeding; or

(b) any agreement by which a solicitor retained or employed to prosecute any action, suit or other contentious proceeding, stipulates for payment only in the event of success in that action, suit or proceeding; or

(c) any disposition, contract, settlement, conveyance, delivery, dealing or transfer which under the law relating to bankruptcy is invalid against a trustee or creditor in any bankruptcy or composition.

Effect of contentious business agreements

60.—(1) Subject to the provisions of this section and to sections 61 to 63, the costs of a solicitor in any case where a contentious business agreement has been made shall not be subject to taxation or (except in the case of an agreement which provides for the solicitor to be remunerated by reference to an hourly rate) to the provisions of section 69.   **D–005**

(2) Subject to subsection (3) a contentious business agreement shall not affect the amount of, or any rights or remedies for the recovery of, any costs payable by the client to, or to the client by, any person other than the solicitor, and that person may, unless he has otherwise agreed, require any such costs to be taxed according to the rules for their taxation for the time being in force.

(3) A client shall not be entitled to recover from any other person under an order for the payment of any costs to which a contentious business agreement relates more than the amount payable by him to his solicitor in respect of those costs under the agreement.

(4) A contentious business agreement shall be deemed to exclude any claim by the solicitor in respect of the business to which it relates other than—

(a) a claim for the agreed costs; or

(b) a claim for such costs as are expressly excepted from the agreement.

(5) A provision in a contentious business agreement that the solicitor shall not be liable for negligence, or that he shall be relieved from any responsibility to which he would otherwise be subject as a solicitor, shall be void.

Enforcement of contentious business agreements

D–006 **61.**—(1) No action shall be brought on any contentious business agreement, but on the application of any person who—

(a) is a party to the agreement or the representative of such a party, or
(b) is or is alleged to be liable to pay, or is or claims to be entitled to be paid, the costs due or alleged to be due in respect of the business to which the agreement relates,

the court may enforce or set aside the agreement and determine every question as to its validity or effect.

(2) On any application under subsection (1) the court—

(a) if it is of the opinion that the agreement is in all respects fair and reasonable, may enforce it;
(b) if it is of the opinion that the agreement is in any respect unfair or unreasonable, may set it aside and order the costs covered by it to be taxed as if it had never been made;
(c) in any case, may make such order as to the costs of the application as it thinks fit.

(3) If the business covered by a contentious business agreement (not being an agreement to which section 62 applies) is business done, or to be done, in any action, a client who is a party to the agreement may make application to a taxing officer of the court for the agreement to be examined.

(4) A taxing officer before whom an agreement is laid under subsection (3) shall examine it and may either allow it, or, if he is of the opinion of the court to be taken on it, and the court may allow the agreement or reduce the amount payable under it, or set it aside and order the costs covered by it to be taxed as if it had never been made.

(4A) Subsection (4B) applies where a contentious business agreement provides for the remuneration of the solicitor to be by reference to an hourly rate.

(4B) If on the taxation of any costs the agreement is relied on by the solicitor and the client objects to the amount of the costs (but is not alleging that the agreement is unfair or unreasonable), the taxing officer may enquire into—

(a) the number of hours worked by the solicitor; and
(b) whether the number of hours worked by him was excessive.

(5) Where the amount agreed under any contentious business agreement is paid by the payment may at any time within twelve months from the date of payment, or within such further time as appears to the court to be reasonable, apply to the court, and, if it appears to the court that the special circumstances of the case require it to be reopened, the court may, on such terms as may be just, re-open it and order the costs covered by the agreement to be taxed and the whole or any part of the amount received by the solicitor to be repaid by him.

(6) In this section and in sections 62 and 63 "the court" means—

(a) in relation to an agreement under which any business has been done in any court having jurisdiction to enforce and set aside agreements, any such court in which any of that business has been done;

(b) in relation to an agreement under which no business has been done in any such court and under which not more than £50 is payable, the High Court;

(c) in relation to an agreement under which no business has been done in any such court and under which not more than £50 is payable, any county court which would, but for the provisions of subsection (1) prohibiting the bringing of an action on the agreement, have had jurisdiction in any action on it;

and for the avoidance of doubt it is hereby declared that in paragraph (a) "court having jurisdiction to enforce and set aside agreements" includes a county court.

Contentious business agreements by certain representatives

62.—(1) Where the client who makes a contentious business agreement makes it **D–007** as a representative of a person whose property will be chargeable with the whole or part of the amount payable under the agreement, the agreement shall be laid before a taxing officer of the court before payment.

(2) A taxing officer before whom an agreement is laid under subsection (1) shall examine it and may either allow it, or, if he is of the opinion that it is unfair or unreasonable, require the opinion of the court to be taken on it and the court may allow the agreement or reduce the amount payable under it, or set it aside and order the costs covered by it to be taxed as if it had never been made.

(3) A client who makes a contentious business agreement as mentioned in subsection (1) and pays the whole or any part of the amount payable under the agreement without it being allowed by the officer or by the court shall be liable at any time to account to the person whose property is charged with the whole or any part of the amount so paid for the sum so charged, and the solicitor who accepts the payment may be ordered by the court to refund the amount received by him.

(4) A client makes a contentious business agreement as the representative of another person if he makes it—

(a) as his guardian,

(b) as a trustee for him under a deed or will,

(c) as his receiver appointed under Part VII of the Mental Health Act 1983, or

(d) as a person other than a receiver authorised under that Part of that Act to act on his behalf.

Effect on contentious business agreement of death, incapability or change of solicitor

63.—(1) If, after some business has been done under a contentious business **D–008** agreement but before the solicitor has wholly performed it—

(a) the solicitor dies, or becomes incapable of acting; or

(b) the client changes his solicitor (as, notwithstanding the agreement, he shall be entitled to do)

any party to, or the representative of any party to, the agreement may apply to the court, and the court shall have the same jurisdiction as to enforcing the agreement so far as it has been performed, or setting it aside, as the court would have had if the solicitor had not died or become incapable of acting, or the client had not changed his solicitor.

(2) The court, notwithstanding that it is of the opinion that the agreement is in all respects fair and reasonable, may order the amount due in respect of business under the agreement to be ascertained by taxation, and in that case—

    (a) the taxing officer, in ascertaining that amount, shall have regard so far as may be to the terms of the agreement; and

    (b) payment of the amount found by him to be due may be enforced in the same manner as if the agreement had been completely performed.

If in such a case as is mentioned in subsection (1)(b) an order is made for the taxation of the amount due to the solicitor in respect of the business done under the agreement, the court shall direct the taxing officer to have regard to the circumstances under which the change of solicitor has taken place, and the taxing officer, unless h is of the opinion that there has been no default, negligence, improper delay or other conduct on the part of the solicitor affording the client reasonable ground for changing his solicitor, shall not allow to the solicitor the full amount of the remuneration agreed to be paid to him.

Form of bill of costs for contentious business

D–009   **64.**—(1) Where the remuneration of a solicitor in respect of contentious business done by him is not the subject of contentious business agreement, then, subject to subsections (2) to (4) the solicitor's bill of costs may at the option of the solicitor be either a bill containing detailed items or a gross sum bill.

(2) The party chargeable with a gross sum bill may at any time—

    (a) before he is served with a writ or other originating process for the recovery of costs included in the bill, and

    (b) before the expiration of three months from the date on which the bill was delivered to him,

require the solicitor to deliver, in lieu of that bill, a bill containing detailed items; and on such a requirement being made the gross sum bill shall be of no effect.

(3) Where an action is commenced on a gross sum bill, the court shall, if so requested by the party chargeable with the bill before the expiration of one month from the service on that party of the writ or other originating process, order that the bill be taxed.

(4) If a gross sum bill is taxed, whether under this section or otherwise, nothing in this section shall prejudice any rules of court with respect to taxation, and the solicitor shall furnish the taxing officer with such details of any of the costs covered by the bill as the taxing officer may require.

Security for costs and termination of retainer

D–010   **65.**—(1) A solicitor may take security from his client for his costs, to be ascertained by taxation or otherwise, in respect of any contentious business to be done by him.

(2) If a solicitor who has been retained by a client to conduct contentious business requests the client to make a payment of a sum of money, being a reasonable sum on account of the costs incurred or to be incurred in the conduct of that business and the client refuses or fails within a reasonable time to make that payment, the refusal

or failure shall be deemed to be a good cause whereby the solicitor may, upon giving reasonable notice to the client, withdraw from the retainer.

Taxation with respect to contentious business

66.—Subject to the provisions of any rules of court, on every taxation of costs in respect of any contentious business, the taxing officer may— **D–011**

(a) allow interest at such rate and from such time as he thinks just on money disbursed by the solicitor for the client, and on money of the client in the hands of, and improperly retained by, the solicitor; and

(b) in determining the remuneration of the solicitor, have regard to the skill, labour and responsibility involved in the business done by him.

Inclusion of disbursements in bill of costs

67.—A solicitor's bill of costs may include costs payable in discharge of a liability properly incurred by him on behalf of the party to be charged with the bill (including counsel's fees) notwithstanding that those costs have not been paid before the delivery of the bill to that party; but those costs— **D–012**

(a) shall be described in the bill as not then paid; and

(b) if the bill is taxed, shall not be allowed by the taxing officer unless they are paid before the taxation is completed.

Power of court to order solicitor to deliver bill, etc.

68.—(1) The jurisdiction of the High Court to make orders for the delivery by a solicitor of a bill of costs, and for the delivery up of, or otherwise in relation to, any documents in his possession, custody or power, is hereby declared to extend to cases in which no business has been done by him in the High Court. **D–013**

(2) A county court shall have the same jurisdiction as the High Court to make orders making such provision as is mentioned in subsection (1) in cases where the bill of costs or the documents relate wholly or partly to contentious business done by the solicitor in that county court.

(3) In this section and in sections 69 to 71 "solicitor" includes the executors, administrators and assignees of a solicitor.

Action to recover solicitor's costs

69.—(1) Subject to the provisions of this Act, no action shall be brought to recover any costs due to a solicitor before the expiration of one month from the date on which a bill of those costs is delivered in accordance with the requirements mentioned in subsection (2); but if there is probable cause for believing that the party chargeable with the costs— **D–014**

(a) is about to quit England and Wales, to become bankrupt or to compound with his creditors, or

(b) is about to do any other act which would tend to prevent or delay the solicitor obtaining payment,

the High Court may, notwithstanding that one month has not expired from the delivery of the bill, order that the solicitor be at liberty to commence an action to recover his costs and may order that those costs be taxed.

(2) The requirements referred to in subsection (1) are that the bill—

    (a) must be signed by the solicitor, or if the costs are due to a firm, by one of the partners of that firm, either in his own name or in the name of the firm, or be enclosed in, or accompanied by, a letter which is so signed and refers to the bill; and

    (b) must be delivered to the party to be charged with the bill, either personally or by being sent to him by post to, or left for him at, his place of business, dwelling-house, or last known place of abode;

and, where a bill is proved to have been delivered in compliance with those requirements, it shall not be necessary in the first instance for the solicitor to prove the contents of the bill and it shall be presumed, until the contrary is shown, to be a bill bona fide complying with this Act.

(3) Where a bill of costs relates wholly or party to contentious business done in a county court and the amount of the bill does not exceed £5,000, the powers and duties of the High Court under this section and sections 70 and 71 in relation to that bill may be exercised and performed by any county court in which any part of the business was done.

(4) [Repealed by S.I. 1991 No. 724.]

Taxation on application of party chargeable or solicitor

D–015   70.—(1) Where before the expiration of one month from the delivery of a solicitor's bill an application is made by the party chargeable with the bill, the High Court shall, without requiring any sum to be paid into court, order that the bill be taxed and that no action be commenced on the bill until the taxation is completed.

(2) Where no such application is made before the expiration of the period mentioned in subsection (1) then, on an application being made by the solicitor or, subject to subsections (3) and (4) by the party chargeable with the bill, the court may on such terms, if any, as it thinks fit (not being terms as to the costs of the taxation) order—

    (a) that the bill be taxed; and

    (b) that no action be commenced on the bill, and that any action already commenced be stayed, until the taxation is completed.

(3) Where an application under subsection (2) is made by the party chargeable with the bill—

    (a) after the expiration of 12 months from the delivery of the bill, or

    (b) after a judgment has been obtained for the recovery of the costs covered by the bill, or

    (c) after the bill has been paid, but before the expiration of 12 months from the payment of the bill,

no order shall be made except in special circumstances and, if an order is made, it may contain such terms as regards the costs of the taxation as the court may think fit.

(4) The power to order taxation conferred by subsection (2) shall not be exercisable on an application made by the party chargeable with the bill after the expiration of 12 months from the payment of the bill.

(5) An order for the taxation of a bill made on an application under this section by the party chargeable with the bill shall, if he so requests, be an order for the taxation of the profit costs covered by the bill.

(6) Subject to subsection (5) the court may under this section order the taxation of all the costs, or of the profit costs, or of the costs other than profit costs and, where part of the costs is not to be taxed, may allow an action to be commenced or to be continued for that part of the costs.

(7) Every order for the taxation of a bill shall require the taxing officer to tax not only the bill but also the costs of the taxation and to certify what is due to or by the solicitor in respect of the bill and in respect of the costs of the taxation.

(8) If after due notice of any taxation either party to it fails to attend, the officer may proceed with the taxation ex parte.

(9) Unless—

(a) the order for taxation was made on the application of the solicitor and the party chargeable does not attend the taxation, or
(b) the order for taxation or an order under subsection (10) otherwise provides,

the costs of a taxation shall be paid according to the event of the taxation, that is to say, if one-fifth of the amount of the bill is taxed off, the solicitor shall pay the costs, but otherwise the party chargeable shall pay the costs.

(10) The taxing officer may certify to the court any special circumstances relating to a bill or to the taxation of a bill, and the court may make such order as respects the costs of the taxation as it may think fit.

(11) Subsection (9) shall have effect in any case where the application for an order for taxation was made before the passing of the Solicitors (Amendment) Act 1974 and—

(a) the bill is a bill for contentious business, or
(b) more than half of the amount of the bill before taxation consists of costs for which a scale charge is provided by an order for the time being in operation under section 56.

as if for the reference to one-fifth of the amount of the bill there were substituted a reference to one-sixth of that amount.

(12) In this section "profit costs" means costs other than counsel's fees or costs paid or payable in the discharge of a liability incurred by the solicitor on behalf of the party chargeable, and the reference in subsection (9) to the fraction of the amount of the bill taxed off shall be taken, where the taxation concerns only part of the costs covered by the bill, as a reference to that fraction of the amount of those costs which is being taxed.

Taxation on application of third parties

71.—(1) Where a person other than the party chargeable with the bill for the **D–016** purposes of section 70 has paid, or is or was liable to pay, a bill either to the solicitor or to the party chargeable with the bill, that person or his executors, administrators or assignees may apply to the High Court for an order for the taxation of the bill as if he were the party chargeable with it, and the court may make the same order (if any) as it might have been if the application had been made by the party chargeable with the bill.

(2) Where the court has no power to make an order by virtue of subsection (1) except in special circumstances it may, in considering whether there are special

circumstances sufficient to justify the making of an order, take into account circumstances which affect the applicant but do not affect the party chargeable with the bill.

(3) Where a trustee, executor or administrator has become liable to pay a bill of a solicitor, then, on the application of any person interested in any property out of which the trustee, executor or administrator has paid, or is entitled to pay, the bill, the court may order—

    (a) that the bill be taxed on such terms, if any, as it thinks fit; and

    (b) that such payments, in respect of the amount found to be due to or by a solicitor and in respect of the costs of the taxation, be made to or by the applicant, to or by the solicitor, or to or by the executor, administrator or trustee, as it thinks fit.

(4) In considering any application under subsection (3) the court shall have regard—

    (a) to the provisions of section 70 as to applications by the party chargeable for the taxation of a solicitor's bill so far as they are capable of being applied to an application made under that subsection;

    (b) to the extent and nature of the interest of the applicant.

(5) If an applicant under subsection (3) pays any money to the solicitor, he shall have the same right to be paid that money by the trustee, executor or administrator chargeable with the bill as the solicitor had.

(6) Except in special circumstances, no order shall be made on an application under this section for the taxation of a bill which has already been taxed.

(7) If the court on an application under this section orders a bill to be taxed, it may order the solicitor to deliver to the applicant a copy of the bill on payment of the costs of that copy.

Supplementary provisions as to taxations

D–017   72.—(1) Every application for an order for the taxation of a solicitor's bill or for the delivery of a solicitor's bill and for the delivery up by a solicitor of any documents in his possession, custody or power shall be made in the matter of that solicitor.

(2) Where a taxing officer is in the course of taxing a bill of costs, he may request the taxing officer of any other court to assist him in taxing any part of the bill, and the taxing officer so requested shall tax that part of the bill and shall return the bill with his opinion on it to the taxing officer making the request.

(3) Where a request is made as mentioned in subsection (2) the taxing officer who is requested to tax part of a bill shall have such powers, and may take such fees, in respect of that part of the bill, as he would have or be entitled to take if he were taxing that part of the bill in pursuance of an order of the court of which he is an officer; and the taxing officer who made the request shall not take any fee in respect of that part of the bill.

(4) The certificate of the taxing officer by whom any bill has been taxed shall, unless it is set aside or altered by the court, be final as to the amount of the costs covered by it, and the court may make such order in relation to the certificate as it thinks fit, including, in a case where the retainer is not disputed, an order that judgment be entered for the sum certified to be due with costs.

412

Charging orders

73.—(1) Subject to subsection (2) any court in which a solicitor has been **D–018** employed to prosecute or defend any suit, matter or proceeding may at any time—

(a) declare the solicitor entitled to a charge on any property recovered or preserved through his instrumentality for his taxed costs in relation to that suit, matter or proceeding; and

(b) make such orders for the taxation of those costs and for raising money to pay or for paying them out of the property recovered or preserved as the court thinks fit;

and all conveyances and acts done to defeat, or operating to defeat, that charge shall, except in the case of a conveyance to a bona fide purchaser for value without notice, be void as against the solicitor.

(2) No order shall be made under subsection (1) if the right to recover the costs is barred by any statute of limitations.

Special provisions as to contentious business done in county courts

74.—(1) The remuneration of a solicitor in respect of contentious business done **D–019** by him in a county court shall be regulated in accordance with sections 59 to 73, and for that purpose those sections shall have effect subject to the following provisions of this section.

(2) The registrar of a county court shall be the taxing officer of that court but any taxation of costs by him may be reviewed by a judge assigned to the county court district, or by a judge acting as a judge so assigned, on the application of any part to the taxation.

(3) The amount which may be allowed on the taxation of any costs or bill of costs in respect of any item relating to proceedings in a county court shall not, except in so far as rules of court may otherwise provide, exceed the amount which could have been allowed in respect of that item as between party and party in those proceedings, having regard to the nature of the proceedings and the amount of the claim and of any counterclaim.

Saving for certain enactments

75.—Nothing in this Part of this Act shall affect the following enactments, that is **D–020** to say—

(a) [Repealed by Statute Law Repeals Act 1989.];

(b) section 144 of the Land Registration Act 1925 (which enables rules to be made regulating, among other things, the taxation and incidence of the costs of the registration of land and other matters done under that Act);

(c) any of the provisions of the Costs in Criminal Cases Act 1973;

(d) [Repealed by Legal Aid Act 1988, Sched. 6.];

(e) any other enactment not expressly repealed by this Act which authorizes the making of rules or orders or the giving of directions with respect to costs, or which provides that any such rule, order or direction made or given under a previous enactment shall continue in force.

* * *

Interpretation

D–021   87.—(1) In this Act, except where the context otherwise requires,—
"articles" means written articles of clerkship binding a person to serve a solicitor as an articled clerk;
"authorised insurer" means a person who—

(a) is permitted under the Insurance Companies Act 1982 on insurance business of class 13 in Schedule 2 to that Act or, being an insurance company the head office of which is in a member State, is permitted under the law of a member State other than the United Kingdom to carry on business of a corresponding class; or

(b) is permitted under the Insurance Companies Act 1982 to carry on insurance business of class 1, 2, 14, 15, 16 and 17 in that Schedule or, being an insurance company the head office of which is in a member State, is permitted under the law of a member State other than the United Kingdom to carry on insurance business of corresponding classes.

"bank" means—

(a) the Bank of England, the Post Office, in the exercise of its power to provide banking services, or an institution authorised under the Banking Act 1987.

(b) [. . .]

(c) [. . .]

"building society" means a building society within the meaning of the Building Societies Act 1986; and a reference to an account is a reference to a deposit account.
"the Charter" means the Royal Charter dated 26th February 1845, whereby the Society was incorporated, together with the Royal Charters supplemental to it dated respectively, 26th November 1872, 4th June 1903, 2nd June 1909 and 10th March 1954;
"client"—includes

(a) in relation to contentious business, any person who as principal or on behalf of another person retains or employs, or is about to retain or employ, a solicitor, and any person who is or may be liable to pay a solicitor's costs;

(b) in relation to non-contentious business, any person who, as a principal or on behalf of another, or as a trustee or executor, or in any other capacity, has power, express or implied, to retain or employ, and retains or employs or is about to retain or employ a solicitor, and any person for the time being liable to pay to a solicitor for his services any costs;

"client account" means an account in the title of which the word "client" is required by rules under section 32;
"contentious business" means business done, whether as solicitor or advocate, in or for the purposes of proceedings begun before a court or before an arbitrator[1], not being business which falls within the definition of non-contentious or common form probate business contained in section 128 of the Supreme Court Act 1981;

---

1 Repealed by the Arbitration Act 1996 s.107(2) Sch.4.

"contentious business agreement" means an agreement made in pursuance of section 59;

"controlled trust" in relation to a solicitor, means a trust of which he is a sole trustee or co-trustee only with one or more of his partners or employees;

"costs" includes fees, charges, disbursements, expenses and remuneration;

"the Council" means the Council of the Society elected in accordance with the provisions of the Charter and this Act;

"duly certificated notary public" means a notary public who either—

(a) has in force a practising certificate as a solicitor issued under this Act, and duly entered in the court of faculties of the Archbishop of Canterbury in accordance with rules made by the master of the faculties; or

(b) has in force a practising certificate as a notary public issued by the said court of faculties in accordance with rules so made;

"employee" includes an articled clerk;

"indemnity conditions" has the meaning assigned to it by section 28(2)(b);

"indemnity rules" means rules under section 37;

"local law society" means a society which is for the time being recognized by the Council as representative of solicitors in some particular part of England and Wales;

"non-contentious business" means any business done as a solicitor which is not contentious business as defined by this subsection;

"practising certificate" has the meaning assigned to it by section 1;

"replacement date", in relation to a practising certificate, means the date prescribed under section 14(2)(a) or specified by the Society under any regulation made by virtue of section 14(4)(b);

"the roll" means the list of solicitors of the Supreme Court kept by the Society under section 6;

"Secretary" of the Society includes any deputy or person appointed temporarily to perform the duties of that office;

"the Society" means the Law Society, that is to say, the Society incorporated and regulated by the Charter;

"sole solicitor" means a solicitor who is the sole principal in a practice;

"solicitor" means solicitor of the Supreme Court;

"solicitor in Scotland" means a person enrolled or deemed to have been enrolled as a solicitor in pursuance of the Solicitors (Scotland) Act 1933;

"the standard scale" has the meaning given by section 37 of the Criminal Justice Act 1982;

"training conditions" has the meaning assigned to it by section 28(2)(a);

"training regulations" means regulations under section 2;

"the Tribunal" means the Solicitors Disciplinary Tribunal;

"trust" includes an implied or constructive trust and a trust where the trustee has a beneficial interest in the trust property, and also includes the duties incident to the office of a personal representative, and "trustee" shall be construed accordingly;

"Unqualified person" means a person who is not qualified under section 1 to act as a solicitor.

APPENDIX E

Litigants in Person (Costs and Expenses) Act 1975

Costs or expenses recoverable

1.—(1) Where, in any proceedings to which this subsection applies, any costs of E–001
a litigant in person are ordered to be paid by any other party to the proceedings or
in any other way, there may, subject to rules of court, be allowed on the taxation or
other determination of those costs sums in respect of any work done, and any
expenses and losses incurred, by the litigants in or in connection with the
proceedings to which the order relates.

This subsection applies to civil proceedings—

(a) in a county court, in the Supreme Court or in the House of Lords on appeal
from the High Court or the Court of Appeal,

(b) before the Lands Tribunal or the Lands Tribunal for Northern Ireland,
or

(c) in or before any other court or tribunal specified in an order made under
this subsection by the Lord Chancellor.

(2) Where, in any proceedings to which this subsection applies, any costs or
expenses of a party litigant are ordered to be paid by any other party to the
proceedings or in any other way, there may, subject to rules of court, be allowed on
the taxation or other determination of those costs or expenses sums in respect of any
work done, and any outlays and losses incurred, by the litigant or in connection with
the proceedings to which the order relates.

This subsection applies to civil proceedings—

(a) in the sheriff court, the Scottish Land Court, the Court of Session or the
House of Lords on appeal from the Court of Session.

(b) before the Lands Tribunal for Scotland, or

(c) in or before any other court or tribunal specified in an order made under
this subsection by the Lord Advocate.

(3) An order under subsection (1) or (2) above shall be made by statutory
instrument and shall be subject to annulment in pursuance of the resolution of either
House of Parliament.

(4) In this section "rules of court"—

(a) in relation to the Lands Tribunal or the Lands Tribunal for Scotland, means
rules made under section 3 of the Lands Tribunal Act 1949,

(b) in relation to the Lands Tribunal for Northern Ireland means rules made
under section 9 of the Lands Tribunal and Compensation Act (Northern
Ireland) 1964, and

(c) in relation to any other tribunal specified in an order made under
subsection (1) or (2) above, shall have the meaning given by the order as
respects that tribunal.

(5) In the application of subsection (1) above to Northern Ireland, the expression
"county court", "the Supreme Court", "the High Court" and "the Court of Appeal"
shall have the meanings respectively assigned to them by section 29(1) of the
Northern Ireland Act 1962.

Short title, commencement and extent

E–002   2.—(1) This Act may be cited as the Litigants in Person (Costs and Expenses) Act 1975.

(2) This Act shall come into operation—

(a) in relation to England and Wales and Northern Ireland, on such day as the Lord Chancellor may by order made by statutory instrument appoint, and

(b) in relation to Scotland, on such day as the Lord Advocate may by order made by statutory instrument appoint.

(3) An order under subsection (2) above—

(a) may appoint different days for different purposes, and

(b) may make such transitional provisions as appears to the Lord Chancellor or, as the case may be, the Lord Advocate to be necessary or expedient.

Note: The Litigants in Person (Costs and Expenses) Order 1980 (S.I. 1980 No. 1159) extends the scope of the Act to the Employment Appeal Tribunal.

APPENDIX F

Part 8

Alternative Procedure for Claims

CONTENTS OF THIS PART

Types of claim in which Part 8 procedure may be followed

8.1

(1) The Part 8 procedure is the procedure set out in this Part.   **F–001**

(2) A claimant may use the Part 8 procedure where—

     (a) he seeks the court's decision on a question which is unlikely to involve a substantial dispute of fact; or

     (b) paragraph (6) applies.

(3) The court may at any stage order the claim to continue as if the claimant had not used the Part 8 procedure and, if it does so, the court may give any directions it considers appropriate.

(4) Paragraph (2) does not apply if a practice direction provides that the Part 8 procedure may not be used in relation to the type of claim in question.

(5) Where the claimant uses the Part 8 procedure he may not obtain default judgment under Part 12.

(6) A rule or practice direction may, in relation to a specified type of proceedings—

     (a) require or permit the use of the Part 8 procedure; and

     (b) disapply or modify any of the rules set out in this Part as they apply to those proceedings.

(Rule 8.9 provides for other modifications to the general rules where the Part 8 procedure is being used)

Contents of the claim form

F–002   8.2 Where the claimant uses the Part 8 procedure the claim form must state—

(a) that this Part applies;
(b) (i) the question which the claimant wants the court to decide; or
     (ii) the remedy which the claimant is seeking and the legal basis for the claim to that remedy;
(c) if the claim is being made under an enactment, what that enactment is;
(d) if the claimant is claiming in a representative capacity, what that capacity is; and
(e) if the defendant is sued in a representative capacity, what that capacity is.

(Part 22 provides for the claim form to be verified by a statement of truth)
(Rule 7.5 provides for service of the claim form)
 (The costs practice direction sets out the information about a funding arrangement to be provided with the claim form where the claimant intends to seek to recover an additional liability)
 ("Funding arrangement" and "additional liability" are defined in rule 43.2)

Issue of claim form without naming defendants

8.2A

(1) A practice direction may set out the circumstances in which the court may give permission for a claim form to be issued under this Part without naming a defendant.
(2) An application for permission must be made by application notice before the claim form is issued.
(3) The application notice for permission—

(a) need not be served on any other person; and
(b) must be accompanied by a copy of the claim form that the applicant proposes to issue.

(4) Where the court gives permission it will give directions about the future management of the claim.

Acknowledgment of service

8.3

F–003   (1) The defendant must—

(a) file an acknowledgment of service in the relevant practice form not more than 14 days after service of the claim form; and
(b) serve the acknowledgment of service on the claimant and any other party.

(2) The acknowledgment of service must state—

(a) whether the defendant contests the claim; and
(b) if the defendant seeks a different remedy from that set out in the claim form, what that remedy is.

(3) The following rules of Part 10 (acknowledgment of service) apply—

(a) rule 10.3(2) (exceptions to the period for filing an acknowledgment of service); and

(b) rule 10.5 (contents of acknowledgment of service).

(4) Revoked.

(The costs practice direction sets out the information about a funding arrangement to be provided with the acknowledgment of service where the defendant intends to seek to recover an additional liability)

("Funding arrangement" and "additional liability" are defined in rule 43.2)

Consequence of not filing an acknowledgment of service

8.4

(1) This rule applies where—   **F–004**

(a) the defendant has failed to file an acknowledgment of service; and

(b) the time period for doing so has expired.

(2) The defendant may attend the hearing of the claim but may not take part in the hearing unless the court gives permission.

Filing and serving written evidence

8.5

(1) The claimant must file any written evidence on which he intends to rely   **F–005**
when he files his claim form.

(2) The claimant's evidence must be served on the defendant with the claim form.

(3) A defendant who wishes to rely on written evidence must file it when he files his acknowledgment of service.

(4) If he does so, he must also, at the same time, serve a copy of his evidence on the other parties.

(5) The claimant may, within 14 days of service of the defendant's evidence on him, file further written evidence in reply.

(6) If he does so, he must also, within the same time limit, serve a copy of his evidence on the other parties.

(7) The claimant may rely on the matters set out in his claim form as evidence under this rule if the claim form is verified by a statement of truth.

Evidence—general

8.6

(1) No written evidence may be relied on at the hearing of the claim   **F–006**
unless—

(a) it has been served in accordance with rule 8.5; or

(b) the court gives permission.

(2) The court may require or permit a party to give oral evidence at the hearing.

(3) The court may give directions requiring the attendance for cross-examination (gl) of a witness who has given written evidence.

(Rule 32.1 contains a general power for the court to control evidence)

Part 20 claims

F–007   8.7 Where the Part 8 procedure is used, Part 20 (counterclaims and other additional claims) applies except that a party may not make a Part 20 claim (as defined by rule 20.2) without the court's permission.

Procedure where defendant objects to use of the Part 8 procedure

8.8

F–008   (1) Where the defendant contends that the Part 8 procedure should not be used because—

(a) there is a substantial dispute of fact; and
(b) the use of the Part 8 procedure is not required or permitted by a rule or practice direction,

he must state his reasons when he files his acknowledgment of service.

(Rule 8.5 requires a defendant who wishes to rely on written evidence to file it when he files his acknowledgment of service)

        (2) When the court receives the acknowledgment of service and any written evidence it will give directions as to the future management of the case.

(Rule 8.1(3) allows the court to make an order that the claim continue as if the claimant had not used the Part 8 procedure)

Modifications to the general rules

F–009   8.9 Where the Part 8 procedure is followed—

(a) provision is made in this Part for the matters which must be stated in the claim form and the defendant is not required to file a defence and therefore—

(i) Part 16 (statements of case) does not apply;
(ii) Part 15 (defence and reply) does not apply;
(iii) any time limit in these Rules which prevents the parties from taking a step before a defence is filed does not apply;
(iv) the requirement under rule 7.8 to serve on the defendant a form for defending the claim does not apply;

(b) the claimant may not obtain judgment by request on an admission and therefore—

(i) rules 14.4 to 14.7 do not apply; and
(ii) the requirement under rule 7.8 to serve on the defendant a form for admitting the claim does not apply; and

(c) the claim shall be treated as allocated to the multi-track and therefore Part 26 does not apply.

APPENDIX G

Practice direction—alternative procedure for claims

THIS PRACTICE DIRECTION SUPPLEMENTS CPR PART 8

Types of claim in which Part 8 procedure may be used

1.1 A claimant may use the Part 8 procedure where he seeks the court's **G–001** decision on a question which is unlikely to involve a substantial dispute of fact.

1.2 A claimant may also use the Part 8 procedure if a practice direction permits or requires its use for the type of proceedings in question.

1.3 The practice directions referred to in paragraph 1.2 above may in some respects modify or disapply the Part 8 procedure and, where that is so, it is those practice directions that must be complied with.

1.4 The types of claim for which the Part 8 procedure may be used include:

   (1) a claim by or against a child or patient which has been settled before the commencement of proceedings and the sole purpose of the claim is to obtain the approval of the court to the settlement,

   (2) a claim for provisional damages which has been settled before the commencement of proceedings and the sole purpose of the claim is to obtain a consent judgment, and

   (3) provided there is unlikely to be a substantial dispute of fact, a claim for a summary order for possession against named or unnamed defendants occupying and or premises without the licence or consent of the person claiming possession.

1.5 Where it appears to a court officer that a claimant is using the Part 8 procedure inappropriately, he may refer the claim to a judge for the judge to consider the point.

1.6 The court may at any stage order the claim to continue as if the claimant had not used the Part 8 procedure and, if it does so, the court will allocate the claim to a track and give such directions as it considers appropriate[1].

Issuing the claim

2.1 Part 7 and the practice direction which supplements it contain a number **G–002** of rules and directions applicable to all claims, including those to which Part 8 applies. Those rules and directions should be applied where appropriate.

2.2 Where a claimant uses the Part 8 procedure, the claim form (practice form N208) should be used and must state the matters set out in rule 8.2 and, if paragraphs 1.2 or 1.3 apply, must comply with the requirements of the practice direction in question. In particular, the claim form must state that Part 8 applies; a Part 8 claim form means a claim form which so states.

(The Costs Practice Direction supplementing Parts 43 to 48 contains details of the information required to be filed with a claim form to comply with rule 44.15 (providing information about funding arrangements))

---

[1] R.8.1(3).

Responding to the claim

G–003

3.1 The provisions of Part 15 (defence and reply) do not apply where the claim form is a Part 8 claim form.

3.2 Where a defendant who wishes to respond to a Part 8 claim form is required to file an acknowledgment of service, that acknowledgment of service should be in practice form N210[2] but can, alternatively, be given in an informal document such as a letter.

3.3 Rule 8.3 sets out provisions relating to an acknowledgment of service of a Part 8 claim form.

3.4 Rule 8.4 sets out the consequence of failing to file an acknowledgment of service.

3.5 The provisions of Part 12 (obtaining default judgment) do not apply where the claim form is a Part 8 claim form.

3.6 Where a defendant believes that the Part 8 procedure should not be used because there is a substantial dispute of fact or, as the case may be, because its use is not authorised by any rule or practice direction, he must state his reasons in writing when he files his acknowledgment of service.[3] If the statement of reasons includes matters of evidence it should be verified by a statement of truth.

Managing the claim

G–004

4.1 The court may give directions immediately a Part 8 claim form is issued either on the application of a party or on its own initiative. The directions may include fixing a hearing date where:

(1) there is no dispute, such as in child and patient settlements, or

(2) where there may be a dispute, such as in claims for mortgage possession or appointment of trustees, but a hearing date could conveniently be given.

4.2 Where the court does not fix a hearing date when the claim form is issued, it will give directions for the disposal of the claim as soon as practicable after the defendant has acknowledged service of the claim form or, as the case may be, after the period for acknowledging service has expired.

4.3 Certain applications, such as a consent application under section 38 of the Landlord and Tenant Act 1954, may not require a hearing.

4.4 The court may convene a directions hearing before giving directions.

Evidence

G–005

5.1 A claimant wishing to rely on written evidence should file it when his Part 8 claim form is issued[4] (unless the evidence is contained in the claim form itself).

5.2 Evidence will normally be in the form of a witness statement or an affidavit but a claimant may rely on the matters set out in his claim form provided that it has been verified by a statement of truth.
(For information about (1) statements of truth see Part 22 and the practice direction that supplements it, and (2) written evidence see Part 32 and the practice direction that supplements it.)

---

[2] R.8.3(1)(a).
[3] R.8.8(1).
[4] R.8.5

5.3 A defendant wishing to rely on written evidence, should file it with his acknowledgment of service.[5]

5.4 Rule 8.5 sets out the times and provisions for filing and serving written evidence.

5.5 A party may apply to the court for an extension of time to serve and file evidence under Rule 8.5 or for permission to serve and file additional evidence under Rule 8.6(1).

(For information about applications see Part 23 and the practice direction that supplements it)

5.6 (1) The parties may, subject to the following provisions, agree in writing on an extension of time for serving and filing evidence under Rule 8.5(3) or Rule 8.5(5).

(2) An agreement extending time for a defendant to file evidence under Rule 8.5(3)—

(a) must be filed by the defendant at the same time as he files his acknowledgment of service; and

(b) must not extend time by more than 14 days after the defendant files his acknowledgment of service.

(3) An agreement extending time for a claimant to file evidence in reply under Rule 8.5(5) must not extend time to more than 28 days after service of the defendant's evidence on the claimant.

Practice direction—Part 8

THIS PRACTICE DIRECTION SUPPLEMENTS CPR PART 8, AND SCHEDULE 1 AND SCHEDULE 2 TO THE CPR

Terminology

1.1 In this practice direction "Schedule rules" means provisions contained in the Schedules to the CPR, which were previously contained in the Rules of the Supreme Court (1965) or the County Court Rules (1981).   G–009

Contents of this Practice Direction

2.1 This practice direction explains—   G–010

(1) how to start the claims referred to in Sections A and B;

---

[5] R.8.5(3).

(2) which form to use as the claim form;

(3) the procedure which those claims will follow; and

(4) how to start the appeals referred to in Section C.

(Further guidance about Forms other than claim forms can be found in the practice direction supplementing Part 4.)

(Forms to be used when making applications under Schedule 1, RSC.0.53 for judicial review and under Schedule RSC.0.54 for writs of habeas corpus are forms 86 and 87 (modified as necessary). Reference should be made to the relevant existing Crown Office practice directions for further guidance on procedure).

How to use this Practice Direction

G–011
3.1 This Practice direction is divided into three sections—Section A, Section B and Section C. Only one section will be relevant to how to make a particular claim or appeal.

3.2 If the claim is described in paragraph A.1—use section A.

3.3 If the claim is described in paragraph B.1—use section B.

3.4 If the claim is described in paragraph C.1—use section C.

SECTION A

Application

G–012
A.1 Section A applies if—

(1) the claim is listed in Table 1 below;

(2) an Act provides that a claim or application in the High Court is to be brought by originating summons; or

(3) before 26 April 1999, a claim or application in the High Court would have been brought by originating summons, and is not listed in Section C, and no other method for bringing the claim or application on and after 26 April 1999 is specified in a Schedule rule or practice direction.

A.2 (1) The claimant must use the Part 8 procedure unless an Act, Schedule rule, or practice direction, makes any additional or contrary provision.

(2) Where such additional or contrary provision is made the claimant must comply with it and modify the Part 8 procedure accordingly.

Claim form

G–013
A.3 The claimant must use the Part 8 claim form.

Table 1	
RSC 0.17, r.3(1)	Interpleader (Mode of application)
RSC 0.77, r.11	Proceedings by and against the Crown (Interpleader: Application for order against Crown)

Table 1—*continued*

RSC O.77, r.16(2)	Proceedings by and against the Crown (Attachment of debts, etc.)
RSC O.77, r.17(1)	Proceedings by and against the Crown (Proceedings relating to postal packets)
RSC O.77, r.18(1)	Proceedings by and against the Crown (Applications under sections 17 and 29 of Crown Proceedings Act)
RSC O.79, r.8(2)	Criminal Proceedings (Estreat of recognizances)
RSC O.79, r.9(2)	Criminal Proceedings (Bail)
RSC O.81, r.10(1)	Partners (Applications for orders charging partner's interest in partnership property)
RSC O.93, r.5(2)	Applications and Appeals to High Court under Various Acts: Chancery Division (Applications under section 2(3) of the Public Order Act 1936)
RSC O.93, r.18(2)	Applications and Appeals to High Court under Various Acts: Chancery Division (Proceedings under section 86 of the Civil Aviation Act 1982)
RSC O.94, r.5	Applications and Appeals to High Court under Various Acts: Queen's Bench Division (Exercise of jurisdiction under Representation of the People Acts)
RSC O.95, r.2(1)	Bills of Sale Acts 1878 and 1882 and the Industrial and Provident Societies Act 1967 (Entry of satisfaction)
RSC O.95, r.3	Bills of Sale Acts 1878 and 1882 and the Industrial and Provident Societies Act 1967 (Restraining removal on sale of goods seized)
RSC O.96, r.1	The Mines (Working Facilities and Support) Act 1996 etc. (Assignment to Chancery Division)
RSC O.96, r.3	The Mines (Working Facilities and Support) Act 1966 etc. (Issue of claim form)
RSC O.106, r.3(2)	Proceedings Relating to Solicitors: The Solicitors Act 1974 (Power to order solicitor to deliver cash account etc.)
RSC O.106, r.6(2)	Proceedings Relating to Solicitors: The Solicitors Act 1974 (Applications under schedule 1 to the Act)
RSC O.106, r.8	Proceedings Relating to Solicitors: The Solicitors Act 1974 (Interim order restricting payment out of banking account)
RSC O.109, r.1(3)	Administration Act 1960 (Applications under Act)

SECTION B

Application

G–014   B.1   Section B applies if the claim—

(1) is listed in Table 2;

(2) in the county court is for, or includes a claim for:

(a) the recovery of possession of land; or

(b) for damages for harassment under Section 3 of the Protection from Harassment Act 1997

(3) would have been brought before 26 April 1999—

(a) in the High Court, by originating motion;

(b) in the county court—

(i) by originating application; or

(ii) by petition, and

no other procedure is prescribed in an Act, a Schedule rule or a practice direction.

Table 2

Schedule Rule		Claim Form
RSC O.77, r.8(2)[1]	Proceedings by and against the Crown (Summary applications to the court in certain revenue matters)	
RSC O.93, r.19(1)	Applications and Appeals to High Court under Various Acts: (Proceedings under section 85(7) of the Fair Trading Act 1973 and the Control of Misleading Advertisements Regulations 1988)	
RSC O.93, r.22(3)	Applications and Appeals to High Court under Various Acts: Chancery Division (Proceedings under the Financial Services Act 1986) (Applications by inspectors under section 94 or 178)	
RSC O.94, r.1(2)	Applications and Appeals to High Court under Various Acts: Queens Bench Division (Jurisdiction of High Court to Quash Certain Orders, Schemes etc.)	
RSC O.94, r.7(2)	Applications and Appeals to High Court under Various Acts: Queens Bench Division (Reference of Question of Law by Agricultural Land Tribunal)	

[1] This type of claim may also be brought by the Part 8 procedure.

Table 2 (*continued*)

RSC O.94, r.11(4)	Applications and Appeals to High Court under Various Acts: Queens Bench Division (Case stated by Mental Health Review Tribunal)
RSC O.94, r.12(5)(c)	Applications and Appeals to High Court under Various Acts: Queens Bench Division Applications for Permission under section 289(6) of the Town and Country Planning Act 1990 and section 65(5) of the Planning (Listed Buildings and Conservation Areas) Act 1990
RSC O.94, r.13(5)	Applications and Appeals to High Court under Various Acts: Queens Bench Division Proceedings under sections 289 and 290 of the Town and Country Planning Act 1990 and under section 65 of the Planning (Listed Buildings and Conservation Areas) Act 1990
RSC O.94, r.14(2)	Applications and Appeals to High Court under Various Acts; Queens Bench Division Applications under section 13 of the Coroners Act 1988
RSC O.94, r.15(2)	Applications and Appeals to High Court under Various Acts: Queens Bench Division Applications under section 42 of the Supreme Court Act 1981
RSC O.109, r.2(4)	Administration of Justice Act 1960 (Appeals under section 13 of Act)
RSC O.115, r.2B(1)	Confiscation and Forfeiture in Connection with Criminal Proceedings (I. Drug Trafficking Act 1994 and Criminal Justice (International Co-operation) Act 1990 — Application for confiscation Order)
RSC O.115, r.3(1)	Confiscation and Forfeiture in Connection with Criminal Proceedings (I. Drug Trafficking Act 1994 and Criminal Justice (International Co-operation) Act 1990 — Application for restraint order or charging order)
RSC O.115, r.7(1)	Confiscation and Forfeiture in Connection with Criminal Proceedings (I. Drug Trafficking Act 1994 and Criminal Justice (International Co-operation) Act 1990 — Realisation of property)

	Table 2 (*continued*)	
RSC O.115, r.26(1)	Confiscation and Forfeiture in Connection with Criminal Proceedings (III. Prevention of Terrorism (Temporary Provisions) Act 1989—Application for restraint order)	
RSC O.116, r.5(1)	The Criminal Procedure and Investigations Act 1996 (Application under section 54(3))	
CCR O.44, r.1(1)	The Agricultural Holdings Act 1986 (Special case stated by arbitrator)	
CCR O.44, r.3(1)	The Agricultural Holdings Act 1986 (Removal of arbitrator or setting aside award)	
CCR O.45, r.1(1)	The Representation of the People Act 1983 (Application for detailed assessment of returning officer's account)	N408
CCR O.46, r.1(1)	The Legitimacy Act 1976 (Manner of application)	
CCR O.49, r.7(2)	Miscellaneous Statutes: Injunctions to Prevent Environmental Harm: Town and Country Planning Act 1990 etc. (Application for injunction)	
CCR O.49, r.12(2)	Miscellaneous Statutes: Mental Health Act 1983 (Application)	
CCR O.49, r.15(1)	Miscellaneous Statutes: Post Office Act 1969 (Application under section 30(5))	

The Local Government Act 1972 (claims under section 92—proceedings for disqualification)

Special provisions take precedence

G–015   B.2 The claimant must first comply with any special provision set out in the Schedule rules, practice direction or any Act relating to the claim. (In Schedule 2, CCR 0.6 makes special provisions about particulars of claim and CCR 0.7 makes special provision for service, for certain types of claim.)

B.3 Special provisions contained in Schedule rules or an Act may set out—

(1) where the claim may be started;
(2) the contents of the claim form;
(3) whether a hearing is required;
(4) the nature of evidence required in support of the claim, and when it must be filed or served;
(5) the method of service of the claim form and evidence;
(6) persons on whom service must or may be effected;

(7) the form and content of Notices, and when they must or may be filed, and on whom served;

(8) the form and content of any affidavit, answer, or reply and when they must or may be filed or served;

(9) persons who may apply to be joined as parties to the claim;

(10) minimum periods of notice before the hearing date.

B.4 Where a Schedule rule makes special provision for the contents of particulars of claim, those particulars must be attached to the claim form and served with it.

B.5 Subject to any special or contrary provision in an Act or Schedule rule, the claimant must use the procedure set out in the remainder of this section.

Restrictions on where to start the claim

B.6 Where the claimant is bringing a claim in a county court that claim may only be started — **G–016**

(1) in the county court for the district in which —

(a) the defendants or one of the defendants lives or carries on business; or

(b) the subject matter of the claim is situated; or

(2) if there is no defendant named in the claim form, in the county court for the district in which the claimant or one of the claimants lives or carries on business.

B.7 Where the claimant is making a claim in the county court for —

(1) enforcing any charge or lien on land;

(2) the recovery of moneys secured by a mortgage or charge on land, the claim must be started in the court for the district in which the land, or any part of it, is situated.

Claim form

B.8 This paragraph sets out which Form is to be used as the claim form — **G–017**

(1) where a claim form number is listed against a particular claim in Table 2, the claimant must use that numbered form as the claim form;

(2) in every other claim, the claimant must use the Part 8 claim form.

Court will fix a date

B.9 When the court issues the claim form it will — **G–018**

(1) fix a date for the hearing; and

(2) prepare a notice of the hearing date for each party.

Service of the claim form

B.10 The claim form must be served not less than 21 days before the hearing date. **G–019**

B.11 Where the claimant serves the claim form, he must serve notice of the hearing date at the same time, unless the hearing date is specified in the claim form.

(CPR Rule 3.1(2)(a) and (b) provide for the court to extend or shorten the time for compliance with any rule or practice direction, and to adjourn or bring forward a hearing)

Defendant is not required to respond

G–020   B.12 The defendant is not required to serve an acknowledgment of service.

At the hearing

G–021–
G–022   B.13 The court may on the hearing date—

         (1) proceed to hear the case and dispose of the claim; or
         (2) give case management directions.

     B.14 Case management directions given under paragraph B.13 will, if the defendant has filed a defence, include the allocation of a case to a track, or directions to enable the case to be allocated.

     B.15 CPR rule 26.5(3) to (5) and CPR rules 26.6 to 26.10 apply to the allocation of a claim under paragraph B.14.

CPR Part 19

III Group Litigation

Definition

19.10 A Group Litigation Order ("GLO") means an order made under rule 19.11   **G–023**
to provide for the case management of claims which give rise to common or related
issues of fact or law (the "GLO issues").

Group Litigation Order

19.11   **G–024**

  (1) The court may make a GLO where there are or are likely to be a number
      of claims giving rise to the GLO issues.

(The practice direction provides the procedure for applying for a GLO)

  (2) A GLO must—

    (a) contain directions about the establishment of a register (the "group
        register") on which the claims managed under the GLO will be
        entered;
    (b) specify the GLO issues which will identify the claims to be managed as
        a group under the GLO; and
    (c) specify the court (the "management court") which will manage the
        claims on the group register.

  (3) A GLO may—

    (a) in relation to claims which raise one or more of the GLO issues—
      (i) direct their transfer to the management court;
      (ii) order their stay (GL) until further order; and
      (iii) direct their entry on the group register;
    (b) direct that from a specified date claims which raise one or more of the
        GLO issues should be started in the management court and entered on
        the group register; and
    (c) give directions for publicising the GLO.

Effect of the GLO

19.12   **G–025**

  (1) Where a judgment or order is given or made in a claim on the group
      register in relation to one or more GLO issues—

    (a) that judgment or order is binding on the parties to all other claims that
        are on the group register at the time the judgment is given or the order
        is made unless the court orders otherwise; and
    (b) the court may give directions as to the extent to which that judgment
        or order is binding on the parties to any claim which is subsequently
        entered on the group register.

  (2) Unless paragraph (3) applies, any party who is adversely affected by a
      judgment or order which is binding on him may seek permission to appeal
      the order.

(3) A party to a claim which was entered on the group register after a judgment or order which is binding on him was given or made may not—

    (a) apply for the judgment or order to be set aside (GL), varied or stayed (GL); or

    (b) appeal the judgment or order,

but may apply to the court for an order that the judgment or order is not binding on him.

(4) Unless the court orders otherwise, disclosure of any document relating to the GLO issues by a party to a claim on the group register is disclosure of that document to all parties to claims—

    (a) on the group register; and

    (b) which are subsequently entered on the group register.

Case Management

G–026   **19.13**

Directions given by the management court may include directions—

    (a) varying the GLO issues;

    (b) providing for one or more claims on the group register to proceed as test claims;

    (c) appointing the solicitor of one or more parties to be the lead solicitor for the claimants or defendants;

    (d) specifying the details to be included in a statement of case in order to show that the criteria for entry of the claim on the group register have been met;

    (e) specifying a date after which no claim may be added to the group register unless the court gives permission; and

    (f) for the entry of any particular claim which meets one or more of the GLO issues on the group register.

(Part 3 contains general provisions about the case management powers of the court)

Removal from the Register

G–027   **19.14**

(1) A party to a claim entered on the group register may apply to the management court for the claim to be removed from the register.

(2) If the management court orders the claim to be removed from the register it may give directions about the future management of the claim.

Test Claims

G–028   **19.15**

(1) Where a direction has been given for a claim on the group register to proceed as a test claim and that claim is settled, the management court may order that another claim on the group register be substituted as the test claim.

(2) Where an order is made under paragraph (1), any order made in the test claim before the date of substitution is binding on the substituted claim unless the court orders otherwise.

Practice Direction — Group Litigation

THIS PRACTICE DIRECTION SUPPLEMENTS SECTION III OF PART 19

COSTS

Introduction

1 This practice direction deals with group litigation where the multiple parties are claimants. Section III of Part 19 (group litigation orders) also applies where the multiple parties are defendants. The court will give such directions in such a case as are appropriate.

G–029.1

Preliminary steps

2.1 Before applying for a Group Litigation Order ('GLO') the solicitor acting for the proposed applicant should consult the Law Society's Multi Party Action Information Service in order to obtain information about other cases giving rise to the proposed GLO issues.

G–029.2

2.2 It will often be convenient for the claimants' solicitors to form a Solicitors' Group and to choose one of their number to take the lead in applying for the GLO and in litigating the GLO issues. The lead solicitor's role and relationship with the other members of the Solicitors' Group should be carefully defined in writing and will be subject to any directions given by the court under CPR 19.13(c).

2.3 In considering whether to apply for a GLO, the applicant should consider whether any other order would be more appropriate. In particular he should consider whether, in the circumstances of the case, it would be more appropriate for—

(1) the claims to be consolidated; or
(2) the rules in Section II of Part 19 (representative parties) to be used.

Application for a GLO

3.1 An application for a GLO must be made in accordance with CPR Part 23, may be made at any time before or after any relevant claims have been issued and may be made either by a claimant or by a defendant.

G–029.3

3.2 The following information should be included in the application notice or in written evidence filed in support of the application:

(1) a summary of the nature of the litigation;
(2) the number and nature of claims already issued;
(3) the number of parties likely to be involved;
(4) the common issues of fact or law (the 'GLO issues') that are likely to arise in the litigation; and

(5) whether there are any matters that distinguish smaller groups of claims within the wider group.

3.3 A GLO may not be made—

(1) in the Queen's Bench Division, without the consent of the Lord Chief Justice,
(2) in the Chancery Division, without the consent of the Vice-Chancellor, or
(3) in a county court, without the consent of the Head of Civil Justice.

3.4 The court to which the application for a GLO is made will, if minded to make the GLO, send to the Lord Chief Justice, the Vice-Chancellor, or the Head of Civil Justice, as appropriate—

(1) a copy of the application notice,
(2) a copy of any relevant written evidence, and
(3) a written statement as to why a GLO is considered to be desirable.

These steps may be taken either before or after a hearing of the application.

High Court in London

G–029.4   3.5 The application for the GLO should be made to the Senior Master in the Queen's Bench Division or the Chief Chancery Master in the Chancery Division. For claims that are proceeding or are likely to proceed in a specialist list, the application should be made to the senior judge of that list.

High Court outside London

G–029.5   3.6 Outside London, the application should be made to a Presiding Judge or a Chancery Supervising Judge of the Circuit in which the District Registry which has issued the application notice is situated.

County courts

G–029.6   3.7 The application should be made to the Designated Civil Judge for the area in which the county court which has issued the application notice is situated.

3.8 The applicant for a GLO should request the relevant court to refer the application notice to the judge by whom the application will be heard as soon as possible after the application notice has been issued. This is to enable the judge to consider whether to follow the practice set out in paragraph 3.4 above prior to the hearing of the application.

3.9 The directions under paragraphs 3.5, 3.6 and 3.7 above do not prevent the judges referred to from making arrangements for other judges to hear applications for GLOs when they themselves are unavailable.

GLO made by court of its own initiative

G–029.7   4 Subject to obtaining the appropriate consent referred to in paragraph 3.3 and the procedure set out in paragraph 3.4, the court may make a GLO of its own initiative.

(CPR 3.3 deals with the procedure that applies when a court proposes to make an order of its own initiative)

442

The GLO

5 CPR 19.11(2) and (3) set out rules relating to the contents of GLOs.   G–029.8

The group register

6.1 Once a GLO has been made a Group Register will be established on which   G–029.9
will be entered such details as the court may direct of the cases which are to be
subject to the GLO.

6.1A A claim must be issued before it can be entered on a Group Register.

6.2 An application for details of a case to be entered on a Group Register may be
made by any party to the case.

6.3 An order for details of the case to be entered on the Group Register will not
be made unless the case gives rise to at least one of the GLO issues.
(CPR 19.10 defines GLO issues)

6.4 The court, if it is not satisfied that a case can be conveniently case managed
with the other cases on the Group Register, or if it is satisfied that the entry of the
case on the Group Register would adversely affect the case management of the other
cases, may refuse to allow details of the case to be entered on the Group Register, or
order their removal from the Register if already entered, although the case gives rise
to one or more of the Group issues.

6.5 The Group Register will normally be maintained by and kept at the court but
the court may direct this to be done by the solicitor for one of the parties to a case
entered on the Register.

6.6

   (1) Rule 5.4 (supply of documents from court records) applies where the
       register is maintained by the court. A party to a claim on the group register
       may request documents relating to any other claim on the group register
       in accordance with rule 5.4(1) as if he were a party to those proceed-
       ings.
   (2) Where the register is maintained by a solicitor, any person may inspect the
       Group Register during normal business hours and upon giving reasonable
       notice to the solicitor; the solicitor may charge a fee not exceeding the fee
       prescribed for a search at the court office.

6.7 In this paragraph, 'the court' means the management court specified in the
GLO.

Allocation to track

7 Once a GLO has been made and unless the management court directs other-   G–029.10
wise:

   (1) every claim in a case entered on the Group Register will be automatically
       allocated, or re-allocated (as the case may be), to the multi-track;
   (2) any case management directions that have already been given in any such
       case otherwise than by the management court will be set aside; and
   (3) any hearing date already fixed otherwise than for the purposes of the
       group litigation will be vacated.

Managing judge

8 A judge ('the managing judge') will be appointed for the purpose of the GLO as   G–029.11
soon as possible. He will assume overall responsibility fo the management of the

claims and will generally hear the GLO issues. A Master or a District Judge may be appointed to deal with procedural matters, which he will do in accordance with any directions given by the managing judge. A costs judge may be appointed and may be invited to attend case management hearings.

Claims to be started in management court

G–029.12   9.1 The management court may order that as from a specified date all claims that raise one or more of the GLO issues shall be started in the management court.

9.2 Failure to comply with an order made under paragraph 9.1 will not invalidate the commencement of the claim but the claim should be transferred to the management court and details entered on the Group Register as soon as possible. Any party to the claim may apply to the management court for an order under CPR 19.14 removing the case from the Register or, as the case may be, for an order that details of the case be not entered on the Register.

Transfer

G–029.13   10 Where the management court is a county court and a claim raising one or more of the GLO issues is proceeding in the High Court, an order transferring the case to the management court and directing the details of the case to be entered on the Group Register can only be made in the High Court.

Publicising the GLO

G–029.14   11 After a GLO has been made, a copy of the GLO should be supplied—

    (1) to the Law Society, 113 Chancery Lane, London WC2A 1PL; and
    (2) to the Senior Master, Queen's Bench Division, Royal Courts of Justice, Strand, London WC2A 2LL.

Case management

G–029.15   12.1 The management court may give case management directions at the time the GLO is made or subsequently. Directions given at a case management hearing will generally be binding on all claims that are subsequently entered on the Group Register (see CPR 19.12(1)).

12.2 Any application to vary the terms of the GLO must be made to the management court.

12.3 The management court may direct that one or more of the claims are to proceed as test claims.

12.4 The management court may give directions about how the costs of resolving common issues or the costs of claims proceeding as test claims are to be borne or shared as between the claimants on the Group Register.

Cut-off dates

G–029.16   13 The management court may specify a date after which no claim may be added to the Group Register unless the court gives permission. An early cut-off date may be appropriate in the case of 'instant disasters' (such as transport accidents). In the case of consumer claims, and particularly pharmaceutical claims, it may be necessary to delay the ordering of a cut-off date.

Statements of case

14.1 The management court may direct that the GLO claimants serve 'Group Particulars of Claim' which set out the various claims of all the claimants on the Group Register at the time the particulars are filed. Such particulars of claim will usually contain—

    (1) general allegations relating to all claims; and

    (2) a schedule containing entries relating to each individual claim specifying which of the general allegations are relied on and any specific facts relevant to the claimant.

G–029.17

14.2 The directions given under paragraph 14.1 should include directions as to whether the Group Particulars should be verified by a statement or statements of truth and, if so, by whom.

14.3 The specific facts relating to each claimant on the Group Register may be obtained by the use of a questionnaire. Where this is proposed, the management court should be asked to approve the questionnaire. The management court may direct that the questionnaires completed by individual claimants take the place of the schedule referred to in paragraph 14.1(2).

14.4 The management court may also give directions about the form that particulars of claim relating to claims which are to be entered on the Group Register should take.

The trial

15.1 The management court may give directions—

    (1) for the trial of common issues; and

    (2) for the trial of individual issues.

G–029.18

15.2 Common issues and test claims will normally be tried at the management court. Individual issues may be directed to be tried at other courts whose locality is convenient for the parties.

Costs

16.1 CPR 48 contains rules about costs where a GLO has been made.

16.2 Where the court has made an order about costs in relation to any application or hearing which involved both—

    (1) one or more of the GLO issues; and

    (2) an issue or issues relevant only to individual claims;

G–029.19

and the court has not directed the proportion of the costs that is to relate to common costs and the proportion that is to relate to individual costs in accordance with rule 48.6A(5), the costs judge will make a decision as to the relevant proportions at or before the commencement of the detailed assessment of costs.

CPR Part 25

Security for costs

G–030   25.12

(1) A defendant to any claim may apply under this Section of this Part for security for his costs of the proceedings.

(Part 3 provides for the court to order payment of sums into court in other circumstances. Rule 20.3 provides for this Section of this Part to apply to Part 20 claims)

(2) An application for security for costs must be supported by written evidence.

(3) Where the court makes an order for security for costs, it will—

    (a) determine the amount of security; and

    (b) direct—

        (i) the manner in which; and

        (ii) the time within which

    the security must be given.

Conditions to be Satisfied

G–031   25.13

(1) The court may make an order for security for costs under rule 25.12 if—

    (a) it is satisfied, having regard to all the circumstances of the case, that it is just to make such an order; and

    (b) (i) one or more of the conditions in paragraph (2) applies, or

        (ii) an enactment permits the court to require security for costs.

(2) The conditions are—

    (a) the claimant is an individual—

        (i) who is ordinarily resident out of the jurisdiction; and

        (ii) is not a person against whom a claim can be enforced under the Brussels Conventions of the Lugano Convention, as defined by section 1(1) of the Civil Jurisdiction and Judgments Act 1982 [43];

    (b) the claimant is a company or other incorporated body—

        (i) which is ordinarily resident out of the jurisdiction; and

        (ii) is not a body against whom a claim can be enforced under the Brussels Conventions or the Lugano Convention;

    (c) the claimant is a company or other body (whether incorporated inside or outside Great Britain) and there is reason to believe that it will be unable to pay the defendant's costs if ordered to do so;

    (d) the claimant has changed his address since the claim was commenced with a view to evading the consequences of the litigation;

    (e) the claimant failed to give his address in the claim form, or gave an incorrect address in that form;

    (f) the claimant is acting as a nominal claimant, other than as a representative claimant under Part 19, and there is reason to believe that he will be unable to pay the defendant's costs if ordered to do so;

(g) the claimant has taken steps in relation to his assets that would make it difficult to enforce an order for costs against him.

(Rule 3.4 allows the court to strike out a statement of case and Part 24 for it to give summary judgment)

Security for costs other than from the claimant

25.14   G–032

(1) The defendant may seek an order against someone other than the claimant, and the court may make an order for security for costs against that person if—

(a) it is satisfied, having regard to all the circumstances of the case, that it is just to make such an order; and

(b) one or more of the conditions in paragraph (2) applies.

(2) The conditions are that the person—

(a) has assigned the right to the claim to the claimant with a view to avoiding the possibility of a costs order being made against him; or

(b) has contributed or agreed to contribute to the claimant's costs in return for a share of any money or property which the claimant may recover in the proceedings; and

is a person against whom a costs order may be made.
(Rule 48.2 makes provision for costs orders against non-parties)

Security for costs of an appeal

25.15   G–033

(1) The court may order security for costs of an appeal against—

(a) an appellant;

(b) a respondent who also appeals,

on the same grounds as it may order security for costs against a claimant under this Part.

(2) The court may also make an order under paragraph (1) where the appellant, or the respondent who also appeals, is a limited company and there is reason to believe it will be unable to pay the costs of the other parties to the appeal should its appeal be unsuccessful.

APPENDIX H

Part 36 Offers to Settle and Payments into Court

CONTENTS OF THIS PART

451

Interest	Rule 36.22
Deduction of benefits	Rule 36.23

Scope of this Part

H–001   36.1—(1) This Part contains rules about—

(a) offers to settle and payments into court; and
(b) the consequences where an offer to settle or payment into court is made in accordance with this Part.

(2) Nothing in this Part prevents a party making an offer to settle in whatever way he chooses, but if that offer is not made in accordance with this Part, it will only have the consequences specified in this Part if the court so orders.
(Part 36 applies to Part 20 claims by virtue of rule 20.3)

Part 36 offers and Part 36 payments—general provisions

H–002   36.2—(1) An offer made in accordance with the requirements of this Part is called—

(a) if made by way of a payment into court, 'a Part 36 payment';
(b) otherwise 'a Part 36 offer'.

(Rule 36.3 sets out when an offer has to be made by way of a payment into court)
(2) The party who makes an offer is the 'offeror'.
(3) The party to whom an offer is made is the 'offeree'.
(4) A Part 36 offer or a Part 36 payment—

(a) may be made at any time after proceedings have started; and
(b) may be made in appeal proceedings.

(5) A Part 36 offer or a Part 36 payment shall not have the consequences set out in this Part while the claim is being dealt with on the small claims track unless the court orders otherwise.
(Part 26 deals with allocation to the small claims track)
(Rule 27.2 provides that Part 36 does not apply to small claims)

A defendant's offer to settle a money claim requires a Part 36 payment

H–003   36.3—(1) Subject to rules 36.5(5) and 36.23, an offer by a defendant to settle a money claim will not have the consequences set out in this Part unless it is made by way of a Part 36 payment.
(2) A Part 36 payment may only be made after proceedings have started.
(Rule 36.5(5) permits a Part 36 offer to be made by reference to an interim payment)
(Rule 36.10 makes provision for an offer to settle a money claim before the commencement of proceedings)
(Rule 36.23 makes provision for where benefit is recoverable under the Social Security (Recovery of Benefit) Act 1997[1])

---

[1] 1997 c.27.

Defendant's offer to settle the whole of a claim which includes both a money claim and a non-money claim

36.4—(1) This rule applies where a defendant to a claim which includes both a money claim and a non-money claim wishes—   H–004

    (a) to make an offer to settle the whole claim which will have the consequences set out in this Part; and

    (b) to make a money offer in respect of the money claim and a non-money offer in respect of the non-money claim.

(2) The defendant must—

    (a) make a Part 36 payment in relation to the money claim; and

    (b) make a Part 36 offer in relation to the non-money claim.

(3) The Part 36 payment notice must—

    (a) identify the document which sets out the terms of the Part 36 offer; and

    (b) state that if the claimant gives notice of acceptance of the Part 36 payment he will be treated as also accepting the Part 36 offer.

(Rule 36.6 makes provision for a Part 36 payment notice)

(4) If the claimant gives notice of acceptance of the Part 36 payment, he shall also be taken as giving notice of acceptance of the Part 36 offer in relation to the non-money claim.

Form and content of a Part 36 offer

36.5—(1) A Part 36 offer must be in writing.   H–005

(2) A Part 36 offer may relate to the whole claim or to part of it or to any issue that arises in it.

(3) A Part 36 offer must—

    (a) state whether it relates to the whole of the claim or to part of it or to an issue that arises in it and if so to which part or issue;

    (b) state whether it takes into account any counterclaim; and

    (c) if it is expressed not to be inclusive of interest, give the details relating to interest set out in rule 36.22(2).

(4) A defendant may make a Part 36 offer limited to accepting liability up to a specified proportion.

(5) A Part 36 offer may be made by reference to an interim payment.

(Part 25 contains provisions relating to interim payments)

(6) A Part 36 offer made not less than 21 days before the start of the trial must—

    (a) be expressed to remain open for acceptance for 21 days from the date it is made; and

    (b) provide that after 21 days the offeree may only accept it if—

        (i) the parties agree the liability for costs; or

        (ii) the court gives permission.

(7) A Part 36 offer made less than 21 days before the start of the trial must state that the offeree may only accept it if—

(a) the parties agree the liability for costs; or

(b) the court gives permission.

(Rule 36.8 makes provision for when a Part 36 offer is treated as being made)

(8) If a Part 36 offer is withdrawn it will not have the consequences set out in this Part.

Notice of a Part 36 payment

H–006   36.6—(1) A Part 36 payment may relate to the whole claim or part of it or to an issue that arises in it.

(2) A defendant who makes a Part 36 payment must file with the court a notice ('Part 36 payment notice') which—

(a) states the amount of the payment;

(b) states whether the payment relates to the whole claim or to part of it or to any issue that arises in it and if so to which part or issue;

(c) states whether it takes into account any counterclaim;

(d) if an interim payment has been made, states that the defendant has taken into account the interim payment; and

(e) if it is expressed not to be inclusive of interest, gives the details relating to interest set out in rule 36.22(2).

(Rule 25.6 makes provision for an interim payment)

(Rule 36.4 provides for further information to be included where a defendant wishes to settle the whole of a claim which includes a money claim and a non-money claim)

(Rule 36.23 makes provision for extra information to be included in the payment notice in a case where benefit is recoverable under the Social Security (Recovery of Benefit) Act 1997)

(3) The offeror must—

(a) serve the Part 36 payment notice on the offeree; and

(b) file a certificate of service of the notice.

(5) A Part 36 payment may be withdrawn or reduced only with the permission of the court.

Offer to settle a claim for provisional damages

H–007   36.7—(1) A defendant may make a Part 36 payment in respect of a claim which includes a claim for provisional damages.

(2) Where he does so, the Part 36 payment notice must specify whether or not the defendant is offering to agree to the making of an award of provisional damages.

(3) Where the defendant is offering to agree to the making of an award of provisional damages the payment notice must also state—

(a) that the sum paid into court is in satisfaction of the claim for damages on the assumption that the injured person will not develop the disease or suffer the type of deterioration specified in the notice;

(b) that the offer is subject to the condition that the claimant must make any claim for further damages within a limited period; and

(c) what that period is.

(4) Where a Part 36 payment is—

(a) made in accordance with paragraph (3); and

(b) accepted within the relevant period in rule 36.11,

the Part 36 payment will have the consequences set out in rule 36.13, unless the court orders otherwise.

(5) If the claimant accepts the Part 36 payment he must, within 7 days of doing so, apply to the court for an order for an award of provisional damages under rule 41.2.

(Rule 41.2 provides for an order for an award of provisional damages)

(6) The money in court may not be paid out until the court has disposed of the application made in accordance with paragraph (5).

Time when a Part 36 offer or a Part 36 payment is made and accepted

36.8—(1) A Part 36 offer is made when received by the offeree.　　　　　　　**H–008**

(2) A Part 36 payment is made when written notice of the payment into court is served on the offeree.

(3) An improvement to a Part 36 offer will be effective when its details are received by the offeree.

(4) An increase in a Part 36 payment will be effective when notice of the increase is served on the offeree.

(5) A Part 36 offer or Part 36 payment is accepted when notice of its acceptance is received by the offeror.

Clarification of a Part 36 offer or a Part 36 payment notice

36.9—(1) The offeree may, within 7 days of a Part 36 offer or payment being made, **H–009** request the offeror to clarify the offer or payment notice.

(2) If the offeror does not give the clarification requested under paragraph (1) within 7 days of receiving the request, the offeree may, unless the trial has started, apply for an order that he does so.

(3) If the court makes an order under paragraph (2), it must specify the date when the Part 36 offer or Part 36 payment is to be treated as having been made.

Court to take into account offer to settle made before commencement of proceedings

36.10—(1) If a person makes an offer to settle before proceedings are begun which **H–010** complies with the provisions of this rule, the court will take that offer into account when making any order as to costs.

(2) The offer must—

(a) be expressed to be open for at least 21 days after the date it was made;

(b) if made by a person who would be a defendant were proceedings commenced, include an offer to pay the costs of the offeree incurred up to the date 21 days after the date it was made; and

(c) otherwise comply with this Part.

(3) If the offeror is a defendant to a money claim—

(a) he must make a Part 36 payment within 14 days of service of the claim form; and

(b) the amount of the payment must be not less than the sum offered before proceedings began.

(4) An offeree may not, after proceedings have begun, accept—

(a) an offer made under paragraph (2); or
(b) a Part 36 payment made under paragraph (3),

without the permission of the court.

(5) An offer under this rule is made when it is received by the offeree.

Time for acceptance of a defendant's Part 36 offer or Part 36 payment

H–011 36.11—(1) A claimant may accept a Part 36 offer or a Part 36 payment made not less than 21 days before the start of the trial without needing the court's permission if he gives the defendant written notice of acceptance not later than 21 days after the offer or payment was made.

(Rule 36.13 sets out the costs consequences of accepting a defendant's offer or payment without needing the permission of the court)

(2) If—

(a) a defendant's Part 36 offer or Part 36 payment is made less than 21 days before the start of the trial; or
(b) the claimant does not accept it within the period specified in paragraph (1)—

(i) if the parties agree the liability for costs, the claimant may accept the offer or payment without needing the permission of the court;
(ii) if the parties do not agree the liability for costs the claimant may only accept the offer or payment with the permission of the court.

(3) Where the permission of the court is needed under paragraph (2) the court will, if it gives permission, make an order as to costs.

Time for acceptance of a claimant's Part 36 offer

H–012 36.12—(1) A defendant may accept a Part 36 offer made not less than 21 days before the start of the trial without needing the court's permission if he gives the claimant written notice of acceptance not later than 21 days after the offer was made.

(Rule 36.14 sets out the costs consequences of accepting a claimant's offer without needing the permission of the court)

(2) If—

(a) a claimant's Part 36 offer is made less than 21 days before the start of the trial; or
(b) the defendant does not accept it within the period specified in paragraph (1)—

(i) if the parties agree the liability for costs, the defendant may accept the offer without needing the permission of the court;
(ii) if the parties do not agree the liability for costs the defendant may only accept the offer with the permission of the court.

(3) Where the permission of the court is needed under paragraph (2) the court will, if it gives permission, make an order as to costs.

Costs consequences of acceptance of a defendant's Part 36 offer or Part 36 payment

36.13—(1) Where a Part 36 offer or a Part 36 payment is accepted without needing **H–013** the permission of the court the claimant will be entitled to his costs of the proceedings up to the date of serving notice of acceptance.
   (2) Where—

(a) a Part 36 offer or a Part 36 payment relates to part only of the claim; and

(b) at the time of serving notice of acceptance the claimant abandons the balance of the claim,

the claimant will be entitled to his costs of the proceedings up to the date of serving notice of acceptance, unless the court orders otherwise.
   (3) The claimant's costs include any costs attributable to the defendant's counterclaim if the Part 36 offer or the Part 36 payment notice states that it takes into account the counterclaim.
   (4) Costs under this rule will be payable on the standard basis if not agreed.

Costs consequences of acceptance of a claimant's Part 36 offer

36.14 Where a claimant's Part 36 offer is accepted without needing the permission **H–014** of the court the claimant will be entitled to his costs of the proceedings up to the date upon which the defendant serves notice of acceptance.

The effect of acceptance of a Part 36 offer or a Part 36 payment

36.15—(1) If a Part 36 offer or Part 36 payment relates to the whole claim and is **H–015** accepted, the claim will be stayed (GL).
   (2) In the case of acceptance of a Part 36 offer which relates to the whole claim—

(a) the stay (GL) will be upon the terms of the offer; and

(b) either party may apply to enforce those terms without the need for a new claim.

(3) If a Part 36 offer or a Part 36 payment which relates to part only of the claim is accepted—

(a) the claim will be stayed (GL) as to that part; and

(b) unless the parties have agreed costs, the liability for costs shall be decided by the court.

(4) If the approval of the court is required before a settlement can be binding, any stay (GL) which would otherwise arise on the acceptance of a Part 36 offer or a Part 36 payment will take effect only when that approval has been given.
   (5) Any stay (GL) arising under this rule will not affect the power of the court—

(a) to enforce the terms of a Part 36 offer;

(b) to deal with any question of costs (including interest on costs) relating to the proceedings;

(c) to order payment out of court of any sum paid into court.

(6) Where—

(a) a Part 36 offer has been accepted; and

(b) a party alleges that—

(i) the other party has not honoured the terms of the offer; and

(ii) he is therefore entitled to a remedy for breach of contract,

the party may claim the remedy by applying to the court without the need to start a new claim unless the court orders otherwise.

Payment out of a sum in court on the acceptance of a Part 36 payment

H–016   36.16 Where a Part 36 payment is accepted the claimant obtains payment out of the sum in court by making a request for payment in the practice form.

Acceptance of a Part 36 offer or a Part 36 payment made by one or more, but not all, defendants

H–017   36.17—(1) This rule applies where the claimant wishes to accept a Part 36 offer or a Part 36 payment made by one or more, but not all, of a number of defendants.

(2) If the defendants are sued jointly or in the alternative, the claimant may accept the offer or payment without needing the permission of the court in accordance with rule 36.11(1) if—

(a) he discontinues his claim against those defendants who have not made the offer or payment; and

(b) those defendants give written consent to the acceptance of the offer or payment.

(3) If the claimant alleges that the defendants have a several liability ^(GL) to him the claimant may—

(a) accept the offer or payment in accordance with rule 36.11(1); and

(b) continue with his claims against the other defendants if he is entitled to do so.

(4) In all other cases the claimant must apply to the court for—

(a) an order permitting a payment out to him of any sum in court; and

(b) such order as to costs as the court considers appropriate.

Other cases where a court order is required to enable acceptance of a Part 36 offer or a Part 36 payment

H–018   36.18—(1) Where a Part 36 offer or a Part 36 payment is made in proceedings to which rule 21.10 applies—

(a) the offer or payment may be accepted only with the permission of the court; and

(b) no payment out of any sum in court shall be made without a court order.

(Rule 21.10 deals with compromise etc. by or on behalf of a child or patient)

(2) Where the court gives a claimant permission to accept a Part 36 offer or payment after the trial has started—

(a) any money in court may be paid out only with a court order; and
(b) the court must, in the order, deal with the whole costs of the proceedings.

(3) Where a claimant accepts a Part 36 payment after a defence of tender before claim (GL) has been put forward by the defendant, the money in court may be paid out only after an order of the court.
(Rule 37.3 requires a defendant who wishes to rely on a defence of tender before claim (GL) to make a payment into court)

Restriction on disclosure of a Part 36 offer or a Part 36 payment

36.19—(1) A Part 36 offer will be treated as 'without prejudice (GL) except as to costs'.   **H–019**
(2) The fact that a Part 36 payment has been made shall not be communicated to the trial judge until all questions of liability and the amount of money to be awarded have been decided.
(3) Paragraph (2) does not apply—

(a) where the defence of tender before claim (GL) has been raised;
(b) where the proceedings have been stayed (GL) under rule 36.15 following acceptance of a Part 36 offer or Part 36 payment; or
(c) where—
    (i) the issue of liability has been determined before any assessment of the money claimed; and
    (ii) the fact that there has or has not been a Part 36 payment may be relevant to the question of the costs of the issue of liability.

Costs consequences where claimant fails to do better than a Part 36 offer or a Part 36 payment

36.20—(1) This rule applies where at trial a claimant—   **H–020**

(a) fails to better a Part 36 payment; or
(b) fails to obtain a judgment which is more advantageous than a defendant's Part 36 offer.

(2) Unless it considers it unjust to do so, the court will order the claimant to pay any costs incurred by the defendant after the latest date on which the payment or offer could have been accepted without needing the permission of the court.
(Rule 36.11 sets out the time for acceptance of a defendant's Part 36 offer or Part 36 payment)

Costs and other consequences where claimant does better than he proposed in his Part 36 offer

36.21—(1) This rule applies where at trial—   **H–021**

(a) a defendant is held liable for more; or
(b) the judgment against a defendant is more advantageous to the claimant,

than the proposals contained in a claimant's Part 36 offer.
(2) The court may order interest on the whole or part of any sum of money (excluding interest) awarded to the claimant at a rate not exceeding 10% above base

rate (GL) for some or all of the period starting with the latest date on which the defendant could have accepted the offer without needing the permission of the court.

(3) The court may also order that the claimant is entitled to—

    (a) his costs on the indemnity basis from the latest date when the defendant could have accepted the offer without needing the permission of the court; and

    (b) interest on those costs at a rate not exceeding 10% above base rate (GL).

(4) Where this rule applies, the court will make the orders referred to in paragraphs (2) and (3) unless it considers it unjust to do so.

(Rule 36.12 sets out the latest date when the defendant could have accepted the offer)

(5) In considering whether it would be unjust to make the orders referred to in paragraphs (2) and (3) above, the court will take into account all the circumstances of the case including—

    (a) the terms of any Part 36 offer;

    (b) the stage in the proceedings when any Part 36 offer or Part 36 payment was made;

    (c) the information available to the parties at the time when the Part 36 offer or Part 36 payment was made; and

    (d) the conduct of the parties with regard to the giving or refusing to give information for the purposes of enabling the offer or payment into court to be made or evaluated.

(6) Where the court awards interest under this rule and also awards interest on the same sum and for the same period under any other power, the total rate of interest may not exceed 10% above base rate (GL).

Interest

H–022 36.22—(1) Unless—

    (a) a claimant's Part 36 offer which offers to accept a sum of money; or

    (b) a Part 36 payment notice,

indicates to the contrary, any such offer or payment will be treated as inclusive of all interest until the last date on which it could be accepted without needing the permission of the court.

(2) Where a claimant's Part 36 offer or Part 36 payment notice is expressed not to be inclusive of interest, the offer or notice must state—

    (a) whether interest is offered; and

    (b) if so, the amount offered, the rate or rates offered and the period or periods for which it is offered.

Deduction of benefits

H–023 36.23—(1) This rule applies where a payment to a claimant following acceptance of a Part 36 offer or Part 36 payment into court would be a compensation payment as defined in section 1 of the Social Security (Recovery of Benefits) Act 1997([2]).

---

[2] 1997 c.27.

(2) A defendant to a money claim may make an offer to settle the claim which will have the consequences set out in this Part, without making a Part 36 payment if—

    (a) at the time he makes the offer he has applied for, but not received, a certificate of recoverable benefit; and

    (b) he makes a Part 36 payment not more than 7 days after he receives the certificate.

(Section 1 of the 1997 Act defines 'recoverable benefit')

    (3) A Part 36 payment notice must state—

    (a) the amount of gross compensation;

    (b) the name and amount of any benefit by which that gross amount is reduced in accordance with section 8 and Schedule 2 to the 1997 Act; and

    (c) that the sum paid in is the net amount after deduction of the amount of benefit.

(4) For the purposes of rule 36.20, a claimant fails to better a Part 36 payment if he fails to obtain judgment for more than the gross sum specified in the Part 36 payment notice.

    (5) Where—

    (a) a Part 36 payment has been made; and

    (b) application is made for the money remaining in court to be paid out,

the court may treat the money in court as being reduced by a sum equivalent to any further recoverable benefits paid to the claimant since the date of payment into court and may direct payment out accordingly.

APPENDIX I

PRACTICE DIRECTION—OFFERS TO SETTLE AND PAYMENTS INTO COURT

THIS PRACTICE DIRECTION SUPPLEMENTS CPR PART 36

CONTENTS OF THIS PRACTICE DIRECTION

Part 36 offers and Part 36 Payments

Parties and Part 36 offers

Parties and Part 36 payments

Making a Part 36 payment

Part 36 offers and Part 36 payments—general provisions

Clarification of Part 36 offer or payment

Acceptance of a Part 36 offer or payment

Payment out of court

Foreign currency

Compensation recovery

General

PART 36 OFFERS AND PART 36 PAYMENTS

1.1 A written offer to settle a claim[1] or part of a claim or any issue that arises   I–001
in it made in accordance with the provisions of Part 36 is called:

(1) if made by way of a payment into court, a Part 36 payment,[2] or
(2) if made otherwise, a Part 36 offer.[3]

1.2 A Part 36 offer or Part 36 payment has the costs and other consequences
set out in rules 36.13, 36.14, 36.20 and 36.21.

1.3 An offer to settle which is not made in accordance with Part 36 will only
have the consequences specified in that Part if the court so orders and will
be given such weight on any issue as to costs as the court thinks appropriate.[4]

PARTIES AND PART 36 OFFERS

2.1 A Part 36 offer, subject to paragraph 3 below, may be made by any   I–002
party.

---

[1] Includes Part 20 claims.
[2] See rule 36.2(1)(a).
[3] See rule 36.2(1)(b).
[4] See rule 36.1(2).

2.2 The party making an offer is the 'offeror' and the party to whom it is made is the 'offeree'.

2.3 A Part 36 offer may consist of a proposal to settle for a specified sum or for some other remedy.

2.4 A Part 36 offer is made when received by the offeree.[5]

2.5 An improvement to a Part 36 offer is effective when its details are received by the offeree.[6]

PARTIES AND PART 36 PAYMENTS

I–003

3.1 An offer to settle for a specified sum made by a defendant[7] must, in order to comply with Part 36, be made by way of a Part 36 payment into court.[8]

3.2 A Part 36 payment is made when the Part 36 payment notice is served on the claimant.[9]

3.3 An increase to a Part 36 payment will be effective when notice of the increase is served on the claimant.[10]
(For service of the Part 36 payment notice see rule 36.6(3) and (4).)

3.4 A defendant who wishes to withdraw or reduce a Part 36 payment must obtain the court's permission to do so.

3.5 Permission may be obtained by making an application in accordance with Part 23 stating the reasons giving rise to the wish to withdraw or reduce the Part 36 payment.

MAKING A PART 36 PAYMENT

I–004

4.1 Except where paragraph 4.2 applies, to make a Part 36 payment in any court the defendant must[11] —

(1) serve the Part 36 payment notice on the offeree;
(2) file at the court[12] —

    (a) a copy of the payment notice; and
    (b) a certificate of service confirming service on the offeree; and

(3) send to the Court Funds Office —

    (a) the payment, usually a cheque made payable to the Accountant General of the Supreme Court;
    (b) a sealed copy of the claim form; and
    (c) Court Funds Office form 100.

4.2 A litigant in person without a current account may, in a claim proceeding in a county court or District Registry, make a Part 36 payment by —

---

[5] See rule 36.8(1).
[6] See rule 36.8(3).
[7] Includes a respondent to a claim or issue.
[8] See rule 36.3(1).
[9] See rule 36.8(2).
[10] See rule 36.8(4).
[11] Rule 36.4.
[12] Practice form N242A.

(1)lodging the payment in cash with the court;

(2) filing at the court—

(a) the Part 36 payment notice; and

(b) Court Funds Office form 100.

PART 36 OFFERS AND PART 36 PAYMENTS—GENERAL PROVISIONS

5.1 A Part 36 offer or a Part 36 payment notice must: I–005

(1) state that it is a Part 36 offer or that the payment into court is a Part 36 payment, and (2) be signed by the offeror or his legal representative.[13]

5.2 The contents of a Part 36 offer must also comply with the requirements of rule 36.5(3), (5) and (6).

5.3 The contents of a Part 36 payment notice must comply with rule 36.6(2) and, if rule 36.23 applies, with rule 36.23(3).

5.4 A Part 36 offer or Part 36 payment will be taken to include interest unless it is expressly stated in the offer or the payment notice that interest is not included, in which case the details set out in rule 36.22(2) must be given.

5.5 Where a Part 36 offer is made by a company or other corporation, a person holding a senior position in the company or corporation may sign the offer on the offeror's behalf, but must state the position he holds.

5.6 Each of the following persons is a person holding a senior position:

(1) in respect of a registered company or corporation, a director, the treasurer, secretary, chief executive, manager or other officer of the company or corporation, and

(2) in respect of a corporation which is not a registered company, in addition to those persons set out in (1), the mayor, chairman, president, town clerk or similar officer of the corporation.

CLARIFICATION OF PART 36 OFFER OR PAYMENT

6.1 An offeree may apply to the court for an order requiring the offeror to   I–006 clarify the terms of a Part 36 offer or Part 36 payment notice (a clarification order) where the offeror has failed to comply within 7 days with a request for clarification.[14]

6.2 An application for a clarification order should be made in accordance with Part 23.

6.3 The application notice should state the respects in which the terms of the Part 36 offer or Part 36 payment notice, as the case may be, are said to need clarification.

ACCEPTANCE OF A PART 36 OFFER OR PAYMENT

7.1 The times for accepting a Part 36 offer or a Part 36 payment are set out   I–007 in rules 36.11 and 36.12.

---

[13] For the definition of legal representative see rule 2.3.

[14] See rule 36.9(1) and (2).

7.2 The general rule is that a Part 36 offer or Part 36 payment made more than 21 days before the start of the trial may be accepted within 21 days after it was made without the permission of the court. The costs consequences set out in rules 36.13 and 36.14 will then come into effect.

7.3 A Part 36 offer or Part 36 payment made less than 21 days before the start of the trial cannot be accepted without the permission of the court unless the parties agree what the costs consequences of acceptance will be.

7.4 The permission of the court may be sought:

(1) before the start of the trial, by making an application in accordance with Part 23, and

(2) after the start of the trial, by making an application to the trial judge.

7.5 If the court gives permission it will make an order dealing with costs and may order that, in the circumstances, the costs consequences set out in rules 36.13 and 36.14 will apply.

7.6 Where a Part 36 offer or Part 36 payment is accepted in accordance with rule 36.11(1) or rule 36.12(1) the notice of acceptance must be sent to the offeror and filed with the court.

7.7 The notice of acceptance:

(1) must set out—

(a) the claim number, and
(b) the title of the proceedings,

(2) must identify the Part 36 offer or Part 36 payment notice to which it relates, and

(3) must be signed by the offeree or his legal representative (see paragraphs 5.5 and 5.6 above).

7.8 Where:

(1) the court's approval, or
(2) an order for payment of money out of court, or
(3) an order apportioning money in court—

(a) between the Fatal Accidents Act 1976 and the Law Reform (Miscellaneous Provisions) Act 1934, or
(b) between the persons entitled to it under the Fatal Accidents Act 1976, is required for acceptance of a Part 36 offer or Part 36 payment, application for the approval or the order should be made in accordance with Part 23.

7.9 The court will include in any order made under paragraph 7.8 above a direction for;

(1) the payment out of the money in court, and
(2) the payment of interest.

7.10 Unless the parties have agreed otherwise:

(1) interest accruing up to the date of acceptance will be paid to the offeror, and

(2) interest accruing as from the date of acceptance until payment out will be paid to the offeree.

7.11 A claimant may not accept a Part 36 payment which is part of a defendant's offer to settle the whole of a claim consisting of both a money and a non-money claim unless at the same time he accepts the offer to settle the whole of the claim. Therefore:

(1) if a claimant accepts a Part 36 payment which is part of a defendant's offer to settle the whole of the claim, or
(2) if a claimant accepts a Part 36 offer which is part of a defendant's offer to settle the whole of the claim, the claimant will be deemed to have accepted the offer to settle the whole of the claim.[15]
(See paragraph 8 below for the method of obtaining money out of court.)

PAYMENT OUT OF COURT

8.1 To obtain money out of court following acceptance of a Part 36 payment, the claimant should— I–008

(1) file a request for payment in Court Funds Office form 201 with the Court Funds Office; and
(2) file a copy of form 201 at the court.

8.2 The request for payment should contain the following details:

(1) where the party receiving the payment—

(a) is legally represented—

(i) the name, business address and reference of the legal representative, and
(ii) the name of the bank and the sort code number, the title of the account and the account number where the payment is to be transmitted, and

(2) where the party is acting in person—

(a) his name and address, and
(b) his bank account details as in (ii) above.

8.3 Where a trial is to take place at a different court to that where the case is proceeding, the claimant must also file notice of request for payment with the court where the trial is to take place.
8.4 Subject to paragraph 8.5(1) and (2), if a party does not wish the payment to be transmitted into his bank account or if he does not have a bank account, he may send a written request to the Accountant-General for the payment to be made to him by cheque.
8.5 Where a party seeking payment out of court has provided the necessary information, the payment:

---

[15] See rule 36.4.

(1) where a party is legally represented, must be made to the legal representative,

(2) if the party is not legally represented but is, or has been, in receipt of legal aid in respect of the proceedings and a notice to that effect has been filed, should be made to the Legal Aid Board by direction of the court,

(3) where a person entitled to money in court dies without having made a will and the court is satisfied—

(a) that no grant of administration of his estate has been made, and

(b) that the assets of his estate, including the money in court, do not exceed in value the amount specified in any order in force under section 6 of the Administration of Estates (Small Payments) Act 1965, may be ordered to be made to the person appearing to have the prior right to a grant of administration of the estate of the deceased, e.g. a widower, widow, child, father, mother, brother or sister of the deceased.

FOREIGN CURRENCY

I–009   9.1 Money may be paid into court in a foreign currency:

(1) where it is a Part 36 payment and the claim is in a foreign currency, or

(2) under a court order.

9.2 The court may direct that the money be placed in an interest bearing account in the currency of the claim or any other currency.

9.3 Where a Part 36 payment is made in a foreign currency and has not been accepted within 21 days, the defendant may apply for an order that the money be placed in an interest bearing account.

9.4 The application should be made in accordance with Part 23 and should state:

(1) that the payment has not been accepted in accordance with rule 36.11, and

(2) the type of currency on which interest is to accrue.

COMPENSATION RECOVERY

I–010   10.1 Where a defendant makes a Part 36 payment in respect of a claim for a sum or part of a sum:

(1) which falls under the heads of damage set out in column 1 of Schedule 2 of the Social Security (Recovery of Benefits) Act 1997 in respect of recoverable benefits received by the claimant as set out in column 2 of that Schedule, and

(2) where the defendant is liable to pay recoverable benefits to the Secretary of State, the defendant should obtain from the Secretary of State a certificate of recoverable benefits and file the certificate with the Part 36 payment notice.

10.2 If a defendant wishes to offer to settle a claim where he has applied for but not yet received a certificate of recoverable benefits, he may, provided that he makes a Part 36 payment not more than 7 days after he has received the certificate, make a Part 36 offer which will have the costs and other consequences set out in rules 36.13 and 36.20.

10.3 The Part 36 payment notice should state in addition to the requirements set out in rule 36.6(2):

(1) the total amount represented by the Part 36 payment (the gross compensation),

(2) that the defendant has reduced this sum by £ , in accordance with section 8 of and Schedule 2 to the Social Security (Recovery of Benefits) Act 1997, which was calculated as follows:

Name of benefit   Amount

and

(3) that the amount paid in, being the sum of £ is the net amount after the deduction of the amount of benefit.

10.4 On acceptance of a Part 36 payment to which this paragraph relates, a claimant will receive the sum in court which will be net of the recoverable benefits.

10.5 In establishing at trial whether a claimant has bettered or obtained a judgment more advantageous than a Part 36 payment to which this paragraph relates, the court will base its decision on the gross sum specified in the Part 36 payment notice.

GENERAL

11.1 Where a party on whom a Part 36 offer, a Part 36 payment notice or a notice of acceptance is to be served is legally represented, the Part 36 offer, Part 36 payment notice and notice of acceptance must be served on the legal representative. **I–011**

11.2 In a claim arising out of an accident involving a motor vehicle on a road or in a public place:

(1) where the damages claimed include a sum for hospital expenses, and

(2) the defendant or his insurer pays that sum to the hospital under section 157 of the Road Traffic Act 1988, the defendant must give notice of that payment to the court and all the other parties to the proceedings.

11.3 Money paid into court:

(1) as a Part 36 payment[16] which is not accepted by the claimant, or
(2) under a court order,
will be placed after 21 days in a basic account[17] (subject to paragraph 11.4 below) for interest to accrue.

---

[16] In practice form N243.
[17] See rule 26 of the Court Funds Office Rules 1987.

11.4 Where money referred to in paragraph 11.3 above is paid in in respect of a child or patient it will be placed in a special investment account[18] for interest to accrue.

(A practice direction supplementing Part 21 contains information about the investment of money in court in respect of a child or patient.)

(Practice directions supplementing Part 40 contain information about adjustment of the judgment sum in respect of recoverable benefits, and about structured settlements.)

(A practice direction supplementing Part 41 contains information about provisional damages awards.)

---

[18] See rule 26 as above.

APPENDIX J

Part 43

Scope of Cost Rules and Definitions

CONTENTS OF THIS PART

Scope of this part

43.1 This Part contains definitions and interpretation of certain matters set out in   **J–001**
the rules about costs contained in Parts 44 to 48.
(Part 44 contains general rules about costs; Part 45 deals with fixed costs; Part 46
deals with fast track trial costs; Part 47 deals with the detailed assessment of costs
and related appeals and Part 48 deals with costs payable in special cases)

Definitions and application

43.2   **J–002**

(1) In Parts 44 to 48, unless the context otherwise requires—

  (a) "costs" includes fees, charges, disbursements, expenses, remuneration,
reimbursement allowed to a litigant in person under rule 48.6, any
additional liability incurred under a funding arrangement and any fee
or reward charged by a lay representative for acting on behalf of a
party in proceedings allocated to the small claims track;

  (b) "costs judge" means a taxing master of the Supreme Court;

  (c) "costs officer" means—
    (i) a costs judge;
    (ii) a district judge; and
    (iii) an authorised court officer;

  (d) "authorised court officer" means any officer of—
    (i) a county court;
    (ii) a district registry;
    (iii) the Principal Registry of the Family Division; or
    (iv) the Supreme Court Costs Office,
    whom the Lord Chancellor has authorised to assess costs.

  (e) "fund" includes any estate or property held for the benefit of any
person or class of person and any fund to which a trustee or personal
representative is entitled in his capacity as such;

  (f) "receiving party" means a party entitled to be paid costs;

  (g) "paying party" means a party liable to pay costs;

(h) "assisted person" means an assisted person within the statutory provisions relating to legal aid;

(i) "LSC funded client" means an individual who receives services funded by the Legal Services Commission as part of the Community Legal Service within the meaning of Part I of the Access to Justice Act 1999;

(j) "fixed costs" means the amounts which are to be allowed in respect of solicitors' charges in the circumstances set out in Part 45.

(k) "funding arrangement" means an arrangement where a person has—

    (i) entered into a conditional fee agreement or a collective conditional fee agreement which provides for a success fee within the meaning of section 58(2) of the Courts and Legal Services Act 1990[1];

    (ii) taken out an insurance policy to which section 29 of the Access to Justice Act 1999 (recovery of insurance premiums by way of costs) applies; or

    (iii) made an agreement with a membership organisation to meet his legal costs;

(l) "percentage increase" means the percentage by which the amount of a legal representative's fee can be increased in accordance with a conditional fee agreement which provides for a success fee;

(m) "insurance premium" means a sum of money paid or payable for insurance against the risk of incurring a costs liability in the proceedings, taken out after the event that is the subject matter of the claim;

(n) "membership organisation" means a body prescribed for the purposes of section 30 of the Access to Justice Act 1999 (recovery where body undertakes to meet costs liabilities); and

(o) "additional liability" means the percentage increase, the insurance premium, or the additional amount in respect of provision made by a membership organisation, as the case may be.

(The Conditional Fee Agreements Regulations 2000[7], the Collective Conditional Fee Agreements Regulations 2000[8] and the Access to Justice (Membership Organisations) Regulations 2000[9] contain further provisions about conditional fee agreements and arrangements to meet costs liabilities)

(2) The costs to which Parts 44 to 48 apply include—

(a) the following costs where those costs may be assessed by the court—

    (i) costs of proceedings before an arbitrator or umpire;

    (ii) costs of proceedings before a tribunal or other statutory body; and

    (iii) costs payable by a client to his solicitor; and

(b) costs which are payable by one party to another party under the terms of a contract, where the court makes an order for an assessment of those costs.

---

[1] 1990 c. 41. S.58 was substituted by s.27 of the Access to Justice Act 1999 with effect from April 1, 2000 (the Access to Justice Act 1999 (Commencement No. 3, Transitional Provisions and Savings) Order 2000, SI 2000/774 and the Access to Justice Act 1999 (Transitional Provisions) Order 2000, SI 2000/900).

(3) Where advocacy or litigation services are provided to a client under a conditional fee agreement, costs are recoverable under Parts 44 to 48 notwithstanding that the client is liable to pay his legal representative's fees and expenses only to the extent that sums are recovered in respect of the proceedings, whether by way of costs or otherwise.

(4) In paragraph (3), the reference to a conditional fee agreement is to an agreement which satisfies all the conditions applicable to it by virtue of section 58 of the Courts and Legal Services Act 1990([2]).

Meaning of a summary assessment

43.3 "Summary assessment" means the procedure by which the court, when making an order about costs, orders payment of a sum of money instead of fixed costs or "detailed assessment".

J–003

Meaning of detailed assessment

43.4 "Detailed assessment" means the procedure by which the amount of costs is decided by a costs officer in accordance with Part 47.

J–004

---

[2] 1990 c.41, as substituted by s.27(1) of the Access to Justice Act 1999 (c.22).

Part 44

General Rules about Costs

CONTENTS OF THIS PART

Scope of this part

J–005   44.1 This Part contains general rules about costs and entitlement to costs. (The definitions contained in Part 43 are relevant to this Part)

Solicitor's duty to notify client

J–006   44.2 Where—

(a) the court makes a costs order against a legally represented party; and

478

(b) the party is not present when the order is made,

the party's solicitor must notify his client in writing of the costs order no later than 7 days after the solicitor receives notice of the order.

Court's discretion and circumstances to be taken into account when exercising its discretion as to costs

44.3

(1) The court has discretion as to—   **J–007**

   (a) whether costs are payable by one party to another;
   (b) the amount of those costs; and
   (c) when they are to be paid.

(2) If the court decides to make an order about costs—

   (a) the general rule is that the unsuccessful party will be ordered to pay the costs of the successful party; but
   (b) the court may make a different order.

(3) The general rule does not apply to the following proceedings—

   (a) proceedings in the Court of Appeal on an application or appeal made in connection with proceedings in the Family Division; or
   (b) proceedings in the Court of Appeal from a judgment, direction, decision or order given or made in probate proceedings or family proceedings.

(4) In deciding what order (if any) to make about costs, the court must have regard to all the circumstances, including—

   (a) the conduct of all the parties;
   (b) whether a party has succeeded on part of his case, even if he has not been wholly successful; and
   (c) any payment into court or admissible offer to settle made by a party which is drawn to the court's attention (whether or not made in accordance with Part 36).

(Part 36 contains further provisions about how the court's discretion is to be exercised where a payment into court or an offer to settle is made under that Part)

(5) The conduct of the parties includes—

   (a) conduct before, as well as during, the proceedings and in particular the extent to which the parties followed any relevant pre-action protocol;
   (b) whether it was reasonable for a party to raise, pursue or contest a particular allegation or issue;
   (c) the manner in which a party has pursued or defended his case or a particular allegation or issue; and
   (d) whether a claimant who has succeeded in his claim, in whole or in part, exaggerated his claim.

(6) The orders which the court may make under this rule include an order that a party must pay—

   (a) a proportion of another party's costs;

(b) a stated amount in respect of another party's costs;

(c) costs from or until a certain date only;

(d) costs incurred before proceedings have begun;

(e) costs relating to particular steps taken in the proceedings;

(f) costs relating only to a distinct part of the proceedings; and

(g) interest on costs from or until a certain date, including a date before judgment.

(7) Where the court would otherwise consider making an order under paragraph (6)(f), it must instead, if practicable, make an order under paragraph (6)(a) or (c).

(8) Where the court has ordered a party to pay costs, it may order an amount to be paid on account before the costs are assessed.

(9) Where a party entitled to costs is also liable to pay costs the court may assess the costs which that party is liable to pay and either—

(a) set off the amount assessed against the amount the party is entitled to be paid and direct him to pay any balance; or

(b) delay the issue of a certificate for the costs to which the party is entitled until he has paid the amount which he is liable to pay.

Costs orders relating to funding arrangements

44.3A

(1) The court will not assess any additional liability until the conclusion of the proceedings, or the part of the proceedings, to which the funding arrangement relates.

("Funding arrangement" and "additional liability" are defined in rule 43.2)

(2) At the conclusion of the proceedings, or the part of the proceedings, to which the funding arrangement relates the court may—

(a) make a summary assessment of all the costs, including any additional liability;

(b) make an order for detailed assessment of the additional liability but make a summary assessment of the other costs; or

(c) make an order for detailed assessment of all the costs.

(Part 47 sets out the procedure for the detailed assessment of costs)

Limits on recovery under funding arrangements

44.3B

(1) A party may not recover as an additional liability—

(a) any proportion of the percentage increase relating to the cost to the legal representative of the postponement of the payment of his fees and expenses;

(b) any provision made by a membership organisation which exceeds the likely cost to that party of the premium of an insurance policy against the risk of incurring a liability to pay the costs of other parties to the proceedings;

(c) any additional liability for any period in the proceedings during which he failed to provide information about a funding arrangement in accordance with a rule, practice direction or court order;

(d) any percentage increase where a party has failed to comply with—
  (i) a requirement in the costs practice direction; or
  (ii) a court order,
to disclose in any assessment proceedings the reasons for setting the percentage increase at the level stated in the conditional fee agreement.

(2) his rule does not apply in an assessment under rule 48.9 (assessment of a solicitor's bill to his client).

(Rule 3.9 sets out the circumstances the court will consider on an application for relief from a sanction for failure to comply with any rule, practice direction or court order)

Basis of assessment

44.4   J–008

(1) Where the court is to assess the amount of costs (whether by summary or detailed assessment) it will assess those costs—

(a) on the standard basis; or
(b) on the indemnity basis,

but the court will not in either case allow costs which have been unreasonably incurred or are unreasonable in amount.

(Rule 48.3 sets out how the court decides the amount of costs payable under a contract)

(2) Where the amount of costs is to be assessed on the standard basis, the court will—

(a) only allow costs which are proportionate to the matters in issue; and
(b) resolve any doubt which it may have as to whether costs were reasonably incurred or reasonable and proportionate in amount in favour of the paying party.

(Factors which the court may take into account are set out in rule 44.5)

(3) Where the amount of costs is to be assessed on the indemnity basis, the court will resolve any doubt which it may have as to whether costs were reasonably incurred or were reasonable in amount in favour of the receiving party.
(4) Where—

(a) the court makes an order about costs without indicating the basis on which the costs are to be assessed; or
(b) the court makes an order for costs to be assessed on a basis other than the standard basis or the indemnity basis,

the costs will be assessed on the standard basis.
(6) Where the amount of a solicitor's remuneration in respect of non-contentious business is regulated by any general orders made under the Solicitors Act 1974([1]), the amount of the costs to be allowed in respect of

---

[1] 1974 c. 47.

any such business which falls to be assessed by the court will be decided in accordance with those general orders rather than this rule and rule 44.5.

Factors to be taken into account in deciding the amount of costs

44.5

J–009

(1) The court is to have regard to all the circumstances in deciding whether costs were—

    (a) if it is assessing costs on the standard basis—

        (i) proportionately and reasonably incurred; or
        (ii) were proportionate and reasonable in amount, or

    (b) if it is assessing costs on the indemnity basis—

        (i) unreasonably incurred; or
        (ii) unreasonable in amount.

(2) In particular the court must give effect to any orders which have already been made.

(3) The court must also have regard to—

    (a) the conduct of all the parties, including in particular—

        (i) conduct before, as well as during, the proceedings; and
        (ii) the efforts made, if any, before and during the proceedings in order to try to resolve the dispute;

    (b) the amount or value of any money or property involved;
    (c) the importance of the matter to all the parties;
    (d) the particular complexity of the matter or the difficulty or novelty of the questions raised;
    (e) the skill, effort, specialised knowledge and responsibility involved;
    (f) the time spent on the case; and
    (g) the place where and the circumstances in which work or any part of it was done.

(Rule 35.4(4) gives the court power to limit the amount that a party may recover with regard to the fees and expenses of an expert)

Fixed costs

J–010   44.6 A party may recover the fixed costs specified in Part 45 in accordance with that Part.

Procedure for assessing costs

J–011   44.7 Where the court orders a party to pay costs to another party (other than fixed costs) it may either—

    (a) make a summary assessment of the costs; or
    (b) order detailed assessment of the costs by a costs officer,

unless any rule, practice direction or other enactment provides otherwise.

(The costs practice direction sets out the factors which will affect the court's decision under this rule)

Time for complying with an order for costs

44.8   J–012

A party must comply with an order for the payment of costs within 14 days of—

  (a) the date of the judgment or order if it states the amount of those costs; or
  (b) if the amount of those costs (or part of them) is decided later in accordance with Part 47, the date of the certificate which states the amount.
  (c) in either case, such later date as the court may specify.

(Part 47 sets out the procedure for detailed assessment of costs)

Costs on the small claims track and fast track

44.9

  (1) Part 27 (small claims) and Part 46 (fast track trial costs) contain special   J–013
      rules about—

    (a) liability for costs;
    (b) the amount of costs which the court may award; and
    (c) the procedure for assessing costs.

  (2) Those special rules do not apply until a claim is allocated to a particular track.

Limitation on amount court may allow where a claim allocated to the fast track settles before trial

44.10

  (1) Where the court—   J–014

    (a) assesses costs in relation to a claim which—

      (i) has been allocated to the fast track; and
      (ii) settles before the start of the trial; and

    (b) is considering the amount of costs to be allowed in respect of a party's advocate for preparing for the trial,

      it may not allow, in respect of those advocate's costs, an amount that exceeds the amount of fast track trial costs which would have been payable in relation to the claim had the trial taken place.

  (2) When deciding the amount to be allowed in respect of the advocate's costs, the court shall have regard to—

    (a) when the claim was settled; and
    (b) when the court was notified that the claim had settled.

  (3) In this rule, "advocate" and "fast track trial costs" have the meanings given to them by Part 46.

(Part 46 sets out the amount of fast track trial costs which may be awarded)

Costs following allocation and re-allocation

44.11

J–015

(1) Any costs orders made before a claim is allocated will not be affected by allocation.

(2) Where—

(a) a claim is allocated to a track; and

(b) the court subsequently re-allocates that claim to a different track, then unless the court orders otherwise, any special rules about costs applying—

(i) to the first track, will apply to the claim up to the date of re-allocation; and

(ii) to the second track, will apply from the date of re-allocation.

(Part 26 deals with the allocation and re-allocation of claims between tracks)

Cases where costs orders deemed to have been made

44.12

J–016

(1) Where a right to costs arises under—

(a) rule 3.7 (defendant's right to costs where claim struck out for non-payment of fees);

(b) rule 36.13(1) (claimant's right to costs where he accepts defendant's Part 36 offer or Part 36 payment);

(c) rule 36.14 (claimant's right to costs where defendant accepts the claimant's Part 36 offer); or

(d) rule 38.6 (defendant's right to costs where claimant discontinues), a costs order will be deemed to have been made on the standard basis.

(2) Interest payable pursuant to section 17 of the Judgments Act 1838[2] or section 74 of the County Courts Act 1984[3] on the costs deemed to have been ordered under paragraph (1) shall begin to run from the date on which the event which gave rise to the entitlement to costs occurred.

Costs-only proceedings

44.12A

(1) This rule sets out a procedure which may be followed where—

(a) the parties to a dispute have reached an agreement on all issues (including which party is to pay the costs) which is made or confirmed in writing; but

(b) they have failed to agree the amount of those costs; and

(c) no proceedings have been started.

(1A) The procedure set out in this rule may be followed if the only proceedings that have been started are proceedings under rule 21.10 or any other proceedings necessitated solely by reason of one or more of the parties being a child or patient.

(Rule 21.10 makes provision for compromise, etc. by or on behalf of a child or patient).

---

[2] 1838 c.110. Section 7 was amended by S.I. 1998/2940.
[3] 1984 c.28. Section 74 was amended by section 2 of the Private International Law Miscellaneous Provisions Act 1995 (c.42).

(2) Either party to the agreement may start proceedings under this rule by issuing a claim form in accordance with Part 8.

(3) The claim form must contain or be accompanied by the agreement or confirmation.

(4) In proceedings to which this rule applies the court—

    (a) may

        (i) make an order for costs; or

        (ii) dismiss the claim; and

    (b) must dismiss the claim if it is opposed.

(4A) in proceedings to which Section 11 of Part 45 applies, the court shall assess the costs in the manner set out in that section.

(5) Rule 48.3 (amount of costs where costs are payable pursuant to a contract) does not apply to claims started under the procedure in this rule. (Rule 7.2 provides that proceedings are started when the court issues a claim form at the request of the claimant)

(Rule 8.1(6) provides that a practice direction may modify the Part 8 procedure)

Special situations

44.13

    (1) Where the court makes an order which does not mention costs—   J–017

        (a) the general rule is that no party is entitled to costs in relation to that order; but

        (b) this does not affect any entitlement of a party to recover costs out of a fund held by him as trustee or personal representative, or pursuant to any lease, mortgage or other security.

    (2) The court hearing an appeal may, unless it dismisses the appeal, make orders about the costs of the proceedings giving rise to the appeal as well as the costs of the appeal.

    (3) Where proceedings are transferred from one court to another, the court to which they are transferred may deal with all the costs, including the costs before the transfer.

    (4) Paragraph 3 is subject to any order of the court which ordered the transfer.

Court's powers in relation to misconduct

44.14   J–018

    (1) The court may make an order under this rule where—

        (a) a party or his legal representative fails to conduct detailed assessment proceedings in accordance with Part 47 or any direction of the court; or

        (b) it appears to the court that the conduct of a party or his legal representative, before or during the proceedings which gave rise to the assessment proceedings, was unreasonable or improper.

    (2) Where paragraph (1) applies, the court may—

        (a) disallow all or part of the costs which are being assessed; or

        (b) order the party at fault or his legal representative to pay costs which he has caused any other party to incur.

    (3) Where—

        (a) the court makes an order under paragraph (2) against a legally represented party; and

(b) the party is not present when the order is made,

the party's solicitor must notify his client in writing of the order no later than 7 days after the solicitor receives notice of the order.

(Other rules about costs can be found—

(a) in Schedule 1, in the following RSC—O.45 (court may order act to be done at the expense of disobedient party); O.47 (writ of fieri facias to enforce payment of costs); and

(b) in Schedule 2, in the following CCR—O.27 (attachment of earnings—judgment creditor's entitlement to costs); O.28 (costs on judgment summons); O.30 (garnishee proceedings—judgment creditor's entitlement to costs); O.49 (costs incurred in making a payment in under section 63 of the Trustee Act 1925 to be assessed by the detailed procedure)).

Providing information about funding arrangements

J–018/1   44.15

(1) A party who seeks to recover an additional liability must provide information about the funding arrangement to the court and to other parties as required by a rule, practice direction or court order.

(2) Where the funding arrangement has changed, and the information a party has previously provided in accordance with paragraph (1) is no longer accurate, that party must file notice of the change and serve it on all other parties within 7 days.

(3) Where paragraph (2) applies, and a party has already filed—

(a) an allocation questionnaire; or
(b) a listing questionnaire,

he must file and serve a new estimate of costs with the notice.
    (The costs practice direction sets out—

- the information to be provided when a party issues or responds to a claim form, files an allocation questionaire, a listing questionnaire, and a claim for costs;
- the meaning of estimate of costs and the information required in it (Rule 44.3B sets out situations where a party will not recover a sum representing any additional liability)

Adjournment where legal representative seeks to challenge disallowance of any amount of percentage increase

J–018/2   44.16

Where—

(a) the court disallows any amount of a legal representative's percentage increase in summary or detailed assessment proceedings; and

(b) the legal representative applies for an order that the disallowed amount should continue to be payable by his client,

the court may adjourn the hearing to allow the legally represented party to be notified of the order sought.
(Regulation 3(2)(b) of the Conditional Fee Agreements Regulations 2000 provides that a conditional fee agreement which provides for a success fee

must state that any amount of a percentage increase disallowed on assessment ceases to be payable unless the court is satisfied that it should continue to be so payable. Regulation 5(2)(b) of the Collective Conditional Fee Agreements Regulations 2000 makes similar provision in relation to collective conditional fee agreements)

Application of costs rules

44.17   J–018/3

This Part and Part 45 (fixed costs), Part 46 (fast track trial costs), Part 47 (procedure for detailed assessment of costs and default provisions) and Part 48 (special cases), do not apply to the assessment of costs in proceedings to the extent that—

(a) section 11 of the Access to Justice Act 1999, and provisions made under that Act, or
(b) regulations made under the Legal Aid Act 1989[9],

make different provision. (The costs practice direction sets out the procedure to be followed where a party was wholly or partially funded by the Legal Services Commission).

---

[9] 1998 c. 34.

Part 45

Fixed Costs

CONTENTS OF THIS PART

Scope of this part

45.1

J–019

(1) This Part sets out the amounts which, unless the court orders otherwise, are to be allowed in respect of solicitors' charges in the cases to which this Part applies.
(The definitions contained in Part 43 are relevant to this Part)

(2) This part applies where—

(a) the only claim is a claim for a specified sum of money where the value of the claim exceeds £25 and—

(i) judgment in default is obtained under rule 12.4(1);

(ii) judgment on admission is obtained under rule 14.4(3);

(iii) judgment on admission on part of the claim is obtained under rule 14.5(6);

(iv) summary judgment is given under Part 24;

(v) the court has made an order to strike out (GL) a defence under rule 3.4(2)(a) as disclosing no reasonable grounds for defending the claim; or

(vi) rule 45.3 applies; or

(b) the only claim is a claim where the court gave a fixed date for the hearing when it issued the claim and judgment is given for the delivery of goods, and the value of the claim exceeds £25; or;

(c) a judgment creditor has taken steps under Parts 70 to 73 to enforce a judgment or order.
(The practice direction supplementing rule 7.9 sets out the types of case where a court may give a fixed date for a hearing when it issues a claim)
(The practice direction supplementing rule 7.9 sets out the types of case where a court may give a fixed date for a hearing when it issues a claim)

(3) Any appropriate court fee will be allowed in addition to the costs set out in this Part.

Amount of fixed commencement costs

45.2

J–020

(1) The claim form may include a claim for fixed commencement costs.

(2) The amount of fixed commencement costs which the claim form may include shall be calculated by reference to the following table (Table 1).

(3) Additional costs may also be claimed in the circumstances specified in Table 3.

(4) The amount claimed, or the value of the goods claimed if specified, in the claim form is to be used for determining the band in the table that applies to the claim.

TABLE 1

FIXED COSTS ON COMMENCEMENT OF A CLAIM

Relevant band	Where the claim form is served by the court or by any method other than personal service by the claimant	Where • the claim form is served personally by the claimant; and • there is only one defendant	Where there is more than one defendant, for each additional defendant personally served at separate addresses by the claimant
Where— • the value of the claim exceeds £25 but does not exceed £500	£50	£60	£15
Where— • the value of the claim exceeds £500 but does not exceed £1,000	£70	£80	£15
Where— • the value of the claim exceeds £1,000 but does not exceed £5,000; or • the only claim is for delivery of goods and no value is specified or stated on the claim form	£80	£90	£15
Where— • the value of the claim exceeds £5,000	£100	£110	£15

When defendant only liable for fixed commencement costs

45.3

J–021   (1) Where—

(a) the only claim is for a specified sum of money; and
(b) the defendant pays the money claimed within 14 days after service of particulars of claim on him, together with the fixed commencement costs stated in the claim form,

the defendant is not liable for any further costs unless the court orders otherwise.

(2) Where—

(a) the claimant gives notice of acceptance of a payment into court in satisfaction of the whole claim;
(b) the only claim is for a specified sum of money; and
(c) the defendant made the payment into court within 14 days after service of the particulars of claim on him, together with the fixed costs stated in the claim form,

the defendant is not liable for any further costs unless the court orders otherwise.

Costs on entry of judgment

J–022   45.4 Where—

(a) the claimant has claimed fixed commencement costs under rule 45.2; and
(b) judgment is entered in the circumstances specified in the table in this rule (Table 2),

the amount to be included in the judgment in respect of the claimant's solicitor's charges is the aggregate of—

(i) the fixed commencement costs; and
(ii) the relevant amount shown in Table 2.

TABLE 2
FIXED COSTS ON ENTRY OF JUDGMENT

	Where the amount of the judgment exceeds £25 but does not exceed £5,000	Where the amount of the judgment exceeds £5,000
Where judgment in default of an acknowledgment of service is entered under rule 12.4(1) (entry of judgment by request on claim for money only)	£22	£30

	Where the amount of the judgment exceeds £25 but does not exceed £5,000	Where the amount of the judgment exceeds £5,000
Where judgment in default of a defence is entered under rule 12.4(1) (entry of judgment by request on claim for money only)	£25	£35
Where judgment is entered under rule 14.4 (judgment on admission), or rule 14.5 (judgment on admission of part of claim) and claimant accepts the defendant's proposal as to the manner of payment	£40	£55
Where judgment is entered under rule 14.4 (judgment on admission), or rule 14.5 (judgment on admission on part of claim) and court decides the date or times of payment	£55	£70
Where summary judgment is given under Part 24 or the court strikes out a defence under rule 3.4(2)(a), in either case, on application by a party	£175	£210
Where judgment is given on a claim for delivery of goods under a regulated agreement within the meaning of the Consumer Credit Act 1974([59]) and no other entry in this table applies	£60	£85

Miscellaneous fixed costs

45.5 The table in this rule (Table 3) shows the amount to be allowed in respect of solicitor's charges in the circumstances mentioned. **J–023**

491

TABLE 3
MISCELLANEOUS FIXED COSTS

For service by a party of any document required to be served personally including preparing and copying a certificate of service for each individual served	£15
Where service by an alternative method is permitted by an order under rule 6.8 for each individual served	£25
Where a document is served out of the jurisdiction— (a) in Scotland, Northern Ireland, the Isle of Man or the Channel Islands;	£65
(b) In any other place	£75

(Other rules which provide for situations where fixed costs may be allowed can be found in Schedule 1 in RSC Order 62 and in Schedule 2 in CCR Order 38, Appendix B)

Fixed enforcement costs

45.6 The table in this rule (Table 4) shows the amount to be allowed in respect of solicitors' costs in the circumstances mentioned. The amounts shown in Table 3 are to be allowed in addition, if applicable.

TABLE 4 *FIXED ENFORCEMENT COSTS*

For an application under rule 70.5(4) that an award may be enforced as if payable under a court order, where the amount outstanding under the award:

exceeds £25 but does not exceed £250	£30.75
exceeds £250 but does not exceed £600	£41.00
exceeds £600 but does not exceed £2,000	£69.50
exceeds £2,000	£75.50

On attendance to question a judgment debtor (or officer of a company or other corporation) who has been ordered to attend court under rule 71.2 where the questioning takes place before a court officer, including attendance by a responsible representative of the solicitor:	for each half-hour or part, £15.00

(When the questioning takes place before a judge, he may summarily assess any costs allowed.)

On the making of a final third party debt order under rule 72.8(6)(a) or an order for the payment to the judgment creditor of money in court under rule 72.10(1)(b):	
if the amount recovered is less than £150	one-half of the amount recovered
otherwise	£98.50
On the making of a final charging order under rule 73.8(2)(a):	£110.00

The court may also allow reasonable disbursements in respect of search fees and the registration of the order.

II ROAD TRAFFIC ACCIDENTS—FIXED RECOVERABLE COSTS IN COSTS-ONLY PROCEEDINGS

Scope and interpretation

45.7   J–024

(1) This Section sets out the costs which are to be allowed in costs-only proceedings in cases to which this Section applies.
(Costs-only proceedings are issued using the procedure set out in rule 44.12A)
(2) This Section applies where—

(a) the dispute arises from a road traffic accident;
(b) the agreed damages include damages in respect of personal injury, damage to property, or both;
(c) the total value of the agreed damages does not exceed £10,000; and
(d) if a claim had been issued for the amount of the agreed damages, the small claims track would not have been the normal track for that claim.

(3) This Section does not apply where the claimant is a litigant in person.
(Rule 2.3 defines 'personal injuries' as including any disease and any impairment of a person's physical or mental condition)
(Rule 26.6 provides for when the small claims track is the normal track)

493

(4) In this Section—

(a) 'road traffic accident' means an accident resulting in bodily injury to any person or damage to property caused by, or arising out of, the use of a motor vehicle on a road or other public place in England and Wales;

(b) 'motor vehicle' means a mechanically propelled vehicle intended for use on roads; and

(c) 'road' means any highway and any other road to which the public has access and includes bridges over which a road passes.

Application of fixed recoverable costs

J–025 45.8 Subject to rule 45.12, the only costs which are to be allowed are—

(a) fixed recoverable costs calculated in accordance with rule 45.9;
(b) disbursements allowed in accordance with rule 45.10; and
(c) a success fee allowed in accordance with rule 45.11.

(Rule 45.12 provides for where a party issues a claim for more than the fixed recoverable costs)

Amount of fixed recoverable costs

J–026 45.9

(1) Subject to paragraphs (2) and (3), the amount of fixed recoverable costs is the total of—

(a) £800;
(b) 20% of the damages agreed up to £5,000; and
(c) 15% of the damages agreed between £5,000 and £10,000.

(2) Where the claimant—

(a) lives or works in an area set out in the relevant practice direction; and
(b) instructs a solicitor or firm of solicitors who practise in that area,

the fixed recoverable costs shall include, in addition to the costs specified in paragraph (1), an amount equal to 12.5% of the costs allowable under that paragraph.

(3) Where appropriate, value added tax (VAT) may be recovered in addition to the amount of fixed recoverable costs and any reference in this Section to fixed recoverable costs is a reference to those costs net of any such VAT.

Disbursements

J–027 45.10

(1) The court—

(a) may allow a claim for a disbursement of a type mentioned in paragraph (2); but
(b) must not allow a claim for any other type of disbursement.

(2) The disbursements referred to in paragraph (1) are—

    (a) the cost of obtaining—

        (i) medical records;

        (ii) a medical report;

        (iii) a police report;

        (iv) an engineer's report; or

        (v) a search of the records of the Driver Vehicle Licensing Authority;

    (b) the amount of an insurance premium; or, where a membership organisation undertakes to meet liabilities incurred to pay the costs of other parties to proceedings, a sum not exceeding such additional amount of costs as would be allowed under section 30 in respect of provision made against the risk of having to meet such liabilities;

('membership organisation' is defined in rule 43.2(1)(n))

    (c) where they are necessarily incurred by reason of one or more of the claimants being a child or patient as defined in Part 21—

        (i) fees payable for instructing counsel; or

        (ii) court fees payable on an application to the court;

    (d) any other disbursement that has arisen due to a particular feature of the dispute.

('insurance premium' is defined in rule 43.2)

Success fee

45.11   J–028

(1) A claimant may recover a success fee if he has entered into a funding arrangement of a type specified in rule 43.2(k)(i).

(2) The amount of the success fee shall be 12.5% of the fixed recoverable costs calculated in accordance with rule 45.9(1), disregarding any additional amount which may be included in the fixed recoverable costs by virtue of rule 45.9(2).

(Rule 43.2(k)(i) defines as funding arrangement as including a conditional fee agreement or collective conditional fee agreement which provides for a success fee)

Claims for an amount of costs exceeding fixed recoverable costs

45.12   J–029

(1) The court will entertain a claim for an amount of costs (excluding any success fee or disbursements) greater than the fixed recoverable costs but only if it considers that there are exceptional circumstances making it appropriate to do so.

(2) If the court considers such a claim appropriate, it may—

    (a) assess the costs; or

    (b) make an order for the costs to be assessed.

(3) If the court does not consider the claim appropriate, it must make an order for fixed recoverable costs only.

Failure to achieve costs greater than fixed recoverable costs

J–030   45.13

(1) This rule applies where—

(a) costs are assessed in accordance with rule 45.12(2); and
(b) the court assesses the costs (excluding any VAT) as being an amount which is less than 20% greater than the amount of the fixed recoverable costs.

(2) The court must order the defendant to pay to the claimant the lesser of—

(a) the fixed recoverable costs; and
(b) the assessed costs.

Costs of the costs-only proceedings

J–031   45.14
Where—

(a) the court makes an order for fixed recoverable costs in accordance with rule 45.12(3); or
(b) rule 45.13 applies,

the court must—

(i) make no award for the payment of the claimant's costs in bringing the proceedings under rule 44.12A; and
(ii) order that the claimant pay the defendant's costs of defending those proceedings.

III FIXED PERCENTAGE INCREASE IN ROAD TRAFFIC ACCIDENT CLAIMS

Scope and interpretation

J–032   45.15

(1) This Section sets out the percentage increase which is to be allowed in the cases to which this Section applies.
(Rule 43.2(1)(l) defines 'percentage increase' as the percentage by which the amount of a legal representative's fee can be increased in accordance with a conditional fee agreement which provides for a success fee)
(2) This Section applies where—

(a) the dispute arises from a road traffic accident; and
(b) the claimant has entered into a funding arrangement of a type specified in rule 43.2(k)(i).

(Rule 43.2(k)(i) defines a funding arrangement as including an arrangement where a person has entered into a conditional fee agreement or collective conditional fee agreement which provides for a success fee).

(3) This Section does not apply if the proceedings are costs only proceedings to which Section II of this Part applies.

(4) This Section does not apply—

    (a) to a claim which has been allocated to the small claims track;

    (b) to a claim not allocated to a track, but for which the small claims track is the normal track; or

    (c) where the road traffic accident which gave rise to the dispute occurred before 6th October 2003.

(5) The definitions in rule 45.7(4) apply to this Section as they apply to Section II.

(6) In this Section—

    (a) a reference to 'fees' is a reference to fees for work done under a conditional fee agreement or collective conditional fee agreement;

    (b) a reference to 'trial' is a reference to the final contested hearing or to the contested hearing of any issue ordered to be tried separately;

    (c) a reference to a claim concluding at trial is a reference to a claim concluding by settlement after the trial has commenced or by judgment; and

    (d) 'trial period' means a period of time fixed by the court within which the trial is to take place and where the court fixes more than one such period in relation to a claim, means the most recent period to be fixed.

Percentage increase of solicitors' fees

45.16 Subject to rule 45.18, the percentage increase which is to be allowed in relation to solicitors' fees is—   **J–033**

    (a) 100% where the claim concludes at trial; or

    (b) 12.5% where—

        (i) the claim concludes before a trial has commenced; or

        (ii) the dispute is settled before a claim is issued.

Percentage increase of counsel's fees

45.17   **J–034**

(1) Subject to rule 45.18, the percentage increase which is to be allowed in relation to counsel's fees is—

    (a) 100% where the claim concludes at trial;

    (b) if the claim has been allocated to the fast track—

        (i) 50% if the claim concludes 14 days or less before the date fixed for the commencement of the trial; or

        (ii) 12.5% if the claim concludes more than 14 days before the date fixed for the commencement of the trial or before any such date has been fixed;

    (c) if the claim has been allocated to the multi-track—

        (i) 75% if the claim concludes 21 days or less before the date fixed for the commencement of the trial; or

        (ii) 12.5% if the claim concludes more than 21 days before the date fixed for the commencement of the trial or before any such date has been fixed;

(d) 12.5% where—

    (i) the claim has been issued but concludes before it has been allocated to a track; or

    (ii) in relation to costs-only proceedings, the dispute is settled before a claim is issued.

(2) Where a trial period has been fixed, if—

    (a) the claim concludes before the first day of that period; and

    (b) no trial date has been fixed within that period before the claim concludes,

the first day of that period is treated as the date fixed for the commencement of the trial for the purposes of paragraph (1).

(3) Where a trial period has been fixed, if

    (a) the claim concludes before the first day of that period; but

    (b) before the claim concludes, a trial date had been fixed within that period,

the trial date is the date fixed for the commencement of the trial for the purposes of paragraph (1).

(4) Where a trial period has been fixed and the claim concludes—

    (a) on or after the first day of that period; but

    (b) before commencement of the trial,

the percentage increase in paragraph (1)(b)(i) or (1)(c)(i) shall apply as appropriate, whether or not a trial date has been fixed within that period.

(5) For the purposes of this rule, in calculating the periods of time, the day fixed for the commencement of the trial (or the first day of the trial period, where appropriate) is not included.

Application for an alternative percentage increase where the fixed increase is 12.5%

J–035   45.18

(1) This rule applies where the percentage increase to be allowed—

    (a) in relation to solicitors' fees under the provisions of rule 45.16; or

    (b) in relation to counsel's fees under rule 45.17, is 12.5%.

(2) A party may apply for a percentage increase greater or less than that amount if—

    (a) the parties agree damages of an amount greater than £500,000 or the court awards damages of an amount greater than £500,000; or

    (b) the court awards damages of £500,000 or less but would have awarded damages greater than £500,000 if it had not made a finding of contributory negligence; or

    (c) the parties agree damages of £500,000 or less and it is reasonable to expect that, but for any finding of contributory negligence, the court would have awarded damages greater than £500,000.

(3) In paragraph (2), a reference to a lump sum of damages includes a reference to periodical payments of equivalent value.

(4) If the court is satisfied that the circumstances set out in paragraph (2) apply it must—

(a) assess the percentage increase; or

(b) make an order for the percentage increase to be assessed.

Assessment of alternative percentage increase

45.19   J–036

(1) This rule applies where the percentage increase of fees is assessed under rule 45.18(4).

(2) If the percentage increase is assessed as greater than 20% or less than 7.5%, the percentage increase to be allowed shall be that assessed by the court.

(3) If the percentage increase is assessed as no greater than 20% and no less than 7.5% —

(a) the percentage increase to be allowed shall be 12.5%; and

(b) the costs of the application and assessment shall be paid by the applicant.

IV FIXED PERCENTAGE INCREASE IN EMPLOYERS LIABILITY CLAIMS

Scope and interpretation

45.20   J–037

(1) Subject to paragraph (2), this Section applies where —

(a) the dispute is between an employee and his employer arising from a bodily injury sustained by the employee in the course of his employment; and

(b) the claimant has entered into a funding arrangement of a type specified in rule 43.2(1)(k)(i).

(2) This Section does not apply —

(a) where the dispute —

(i) relates to a disease;

(ii) relates to an injury sustained before 1st October 2004; or

(iii) arises from a road traffic accident (as defined in rule 45.7(4)(a)); or

(b) to a claim —

(i) which has been allocated to the small claims track; or

(ii) not allocated to a track, but for which the small claims track is the normal track.

(3) For the purposes of this Section —

(a) 'employee' has the meaning given to it by section 2(1) of the Employers' Liability (Compulsory Insurance) Act 1969(2); and

(b) a reference to 'fees' is a reference to fees for work done under a conditional fee agreement or collective conditional fee agreement.

Percentage increase of solicitors' and counsel's fees

J–038   45.21 In the cases to which this Section applies, subject to rule 45.22 the percentage increase which is to be allowed in relation to solicitors' and counsel's fees is to be determined in accordance with rules 45.16 and 45.17, subject to the modifications that—

    (a) the percentage increase which is to be allowed in relation to solicitors' fees under rule 45.16(b) is—

        (i) 27.5% if a membership organisation has undertaken to meet the claimant's liabilities for legal costs in accordance with section 30 of the Access to Justice Act 1999; and

        (ii) 25% in any other case; and

    (b) the percentage increase which is to be allowed in relation to counsel's fees under rule 45.17(1)(b)(ii), (1)(c)(ii) or (1)(d) is 25%.

('membership organisation' is defined in rule 43.2(1)(n))

Alternative percentage increase

J–039   45.22

    (1) In the cases to which this Section applies, rule 45.18(2)–(4) applies where—

        (a) the percentage increase of solicitors' fees to be allowed in accordance with rule 45.21 is 25% or 27.5%; or

        (b) the percentage increase of counsel's fees to be allowed is 25%.

    (2) Where the percentage increase of fees is assessed by the court under rule 45.18(4) as applied by paragraph (1) above—

        (a) if the percentage increase is assessed as greater than 40% or less than 15%, the percentage increase to be allowed shall be that assessed by the court; and

        (b) if the percentage increase is assessed as no greater than 40% and no less than 15%—

            (i) the percentage increase to be allowed shall be 25% or 27.5% (as the case may be); and

            (ii) the costs of the application and assessment shall be paid by the applicant.

Part 46

Fast track trial costs

CONTENTS OF THIS PART

Scope of this part

46.1

   (1) This Part deals with the amount of costs which the court may award as the   **J–040**
       costs of an advocate for preparing for and appearing at the trial of a claim
       in the fast track (referred to in this rule as "fast track trial costs").
   (2) For the purposes of this Part—

      (a) "advocate" means a person exercising a right of audience as a
          representative of, or on behalf of, a party;
      (b) "fast track trial costs" means the costs of a party's advocate for
          preparing for and appearing at the trial, but does not include—

         (i) any other disbursements; or
         (ii) any value added tax payable on the fees of a party's advocate;
             and

      (c) "trial" includes a hearing where the court decides an amount of money
          or the value of goods following a judgment under Part 12 (default
          judgment) or Part 14 (admissions) but does not include—

         (i) the hearing of an application for summary judgment under Part
             24; or
         (ii) the court's approval of a settlement or other compromise under
             rule 21.10.

(Part 21 deals with claims made by or on behalf of, or against, children and patients)

Amount of fast track trial costs

46.2

   (1) The following table shows the amount of fast track trial costs which the   **J–041**
       court may award (whether by summary or detailed assessment).

VALUE OF THE CLAIM	AMOUNT OF FAST TRACK TRIAL COSTS WHICH THE COURT MAY AWARD
Up to £3,000	£350
More than £3,000 but not more than £10,000	£500
More than £10,000	£750

(2) The court may not award more or less than the amount shown in the table except where—

(a) it decides not to award any fast track trial costs; or
(b) rule 46.3 applies,

but the court may apportion the amount awarded between the parties to reflect their respective degrees of success on the issues at trial.

(3) Where the only claim is for the payment of money—

(a) for the purpose of quantifying fast track trial costs awarded to a claimant, the value of the claim is the total amount of the judgment excluding—

(i) interest and costs; and
(ii) any reduction made for contributory negligence.

(b) for the purpose of the quantifying fast track trial costs awarded to a defendant, the value of the claim is—

(i) the amount specified in the claim form (excluding interest and costs);
(ii) if no amount is specified, the maximum amount which the claimant reasonably expected to recover according to the statement of value included in the claim form under rule 16.3; or
(iii) more than £10,000, if the claim form states that the claimant cannot reasonably say how much he expects to recover.

(4) Where the claim is only for a remedy other than the payment of money the value of the claim is deemed to be more than £3,000 but not more than £10,000, unless the court orders otherwise.

(5) Where the claim includes both a claim for the payment of money and for a remedy other than the payment of money, the value of the claim is deemed to be the higher of—

(a) the value of the money claim decided in accordance with paragraph (3); or
(b) the deemed value of the other remedy decided in accordance with paragraph (4),

unless the court orders otherwise.

(6) Where—

(a) a defendant has made a counterclaim against the claimant;
(b) the counterclaim has a higher value than the claim; and

(c) the claimant succeeds at trial both on his claim and the counter-claim,

for the purpose of quantifying fast track trial costs awarded to the claimant, the value of the claim is the value of the defendant's counter-claim calculated in accordance with this rule.

(Rule 20.4 sets out how a defendant may make a counterclaim)

Power to award more or less than the amount of fast track trial costs

46.3   J–042

(1) This rule sets out when a court may award—

(a) an additional amount to the amount of fast track trial costs shown in the table in rule 46.2(1); and
(b) less than those amounts.

(2) If—

(a) in addition to the advocate, a party's legal representative attends the trial;
(b) the court considers that it was necessary for a legal representative to attend to assist the advocate; and
(c) the court awards fast track trial costs to that party,

the court may award an additional £250 in respect of the legal representa-tive's attendance at the trial.

(Legal representative is defined in rule 2.3)
(2A) The court may in addition award a sum representing an additional liabil-ity.
(The requirements to provide information about a funding arrangement where a party wishes to recover any additional liability under a funding arrangement are set out in the costs practice direction)
("Additional liability" is defined in rule 43.2)

(3) If the court considers that it is necessary to direct a separate trial of an issue then the court may award an additional amount in respect of the separate trial but that amount is limited in accordance with paragraph (4) of this rule.
(4) The additional amount the court may award under paragraph 3 must not exceed two-thirds of the amount payable for that claim, subject to a minimum award of £350.
(5) Where the party to whom fast track trial costs are to be awarded is a litigant in person, the court will award—

(a) if the litigant in person can prove financial loss, two-thirds of the amount that would otherwise be awarded; or
(b) if the litigant in person fails to prove financial loss, an amount in respect of the time spent reasonably doing the work at the rate specified in the costs practice direction.

(6) Where a defendant has made a counterclaim against the claimant, and—

(a) the claimant has succeeded on his claim; and

(b) the defendant has succeeded on his counterclaim,

the court will quantify the amount of the award of fast track trial costs to which—

    (i) but for the counterclaim, the claimant would be entitled for succeeding on his claim; and

    (ii) but for the claim, the defendant would be entitled for succeeding on his counterclaim,

and make one award of the difference, if any, to the party entitled to the higher award of costs.

(7) Where the court considers that the party to whom fast track trial costs are to be awarded has behaved unreasonably or improperly during the trial, it may award that party an amount less than would otherwise be payable for that claim, as it considers appropriate.

(8) Where the court considers that the party who is to pay the fast track trial costs has behaved improperly during the trial the court may award such additional amount to the other party as it considers appropriate.

Fast track trial costs where there is more than one claimant or defendant

46.4

J–043

(1) Where the same advocate is acting for more than one party—

    (a) the court may make only one award in respect of fast track trial costs payable to that advocate; and

    (b) the parties for whom the advocate is acting are jointly entitled to any fast track trial cost awarded by the court.

(2) Where—

    (a) the same advocate is acting for more than one claimant; and

    (b) each claimant has a separate claim against the defendant,

the value of the claim, for the purpose of quantifying the award in respect of fast track trial costs is to be ascertained in accordance with paragraph (3).

(3) The value of the claim in the circumstances mentioned in paragraph (2) is—

    (a) where the only claim of each claimant is for the payment of money—

        (i) if the award of fast track trial costs is in favour of the claimants, the total amount of the judgment made in favour of all the claimants jointly represented; or

        (ii) if the award is in favour of the defendant, the total amount claimed by the claimants,

    and in either case, quantified in accordance with rule 46.2(3);

    (b) where the only claim of each claimant is for a remedy other than the payment of money, deemed to be more than £3,000 but not more than £10,000; and

    (c) where claims of the claimants include both a claim for the payment of money and for a remedy other than the payment of money, deemed to be—

        (i) more than £3,000 but not more than £10,000; or

      (ii) if greater, the value of the money claims calculated in accordance with sub paragraph (a) above.

(4) Where—

(a) there is more than one defendant; and
(b) any or all of the defendants are separately represented,
the court may award fast track trial costs to each party who is separately represented.

(5) Where—

(a) there is more than one claimant; and
(b) a single defendant,
the court may make only one award to the defendant of fast track trial costs, for which the claimants are jointly and severally liable;(ᵍˡ;).

(6) For the purpose of quantifying the fast track trial costs awarded to the single defendant under paragraph (5), the value of the claim is to be calculated in accordance with paragraph (3) of this rule.

Part 47

Procedure for Detailed Assessment of Costs and Default Provisions

CONTENTS OF THIS PART

(The definitions contained in Part 43 are relevant to this Part)

I GENERAL RULES ABOUT DETAILED ASSESSMENT

Time when detailed assessment may be carried out

47.1 The general rule is that the costs of any proceedings or any part of the proceedings are not to be assessed by the detailed procedure until the conclusion of the proceedings but the court may order them to be assessed immediately.   **J–044**

(The costs practice direction gives further guidance about when proceedings are concluded for the purpose of this rule)

No stay of detailed assessment where there is an appeal

47.2 Detailed assessment is not stayed pending an appeal unless the court so orders.   **J–045**

Powers of an authorised court officer

47.3

(1) An authorised court officer has all the powers of the court when making   **J–046**
a detailed assessment, except—

(a) power to make a wasted costs order as defined in rule 48.7;
(b) power to make an order under—

(i) rule 44.14 (powers in relation to misconduct);

507

(ii) rule 47.8 (sanction for delay in commencing detailed assessment proceedings);

(iii) paragraph (2) (objection to detailed assessment by authorised court officer); and

(c) power to make a detailed assessment of costs payable to a solicitor by his client, unless the costs are being assessed under rule 48.5 (costs where money is payable to a child or patient).

(2) Where a party objects to the detailed assessment of costs being made by an authorised court officer, the court may order it to be made by a costs judge or a district judge.

(The costs practice direction sets out the relevant procedure)

Venue for detailed assessment proceedings

47.4

J–047

(1) All applications and requests in detailed assessment proceedings must be made to or filed at the appropriate office.

(The costs practice direction sets out the meaning of "appropriate office" in any particular case)

(2) The court may direct that the appropriate office is to be the Supreme Court Costs Office.

(3) A county court may direct that another county court is to be the appropriate office.

(4) A direction under paragraph (3) may be made without proceedings being transferred to that court.

(Rule 30.2 makes provision for any county court to transfer the proceedings to another county court for detailed assessment of costs)

II COSTS PAYABLE BY ONE PARTY TO ANOTHER —COMMENCEMENT OF DETAILED ASSESSMENT PROCEEDINGS

Application of this section

J–048

47.5 This section of Part 47 applies where a costs officer is to make a detailed assessment of costs which are payable by one party to another.

Commencement of detailed assessment proceedings

47.6

J–049

(1) Detailed assessment proceedings are commenced by the receiving party serving on the paying party—

(a) notice of commencement in the relevant practice form; and

(b) a copy of the bill of costs.

(Rule 47.7 sets out the period for commencing detailed assessment proceedings)

(2) The receiving party must also serve a copy of the notice of commencement and the bill on any other relevant persons specified in the costs practice direction.

(3) A person on whom a copy of the notice of commencement is served under paragraph (2) is a party to the detailed assessment proceedings (in addition to the paying party and the receiving party).

(The costs practice direction deals with—

- other documents which the party must file when he requests detailed assessment;
- the court's powers where it considers that a hearing may be necessary;
- the form of a bill; and
- the length of notice which will be given if a hearing date is fixed)

Period for commencing detailed assessment proceedings

47.7 The following table shows the period for commencing detailed assessment proceedings. J–050

SOURCE OF RIGHT TO DETAILED ASSESSMENT	TIME BY WHICH DETAILED ASSESSMENT PROCEEDINGS MUST BE COMMENCED
Judgment, direction, order, award or other determination	3 months after the date of the judgment etc. Where detailed assessment is stayed pending an appeal, 3 months after the date of the order lifting the stay
Discontinuance under Part 38	3 months after the date of service of notice of discontinuance under rule 38.3; or 3 months after the date of the dismissal of application to set the notice of discontinuance aside under rule 38.4
Acceptance of an offer to settle or a payment into court under Part 36	3 months after the date when the right to costs arose

Sanction for delay in commencing detailed assessment proceedings

47.8 J–051

(1) Where the receiving party fails to commence detailed assessment proceedings within the period specified—

(a) in rule 47.7; or
(b) by any direction of the court,

the paying party may apply for an order requiring the receiving party to commence detailed assessment proceedings within such time as the court may specify.

(2) On an application under paragraph (1), the court may direct that, unless the receiving party commences detailed assessment proceedings within the time specified by the court, all or part of the costs to which the receiving party would otherwise be entitled will be disallowed.

(3) If—

(a) the paying party has not made an application in accordance with paragraph (1); and

(b) the receiving party commences the proceedings later than the period specified in rule 47.7,

the court may disallow all or part of the interest otherwise payable to the receiving party under—

(i) section 17 of the Judgments Act 1838[1]; or

(ii) section 74 of the County Courts Act 1984[2],

but must not impose any other sanction except in accordance with rule 44.14 (powers in relation to misconduct).

(4) Where the costs to be assessed in a detailed assessment are payable out of the Community Legal Service Fund, this rule applies as if the receiving party were the solicitor to whom the costs are payable and the paying party were the Legal Services Commission.

Points of dispute and consequence of not serving

47.9

J–052

(1) The paying party and any other party to the detailed assessment proceedings may dispute any item in the bill of costs by serving points of dispute on—

(a) the receiving party; and

(b) every other party to the detailed assessment proceedings.

(2) The period for serving points of dispute is 21 days after the date of service of the notice of commencement.

(3) If a party serves points of dispute after the period set out in paragraph (2), he may not be heard further in the detailed assessment proceedings unless the court gives permission.

(The costs practice direction sets out requirements about the form of points of dispute)

(4) The receiving party may file a request for a default costs certificate if—

(a) the period set out in rule 47.9(2) for serving points of dispute has expired; and

(b) he has not been served with any points of dispute.

(5) If any party (including the paying party) serves points of dispute before the issue of a default costs certificate the court may not issue the default costs certificate.

---

[1] 1838 c. 110. S.17 was amended by SI 1998/2940.

[2] 1984 c. 28. S.74 was amended by s.2 of the Private International Law (Miscellaneous Provisions) Act 1995 (c. 42).

(Section IV of this Part sets out the procedure to be followed after points of dispute have been filed)

Procedure where costs are agreed

47.10

    (1) the paying party and the receiving party agree the amount of costs, either party may apply for a costs certificate (either interim or final) in the amount agreed.   J–053

(Rule 47.15 and rule 47.16 contain further provisions about interim and final costs certificates respectively)

    (2) An application for a certificate under paragraph (1) must be made to the court which would be the venue for detailed assessment proceedings under rule 47.4.

        (a) where the right to detailed assessment arises from a judgment or court order—

           (i) to the court where the judgment or order was given or made, if the proceedings have not been transferred since then; or

           (ii) to the court to which the proceedings have been transferred; and

        (b) in any other case, to the court which would be the venue for detailed assessment proceedings under rule 47.4.

III COSTS PAYABLE BY ONE PARTY TO ANOTHER —DEFAULT PROVISIONS

Default costs certificate

47.11

    (1) Where the receiving party is permitted by rule 47.9 to obtain a default costs certificate, he does so by filing a request in the relevant practice form.   J–054

(The costs practice direction deals with the procedure by which the receiving party may obtain a default costs certificate)

    (2) A default costs certificate will include an order to pay the costs to which it relates.

Setting aside default costs certificate

47.12

    (1) The court must set aside a default costs certificate if the receiving party was not entitled to it.   J–055

    (2) In any other case, the court may set aside or vary a default costs certificate if it appears to the court that there is some good reason why the detailed assessment proceedings should continue.

(3) Where—

(a) the receiving party has purported to serve the notice of commencement on the paying party;

(b) a default costs certificate has been issued; and

(c) the receiving party subsequently discovers that the notice of commencement did not reach the paying party at least 21 days before the default costs certificate was issued,

the receiving party must—

(i) file a request for the default costs certificate to be set aside; or

(ii) apply to the court for directions.

(4) Where paragraph (3) applies, the receiving party may take no further step in—

(a) the detailed assessment proceedings; or

(b) the enforcement of the default costs certificate,

until the certificate has been set aside or the court has given directions.

(The costs practice direction contains further details about the procedure for setting aside a default costs certificate and the matters which the court must take into account)

IV COSTS PAYABLE BY ONE PARTY TO ANOTHER —PROCEDURE WHERE POINTS OF DISPUTE ARE SERVED

Optional reply

J–056 **47.13**

(1) Where any party to the detailed assessment proceedings serves points of dispute, the receiving party may serve a reply on the other parties to the assessment proceedings.

(2) He may do so within 21 days after service on him of the points of dispute to which his reply relates.

(The costs practice direction sets out the meaning of reply)

Detailed assessment hearing

47.14

J–057

(1) Where points of dispute are served in accordance with this Part, the receiving party must file a request for a detailed assessment hearing.

(2) He must file the request within 3 months of the expiry of the period for commencing detailed assessment proceedings as specified—

(a) in rule 47.7; or

(b) by any direction of the court.

(3) Where the receiving party fails to file a request in accordance with paragraph (2), the paying party may apply for an order requiring the

receiving party to file the request within such time as the court may specify.

(4) On an application under paragraph (3), the court may direct that, unless the receiving party requests a detailed assessment hearing within the time specified by the court, all or part of the costs to which the receiving party would otherwise be entitled will be disallowed.

(5) If—

(a) the paying party has not made an application in accordance with paragraph (3); and

(b) the receiving party files a request for a detailed assessment hearing later than the period specified in paragraph (2),

the court may disallow all or part of the interest otherwise payable to the receiving party under—

(i) section 17 of the Judgments Act 1838[3] or

(ii) section 74 of the County Courts Act 1984[4],

but must not impose any other sanction except in accordance with rule 44.14 (powers in relation to misconduct).

(6) No person other than—

(a) the receiving party;

(b) the paying party; and

(c) any party who has served points of dispute under rule 47.9,

may be heard at the detailed assessment hearing unless the court gives permission.

(7) Only items specified in the points of dispute may be raised at the hearing, unless the court gives permission.

(The costs practice direction specifies other documents which must be filed with the request for hearing and the length of notice which the court will give when it fixes a hearing date.)

V INTERIM COSTS CERTIFICATE AND FINAL COSTS CERTIFICATE

Power to issue an interim certificate

47.15

(1) The court may at any time after the receiving party has filed a request for a detailed assessment hearing—   J–058

(a) issue an interim costs certificate for such sums as it considers appropriate;

(b) amend or cancel an interim certificate.

(2) An interim certificate will include an order to pay the costs to which it relates, unless the court orders otherwise.

---

[3] 1838 c. 110. S.17 was amended by SI 1998/2940.

[4] 1984 c. 28. S.74 was amended by s.2 of the Private International Law (Miscellaneous Provisions) Act 1995 (c. 42).

(3) The court may order the costs certified in an interim certificate to be paid into court.

Final costs certificate

47.16

J–059

(1) In this rule a completed bill means a bill calculated to show the amount due following the detailed assessment of the costs.

(2) The period for filing the completed bill is 14 days after the end of the detailed assessment hearing.

(3) When a completed bill is filed the court will issue a final costs certificate and serve it on the parties to the detailed assessment proceedings.

(4) Paragraph (3) is subject to any order made by the court that a certificate is not to be issued until other costs have been paid.

(5) A final costs certificate will include an order to pay the costs to which it relates, unless the court orders otherwise.

(The costs practice direction deals with the form of a final costs certificate)

VI DETAILED ASSESSMENT PROCEDURE FOR COSTS OF AN ASSISTED PERSON WHERE COSTS ARE PAYABLE OUT OF THE LEGAL AID FUND

Detailed assessment procedure for costs of an assisted person where costs are payable out of the legal aid fund

47.17

J–060

(1) Where the court is to assess costs of an assisted person which are payable out of the legal aid fund, the assisted person's solicitor may commence detailed assessment proceedings by filing a request in the relevant practice form.

(2) A request under paragraph (1) must be filed within 3 months after the date when the right to detailed assessment arose.

(3) The solicitor must also serve a copy of the request for detailed assessment on the LSC funded client or the assisted person, if notice of that person's interest has been given to the court in accordance with Community Legal Service or legal aid regulations.

(4) Where the solicitor has certified that the assisted person wishes to attend an assessment hearing, the court will, on receipt of the request for assessment, fix a date for the assessment hearing.

(5) Where paragraph (3) does not apply, the court will, on receipt of the request for assessment provisionally assess the costs without the attendance of the solicitor, unless it considers that a hearing is necessary.

(6) After the court has provisionally assessed the bill, it will return the bill to the solicitor.

(7) The court will fix a date for an assessment hearing if the solicitor informs the court, within 14 days after he receives the provisionally assessed bill, that he wants the court to hold such a hearing.

Detailed assessment procedure where costs are payable out of a fund other than the community legal service fund

47.17A J–061

(1) Where the court is to assess costs which are payable out of a fund other than the Community Legal Service Fund, the receiving party may commence detailed assessment proceedings by filing a request in the relevant practice form.

(2) A request under paragraph (1) must be filed within 3 months after the date when the right to detailed assessment arose.

(3) The court may direct that the party seeking assessment serve a copy of the request on any person who has a financial interest in the outcome of the assessment.

(4) The court will, on receipt of the request for assessment, provisionally assess the costs without the attendance of the receiving party, unless it considers that a hearing is necessary.

(5) After the court has provisionally assessed the bill, it will return the bill to the receiving party.

(6) The court will fix a date for an assessment hearing if the party informs the court, within 14 days after he receives the provisionally assessed bill, that he wants the court to hold such a hearing.

VII COSTS OF DETAILED ASSESSMENT PROCEEDINGS

Liability for costs of detailed assessment proceedings

47.18

(1) The receiving party is entitled to his costs of the detailed assessment proceedings except where— J–062

   (a) the provisions of any Act, any of these Rules or any relevant practice direction provide otherwise; or

   (b) the court makes some other order in relation to all or part of the costs of the detailed assessment proceedings.

(2) In deciding whether to make some other order, the court must have regard to all the circumstances, including—

   (a) the conduct of all the parties;

   (b) the amount, if any, by which the bill of costs has been reduced; and

   (c) whether it was reasonable for a party to claim the costs of a particular item or to dispute that item.

Offers to settle without prejudice save as to costs of the detailed assessment proceedings

47.19

(1) Where— J–063

   (a) a party (whether the paying party or the receiving party) makes a written offer to settle the costs of the proceedings which gave rise to the assessment proceedings; and

(b) the offer is expressed to be without prejudice (GL) save as to the costs of the detailed assessment proceedings,

the court will take the offer into account in deciding who should pay the costs of those proceedings.

(2) The fact of the offer must not be communicated to the costs officer until the question of costs of the detailed assessment proceedings falls to be decided.

(The costs practice direction provides that rule 47.19 does not apply where the receiving party is a LSC funded client or an assisted person)

VIII APPEALS FROM AUTHORISED COURT OFFICERS IN DETAILED ASSESSMENT PROCEEDINGS

Right to appeal

J–064   47.20

(1) Any party to detailed assessment proceedings may appeal against a decision of an authorised court officer in those proceedings.
(2) For the purposes of this Section, a LSC funded client or an assisted person is not a party to detailed assessment proceedings.

(Part 52 sets out general rules about appeals)

Court to hear appeal

J–065   47.21 An appeal against a decision of an authorised court officer is to a costs judge or a district judge of the High Court.

Appeal procedure

J–066   47.22

(1) The appellant must file an appeal notice within 14 days after the date of the decision he wishes to appeal against.
(2) On receipt of the appeal notice, the court will—

(a) serve a copy of the notice on the parties to the detailed assessment proceedings; and
(b) give notice of the appeal hearing to those parties.

Powers of the court on appeal

J–067   47.23
On an appeal from an authorised court officer the court will—

(a) re-hear the proceedings which gave rise to the decision appealed against; and
(b) make any order and give any directions as it considers appropriate.

PRACTICE DIRECTION—PILOT SCHEME FOR DETAILED ASSESSMENT BY THE SUPREME COURT COSTS OFFICE OF COSTS OF CIVIL PROCEEDINGS IN LONDON COUNTY COURTS

THIS PRACTICE DIRECTION SUPPLEMENTS CPR PART 47

1. This practice direction applies, instead of paragraph 31.1 of the CPR Costs Practice Direction, to requests for a detailed assessment hearing which are filed between 6th July 2004 and 5th July 2005, pursuant to a judgment or order for the payment of costs by one party to another in civil proceedings in any of the following County Courts:
Barnet, Bow, Brentford, Central London, Clerkenwell, Croydon, Edmonton, Ilford, Lambeth, Mayors and City of London, Romford, Shoreditch, Wandsworth, West London, Willesden and Woolwich.

2. Where this practice direction applies, unless the court orders otherwise—

    (1) the receiving party must file any request for a detailed assessment hearing in the Supreme Court Costs Office, Cliffords Inn, Fetter Lane, London EC4A 1DQ, DX 44454 Strand; and

    (2) the Supreme Court Costs Office is the appropriate office for the purpose of CPR 47.4(1), and therefore all applications and requests in the detailed assessment proceedings must be made to that Office.

Part 48

Costs—Special Cases

CONTENTS OF THIS PART

I COSTS PAYABLE BY OR TO PARTICULAR PERSONS

II COSTS RELATING TO SOLICITORS AND OTHER LEGAL REPRESENTATIVES

(The definitions contained in Part 43 are relevant to this Part)

I COSTS PAYABLE BY OR TO PARTICULAR PERSONS

Pre-commencement disclosure and orders for disclosure against a person who is not a party

48.1

J–068   (1) This paragraph applies where a person applies—

         (a) for an order under—

             (i) section 33 of the Supreme Court Act 1981[1]; or

---

[1] 1981 c. 54. S.33 was amended by SI 1998/2940.

(ii) section 52 of the County Courts Act (1984)[2],
(which give the court powers exercisable before commencement of
proceedings); or

(b) for an order under—

(i) section 34 of the Supreme Court Act 1981[3]; or
(ii) section 53 of the County Courts Act 1984[4],
(which give the court power to make an order against a non-party for
disclosure of documents, inspection of property etc.).

(2) The general rule is that the court will award the person against whom the
order is sought his costs—

(a) of the application; and
(b) of complying with any order made on the application.

(3) The court may however make a different order, having regard to all the
circumstances, including—

(a) the extent to which it was reasonable for the person against whom the
order was sought to oppose the application; and
(b) whether the parties to the application have complied with any relevant
pre-action protocol.

Costs orders in favour of or against non-parties

48.2

(1) Where the court is considering whether to exercise its power under section   **J–069**
51 of the Supreme Court Act 1981[5] (costs are in the discretion of the
court) to make a costs order in favour of or against a person who is not
a party to proceedings—

(a) that person must be added as a party to the proceedings for the
purposes of costs only; and
(b) he must be given a reasonable opportunity to attend a hearing at
which the court will consider the matter further.

(2) This rule does not apply—

(a) where the court is considering whether to—
(i) make an order against the Legal Services Commission;
(ii) make a wasted costs order (as defined in 48.7); and
(b) in proceedings to which rule 48.1 applies (pre-commencement disclosure and orders for disclosure against a person who is not a
party).

Amount of costs where costs are payable pursuant to a contract

48.3

---

[2] 1984 c. 28. S.52 was amended by the Courts and Legal Services Act 1990 (c. 41), Sch.18,
para.43 and SI 1998/2940.
[3] 1981 c. 54. S.34 was amended by SI 1998/2940.
[4] 1984 c. 28. S.53 was amended by the Courts and Legal Services Act 1990 (c. 41), Sch.18,
para.44 and by SI 1998/2940.
[5] 1981 c. 54. S.51 was substituted by s.4(1) of the Courts and Legal Services Act 1990
(c. 41).

J–070   (1) Where the court assesses (whether by the summary or detailed procedure) costs which are payable by the paying party to the receiving party under the terms of a contract, the costs payable under those terms are, unless the contract expressly provides otherwise, to be presumed to be costs which—

(a) have been reasonably incurred; and
(b) are reasonable in amount,

and the court will assess them accordingly.

(The costs practice direction sets out circumstances where the court may order otherwise)

(2) This rule does not apply where the contract is between a solicitor and his client.

Limitations on court's power to award costs in favour of trustee or personal representative

48.4

J–071   (1) This rule applies where—

(a) a person is or has been a party to any proceedings in the capacity of trustee or personal representative; and
(b) rule 48.3 does not apply.

(2) The general rule is that he is entitled to be paid the costs of those proceedings, insofar as they are not recovered from or paid by any other person, out of the relevant trust fund or estate.
(3) Where he is entitled to be paid any of those costs out of the fund or estate, those costs will be assessed on the indemnity basis.

Costs where money is payable by or to a child or patient

48.5

J–072   (1) This rule applies to any proceedings where a party is a child or patient and—

(a) money is ordered or agreed to be paid to, or for the benefit of, that party; or
(b) money is ordered to be paid by him or on his behalf.

("Child" and "patient" are defined in rule 2.3)

(2) The general rule is that—

(a) the court must order a detailed assessment of the costs payable by any party who is a child or patient to his solicitor; and
(b) on an assessment under paragraph (a), the court must also assess any costs payable to that party in the proceedings, unless the court has

issued a default costs certificate in relation to those costs under rule 47.11.

(3) The court need not order detailed assessment of costs in the circumstances set out in the costs practice direction.

(4) Where—

(a) a claimant is a child or patient; and

(b) a detailed assessment has taken place under paragraph (2)(a), the only amount payable by the child or patient to his solicitor is the amount which the court certifies as payable.

(This rule applies to a counterclaim by or on behalf of a child or patient by virtue of rule 20.3)

Litigants in person

48.6

(1) This rule applies where the court orders (whether by summary assessment or detailed assessment) that the costs of a litigant in person are to be paid by any other person.   J–073

(2) The costs allowed under this rule must not exceed, except in the case of a disbursement, two-thirds of the amount which would have been allowed if the litigant in person had been represented by a legal representative.

(3) The litigant in person shall be allowed—

(a) costs for the same categories of—

(i) work; and

(ii) disbursements,

which would have been allowed if the work had been done or the disbursements had been made by a legal representative on the litigant in person's behalf;

(b) the payments reasonably made by him for legal services relating to the conduct of the proceedings; and

(c) the costs of obtaining expert assistance in assessing the costs claim.

(4) The amount of costs to be allowed to the litigant in person for any item of work claimed shall be—

(a) where the litigant can prove financial loss, the amount that he can prove he has lost for time reasonably spent on doing the work; or

(b) where the litigant cannot prove financial loss, an amount for the time reasonably spent on doing the work at the rate set out in the practice direction.

(5) A litigant who is allowed costs for attending at court to conduct his case is not entitled to a witness allowance in respect of such attendance in addition to those costs.

(6) For the purposes of this rule, a litigant in person includes—

(a) a company or other corporation which is acting without a legal representative; and

(b) a barrister, solicitor, solicitor's employee or other authorised litigator (as defined in the Courts and Legal Services Act 1990[6] who is acting for himself.

Costs where the court has made a Group Litigation Order

J–074   48.6A

(1) This rule applied where the court has made a Group Litigation Order ("GLO").
(2) In this rule—

   (a) "individual costs" means costs incurred in relation to an individual claim on the group register;
   (b) "common costs" means—
      (i) costs incurred in relation to the GLO issues;
      (ii) individual costs incurred in a claim while it is proceeding as a test claim, and
      (iii) costs incurred by the lead solicitor in administering the group litigation; and
   (c) "group litigant" means a claimant or defendant, as the case may be, whose claim is entered on the group register.

(3) Unless the court orders otherwise, any order for common costs against group litigants imposes on each group litigant several liability (GL) for an equal proportion of those common costs.
(4) The general rule is that where a group litigant is the paying party, he will, in addition to any costs he is liable to pay to the receiving party, be liable for—

   (a) the individual costs of his claim; and
   (b) an equal proportion, together with all the other group litigants, of the common costs.

(5) Where the court makes an order about costs in relation to any application or hearing which involved—

   (a) one or more GLO issues; and
   (b) issues relevant only to individual claims,

   the court will direct the proportion of the costs that is to relate to common costs and the proportion that is to relate to individual costs.
(6) Where common costs have been incurred before a claim is entered on the group register, the court may order the group litigant to be liable for a proportion of those costs.
(7) Where a claim is removed from the group register, the court may make an order for costs in that claim which includes a proportion of the common costs incurred up to the date on which the claim is removed from the group register. (Part 19 sets out rules about group litigation).

---

[6] 1990 c. 41.

II COSTS RELATING TO SOLICITORS AND OTHER LEGAL REPRESENTATIVES

Personal liability of legal representative for costs—wasted costs orders

48.7   J–075

(1) This rule applies where the court is considering whether to make an order under section 51(6) of the Supreme Court Act 1981[7] (court's power to disallow or (as the case may be) order a legal representative to meet, "wasted costs").

(2) The court must give the legal representative a reasonable opportunity to attend a hearing to give reasons why it should not make such an order.

(4) When the court makes a wasted costs order, it must—

    (a) specify the amount to be disallowed or paid; or

    (b) direct a costs judge or a district judge to decide the amount of costs to be disallowed or paid.

(5) The court may direct that notice must be given to the legal representative's client, in such manner as the court may direct—

    (a) of any proceedings under this rule; or

    (b) of any order made under it against his legal representative.

(6) Before making a wasted costs order, the court may direct a costs judge or a district judge to inquire into the matter and report to the court.

(7) The court may refer the question of wasted costs to a costs judge or a district judge, instead of making a wasted costs order.

Basis of detailed assessment of solicitor and client costs

48.8

(1) This rule applies to every assessment of a solicitor's bill to his client except a bill which is to be paid out of the Community Legal Service Fund under the Legal Aid Act 1988[8] or the Access to Justice Act 1999[9]; and

(1A) Section 74(3) of the Solicitors Act 1974(a) applies unless the solicitor and client have entered into a written agreement which expressly permits payment to the solicitor of an amount of costs greater than that which the client could have recovered from another party to the proceedings.

(2) Subject to paragraph (1A), costs are to be assessed on the indemnity basis but are to be presumed—

    (a) to have been reasonably incurred if they were incurred with the express or implied approval of the client;

    (b) to be reasonable in amount if their amount was expressly or impliedly approved by the client;

    (c) to have been unreasonably incurred if—

        (i) they are of an unusual nature or amount; and

---

[7] 1981 c. 54. S.51 was substituted by s.4(1) of the Courts and Legal Services Act 1990 (c. 41).

[8] 1988, c. 34.

[9] 1999 c. 22.

> (ii) the solicitor did not tell his client that as a result he might not recover all of them from the other party.

(3) Where the court, is considering a percentage increase, whether on the application of the legal representative under rule 44.16 or on the application of the client, the court will have regard to all the relevant factors as they reasonably appeared to the solicitor or counsel when the conditional fee agreement was entered into or varied.

(4) In paragraph (3), "conditional fee agreement" means an agreement enforceable under section 58 of the Courts and Legal Services Act 1990[10] at the date on which that agreement was entered into or varied.

Assessment procedure

48.9 Revoked.

J–076 48.10

(1) This rule sets out the procedure to be followed where the court has made an order under Part III of the Solicitors Act 1974(10)for the assessment of costs payable to a solicitor by his client.

(2) The solicitor must serve a breakdown of costs within 28 days of the order for costs to be assessed.

(3) The client must serve points of dispute within 14 days after service on him of the breakdown of costs.

(4) If the solicitor wishes to serve a reply, he must do so within 14 days of service on him of the points of dispute.

(5) Either party may file a request for a hearing date—

> (a) after points of dispute have been served; but
> (b) no later than 3 months after the date of the order for the costs to be assessed.

(6) This procedure applies subject to any contrary order made by the court.

(Other rules about costs payable in special cases can be found in Schedule 1, in the following RSC—O.30 (remuneration of receivers); O.49 (costs of garnishee))

---

[10] 1990, c. 41. S.58 was substituted by s.27 of the Access to Justice Act 1999 (c. 22) with effect from April 1, 2000 (the Access to Justice Act 1999 (Commencement No. 3, Transitional Provisions and Savings) Order 2000, SI 2000/774, and the Access to Justice Act 1999 (Transitional Provisions) Order 2000, SI 2000/900).

APPENDIX K

PRACTICE DIRECTION SUPPLEMENTING PARTS 43 TO 48 OF THE CIVIL PROCEDURE RULES

Directions Relating To Part 44—General Rules About Costs

Directions Relating To Part 45—Fixed Costs

Directions Relating to Part 46—Fast Track Trial Costs

K–004
- SECTION 26 SCOPE OF PART 46: RULE 46.1
- SECTION 27 POWER TO AWARD MORE OR LESS THAN THE AMOUNT OF FAST TRACK TRIAL COSTS: RULE 46.3

Directions Relating to Part 47—Procedure for Detailed Assessment of Costs and Default Provisions

K–005
- SECTION 28 TIME WHEN ASSESSMENT MAY BE CARRIED OUT: RULE 47.1
- SECTION 29 NO STAY OF DETAILED ASSESSMENT WHERE THERE IS AN APPEAL: RULE 47.2
- SECTION 30 POWERS OF AN AUTHORISED COURT OFFICER: RULE 47.3
- SECTION 31 VENUE FOR DETAILED ASSESSMENT PROCEEDINGS: RULE 47.4
- SECTION 32 COMMENCEMENT OF DETAILED ASSESSMENT PROCEED-INGS: RULE 47.6
- SECTION 33 PERIOD FOR COMMENCING DETAILED ASSESSMENT PRO-CEEDINGS: RULE 47.7
- SECTION 34 SANCTION FOR DELAY IN COMMENCING DETAILED ASSESSMENT PROCEEDINGS: RULE 47.8
- SECTION 35 POINTS OF DISPUTE AND CONSEQUENCES OF NOT SERV-ING: RULE 47.9
- SECTION 36 PROCEDURE WHERE COSTS ARE AGREED: RULE 47.10
- SECTION 37 DEFAULT COSTS CERTIFICATE: RULE 47.11
- SECTION 38 SETTING ASIDE DEFAULT COSTS CERTIFICATE: RULE 47.12
- SECTION 39 OPTIONAL REPLY: RULE 47.13
- SECTION 40 DETAILED ASSESSMENT HEARING: RULE 47.14
- SECTION 41 POWER TO ISSUE AN INTERIM CERTIFICATE: RULE 47.15
- SECTION 42 FINAL COSTS CERTIFICATE: RULE 47.16
- SECTION 43 DETAILED ASSESSMENT PROCEDURE WHERE COSTS ARE PAYABLE OUT OF THE COMMUNITY LEGAL SERVICE FUND: RULE 47.17
- SECTION 44 COSTS OF DETAILED ASSESSMENT PROCEEDINGS WHERE COSTS ARE PAYABLE OUT OF A FUND OTHER THAN THE COMMUNITY LEGAL SERVICE FUND: RULE 47.17A
- SECTION 45 LIABILITY FOR COSTS OF DETAILED ASSESSMENT PRO-CEEDINGS: RULE 47.18
- SECTION 46 OFFERS TO SETTLE WITHOUT PREJUDICE SAVE AS TO THE COSTS OF THE DETAILED ASSESSMENT PROCEEDINGS: RULE 47.19
- SECTION 47 APPEALS FROM AUTHORISED COURT OFFICERS IN DETAILED ASSESSMENT PROCEEDINGS: RIGHT TO APPEAL: RULE 47.20
- SECTION 48 PROCEDURE ON APPEAL FROM AUTHORISED COURT OFFICERS: RULE 47.22
- SECTION 49 COSTS PAYABLE BY THE LSC AT PRESCRIBED RATES

Directions Relating To Part 48 Costs—Special Cases

- SECTION 50 AMOUNT OF COSTS WHERE COSTS ARE PAYABLE PURSU- **K–006**
  ANT TO CONTRACT: RULE 48.3
- SECTION 51 COSTS WHERE MONEY IS PAYABLE BY OR TO A CHILD OR
  PATIENT: RULE 48.5
- SECTION 52 LITIGANTS IN PERSON: RULE 48.6
- SECTION 53 PERSONAL LIABILITY OF LEGAL REPRESENTATIVE FOR
  COSTS—WASTED COSTS ORDERS: RULE 48.7
- SECTION 54 BASIS OF DETAILED ASSESSMENT OF SOLICITOR AND
  CLIENT COSTS: RULE 48.8
- SECTION 55 CONDITIONAL FEES: RULE 48.9
- SECTION 56 PROCEDURE ON ASSESSMENT OF SOLICITOR AND CLIENT
  COSTS: RULE 48.10
- SECTION 57 TRANSITIONAL ARRANGEMENTS

Schedule Of Costs Precedents

A: Model form of bill of costs (receiving party's solicitor and counsel on CFA **K–007**
   terms)
B: Model form of bill of costs (detailed assessment of additional liability only)
C: Model form of bill of costs (payable by Defendant and the LSC)
D: Model form of bill of costs (alternative form, single column for amounts
   claimed, separate parts for costs payable by the LSC only)
E: Legal Aid/ LSC Schedule of Costs
F: Certificates for inclusion in bill of costs
G: Points of Dispute
H: Estimate of costs served on other parties
J: Solicitors Act 1974: Part 8 claim form under Part III of the Act
K: Solicitors Act 1974: order for delivery of bill
L: Solicitors Act 1974: order for detailed assessment (client)
M: Solicitors Act 1974: order for detailed assessment (solicitors)
P: Solicitors Act 1974: breakdown of costs

SECTION 1 Introduction

1.1   This Practice Direction supplements Parts 43 to 48 of the Civil Procedure **K–008**
      Rules. It applies to all proceedings to which those Parts apply.
*1.2   Paragraphs 57.1 to 57.9 of this Practice Direction deal with various
      transitional provisions affecting proceedings about costs.
1.3   Attention is drawn to the powers to make orders about costs conferred on
      the Supreme Court and any county court by Section 51 of the Supreme
      Court Act 1981.
*1.4   In these Directions:

      "counsel" means a barrister or other person with a right of audience in
      relation to proceedings in the High Court or in the County Courts in which
      he is instructed to act.

      "LSC" means Legal Services Commission.

      "solicitor" means a solicitor of the Supreme Court or other person with a
      right of audience in relation to proceedings, who is conducting the claim or
      defence (as the case may be) on behalf of a party to the proceedings and,
      where the context admits, includes a patent agent.

1.5 In respect of any document which is required by these Directions to be signed by a party or his legal representative the Practice Direction supplementing Part 22 will apply as if the document in question was a statement of truth. (The Practice Direction supplementing Part 22 makes provision for cases in which a party is a child, a patient or a company or other corporation and cases in which a document is signed on behalf of a partnership).

SECTION 2 Scope of costs rules and definitions

Rule 43.2 Definitions and Application

K–009 *2.1 Where the court makes an order for costs and the receiving party has entered into a funding arrangement as defined in rule 43.2, the costs payable by the paying party include any additional liability (also defined in rule 43.2) unless the court orders otherwise.

*2.2 In the following paragraphs—

"funding arrangement", "percentage increase", "insurance premium", "membership organisation" and "additional liability" have the meanings given to them by rule 43.2.
* A "conditional fee agreement" is an agreement with a person providing advocacy or litigation services which provides for his fees and expenses, or part of them, to be payable only in specified circumstances, whether or not it provides for a success fee as mentioned in section 58(2)(b) of the Courts and Legal Services Act 1990.
"base costs" means costs other than the amount of any additional liability.

*2.3 Rule 44.3A(1) provides that the court will not assess any additional liability until the conclusion of the proceedings or the part of the proceedings to which the funding arrangement relates. (As to the time when detailed assessment may be carried out see paragraph 27.1 below).

*2.4 For the purposes of the following paragraphs of this practice direction and rule 44.3A proceedings are concluded when the court has finally determined the matters in issue in the claim, whether or not there is an appeal. The making of an award of provisional damages under Part 41 will also be treated as a final determination of the matters in issue.

*2.5 The court may order or the parties may agree in writing that, although the proceedings are continuing, they will nevertheless be treated as concluded.

SECTION 3 Model forms for claims for costs

Rule 43.3 Meaning of summary assessment

K–010 *3.1 Rule 43.3 defines summary assessment. When carrying out a summary assessment of costs where there is an additional liability the court may assess the base costs alone, or the base costs and the additional liability.

*3.2 Form N260 is a model form of Statement of Costs to be used for summary assessments.

*3. Further details about Statements of Costs are given in paragraph 13.5 below.

Rule 43.4 Meaning of detailed assessment

*3.4 Rule 43.4 defines detailed assessment. When carrying out a detailed **K–011** assessment of costs where there is an additional liability the court will assess both the base costs and the additional liability, or, if the base costs have already been assessed, the additional liability alone.

*3.5 Precedents A, B, C and D in the Schedule of Costs Precedents annexed to this Practice Direction are model forms of bills of costs to be used for detailed assessments.

*3.6 Further details about bills of costs are given in the next section of these Directions and in paragraphs 28.1 to 49.1, below.

*3.7 Precedents A, B, C and D in the Schedule of Costs Precedents and the next section of this Practice Direction all refer to a model form of bill of costs. The use of a model form is not compulsory, but is encouraged. A party wishing to rely upon a bill which departs from the model forms should include in the background information of the bill an explanation for that departure.

3.8 In any order of the court (whether made before or after 26 April 1999) the word "taxation" will be taken to mean "detailed assessment" and the words "to be taxed" will be taken to mean "to be decided by detailed assessment" unless in either case the context otherwise requires.

SECTION 4 Form and contents of bills of costs

4.1 A bill of costs may consist of such of the following sections as may be **K–012** appropriate–

(1) title page;
(2) background information;
(3) items of costs claimed under the headings specified in paragraph 4.6;
(4) summary showing the total costs claimed on each page of the bill;
(5) schedules of time spent on non-routine attendances; and
(6) the certificates referred to in paragraph 4.15.

*4.2 Where it is necessary or convenient to do so, a bill of costs may be divided into two or more parts, each part containing sections (2), (3) and (4) above. A division into parts will be necessary or convenient in the following circumstances–

(1) Where the receiving party acted in person during the course of the proceedings (whether or not he also had a legal representative at that time) the bill should be divided into different parts so as to distinguish between;
(a) the costs claimed for work done by the legal representative; and
(b) the costs claimed for work done by the receiving party in person.

(2) Where the receiving party was represented by different solicitors during the course of the proceedings, the bill should be divided into different parts so as to distinguish between the costs payable in respect of each solicitor.

(3) Where the receiving party obtained legal aid or LSC funding in respect of all or part of the proceedings the bill should be divided into separate parts so as to distinguish between;
(a) costs claimed before legal aid or LSC funding was granted;
(b) costs claimed after legal aid or LSC funding was granted; and

(c) any costs claimed after legal aid or LSC funding ceased.

(4) Where value added tax (VAT) is claimed and there was a change in the rate of VAT during the course of the proceedings, the bill should be divided into separate parts so as to distinguish between;

(a) costs claimed at the old rate of VAT; and

(b) costs claimed at the new rate of VAT.

(5) Where the bill covers costs payable under an order or orders under which there are different paying parties the bill should be divided into parts so as to deal separately with the costs payable by each paying party.

(6) Where the bill covers costs payable under an order or orders, in respect of which the receiving party wishes to claim interest from different dates, the bill should be divided to enable such interest to be calculated.

*4.3 Where a party claims costs against another party and also claims costs against the LSC only for work done in the same period, the costs claimed against the LSC only can be claimed either in a separate part of the bill or in additional columns in the same part of the bill. Precedents C and D in the Schedule of Costs Precedents annexed to this Practice Direction show how bills should be drafted when costs are claimed against the LSC only.

*4.4 The title page of the bill of costs must set out–

(1) the full title of the proceedings;

(2) the name of the party whose bill it is and a description of the document showing the right to assessment (as to which see paragraph 40.4, below);

(3) if VAT is included as part of the claim for costs, the VAT number of the legal representative or other person in respect of whom VAT is claimed;

(4) details of all legal aid certificates, LSC certificates and relevant amendment certificates in respect of which claims for costs are included in the bill.

4.5 The background information included in the bill of costs should set out–

(1) a brief description of the proceedings up to the date of the notice of commencement;

(2) A statement of the status of the solicitor or solicitor's employee in respect of whom costs are claimed and (if those costs are calculated on the basis of hourly rates) the hourly rates claimed for each such person.

It should be noted that "legal executive" means a Fellow of the Institute of Legal Executives.

Other clerks, who are fee earners of equivalent experience, may be entitled to similar rates. It should be borne in mind that Fellows of the Institute of Legal Executives will have spent approximately 6 years in practice, and taken both general and specialist examinations. The Fellows have therefore acquired considerable practical and academic experience. Clerks without the equivalent experience of legal executives will normally be treated as being the equivalent of trainee solicitors and para-legals.

(3) a brief explanation of any agreement or arrangement between the receiving party and his solicitors, which affects the costs claimed in the bill.

*4.6 The bill of costs may consist of items under such of the following heads as may be appropriate–

(1) attendances on the court and counsel up to the date of the notice of commencement;
(2) attendances on and communications with the receiving party;
(3) attendances on and communications with witnesses including any expert witness;
(4) attendances to inspect any property or place for the purposes of the proceedings;
(5) attendances on and communications with other persons, including offices of public records;
(6) communications with the court and with counsel;
(7) work done on documents: preparing and considering documentation, including documentation relating to pre-action protocols where appropriate, work done in connection with arithmetical calculations of compensation and/or interest and time spent collating documents;
(8) work done in connection with negotiations with a view to settlement if not already covered in the heads listed above;
(9) attendances on and communications with London and other agents and work done by them;
(10) other work done which was of or incidental to the proceedings and which is not already covered in the heads listed above.

4.7 In respect of each of the heads of costs–

(1) "communications" means letters out and telephone calls;
(2) communications, which are not routine communications, must be set out in chronological order;
(3) routine communications should be set out as a single item at the end of each head;

*4.8 Routine communications are letters out, e mails out and telephone calls which because of their simplicity should not be regarded as letters or e mails of substance or telephone calls which properly amount to an attendance.

4.9 Each item claimed in the bill of costs must be consecutively numbered.

4.10 In each part of the bill of costs which claims items under head (1) (attendances on court and counsel) a note should be made of:

(1) all relevant events, including events which do not constitute chargeable items;
(2) any orders for costs which the court made (whether or not a claim is made in respect of those costs in this bill of costs).

*4.11 The numbered items of costs may be set out on paper divided into columns. Precedents A, B, C and D in the Schedule of Costs Precedents annexed to this Practice Direction illustrate various model forms of bills of costs.

4.12 In respect of heads (2) to (10) in paragraph 4.6 above, if the number of attendances and communications other than routine communications is twenty or more, the claim for the costs of those items in that section of the bill of costs should be for the total only and should refer to a schedule in which the full record of dates and details is set out. If the bill of costs contains more than one schedule each schedule should be numbered consecutively.

4.13 The bill of costs must not contain any claims in respect of costs or court fees which relate solely to the detailed assessment proceedings other than costs claimed for preparing and checking the bill.

4.14 The summary must show the total profit costs and disbursements claimed separately from the total VAT claimed. Where the bill of costs is divided into parts the summary must also give totals for each part. If each page of the bill gives a page total the summary must also set out the page totals for each page.

*4.15 The bill of costs must contain such of the certificates, the texts of which are set out in Precedent F of the Schedule of Costs Precedents annexed to this Practice Direction, as are appropriate.

*4.16 The following provisions relate to work done by solicitors:

(1) Routine letters out and routine telephone calls will in general be allowed on a unit basis of 6 minutes each, the charge being calculated by reference to the appropriate hourly rate. The unit charge for letters out will include perusing and considering the relevant letters in and no separate charge should be made for in-coming letters.

(2) E-mails received by solicitors will not normally be allowed. The court may, in its discretion, allow an actual time charge for preparation of e-mails sent by solicitors, which properly amount to attendances provided that the time taken has been recorded. The court may also, in its discretion, allow a sum in respect of routine e-mails sent to the client or others on a unit basis of 6 minutes each, the charge being calculated by reference to the appropriate hourly rate.

(3) Local travelling expenses incurred by solicitors will not be allowed. The definition of "local" is a matter for the discretion of the court. While no absolute rule can be laid down, as a matter of guidance, "local" will, in general, be taken to mean within a radius of 10 miles from the court dealing with the case at the relevant time. Where travelling and waiting time is claimed, this should be allowed at the rate agreed with the client unless this is more than the hourly rate on the assessment.

(4) The cost of postage, couriers, out-going telephone calls, fax and telex messages will in general not be allowed but the court may exceptionally in its discretion allow such expenses in unusual circumstances or where the cost is unusually heavy.

(5) The cost of making copies of documents will not in general be allowed but the court may exceptionally in its discretion make an allowance for copying in unusual circumstances or where the documents copied are unusually numerous in relation to the nature of the case. Where this discretion is invoked the number of copies made, their purpose and the costs claimed for them must be set out in the bill.

(6) Agency charges as between a principal solicitor and his agent will be dealt with on the principle that such charges, where appropriate, form part of the principal solicitor's charges. Where these charges relate to head (1) in paragraph 4.6 (attendances at court and on counsel) they should be included in their chronological order in that head. In other cases they should be included in head (9) (attendances on London and other agents).

*4.17

(1) Where a claim is made for a percentage increase in addition to an hourly rate or base fee, the amount of the increase must be shown separately, either in the appropriate arithmetic column or in the narrative column. (For an example see Precedent A or Precedent B.)

(2) Where a claim is made against the LSC only and includes enhancement and where a claim is made in family proceedings and includes a claim for uplift or general care and conduct, the amount of enhancement uplift and general care and conduct must be shown, in respect of each item upon which it is claimed, as a separate amount either in the appropriate arithmetic column or in the narrative column. (For an example, see Precedent C.)

"Enhancement" means the increase in prescribed rates which may be allowed by a costs officer in accordance with the Legal Aid in Civil Proceedings (Remuneration) Regulations 1994 or the Legal Aid in Family Proceedings Regulations 1991.

Costs of preparing the bill

4.18   A claim may be made for the reasonable costs of preparing and checking the bill of costs.   **K–013**

SECTION 5 Special provisions relating to VAT

5.1   This section deals with claims for value added tax (VAT) which are made in respect of costs being dealt with by way of summary assessment or detailed assessment.   **K–014**

VAT Registration Number

5.2   The number allocated by HM Customs and Excise to every person registered under the Value Added Tax Act 1983 except a Government Department) must appear in a prominent place at the head of every statement, bill of costs, fee sheet, account or voucher on which VAT is being included as part of a claim for costs.   **K–015**

Entitlement to VAT on Costs

5.3   VAT should not be included in a claim for costs if the receiving party is able to recover the VAT as input tax. Where the receiving party is able to obtain credit from HM Customs and Excise for a proportion of the VAT as input tax, only that proportion which is not eligible for credit should be included in the claim for costs.   **K–016**

5.4   The receiving party has responsibility for ensuring that VAT is claimed only when the receiving party is unable to recover the VAT or a proportion thereof as input tax.

*5.5   Where there is a dispute as to whether VAT is properly claimed the receiving party must provide a certificate signed by the solicitors or the auditors of the receiving party substantially in the form illustrated in Precedent F in the Schedule of Costs Precedents annexed to this Practice Direction. Where the receiving party is a litigant in person who is claiming VAT, reference should be made by him to HM Customs and Excise and wherever possible a Statement to similar effect produced at the hearing at which the costs are assessed.

5.6   Where there is a dispute as to whether any service in respect of which a charge is proposed to be made in the bill is zero rated or exempt, reference should be made to HM Customs and Excise and wherever possible the view of HM Customs and Excise obtained and made known at the hearing at which the costs are assessed. Such application should be made by the receiving party. In the case of a bill from a solicitor to his own client, such application should be made by the client.

Form of bill of costs where VAT rate changes

K–017 5.7 Where there is a change in the rate of VAT, suppliers of goods and services are entitled by ss.88(1) and (2) of the VAT Act 1994 in most circumstances to elect whether the new or the old rate of VAT should apply to a supply where the basic and actual tax points span a period during which there has been a change in VAT rates.

5.8 It will be assumed, unless a contrary indication is given in writing, that an election to take advantage of the provisions mentioned in paragraph 5.7 above and to charge VAT at the lower rate has been made. In any case in which an election to charge at the lower rate is not made, such a decision must be justified to the court assessing the costs.

Apportionment

K–018 5.9 All bills of costs, fees and disbursements on which VAT is included must be divided into separate parts so as to show work done before, on and after the date or dates from which any change in the rate of VAT takes effect. Where, however, a lump sum charge is made for work which spans a period during which there has been a change in VAT rates, and paragraphs 5.7 and 5.8 above do not apply, reference should be made to paragraphs 8 and 9 of Appendix F of Customs' Notice 700 (or any revised edition of that notice), a copy of which should be in the possession of every registered trader. If necessary, the lump sum should be apportioned. The totals of profit costs and disbursements in each part must be carried separately to the summary.

5.10 Should there be a change in the rate between the conclusion of a detailed assessment and the issue of the final costs certificate, any interested party may apply for the detailed assessment to be varied so as to take account of any increase or reduction in the amount of tax payable. Once the final costs certificate has been issued, no variation under this paragraph will be permitted.

Disbursements

K–019 5.11 Petty (or general) disbursements such as postage, fares etc which are normally treated as part of a solicitor's overheads and included in his profit costs should be charged with VAT even though they bear no tax when the solicitor incurs them. The cost of travel by public transport on a specific journey for a particular client where it forms part of the service rendered by a solicitor to his client and is charged in his bill of costs, attracts VAT.

5.12 Reference is made to the criteria set out in the VAT Guide (Customs and Excise Notice 700—1st August 1991 edition paragraph 83, or any revised edition of that Notice), as to expenses which are not subject to VAT. Charges for the cost of travel by public transport, postage, telephone calls and telegraphic transfers where these form part of the service rendered by the solicitor to his client are examples of charges which do not satisfy these criteria and are thus liable to VAT at the standard rate.

Legal Aid/LSC Funding

*5.13

K–020

   (1) VAT will be payable in respect of every supply made pursuant to a legal aid/LSC certificate where—
     (a) the person making the supply is a taxable person; and
     (b) the assisted person/LSC funded client—
       (i) belongs in the United Kingdom or another member state of the European Union; and
       (ii) is a private individual or receives the supply for non-business purposes.
   (2) Where the assisted person/LSC funded client belongs outside the European Union, VAT is generally not payable unless the supply relates to land in the United Kingdom.
   (3) For the purpose of sub-paragraphs (1) and (2), the place where a person belongs is determined by section 9 of the Value Added Tax Act 1994.
   (4) Where the assisted person/LSC funded client is registered for VAT and the legal services paid for by the LSC are in connection with that person's business, the VAT on those services will be payable by the LSC only.

*5.14   Any summary of costs payable by the LSC must be drawn so as to show the total VAT on Counsel's fees as a separate item from the VAT on other disbursements and the VAT on profit costs.

Tax invoice

5.15   A bill of costs filed for detailed assessment is always retained by the Court. Accordingly if a solicitor waives his solicitor and client costs and accepts the costs certified by the court as payable by the unsuccessful party in settlement, it will be necessary for a short statement as to the amount of the certified costs and the VAT thereon to be prepared for use as the tax invoice.

K–021

Vouchers

5.16   Where receipted accounts for disbursements made by the solicitor or his client are retained as tax invoices a photostat copy of any such receipted account may be produced and will be accepted as sufficient evidence of payment when disbursements are vouched.

K–022

Certificates

*5.17   In a costs certificate payable by the LSC, the VAT on solicitor's costs, Counsel's fees and disbursements will be shown separately.

K–023

Litigants acting in person

*5.18   Where a litigant acts in litigation on his own behalf he is not treated for the purposes of VAT as having supplied services and therefore no VAT is chargeable in respect of work done by that litigant (even where, for example, that litigant is a solicitor or other legal representative).

K–024

5.19 Consequently in the circumstances described in the preceding paragraph, a bill of costs presented for agreement or assessment should not claim any VAT which will not be allowed on assessment.

Government Departments

K–025   5.20 On an assessment between parties, where costs are being paid to a Government Department in respect of services rendered by its legal staff, VAT should not be added.

SECTION 6 Estimates of costs

K–026   6.1*   This section sets out certain steps which parties and their legal representatives must take in order to keep the parties informed about their potential liability in respect of costs and in order to assist the court to decide what, if any, order to make about costs and about case management.

*6.2

(1) In this section an "estimate of costs" means—
   (a) an estimate of base costs (including disbursements) already incurred; and
   (b) an estimate of base costs (including disbursements) to be incurred,
   which a party intends to seek to recover from any other party under an order for costs if he is successful in the case. ("Base costs" are defined in paragraphs 2.2 of this Practice Direction.)
(2) A party who intends to recover an additional liability (defined in rule 43.2) need not reveal the amount of that liability in the estimate.

6.3   The court may at any stage in a case order any party to file an estimate of base costs and to serve copies of the estimate on all other parties. The court may direct that the estimate be prepared in such a way as to demonstrate the likely effects of giving or not giving a particular case management direction which the court is considering, for example a direction for a split trial or for the trial of a preliminary issue. The court may specify a time limit for filing and serving the estimate. However, if no time limit is specified the estimate should be filed and served within 28 days of the date of the order.

*6.4

(1) When a party to a claim which is outside the financial scope of the small claims track, files an allocation questionnaire, he must also file an estimate of base costs and serve a copy of it on every other party, unless the court otherwise directs. The legal representative must in addition serve an estimate upon the party he represents.
(2) Where a party to a claim which is being dealt with on the fast track or the multi track, or under Part 8, files a listing questionnaire, he must also file an estimate of base costs and serve a copy of it on every other party, unless the court otherwise directs. Where a party is represented, the legal representative must in addition serve an estimate on the party he represents.
(3) This paragraph does not apply to litigants in person.

*6.5   An estimate of base costs should be substantially in the form illustrated in Precedent H in the Schedule of Costs Precedents annexed to the Practice Direction.

*6.6   On an assessment of the costs of a party the court may have regard to any estimate previously filed by that party, or by any other party in the same proceedings. Such an estimate may be taken into account as a factor among others, when assessing the reasonableness of any costs claimed.

Directions Relating To Part 44

General rules about costs

SECTION 7 Solicitor's duty to notify client: rule 44.2

*7.1   For the purposes of rule 44.2 "client" includes a party for whom a solicitor is acting and any other person (for example, an insurer, a trade union or the LSC) who has instructed the solicitor to act or who is liable to pay his fees.   **K–027**

7.2   Where a solicitor notifies a client of an order under that rule, he must also explain why the order came to be made.

7.3   Although rule 44.2 does not specify any sanction for breach of the rule the court may, either in the order for costs itself or in a subsequent order, require the solicitor to produce to the court evidence showing that he took reasonable steps to comply with the rule.

SECTION 8 Court's discretion and circumstances to be taken into account when exercising its discretion as to costs: rule 44.3

8.1   Attention is drawn to the factors set out in this rule which may lead the court to depart from the general rule stated in rule 44.3(2) and to make a different order about costs.   **K–028**

8.2   In a probate claim where a defendant has in his defence given notice that he requires the will to be proved in solemn form (see paragraph 8.3 of the practice direction supplementing Part 57), the court will not make an order for costs against the defendant unless it appears that there was no reasonable ground for opposing the will. The term 'probate claim' is defined in rule 57.1(2).

*8.3

(1) The court may make an order about costs at any stage in a case.

(2) In particular the court may make an order about costs when it deals with any application, makes any order or holds any hearing and that order about costs may relate to the costs of that application, order or hearing.

(3) * Rule 44.3A(1) provides that the court will not assess any additional liability until the conclusion of the proceedings or the part of the proceedings to which the funding arrangement relates. (Paragraphs 2.4 and 2.5 above explain when proceedings are concluded. As to the time when detailed assessment may be carried out see paragraphs 28.1, below.)

8.4   In deciding what order to make about costs the court is required to have regard to all the circumstances including any payment into court or admissible offer to settle made by a party which is drawn to the court's attention (whether or not it is made in accordance with Part 36). Where a claimant has made a Part 36 offer and fails to obtain a judgment which is more advantageous than that offer, that circumstance alone will not lead to a reduction in the costs awarded to the claimant under this rule.

8.5   There are certain costs orders which the court will commonly make in proceedings before trial. The following table sets out the general effect of these orders. The table is not an exhaustive list of the orders which the court may make.

K–029

Term	Effect
• Costs • Costs in any event	The party in whose favour the order is made is entitled to the costs in respect of the part of the proceedings to which the order relates, whatever other costs orders are made in the proceedings.
• Costs in the case • Costs in the application	The party in whose favour the court makes an order for costs at the end of the proceedings is entitled to his costs of the part of the proceedings to which the order relates.
• Costs reserved	The decision about costs is defered to a later occasion, but if no later order is made the costs will be costs in the case.
• Claimant's/Defendant's costs in the case/application	If the party in whose favour the costs order is made is awarded costs at the end of the proceedings, that party is entitled to his costs of the part of the proceedings to which the order relates. If any other party is awarded costs at the end of the proceedings, the party in whose favour the final costs order is made is not liable to pay the costs of any other party in respect of the part of the proceedings to which the order relates.
• Costs thrown away	Where, for example, a judgment or order is set aside, the party in whose favour the costs order is made is entitled to the costs which have been incurred as a consequence. This includes the costs of— a) preparing for and attending any hearing at which the judgment or order which has been set aside was made; b) preparing for and attending any hearing to set aside the judgment or order in question; c) preparing for and attending any hearing at which the court orders the proceedings or the part in question to be adjourned; d) any steps taken to enforce a judgment or order which has subsequently been set aside.
• Costs of and caused by	Where, for example, the court makes this order on an application to amend a statement of case, the party in whose favour the costs order is made is entitled to the costs of preparing for and attending the application and the costs of any consequential amendment to his own statement of case.
• Costs here and below	The party in whose favour the costs order is made is entitled not only to his costs in respect of the proceedings in which the court makes the order but also to his costs of the proceedings in any lower court. In the case of an appeal from a Divisional Court the party is not entitled to any costs incurred in any court below the Divisional Court.

Term	Effect
• No order as to costs • Each party to pay his own costs	Each party is to bear his own costs of the part of the proceedings to which the order relates whatever costs order the court makes at the end of the proceedings.

8.6 Where, under rule 44.3(8), the court orders an amount to be paid before costs are assessed—

    (1) the order will state that amount, and

    (2) if no other date for payment is specified in the order rule 44.8 (Time for complying with an order for costs) will apply.

Fees of counsel

*8.7   K–030

    (1) This paragraph applies where the court orders the detailed assessment of the costs of a hearing at which one or more counsel appeared for a party.

    (2) Where an order for costs states the opinion of the court as to whether or not the hearing was fit for the attendance of one or more counsel, a costs officer conducting a detailed assessment of costs to which that order relates will have regard to the opinion stated.

    (3) The court will generally express an opinion only where:

        (a) the paying party asks it to do so;

        (b) more than one counsel appeared for a party or,

        (c) the court wishes to record its opinion that the case was not fit for the attendance of counsel.

Fees payable to conveyancing counsel appointed by the court to assist it

*8.8   K–031

    (1) Where the court refers any matter to the conveyancing counsel of the court the fees payable to counsel in respect of the work done or to be done will be assessed by the court in accordance with rule 44.3.

    (2) An appeal from a decision of the court in respect of the fees of such counsel will be dealt with under the general rules as to appeals set out in Part 52. If the appeal is against the decision of an authorised court officer, it will be dealt with in accordance with rules 47.20 to 47.23.

SECTION 9 Costs orders relating to funding arrangements: Rule 44.3A

*9.1 Under an order for payment of "costs" the costs payable will include an   K–032
additional liability incurred under a funding arrangement.

*9.2

    (1) If before the conclusion of the proceedings the court carries out a summary assessment of the base costs it may identify separately the amount allowed in respect of: solicitors' charges; counsels' fees; other disbursements; and any value added tax (VAT). (Sections 13 and 14 of this Practice Direction deal with summary assessment.)

(2) If an order for the base costs of a previous application or hearing did not identify separately the amounts allowed for solicitor's charges, counsel's fees and other disbursements, a court which later makes an assessment of an additional liability may apportion the base costs previously ordered.

SECTION 10 Limits on recovery under funding arrangements: Rule 44.3B

K–033   *10.1   In a case to which rule 44.3B(1)(c) or (d) applies the party in default may apply for relief from the sanction. He should do so as quickly as possible after he becomes aware of the default. An application, supported by evidence, should be made under Part 23 to a costs judge or district judge of the court which is dealing with the case. (Attention is drawn to rules 3.8 and 3.9 which deal with sanctions and relief from sanctions).

    *10.2   Where the amount of any percentage increase recoverable by counsel may be affected by the outcome of the application, the solicitor issuing the application must serve on counsel a copy of the application notice and notice of the hearing as soon as practicable and in any event at least 2 days before the hearing. Counsel may make written submissions or may attend and make oral submissions at the hearing. (Paragraph 1.4 contains definitions of the terms "counsel" and "solicitor".)

SECTION 11 Factors to be taken into account in deciding the amount of costs: Rule 44.5

K–034   11.1   In applying the test of proportionality the court will have regard to rule 1.1(2)(c). The relationship between the total of the costs incurred and the financial value of the claim may not be a reliable guide. A fixed percentage cannot be applied in all cases to the value of the claim in order to ascertain whether or not the costs are proportionate.

    11.2   In any proceedings there will be costs which will inevitably be incurred and which are necessary for the successful conduct of the case. Solicitors are not required to conduct litigation at rates which are uneconomic. Thus in a modest claim the proportion of costs is likely to be higher than in a large claim, and may even equal or possibly exceed the amount in dispute.

    11.3   Where a trial takes place, the time taken by the court in dealing with a particular issue may not be an accurate guide to the amount of time properly spent by the legal or other representatives in preparation for the trial of that issue.

    *11.4   Where a party has entered into a funding arrangement the costs claimed may, subject to rule 44.3B include an additional liability.

    *11.5   In deciding whether the costs claimed are reasonable and (on a standard basis assessment) proportionate, the court will consider the amount of any additional liability separately from the base costs.

    *11.6   In deciding whether the base costs are reasonable and (if relevant) proportionate the court will consider the factors set out in rule 44.5.

    *11.7   Subject to paragraph 17.8(2), when the court is considering the factors to be taken into account in assessing an additional liability, it will have regard to the facts and circumstances as they reasonably appeared to the solicitor or counsel when the funding arrangement was entered into and at the time of any variation of the arrangement.

    *11.8

(1) In deciding whether a percentage increase is reasonable relevant factors to be taken into account may include–

    (a) the risk that the circumstances in which the costs, fees or expenses would be payable might or might not occur;

    (b) the legal representative's liability for any disbursements;

    (c) what other methods of financing the costs were available to the receiving party.

(2) The court has the power, when considering whether a percentage increase is reasonable, to allow different percentages for different items of costs or for different periods during which costs were incurred.

*11.9 A percentage increase will not be reduced simply on the ground that, when added to base costs which are reasonable (where relevant) proportionate, the total appears disproportionate.

*11.10 In deciding whether the cost of insurance cover is reasonable, relevant factors to be taken into account include:

(1) where the insurance cover is not purchased in support of a conditional fee agreement with a success fee, how its cost compares with the likely cost of funding the case with a conditional fee agreement with a success fee and supporting insurance cover;

(2) the level and extent of the cover provided;

(3) the availability of any pre-existing insurance cover;

(4) whether any part of the premium would be rebated in the event of early settlement;

(5) the amount of commission payable to the receiving party or his legal representatives or other agents.

*11.11 Where the court is considering a provision made by a membership organisation, rule 44.3B(1)(b) provides that any such provision which exceeds the likely cost to the receiving party of the premium of an insurance policy against the risk of incurring a liability to pay the costs of other parties to the proceedings is not recoverable. In such circumstances the court will, when assessing the additional liability, have regard to the factors set out in paragraph 11.10 above, in addition to the factors set out in rule 44.5.

SECTION 12 Procedure for assessing costs: Rule 44.7

12.1 Where the court does not order fixed costs (or no fixed costs are provided   **K–035** for) the amount of costs payable will be assessed by the court. This rule allows the court making an order about costs either

    (a) to make a summary assessment of the amount of the costs, or

    (b) to order the amount to be decided in accordance with Part 47 (a detailed assessment).

12.2 An order for costs will be treated as an order for the amount of costs to be decided by a detailed assessment unless the order otherwise provides.

12.3 Whenever the court awards costs to be assessed by way of detailed assessment it should consider whether to exercise the power in rule 44.3(8) (Courts Discretion as to Costs) to order the paying party to pay such sum of money as it thinks just on account of those costs.

SECTION 13 Summary assessment: general provisions

13.1 Whenever a court makes an order about costs which does not provide for   **K–036** fixed costs to be paid the court should consider whether to make a summary assessment of costs.

*13.2 The general rule is that the court should make a summary assessment of the costs:

(1) at the conclusion of the trial of a case which has been dealt with on the fast track, in which case the order will deal with the costs of the whole claim, and

(2) at the conclusion of any other hearing, which has lasted not more than one day, in which case the order will deal with the costs of the application or matter to which the hearing related. If this hearing disposes of the claim, the order may deal with the costs of the whole claim;

(3) in hearings in the Court of Appeal to which Paragraph 14 of the Practice Direction supplementing Part 52 (Appeals) applies;

unless there is good reason not to do so e.g. where the paying party shows substantial grounds for disputing the sum claimed for costs that cannot be dealt with summarily or there is insufficient time to carry out a summary assessment.

13.3 The general rule in paragraph 13.2 does not apply to a mortgagee's costs incurred in mortgage possession proceedings or other proceedings relating to a mortgage unless the mortgagee asks the court to make an order for his costs to be paid by another party. Paragraphs 50.3 and 50.4 deal in more detail with costs relating to mortgages.

13.4 Where an application has been made and the parties to the application agree an order by consent without any party attending, the parties should agree a figure for costs to be inserted in the consent order or agree that there should be no order for costs. If the parties cannot agree the costs position, attendance on the appointment will be necessary but, unless good reason can be shown for the failure to deal with costs as set out above, no costs will be allowed for that attendance.

*13.5

(1) It is the duty of the parties and their legal representatives to assist the judge in making a summary assessment of costs in any case to which paragraph 13.2 above applies, in accordance with the following paragraphs.

(2) Each party who intends to claim costs must prepare a written statement of the costs he intends to claim showing separately in the form of a schedule:

(a) the number of hours to be claimed,

(b) the hourly rate to be claimed,

(c) the grade of fee earner;

(d) the amount and nature of any disbursement to be claimed, other than counsel's fee for appearing at the hearing,

(e) the amount of solicitor's costs to be claimed for attending or appearing at the hearing,

(f) the fees of counsel to be claimed in respect of the hearing, and

(g) any value added tax (VAT) to be claimed on these amounts.

*(3) The statement of costs should follow as closely as possible Form N260 and must be signed by the party or his legal representative. Where a litigant is an assisted person or is a LSC funded client or is represented by a solicitor in the litigant's employment the statement of costs need not include the certificate appended at the end of Form N260.

(4) The statement of costs must be filed at court and copies of it must be served on any party against whom an order for payment of those costs

is intended to be sought. The statement of costs should be filed and the copies of it should be served as soon as possible and in any event not less than 24 hours before the date fixed for the hearing.

(5) *Where the litigant is or may be entitled to claim an additional liability the statement filed and served need not reveal the amount of that liability.

13.6 The failure by a party, without reasonable excuse, to comply with the foregoing paragraphs will be taken into account by the court in deciding what order to make about the costs of the claim, hearing or application, and about the costs of any further hearing or detailed assessment hearing that may be necessary as a result of that failure.

*13.7 If the court makes a summary assessment of costs at the conclusion of proceedings the court will specify separately

(1) the base costs, and if appropriate, the additional liability allowed as solicitor's charges, counsel's fees, other disbursements and any VAT; and

(2) the amount which is awarded under Part 46 (Fast Track Trial Costs).

*13.8 The court awarding costs cannot make an order for a summary assessment of costs by a costs officer. If a summary assessment of costs is appropriate but the court awarding costs is unable to do so on the day, the court must give directions as to a further hearing before the same judge.

13.9* The court will not make a summary assessment of the costs of a receiving party who is an assisted person or LSC funded client.

13.10*A summary assessment of costs payable by an assisted person or LSC funded client is not by itself a determination of that person's liability to pay those costs (as to which see rule 44.17 and paragraphs 21.1 to 23.17 of this Practice Direction).

*13.11

(1) The court will not make a summary assessment of the costs of a receiving party who is a child or patient within the meaning of Part 21 unless the solicitor acting for the child or patient has waived the right to further costs (see paragraph 51.1 below).

(2) The court may make a summary assessment of costs payable by a child or patient.

13.12*

(1) Attention is drawn to rule 44.3A which prevents the court from making a summary assessment of an additional liability before the conclusion of the proceedings or the part of the proceedings to which the funding arrangement relates. Where this applies, the court should nonetheless make a summary assessment of the base costs of the hearing or application unless there is a good reason not to do so.

(2) Where the court makes a summary assessment of the base costs all statements of costs and costs estimates put before the judge will be retained on the court file.

13.13 The court will not give its approval to disproportionate and unreasonable costs. Accordingly:

(a) When the amount of the costs to be paid has been agreed between the parties the order for costs must state that the order is by consent.

(b) If the judge is to make an order which is not by consent, the judge will, so far as possible, ensure that the final figure is not disproportionate and/or unreasonable having regard to Part 1 of the CPR. The judge will retain this responsibility notwithstanding the absence of challenge to individual items in the make-up of the figure sought. The fact that the paying party is not disputing the amount of costs can however be taken as some indication that the amount is proportionate and reasonable. The judge will therefore intervene only if satisfied that the costs are so disproportionate that it is right to do so.

SECTION 14 Summary assessment where costs claimed include an additional liability

Orders made before the conclusion of the proceedings

K–037   *14.1   The existence of a conditional fee agreement or other funding arrangement within the meaning of rule 43.2 is not by itself a sufficient reason for not carrying out a summary assessment.

*14.2   Where a legal representative acting for the receiving party has entered into a conditional fee agreement the court may summarily assess all the costs (other than any additional liability).

*14.3   Where costs have been summarily assessed an order for payment will not be made unless the court has been satisfied that in respect of the costs claimed, the receiving party is at the time liable to pay to his legal representative an amount equal to or greater than the costs claimed. A statement in the form of the certificate appended at the end of Form N260 may be sufficient proof of liability. The giving of information under rule 44.15 (where that rule applies) is not sufficient.

*14.4   The court may direct that any costs, for which the receiving party may not in the event be liable, shall be paid into court to await the outcome of the case, or shall not be enforceable until further order, or it may postpone the receiving party's right to receive payment in some other way.

Orders made at the conclusion of the proceedings

K–038   *14.5   Where there has been a trial of one or more issues separately from other issues, the court will not normally order detailed assessment of the additional liability until all issues have been tried unless the parties agree.

*14.6   Rule 44.3A(2) sets out the ways in which the court may deal with the assessment of the costs where there is a funding arrangement. Where the court makes a summary assessment of the base costs:

(1) The order may state separately the base costs allowed as (a) solicitor's charges, (b) counsel's fees, (c) any other disbursements and (d) any VAT;

(2) the statements of costs upon which the judge based his summary assessment will be retained on the court file.

*14.7   Where the court makes a summary assessment of an additional liability at the conclusion of proceedings, that assessment must relate to the whole of the proceedings; this will include any additional liability relating to base costs allowed by the court when making a summary assessment on a previous application or hearing.

*14.8   Paragraph 13.13 applies where the parties are agreed about the total amount to be paid by way of costs, or are agreed about the amount of the base costs that will be paid. Where they disagree about the additional liability the court may summarily assess that liability or make an order for a detailed assessment.

*14.9 In order to facilitate the court in making a summary assessment of any additional liability at the conclusion of the proceedings the party seeking such costs must prepare and have available for the court a bundle of documents which must include—

(1) a copy of every notice of funding arrangement (Form N251) which has been filed by him;

(2) a copy of every estimate and statement of costs filed by him;

(3) a copy of the risk assessment prepared at the time any relevant funding arrangement was entered into and on the basis of which the amount of the additional liability was fixed.

SECTION 15 Costs on the small claims track and fast track: Rule 44.9

15.1   K–039

(1) Before a claim is allocated to one of those tracks the court is not restricted by any of the special rules that apply to that track.

(2) Where a claim has been allocated to one of those tracks, the special rules which relate to that track will apply to work done before as well as after allocation save to the extent (if any) that an order for costs in respect of that work was made before allocation.

(3) (i) This paragraph applies where a claim, issued for a sum in excess of the normal financial scope of the small claims track, is allocated to that track only because an admission of part of the claim by the defendant reduces the amount in dispute to a sum within the normal scope of that track.
       See also paragraph 7.4 of the practice direction supplementing CPR Part 26)

     (ii) On entering judgment for the admitted part before allocation of the balance of the claim the court may allow costs in respect of the proceedings down to that date.

SECTION 16 Costs following allocation and re-allocation: Rule 44.11

16.1 This paragraph applies where the court is about to make an order to   K–040
reallocate a claim from the small claims track to another track.

16.2 Before making the order to re-allocate the claim, the court must decide whether any party is to pay costs to any other party down to the date of the order to re-allocate in accordance with the rules about costs contained in Part 27 (The Small Claims Track).

16.3 If it decides to make such an order about costs, the court will make a summary assessment of those costs in accordance with that Part.

SECTION 17 Costs—only proceedings: Rule 44.12A

*17.1 A claim form under this rule should be issued in the court which would have   K–041
been the appropriate office in accordance with rule 47.4 had proceedings been brought in relation to the substantive claim. A claim form under this rule should not be issued in the High Court unless the dispute to which the agreement relates was of such a value or type that had proceedings been begun they would have been commenced in the High Court.

*17.2 A claim form which is to be issued in the High Court at the Royal Courts of Justice will be issued in the Supreme Court Costs Office.

*17.3 Attention is drawn to rule 8.2 (in particular to paragraph (b)(ii)) and to rule 44.12A(3). The claim form must:

(1) identify the claim or dispute to which the agreement to pay costs relates;

(2) state the date and terms of the agreement on which the claimant relies;

(3) set out or have attached to it a draft of the order which the claimant seeks;

(4) state the amount of the costs claimed; and,

(5) state whether the costs are claimed on the standard or indemnity basis. If no basis is specified the costs will be treated as being claimed on the standard basis.

*17.4 The evidence to be filed and served with the claim form under Rule 8.5 must include copies of the documents on which the claimant relies to prove the defendant's agreement to pay costs.

*17.5 A costs judge or a district judge has jurisdiction to hear and decide any issue which may arise in a claim issued under this rule irrespective of the amount of the costs claimed or of the value of the claim to which the agreement to pay costs relates. A costs officer may make an order by consent under paragraph 17.7, or an order dismissing a claim under paragraph 17.9 below.

*17.6 When the time for filing the defendant's acknowledgement of service has expired, the claimant may by letter request the court to make an order in the terms of his claim, unless the defendant has filed an acknowledgement of service stating that he intends to contest the claim or to seek a different order.

*17.7 Rule 40.6 applies where an order is to be made by consent. An order may be made by consent in terms which differ from those set out in the claim form.

*17.8

(1) An order for costs made under this rule will be treated as an order for the amount of costs to be decided by a detailed assessment to which Part 47 and the practice directions relating to it apply. Rule 44.4(4) (determination of basis of assessment) also applies to the order.

(2) In cases in which an additional liability is claimed, the costs judge or district judge should have regard to the time when and the extent to which the claim has been settled and to the fact that the claim has been settled without the need to commence proceedings.

*17.9

(1) For the purposes of rule 44.12A(4)(b)—

(a) a claim will be treated as opposed if the defendant files an acknowledgment of service stating that he intends to contest the making of an order for costs or to seek a different remedy; and

(b) a claim will not be treated as opposed if the defendant files an acknowledgment of service stating that he disputes the amount of the claim for costs.

(2) An order dismissing the claim will be made as soon as an acknowledgment of service opposing the claim is filed. The dismissal of a claim

under rule 44.12A(4) does not prevent the claimant from issuing another claim form under Part 7 or Part 8 based on the agreement or alleged agreement to which the proceedings under this rule related.

*17.10

(1) Rule 8.9 (which provides that claims issued under Part 8 shall be treated as allocated to the multi-track) shall not apply to claims issued under this rule. A claim issued under this rule may be dealt with without being allocated to a track.

(2) Rule 8.1(3) and Part 24 do not apply to proceedings brought under rule 44.12A.

*17.11 Nothing in this rule prevents a person from issuing a claim form under Part 7 or Part 8 to sue on an agreement made in settlement of a dispute where that agreement makes provision for costs, nor from claiming in that case an order for costs or a specified sum in respect of costs.

SECTION 18 Court's powers in relation to misconduct: Rule 44.14

18.1 Before making an order under rule 44.14 the court must give the party or legal representative in question a reasonable opportunity to attend a hearing to give reasons why it should not make such an order.   K–042

18.2 Conduct before or during the proceedings which gave rise to the assessment which is unreasonable or improper includes steps which are calculated to prevent or inhibit the court from furthering the overriding objective.

18.3 Although rule 44.14(3) does not specify any sanction for breach of the obligation imposed by the rule the court may, either in the order under paragraph (2) or in a subsequent order, require the solicitor to produce to the court evidence that he took reasonable steps to comply with the obligation.

SECTION 19 Providing information about funding arrangements: Rule 44.15

*19.1   K–043

(1) A party who wishes to claim an additional liability in respect of a funding arrangement must give any other party information about that claim if he is to recover the additional liability. There is no requirement to specify the amount of the additional liability separately nor to state how it is calculated until it falls to be assessed. That principle is reflected in rules 44.3A and 44.15, in the following paragraphs and in Sections 6, 13, 14 and 31 of this Practice Direction. Section 6 deals with estimates of costs, Sections 13 and 14 deal with summary assessment and Section 31 deals with detailed assessment.

(2) In the following paragraphs a party who has entered into a funding arrangement is treated as a person who intends to recover a sum representing an additional liability by way of costs.

(3) Attention is drawn to paragraph 57.9 of this Practice Direction which sets out time limits for the provision of information where a funding arrangement is entered into between 31 March and 2 July 2000 and proceedings relevant to that arrangement are commenced before 3 July 2000.

Method of giving information

K–044 *19.2

(1) In this paragraph, "claim form" includes petition and application notice, and the notice of funding to be filed or served is a notice containing the information set out in Form N251.

(2) (a) A claimant who has entered into a funding arrangement before starting the proceedings to which it relates must provide information to the court by filing the notice when he issues the claim form.

    (b) He must provide information to every other party by serving the notice. If he serves the claim form himself he must serve the notice with the claim form. If the court is to serve the claim form, the court will also serve the notice if the claimant provides it with sufficient copies for service.

(3) A defendant who has entered into a funding arrangement before filing any document

    (a) must provide information to the court by filing notice with his first document. A "first document" may be an acknowledgement of service, a defence, or any other document, such as an application to set aside a default judgment.

    (b) must provide information to every party by serving notice. If he serves his first document himself he must serve the notice with that document. If the court is to serve his first document the court will also serve the notice if the defendant provides it with sufficient copies for service.

(4) In all other circumstances a party must file and serve notice within 7 days of entering into the funding arrangement concerned.

(5) There is no requirement in this Practice Direction for the provision of information about funding arrangements before the commencement of proceedings. Such provision is however recommended and may be required by a pre-action protocol.

Notice of change of information

K–045 *19.3

(1) Rule 44.15 imposes a duty on a party to give notice of change if the information he has previously provided is no longer accurate. To comply he must file and serve notice containing the information set out in Form N251. Rule 44.15(3) may impose other duties in relation to new estimates of costs.

(2) Further notification need not be provided where a party has already given notice:

    (a) that he has entered into a conditional fee agreement with a legal representative and during the currency of that agreement either of them enters into another such agreement with an additional legal representative; or

    (b) of some insurance cover, unless that cover is cancelled or unless new cover is taken out with a different insurer.

(3) Part 6 applies to the service of notices.

(4) The notice must be signed by the party or by his legal representative.

Information which must be provided

*19.4   K–046

    (1) Unless the court otherwise orders, a party who is required to supply information about a funding arrangement must state whether he has—

        entered into a conditional fee agreement which provides for a success fee within the meaning of section 58(2) of the Courts and Legal Services Act 1990;

        taken out an insurance policy to which section 29 of the Access to Justice Act 1999 applies;

        made an arrangement with a body which is prescribed for the purpose of section 30 of that Act;

        or more than one of these.

    (2) Where the funding arrangement is a conditional fee agreement, the party must state the date of the agreement and identify the claim or claims to which it relates (including Part 20 claims if any).

    (3) Where the funding arrangement is an insurance policy the party must state the name of the insurer, the date of the policy and must identify the claim or claims to which it relates (including Part 20 claims if any).

    (4) Where the funding arrangement is by way of an arrangement with a relevant body the party must state the name of the body and set out the date and terms of the undertaking it has given and must identify the claim or claims to which it relates (including Part 20 claims if any).

    (5) Where a party has entered into more than one funding arrangement in respect of a claim, for example a conditional fee agreement and an insurance policy, a single notice containing the information set out in Form N251 may contain the required information about both or all of them

*19.5 Where the court makes a Group Litigation Order, the court may give directions as to the extent to which individual parties should provide information in accordance with rule 44.15. (Part 19 deals with Group Litigation Orders.)

SECTION 20 Procedure where legal representative wishes to recover from his client an agreed percentage increase which has been disallowed or reduced on assessment: Rule 44.16

*20.1   K–047

    (1) Attention is drawn to Regulation 3(2)(b) of the Conditional Fee Agreements Regulations 2000 and to Regulation 5(2)(b) of the Collective Conditional Fee Agreements Regulations 2000, which provide that some or all of a success fee ceases to be payable in certain circumstances.

    (2) Rule 44.16 allows the court to adjourn a hearing at which the legal representative acting for the receiving party applies for an order that a disallowed amount should continue to be payable under the agreement.

*20.2 In the following paragraphs "counsel" means counsel who has acted in the case under a conditional fee agreement which provides for a success fee. A reference to counsel includes a reference to any person who appeared as an advocate in the case and who is not a partner or employee of the solicitor or firm which is conducting the claim or defence (as the case may be) on behalf of the receiving party.

Procedure following Summary Assessment

K–048 *20.3

(1) If the court disallows any amount of a legal representative's percentage increase, the court will, unless sub-paragraph (2) applies, give directions to enable an application to be made by the legal representative for the disallowed amount to be payable by his client, including, if appropriate, a direction that the application will be determined by a costs judge or district judge of the court dealing with the case.

(2) The court that has made the summary assessment may then and there decide the issue whether the disallowed amount should continue to be payable, if:

(a) the receiving party and all parties to the relevant agreement consent to the court doing so;

(b) the receiving party (or, if corporate, an officer) is present in court; and

(c) the court is satisfied that the issue can be fairly decided then and there.

Procedure following Detailed Assessment

K–049 *20.4

(1) Where detailed assessment proceedings have been commenced, and the paying party serves points of dispute (as to which see Section 34 of this Practice Direction), which show that he is seeking a reduction in any percentage increase charged by counsel on his fees, the solicitor acting for the receiving party must within 3 days of service deliver to counsel a copy of the relevant points of dispute and the bill of costs or the relevant parts of the bill.

(2) Counsel must within 10 days thereafter inform the solicitor in writing whether or not he will accept the reduction sought or some other reduction. Counsel may state any points he wishes to have made in a reply to the points of dispute, and the solicitor must serve them on the paying party as or as part of a reply.

(3) Counsel who fails to inform the solicitor within the time limits set out above will be taken to accept the reduction unless the court otherwise orders.

*20.5 Where the paying party serves points of dispute seeking a reduction in any percentage increase charged by a legal representative acting for the receiving party, and that legal representative intends, if necessary, to apply for an order that any amount of the percentage disallowed as against the paying party shall continue to be payable by his client, the solicitor acting for the receiving party must, within 14 days of service of the points of dispute, give to his client a clear written explanation of the nature of the relevant point of dispute and the effect it will have if it is upheld in whole or in part by the court, and of the client's right to attend any subsequent hearings at court when the matter is raised.

*20.6 Where the solicitor acting for a receiving party files a request for a detailed assessment hearing it must if appropriate, be accompanied by a certificate signed by him stating:

(1) that the amount of the percentage increase in respect of counsel's fees or solicitor's charges is disputed;
(2) whether an application will be made for an order that any amount of that increase which is disallowed should continue to be payable by his client;
(3) that he has given his client an explanation in accordance with paragraph 20.5; and,
(4) whether his client wishes to attend court when the amount of any relevant percentage increase may be decided.

*20.7

(1) The solicitor acting for the receiving party must within 7 days of receiving from the court notice of the date of the assessment hearing, notify his client, and if appropriate, counsel in writing of the date, time and place of the hearing.
(2) Counsel may attend or be represented at the detailed assessment hearing and may make oral or written submissions.

*20.8

(1) At the detailed assessment hearing, the court will deal with the assessment of the costs payable by one party to another, including the amount of the percentage increase, and give a certificate accordingly.
(2) The court may decide the issue whether the disallowed amount should continue to be payable under the relevant conditional fee agreement without an adjournment if:

(a) the receiving party and all parties to the relevant agreement consent to the court deciding the issue without an adjournment,
(b) the receiving party (or, if corporate, an officer or employee who has authority to consent on behalf of the receiving party) is present in court, and
(c) the court is satisfied that the issue can be fairly decided without an adjournment.

(3) In any other case the court will give directions and fix a date for the hearing of the application.

SECTION 21 Application of costs rules: Rule 44.17

*21.1 Rule 44.17(b) excludes the costs rules to the extent that regulations under the Legal Aid Act 1988 make different provision. The primary examples of such regulations are the regulations providing prescribed rates (with or without enhancement). **K–050**

*21.2 Rule 44.17(a) also excludes the procedure for the detailed assessment of costs in cases to which Section 11 of the Access to Justice Act 1999 applies, whether it applies in whole or in part. In these excluded cases the procedure for determination of costs is set out in Section 22 of this Practice Direction.

*21.3 Section 11 of the Access to Justice Act 1999 provides special protection against liability for costs for litigants who receive funding by the LSC (Legal Services Commission) as part of the Community Legal Service. Any costs ordered to be paid by a LSC funded client must not exceed the amount

553

which is reasonable for him to pay having regard to all the circumstances including:

    (a) the financial resources of all the parties to the proceedings, and

    (b) their conduct in connection with the dispute to which the proceedings relate.

*21.4 In this Practice Direction

"cost protection" means the limit on costs awarded against a LSC funded client set out in Section 11(1) of the Access to Justice Act 1999.

"partner" has the meaning given by the Community Legal Service (Costs) Regulations 2000.

K–051 *21.5 Whether or not cost protection applies depends upon the "level of service" for which funding was provided by the LSC in accordance with the Funding Code approved under section 9 of the Access to Justice Act 1999. The levels of service referred to are:

(1) **Legal Help**—advice and assistance about a legal problem, not including representation or advocacy in proceedings.

(2) **Help at Court**—advocacy at a specific hearing, where the advocate is not formally representing the client in the proceedings.

(3) **Family Mediation.**

(4) **Legal Representation**—representation in actual or contemplated proceedings. Legal Representation can take the form of **Investigative Help** (limited to investigating the merits of a potential claim) or **Full Representation.**

(5) **Approved Family Help**—this can take the form of **Help with Mediation** (legal advice in support of the family mediation process) or **General Family Help** (help negotiating a settlement to a family dispute without recourse to adversarial litigation).

(6) **Support Funding**—partial funding in expensive cases that are primarily being funded privately, under or with a view to a conditional fee agreement. Support Funding can take the form of **Investigative Support** (equivalent to *Investigative Help*) or **Litigation Support** (equivalent to *Full Representation*).

*21.6 Levels of service (4) (5) and (6) are provided under a certificate (similar to a legal aid certificate). The certificate will state which level of service is covered. Where there are proceedings, a copy of the certificate will be lodged with the court.

*21.7 Cost protection does not apply where:

    (1) The LSC funded client receives Help at Court;

    (2) the LSC funded client receives Litigation Support (but see further, paragraph 21.8);

    (3) the LSC funded client receives Investigative Support (except where the proceedings for which Investigative Support was given are not pursued after the certificate is discharged). Investigative Support will not normally cover the issue of proceedings (except for disclosure), but cost protection may be relevant if the defendant seeks an assessment of pre-action costs;

    (4) the LSC funded client receives Legal Help only i.e. where the solicitor is advising, but not representing a litigant in person. However, where the LSC funded client receives Legal Help e.g. to write a letter before action, but later receives Legal Representation or Approved Family Help in respect of the same dispute, cost protection does apply to all

554

costs incurred by the receiving party in the funded proceedings or prospective proceedings.

*21.8 Where cost protection does not apply, the court may award costs in the normal way. In the case of Litigation Support, costs that are not covered by the LSC funded client's insurance are usually payable by the LSC rather than the funded client, and the court should order accordingly (see Regulation. 6 of the Community Legal Service (Cost Protection) Regulations 2000).

*21.9 Where work is done before the issue of a certificate, cost protection does not apply to those costs, except where:

(1) pre-action Legal Help is given and the LSC funded client subsequently receives Legal Representation or Approved Family Help in the same dispute; or

(2) where urgent work is undertaken immediately before the grant of an emergency certificate when no emergency application could be made as the LSC's offices were closed, provided that the solicitor seeks an emergency certificate at the first available opportunity and the certificate is granted.

*21.10 If a LSC funded client's certificate is revoked, costs protection does not apply to work done before or after revocation.

*21.11 If a LSC funded client's certificate is discharged, costs protection only applies to costs incurred before the date on which funded services ceased to be provided under the certificate. This may be a date before the date on which the certificate is formally discharged by the LSC (Burridge v Stafford: Khan v Ali [2000] 1 WLR 927, [1999] 4 All ER 660 C.A.).

Assessing a LSC Funded Client's Resources

*21.12 The first £100,000 of the value of the LSC funded client's interest in the main or only home is disregarded when assessing his or her financial resources for the purposes of S.11 and cannot be the subject of any enforcement process by the receiving party. The receiving party cannot apply for an order to sell the LSC funded client's home, but could secure the debt against any value exceeding £100,000 by way of a charging order.

*21.13 The court may only take into account the value of the LSC funded client's clothes, household furniture, tools and implements of trade to the extent that it considers that having regard to the quantity or value of the items, the circumstances are exceptional.

*21.14 The LSC funded client's resources include the resources of his partner, unless the partner has a contrary interest in the dispute in respect of which funded services are provided.

Party acting in a Representative, Fiduciary or Official Capacity

*21.15   K–052

(1) Where a LSC funded client is acting in a representative, fiduciary or official capacity, the court shall not take the personal resources of the party into account for the purposes of either a Section 11 order or costs against the Commission, but shall have regard to the value of any property or estate or the amount of any fund out of which the party is entitled to be indemnified, and may also have regard to the resources of any persons who are beneficially interested in the property, estate or fund.

(2) The purpose of this provision is to ensure that any liability is determined with reference to the value of the property or fund being used to pay for the litigation, and the financial position of those who may benefit from or rely on it.

Costs against the LSC

K–053   *21.16 Regulation 5 of the Community Legal Service (Cost Protection) Regulations 2000 governs when costs can be awarded against the LSC. This provision only applies where cost protection applies and the costs ordered to be paid by the LSC funded client do not fully meet the costs that would have been ordered to be paid by him if cost protection did not apply.

*21.17 In this Section and the following two Sections of this Practice Direction "non-funded party" means a party to proceedings who has not received LSC funded services in relation to these proceedings under a legal aid certificate or a certificate issued under the LSC Funding Code other than a certificate which has been revoked.

*21.18 The following criteria set out in Regulation 5 must be satisfied before the LSC can be ordered to pay the whole or any part of the costs incurred by a non-funded party:

(1) the proceedings are finally decided in favour of a non-funded party;
(2) the non-funded party provides written notice of intention to seek an order against the LSC within three months of the making of the section 11(1) costs order;
(3) the court is satisfied that it is just and equitable in the circumstances that provision for the costs should be made out of public funds; and
(4) where costs are incurred in a court of first instance, the following additional criteria must also be met:

(i) the proceedings were instituted by the LSC funded client; and
(ii) the non-funded party will suffer severe financial hardship unless the order is made.

"Section 11(1) costs order" is defined in paragraph 22.1, below).

*21.19 In determining whether conditions (3) and (4) are satisfied, the court shall take into account the resources of the non-funded party and his partner, unless the partner has a contrary interest.

Effect of Appeals

K–054   *21.20

(1) An order for costs can only be made against the LSC when the proceedings (including any appeal) are finally decided. Therefore, where a court of first instance decides in favour of a non-funded party and an appeal lies, any order made against the LSC shall not take effect unless:

(a) where permission to appeal is required, the time limit for permission to appeal expires, without permission being granted;
(b) where permission to appeal is granted or is not required, the time limit for appeal expires without an appeal being brought.

(2) Accordingly, if the LSC funded client appeals, any earlier order against the LSC can never take effect. If the appeal is unsuccessful, an application can be made to the appeal court for a fresh order.

SECTION 22 Orders for costs to which section 11 of the Access to Justice Act 1999 applies

*22.1   In this Practice Direction: **K–055**

"order for costs to be determined" means an order for costs to which Section 11 of the Access to Justice Act 1999 applies under which the amount of costs payable by the LSC funded client is to be determined by a costs judge or district judge under Section 23 of this Practice Direction.

"order specifying the costs payable" means an order for costs to which Section 11 of the Act applies and which specifies the amount which the LSC funded client is to pay.

"full costs" means, where an order to which Section 11 of the Act applies is made against a LSC funded client, the amount of costs which that person would, had cost protection not applied, have been ordered to pay.

"determination proceedings" means proceedings to which paragraphs 22.1 to 22.10 apply.

"Section 11(1) costs order" means an order for costs to be determined or an order specifying the costs payable other than an order specifying the costs payable which was made in determination proceedings.

"statement of resources" means

(1) a statement, verified by a statement of truth, made by a party to proceedings setting out:
   (a) his income and capital and financial commitments during the previous year and, if applicable, those of his partner;
   (b) his estimated future financial resources and expectations and, if applicable, those of his partner ("partner" is defined in paragraph 21.4, above);
   (c) a declaration that he and, if applicable, his partner, has not deliberately foregone or deprived himself of any resources or expectations;
   (d) particulars of any application for funding made by him in connection with the proceedings; and,
   (e) any other facts relevant to the determination of his resources; or

(2) a statement, verified by a statement of truth, made by a client receiving funded services, setting out the information provided by the client under Regulation 6 of the Community Legal Service (Financial) Regulations 2000, and stating that there has been no significant change in the client's financial circumstances since the date on which the information was provided or, as the case may be, details of any such change.

"Regional Director" means any Regional Director appointed by the LSC and any member of his staff authorised to act on his behalf.

*22.2   Regulations 8 to 13 of the Community Legal Service (Costs) Regulations 2000 set out the procedure for seeking costs against a funded client and the LSC. The effect of these Regulations is set out in this section and the next section of this Practice Direction.

*22.3   As from 5 June 2000, Regulations 9 to 13 of the Community Legal Service (Costs) Regulations 2000 also apply to certificates issued under the Legal Aid Act 1988 where costs against the assisted person fall to be assessed under Regulation 124 of the Civil Legal Aid (General) Regulations 1989. In this section and the next section of this Practice Direction the expression "LSC funded client" includes an assisted person (defined in rule 43.2).

*22.4 Regulation 8 of the Community Legal Service (Costs) Regulations 2000 provides that a party intending to seek an order for costs against a LSC funded client may at any time file and serve on the LSC funded client a statement of resources. If that statement is served 7 or more days before a date fixed for a hearing at which an order for costs may be made, the LSC funded client must also make a statement of resources and produce it at the hearing.

*22.5 If the court decides to make an order for costs against a LSC funded client to whom cost protection applies it may either:

(1) make an order for costs to be determined, or

(2) make an order specifying the costs payable.

*22.6 If the court makes an order for costs to be determined it may also

(1) state the amount of full costs, or

(2) make findings of facts, e.g., concerning the conduct of all the parties which are to be taken into account by the court in the subsequent determination proceedings.

*22.7 The court will not make an order specifying the costs payable unless:

(1) it considers that it has sufficient information before it to decide what amount is a reasonable amount for the LSC funded client to pay in accordance with Section 11 of the Act, and

(2) either

(a) the order also states the amount of full costs, or

(b) the court considers that it has sufficient information before it to decide what amount is a reasonable amount for the LSC funded client to pay in accordance with Section 11 of the Act and is satisfied that, if it were to determine the full costs at that time, they would exceed the amounts specified in the order.

*22.8 Where an order specifying the costs payable is made and the LSC funded client does not have cost protection in respect of all of the costs awarded in that order, the order must identify the sum payable (if any) in respect of which the LSC funded client has cost protection and the sum payable (if any) in respect of which he does not have cost protection.

*22.9 The court cannot make an order under Regulations 8 to 13 of the Community Legal Service (Costs) Regulations 2000 except in proceedings to which the next section of this Practice Direction applies.

SECTION 23 Determination proceedings and similar proceedings under the Community Legal Service (Costs) Regulations 2000

K–056 *23.1 This section of this Practice Direction deals with

(1) proceedings subsequent to the making of an order for costs to be determined,

(2) variations in the amount stated in an order specifying the amount of costs payable and

(3) the late determination of costs under an order for costs to be determined.

*23.2 In this section of this Practice Direction "appropriate court office" means:

(1) the district registry or county court in which the case was being dealt with when the Section 11(1) order was made, or to which it has subsequently been transferred; or

(2) in all other cases, the Supreme Court Costs Office.

*23.3

(1) A receiving party seeking an order specifying costs payable by an LSC funded client and/or by the LSC may within 3 months of an order for costs to be determined, file in the appropriate court office an application in Form N244 accompanied by

(a) the receiving party's bill of costs (unless the full costs have already been determined);

(b) the receiving party's statement of resources; and

(c) if the receiving party intends to seek costs against the LSC, written notice to that effect.

(2) If the LSC funded client's liability has already been determined and is less than the full costs, the application will be for costs against the LSC only. If the LSC funded client's liability has not yet been determined, the receiving party must indicate if costs will be sought against the LSC if the funded client's liability is determined as less than the full costs.

(The LSC funded client's certificate will contain the addresses of the LSC funded client, his solicitor, and the relevant Regional Office of the LSC.)

*23.4 The receiving party must file the above documents in the appropriate court office and (where relevant) serve copies on the LSC funded client and the Regional Director. Failure to file a request within the 3 months time limit specified in Regulation 10(2) is an absolute bar to the making of a costs order against the LSC.

*23.5 On being served with the application, the LSC funded client must respond by filing a statement of resources and serving a copy of it on the receiving party (and the Regional Director where relevant) within 21 days. The LSC funded client may also file and serve written points disputing the bill within the same time limit. (Under rule 3.1 the court may extend or shorten this time limit.)

*23.6 If the LSC funded client fails to file a statement of resources without good reason, the court will determine his liability (and the amount of full costs if relevant) and need not hold an oral hearing for such determination.

*23.7 When the LSC funded client files a statement or the 21 day period for doing so expires, the court will fix a hearing date and give the relevant parties at least 14 days notice. The court may fix a hearing without waiting for the expiry of the 21 day period if the application is made only against the LSC.

*23.8 Determination proceedings will be listed for hearing before a costs judge or district judge.

*23.9 Where the LSC funded client does not have cost protection in respect of all of the costs awarded, the order made by the costs judge or district judge must in addition to specifying the costs payable, identify the full costs in respect of which cost protection applies and the full costs in respect of which cost protection does not apply.

*23.10 The Regional Director may appear at any hearing at which a costs order may be made against the LSC. Instead of appearing, he may file a written statement at court and serve a copy on the receiving party. The written statement should be filed and a copy served, not less than 7 days before the hearing.

Variation of an order specifying the costs payable

K–057 *23.11

(1) This paragraph applies where the amount stated in an order specifying the costs payable plus the amount ordered to be paid by the LSC is less than the full costs to which cost protection applies.

(2) The receiving party may apply to the court for a variation of the amount which the LSC funded client is required to pay on the ground that there has been a significant change in the client's circumstances since the date of the order.

*23.12 On an application under paragraph 23.11, where the order specifying the costs payable does not state the full costs

(1) the receiving party must file with his application the receiving party's statement of resources and bill of costs and copies of these documents should be served with the application.

(2) The LSC funded client must respond to the application by making a statement of resources which must be filed at court and served on the receiving party within 21 days thereafter. The LSC funded client may also file and serve written points disputing the bill within the same time limit.

(3) The court will, when determining the application assess the full costs identifying any part of them to which cost protection does apply and any part of them to which cost protection does not apply.

*23.13 On an application under paragraph 23.11 the order specifying the costs payable may be varied as the court thinks fit. That variation must not increase:

(1) the amount of any costs ordered to be paid by the LSC, and

(2) the amount payable by the LSC funded client,

to a sum which is greater than the amount of the full costs plus the costs of the application.

*23.14

(1) Where an order for costs to be determined has been made but the receiving party has not applied, within the three month time limit under paragraph 23.2, the receiving party may apply on any of the following grounds for a determination of the amount which the funded client is required to pay:

(a) there has been a significant change in the funded client's circumstances since the date of the order for costs to be determined; or

(b) material additional information about the funded client's financial resources is available which could not with reasonable diligence have been obtained by the receiving party at the relevant time; or

(c) there were other good reasons for the failure by the receiving party to make an application within the time limit.

(2) An application for costs payable by the LSC cannot be made under this paragraph.

*23.15

(1) Where the receiving party has received funded services in relation to the proceedings, the LSC may make an application under paragraphs 23.11 and 23.14 above.

(2) In respect of an application under paragraph 23.11 made by the LSC, the LSC must file and serve copies of the documents described in paragraph 23.12(1)

*23.16 An application under paragraph 23.11, 23.14 and 23.15 must be commenced before the expiration of 6 years from the date on which the court made the order specifying the costs payable, or (as the case may be) the order for costs to be determined.

*23.17 Applications under paragraphs 23.11, 23.14 and 23.15 should be made in the appropriate court office and should be made in Form N244 to be listed for a hearing before a costs judge or district judge.

Directions Relating to Part 45

Fixed Costs

SECTION 24 Fixed costs in small claims

24.1 Under Rule 27.14 the costs which can be awarded to a claimant in a small claims track case include the fixed costs payable under Part 45 attributable to issuing the claim.   K–058

24.2 Those fixed costs shall be the sum of

(a) the fixed commencement costs calculated in accordance with Table 1 of Rule 45.2 and;

(b) the appropriate court fee or fees paid by the claimant.

SECTION 25 Fixed costs on the issue of a default costs certificate

25.1 Unless paragraph 24.2 applies or unless the court orders otherwise, the fixed costs to be included in a default costs certificate are £80 plus a sum equal to any appropriate court fee payable on the issue of the certificate.   K–059

25.2 The fixed costs included in a certificate must not exceed the maximum sum specified for costs and court fee in the notice of commencement.

SECTION 25A Road traffic accidents: fixed recoverable costs in costs-only proceedings

Scope

25A.1 Section II of Part 45 ('the Section') provides for certain fixed costs to be recoverable between parties in respect of costs incurred in disputes which are settled prior to proceedings being issued. The Section applies to road traffic accident disputes as defined in rule 45.7(4)(a), where the accident which gave rise to the dispute occurred on or after 6th October 2003.

25A.2 The Section does not apply to diputes where the total agreed value of the damages is within the small claims limit or exceeds £10,000. Rule 26.8(2) sets out how the financial value of a claim is assessed for the purposes of allocation to track.

25A.3 Fixed recoverable costs are to be calculated by reference to the amount of agreed damages which are payable to the receiving party. In calculating the amount of these damages—

(a) account must be taken of both general and special damages and interest;

(b) any interim payments made must be included;

(c) where the parties have agreed an element of contributory negligence, the amount of damages attributed to that negligence must be deducted;

(d) any amount required by statute to be paid by the compensating party directly to a third party (such as sums paid by way of compensation recovery payments and National Health Service expenses) must not be included.

25A.4 The Section applies to cases which fall within the scope of the Uninsured Drivers Agreement dated 13 August 1999. The section does not apply to cases which fall within the scope of the Untraced Drivers Agreement dated 14 February 2003.

Directions Relating to Part 46

Fast track trial costs

SECTION 26 Scope of Part 46: Rule 46.1

K–060   26.1   Part 46 applies to the costs of an advocate for preparing for and appearing at the trial of a claim in the fast track.

26.2   It applies only where, at the date of the trial, the claim is allocated to the fast track. It does not apply in any other case, irrespective of the final value of the claim.

26.3   In particular it does not apply to:

(a) the hearing of a claim which is allocated to the small claims track with the consent of the parties given under rule 26.7(3); or

(b) a disposal hearing at which the amount to be paid under a judgment or order is decided by the court (see paragraph 12.8 of the Practice Direction which supplements Part 26 (Case Management—Preliminary Stage)).

Cases which settle before trial

K–061   26.4   Attention is drawn to rule 44.10 (limitation on amount court may award where a claim allocated to the fast track settles before trial).

SECTION 27 Power to award more or less than the amount of fast track trial costs: Rule 46.3

K–062   *27.1   Rule 44.15 (providing information about funding arrangements) sets out the requirement to provide information about funding arrangements to the court and other parties. Section 19 of this Practice Direction sets out the information to be provided and when this is to be done.

*27.2   Section 11, of this Practice Direction explains how the court will approach the question of what sum to allow in respect of additional liability.

*27.3   The court has the power, when considering whether a percentage increase is reasonable, to allow different percentages for different items of costs or for different periods during which costs were incurred.

Directions Relating to Part 47

Procedure for detailed assessment of costs and default provisions

SECTION 28 Time when assessment may be carried out: Rule 47.1

*28.1   K–063

(1) For the purposes of rule 47.1, proceedings are concluded when the court has finally determined the matters in issue in the claim, whether or not there is an appeal.

(2) For the purposes of this rule, the making of an award of provisional damages under Part 41 will be treated as a final determination of the matters in issue.

(3) The court may order or the parties may agree in writing that, although the proceedings are continuing, they will nevertheless be treated as concluded.

(4) (a) A party who is served with a notice of commencement (see paragraph 32.3 below) may apply to a costs judge or a district judge to determine whether the party who served it is entitled to commence detailed assessment proceedings.

    (b) On hearing such an application the orders which the court may make include: an order allowing the detailed assessment proceedings to continue, or an order setting aside the notice of commencement.

(5) A costs judge or a district judge may make an order allowing detailed assessment proceedings to be commenced where there is no realistic prospect of the claim continuing.

SECTION 29 No stay of detailed assessment where there is an appeal: Rule 47.2

29.1   K–064

(1) Rule 47.2 provides that detailed assessment is not stayed pending an appeal unless the court so orders.

(2) An application to stay the detailed assessment of costs pending an appeal may be made to the court whose order is being appealed or to the court who will hear the appeal.

SECTION 30 Powers of an authorised court officer: Rule 47.3

*30.1   K–065

(1) The court officers authorised by the Lord Chancellor to assess costs in the Supreme Court Costs Office and the Principal Registry of the Family Division are authorised to deal with claims for costs not exceeding £17,500 (excluding VAT) in the case of senior executive officers and £35,000 (excluding VAT) in the case of principal officers.

(2) In calculating whether or not a bill of costs is within the authorised amounts, the figure to be taken into account is the total claim for costs including any additional liability.

(3) Where the receiving party, paying party and any other party to the detailed assessment proceedings who has served points of dispute are

agreed that the assessment should not be made by an authorised court officer, the receiving party should so inform the court when requesting a hearing date. The court will then list the hearing before a costs judge or a district judge.

(4) In any other case a party who objects to the assessment being made by an authorised court officer must make an application to the costs judge or district judge under Part 23 (General Rules about Applications for Court Orders) setting out the reasons for the objection and if sufficient reason is shown the court will direct that the bill be assessed by a costs judge or district judge.

SECTION 31 Venue for detailed assessment proceedings: Rule 47.4

K–066 *31.1 For the purposes of rule 47.4(1) the "appropriate office" means

(1) the district registry or county court in which the case was being dealt with when the judgment or order was made or the event occurred which gave rise to the right to assessment, or to which it has subsequently been transferred; or

(2) in all other cases, the Supreme Court Costs Office.

31.2

(1) A direction under rule 47.4(2) or (3) specifying a particular court, registry or office as the appropriate office may be given on application or on the court's own initiative.

(2) Before making such a direction on its own initiative the court will give the parties the opportunity to make representations.

(3) Unless the Supreme Court Costs Office is the appropriate office for the purposes of Rule 47.4(1) an order directing that an assessment is to take place at the Supreme Court Costs Office will be made only if it is appropriate to do so having regard to the size of the bill of costs, the difficulty of the issues involved, the likely length of the hearing, the cost to the parties and any other relevant matter.

SECTION 32 Commencement of detailed assessment proceedings: Rule 47.6

K–067 32.1 * Precedents A, B, C and D in the Schedule of Costs Precedents annexed to this Practice Direction are model forms of bills of costs for detailed assessment. Further information about bills of costs is set out in Section 4.

*32.2 A detailed assessment may be in respect of:

(1) base costs, where a claim for additional liability has not been made or has been agreed;

(2) a claim for additional liability only, base costs having been summarily assessed or agreed; or

(3) both base costs and additional liability.

*32.3 If the detailed assessment is in respect of costs without any additional liability, the receiving party must serve on the paying party and all the other relevant persons the following documents:

(a) a notice of commencement;

(b) a copy of the bill of costs;

(c) copies of the fee notes of counsel and of any expert in respect of fees claimed in the bill;

    (d) written evidence as to any other disbursement which is claimed and which exceeds £250;

    (e) a statement giving the name and address for service of any person upon whom the receiving party intends to serve the notice of commencement.

*32.4 If the detailed assessment is in respect of an additional liability only, the receiving party must serve on the paying party and all other relevant persons the following documents:

    (a) a notice of commencement;

    (b) a copy of the bill of costs;

    (c) the relevant details of the additional liability;

    (d) a statement giving the name and address of any person upon whom the receiving party intends to serve the notice of commencement.

*32.5 The relevant details of an additional liability are as follows:

    (1) In the case of a conditional fee agreement with a success fee:

        (a) a statement showing the amount of costs which have been summarily assessed or agreed, and the percentage increase which has been claimed in respect of those costs;

        (b) a statement of the reasons for the percentage increase given in accordance with Regulation 3 of the Conditional Fee Agreement Regulations 2000.

    (2) If the additional liability is an insurance premium: a copy of the insurance certificate showing whether the policy covers the receiving party's own costs; his opponents costs; or his own costs and his opponent's costs; and the maximum extent of that cover, and the amount of the premium paid or payable.

    (3) If the receiving party claims an additional amount under Section 30 of the Access of Justice Act 1999: a statement setting out the basis upon which the receiving party's liability for the additional amount is calculated.

*32.6 Attention is drawn to the fact that the additional amount recoverable pursuant to section 30 of the Access to Justice Act 1999 in respect of a membership organisation must not exceed the likely cost of the premium of an insurance policy against the risk of incurring a liability to pay the costs of other parties to the proceedings as provided by the Access to Justice (Membership Organisation) Regulations 2000 Regulation 4.

*32.7 If a detailed assessment is in respect of both base costs and an additional liability, the receiving party must serve on the paying party and all other relevant persons the documents listed in paragraph 32.3 and the documents giving relevant details of an additional liability listed in paragraph 32.5.

*32.8

    (1) The Notice of Commencement should be in Form N252.

    (2) Before it is served, it must be completed to show as separate items;

        (a) the total amount of the costs claimed in the bill;

        (b) the extra sum which will be payable by way of fixed costs and court fees if a default costs certificate is obtained.

*32.9

    (1) This paragraph applies where the notice of commencement is to be served outside England and Wales.

(2) The date to be inserted in the notice of commencement for the paying party to send points of dispute is a date (not less than 21 days from the date of service of the notice) which must be calculated by reference to Part 6 Section III as if the notice were a claim form and as if the date to be inserted was the date for the filing of a defence.

32.10

(1) For the purposes of rule 47.6(2) a "relevant person" means:

    (a) any person who has taken part in the proceedings which gave rise to the assessment and who is directly liable under an order for costs made against him;

    (b) any person who has given to the receiving party notice in writing that he has a financial interest in the outcome of the assessment and wishes to be a party accordingly;

    (c) any other person whom the court orders to be treated as such.

(2) Where a party is unsure whether a person is or is not a relevant person, that party may apply to the appropriate office for directions.

(3) The court will generally not make an order that the person in respect of whom the application is made will be treated as a relevant person, unless within a specified time he applies to the court to be joined as a party to the assessment proceedings in accordance with Part 19 (Parties and Group Litigation).

32.11

(1) This paragraph applies in cases in which the bill of costs is capable of being copied onto a computer disk.

(2) If, before the detailed assessment hearing, a paying party requests a disk copy of a bill to which this paragraph applies, the receiving party must supply him with a copy free of charge not more than 7 days after the date on which he received the request.

SECTION 33 Period for commencing detailed assessment proceedings: Rule 47.7

K–068   33.1 The parties may agree under rule 2.11 (Time limits may be varied by parties) to extend or shorten the time specified by rule 47.7 for commencing the detailed assessment proceedings.

    33.2 A party may apply to the appropriate office for an order under rule 3.1(2)(a) to extend or shorten that time.

    33.3 Attention is drawn to rule 47.6(1). The detailed assessment proceedings are commenced by service of the documents referred to.

    33.4 Permission to commence assessment proceedings out of time is not required.

SECTION 34 Sanction for delay in commencing detailed assessment proceedings: Rule 47.8

K–069   34.1

(1) An application for an order under rule 47.8 must be made in writing and be issued in the appropriate office.

(2) The application notice must be served at least 7 days before the hearing.

SECTION 35 Points of dispute and consequences of not serving: Rule 47.9

35.1 The parties may agree under rule 2.11 (Time limits may be varied by parties) **K–070**
to extend or shorten the time specified by rule 47.9 for service of points of
dispute. A party may apply to the appropriate office for an order under rule
3.1(2)(a) to extend or shorten that time.

*35.2 Points of dispute should be short and to the point and should follow as
closely as possible Precedent G of the Schedule of Costs Precedents annexed
to this Practice Direction.

35.3 Points of dispute must—

(1) identify each item in the bill of costs which is disputed,
(2) in each case, state concisely the nature and grounds of dispute,
(3) where practicable suggest a figure to be allowed for each item in
respect of which a reduction is sought, and
(4) be signed by the party serving them or his solicitor.

*35.4

(1) The normal period for serving points of dispute is 21 days after the
date of service of the notice of commencement.
(2) Where a notice of commencement is served on a party outside England
and Wales the period within which that party should serve points of
dispute is to be calculated by reference to Part 6 Section III as if the
notice of commencement was a claim form and as if the period for
serving points of dispute were the period for filing a defence.

35.5 A party who serves points of dispute on the receiving party must at the same
time serve a copy on every other party to the detailed assessment proceedings, whose name and address for service appears on the statement served by
the receiving party in accordance with paragraph 32.3 or 32.4 above.

35.6

(1) This paragraph applies in cases in which Points of Dispute are capable
of being copied onto a computer disk.
(2) If, within 14 days of the receipt of the Points of Dispute, the receiving
party requests a disk copy of them, the paying party must supply him
with a copy free of charge not more than 7 days after the date on
which he received the request.

*35.7

(1) Where the receiving party claims an additional liability, a party who
serves points of dispute on the receiving party may include a request
for information about other methods of financing costs which were
available to the receiving party.
(2) Part 18 (further information) and the Practice Direction Supplementing that part apply to such a request.

SECTION 36 Procedure where costs are agreed: Rule 47.10

36.1 Where the parties have agreed terms as to the issue of a costs certificate **K–071**
(either interim or final) they should apply under rule 40.6 (Consent
judgments and orders) for an order that a certificate be issued in terms set
out in the application. Such an application may be dealt with by a court
officer, who may issue the certificate.

*36.2 Where in the course of proceedings the receiving party claims that the
paying party has agreed to pay costs but that he will neither pay those costs

nor join in a consent application under paragraph 36.1, the receiving party may apply under Part 23 (General Rules about Applications for Court Orders) for a certificate either interim or final to be issued.

36.3 An application under paragraph 36.2 must be supported by evidence and will be heard by a costs judge or a district judge. The respondent to the application must file and serve any evidence he relies on at least two days before the hearing date.

36.4 Nothing in rule 47.10 prevents parties who seek a judgment or order by consent from including in the draft a term that a party shall pay to another party a specified sum in respect of costs.

36.5

(1) The receiving party may discontinue the detailed assessment proceedings in accordance with Part 38 (Discontinuance).

(2) Where the receiving party discontinues the detailed assessment proceedings before a detailed assessment hearing has been requested, the paying party may apply to the appropriate office for an order about the costs of the detailed assessment proceedings.

(3) Where a detailed assessment hearing has been requested the receiving party may not discontinue unless the court gives permission.

(4) A bill of costs may be withdrawn by consent whether or not a detailed assessment hearing has been requested.

SECTION 37 Default costs certificate: Rule 47.11

K–072 37.1 A request for the issue of a default costs certificate must be made in Form N254 and must be signed by the receiving party or his solicitor.

37.2 The request must be filed at the appropriate office.

37.3 A default costs certificate will be in Form N255.

37.4 Attention is drawn to Rules 40.3 (Drawing up and Filing of Judgments and Orders) and 40.4 (Service of Judgments and Orders) which apply to the preparation and service of a default costs certificate. The receiving party will be treated as having permission to draw up a default costs certificate by virtue of this Practice Direction.

*37.5 The issue of a default costs certificate does not prohibit, govern or affect any detailed assessment of the same costs which are payable out of the Community Legal Service Fund.

37.6 An application for an order staying enforcement of a default costs certificate may be made either—

(1) to a costs judge or district judge of the court office which issued the certificate; or

(2) to the court (if different) which has general jurisdiction to enforce the certificate.

37.7 Proceedings for enforcement of default costs certificates may not be issued in the Supreme Court Costs Office.

37.8* The fixed costs payable in respect of solicitor's charges on the issue of the default costs certificate are £80.

SECTION 38 Setting aside default costs certificate: Rule 47.12

K–073 38.1

(1) A court officer may set aside a default costs certificate at the request of the receiving party under rule 47.12(3).

568

(2) A costs judge or a district judge will make any other order or give any directions under this rule.

*38.2

(1) An application for an order under rule 47.12(2) to set aside or vary a default costs certificate must be supported by evidence.

(2) In deciding whether to set aside or vary a certificate under rule 47.12(2) the matters to which the court must have regard include whether the party seeking the order made the application promptly.

(3) As a general rule a default costs certificate will be set aside under rule 47.12(2) only if the applicant shows a good reason for the court to do so and if he files with his application a copy of the bill and a copy of the default costs certificate, and a draft of the points of dispute he proposes to serve if his application is granted.

38.3

(1) Attention is drawn to rule 3.1(3) (which enables the court when making an order to make it subject to conditions) and to rule 44.3(8) (which enables the court to order a party whom it has ordered to pay costs to pay an amount on account before the costs are assessed).

(2) A costs judge or a district judge may exercise the power of the court to make an order under rule 44.3(8) although he did not make the order about costs which led to the issue of the default costs certificate.

38.4 If a default costs certificate is set aside the court will give directions for the management of the detailed assessment proceedings.

SECTION 39 Optional reply: Rule 47.13

39.1   **K–074**

(1) Where the receiving party wishes to serve a reply, he must also serve a copy on every other party to the detailed assessment proceedings. The time for doing so is within 21 days after service of the points of dispute.

(2) A reply means:—

(i) a separate document prepared by the receiving party; or
(ii) his written comments added to the points of dispute.

(3) A reply must be signed by the party serving it or his solicitor.

SECTION 40 Detailed assessment hearing: Rule 47.14

40.1 The time for requesting a detailed assessment hearing is within 3 months of   **K–075**
the expiry of the period for commencing detailed assessment proceedings.

*40.2 The request for a detailed assessment hearing must be in Form N258. The request must be accompanied by:

(a) a copy of the notice of commencement of detailed assessment proceedings;

(b) a copy of the bill of costs;

(c) the document giving the right to detailed assessment (see paragraph 40.4 below);

(d) a copy of the points of dispute, annotated as necessary in order to show which items have been agreed and their value and to show which items remain in dispute and their value;

     (e) as many copies of the points of dispute so annotated as there are persons who have served points of dispute;

     (f) a copy of any replies served;

     (g) a copy of all orders made by the court relating to the costs which are to be assessed;

     (h) copies of the fee notes and other written evidence as served on the paying party in accordance with paragraph 32.3 above;

     (i) where there is a dispute as to the receiving party's liability to pay costs to the solicitors who acted for the receiving party, any agreement, letter or other written information provided by the solicitor to his client explaining how the solicitor's charges are to be calculated;

     (j) a statement signed by the receiving party or his solicitor giving the name, address for service, reference and telephone number and fax number, if any, of—

        (i) the receiving party;

        (ii) the paying party;

        (iii) any other person who has served points of dispute or who has given notice to the receiving party under paragraph 32.10(1)(b) above;

     and giving an estimate of the length of time the detailed assessment hearing will take;

     (k) where the application for a detailed assessment hearing is made by a party other than the receiving party, such of the documents set out in this paragraph as are in the possession of that party;

     (l) where the court is to assess the costs of an assisted person or LSC funded client—

        (i) the legal aid certificate, LSC certificate and relevant amendment certificates, any authorities and any certificates of discharge or revocation.

        (ii) a certificate, in Precedent F(3) of the Schedule of Costs Precedents;

        (iii) if the assisted person has a financial interest in the detailed assessment hearing and wishes to attend, the postal address of that person to which the court will send notice of any hearing;

        (iv) if the rates payable out of the LSC fund are prescribed rates, a schedule to the bill of costs setting out all the items in the bill which are claimed against other parties calculated at the legal aid prescribed rates with or without any claim for enhancement: (further information as to this schedule is set out in Section 48 of this Practice Direction);

        (v) a copy of any default costs certificate in respect of costs claimed in the bill of costs.

40.3

     (1) This paragraph applies to any document described in paragraph 40.2(i) above which the receiving party has filed in the appropriate office. The document must be the latest relevant version and in any event have been filed not more than 2 years before filing the request for a detailed assessment hearing.

     (2) In respect of any documents to which this paragraph applies, the receiving party may, instead of filing a copy of it, specify in the request for a detailed assessment hearing the case number under which a copy of the document was previously filed.

40.4 "The document giving the right to detailed assessment" means such one or more of the following documents as are appropriate to the detailed assessment proceedings:

    (a) a copy of the judgment or order of the court giving the right to detailed assessment;

    (b) a copy of the notice served under rule 3.7 (sanctions for non-payment of certain fees) where a claim is struck out under that rule;

    (c) a copy of the notice of acceptance where an offer to settle is accepted under Part 36 (Offers to settle and payments into court);

    (d) a copy of the notice of discontinuance in a case which is discontinued under Part 38 (Discontinuance);

    (e) a copy of the award made on an arbitration under any Act or pursuant to an agreement, where no court has made an order for the enforcement of the award;

    (f) a copy of the order, award or determination of a statutorily constituted tribunal or body;

    (g) in a case under the Sheriffs Act 1887, the sheriff's bill of fees and charges, unless a court order giving the right to detailed assessment has been made;

    (h) a notice of revocation or discharge under Regulation 82 of the Civil Legal Aid (General) Regulations 1989.

    (j) In the county courts certain Acts and Regulations provide for costs incurred in proceedings under those Acts and Regulations to be assessed in the county court if so ordered on application. Where such an application is made, a copy of the order.

40.5 On receipt of the request for a detailed assessment hearing the court will fix a date for the hearing, or, if the costs officer so decides, will give directions or fix a date for a preliminary appointment.

40.6

    (1) The court will give at least 14 days notice of the time and place of the detailed assessment hearing to every person named in the statement referred to in paragraph 40.2(j) above.

    (2) The court will when giving notice, give each person who has served points of dispute a copy of the points of dispute annotated by the receiving party in compliance with paragraph 40.2(d) above.

    (3) Attention is drawn to rule 47.14(6)&(7): apart from the receiving party, only those who have served points of dispute may be heard on the detailed assessment unless the court gives permission, and only items specified in the points of dispute may be raised unless the court gives permission.

*40.7

    (1) If the receiving party does not file a request for a detailed assessment hearing within the prescribed time, the paying party may apply to the court to fix a time within which the receiving party must do so. The sanction, for failure to commence detailed assessment proceedings within the time specified by the court, is that all or part of the costs may be disallowed (see rule 47.8(2)).

    (2) Where the receiving party commences detailed assessment proceedings after the time specified in the rules but before the paying party has made an application to the court to specify a time, the only sanction which the court may impose is to disallow all or part of the interest which would otherwise be payable for the period of delay, unless the

court exercises its powers under rule 44.14 (court's powers in relation to misconduct).

40.8 If either party wishes to make an application in the detailed assessment proceedings the provisions of Part 23 (General Rules about Applications for Court Orders) apply.

40.9

(1) This paragraph deals with the procedure to be adopted where a date has been given by the court for a detailed assessment hearing and

(a) the detailed assessment proceedings are settled; or
(b) a party to the detailed assessment proceedings wishes to apply to vary the date which the court has fixed; or
(c) the parties to the detailed assessment proceedings agree about changes they wish to make to any direction given for the management of the detailed assessment proceedings.

(2) If detailed assessment proceedings are settled, the receiving party must give notice of that fact to the court immediately, preferably by fax.

(3) A party who wishes to apply to vary a direction must do so in accordance with Part 23 (General Rules about Applications for Court Orders).

(4) If the parties agree about changes they wish to make to any direction given for the management of the detailed assessment proceedings —

(a) they must apply to the court for an order by consent; and
(b) they must file a draft of the directions sought and an agreed statement of the reasons why the variation is sought; and
(c) the court may make an order in the agreed terms or in other terms without a hearing, but it may direct that a hearing is to be listed.

40.10

(1) If a party wishes to vary his bill of costs, points of dispute or a reply, an amended or supplementary document must be filed with the court and copies of it must be served on all other relevant parties.

(2) Permission is not required to vary a bill of costs, points of dispute or a reply but the court may disallow the variation or permit it only upon conditions, including conditions as to the payment of any costs caused or wasted by the variation.

40.11 Unless the court directs otherwise the receiving party must file with the court the papers in support of the bill not less than 7 days before the date for the detailed assessment hearing and not more than 14 days before that date.

*40.12 The following provisions apply in respect of the papers to be filed in support of the bill;

(a) If the claim is for costs only without any additional liability the papers to be filed, and the order in which they are to be arranged are as follows:

(i) instructions and briefs to counsel arranged in chronological order together with all advices, opinions and drafts received and response to such instructions;
(ii) reports and opinions of medical and other experts;
(iii) any other relevant papers;
(iv) a full set of any relevant pleadings to the extent that they have not already been filed in court.
(v) correspondence, files and attendance notes;

(b) where the claim is in respect of an additional liability only, such of the papers listed at (a) above, as are relevant to the issues raised by the claim for additional liability;

(c) where the claim is for both base costs and an additional liability, the papers listed at (a) above, together with any papers relevant to the issues raised by the claim for additional liability.

40.13 The provisions set out in Section 20 of this Practice Direction apply where the court disallows any amount of a legal representative's percentage increase, and the legal representative applies for an order that the disallowed amount should continue to be payable by the client in accordance with Rule 44.16.

40.14 The court may direct the receiving party to produce any document which in the opinion of the court is necessary to enable it to reach its decision. These documents will in the first instance be produced to the court, but the court may ask the receiving party to elect whether to disclose the particular document to the paying party in order to rely on the contents of the document, or whether to decline disclosure and instead rely on other evidence.

*40.15 Costs assessed at a detailed assessment at the conclusion of proceedings may include an assessment of any additional liability in respect of the costs of a previous application or hearing.

40.16 Once the detailed assessment hearing has ended it is the responsibility of the legal representative appearing for the receiving party or, as the case may be, the receiving party in person to remove the papers filed in support of the bill.

SECTION 41 Power to issue an interim certificate: Rule 47.15

41.1   K–076

(1) A party wishing to apply for an interim certificate may do so by making an application in accordance with Part 23 (General Rules about Applications for Court Orders).

(2) Attention is drawn to the fact that the court's power to issue an interim certificate arises only after the receiving party has filed a request for a detailed assessment hearing.

SECTION 42 Final costs certificate: Rule 47.16

42.1 At the detailed assessment hearing the court will indicate any disallowance   K–077 or reduction in the sums claimed in the bill of costs by making an appropriate note on the bill.

*42.2 The receiving party must, in order to complete the bill after the detailed assessment hearing make clear the correct figures agreed or allowed in respect of each item and must re-calculate the summary of the bill appropriately.

42.3 The completed bill of costs must be filed with the court no later than 14 days after the detailed assessment hearing.

*42.4 At the same time as filing the completed bill of costs, the party whose bill it is must also produce receipted fee notes and receipted accounts in respect of all disbursements except those covered by a certificate in Precedent F(5) in the Schedule of Costs Precedents annexed to this Practice Direction.

42.5 No final costs certificate will be issued until all relevant court fees payable on the assessment of costs have been paid.

42.6   If the receiving party fails to file a completed bill in accordance with rule
        47.16 the paying party may make an application under Part 23 (General
        Rules about Applications for Court Orders) seeking an appropriate order
        under rule 3.1 (The court's general powers of management).

42.7   A final costs certificate will show:

    (a) the amount of any costs which have been agreed between the parties or
        which have been allowed on detailed assessment;

    (b) where applicable the amount agreed or allowed in respect of VAT on
        the costs agreed or allowed.
        This provision is subject to any contrary provision made by the
        statutory provisions relating to costs payable out of the Community
        Legal Service Fund.

42.8   A final costs certificate will include disbursements in respect of the fees of
        counsel only if receipted fee notes or accounts in respect of those disburse-
        ments have been produced to the court and only to the extent indicated by
        those receipts.

42.9   Where the certificate relates to costs payable between parties a separate
        certificate will be issued for each party entitled to costs.

42.10   Form N257 is a model form of interim costs certificate and Form N256 is
        a model form of final costs certificate.

42.11   An application for an order staying enforcement of an interim costs
        certificate or final costs certificate may be made either:

    (1) to a costs judge or district judge of the court office which issued the
        certificate; or

    (2) to the court (if different) which has general jurisdiction to enforce the
        certificate.

42.12   Proceedings for enforcement of interim costs certificates or final costs
        certificates may not be issued in the Supreme Court Costs Office.

**SECTION 43 Detailed assessment procedure where costs are payable out of the
community legal service fund: Rule 47.17**

K–078   43.1   The provisions of this section apply where the court is to assess costs which
                are payable only out of the community legal service fund. Paragraphs 39.1
                to 40.16 and 49.1 to 49.8 apply in cases involving costs payable by another
                person as well as costs payable only out of the community legal service
                fund.

        43.2   The time for requesting a detailed assessment under rule 47.17 is within 3
                months after the date when the right to detailed assessment arose.

       *43.3   The request for a detailed assessment of costs must be in Form N258A. The
                request must be accompanied by:

            (a) a copy of the bill of costs;

            (b) the document giving the right to detailed assessment (for further
                information as to this document, see paragraph 40.4 above);

            (c) a copy of all orders made by the court relating to the costs which are
                to be assessed;

            (d) copies of any fee notes of counsel and any expert in respect of fees
                claimed in the bill;

            (e) written evidence as to any other disbursement which is claimed and
                which exceeds £250;

            (f) the legal aid certificates, LSC certificates, any relevant amendment
                certificates, any authorities and any certificates of discharge or revo-
                cation;

(g) In the Supreme Court Costs Office the relevant papers in support of the bill as described in paragraph 40.12 above; in cases proceeding in District Registries and county courts this provision does not apply and the papers should only be lodged if requested by the costs officer.

(h) a statement signed by the solicitor giving his name, address for service, reference, telephone number, fax number and, if the assisted person has a financial interest in the detailed assessment and wishes to attend, giving the postal address of that person, to which the court will send notice of any hearing.

43.4 Rule 47.17 provides that the court will hold a detailed assessment hearing if the assisted person has a financial interest in the detailed assessment and wishes to attend. The court may also hold a detailed assessment hearing in any other case, instead of provisionally assessing a bill of costs, where it considers that a hearing is necessary. Before deciding whether a hearing is necessary under this rule, the court may require the solicitor whose bill it is, to provide further information relating to the bill.

43.5 Where the court has provisionally assessed a bill of costs it will send to the solicitor a notice, in Form N253 annexed to this practice direction, of the amount of costs which the court proposes to allow together with the bill itself. The legal representative should, if the provisional assessment is to be accepted, then complete the bill.

43.6 The court will fix a date for a detailed assessment hearing if the solicitor informs the court within 14 days after he receives the notice of the amount allowed on the provisional assessment that he wants the court to hold such a hearing.

43.7 The court will give at least 14 days notice of the time and place of the detailed assessment hearing to the solicitor and, if the assisted person has a financial interest in the detailed assessment and wishes to attend, to the assisted person.

43.8 If the solicitor whose bill it is, or any other party wishes to make an application in the detailed assessment proceedings, the provisions of Part 23 (General Rules about Applications for Court Orders) applies.

*43.9 It is the responsibility of the legal representative to complete the bill by entering in the bill the correct figures allowed in respect of each item, recalculating the summary of the bill appropriately and completing the Community Legal Service assessment certificate (Form EX80A).

SECTION 44 Costs of detailed assessment proceedings where costs are payable out of a fund other than the community legal service fund: Rule 47.17A

44.1* Rule 47.17A provides that the court will make a provisional assessment of   K–079
a bill of costs payable out of a fund (other than the Community Legal Service Fund) unless it considers that a hearing is necessary. It also enables the court to direct under rule 47.17A(3) that the receiving party must serve a copy of the request for assessment and copies of the documents which accompany it, on any person who has a financial interest in the outcome of the assessment.

*44.2

(a) A person has a financial interest in the outcome of the assessment if the assessment will or may affect the amount of money or property to which he is or may become entitled out of the fund.

(b) Where an interest in the fund is itself held by a trustee for the benefit of some other person, that trustee will be treated as the person having such a financial interest.

(c) "Trustee" includes a personal representative, receiver or any other person acting in a fiduciary capacity.

*44.3   The request for a detailed assessment of costs out of the fund should be in Form N258B, be accompanied by the documents set out at paragraph 43.3(a) to (e) and (g) above and the following;

(a) a statement signed by the receiving party giving his name, address for service, reference, telephone number, fax number and,
(b) a statement of the postal address of any person who has a financial interest in the outcome of the assessment, to which the court may send notice of any hearing; and
(c) in respect of each person stated to have such an interest if such person is a child or patient, a statement to that effect.

*44.4   The court will decide, having regard to the amount of the bill, the size of the fund and the number of persons who have a financial interest, which of those persons should be served. The court may dispense with service on all or some of them.

*44.5   Where the court makes an order dispensing with service on all such persons it may proceed at once to make a provisional assessment, or, if it decides that a hearing is necessary, give appropriate directions. Before deciding whether a hearing is necessary under this rule, the court may require the receiving party to provide further information relating to the bill.

*44.6

(1) Where the court has provisionally assessed a bill of costs, it will send to the receiving party, a notice in Form N253 of the amount of costs which the court proposes to allow together with the bill itself. If the receiving party is legally represented the legal representative should, if the provisional assessment is to be accepted, then complete the bill.
(2) The court will fix a date for a detailed assessment hearing, if the receiving party informs the court within 14 days after he receives the notice in Form N253 of the amount allowed on the provisional assessment, that he wants the court to hold such a hearing.

*44.7   Where the court makes an order that a person who has a financial interest is to be served with a copy of the request for assessment, it may give directions about service and about the hearing.

*44.8   The court will give at least 14 days notice of the time and place of the detailed assessment hearing to the receiving party and, to any person who has a financial interest in the outcome of the assessment and has been served with a copy of the request for assessment.

*44.9   If the receiving party, or any other party or any person who has a financial interest in the outcome of assessment, wishes to make an application in the detailed assessment proceedings, the provisions of Part 23 (General Rules about Applications for Court Orders) applies.

*44.10 If the receiving party is legally represented the legal representative must in order to complete the bill after the assessment make clear the correct figures allowed in respect of each item and must recalculate the summary of the bill if appropriate.

SECTION 45 Liability for costs of detailed assessment proceedings: Rule 47.18

K–080   45.1   As a general rule the court will assess the receiving party's costs of the detailed assessment proceedings and add them to the bill of costs

45.2　If the costs of the detailed assessment proceedings are awarded to the paying party, the court will either assess those costs by summary assessment or make an order for them to be decided by detailed assessment

*45.3　No party should file or serve a statement of costs of the detailed assessment proceedings unless the court orders him to do so.

45.4　Attention is drawn to the fact that in deciding what order to make about the costs of detailed assessment proceedings the court must have regard to the conduct of all parties, the amount by which the bill of costs has been reduced and whether it was reasonable for a party to claim the costs of a particular item or to dispute that item.

> (1) In respect of interest on the costs of detailed assessment proceedings, the interest shall begin to run from the date of the default, interim or final costs certificate as the case may be.
> (2) This provision applies only to the costs of the detailed assessment proceedings themselves. The costs of the substantive proceedings are governed by rule 40.8(1).

SECTION 46 Offers to settle without prejudice save as to the costs of the detailed assessment proceedings: Rule 47.19

46.1　Rule 47.19 allows the court to take into account offers to settle, without prejudice save as to the costs of detailed assessment proceedings, when deciding who is liable for the costs of those proceedings. The rule does not specify a time within which such an offer should be made. An offer made by the paying party should usually be made within 14 days after service of the notice of commencement on that party. If the offer is made by the receiving party, it should normally be made within 14 days after the service of points of dispute by the paying party. Offers made after these periods are likely to be given less weight by the court in deciding what order as to costs to make unless there is good reason for the offer not being made until the later time.　**K–081**

*46.2　Where an offer to settle is made it should specify whether or not it is intended to be inclusive of the cost of preparation of the bill, interest and value added tax (VAT). The offer may include or exclude some or all of these items but the position must be made clear on the face of the offer so that the offeree is clear about the terms of the offer when it is being considered. Unless the offer states otherwise, the offer will be treated as being inclusive of all these items.

46.3　Where an offer to settle is accepted, an application may be made for a certificate in agreed terms, or the bill of costs may be withdrawn, in accordance with rule 47.10 (Procedure where costs are agreed).

46.4　Where the receiving party is an assisted person or an LSC funded client, an offer to settle without prejudice save as to the costs of the detailed assessment proceedings will not have the consequences specified under rule 47.19 unless the court so orders.

SECTION 47 Appeals from authorised court officers in detailed assessment proceedings: right to appeal: Rule 47.20

*47.1　This Section and the next Section of this Practice Direction relate only to appeals from authorised court officers in detailed assessment proceedings. All other appeals arising out of detailed assessment proceedings (and arising out of summary assessments) are dealt with in accordance with Part 52 and　**K–082** the Practice Direction which supplements that Part. The destination of appeals is dealt with in accordance with the Access to Justice Act 1999 (Destination of Appeals) Order 2000.

*47.2   In respect of appeals from authorised court officers, there is no requirement to obtain permission, or to seek written reasons.

SECTION 48 Procedure on appeal from authorised court officers: Rule 47.22

K–083   *48.1   The appellant must file a notice which should be in Form N161 (an appellant's notice).

*48.2   The appeal will be heard by a costs judge or a district judge of the High Court, and is a re-hearing.

*48.3   The appellant's notice should, if possible, be accompanied by a suitable record of the judgment appealed against. Where reasons given for the decision have been officially recorded by the court an approved transcript of that record should accompany the notice. Photocopies will not be accepted for this purpose. Where there is no official record the following documents will be acceptable:

(1) The officer's comments written on the bill.
(2) Advocates' notes of the reasons where the appellant is unrepresented.

When the appellant was unrepresented before the authorised court officer, it is the duty of any advocate for the respondent to make his own note of the reasons promptly available, free of charge to the appellant where there is no official record or if the court so directs. Where the appellant was represented before the authorised court officer, it is the duty of his/her own former advocate to make his/her notes available. The appellant should submit the note of the reasons to the costs judge or district judge hearing the appeal.

*48.4   The appellant may not be able to obtain a suitable record of the authorised court officer's decision within the time in which the appellant's notice must be filed. In such cases, the appellant's notice must still be completed to the best of the appellant's ability. It may however be amended subsequently with the permission of the costs judge or district judge hearing the appeal.

SECTION 49 Costs payable by the LSC at prescribed rates:

K–084   *49.1   This section applies to a bill of costs of an assisted person or LSC funded client which is payable by another person where the costs which can be claimed against the LSC are restricted to prescribed rates (with or without enhancement).

*49.2   Where this section applies, the solicitor of the assisted person or LSC funded client must file a legal aid/ LSC schedule in accordance with Paragraph 40.2(l) above. The schedule should follow as closely as possible Precedent E of the Schedule of Costs Precedents annexed to this Practice Direction.

49.3   The schedule must set out by reference to the item numbers in the bill of costs, all the costs claimed as payable by another person, but the arithmetic in the schedule should claim those items at prescribed rates only (with or without any claim for enhancement).

49.4   Where there has been a change in the prescribed rates during the period covered by the bill of costs, the schedule (as opposed to the bill) should be divided into separate parts, so as to deal separately with each change of rate. The schedule must also be divided so as to correspond with any divisions in the bill of costs.

49.5* If the bill of costs contains additional columns setting out costs claimed against the LSC only, the schedule may be set out in a separate document or, alternatively, may be included in the additional columns of the bill.

*49.6 The detailed assessment of the legal aid/ LSC schedule will take place immediately after the detailed assessment of the bill of costs.

*49.7 Attention is drawn to the possibility that, on occasions, the court may decide to conduct the detailed assessment of the legal aid/ LSC schedule separately from any detailed assessment of the bill of costs. This will occur, for example, where a default costs certificate is obtained as between the parties but that certificate is not set aside at the time of the detailed assessment pursuant to the Legal Aid Act 1988 or regulations thereunder.

*49.8 Where costs have been assessed at prescribed rates it is the responsibility of the legal representative to enter the correct figures allowed in respect of each item and to recalculate the summary of the legal aid/ LSC schedule.

Directions Relating to Part 48

Costs—special cases

SECTION 50 Amount of costs where costs are payable pursuant to contract: Rule 48.3

50.1 Where the court is assessing costs payable under a contract, it may make an order that all or part of the costs payable under the contract shall be disallowed if it is satisfied by the paying party that costs have been unreasonably incurred or are unreasonable in amount.

K–085

50.2 Rule 48.3 only applies if the court is assessing costs payable under a contract. It does not—

  (1) require the court to make an assessment of such costs; or

  (2) require a mortgagee to apply for an order for those costs that he has a contractual right to recover out of the mortgage funds.

50.3 The following principles apply to costs relating to a mortgage—

  (1) An order for the payment of costs of proceedings by one party to another is always a discretionary order: section 51 of the Supreme Court Act 1981

  (2) Where there is a contractual right to the costs the discretion should ordinarily be exercised so as to reflect that contractual right.

  (3) The power of the court to disallow a mortgagee's costs sought to be added to the mortgage security is a power that does not derive from section 51, but from the power of the courts of equity to fix the terms on which redemption will be allowed.

  (4) A decision by a court to refuse costs in whole or in part to a mortgagee litigant may be—

    (a) a decision in the exercise of the section 51 discretion;

    (b) a decision in the exercise of the power to fix the terms on which redemption will be allowed;

    (c) a decision as to the extent of a mortgagee's contractual right to add his costs to the security; or

    (d) a combination of two or more of these things.

  The statements of case in the proceedings or the submissions made to the court may indicate which of the decisions has been made.

579

(5) A mortgagee is not to be deprived of a contractual or equitable right to add costs to the security merely by reason of an order for payment of costs made without reference to the mortgagee's contractual or equitable rights, and without any adjudication as to whether or not the mortgagee should be deprived of those costs.

50.4

(1) Where the contract entitles a mortgagee to—

(a) add the costs of litigation relating to the mortgage to the sum secured by it;
(b) require a mortgagor to pay those costs, or
(c) both,

the mortgagor may make an application for the court to direct that an account of the mortgagee's costs be taken.
(Rule 25.1(1)(n) provides that the court may direct that a party file an account)

(2) The mortgagor may then dispute an amount in the mortgagee's account on the basis that is has been unreasonably incurred or is unreasonable in amount.

(3) Where a mortgagor disputes an amount, the court may make an order that the disputed costs are assessed under rule 48.3

SECTION 50A Limitation on court's power to award costs in favour of trustee or personal representative: Rule 48.4

50A.1 A trustee or personal representative is entitled to an indemnity out of the relevant trust fund or estate for costs properly incurred, which may include costs awarded against the trustee or personal representative in favour of another party.

50A.2 Whether costs were properly incurred depends on all the circumstances of the case, and may, for example, depend on—

(1) whether the trustee or personal representative obtained directions from the court before bringing or defending the proceedings;

(2) whether the trustee or personal representative acted in the interests of the fund or estate or in substance for a benefit other than that of the estate, including his own; and

(3) whether the trustee or personal representative acted in some way unreasonably in bringing or defending, or in the conduct of, the proceedings.

50A.3 The trustee or personal representative is not to be taken to have acted in substance for a benefit other than that of the fund by reason only that he has defended a claim in which relief is sought against him personally.

SECTION 51 Costs where money is payable by or to a child or patient: Rule 48.5

K–086   51.1   The circumstances in which the court need not order the assessment of costs under rule 48.5(3) are as follows:

(a) where there is no need to do so to protect the interests of the child or patient or his estate;

(b) where another party has agreed to pay a specified sum in respect of the costs of the child or patient and the solicitor acting for the child or patient has waived the right to claim further costs;

580

(c) where the court has decided the costs payable to the child or patient by way of summary assessment and the solicitor acting for the child or patient has waived the right to claim further costs;

(d) where an insurer or other person is liable to discharge the costs which the child or patient would otherwise be liable to pay to his solicitor and the court is satisfied that the insurer or other person is financially able to discharge those costs.

SECTION 52 Litigants in person: Rule 48.6

52.1   In order to qualify as an expert for the purpose of rule 48.6(3)(c) (expert assistance in connection with assessing the claim for costs), the person in question must be a   **K–087**

(1) barrister,
(2) solicitor,
(3) Fellow of the Institute of Legal Executives,
(4) Fellow of the Association of Law Costs Draftsmen,
(5) law costs draftsman who is a member of the Academy of Experts,
(6) law costs draftsman who is a member of the Expert Witness Institute.

52.2   Where a litigant in person wishes to prove that he has suffered financial loss he should produce to the court any written evidence he relies on to support that claim, and serve a copy of that evidence on any party against whom he seeks costs at least 24 hours before the hearing at which the question may be decided.

52.3   Where a litigant in person commences detailed assessment proceedings under rule 47.6 he should serve copies of that written evidence with the notice of commencement.

52.4   The amount, which may be allowed to a litigant in person under rule 46.3(5)(b) and rule 48.6(4), is £9.25 per hour.

52.5   Attention is drawn to rule 48.6(6)(b). A solicitor who, instead of acting for himself, is represented in the proceedings by his firm or by himself in his firm name, is not, for the purpose of the Civil Procedure Rules, a litigant in person.

SECTION 53 Personal liability of legal representative for costs—wasted costs orders: Rule 48.7

53.1   Rule 48.7 deals with wasted costs orders against legal representatives. Such orders can be made at any stage in the proceedings up to and including the proceedings relating to the detailed assessment of costs. In general, applications for wasted costs are best left until after the end of the trial.   **K–088**

53.2   The court may make a wasted costs order against a legal representative on its own initiative.

53.3   A party may apply for a wasted costs order—

(1) by filing an application notice in accordance with Part 23; or
(2) by making an application orally in the course of any hearing.

53.4   It is appropriate for the court to make a wasted costs order against a legal representative, only if—

(1) the legal representative has acted improperly, unreasonably or negligently;

(2) his conduct has caused a party to incur unnecessary costs, and

(3) it is just in all the circumstances to order him to compensate that party for the whole or part of those costs.

53.5 The court will give directions about the procedure that will be followed in each case in order to ensure that the issues are dealt with in a way which is fair and as simple and summary as the circumstances permit.

53.6 As a general rule the court will consider whether to make a wasted costs order in two stages—

(1) in the first stage, the court must be satisfied—

(a) that it has before it evidence or other material which, if unanswered, would be likely to lead to a wasted costs order being made; and

(b) the wasted costs proceedings are justified notwithstanding the likely costs involved.

(2) at the second stage (even if the court is satisfied under paragraph (1)) the court will consider, after giving the legal representative an opportunity to give reasons why the court should not make a wasted costs order, whether it is appropriate to make a wasted costs order in accordance with paragraph 53.4 above.

53.7 On an application for a wasted costs order under Part 23 the court may proceed to the second stage described in paragraph 53.6 without first adjourning the hearing if it is satisfied that the legal representative has already had a reasonable opportunity to give reasons why the court should not make a wasted costs order. In other cases the court will adjourn the hearing before proceeding to the second stage.

53.8 On an application for a wasted costs order under Part 23 the application notice and any evidence in support must identify—

(1) what the legal representative is alleged to have done or failed to do; and

(2) the costs that he may be ordered to pay or which are sought against him.

53.9 A wasted costs order is an order—

(1) that the legal representative pay a specified sum in respect of costs to a party; or

(2) for costs relating to a specified sum or items of work to be disallowed.

*53.10 Attention is drawn to rule 44.3A(1) and (2) which respectively prevent the court from assessing any additional liability until the conclusion of the proceedings (or the part of the proceedings) to which the funding arrangement relates, and set out the orders the court may make at the conclusion of the proceedings.

SECTION 54 Basis of detailed assessment of solicitor and client costs: Rule 48.8

K–089   54.1 A client and his solicitor may agree whatever terms they consider appropriate about the payment of the solicitor's charges for his services. If however, the costs are of an unusual nature (either in amount or in the type of costs incurred) those costs will be presumed to have been unreasonably incurred unless the solicitor satisfies the court that he informed the client that they were unusual and, where the costs relate to litigation, that he informed the client they might not be allowed on an assessment of costs between the parties. That information must have been given to the client before the costs were incurred.

54.2

    (1) Costs as between a solicitor and client are assessed on the indemnity basis as defined by rule 44.4.

    (2) Attention is drawn to the presumptions set out in rule 48.8(2). These presumptions may be rebutted by evidence to the contrary.

*54.3   Rule 48.10 and Section 56 of this Practice Direction deal with the procedure to be followed for obtaining the assessment of a solicitor's bill pursuant to an order under Part III of the Solicitors Act 1974.

54.4   If a party fails to comply with the requirements of rule 48.10 concerning the service of a breakdown of costs or points of dispute, any other party may apply to the court in which the detailed assessment hearing should take place for an order requiring compliance with rule 48.10. If the court makes such an order, it may—

    (a) make it subject to conditions including a condition to pay a sum of money into court; and

    (b) specify the consequence of failure to comply with the order or a condition.

54.5   (1) A client who has entered into a conditional fee agreement with a solicitor may apply for assessment of the base costs (which is carried out in accordance with rule 48.8(2) as if there were no conditional fee agreement) or for assessment of the percentage increase (success fee) or both.

    (2) Where the court is to assess the percentage increase the court will have regard to all the relevant factors as they appeared to the solicitor or counsel when the conditional fee agreement was entered into.

54.6   Where the client applies to the court to reduce the percentage increase which the solicitor has charged the client under the conditional fee agreement, the client must set out in his application notice:

    (a) the reasons why the percentage increase should be reduced; and

    (b) what the percentage increase should be.

54.7   The factors relevant to assessing the percentage increase include—

    (a) the risk that the circumstances in which the fees or expenses would be payable might not occur;

    (b) the disadvantages relating to the absence of payment on account;

    (c) whether there is a conditional fee agreement between the solicitor and counsel;

    (d) the solicitor's liability for any disbursements.

54.8   When the court is considering the factors to be taken into account, it will have regard to the circumstances as they reasonably appeared to the solicitor or counsel when the conditional fee agreement was entered into.

SECTION 55 Conditional fees: Rule 48.9

*55.1   K–090

    (1) Attention is drawn to rule 48.9(1) as amended by the Civil Procedure (Amendment No.3) Rules 2000 (SI 2000/1317) with effect from 3 July 2000. Rule 48.9 applies only where the solicitor and the client have

entered into a conditional fee agreement as defined in section 58 of the Courts and Legal Services Act 1990 as it was in force before 1 April 2000. A client who has entered into a conditional fee agreement with a solicitor may apply for assessment of the base costs (which is carried out in accordance with rule 48.8(2) as if there were no conditional fee agreement) or for assessment of the percentage increase (success fee) or both.

(2) Where the court is to assess the percentage increase the court will have regard to all the relevant factors as they appeared to the solicitor or counsel when the conditional fee agreement was entered into.

55.2 Where the client applies to the court to reduce the percentage increase which the solicitor has charged the client under the conditional fee agreement, the client must set out in his application notice:

(a) the reasons why the percentage increase should be reduced; and
(b) what the percentage increase should be.

55.3 The factors relevant to assessing the percentage increase include—

(a) the risk that the circumstances in which the fees or expenses would be payable might not occur;
(b) the disadvantages relating to the absence of payment on account;
(c) whether the amount which might be payable under the conditional fee agreement is limited to a certain proportion of any damages recovered by the client;
(d) whether there is a conditional fee agreement between the solicitor and counsel;
(e) the solicitor's liability for any disbursements.

*55.4 When the court is considering the factors to be taken into account, it will have regard to the circumstances as they reasonably appeared to the solicitor or counsel when the conditional fee agreement was entered into.

SECTION 56 Procedure on assessment of solicitor and client costs: Rule 48.10

K–091   *56.1 The paragraphs in this section apply to orders made under Part III of the Solicitors Act 1974 for the assessment of costs. In these paragraphs "client" includes any person entitled to make an application under Part III of that Act.

*56.2 The procedure for obtaining an order under Part III of the Solicitors Act 1974 is by the alternative procedure for claims under Part 8. The provisions of RSC Order 106 appear, appropriately amended, in Schedule 1 to the CPR. Precedent J of the Schedule of Costs Precedents annexed to this Practice Direction is a model form of claim form. The application must be accompanied by the bill or bills in respect of which assessment is sought, and, if the claim concerns a conditional fee agreement, a copy of that agreement. If the original bill is not available a copy will suffice.

*56.3 Model forms of order, which the court may make, are set out in Precedents K, L and M of the Schedule of Costs Precedents annexed to this Practice Direction.

56.4 Attention is drawn to the time limits within which the required steps must be taken: i.e. the solicitor must serve a breakdown of costs within 28 days of the order for costs to be assessed, the client must serve points of dispute within 14 days after service on him of the breakdown, and any reply must be served within 14 days of service of the points of dispute.

56.5 The breakdown of costs referred to in rule 48.10 is a document which contains the following information:

(a) details of the work done under each of the bills sent for assessment; and

(b) in applications under Section 70 of the Solicitors Act 1974, an account showing money received by the solicitor to the credit of the client and sums paid out of that money on behalf of the client but not payments out which were made in satisfaction of the bill or of any items which are claimed in the bill.

*56.6 Precedent P of the Schedule of Costs Precedents annexed to this Practice Direction is a model form of breakdown of costs. A party who is required to serve a breakdown of costs must also serve—

(1) copies of the fee notes of counsel and of any expert in respect of fees claimed in the breakdown, and

(2) written evidence as to any other disbursement which is claimed in the breakdown and which exceeds £250.

56.7 The provisions relating to default costs certificates (rule 47.11) do not apply to cases to which rule 48.10 applies.

56.8 Points of dispute should, as far as practicable, be in the form complying with paragraphs 35.1 to 35.7.

56.9 The time for requesting a detailed assessment hearing is within 3 months after the date of the order for the costs to be assessed.

*56.10 The form of request for a hearing date must be in Form N258C. The request must be accompanied by copies of—

(a) the order sending the bill or bills for assessment;

(b) the bill or bills sent for assessment;

(c) the solicitor's breakdown of costs and any invoices or accounts served with that breakdown;

(d) a copy of the points of dispute, annotated as necessary in order to show which items have been agreed and their value and to show which items remain in dispute;

(e) as many copies of the points of dispute so annotated as there are other parties to the proceedings to whom the court should give details of the assessment hearing requested;

(f) a copy of any replies served;

(g) a statement signed by the party filing the request or his legal representative giving the names and addresses for service of all parties to the proceedings.

56.11 The request must include an estimate of the length of time the detailed assessment hearing will take.

56.12 On receipt of the request for a detailed assessment hearing the court will fix a date for the hearing or if the costs judge or district judge so decides, will give directions or fix a date for a preliminary appointment.

56.13

(1) The court will give at least 14 days notice of the time and place of the detailed assessment hearing to every person named in the statement referred to in paragraph 56.10(g) above.

(2) The court will when giving notice, give all parties other than the party who requested the hearing a copy of the points of dispute annotated by the party requesting the hearing in compliance with paragraph 56.10(e) above.

(3) Attention is drawn to rule 47.14(6) and (7): apart from the solicitor whose bill it is, only those parties who have served points of dispute may be heard on the detailed assessment unless the court gives permission, and only items specified in the points of dispute may be raised unless the court gives permission.

56.14

(1) If a party wishes to vary his breakdown of costs, points of dispute or reply, an amended or supplementary document must be filed with the court and copies of it must be served on all other relevant parties.

(2) Permission is not required to vary a breakdown of costs, points of dispute or a reply but the court may disallow the variation or permit it only upon conditions, including conditions as to the payment of any costs caused or wasted by the variation.

56.15 Unless the court directs otherwise the solicitor must file with the court the papers in support of the bill not less than 7 days before the date for the detailed assessment hearing and not more than 14 days before that date.

56.16 Once the detailed assessment hearing has ended it is the responsibility of the legal representative appearing for the solicitor or, as the case may be, the solicitor in person to remove the papers filed in support of the bill.

56.17

(1) Attention is drawn to rule 47.15 (power to issue an interim certificate).

(2) If, in the course of a detailed assessment hearing of a solicitor's bill to his client, it appears to the costs judge or district judge that in any event the solicitor will be liable in connection with that bill to pay money to the client, he may issue an interim certificate specifying an amount which in his opinion is payable by the solicitor to his client. Such a certificate will include an order to pay the sum it certifies unless the court orders otherwise.

*56.18

(1) Attention is drawn to rule 47.16 which requires the solicitor to file a completed bill within 14 days after the end of the detailed assessment hearing. The court may dispense with the requirement to file a completed bill.

(2) After the detailed assessment hearing is concluded the court will—

(a) complete the court copy of the bill so as to show the amount allowed;

(b) determine the result of the cash account;

(c) award the costs of the detailed assessment hearing in accordance with Section 70(8) of the Solicitors Act 1974; and

(d) issue a final costs certificate showing the amount due following the detailed assessment hearing.

56.19 A final costs certificate will include an order to pay the sum it certifies unless the court orders otherwise.

SECTION 57 Transitional arrangements:

K–092   57.1   In this section "the previous rules" means the Rules of the Supreme Court 1965 ("RSC") or County Court Rules 1981 ("CCR"), as appropriate.

General Scheme of Transitional Arrangements concerning Costs Proceedings

*57.2   K–093

    (1) Paragraph 18 of the Practice Direction which supplements Part 51 (Transitional Arrangements) provides that the CPR govern any assessments of costs which take place on or after 26th April 1999 and states a presumption to be applied in respect of costs for work undertaken before 26th April 1999.

    (2) The following paragraphs provide five further transitional arrangements:

        (a) to provide an additional presumption to be applied when assessing costs which were awarded by an order made in a county court before 26th April 1999 which allowed costs "on Scale 1" to be determined in accordance with CCR Appendix A, or "on the lower scale" to be determined in accordance with CCR Appendix C.

        (b) to preserve the effect of CCR Appendix B Part III, paragraph 2;

        (c) to clarify the approach to be taken where a bill of costs was provisionally taxed before 26th April 1999 and the receiving party is unwilling to accept the result of the provisional taxation.

        (d) to preserve the right to carry in objections or apply for a reconsideration in all taxation proceedings commenced before 26th April 1999.

        (e) to deal with funding arrangements made before 3 July 2000.

Scale 1 or lower scale costs

57.3   Where an order was made in county court proceedings before 26th April   **K–094**
1999 under which the costs were allowed on Scale 1 or the lower scale, the general presumption is that no costs will be allowed under that order which would not have been allowed in a taxation before 26th April 1999.

Fixed costs on the lower scale

57.4   The amount to be allowed as fixed costs for making or opposing an   **K–095**
application for a rehearing to set aside a judgment given before 26th April 1999 where the costs are on lower scale is £11.25.

Bills provisionally taxed before 26th April 1999

57.5   In respect of bills of costs provisionally taxed before 26th April 1999:   **K–096**

    (1) The previous rules apply on the question who can request a hearing and the time limits for doing so; and

    (2) The CPR govern any subsequent hearing in that case.

Bills taxed before 26th April 1999

57.6   Where a bill of costs was taxed before 26th April 1999, the previous rules   **K–097**
govern the steps which can be taken to challenge that taxation.

Other taxation proceedings

*57.7   K–098

    (1) This paragraph applies to taxation proceedings which were commenced before 26th April 1999, were assigned for taxation to a Taxing

Master or District Judge, and which were still pending on 26th April 1999.

(2) Any assessment of costs that takes place in cases to which this paragraph applies which is conducted on or after 26th April 1999, will be conducted in accordance with the CPR.

(3) In addition to the possibility of appeal under rules 47.20 to 47.23 and Part 52 any party to a detailed assessment who is dissatisfied with any decision on a detailed assessment made by a costs judge or district judge may apply to that costs judge or district judge for a review of the decision. The review shall, for procedural purposes, be treated as if it were an appeal from an authorised court officer.

(4) The right of review provided by paragraph (3) above, will not apply in cases in which, at least 28 days before the date of the assessment hearing, all parties were served with notice that the rights of appeal in respect of that hearing would be governed by Part 47 Section VIII (Appeals from Authorised Court Officers in Detailed Assessment Proceedings) and Part 52 (Appeals).

(5) An order for the service of notice under sub-paragraph (4) above may be made on the application of any party to the detailed assessment proceedings or may be made by the court of its own initiative.

Transitional provisions concerning the Access to Justice Act 1999 sections 28 to 31

K–099   *57.8

(1) Sections 28 to 31 of the Access to Justice Act 1999, the Conditional Fee Agreements Regulations 2000, the Access to Justice (Membership Organisations) Regulations 2000, and the Access to Justice Act 1999 (Transitional Provisions) Order 2000 came into force on 1 April 2000. The Civil Procedure (Amendment No.3) Rules come into force on 3 July 2000.

(2) The Access to Justice Act 1999 (Transitional Provisions) Order 2000 provides that no conditional fee agreement or other arrangement about costs entered into before 1 April 2000 can be a funding arrangement, as defined in rule 43.2 The order also has the effect that where an conditional fee agreement or other funding arrangement has been entered into before 1 April 2000 and a second or subsequent funding arrangement is entered into on or after 1 April 2000, the second or subsequent funding arrangement does not give rise to an additional liability which is recoverable from a paying party.

*57.9

(1) Rule 39 of the Civil Procedure (Amendment No 3) Rules 2000 applies where between 1 April and 2 July 2000 (including both dates) —

a funding arrangement is entered into, and
proceedings are started in respect of a claim which is the subject of that agreement.

(2) Attention is drawn to the need to act promptly so as to comply with the requirements of the Rules and the Practice Directions by 31 July 2000 (i.e. within the 28 days from 3 July 2000 permitted by Rule 39) if that compliance is to be treated as compliance with the relevant provision. Attention is drawn in particular to Rule 44.15 (Providing

Information about Funding Arrangements) and Section 19 of this Practice Direction.

(3) Nothing in the legislation referred to above makes provision for a party who has entered into a funding arrangement to recover from another party any amount of an additional liability which relates to anything done or any costs incurred before the arrangement was entered into.

APPENDIX L

RSC Order 106

Proceedings relating to solicitors: the solicitors act, 1974

Interpretation

Rule 1

(1) In this order—   L–001
'the Act' means the Solicitors Act 1974 and a section referred to by number means the section so numbered in that Act;
'appeal' means an appeal to the High Court against an order made by the tribunal on an application or complaint under the Act.

(2) Expressions used in this order which are used in the Act have the same meanings in this order as in the Act.

Jurisdiction under part III of act

Rule 2

(2) The jurisdiction of the High Court under Part III of the Act may be   L–002
exercised by—

(a) A judge;

(b) A master, a taxing master or a district judge of the Family Division; or

(c) A district judge if the costs are for contentious business done in proceedings in the district registry of which he is the district judge or for non contentious business.

Power to order solicitor to deliver cash account, etc.

Rule 3

(1) Where the relationship of solicitor and client exists or has existed the   L–003
court may, on the application of the client or his personal representatives, make an order for—

(a) the delivery by the solicitor of a cash account;

(b) the payment or delivery up by the solicitor of money or securities;

(c) the delivery to the claimant of a list of the moneys or securities which the solicitor has in his possession or control on behalf of the claimant;

(d) the payment into or lodging in court of any such moneys or securities.

(2) An application for an order under this rule must be made by the issue of a claim form, or if in proceedings by an application in accordance with CPR Part 23.

(3) If the defendant alleges that he has a claim for costs, the court may make such order for detailed assessment in accordance with CPR Part 47 and payment, or securing the payment, thereof and the protection of the defendant's lien, if any, as the court thinks fit.

Certificate to be submitted with solicitor's application for detailed assessment

Rule 5A

L–004 A solicitor who applies for an order under the Act for the detailed assessment in accordance with CPR Part 47 of his bill of costs shall lodge with his application a certificate that all the relevant requirements of the Act have been satisfied.

Applications under schedule 1 to act

Rule 6

L–005 (1) Proceedings in the High Court under Schedule 1 to the Act shall be assigned to the Chancery Division.

(2) The claim form by which an application for an order under the said Schedule is made must be entitled in the matter of a solicitor, or a deceased solicitor, as the case may be (without naming him) and in the matter of the Act.

(3) Where an order has been made under paragraph 9(4), 9(5) or 10 of the said Schedule an application for an order under paragraph 9(8) or 9(10) may be made in accordance with CPR Part 23 in the proceedings in which the first mentioned order was made.

Defendants to applications under schedule 1 to act

Rule 7

L–006 The defendant to a claim by which an application for an order under Schedule 1 to the Act is made shall be—

(a) if the application is for an order under paragraph 5 thereof, the solicitor or, as the case may be, every member of the firm, on whose behalf the money in respect of which the order is sought is held;

(b) if the application is for an order under paragraph 6(4) or 9(8) thereof, the Law Society;

(c) if the application is for an order under paragraph 8, 9(4) or 9(5) thereof, the person against whom the order is sought;

(d) if the application is for an order under paragraph 9(10) thereof, the person from whom the Law Society obtained possession of the documents by virtue of paragraph 9 or 10;

(e) if the application is for an order under paragraph 10 thereof for the redirection of postal packets addressed to a solicitor or his firm, the solicitor or, as the case may be, every member of the firm;

(f) if the application is for an order under paragraph 11 thereof, the solicitor or personal representative in substitution for whom the appointment of a new trustee is sought and, if he is a co-trustee, the other trustee or trustees.

Interim order restricting payment out of banking account

Rule 8

L–007 At any time after the issue of a claim form by which an application for an order under paragraph 5 of Schedule 1 to the Act is made, the court may, on the application of the claimant made without notice in accordance with CPR Part 23 make an interim order under that paragraph to have effect until the hearing of the application and include therein a further order requiring the defendant to show cause at the hearing why an order under that paragraph should not be made.

Adding parties, etc.

Rule 9

The court may, at any stage of proceedings under Schedule 1 to the Act, order any person to be added as a party to the proceedings or to be given notice thereof. **L–008**

Service of documents

Rule 10

(1) Any document required to be served on the Law Society in proceedings **L–009** under this order shall be served by sending it by prepaid post to the secretary of the Law Society.

(2) Subject to paragraph (1) a claim form by which an application under Schedule 1 to the Act is made, an order under paragraph 5 of that Schedule or rule 8 and any other document not required to be served personally which is to be served on a defendant to proceedings under the said Schedule shall, unless the court otherwise directs, be deemed to be properly served by sending it by prepaid post to the defendant at his last known address.

Constitution of divisional court to hear appeals

Rule 11

Every appeal shall be heard by a Divisional Court of the Queen's Bench Division **L–010** consisting, unless the Lord Chief Justice otherwise directs, of not less than three judges.

Title, service, etc., of notice of appeal

Rule 12

(1) The appellant's notice by which an appeal is brought must be entitled in **L–011** the matter of a solicitor, or, as the case may be, a solicitor's clerk, without naming him, and in the matter of the Act.

(2) Unless the court otherwise orders, the persons to be served with such notice are every party to the proceedings before the tribunal and the Law Society.

(3) The appellant's notice must be filed at the court within 14 days after the date on which a statement of the tribunal's findings was filed pursuant to section 48(1) of the Act.

Law society to produce certain documents

Rule 13

(1) Within 7 days after being served with the appellant's notice the Law **L–012** Society must lodge in the Crown Office three copies of each of the following documents—

(a) the order appealed against, together with the statement of the tribunal's findings required by section 48(1) of the Act;

(b) any document lodged by a party with the tribunal which is relevant to a matter in issue on the appeal; and

(c) the transcript of the shorthand note, or, as the case may be, the note taken by the chairman of the tribunal of the evidence in the proceedings before the tribunal.

(2) At the hearing of the appeal the court shall direct by whom the costs incurred in complying with paragraph (1) are to be borne and may order them to be paid to the Law Society by one of the parties notwithstanding that the Society does not appear at the hearing.

Restriction on requiring security for costs

Rule 14

L–013 No person other than an appellant who was the applicant in the proceedings before the tribunal, shall be ordered to give security for the costs of an appeal.

Disciplinary committee's opinion may be required

Rule 15

L–014 The court may direct the tribunal to furnish the court with a written statement of their opinion on the case which is the subject-matter of an appeal or on any question arising therein, and where such a direction is given, the clerk to the tribunal must as soon as may be lodge three copies of such statement in the Crown Office and at the same time send a copy to each of the parties to the appeal.

Persons entitled to be heard on appeal

Rule 16

L–015 A person who has not been served with the appellant's notice but who desires to be heard in opposition to the appeal shall, if he appears to the court to be a proper person to be so heard, be entitled to be so heard.

Discontinuance of appeal

Rule 17

(1) An appellant may at any time discontinue his appeal by serving notice of discontinuance on the clerk to the tribunal and every other party to the appeal and, if the appeal has been entered, by lodging a copy of the notice in the Crown Office.

(2) Where an appeal has been discontinued in accordance with paragraph (1) it shall be treated as having been dismissed with an order for payment by the appellant of the costs of and incidental to the appeal, including any costs incurred by the Law Society in complying with rule 13(1).

APPENDIX M

The Family Proceedings (Miscellaneous Amendments) Rules 1999

(S.I. 1999 No. 1012 (L. 9))

We, the authority having power under section 40(1) of the Matrimonial and **Family Proceedings** Act 1984[1] to make rules of court for the purposes of **family proceedings** in the High Court and county courts, in the exercise of the powers conferred by section 40, make the following Rules—

M–001

1. These Rules may be cited as the **Family Proceedings** (Miscellaneous Amendments) Rules 1999 and shall come into force on 26 April 1999.

M–002

Amendments to the Family Proceedings Rules 1991[2]

2. The **Family Proceedings** Rules 1991 shall be amended in accordance with these rules and a reference to a rule by number alone is a reference to the rule so numbered in the **Family Proceedings** Rules.

M–003

3.—(1) In rules 1.2(5), 1.3 and 1.4, references to "the County Court Rules 1981"[3] and "the Rules of the Supreme Court 1965"[4] are references to the County Court Rules and the Rules of the Supreme Court in force immediately before 26 April 1999 and references to provisions of those Rules in the **Family Proceedings** Rules 1991 shall be read accordingly.

M–004

(2) In rule 1.3(1), after "shall" insert "continue to".

Costs in Family Proceedings

4.—(1) Order 38 of the County Court Rules 1981 and Order 62 of the Rules of the Supreme Court 1965 shall not apply to the assessment of costs in **family proceedings** and **proceedings** in the **Family** Division, and Parts 43, 44 (except rules 44.9 to 44.12), 47 and 48 of the Civil Procedure Rules 1998[5] ("the 1998 Rules") shall apply to the assessment of costs in those **proceedings**, with the following modifications:

M–005

- (a) in rule 43.2(1)(c)(ii) of the 1998 Rules, "district judge" includes a district judge of the Principal Registry of the **Family** Division;
- (b) rule 44.3(2) of the 1998 Rules (costs follow the event) shall not apply.

(2) The **Family Proceedings** (Costs) Rules 1991[6] are revoked.

(3) This rule applies to any assessment of costs that takes place on or after 26 April 1999, but so that, as a general rule, no costs for work done before that date shall be disallowed if they would have been allowed on taxation before that date.

Irvine of Lairg, C.
Stephen Brown, P
Nicholas Wall

---

[1] 1984 c. 42; as amended by the Courts and Legal Services Act 1990 (c. 41), Sch.18, para.50 and the Civil Procedure Act 1997 (c. 12), Sch.2, para.3.
[2] SI 1991/1247.
[3] SI 1981/1687.
[4] SI 1965/1776.
[5] SI 1998/3132; as amended by SI 1999/1008.
[6] SI 1991/1832.

Gerald Angel
A.N. Fricker
L.A. Newton
Jennifer Roberts
I.M. Robertson
D.M. Hodson
Dated 25 March 1999

EXPLANATORY NOTE

(This note is not part of the Rules)

M–006   The **Family Proceedings** Rules 1991 apply the County Court Rules 1981 and the Rules of the Supreme Court 1965. On 26 April 1999, the Civil Procedure Rules 1998 come into force in respect of civil **proceedings**; they supersede the County Court Rules and the Rules of the Supreme Court, which will cease to have effect. These Rules provide for the County Court Rules and Rules of the Supreme Court generally to continue to apply in the **Family Proceedings** Rules. The exception is the assessment of costs, where the relevant provisions of the Civil Procedure Rules will apply instead.

APPENDIX N

Practice Directions, Family Division, 22 April 1999, 24 July 2000

Civil Procedure Rules 1998   *President's Direction*

Allocation of cases—Costs   *22 April 1999*

It is directed that upon the coming to force on the 26 April 1999 of the Civil **N–001** Procedure Rules 1998 ("the 1998 Rules") and the Family Proceedings (Miscellaneous Amendments) Rules 1999:

    a. Paragraph 3.2 of the (Civil Procedure) Practice Direction "Allocation of Cases to Levels of Judiciary" shall apply to the Family Division. District Judges (including District Judges of the Principal Registry) shall have jurisdiction to hear and dispose of proceedings under the Inheritance (Provision for Family & Dependants) Act 1975 and under s 14 of the Trusts of Land and Appointment of Trustees Act 1996.

    b. The (Civil Procedure) Practice Direction about Costs "Supplementing Parts 43 to 48 of the Civil Procedure Rules" ("the costs direction") shall apply to family proceedings to which the Family Proceedings Rules 1991 apply and to proceedings in the Family Division. References in the costs direction to "claimant" and "defendant" are to be read as references to the equivalent terms used in family proceedings and other terms and expressions used in the costs direction shall be similarly treated. References to procedural steps and to other Parts of the 1998 Rules which have not yet been applied to family proceedings are to be read as referring to equivalent or similar procedures under the rules applicable to family proceedings, as the context may permit. The previous practice in relation to "costs reserved" will no longer be followed and such an order will have the effect specified in the costs direction. It should also be noted that the period for commencing detailed assessment proceedings will be as specified in Part 47.7 (3 months) in substitution for the period of 6 months previously applicable.

Issued with the approval and concurrence of the Lord Chancellor

Signed
Stephen Brown
President

THE PRINCIPAL REGISTRY OF THE FAMILY DIVISION

Costs   **President's Direction**

Civil Procedure Rules 1998   **24 July 2000**

The President's Direction dated the 22nd April 1999 applied the (Civil Procedure) **N–002** Practice Direction about Costs Supplementing Parts 43 to 48 of the Civil Procedure Rules ("the costs direction") to family proceedings (within the Family Proceedings Rules 1991) and to proceedings in the Family Division. A further edition of the costs direction (effective from the 3rd July 2000) has been published and it is hereby directed that the further edition (and all subsequent editions as and when they are published and come into effect) shall extend to family proceedings and to proceedings in the Family Division in the same way as did the costs direction and to the extent applicable to such proceedings.

    The further edition of the costs direction includes provisions applicable to proceedings following changes in the manner in which legal services are funded pursuant to the Access to Justice Act 1999. It should be noted that although the cost of the premium in respect of legal costs insurance (section 29) or the cost of funding by a prescribed membership organisation (section 30) may be recoverable, family proceedings (within section 58A(2) of the Courts and Legal Services Act 1990) cannot be the subject of an enforceable conditional fee agreement.

Issued with the approval of the Lord Chancellor

Elizabeth Butler-Sloss
President

APPENDIX O

The Insolvency (Amendment) (No. 2) Rules 1999

(S.I. 1999/1022)

Made	*29th March 1999*
Laid before Parliament	*31st March 1999*
Coming into force	*26th April 1999*

The Lord Chancellor, in the exercise of his powers under sections 411 and 412 of the Insolvency Act 1986[1], with the concurrence of the Secretary of State, and after consulting the committee existing for that purpose under section 413 of that Act, hereby makes the following Rules–

Citation and commencement

1. These Rules may be cited as the Insolvency (Amendment) (No. 2) Rules 1999 and shall come into force on 26th April 1999.

Interpretation

2. In these Rules references to "the principal Rules" are to the Insolvency Rules 1986[2] and a Rule referred to by number means the Rule so numbered in the principal Rules.

Application

3. The principal Rules shall have effect subject to the amendments set out in the Schedule to these Rules.

Irvine of Lairg, C.
25th March 1999

O–001

O–002

O–003

O–004

SCHEDULE

Rule 3

Amendment of Rule 0.2 (Construction and interpretation)

1. For Rule 0.2. substitute—
    "**Construction and interpretation**
    0.2.—(1) In these Rules—
    "the Act" means the Insolvency Act 1986 (any reference to a numbered section being to a section of that Act);
    "the Companies Act" means the Companies Act 1985[3];

O–005

---

[1] 1986 c. 45.
[2] S.I. 1986/1925; amended by S.I. 1987/1919, 1989/397, 1991/495, 1993/602, 1995/586 and 1999/359. The only relevant amending instrument is S.I. 1987/1919.
[3] 1985 c. 6.

"CPR" means the Civil Procedure Rules 1998[4] and "CPR" followed by a Part or rule by number means the Part or rule with that number in those Rules; "RSC" followed by an Order by number means the Order with that number set out in Schedule 1 to the CPR; and "the Rules" means the Insolvency Rules 1986.

(2) References in the Rules to ex parte hearings shall be construed as references to hearings without notice being served on any other party; references to applications made ex parte as references to applications made without notice being served on any other party and other references which include the expression "ex parte" shall be similarly construed.

(3) Subject to paragraphs (1) and (2), Part 13 of the Rules has effect for their interpretation and application.".

Amendment of Rule 6.197 (Claim by mortgagee of land)

O–006   2. In Rule 6.197. in paragraph (3) for "The court may under this paragraph authorise the service of interrogatories on any party." substitute "The court may under this paragraph order any of the parties to clarify any matter which is in dispute in the proceedings or give additional information in relation to any such matter and CPR Part 18 (further information) shall apply to any such order.".

Amendment of Part 7 (Court Procedure and Practice) Chapter 6 (Costs and Taxation)

O–007   3. In Part 7 for Chapter 6 substitute—

"Chapter 6—Costs and Detailed Assessment

Application of the CPR

7.33. Subject to provision to inconsistent effect made as follows in this Chapter, CPR Part 43 (scope of costs rules and definitions), Part 44 (general rules about costs), Part 45 (fixed costs), Part 47 (procedure for detailed assessment of costs and default provisions) and Part 48 (costs—special cases) shall apply to insolvency proceedings with any necessary modifications.

Requirement to assess costs by the detailed procedure

7.34.—(1) Subject as follows, where the costs, charges or expenses of any person are payable out of the insolvent estate, the amount of those costs, charges or expenses shall be decided by detailed assessment unless agreed between the responsible insolvency practitioner and the person entitled to payment, and in the absence of such agreement the responsible insolvency practitioner may serve notice in writing requiring that person to commence detailed assessment proceedings in accordance with CPR Part 47 (procedure for detailed assessment of costs and default provisions) the court to which the insolvency proceedings are allocated or, where in relation to a company there is no such court, that in relation to any court having jurisdiction to wind up the company.

---

[4] S.I. 1998/3132 (L. 17); amended by S.I. 1999/1008 (L. 8).

(2) If a liquidation or creditors' committee established in insolvency proceedings (except administrative receivership) resolves that the amount of any such costs, charges or expenses should be decided by detailed assessment, the insolvency practitioner shall require detailed assessment in accordance with (PR Part 47).

(3) Where the amount of the costs, charges or expenses of any person employed by an insolvency practitioner in insolvency proceedings are required to be decided by detailed assessment or fixed by order of the court this does not preclude the insolvency practitioner from making payments on account to such person on the basis of an undertaking by that person to repay immediately any money which may, when detailed assessment is made, prove to have been overpaid, with interest at the rate specified in section 17 of the Judgments Act 1838[5] on the date payment was made and for the period from the date of payment to that of repayment.

(4) In any proceedings before the court, including proceedings on a petition, the court may order costs to be decided by detailed assessment.

(5) Unless otherwise directed or authorised, the costs of a trustee in bankruptcy or a liquidator are to be allowed on the standard basis for which provision is made in CPR rule 44.4 (basis of assessment) and rule 44.5 (factors to be taken into account in deciding the amount of costs).

(6) This Rule applies additionally (with any necessary modifications) to winding-up and bankruptcy proceedings commenced before the coming into force of the Rules.

Procedure where detailed assessment required

7.35.—(1) Before making a detailed assessment of the costs of any person employed in insolvency proceedings by a responsible insolvency practitioner, the costs officer shall require a certificate of employment, which shall be endorsed on the bill and signed by the insolvency practitioner.

O–008

(2) The certificate shall include—

- (a) the name and address of the person employed,
- (b) details of the functions to be carried out under the employment, and
- (c) a note of any special terms of remuneration which have been agreed.

(3) Every person whose costs in insolvency proceedings are required to be decided by detailed assessment shall, on being required in writing to do so by the insolvency practitioner, commence detailed assessment proceedings in accordance with CPR Part 47 (procedure for detailed assessment of costs and default provisions).

(4) If that person does not commence detailed assessment proceedings within 3 months of the requirement under paragraph (3), or within such further time as the court, on application, may permit, the insolvency practitioner may deal with the insolvent estate without regard to any claim by that person, whose claim is forfeited by such failure to commence proceedings.

(5) Where in any such case such a claim lies additionally against an insolvency practitioner in his personal capacity, that claim is also forfeited by such failure to commence proceedings.

(6) Where costs have been incurred in insolvency proceedings in the High Court and those proceedings are subsequently transferred to a county court, all costs of those proceedings directed by the court or otherwise required to be

---

[5] 1838 c. 110 (1 & 2 Vict.).

assessed may nevertheless, on the application of the person who incurred the costs, be ordered to be decided by detailed assessment in the High Court.

Costs of sheriff

7.36.—(1) Where a sheriff—

    (a) is required under section 184(2) or 346(2) to deliver up goods or money, or

    (b) has under section 184(3) or 346(3) deducted costs from the proceeds of an execution or money paid to him,

the responsible insolvency practitioner may require in writing that the amount of the sheriff's bill of costs be decided by detailed assessment.

(2) Where such a requirement is made, Rule 7.35(4) applies.

(3) Where, in the case of a deduction under paragraph (1)(b), any amount deducted is disallowed at the conclusion of the detailed assessment proceedings, the sheriff shall forthwith pay a sum equal to that disallowed to the insolvency practitioner for the benefit of the insolvent estate.

Petitions presented by insolvents

7.37.—(1) In any case where a petition is presented by a company or individual ("the insolvent") against himself, any solicitor acting for the insolvent shall in his bill of costs give credit for any sum or security received from the insolvent as a deposit on account of the costs and expenses to be incurred in respect of the filing and prosecution of the petition; and the deposit shall be noted by the costs officer on the final costs certificate.

(2) Paragraph (3) applies where a petition is presented by a person other than the insolvent to whom the petition relates and before it is heard the insolvent presents a petition for the same order, and that order is made.

(3) Unless the court considers that the insolvent estate has benefited by the insolvent's conduct, or that there are otherwise special circumstances justifying the allowance of costs, no costs shall be allowed to the insolvent or his solicitor out of the insolvent estate.

Costs paid otherwise than out of the insolvent estate

7.38. Where the amount of costs is decided by detailed assessment under an order of the court directing that those costs are to be paid otherwise than out of the insolvent estate, the costs officer shall note on the final costs certificate by whom, or the manner in which, the costs are to be paid.

Award of costs against official receiver or responsible insolvency practitioner

7.39. Without prejudice to any provision of the Act or Rules by virtue of which the official receiver is not in any event to be liable for costs and expenses, where the official receiver or a responsible insolvency practitioner is made a party to any proceedings on the application of another party to the proceedings, he shall not be personally liable for costs unless the court otherwise directs.

Applications for costs

7.40.—(1) This Rule applies where a party to, or person affected by, any proceedings in an insolvency—

610

(a) applies to the court for an order allowing his costs, or part of them, incidental to the proceedings, and

(b) that application is not made at the time of the proceedings.

(2) The person concerned shall serve a sealed copy of his application on the responsible insolvency practitioner, and, in winding up by the court or bankruptcy, on the official receiver.

(3) The insolvency practitioner and, where appropriate, the official receiver may appear on the application.

(4) No costs of or incidental to the application shall be allowed to the applicant unless the court is satisfied that the application could not have been made at the time of the proceedings.

Costs and expenses of witnesses

7.41.—(1) Except as directed by the court, no allowance as a witness in any examination or other proceedings before the court shall be made to the bankrupt or an officer of the insolvent company to which the proceedings relate.

(2) A person presenting any petition in insolvency proceedings shall not be regarded as a witness on the hearing of the petition, but the costs officer may allow his expenses of travelling and subsistence.

Final costs certificate

7.42.—(1) A final costs certificate of the costs officer is final and conclusive as to all matters which have not been objected to in the manner provided for under the rules of the court.

(2) Where it is proved to the satisfaction of a costs officer that a final costs certificate has been lost or destroyed, he may issue a duplicate.".

Amendment of Rule 7.49 (Procedure on Appeal)

4. For Rule 7.49. substitute—   O–010

"Procedure on appeal"

7.49.—(1) Subject as follows, the procedure and practice of the Supreme Court relating to appeals to the Court of Appeal apply to appeals in insolvency proceedings.

(2) In relation to any appeal to a single judge of the High Court under section 375(2) (individual insolvency) or Rule 7.47(2) above (company insolvency), any reference in the CPR to the Court of Appeal is replaced by a reference to that judge and any reference to the registrar of civil appeals is replaced by a reference to the registrar of the High Court who deals with insolvency proceedings of the kind involved.

(3) In insolvency proceedings, the procedure under RSC Order 59 (appeals to the Court of Appeal) is by ordinary application and not by application notice.".

Amendment of Rule 7.51 (Principal court rules and practice to apply)

5. For Rule 7.51. substitute—   O–011

"Principal court rules and practice to apply

7.51.—(1) The CPR, the practice and procedure of the High Court and of the county court (including any practice direction) apply to insolvency proceedings in the High Court and county court as the case may be, in either case with any necessary modifications, except so far as inconsistent with the Rules.

(2) All insolvency proceedings shall be allocated to the multi-track for which CPR Part 29 (the multi-track) makes provision, accordingly those provisions of the CPR which provide for allocation questionnaires and track allocation will not apply.".

Amendment of Rule 7.57 (Affidavits)

O–012   **6.** For Rule 7.57. substitute—

"Affidavits

7.57.—(1) Subject to the following paragraphs of this Rule the practice and procedure of the High Court with regard to affidavits, their form and contents and the procedure governing their use are to apply to all insolvency proceedings.

(2) Where, in insolvency proceedings, an affidavit is made by the official receiver or the responsible insolvency practitioner, the deponent shall state the capacity in which he makes it, the position which he holds, and the address at which he works.

(3) A creditor's affidavit of debt may be sworn before his own solicitor.

(4) The official receiver, any deputy official receiver, or any officer of the court duly authorised in that behalf, may take affidavits and declarations.

(5) Subject to paragraph (6), where the Rules provide for the use of an affidavit, a witness statement verified by a statement of truth may be used as an alternative.

(6) Paragraph (5) does not apply to Rules 2.12., 3.4., 4.33., 6.60. (statement of affairs), 4.42., 6.66., 6.72. (further disclosure), 4.39., 4.40., 6.65; 6.70. (accounts), 4.73., 4.77., 6.96; 6.99. (claims) and 9.3., 9.4. (examinations).

(7) Where paragraph (5) applies any form prescribed by Rule 12.7 of these Rules shall be modified as necessary.".

Amendment of Rule 7.59 (Payment into court)

O–013   **7.** For Rule 7.59. substitute—

"Payment into court

7.59. The CPR relating to payment into and out of court of money lodged in court as security for costs apply to money lodged in court under the Rules."

Amendment of Rule 7.60 (Discovery)

O–014   **8.** For Rule 7.60. substitute—

"Further Information and Disclosure

7.60.—(1) Any party to insolvency proceedings may apply to the court for an order—

(a) that any other party
   (i) clarify any matter which is in dispute in the proceedings, or
   (ii) give additional information in relation to any such matter; in accordance with CPR Part 18 (further information); or
(b) to obtain disclosure from any other party in accordance with CPR Part 31 (disclosure and inspection of documents).

(2) An application under this Rule may be made without notice being served on any other party."

Amendment of Rule 9.2 (Form and contents of application)

9. In Rule 9.2. for paragraph (3)(b) substitute—

O–015

"(b) to be ordered to clarify any matter which is in dispute in the proceedings or to give additional information in relation to any such matter and if so CPR Part 18 (further information) shall apply to any such order, or)".

Amendment of Rule 9.4 (Procedure for examination)

10. In Rule 9.4. for paragraph (3) substitute—

O–016

"(3) If the respondent is ordered to clarify any matter or to give additional information, the court shall direct him as to the questions which he is required to answer, and as to whether his answers (if any) are to be made on affidavit.".

Amendment of Rule 12.9 (Time-limits)

11. For Rule 12.9. substitute—

O–017

"Time-Limits

12.9.—(1) The provisions of CPR ruled 2.8 (time) apply, as regards computation of time, to anything required or authorised to be done by the Rules.
(2) The provisions of CPR rule 3.1(2)(a) (the court's general powers of management) apply so as to enable the court to extend or shorten the time for compliance with anything required or authorised to be done by the Rules.".

Amendment of Rule 12.11 (General provisions as to service)

12. For Rule 12.11. substitute—

O–018

"**General provisions as to service**

12.11. Subject to Rule 12.10, CPR Part 6 (service of documents) applies as regards any matter relating to the service of documents and the giving of notice in insolvency proceedings."

Amendment of Rule 12.12 (Service outside the jurisdiction)

13. In Rule 12.12. for paragraph (1) substitute—

O–019

"(1) RSC Order 11 (service of process, etc., out of the jurisdiction) does not apply in insolvency proceedings."

Amendment of Rule 13.13 (Definition of certain expressions used generally)

O–020   **14.** In Rule 13.13.—

(a)   for paragraph (1) substitute—

"(1) "Business day" means any day other than a Saturday, a Sunday, Christmas Day, Good Friday or a day which is a bank holiday in any part of Great Britain under or by virtue of the Banking and Financial Dealings Act 1971[6] except in Rules 1.7., 4.10., 4.11., 4.16., 4.20., 5.10. and 6.23. where "business day" shall include any day which is a bank holiday in Scotland but not in England and Wales."; and

(b)   for paragraph (6) substitute—

"(6) "Practice direction" means a direction as to the practice and procedure of any court within the scope of the CPR.

(7) "Prescribed order of priority" means the order of priority of payments laid down by Chapter 20 of Part 4 of the Rules, or Chapter 23 of Part 6."

EXPLANATORY NOTE

(This note is not part of the Rules)

O–021   These Rules further amend the Insolvency Rules 1986 ("the Rules") which provide detailed procedures for the conduct of all company and individual insolvency proceedings in England and Wales under the Insolvency Act 1986.

The amendments come into force on 26th April 1999 to coincide with the coming into force of the Civil Procedure Rules 1998 ("the CPR") which provide a new code of civil procedure for the civil courts which replaces the Rules of the Supreme Court 1965 and the County Court Rules 1981.

Although, by rule 2.1 of the CPR, the new civil procedure does not apply to insolvency proceedings, the Rules themselves apply all those provisions of the CPR and such practice of the High Court and County Court as is not inconsistent with provisions made by the Rules to such proceedings.

In addition to the application of the CPR and court practice, detailed amendment is made of such of the Rules as use language in relation to insolvency proceedings no longer to be used in civil procedure. References to "ex parte hearings" and to the "taxation" of costs are, for example, to be read, respectively, as references to "hearings without notice being given to any other party" and to "detailed assessment".

Consistent with the CPR, the amendments also bring practice in insolvency proceedings into line with the new civil procedure by permitting, for example, the use of a number of statements of truth in situations where affidavit evidence was, before amendment of the Rules, obligatory.

---

[6] 1971 c. 80.

APPENDIX P

Practice Note Remuneration of a Judicial Trustee

July 1, 2003

CHANCERY DIVISION

Trust and trustee—Judicial trustee—Remuneration—Common form of order—Judicial Trustees Act 1896, s 1(5)—Judicial Trustees Rules 1983, r 11.

[1] When dealing with the assignment of remuneration to a judicial trustee under s 1(5) of the Judicial Trustees Act 1896 and r 11 of the Judicial Trustee Rules 1983, SI 1983/370, the court will consider directions as to remuneration based on the common form of order set out below, subject to such modifications as may be required in any particular case.   **P–001**

[2] In general the court when considering reasonable remuneration for the purposes of r 11(1)(a) will need to be satisfied as to the basis upon which the remuneration is claimed, that it is justified and that the amount is reasonable and proportionate and within the limit of 15% of the capital value of the trust property specified in the rule.

[3] The court may, before determining the amount of remuneration, require the judicial trustee to provide further information, alternatively refer the matter to a costs judge for him to assess remuneration.

[4] When an application is made to the court for the appointment of a judicial trustee or when the court gives directions under r 8 practitioners should produce to the court a draft order which should take account of the common form of the order.

DRAFT PARAGRAPHS OF ORDER

'[IT IS ORDERED]   **P–002**

. . . that the remuneration of the Judicial Trustee shall be in such amount as may be approved from time to time by this court upon application for payment on examination of his accounts.

. . . that the Judicial Trustees accounts shall be endorsed by him with a certificate of the approximate capital value of the trust property at the commencement of the year of account.

. . . that every application for payment by the Judicial Trustee shall be in the form of a letter to the court (with a copy to the beneficiaries) which shall (a) set out the basis of the claim to remuneration, the scales or rates of any professional charges, the work done and time spent, any information concerning the complexity of the trusteeship that may be relied on and any other matters which the court shall be invited by the Judicial Trustee to take account and (b) certify that he considers that the claim for remuneration is reasonable and proportionate.'

Taken from: [2003] 3 All ER 974

APPENDIX Q

The Conditional Fee Agreements Order 2000

(SI 2000/823)

The Lord Chancellor, in exercise of the powers conferred upon him by section 58(4)(a) and (c) of the Courts and Legal Services Act 1990;[1;], and all other powers enabling him in that behalf, having consulted in accordance with section 58A(5);[2;] of that Act, makes the following Order, a draft of which has been laid before and approved by resolution of each House of Parliament:

Citation, commencement and interpretation

1.—(1) This Order may be cited as the Conditional Fee Agreements Order 2000 and shall come into force on 1st April 2000.   Q–001

(2) In this Order "the Act" means the Courts and Legal Services Act 1990.

Revocation of 1998 Order

2. The Conditional Fee Agreements Order 1998[3] is revoked.   Q–002

Agreements providing for success fees

3. All proceedings which, under section 58 of the Act, can be the subject of an enforceable conditional fee agreement, except proceedings under section 82 of the Environmental Protection Act 1990[4], are proceedings specified for the purposes of section 58(4)(a) of the Act.   Q–003

Amount of for success fees

4. In relation to all proceedings specified in article 3, the percentage specified for the purposes of section 58(4)(c) of the Act shall be 100%.   Q–004

Irvine of Lairg, C.

Dated 20th March 2000

EXPLANATORY NOTE

(This note is not part of the Order)

Under sections 58 and 58A of the Courts and Legal Services Act 1990, all proceedings may be the subject of an enforceable fee agreement except specified family proceedings and criminal proceedings other than those under section 82 of the Environmental Protection Act 1990. This Order specifies the proceedings to which a conditional fee agreement must relate if it is to provide for a success fee. These are all proceedings which may be the subject of a conditional fee agreement

---

[1] 1990 c. 41. Section 58 was substituted by section 27(1) of the Access to Justice Act 1999 (c. 22).back

[2] Section 58A was added by section 27(1) of the Access to Justice Act 1999 (c. 22).back

[3] S.I. 1998/1860.back

[4] 1990 c. 43.back

except criminal proceedings under section 82 of the Environmental Protection Act 1990.

Under section 58(4)(c) of the Courts and Legal Services Act 1990, the Order also sets a maximum success fee percentage of 100% for all conditional fee agreements which provide for such fees.

APPENDIX R

APPENDIX R

The Conditional Fee Agreements Regulations 2000

(SI 2000/692)

The Lord Chancellor, in exercise of the powers conferred on him by sections 58(3)(c), 58A(3) and 119 of the Courts and Legal Services Act 1990[1] and all other powers enabling him hereby makes the following Regulations:

Citation, commencement and interpretation

1.—(1) These Regulations may be cited as the Conditional Fee Agreements Regulations 2000.   **R–001**

(2) These Regulations come into force on 1st April 2000.

(3) In these Regulations—

"client" includes, except where the context otherwise requires, a person who—

(a) has instructed the legal representative to provide the advocacy or litigation services to which the conditional fee agreement relates, or

(b) is liable to pay the legal representative's fees in respect of those services; and

"legal representative" means the person providing the advocacy or litigation services to which the conditional fee agreement relates.

Requirements for contents of conditional fee agreements: general

2.—(1) A conditional fee agreement must specify—   **R–002**

(a) the particular proceedings or parts of them to which it relates (including whether it relates to any appeal, counterclaim or proceedings to enforce a judgement or order),

(b) the circumstances in which the legal representative's fees and expenses, or part of them, are payable,

(c) what payment, if any, is due—

   (i) if those circumstances only partly occur,

   (ii) irrespective of whether those circumstances occur, and

   (iii) on the termination of the agreement for any reason, and

(d) the amounts which are payable in all the circumstances and cases specified or the method to be used to calculate them and, in particular, whether the amounts are limited by reference to the damages which may be recovered on behalf of the client.

(2) A conditional fee agreement to which regulation 4 applies must contain a statement that the requirements of that regulation which apply in the case of that agreement have been complied with.

---

[1] 1990 c.41; sections 58 and 58A are substituted by section 27 of the Access to Justice Act 1999 (c.22); section 119 is an interpretation provision and is cited because of the meaning given to the word "prescribed".

Requirements for contents of conditional fee agreements providing for success fees

R–003   3.—(1) A conditional fee agreement which provides for a success fee—

(a)   must briefly specify the reasons for setting the percentage increase at the level stated in the agreement, and

(b)   must specify how much of the percentage increase, if any, relates to the cost to the legal representative of the postponement of the payment of his fees and expenses.

(2) If the agreement relates to court proceedings, it must provide that where the percentage increase becomes payable as a result of those proceedings, then—

(a)   if—
(i)   any fees subject to the increase are assessed, and
(ii)   the legal representative or the client is required by the court to disclose to the court or any other person the reasons for setting the percentage increase at the level stated in the agreement,

he may do so,

(b)   if—
(i)   any such fees are assessed, and
(ii)   any amount in respect of the percentage increase is disallowed on the assessment on the ground that the level at which the increase was set was unreasonable in view of facts which were or should have been known to the legal representative at the time it was set,

that amount ceases to be payable under the agreement, unless the court is satisfied that it should continue to be so payable, and

(c)   if—
(i)   sub-paragraph (b) does not apply, and
(ii)   the legal representative agrees with any person liable as a result of the proceedings to pay fees subject to the percentage increase that a lower amount than the amount payable in accordance with the conditional fee agreement is to be paid instead,

the amount payable under the conditional fee agreement in respect of those fees shall be reduced accordingly, unless the court is satisfied that the full amount should continue to be payable under it.

(3) In this regulation "percentage increase" means the percentage by which the amount of the fees which would be payable if the agreement were not a conditional fee agreement is to be increased under the agreement.

Information to be given before conditional fee agreements made

R–004   4.—(1) Before a conditional fee agreement is made the legal representative must—

(a)   inform the client about the following matters, and

(b)   if the client requires any further explanation, advice or other information about any of those matters, provide such further explanation, advice or other information about them as the client may reasonably require.

(2) Those matters are—

(a) the circumstances in which the client may be liable to pay the costs of the legal representative in accordance with the agreement,

(b) the circumstances in which the client may seek assessment of the fees and expenses of the legal representative and the procedure for doing so,

(c) whether the legal representative considers that the client's risk of incurring liability for costs in respect of the proceedings to which agreement relates is insured against under an existing contract of insurance,

(d) whether other methods of financing those costs are available, and, if so, how they apply to the client and the proceedings in question,

(e) whether the legal representative considers that any particular method or methods of financing any or all of those costs is appropriate and, if he considers that a contract of insurance is appropriate or recommends a particular such contract—

  (i) his reasons for doing so, and
  (ii) whether he has an interest in doing so.

(3) Before a conditional fee agreement is made the legal representative must explain its effect to the client.

(4) In the case of an agreement where—

(a) the legal representative is a body to which section 30 of the Access to Justice Act 1999[2] (recovery where body undertakes to meet costs liabilities) applies, and

(b) there are no circumstances in which the client may be liable to pay any costs in respect of the proceedings,

paragraph (1) does not apply.

(5) Information required to be given under paragraph (1) about the matters in paragraph (2)(a) to (d) must be given orally (whether or not it is also given in writing), but information required to be so given about the matters in paragraph (2)(e) and the explanation required by paragraph (3) must be given both orally and in writing.

(6) This regulation does not apply in the case of an agreement between a legal representative and an additional legal representative.

Form of agreement

5.—(1) A conditional fee agreement must be signed by the client and the legal representative.   **R–005**

(2) This regulation does not apply in the case of an agreement between a legal representative and an additional legal representative.

Amendment of agreement

6. Where an agreement is amended to cover further proceedings or parts of them—   **R–006**

---

[2] 1999 c.22.

(a) regulations 2, 3 and 5 apply to the amended agreement as if it were a fresh agreement made at the time of the amendment, and

(b) the obligations under regulation 4 apply in relation to the amendments in so far as they affect the matters mentioned in that regulation.

Revocation of 1995 Regulations

R–007   7. The Conditional Fee Agreements Regulations 1995[3] are revoked.
8. Exclusion of Collective conditional fee agreements.
These regulations shall not apply to collective conditional fee agreements within the meaning of regulation 3 of the Collective Conditional Fee Agreements Regulations 2000.[4]

Irvine of Lairg, C

9th March 2000

EXPLANATORY NOTE

(This note is not part of the Regulations)

Section 58(1) of the Courts and Legal Services Act 1990 provides that a conditional fee agreement is not unenforceable if it satisfies certain conditions. These include conditions to be specified in regulations under section 58(3) of that Act. Regulations 2 and 3 specify those conditions. Regulation 2 applies to all conditional fee agreements. Regulation 3 sets out further requirements applying only to agreements which provide for success fees.

Section 58A(3) enables the conditions which may be prescribed for conditional fee agreements to include requirements for the person providing advocacy or litigation services to have provided prescribed information before the agreement is made. Regulation 4 imposes such a requirement and specifies what information is to be given. It does not apply where the agreement is between legal representatives.

Regulation 5 requires that agreements other than those between legal representatives must be signed by the client and the legal representative.

Regulation 6 provides for similar requirements to apply as respects amendments of agreements.

These Regulations replace the Conditional Fee Agreements Regulations 1995, which are revoked.

---

[3] S.I. 1995/1675.
[4] Added by SI 2000/2988 (Collective Conditional Fee Agreements Regulations 2000).

APPENDIX S

The Access to Justice (Membership Organisations) Regulations 2000

(SI 2000/693)

The Lord Chancellor, in exercise of the powers conferred on him by section 30(1) and (3) to (5) of the Access to Justice Act 1999[1] and all other powers enabling him hereby makes the following Regulations:

Citation, commencement and interpretation

1.—(1) These Regulations may be cited as the Access to Justice (Membership Organisations) Regulations 2000.   **S–001**
(2) These Regulations come into force on 1st April 2000.

Bodies of a prescribed description

2. The bodies which are prescribed for the purpose of section 30 of the Access to   **S–002**
Justice Act 1999 (recovery where body undertakes to meet costs liabilities) are those bodies which are for the time being approved by the Lord Chancellor for that purpose.

Requirements for arrangements to meet costs liabilities

3.—(1) Section 30(1) of the Access to Justice Act 1999 applies to arrangements   **S–003**
which satisfy the following conditions.
(2) The arrangements must be in writing.
(3) The arrangements must contain a statement specifying—

   (a) the circumstances in which the member or other party may be liable to pay costs of the proceedings,
   (b) whether such a liability arises—

      (i) if those circumstances only partly occur,
      (ii) irrespective of whether those circumstances occur, and
      (iii) on the termination of the arrangements for any reason,

   (c) the basis on which the amount of the liability is calculated, and
   (d) the procedure for seeking assessment of costs.

(4) A copy of the part of the arrangements containing the statement must be given to the member or other party to the proceedings whose liabilities the body is undertaking to meet as soon as possible after the undertaking is given.

Recovery of additional amount for insurance costs

4.—(1) Where an additional amount is included in costs by virtue of section 30(2) of the Access to Justice Act 1999 (costs payable to a member of a body or other person party to the proceedings to include an additional amount in respect of provision made by the body against the risk of having to meet the member's or other

---

[1] 1999 c.22.

person's liabilities to pay other parties' costs), that additional amount must not exceed the following sum.

(2) That sum is the likely cost to the member of the body or, as the case may be, the other person who is a party to the proceedings in which the costs order is made of the premium of an insurance policy against the risk of incurring a liability to pay the costs of other parties to the proceedings.

Irvine of Lairg, C.
9th March 2000

EXPLANATORY NOTE

(This note is not part of the Regulations)

Section 30 of the Access to Justice Act 1999 applies where a body of a description to be specified in regulations undertakes (in accordance with arrangements satisfying conditions to be so specified) to meet liabilities which members of the body or other persons who are parties to proceedings may incur to pay the costs of other parties. Regulation 2 of these Regulations specifies bodies which are for the time being approved by the Lord Chancellor for this purpose. Regulation 3 specifies the conditions which the arrangements must satisfy.

Under section 30(2) of that Act an additional amount may be included in costs payable to a member of such a body or other person to cover insurance or other provision made by the body against the risk of having to meet those liabilities of the member or other person. Under section 30(3) of that Act that additional amount must not exceed a sum determined in a way specified by regulations. Regulation 4 of these Regulations specifies that sum as the likely cost to the member or other person of the premium of an insurance policy against the risk in question.

APPENDIX T

The Collective Conditional Fee Agreements Regulations 2000

(S.I. 2000/2988)

The Lord Chancellor, in exercise of the powers conferred upon him by sections 58(3)(c), 58A(3) and 119 of the Courts and Legal Services Act 1990[1] hereby makes the following Regulations:

Citation, commencement and interpretation

1.—(1) These regulations may be cited as the Collective Conditional Fee Agreements Regulations 2000, and shall come into force on 30th November 2000.   **T–001**

(2) In these Regulations, except where the context requires otherwise—

> "client" means a person who will receive advocacy or litigation services to which the agreement relates;
> "collective conditional fee agreement" has the meaning given in regulation 3;
> "conditional fee agreement" has the same meaning as in section 58 of the Courts and Legal Services Act 1990;
> "funder" means the party to a collective conditional fee agreement who, under that agreement, is liable to pay the legal representative's fees;
> "legal representative" means the person providing the advocacy or litigation services to which the agreement relates.

Transitional provisions

2. These Regulations shall apply to agreements entered into on or after 30th November 2000, and agreements entered into before that date shall be treated as if these Regulations had not come into force.   **T–002**

Definition of "collective conditional fee agreement"

3.—(1) Subject to paragraph (2) of this regulation, a collective conditional fee agreement is an agreement which—   **T–003**

(a) disregarding section 58(3)(c) of the Courts and Legal Services Act 1990, would be a conditional fee agreement; and

(b) does not refer to specific proceedings, but provides for fees to be payable on a common basis in relation to a class of proceedings, or, if it refers to more than one class of proceedings, on a common basis in relation to each class.

(2) An agreement may be a collective conditional fee agreement whether or not—

(a) the funder is a client; or

(b) any clients are named in the agreement.

---

[1] 1990 c. 41. Sections 58 and 58A are substituted by section 27 of the Access to Justice Act 1999 (c. 22); section 119 is an interpretation provision and is cited because of the meaning given to the word "prescribed".

Requirements for contents of collective conditional fee agreements: general

T–004   4.—(1) A collective conditional fee agreement must specify the circumstances in which the legal representative's fees and expenses, or part of them, are payable.

(2) A collective conditional fee agreement must provide that, when accepting instructions in relation to any specific proceedings the legal representative must—

   (a) inform the client as to the circumstances in which the client may be liable to pay the costs of the legal representative; and
   (b) if the client requires any further explanation, advice or other information about the matter referred to in sub-paragraph (a), provide such further explanation, advice or other information about it as the client may reasonably require.

(3) Paragraph (2) does not apply in the case of an agreement between a legal representative and an additional legal representative.

(4) A collective conditional fee agreement must provide that, after accepting instructions in relation to any specific proceedings, the legal representative must confirm his acceptance of instructions in writing to the client.

Requirements for contents of collective conditional fee agreements providing for success fees

T–005   5.—(1) Where a collective conditional fee agreement provides for a success fee the agreement must provide that, when accepting instructions in relation to any specific proceedings the legal representative must prepare and retain a written statement containing—

   (a) his assessment of the probability of the circumstances arising in which the percentage increase will become payable in relation to those proceedings ("the risk assessment");
   (b) his assessment of the amount of the percentage increase in relation to those proceedings, having regard to the risk assessment; and
   (c) the reasons, by reference to the risk assessment, for setting the percentage increase at that level.

(2) If the agreement relates to court proceedings it must provide that where the success fee becomes payable as a result of those proceedings, then—

   (a) if—

      (i) any fees subject to the increase are assessed, and
      (ii) the legal representative or the client is required by the court to disclose to the court or any other person the reasons for setting the percentage increase at the level assessed by the legal representative,
      he may do so,

   (b) if—

      (i) any such fees are assessed by the court, and
      (ii) any amount in respect of the percentage increase is disallowed on the assessment on the ground that the level at which the increase was set was unreasonable in view of facts which were or should have been known to the legal representative at the time it was set
      that amount ceases to be payable under the agreement, unless the court is satisfied that it should continue to be so payable, and

(c) if—

    (i) sub-paragraph (b) does not apply, and

    (ii) the legal representative agrees with any person liable as a result of the proceedings to pay fees subject to the percentage increase that a lower amount than the amount payable in accordance with the conditional fee agreement is to be paid instead,

    the amount payable under the collective conditional fee agreement in respect of those fees shall be reduced accordingly, unless the court is satisfied that the full amount should continue to be payable under it.

(3) In this regulation "percentage increase" means the percentage by which the amount of the fees which would have been payable if the agreement were not a conditional fee agreement is to be increased under the agreement.

Form and amendment of collective conditional fee agreement

6.—(1) Subject to paragraph (2), a collective conditional fee agreement must be signed by the funder, and by the legal representative.

(2) Paragraph (1) does not apply in the case of an agreement between a legal representative and an additional legal representative.

(3) Where a collective conditional fee agreement is amended, regulations 4 and 5 apply to the amended agreement as if it were a fresh agreement made at the time of the amendment.

T–006

Amendment to the Conditional Fee Agreements Regulations 2000

7. After regulation 7 of the Conditional Fee Agreements Regulations 2000[2] there shall be inserted the following new regulation–

T–007

"Exclusion of collective conditional fee agreements

8. These Regulations shall not apply to collective conditional fee agreements within the meaning of regulation 3 of the Collective Conditional Fee Agreements Regulations 2000.".

T–008

Irvine of Lairg,
C.

Dated 7th November 2000

EXPLANATORY NOTE

(This note is not part of the Regulations)

These regulations prescribe conditions which must be satisfied by a collective conditional fee agreement.

A collective conditional fee agreement is a conditional fee agreement with a legal representative which does not refer to specific proceedings, but provides for fees to be payable on a common basis in relation to a class of proceedings, whether or not the person liable to pay the fees under the agreement is the client of the legal representative.

---

[2] S.I. 2000/692.

APPENDIX U

CPR Part 69

COURT'S POWER TO APPOINT A RECEIVER

Receiver's remuneration

69.7 (1) A receiver may only charge for his services if the court—

U–001

(a) so directs; and
(b) specifies the basis on which the receiver is to be remunerated.

(2) The court may specify—

(a) who is to be responsible for paying the receiver; and
(b) the fund or property from which the receiver is to recover his remuneration.

(3) If the court directs that the amount of a receiver's remuneration is to be determined by the court—

(a) the receiver may not recover any remuneration for his services without a determination by the court; and
(b) the receiver or any party may apply at any time for such a determination to take place.

(4) Unless the court orders otherwise, in determining the remuneration of a receiver the court shall award such sum as is reasonable and proportionate in all the circumstances and which takes into account—

(a) the time properly given by him and his staff to the receivership;
(b) the complexity of the receivership;
(c) any responsibility of an exceptional kind or degree which falls on the receiver in consequence of the receivership;
(d) the effectiveness with which the receiver appears to be carrying out, or to have carried out, his duties; and
(e) the value and nature of the subject matter of the receivership.

(5) The court may refer the determination of a receiver's remuneration to a costs judge.

Accounts

69.8 (1) The court may order a receiver to prepare and serve accounts.

U–002

(The practice direction contains provisions about directions for the preparation and service of accounts.)
(2) A party served with such accounts may apply for an order
(3) Any party may, within 14 days of being served with the

(a) specifying any item in the accounts to which he objects;
(b) giving the reason for such objection; and
(c) requiring the receiver, within 14 days of receipt

of the notice, either—

(i) to notify all the parties who were served with the accounts that he accepts the objection; or

(ii) if he does not accept the objection, to apply for an examination of the accounts in relation to the contested item.

(4) When the receiver applies for the examination of the accounts he must at the same time file—

(a) the accounts; and

(b) a copy of the notice served on him under this rule.

(5) If the receiver fails to comply with paragraph (3)(c) of this rule, any party may apply to the court for an examination of the accounts in relation to the contested item.

(6) At the conclusion of its examination of the accounts the court will certify the result.

(The practice direction supplementing Part 40 provides for inquiries into accounts.)

Non-compliance by receiver

U–003   69.9 (1) If a receiver fails to comply with any rule, practice direction or direction of the court the court may order him to attend a hearing to explain his non-compliance.

(2) At the hearing the court may make any order it considers appropriate, including—

(a) terminating the appointment of the receiver;

(b) reducing the receiver's remuneration or disallowing it altogether; and

(c) ordering the receiver to pay the costs of any party.

(3) Where—

(a) the court has ordered a receiver to pay a sum of money into court; and

(b) the receiver has failed to do so,

the court may order him to pay interest on that sum for the time he is in default at such rate as it considers appropriate.

APPENDIX V

The Solicitors' (Non-Contentious Business) Remuneration Order 1994

(SI 1994/2616)

The Lord Chancellor, the Lord Chief Justice, the Master of the Rolls, the President of the Law Society, the president of Holborn law society and the Chief Land Registrar (in respect of business done under the Land Registration Act 1925[1]), together constituting the committee authorised to make orders under section 56 of the Solicitors Act 1974[2], in exercise of the powers conferred on them by that section and having complied with the requirements of section 56(3), hereby make the following Order—

Citation, Commencement and Revocation

1.—(1) This Order may be cited as the Solicitors' (Non-Contentious Business)   **V–001**
Remuneration Order 1994.

(2) This Order shall come into force on 1st November 1994 and shall apply to all non-contentious business for which bills are delivered on or after that date.

(3) The Solicitors' Remuneration Order 1972[3] is hereby revoked except in its application to business for which bills are delivered before this Order comes into force.

Interpretation

2. In this Order—   **V–002**

"client" means the client of a solicitor;

"costs" means the amount charged in a solicitor's bill, exclusive of disbursements and value added tax, in respect of non-contentious business or common form probate business;

"entitled person" means a client or an entitled third party;

"entitled third party" means a residuary beneficiary absolutely and immediately (and not contingently) entitled to an inheritance, where a solicitor has charged the estate for his professional costs for acting in the administration of the estate, and either

(a) the only personal representatives are solicitors (whether or not acting in a professional capacity); or

(b) the only personal representatives are solicitors acting jointly with partners or employees in a professional capacity;

"paid disbursements" means disbursements already paid by the solicitor;

"recognised body" means a body corporate recognised by the Council under section 9 of the Administration of Justice Act 1985[4];

"remuneration certificate" means a certificate issued by the Council pursuant to this Order;

---

[1] 1925 c.21.

[2] 1974 c.47, as modified by the Administration of Justice Act 1985 (c.61) Schedule 2, paragraphs 22 and 23.

[3] S.I. 1972/1139.

[4] 1985 c.61.

"residuary beneficiary" includes a person entitled to all or part of the residue of an intestate estate;

"solicitor" includes a recognised body;

"the Council" means the Council of the Law Society.

Solicitors' costs

V–003   3. A solicitor's costs shall be such sum as may be fair and reasonable to both solicitor and entitled person, having regard to all the circumstances of the case and in particular to–

(a) the complexity of the matter or the difficulty or novelty of the questions raised;

(b) the skill, labour, specialised knowledge and responsibility involved;

(c) the time spent on the business;

(d) the number and importance of the documents prepared or perused, without regard to length;

(e) the place where and the circumstances in which the business or any part thereof is transacted;

(f) the amount or value of any money or property involved;

(g) whether any land involved is registered land;

(h) the importance of the matter to the client; and

(i) the approval (express or implied) of the entitled person or the express approval of the testator to–

(i) the solicitor undertaking all or any part of the work giving rise to the costs or

(ii) the amount of the costs.

Right to certification

V–004   4.–(1) Without prejudice to the provisions of sections 70, 71, and 72 of the Solicitors Act 1974 (which relate to taxation of costs), an entitled person may, subject to the provisions of this Order, require a solicitor to obtain a remuneration certificate from the Council in respect of a bill which has been delivered where the costs are not more than £50,000.

(2) The remuneration certificate must state what sum, in the opinion of the Council, would be a fair and reasonable charge for the business covered by the bill (whether it be the sum charged or a lesser sum). In the absence of taxation the sum payable in respect of such costs is the sum stated in the remuneration certificate.

Disciplinary and other measures

V–005   5.–(1) If on a taxation the taxing officer allows less than one half of the costs, he must bring the facts of the case to the attention of the Council.

(2) The provisions of this Order are without prejudice to the general powers of the Council under the Solicitors Act 1974.

Commencement of proceedings against a client

V–006   6. Before a solicitor brings proceedings to recover costs against a client on a bill for non-contentious business he must inform the client in writing of the matters specified in article 8, except where the bill has been taxed.

Costs paid by deduction

7.—(1) If a solicitor deducts his costs from monies held for or on behalf of a client V–007
or of an estate in satisfaction of a bill and an entitled person objects in writing to the
amount of the bill within the prescribed time, the solicitor must immediately inform
the entitled person in writing of the matters specified in article 8, unless he has
already done so.

(2) In this article and in article 10, "the prescribed time" means–

    (a) in respect of a client, three months after delivery of the relevant bill, or a
    lesser time (which may not be less than one month) specified in writing to
    the client at the time of delivery of the bill, or

    (b) in respect of an entitled third party, three months after delivery of
    notification to the entitled third party of the amount of the costs, or a lesser
    time (which may not be less than one month) specified in writing to the
    entitled third party at the time of such notification.

Information to be given in writing to entitled person

8. When required by articles 6 or 7, a solicitor must inform an entitled person in V–008
writing of the following matters–

    (a) where article 4(1) applies—

        (i) that the entitled person may, within one month of receiving from the
        solicitor the information specified in this article or (if later) of delivery
        of the bill or notification of the amount of the costs, require the
        solicitor to obtain a remuneration certificate; and

        (ii) that (unless the solicitor has agreed to do so) the Council may waive
        the requirements of article 11(1), if satisfied from the client's written
        application that exceptional circumstances exist to justify granting a
        waiver;

    (b) that sections 70, 71 and 72 of the Solicitors Act 1974 set out the entitled
    person's rights in relation to taxation;

    (c) that (where the whole of the bill has not been paid, by deduction or
    otherwise) the solicitor may charge interest on the outstanding amount of
    the bill in accordance with article 14.

Loss by client of right to certification

9. A client may not require a solicitor to obtain a remuneration certificate– V–009

    (a) after a bill has been delivered and paid by the client, other than by
    deduction;

    (b) where a bill has been delivered, after the expiry of one month from the date
    on which the client was informed in writing of the matters specified in
    article 8 or from delivery of the bill if later;

    (c) after the solicitor and client have entered into a non-contentious business
    agreement in accordance with the provisions of section 57 of the Solicitors
    Act 1974;

    (d) after a court has ordered the bill to be taxed;

    (e) if article 11(2) applies.

Loss by entitled third party of right to certification

V–010   10. An entitled third party may not require a solicitor to obtain a remuneration certificate–

(a) after the prescribed time (within the meaning of article 7(2)(b)) has elapsed without any objection being received to the amount of the costs;

(b) after the expiry of one month from the date on which the entitled third party was (in compliance with article 7) informed in writing of the matters specified in article 8 or from notification of the costs if later;

(c) after a court has ordered the bill to be taxed.

Requirement to pay a sum towards the costs

V–011   11.–(1) On requiring a solicitor to obtain a remuneration certificate a client must pay to the solicitor the paid disbursements and value added tax comprised in the bill together with 50% of the costs unless–

(a) the client has already paid the amount required under this article, by deduction from monies held or otherwise; or

(b) the solicitor or (if the solicitor refuses) the Council has agreed in writing to waive all or part of this requirement.

(2) The Council shall be under no obligation to provide a remuneration certificate, and the solicitor may take steps to obtain payment of his bill, if the client, having been informed of his right to seek a waiver of the requirements of paragraph (1), has not–

(a) within one month of receipt of the information specified in article 8, either paid in accordance with paragraph (1) or applied to the Council in writing for a waiver of the requirements of paragraph (1); or

(b) made payment in accordance with the requirements of paragraph (1) within one month of written notification that he has been refused a waiver of those requirements by the Council.

Miscellaneous provisions

V–012   12.–(1) After an application has been made by a solicitor for a remuneration certificate the client may pay the bill in full without invalidating the application.

(2) A solicitor and entitled person may agree in writing to waive the provisions of sub-paragraphs (a) or (b) of articles 9 or 10.

(3) A solicitor may take from his client security for the payment of any costs, including the amount of any interest to which the solicitor may become entitled under article 14.

Refunds by solicitor

V–013   13.–(1) If a solicitor has received payment of all or part of his costs and a remuneration certificate is issued for less than the sum already paid, the solicitor must immediately pay to the entitled person any refund which may be due (after taking into account any other sums which may properly be payable to the solicitor whether for costs, paid disbursements, value added tax or otherwise) unless the solicitor has applied for an order for taxation within one month of receipt by him of the remuneration certificate.

(2) Where a solicitor applies for taxation, his liability to pay any refund under paragraph (1) shall be suspended for so long as the taxation is still pending.

(3) The obligation of the solicitor to repay costs under paragraph (1) is without prejudice to any liability of the solicitor to pay interest on the repayment by virtue of any enactment, rule of law or professional rule.

Interest

14.—(1) After the information specified in article 8 has been given to an entitled person in compliance with articles 6 or 7, a solicitor may charge interest on the unpaid amount of his costs plus any paid disbursements and value added tax, subject to paragraphs (2) and (3) below.

(2) Where an entitlement to interest arises under paragraph (1), and subject to any agreement made between a solicitor and client, the period for which interest may be charged may run from one month after the date of delivery of a bill, unless the solicitor fails to lodge an application within one month of receipt of a request for a remuneration certificate under article 4, in which case no interest is payable in respect of the period between one month after receiving the request and the actual date on which the application is lodged.

(3) Subject to any agreement made between a solicitor and client, the rate of interest must not exceed the rate for the time being payable on judgment debts.

(4) Interest charged under this article must be calculated, where applicable, by reference to the following–

V–014

    (a) if a solicitor is required to obtain a remuneration certificate, the total amount of the costs certified by the Council to be fair and reasonable plus paid disbursements and value added tax;

    (b) if an application is made for the bill to be taxed, the amount ascertained on taxation;

    (c) if an application is made for the bill to be taxed or a solicitor is required to obtain a remuneration certificate and for any reason the taxation or application for a remuneration certificate does not proceed, the unpaid amount of the costs shown in the bill or such lesser sum as may be agreed between the solicitor and the client, plus paid disbursements and value added tax.

Application by solicitor

15. A solicitor, when making an application for a remuneration certificate in accordance with the provisions of this Order, must deliver to the Council the complete relevant file and working papers, and any other information or documentation which the Council may require for the purpose of providing a remuneration certificate.

V–015

Mackay of Clashfern, C.

Taylor, C.J.

Bingham, M.R.

R C Elly

J Lewis

J Manthorpe

Dated 5th October 1994

EXPLANATORY NOTE

(This note is not part of the Order)

Section 56 of the Solicitors Act 1974 establishes a Committee with power to make general orders regulating the remuneration of solicitors in respect of non-contentious business. Paragraph 22(2) of Schedule 2 to the Administration of Justice Act 1985 modifies the section so that references to solicitors include references to recognised bodies (solicitors' incorporated practices recognised under section 9 of the Administration of Justice Act 1985). This Order sets out the rights of solicitors' clients and residuary beneficiaries of certain estates to require the solicitor charging the client or estate to obtain a certificate from the Law Society as to the reasonableness of his costs. The Order prescribes requirements in relation to information to be given in writing to clients and beneficiaries who are entitled to require a solicitor to obtain a certificate, and lays certain obligations on clients, beneficiaries and solicitors.

APPENDIX W

Solicitors' Practice Rule 7 and Introduction and Referral Code 1990

Rule 7 (Fee sharing, partnership and corporate practice)

Rule 7 of the Solicitors' Practice Rules has been amended, primarily by the insertion of a new paragraph (1A) as follows: **W–001**

"(1A) (Fee sharing—exception for introducing capital or providing services)

Notwithstanding paragraph (1) of this rule a solicitor may share his or her professional fees with a third party ("the fee sharer") provided that **W–002**

- (a) the purpose of the fee sharing arrangement is solely to facilitate the introduction of capital and/or the provision of services to a practice;

- (b) neither the fee sharing agreement between the solicitor and a fee sharer, nor the extent of the fees the solicitor shares with fee sharers, permits any fee sharer to influence or constrain the solicitor's professional judgement in relation to the advice given to any client;

- (c) the operation of the agreement does not result in a partnership prohibited by paragraph (6) of this rule;

- (d) if requested by the Law Society to do so, the solicitor supplies details of all agreements between the solicitor and fee sharers and the percentage of the annual gross fees of the practice which has been paid to each fee sharer; and

- (e) the fee sharing agreement does not involve a breach of the Solicitors' Introduction and Referral Code.

"Fee sharer" means a person who or which shares a solicitor's fees in reliance on the exception contained in this paragraph, and the expression includes any person connected to or associated with the fee sharer."

Annex 11B Solicitors' Intro and Referral Code 1990

[last amended 8 March 2004]

Code dated 18th July 1990 promulgated by the Council of the Law Society with the concurrence of the Master of the Rolls under Rule 3 of the Solicitors' Practice Rules 1990, regulating the introduction of clients to and by solicitors, registered European lawyers, registered foreign lawyers and recognised bodies practising in England and Wales.

Introduction

(1) This code states the principles to be observed in relation to the introduction of clients by third parties to solicitors or by solicitors to third parties. **W–003**

(2) The code does not apply to introductions and referrals between lawyers.

(3) Non-compliance, evasion or disregard of the code could represent not only a breach of Practice Rule 3 (introductions and referrals) but also a breach of Practice Rule 1 (basic principles) or one of the other practice rules, and conduct unbefitting a solicitor of the Supreme Court or other lawyer.

(4) Those wishing to advertise the services of solicitors to whom they refer work should be encouraged to publicise their adherence to the code by means of a notice on the following lines:

"We comply with the Solicitors' Introduction and Referral Code published by the Law Society, and any solicitor [or registered European lawyer] to whom we may refer you is an independent professional from whom you will receive impartial and confidential advice. You are free to choose another solicitor [or registered European lawyer]."

(5) In this code all references to individual practice rules are references to the Solicitors' Practice Rules 1990 and all words have the meanings assigned to them in Rule 18 of those rules.

(6) The code will come into force on 1st September 1990.

Section 1: The basic principles

W–004 (1) Solicitors must always retain their professional independence and their ability to advise their clients fearlessly and objectively. Solicitors should never permit the requirements of an introducer to undermine this independence.

(2) In making or accepting introductions or referrals, solicitors must do nothing which would be likely to compromise or impair any of the principles set out in Practice Rule 1:

(a) the solicitor's independence or integrity;

(b) a person's freedom to instruct a solicitor of his or her choice;

(c) the solicitor's duty to act in the best interests of the client;

(d) the good repute of the solicitor or the solicitor's profession;

(e) the solicitor's proper standard of work;

(f) the solicitor's duty to the Court.

(3) Practice Rule 9 prevents a solicitor from entering into any arrangement with a claims assessor for the introduction of personal injury clients to the solicitor.

(4) Practice Rule 12 makes provision in respect of introductions and referrals in the field of investment business. In particular the rule prevents a solicitor from acting as an appointed representative as defined in the Financial Services and Markets Act 2000 other than by having a separate business which is the appointed representative of an independent financial adviser.

Note

An independent financial adviser is a financial adviser authorised under the Financial Services and Markets Act 2000, or subsequent relevant legislation, who is not constrained to recommend to clients or effect for them transactions in some investments but not others, with some persons but not others; or to refrain from doing so.

Section 2: Introduction or referral of business to solicitors

W–005 (1) Solicitors may discuss and make known to potential introducers the basis on which they would be prepared to accept instructions and the fees they would charge to clients referred.

(2) Solicitors should draw the attention of potential introducers to the provisions of this code and the relevant provisions of the Solicitors' Publicity Code.

(3) Solicitors must not reward introducers by the payment of commission or otherwise except as permitted by Sections 2A and 3A below. However, this does not prevent normal hospitality. A solicitor may refer clients to an introducer provided the solicitor complies with Section 4 below.

(4) Solicitors should not allow themselves to become so reliant on a limited number of sources of referrals that the interests of an introducer affect the advice given by the solicitor to clients.

(5) Solicitors should be particularly conscious of the need to advise impartially and independently clients referred by introducers. They should ensure that the wish to avoid offending the introducer does not colour the advice given to such clients.

(6) Where a tied agent refers to a solicitor a client who is proposing to take out a company life policy, the solicitor should, where necessary, have regard to the suitability of that policy in each particular case.

(7) Solicitors must ensure that they alone are responsible for any decisions taken in relation to the nature, style or extent of their practices.

(8) This code does not affect the need for the solicitor to communicate directly with the client to obtain or confirm instructions, in the process of providing advice and at all appropriate stages of the transaction.

(9) Each firm should keep a record of agreements for the introduction of work.

(10) Each firm should conduct a review at six-monthly intervals, which should check:

(a) that the provisions of this code have been complied with;

(b) that referred clients have received impartial advice which has not been tainted by the relationship between the firm and the introducer; and

(c) the income arising from each agreement for the introduction of business.

(11) Where, so far as can be reasonably ascertained, more than 20 per cent of a firm's income during the period under review arises from a single source of introduction of business, the firm should consider whether steps should be taken to reduce that proportion.

(12) Factors to be taken into account in considering whether to reduce the proportion include:

(a) the percentage of income deriving from that source;

(b) the number of clients introduced by that source;

(c) the nature of the clients and the nature of the work; and

(d) whether the introducer could be affected by the advice given by the solicitor to the client.

Section 2A: Payments for referrals

(1) A solicitor must not make any payment to a third party in relation to the introduction of clients to the solicitor, except as permitted below. **W–006**

(2) Solicitors may enter into agreements under this section for referrals of clients with introducers who undertake in such agreements to comply with the terms of this code.

(3) A solicitor may make a payment to a third party introducer only where immediately upon receiving the referral and before accepting instructions to act the solicitor provides the client with all relevant information concerning the referral and, in particular, the amount of any payment.

(4) The solicitor must also be satisfied that the introducer:

(a) has provided the client with all information relevant to the client concerning the referral before the referral took place and, in particular, the amount of any payment;

(b) has not acquired the client as a consequence of marketing or publicity or other activities which, if done by a solicitor, would be in breach of any of the Solicitors' Practice Rules and in particular by "cold calling"; and

(c) does not, under the arrangement, influence or constrain the solicitor's professional judgement in relation to the advice given to the client.

(5) If the solicitor has reason to believe that the introducer is breaching terms of the agreement required by this section the solicitor must take all reasonable steps to procure that the breach is remedied. If the introducer persists in breaches the solicitor must terminate the agreement in respect of future referrals.

(6) A solicitor must not make a referral payment if at the time of the referral the solicitor intends to act for that person with the benefit of legal aid, or in any criminal proceedings.

(7) For the purpose of sub-section (1) above, a payment includes any other consideration but does not include normal hospitality, proper disbursements or normal business expenses.

Section 3: Solicitor agreeing to be paid by a third party to do work for the third party's customers other than conveyancing work

W–007 (1) In addition to the other provisions of this code the following requirements should be observed in relation to agreements for the introduction of clients/business to solicitors under which the solicitor agrees with the introducer to be paid by the introducer to do work other than conveyancing work for the introducer's customers.

(2) The terms of the agreement should be set out in writing and a copy available for inspection by the Law Society or the Office for the Supervision of Solicitors.

(3) The solicitor may agree to be remunerated by the introducer either on a case by case basis or on a hourly, monthly or any other appropriate basis.

(4) The solicitor should ensure that any agreement between the introducer and customer for the provision of services under this section includes:

(a) express mention of the independence of the solicitor's professional advice;

(b) a provision that control of the professional work should remain in the hands of the solicitor subject to the instructions of the client; and

(c) a provision that information disclosed by the client to the solicitor should not be disclosed to the introducer unless the client consents.

Section 3A: Contractual referrals for conveyancing

W–008 (1) In addition to the other provisions of this code the following requirements must be observed in relation to agreements for the introduction of clients/business to solicitors under which the solicitor agrees with the introducer to be paid by the introducer to provide conveyancing services for the introducer's customers.

Agreements for referrals

(2) Solicitors may enter into agreements under this section for referrals for conveyancing services only with introducers who undertake in such agreements to comply with the terms of this code.

(3) Referrals under this section must not be made where the introducer is a seller or seller's agent and the conveyancing services are to be provided to the buyer.

(4) The agreement between the solicitor and the introducer must be set out in writing. A copy of the agreement and of records of the six-monthly reviews carried out under paragraph 10 of Section 2 of this code in relation to transactions under the agreement must be retained by the solicitor for production on request to the Law Society or the Office for the Supervision of Solicitors.

(5) If the solicitor has reason to believe that the introducer is breaching terms of the agreement required by this section the solicitor must take all reasonable steps to procure that the breach is remedied. If the introducer persists in breaches the solicitor must terminate the agreement in respect of future referrals.

(6) The agreement between the introducer and the solicitor must not include any provisions which would:

(a) compromise, infringe or impair any of the principles set out in Rule 1 of the Solicitors' Practice Rules or any duties owed by the solicitor to the introducer's customer by virtue of the solicitor/client relationship and/or the requirements of professional conduct; or

(b) restrict the scope of the duties which the solicitor owes to the customer in relation to the services agreed to be provided by virtue of the professional relationship between solicitor and client; or

(c) interfere with or inhibit the solicitor's responsibility for the control of the professional work.

Publicity as to conveyancing services

(7) In publicity material of the introducer which includes reference to any service that may be provided by the solicitor, any reference to the charge for conveyancing services must be clearly expressed and must not be misleading. It must be clear whether disbursements and VAT are included.

Notice to customer

(8) Before making a referral the introducer must give the customer in writing:

(a) details of the conveyancing service to be provided under the terms of the referral;

(b) notification of:
  (i) the charge payable by the customer to the introducer for the conveyancing services;
  (ii) the liability for VAT and disbursements and how these are to be discharged; and
  (iii) what charge if any is to be made if the transaction does not proceed to completion or if the solicitor is unable to continue to act;

(c) notification of the amount the introducer will be paying to the solicitor for the provision of conveyancing services relating to the customer's transaction;

(d) a statement to the effect that the charge for conveyancing services will not be affected whether or not the customer takes other products or services offered by the introducer, and that the availability and price of other services will not be affected whether the customer chooses to instruct a solicitor (or registered European lawyer) under the referral or decides to instruct another solicitor or conveyancer; and

(e) a statement to the effect that the advice and service of the solicitor (or registered European lawyer) to whom the customer is to be referred will remain independent and subject to the instructions of the customer.

Solicitor's terms of business

(9) Where a solicitor accepts instructions on referral under this section the solicitor must provide the client with written terms of business which must include:

(a) details of the conveyancing service to be provided under the referral and if appropriate any other services the solicitor is to provide and on what terms;

(b) a statement that any advice given by the solicitor (or registered European lawyer) will be independent and that the client is free to raise questions on all aspects of the transaction;

(c) confirmation that information disclosed by the client to the solicitor (or registered European lawyer) will not be disclosed to the introducer unless the client consents; but that where the solicitor (or registered European lawyer) is also acting for the introducer in the same matter and a conflict of interest arises, the solicitor (or registered European lawyer) might be obliged to cease acting.

Definition

(10) In this section references to a conveyancing service or services include services to be provided to the introducer if the solicitor is also to be instructed to act for the introducer.

Section 4: Referral of clients by solicitors

W–009 (1) If a solicitor recommends that a client use a particular firm, agency or business, the solicitor must do so in good faith, judging what is in the client's best interest. A solicitor should not enter into any agreement or association which would restrict the solicitor's freedom to recommend any particular firm, agency or business.

(2) The referral to a tied agent of a client requiring life insurance would not discharge the solicitor's duty to give his client independent advice. In such circumstances, any referral should be to an independent intermediary.

(3) If the best interests of the client require it, a solicitor may refer a client requiring a mortgage to a tied agent, provided that the client is informed that the agent offers products from only one company.

(4) In relation to commission received for the introduction of clients' business to third parties, Practice Rule 10 applies.

APPENDIX X

Solicitors' Practice Rule 15 and Costs Information and Client Care Code 1999

Rule 15 (Costs information and client care)

Solicitors shall:

(a) give information about costs and other matters, and

(b) operate a complaints handling procedure, in accordance with a Solicitors' Costs Information and Client Care Code made from time to time by the Council of the Law Society with the concurrence of the Master of the Rolls, but subject to the notes.

Notes

(i) A serious breach of the code, or persistent breaches of a material nature, will be a breach of the rule, and may also be evidence of inadequate professional services under section 37A of the Solicitors Act 1974.

(ii) Material breaches of the code which are not serious or persistent will not be a breach of the rule, but may be evidence of inadequate professional services under section 37A.

(iii) The powers of the Office for the Supervision of Solicitors on a finding of inadequate professional services include:

(a) disallowing all or part of the solicitor's costs; and

(b) directing the solicitor to pay compensation to the client up to a limit of £5,000.

(iv) Non-material breaches of the code will not be a breach of the rule, and will not be evidence of inadequate professional services under section 37A.

(v) Registered foreign lawyers practising in partnership with solicitors of the Supreme Court or registered European lawyers, or as members of recognised bodies which are limited liability partnerships, or as directors of recognised bodies which are companies, although subject to Rule 15 as a matter of professional conduct, are not subject to section 37A. However, such solicitors, registered European lawyers and recognised bodies are subject to section 37A for professional services provided by the firm.

Solicitors' Costs Information and Client Care Code 1999
[last amended 9 March 2004]

Code dated 3rd September 1999 made by the Council of the Law Society with the concurrence of the Master of the Rolls under Rule 15 of the Solicitors' Practice Rules 1990, regulating the English and Welsh practices of solicitors, registered European lawyers, registered foreign lawyers and recognised bodies in giving information to clients and operating complaints procedures.

1. Introduction

X–001.2   (a) This code replaces the written professional standards on costs information for clients (see paragraphs 3—6) and the detail previously contained in Practice Rule 15 (client care) (see paragraph 7).

(b) The main object of the code is to make sure that clients are given the information they need to understand what is happening generally and in particular on:

     (i) the cost of legal services both at the outset and as a matter progresses; and

     (ii) responsibility for clients' matters.

(c) The code also requires firms to operate a complaints handling procedure.

(d) It is good practice to record in writing:

     (i) all information required to be given by the code including all decisions relating to costs and the arrangements for updating costs information; and

     (ii) the reasons why the information required by the code has not been given in a particular case.

(e) References to costs, where appropriate, include fees, VAT and disbursements.

2. Application

X–002   (a) The code is of general application, and it applies to registered foreign lawyers as well as to solicitors of the Supreme Court and registered European lawyers (subject to note (v) to Practice Rule 15). However, as set out in paragraph 2(b), parts of the code may not be appropriate in every case, and solicitors should consider the interests of each client in deciding which parts not to apply in the particular circumstances.

(b) The full information required by the code may be inappropriate, for example:

     (i) in every case, for a regular client for whom repetitive work is done, where the client has already been provided with the relevant information, although such a client should be informed of changes; and

     (ii) if compliance with the code may at the time be insensitive or impractical. In such a case relevant information should be given as soon as reasonably practicable.

(c) Employed solicitors should have regard to paragraphs 3—6A of the code where appropriate, e.g. when acting for clients other than their employer. Paragraph 7 does not apply to employed solicitors.

(d) Solicitors should comply with paragraphs 3—6 of the code even where a client is legally aided if the client may have a financial interest in the costs because contributions are payable or the statutory charge may apply or they may become liable for the costs of another party.

(da) If appropriate solicitors should also comply with paragraph 6A of the code where a client is legally aided.

(e) The code also applies to contingency fee and conditional fee arrangements and to arrangements with a client for the solicitor to retain commissions received from third parties.

3. Informing the client about cost

(a) Costs information must not be inaccurate or misleading.

X–003

(b) Any costs information required to be given by the code must be given clearly, in a way and at a level which is appropriate to the particular client. Any terms with which the client may be unfamiliar, for example "disbursement", should be explained.

(c) The information required by paragraphs 4 and 5 of the code should be given to a client at the outset of, and at appropriate stages throughout, the matter. All information given orally should be confirmed in writing to the client as soon as possible.

4. Advance costs information—general

The overall costs

(a) The solicitor should give the client the best information possible about the likely overall costs, including a breakdown between fees, VAT and disbursements.

X–004

(b) The solicitor should explain clearly to the client the time likely to be spent in dealing with a matter, if time spent is a factor in the calculation of the fees.

(c) Giving "the best information possible" includes:

  (i) agreeing a fixed fee; or
  (ii) giving a realistic estimate; or
  (iii) giving a forecast within a possible range of costs; or
  (iv) explaining to the client the reasons why it is not possible to fix, or give a realistic estimate or forecast of, the overall costs, and giving instead the best information possible about the cost of the next stage of the matter.

(d) The solicitor should, in an appropriate case, explain to a privately paying client that the client may set an upper limit on the firm's costs for which the client may be liable without further authority. Solicitors should not exceed an agreed limit without first obtaining the client's consent.

(e) The solicitor should make it clear at the outset if an estimate, quotation or other indication of cost is not intended to be fixed.

Basis of firm's charges

(f) The solicitor should also explain to the client how the firm's fees are calculated except where the overall costs are fixed or clear. If the basis of charging is an hourly charging rate, that must be made clear.

X–005

(g) The client should be told if charging rates may be increased.

Further information

X–006 (h) The solicitor should explain what reasonably foreseeable payments a client may have to make either to the solicitor or to a third party and when those payments are likely to be needed.

(i) The solicitor should explain to the client the arrangements for updating the costs information as set out in paragraph 6.

Client's ability to pay

X–007 (j) The solicitor should discuss with the client how **and when** any costs are to be met, and consider–

    (i) whether the client may be eligible and should apply for legal aid (including advice and assistance);

    (ii) whether the client's liability for their own costs may be covered by insurance;

    (iii) whether the client's liability for another party's costs may be covered by pre-purchased insurance and, if not, whether it would be advisable for the client's liability for another party's costs to be covered by after the event insurance (including in every case where a conditional fee or contingency fee arrangement is proposed); and

    (iv) whether the client's liability for costs (including the costs of another party) may be paid by another person e.g. an employer or trade union.

Cost-benefit and risk

X–008 (k) The solicitor should discuss with the client whether the likely outcome in a matter will justify the expense or risk involved including, if relevant, the risk of having to bear an opponent's costs.

5. Additional information for particular clients

Legally aided clients

X–009 (a) The solicitor should explain to a legally aided client the client's potential liability for the client's own costs and those of any other party, including:

    (i) the effect of the statutory charge and its likely amount;

    (ii) the client's obligation to pay any contribution assessed and the consequences of failing to do so;

    (iii) the fact that the client may still be ordered by the court to contribute to the opponent's costs if the case is lost even though the client's own costs are covered by legal aid; and

    (iv) the fact that even if the client wins, the opponent may not be ordered to pay or be capable of paying the full amount of the client's costs.

Privately paying clients in contentious matters (and potentially contentious matters)

X–010 (b) The solicitor should explain to the client the client's potential liability for the client's own costs and for those of any other party, including:

    (i) the fact that the client will be responsible for paying the firm's bill in full regardless of any order for costs made against an opponent;

(ii) the probability that the client will have to pay the opponent's costs as well as the client's own costs if the case is lost;

(iii) the fact that even if the client wins, the opponent may not be ordered to pay or be capable of paying the full amount of the client's costs; and

(iv) the fact that if the opponent is legally aided the client may not recover costs, even if successful.

Liability for third party costs in non-contentious matters

(c) The solicitor should explain to the client any liability the client may have for the payment of the costs of a third party. When appropriate, solicitors are advised to obtain a firm figure for or agree a cap to a third party's costs.   **X–011**

6. Updating costs information

The solicitor should keep the client properly informed about costs as a matter progresses.   **X–012**
In particular, the solicitor should:

(a) tell the client, unless otherwise agreed, how much the costs are at regular intervals (at least every six months) and in appropriate cases deliver interim bills at agreed intervals;

(b) explain to the client (and confirm in writing) any changed circumstances which will, or which are likely to affect the amount of costs, the degree of risk involved, or the cost-benefit to the client of continuing with the matter;

(c) inform the client in writing as soon as it appears that a costs estimate or agreed upper limit may or will be exceeded; and

(d) consider the client's eligibility for legal aid if a material change in the client's means comes to the solicitor's attention.

6A. Disclosure of solicitor's arrangements with third parties

(a) The solicitor should disclose to the client any relationship with a third party (for example a funder, fee sharer or introducer) which affects the steps which the solicitor can take on the client's behalf.   **X–013**

(b) The solicitor should explain any constraints or conditions which affect the client.

(c) All information given orally concerning (a) and (b) above should be confirmed in writing to the client as soon as possible.

7. Client care and complaints handling

Information for clients

(a) Every solicitor in private practice must ensure that the client: **X–014**

(i) is given a clear explanation of the issues raised in a matter and is kept properly informed about its progress (including the likely timescale);

(ii) is given the name and status of the person dealing with the matter and the name of the principal, or director (in the case of a recognised body which is a company), or member (in the case of a recognised body which is a limited liability partnership) responsible for its overall supervision;

(iii) is told whom to contact about any problem with the service provided; and

    (iv) is given details of any changes in the information required to be given by this paragraph.

Complaints handling

X–015   (b) Every principal in private practice (or, in the case of a recognised body, the body itself) must:

      (i) ensure the client is told the name of the person in the firm to contact about any problem with the service provided;

     (ii) have a written complaints procedure and ensure that complaints are handled in accordance with it; and

    (iii) ensure that the client is given a copy of the complaints procedure on request.

APPENDIX Y

Guidance Notes on the Application of s. 11 Access to Justice Act 1999 issued by the Senior Costs Judge

Introduction

1.1 On April 1, 2000 the Access to Justice Act 1999 (the Act) replaced the former legal aid scheme with Community Legal Service funding under Part 1 of the Act and the Legal Services Commission took over the functions of the Legal Aid Board. Section 11 of the Act (Costs in funded cases) effectively replaces the Legal Aid Act 1988 Section 17 (Limit on costs against assisted party) and Section 18 (Costs of successful unassisted parties). **Y–001**

1.2 Section 11 of the Act and the regulations made thereunder have given rise to a certain amount of confusion and difficulty. These guidance notes (which have been approved by Lord Phillips of Worth Matravers, Master of the Rolls) are intended to assist judges, litigants and lawyers dealing with cases in the Court of Appeal, the High Court or in the County Court.

1.3 In these notes the expression "LSC funded client" includes an assisted person.

Section 11 of the Act

2.1 The full text of Section 11 of the Act is set out in Appendix 1, below: **Y–002**

2.2 Attention is drawn to Section 11(4)(d): the power to require payment by the Commission to a party for whom services are not funded by the Commission, is now governed by the Regulations rather than, as under the former scheme, by the Statute itself. Under these Regulations the function of deciding whether or not a costs order could and should be made against the Commission is now expressly assigned to the Costs Judge or District Judge. He cannot make such an order unless and until the prescribed formalities have been completed. It is not open to the trial court to rule that it is just and equitable to make the order or to direct that the order is to be made before the prescribed formalities have been completed, although the trial court may record findings of fact as to the parties' conduct which must be taken into account in determining what amount the LSC funded client should pay.

The Regulations made under the Act

3.1 The relevant regulations are the Community Legal Service (Costs) Regulations 2000 (S.I. 2000 No. 441 as amended by S.I. 2001 No. 822, the "Costs Regulations") and the Community Legal Service (Cost Protection) Regulations 2000 (S.I. 2000 No. 824 as amended by S.I. 2001 No. 823, the "Cost Protection Regulations"). **Y–003**

3.2 The procedures for ordering costs against client and Commission are set out in Regulations 9 and 10 and 10A of the Costs Regulations 2000. Regulation 10A empowers the court to order a funded party to pay an amount on account of costs in certain circumstances.

3.3 The Cost Protection Regulations set out the circumstances in which costs orders against the LSC may be made. The full text of Regulation 5 is set out in Appendix 2, below.

3.4 The words shown in square brackets underlined in Regulation 5(3), as set out in Appendix 2 below are taken from draft Amendment Regulations, which it is currently proposed, will be laid before Parliament, to come into force on December 3, 2001.

3.5 Unless and until Regulation 5(3) is amended (see above) a formal request under Costs Regulation 10(2) for an order against the LSC cannot validly be made after the expiry of the 3 month deadline (see further, para. 31(ii) of the judgment quoted in para. 4.3 below).

3.6 Regulation 7 has the effect of excluding the possibility of an order for costs being made against the Commission under the broad and general power to order costs under Section 51(3) of the Supreme Court Act 1981.

The Procedure

Y–004   **4.1** The Costs Regulations and the Cost Protection Regulations form a self contained code of substantive law and procedural law governing orders for costs against assisted persons, LSC funded clients and the LSC. The ordinary rules governing the assessment of costs (i.e., CPR Parts 44 to 48) do not apply (see CPR, r.44.17).

4.2 The relevant parts of the Costs Practice Direction are Sections 21 to 23. In order to provide for the division of functions between the court awarding costs and the Costs Judge or District Judge who assesses them, the Costs Practice Direction gives definitions for the following terms (para. 22.1):

> "order for costs to be determined" means an order for costs to which Section 11 of the Access to Justice Act 1999 applies under which the amount of costs payable by the LSC funded client is to be determined by a costs judge or district judge under Section 23 of this Practice Direction.
> "order specifying the costs payable" means an order for costs to which Section 11 of the Act applies and which specifies the amount which the LSC funded client is to pay.
> "full costs" means, where an order to which Section 11 of the Act applies is made against a LSC funded client, the amount of costs which that person would, had cost protection not applied, have been ordered to pay.
> "determination proceedings" means proceedings to which paragraphs 23.1 to 23.10 [of the Costs Practice Direction] apply.
> "Section 11(1) costs order" means an order for costs to be determined or an order specifying the costs payable other than an order specifying the costs payable which was made in determination proceedings."

4.3 In *R v. Secretary of State for the Home Department Ex Parte Gunn* [2001] EWCA Civ 891, the Master of the Rolls gave the judgment of the court and set out the procedure to be followed. The key passages are set out below:

> "27. The new Regulations introduce a two stage process in relation to the recovery of costs in cases to which Section 11(1) of the 1999 Act applies. The procedure to be followed is primarily to be derived from the Costs Regulations. The scheme is as follows.

> #### Stage 1

> 28. The first stage involves the Court dealing with the substance of the dispute, which we shall call the trial Court. The role of the trial Court is as follows:
>
> (i) To decide whether to make an order for costs against a funded litigant ("the client"). (Regulation 9(1))
> (ii) To decide whether it is in a position to specify the amount, if any, to be paid by the client. (Regulation 9(2)).
> (iii) To make a costs order against the client which either

    (a) Specifies the amount, if any, to be paid by the client and states the amount of the full costs, or

    (b) Does not specify the amount to be paid by the client.

(Regulation 9(3) and (4))
The order is described in the Regulations as a Section 11(1) costs order and is defined in both sets of regulations as a "costs order against a client where cost protection applies". "Cost protection" means "the limit set on costs awarded against a client set out in Section 11(1) of the Act".

  (iv) Where the order does not specify the amount to be paid by the client, to make, if it sees fit, findings of fact, as to the parties conduct in the proceedings or otherwise, relevant to the determination of that amount. (Regulations 9(6))

Stage 2

29. Stage 2 consists of the procedure to be followed to ascertain the amount of costs to be paid by the client against whom the trial Court has made an order that does not specify the amount. Stage 2 also includes the procedure for determining whether an order for costs should be made against the Commission. (Regulation 9(5)). The Regulations in relation to Stage 2 allocate certain functions to "the Court". Regulation 10(10) provides that, in relation to proceedings in the Court of Appeal, High Court or County Court, the Court's functions "may be exercised" by a Costs Judge or a District Judge. While it is arguable that the High Court and the Court of Appeal also enjoy jurisdiction to exercise these functions we think it plain that the scheme does not envisage that they should do so.

30. Regulation 2 provides that "Costs Judge" has the same meaning as in the CPR. CPR 43.2(1)(b) provides that "Costs Judge" means a Taxing Master of the Supreme Court.

31. The procedure under Stage 2 is as follows:

   (i) The party in whose favour the costs order has been made ("the receiving party") may, within three months of the making of the costs order, request a hearing to determine the costs payable to him. (Regulation 10(2))

  (ii) The receiving party may, at the same time, seek a costs order against the Commission. (Regulation 10(3)(c)). We wish to take this opportunity to emphasise a fact that we understand is not generally appreciated. The three month time limit for seeking an order against the Commission is mandatory—there is no power to extend it.

 (iii) The receiving party must, when making the request, file with the Court and serve on the client and the Regional Director of the Commission (if an order is sought against the Commission):

    (a) A bill of costs;

    (b) A statement of resources;

    (c) A written notice that a costs order is sought against the Commission.

(Regulation 10(3) and (4))

  (iv) The client must file a statement of resources and serve this on the receiving party and the Regional Director (where a claim is made on the Commission). (Regulation 10(6))

  (v) The Court sets a date for the hearing. (Regulation 19(9))

671

(vi) The Court conducts the hearing, assesses the costs (if any) to be paid by the client and, where appropriate, makes a costs order against the Commission.

32. The Costs Regulations do not, in fact, expressly provide that the Costs Judge/District Judge shall carry out the functions set out under (vi) above, but it is plainly implicit that he should. That this is part of his role is confirmed by the explicit provisions of the Cost Protection Regulations.

33. The Cost Protection Regulations set out the circumstances in which the Costs Judge or District Judge may make a costs order against the Commission. Regulation 5(3) makes it plain that it is for the Costs Judge or District Judge to be satisfied that it is just and equitable (see Section 7 below) that provision for the costs should be made out of public funds and, in respect of proceedings at first instance, that the non-funded party will suffer severe financial hardship unless the order is made. In considering these matters the Costs Judge or District Judge is expressly required to have regard to the resources of the non-funded party and of his partner—Regulation 5(6)."

Note: Statement of resources—The Community Legal Service (Costs) (Amendment) Regulations 2003 (S.I. 2003 No. 649) amends regulation 10 from April 7, 2003 to the effect that the receiving party only has to make a statement of resources when he has to show financial hardship for the purposes of regulation 5(3)(c) of the Cost Protection Regulations (Order for Costs against the LSC in a court of first instance).

What Orders may the Court Awarding Costs Make?

Y–005   5.1 An order for costs against an LSC funded client may or may not specify the amount of full costs and may or may not specify the amount payable by the LSC funded client. The court will not specify the amounts payable unless it has sufficient information before it to decide what is a reasonable amount for the client to pay in accordance with Section 11(1) of the 1999 Act.

5.2 If the order does not specify the amount payable by the LSC funded client it may instead:

(i) make findings of fact relevant to the determination of the amount to be paid (Costs Regulation 9(6)); and/or

(ii) make an order under Costs Regulation 10A ordering the LSC funded client to pay an amount on account of the costs which are the subject of the order.

5.3 The court may order a payment on account under Costs Regulation 10A only if it has sufficient information before it to decide the minimum amount which the client is likely to be ordered to pay on a determination under Regulation 10 (Costs Regulation 10A(2)). An order for a payment on account must order the client to make the payment into court and the money must remain in court pending the determination of proceedings under Regulation 10. If the receiving party fails to commence such proceedings within the time permitted by Regulation 10(2) the payment on account must be repaid to the LSC funded client (see generally, Costs Regulation 10A (4) and (5)).

5.4 A specimen order for costs against a claimant who is an LSC funded client is set out in Appendix 3, below.

Subsequent Applications to a Costs Judge or District Judge

6.1 Subsequent applications to the Costs Judge or District Judge of the relevant **Y–006** court should be made on Form **N244** within three months after a Section 11(1) Costs Order is made. Full details of the procedure is set out in Sections 21 to 23 of the Costs Practice Direction. Since June 5, 2000 this procedure also applies to applications against assisted persons and against the LSC in respect of old legal aid certificates (Access to Justice Act 1999 (Commencement No. 3: Transitional Provisions and Savings) Order 2000, para. 8.3).

6.2 Depending upon the circumstances the application to the Costs Judge or District Judge may request the determination of:

(i) the amount of full costs;
(ii) the amount payable by the LSC funded client;
(iii) the amount payable by the LSC itself.

6.3 A specimen order for costs for use by a Costs Judge or District Judge is set out in Appendix 4, below.

Applying the "Just and Equitable" Test

7.1 How should the Costs Judge or District Judge apply the "just and equitable" **Y–007** test set out in Costs Protection Regulation 5(3)(d)? In *Ex parte Gunn* the Court of Appeal expressed the view that the well established meaning of "just and equitable" did not require change by reason of the introduction of Regulation 5(6) of the Costs Protection Regulations, which requires the court to have regard to the resources of the non funded party. In courts of first instance the court must be satisfied that the proceedings were instituted by the funded client and that the non funded party will suffer severe financial hardship unless the order is made. The statement of resources filed by the non funded party in accordance with Regulation 10(3)(b) of the Costs Regulations may be of relevance to the just and equitable test but the Court of Appeal found that the requirement to provide a statement of resources was not intended to modify the practice based on the authorities in relation to applications in courts other than courts of first instance. The Court of Appeal went on to state:

> "50. It seems to us that this practice reflects reasoning that it will normally be just and equitable that when a costs order is made against a party who has been supported by public funds, the costs covered by the order should, insofar as they cannot be recovered from the funded party, be defrayed out of public funds."

7.2 It is not open to the court awarding costs to make an order for costs against the LSC itself. However Costs Regulation 9(6) does permit the court awarding costs to make findings of fact relevant to the determination of the amount to be paid by the LSC funded client. In *Ex parte Gunn* the Court of Appeal considered that it must also be open to the trial Court to make any findings in relation to the conduct of the parties or facts that have emerged in the course of the proceedings, that have relevance to the application of the just and equitable test.

Costs Orders in Favour of a Public Body

8.1 Is it appropriate for the Costs Judge or District Judge to make an order against **Y–008** the LSC itself in favour of a public body? This question is unlikely to arise in practice as regards costs incurred in a court of first instance since, in such cases the public body is unlikely to be able to satisfy the financial hardship test set out in Costs Protection Regulation 5(3)(c). As regards costs of appeals, the financial hardship test does not apply. In *Ex parte Gunn* the Court of Appeal made it clear that it could detect no change in legislative intent in relation to the jurisdiction to make an order in favour of a public body and concluded that there is jurisdiction to make an order against the Commission in favour of a public body even if it is a Government Department.

8.2 The Court referred to the judgment of Lord Woolf MR in *Re O (A Minor) (Costs: Liability of Legal Aid Board)* [1997] 1 F.L.R. 465 at page 470G:

"If the court comes to a conclusion that in those circumstances it would make the hypothetical order for costs [what is now a section 11(1) order] then in the case of an appeal the court will usually conclude, in the absence of some special circumstance, that for the purposes of s.18(4)(c) [of the 1988 Act], it is just and equitable to make an order. Contrary to Mr Howard's submission, a local authority, because it is a public body, is not at a disadvantage as compared with any other litigant in seeking an order against the Board,"

8.3 The Court of Appeal considered that the practice laid down in *Re O* should be followed by Costs Judges and District Judges when applications are made to them for costs against the Commission, in respect of appeal costs incurred by non funded parties even if they are Government Departments. Costs Judges and District Judges should proceed on the premise that it is just and equitable that the LSC should stand behind the LSC funded client unless there are circumstances which render that result unjust or inequitable.

APPENDIX 1

Full Text of Access to Justice Act 1999, Section 11

Y–009   (1) Except in prescribed circumstances, costs ordered against an individual in relation to any proceedings or part of proceedings funded for him shall not exceed the amount (if any) which is a reasonable one for him to pay having regard to all the circumstances including—

  (a) the financial resources of all the parties to the proceedings, and
  (b) their conduct in connection with the dispute to which the proceedings relate;

and for this purpose proceedings, or a part of proceedings, are funded for an individual if services relating to the proceedings or part are funded for him by the Commission as part of the Community Legal Service.

(2) In assessing for the purposes of subsection (1) the financial resources of an individual for whom services are funded by the Commission as part of the Community Legal Service, his clothes and household furniture and the tools and implements of his trade shall not be taken into account, except so far as may be prescribed.

(3) Subject to subsections (1) and (2), regulations may make provision about costs in relation to proceedings in which services are funded by the Commission for any of the parties as part of the Community Legal Service.

(4) The regulations may, in particular, make provision—

(a) specifying the principles to be applied in determining the amount of any costs which may be awarded against a party for whom services are funded by the Commission as part of the Community Legal Service,

(b) limiting the circumstances in which, or extent to which, an order for costs may be enforced against such a party,

(c) as to the cases in which, and extent to which, such a party may be required to give security for costs and the manner in which it is to be given,

(d) requiring the payment by the Commission of the whole or part of any costs incurred by a party for whom services are not funded by the Commission as part of the Community Legal Service,

(e) specifying the principles to be applied in determining the amount of any costs which may be awarded to a party for whom services are so funded,

(f) requiring the payment to the Commission, or the person or body by which the services were provided, of the whole or part of any sum awarded by way of costs to such a party, and

(g) as to the court, tribunal or other person or body by whom the amount of any costs is to be determined and the extent to which any determination of that amount is to be final.

Costs order against Commission

APPENDIX 2

Full Text of Regulation 5 of the Community Legal Service (Costs) Regulation 2000, as Amended

(1) The following paragraphs of this regulation apply where: **Y–010**

(a) funded services are provided to a client in relation to proceedings;

(b) those proceedings are finally decided in favour of a non-funded party; and

(c) cost protection applies.

(2) The court may, subject to the following paragraphs of this regulation, make an order for the payment by the Commission to the non-funded party of the whole or any part of the costs incurred by him in the proceedings (other than any costs that the client is required to pay under a section 11(1) costs order).

(3) An order under paragraph (2) may only be made if all the conditions set out in sub-paragraphs (a),(b),(c) and (d) are satisfied:

(a) a section 11(1) costs order is made against the client in the proceedings, and the amount (if any) which the client is required to pay under that costs order is less than the amount of the full costs;

(b) unless there is good reason for the delay, the non-funded party makes a request under regulation 10(2) of the Community Legal Service (Costs) Regulations 2000 within three months of the making of the section 11(1) costs order;

(c) as regards costs incurred in a court of first instance, the proceedings were instituted by the client, the non funded party is an individual and the court is satisfied that the non-funded party will suffer financial hardship unless the order is made; and

(d) in any case, the court is satisfied that it is just and equitable in the circumstances that provision for the costs should be made out of public funds.

(3A) An order under paragraph (2) may be made—

(a) in relation to proceedings in the House of Lords, by the Clerk to the Parliaments;
(b) in relation to proceedings in the Court of Appeal, High Court or a county court, by a costs judge or a district judge;
(c) in relation to proceedings in a magistrates' court, by a single justice or by the justices' clerk;
(d) in relation to proceedings in the Employment Appeal Tribunal, by the Registrar of that tribunal.

(4) Where the client receives funded services in connection with part only of the proceedings, the reference in paragraph (2) to the costs incurred by the non-funded party in the relevant proceedings shall be construed as a reference to so much of those costs as is attributable to the part of the proceedings which are funded proceedings.

(5) Where a court decides any proceedings in favour of the non-funded party and an appeal lies (with or without permission) against that decision, any order made under this regulation shall not take effect:

(a) where permission to appeal is required, unless the time limit for applications for permission to appeal expires without permission being granted;
(b) where permission to appeal is granted or is not required, unless the time limit for appeal expires without an appeal being brought.

(6) Subject to paragraph (7), in determining whether the conditions in paragraph (3)(c) and (d) are satisfied, the court shall have regard to the resources of the non-funded party and of his partner.

(7) The court shall not have regard to the resources of the partner of the non-funded party if the partner has a contrary interest in the funded proceedings.

(8) Where the non-funded party is acting in a representative, fiduciary or official capacity and is entitled to be indemnified in respect of his costs from any property, estate or fund, the court shall, for the purposes of paragraph (3), have regard to the value of the property, estate or fund and the resources of the persons, if any, including that party where appropriate, who are beneficially interested in that property, estate or fund.

SPECIMEN ORDER FOR COSTS AGAINST A CLAIMANT WHO IS AN LSC FUNDED CLIENT

APPENDIX 3

IT IS ORDERED THAT

Y–011

1. The claim is dismissed.
2. The full costs of this claim which have been incurred by the defendant are [summarily assessed at £   ] [to be determined by a Costs Judge or District Judge].
3. The claimant (a party who was in receipt of services funded by the Legal Services Commission) do pay to the Defendant [nil] [£   ] [an amount to be determined by a Costs Judge or District Judge]. [When determining such costs the Costs Judge or District Judge should take into account the following facts:
[Here list any findings of fact as to the party's conduct in the proceedings or otherwise which are relevant to the determination of the costs payable by the LSC funded client]

4. On or before (date) the claimant must pay into court £   on account of the costs payable under paragraph 2, above.

5. There be a detailed assessment of the costs of the claimant which are payable out of the Community Legal Service Fund.

SPECIMEN ORDER FOR USE BY A COSTS JUDGE OR DISTRICT JUDGE

APPENDIX 4

IT IS ORDERED THAT

1. The full costs of the [defendant] herein, [including the costs of this application] **Y–012** *are assessed at £*

2. The amount of costs which it is reasonable for the [claimant] to pay to the [defendant] is [nil] [£   which sum is payable to the [defendant] on or before (date)].

3. The sum of £   paid into court on account of the costs specified in paragraph 2 above and any interest accruing thereon shall be paid out to the [defendant in part satisfaction] [claimant] as specified in the payment schedule to this Order.

4. The amount of costs payable by the Legal Services Commission to the [defendant] [including the costs of this application] is £   which sum is payable to the [defendant] on or before (date)

[Schedule in Form **200** *(see Court Funds Rules 1987)]*

Guidance on Payment of Legal Costs to Parties Represented at Public Expense in Public Inquiries

Introduction

Y–018

1. This is intended as an introductory note of guidance for the Secretariat of Public Inquiries. It has been produced by the Treasury Solicitor's Department and approved by the Chief Costs Judge of the Supreme Court Costs Office.

2. There is no statutory authority for the payment of legal costs to interested parties at Inquiries generally. In the case of Inquiries established under the Tribunals of Inquiry (Evidence) Act 1921, s.2(b) of the Act empowers a Tribunal to "authorise the representation before them of any person appearing to them to be interested to be by Counsel or solicitor or otherwise, or to refuse to allow such representation" but is silent to legal costs. The same goes for non statutory tribunals, but there are exceptions such as Formal Investigations pursuant to the Merchant Shipping Act 1995 where the Regulations envisage award of costs.

3. The Royal Commission on Tribunals of Inquiry under Lord Justice Salmon reported in 1966 (Cmnd 3121) dealt with the right to costs in paragraph 59-62 of its Report, which are copied in an annex to this paper. A White Paper issued in 1973 accepted the greater part of the recommendation of the Salmon Inquiry and indicated that legislation would be brought forward to make necessary amendments. No such legislation has been enacted. The Report of the Tribunal established under the 1921 Act to enquire into the operations of the Crown Agents was published in 1982. In an Appendix to the Report the Inquiry disagreed with the recommendation of the 1966 Royal Commission. It said:

> " . . . we are not convinced that it was necessary for payments to be made as of right. The system of ex gratia payments that has been used in the present Inquiry has worked well . . . in the event of a dispute as to the amount, the final decision rested with the Chief Taxing Master, and a few references to the Master have been needed."

4. On January 29, 1990 in answer to a PQ the Attorney General set out the basis upon which the Government would exercise its discretion to pay costs, having regard to the recommendations of Tribunals of Inquiry. The answer was as follows–

> "Tribunals and public inquiries can be set up in a variety of ways . . . So far as ad hoc tribunals and inquiries are concerned (for example, into major accidents) the Government already pays the administrative costs. So far as the costs of legal representation of parties to any inquiry concerned, where the Government have a discretion they always take careful account of the recommendations on costs of the tribunal or inquiry concerned. In general, the Government accept the need to pay out of public funds the reasonable costs of any necessary party to the inquiry who would be prejudiced in seeking representation were he in any doubt about funds available. The Government do not accept that the costs of substantial bodies should be met from public funds unless there are special circumstances."

A copy of a letter from HM Treasury reproducing that answer and giving further guidance is attached.

5. In recent inquiries there have been demands from numerous potential parties at the preliminary hearing and subsequently to be granted rights of representation at

678

public expense. If uncontrolled this could lead to enormous expense. Tribunals have exercised their discretion to limit the grant of such representation to assist the Tribunal. Representation at private expense has been expected where the party concerned is in a position to pay its own costs, including corporations, public authorities and, often, trade unions. The decision as to which party should receive rights of representation, and of those, which should receive it at public expense is likely significantly to affect the length of the hearing and the overall cost, but the Tribunal will balance such considerations with the desirability of allowing representation to individuals or bodies which should be properly represented and of making recommendations for representation at public expense where it considers that this is justified.

The Basis of Representation

6. Those responsible for agreeing the costs need to know the basis on which they are to be considered and solicitors and Counsel are likewise entitled to know the basis upon which they will be paid. These matters should be defined at the earliest opportunity, preferably when granting the right to representation at public expense. It is suggested that the usual definitions from the Civil Procedure Rules should be adopted. The Salmon Report recommended that costs paid out of public funds should be on the common fund basis (paragraph 60). The modern equivalent of the common fund basis is the standard basis defined in CPR Part 44, r.4 as follows:

Y–019

> "(1) Where the Court is to assess the amount of costs (whether by summary or detailed assessment) it will assess those costs —
>
> (a) on the standard basis; or
> (b) on the indemnity basis,
>
> but the court will not in either case allow costs which have been unreasonably incurred or are unreasonable in amount."
> "(2) "Where the amount of costs is to be assessed on the standard basis, the Court will:
>
> (a) only allow costs which are proportionate to the matter in issue; and
> (b) resolve any doubt which it may have as to whether costs were reasonably incurred or reasonable and proportionate in amount in favour of the paying party."

7. Some solicitors and Counsel may press for payment either on the indemnity basis or the solicitor and client basis. It is not believed that this has been conceded in any Inquiry and it is suggested that it would not normally be appropriate to do so. In general, indemnity costs are only awarded where the paying party has been behaving in a way that is deserving of condemnation by the Court: but that should not normally be a criticism that can be levied against the Crown by reason that it has organised an Inquiry into a matter of public concern.

Control of Costs

8. In addition to providing that costs are payable on the standard basis, Tribunals will wish to exercise prudent control in one or more of the following ways–

Y–020

(a) Providing that representation is authorised subject to agreement in advance of hourly rates (including any uplift for care and attention) and daily or other caps. This should avoid wholly excessive rates being after the event.

(b) Providing that representation is authorised subject to approval in advance of such authorisation of brief fees, refreshers, Counsel's hourly rates, etc. and that preparation should not normally be allowed in addition to refreshers.

(c) Providing for a requirement for advance approval of disbursements above, for example, £50. (This may avoid disputes over expensive expert's reports requested by parties).

(d) Providing caps to the grant of representation, to be periodically reviewed (*e.g.* an overall limit of £10,000 for a party) so that they would have to return for further authority if this cap were to be exceeded, and for setting a cap on the number of hours for preparation prior to the start of the Inquiry and hours to be spent on preparation whilst the Inquiry is sitting.

(e) Submission of accounts at monthly intervals to the Inquiry, and in any event, a final account no later than one month after final submissions.

A draft of the letter and schedule to be sent by the Secretary to representatives of those who are to be represented at public expense is annexed.

The Process of Assessment Costs

Y–021
9. In the overwhelming majority of cases, costs are capable of agreement, often following negotiation. It may often be appropriate to invite the Treasury Solicitor's Costs Team to consider bills of costs, negotiate and advise. A charge is made for this service.

10. Occasionally it may not be possible for the Treasury Solicitor's Costs Team and the solicitors or Counsel concerned to reach agreement. In such cases the Senior Costs Judge should be approached and he will normally be willing to arrange for a Costs Judge to conduct contested adjudications upon such bills provided both the Crown and the receiving party are willing to be bound by the decision of the Costs Judge. In any cases where advance approval of costs is required as suggested above, it may be appropriate to build into a procedure an opportunity to "appeal" to a Costs Judge in terms agreed by the Senior Costs Judge, to preserve the independence of the parties and to avoid any suggestion that they were unreasonably refused sufficient funds to provide proper representation.

Conclusion

Y–022
11. Agreement of the basis on which legal costs are to be paid, the management of legal costs and the assessment of them will often be an unwelcome burden to a Tribunal which will regard its primary function to enquire into the subject matter for which it was established. However, the sums involved can be very substantial, the early decisions as to grant of representation and the basis of representation can bind all later freedom of action and prudential spending controls favour advance approval where the sums are likely to be substantial. The Treasury Solicitor's Costs Team are willing to offer advice at any time. In the first instance please contact the Head of the Company/Chancery Group—Robert Aitken—on 020 7210 3233/ 3183: for technical enquiries please contact the Head of the Costs Team—Alan Pattison—on 020 7210 3360

TREASURY SOLICITOR'S DEPARTMENT
APRIL 2002

LETTER TO REPRESENTATIVES OF THOSE TO BE FUNDED AT PUBLIC EXPENSE

THE INQUIRY INTO [   ]

Dear [   ]   Y–023

PROCEDURES FOR ASSESSMENT OF COSTS OF PARTICIPANTS AT PUBLIC EXPENSE

1. The finding of the Chairman is that the reasonable and appropriate legal costs of [   ] be met from public funds on the terms set out in this letter and the Schedule to this letter [see matters to be addressed in schedule attached]. These deal among other matters with what solicitors and Counsel are authorised to do (advise, represent specifying any limitations); whose responsibility it is to fix costs and when and to whom you should report. The relevant statutory provisions with regard to costs may be found in the Civil Procedure Rules and in particular CPR Part 44.

2. In the first instance, costs will be assessed by the Inquiry Secretariat on the standard basis at an agree hourly rate subject to any capping mechanism as to total hours worked including daily or other caps determined by the Secretariat. Those costs will be paid through the Treasury Solicitor/Inquiry. So far as the formal bills of costs are concerned, these should be in the form of fully drawn bills along the lines of a between the parties bill of costs prepared for detailed assessment. Counsel's fees should be in the usual fee note form with clear indications of time spent and identifying the work carried out. Bills should be presented on a monthly basis for consideration. All bills and fee notes will be subject to an audit procedure carried out by the Costs Team and/or the International Audit Service of the Treasury Solicitor's Department.

3. General disbursements above £50 may be disallowed if they are unreasonable or disproportionate unless they have received prior approval from the solicitor to the Inquiry.

4. The Inquiry reserves the right to disallow any costs for good reason: examples of the circumstances in which costs may be disallowed are set out in paragraph 61 of the Report of the Royal Commission on Tribunals of Inquiry (1966 Cmnd 3121).

> "61. It may be helpful if we state how, in our view, the Tribunal's discretion in respect of costs should be exercised. Normally the witness should be allowed his costs. It is only in exceptional circumstances that the Tribunal's discretion should be exercised to disallow costs. We have recommended in paragraph 54 that any witness should be entitled to be legally represented. If the Tribunal came to the conclusion in respect of any witness that there had never been any real ground for supposing that he might be prejudicially affected by the inquiry and that it was therefore unreasonable for him to have gone to the expense of legal representation, the Tribunal should leave him to bear those expenses himself. In any case in which the Tribunal considered it reasonable for the witness to be legally represented, the practice should be to order that he should recover his costs out of public funds on a Common Fund basis, unless the Tribunal considered that there were good grounds for depriving him of all or part of his costs. It is impossible to catalogue what these grounds might be; cases vary infinitely in their facts and the matter must be left entirely to the discretion of the Tribunal. It may be helpful however, to give a few examples of the type of case in which a Tribunal might deprive a witness of all or part of his costs. If the witness during the course of the inquiry sought to obstruct the Tribunal in arriving at the truth or unreasonably delayed the inquiry. This does

not mean that every departure in evidence from strict accuracy even if deliberate should be regarded as necessarily disqualifying a witness from recovering his costs. It would be a question of fact and degree in each case. The mere fact that a witness had committed a criminal offence—even a serious one—or was a disreputable person should not, of itself, be a ground for depriving him of his costs. We have no doubt that Tribunals can safely be left to exercise their discretion over costs wisely and justly."

5. In the event of a bill not being agreed, in full or in part, payment will be on account of costs, pending resolution at the end of the Inquiry, possibly by means of contested adjudication by a Costs Judge at the Supreme Court Costs Office.

6. All bill of costs should be prepared promptly and comply with any timetable which may be indicated by the Solicitor to the Inquiry. In particular any application to the Supreme Court Costs Office for contested adjudication must be made within 3 months of the Treasury Solicitor's Costs Team's decision on the bill. Failure to do this may result in disallowance of the bill.

7. All claims for costs should be sent to [   ].

Solicitor to the Inquiry

MATTERS TO BE ADDRESSED IN THE SCHEDULE TO CORRESPONDENCE WITH SOLICITORS FOR THOSE TO BE REPRESENTED AT PUBLIC EXPENSE

Y–024   **1. Notes–**

It is normally the responsibility of the Chairman/Chairwoman to decide which parties should receive public funding and to what degree. This normally happens after the Chairman has requested submissions from interested parties who consider they should be represented at the Inquiry and should be allowed public funding to do so.

2. At this stage guidance should be given to the Chairman, by the Inquiry Secretariat, as to the basis of and level of funding which should be recommended for each party, which should include some or all of the following matters:

Matters to be addressed–

- The nature of the work for which funding is to be allowed, *e.g.* full representation, provision of statements only etc.
- Depending on the nature and scope of the Inquiry, it may be advisable to recommend that a particular party is only funded for representation on certain "issues", or funding for only certain parts of the Inquiry. For instance in the Stephen Lawrence Inquiry the only party to receive funding for Part 2 was the Lawrence family.
- Capping hours for preparation prior to start of Inquiry for both Solicitors and Counsel.
- Capping hours for preparation once Inquiry begins for both Solicitors and Counsel.
- Consideration as to whether or not to pay 100% of costs or if appropriate, for example only 50% of costs.
- The terms of funding agreed by the Secretariat should be recorded in writing by the Secretariat.
- Hourly rate of Solicitors and Counsel to be determined by the Secretariat on condition of representation at the outset and any travel time where relevant if part of a weekly cap of say 45 hours can be at the hourly rate otherwise it should be, for example, at half the hourly rate.

- Level of fee earner and number of fee earners for Solicitors to be determined by the Secretariat at the outset as a condition of representation. (It may for example be appropriate to allow funding for a particular party for one Assistant Solicitor or it may be appropriate to allow funding for both a Partner and a Trainee Solicitor.)
- The number of Counsel each party is allowed to instruct, whether QC, Junior or both to be determined by the Secretariat at the outset as a condition of representation.
- Date when funding begins and ends should be made clear.
- It should be made clear to all parties that if a cap has been imposed in respect of say the number of hours allowed, that they will not automatically be entitled to all of those hours.
  The Inquiry (on occasion with the assistance of Costs Team) must be satisfied that all work claimed by Counsel and/or Solicitors is reasonable/ necessary. Additionally there may be daily/weekly caps imposed on hours which may be billed (*e.g.* 45 hours per week) and these should be negotiated at the outset.
- Mechanism by which bills are to be delivered and arrangements for checking and payment.

3. These matters should be addressed in correspondence with solicitors for those representing anyone who is acting on behalf of persons receiving public funding. For the avoidance of doubt copies of such correspondence should be made available to Counsel who are instructed by those solicitors. Because public monies are being deployed, an audit may be carried out by the National Audit Office on the expenditure of public monies. Those engaged should be aware of this from the outset as well as the proper constraints which should operate in relation to publicly funded operations. Certainly the conditions should be clear from the outset and if there is to be a review mechanism built in for fees after a set period this should also be made clear (*e.g.* specify a fixed rate of increase or a formula for a cost of living increase).

Dear [   ]

DISASTER INQUIRES: COSTS OF REPRESENTATION

1. Over recent years, there have been a number of ad hoc public inquires and tribunals set up to investigate the circumstances surrounding various disasters and accidents. They include the Fennell inquiry into the King's Cross fire, the Hidden inquiry into the Clapham rail disaster, the Taylor inquiry into the Hillsborough disaster and the May inquiry into the circumstances surrounding the investigation of the Guildford and Woolwich pub bombings. **Y–025**

2. The handling of some of these suggested some confusion about the Government's position on the payment out of public funds of the costs of those granted legal representation at tribunals or inquires of this nature.

3. The position has now been clarified. The Attorney General was recently asked by Mr. MacLennan MP if he would give favourable consideration to the proposal that the legal costs of determining issues of general public importance in tribunals and public inquires should be paid for out of public funds.

4. The Attorney General replied (Hansard, 29 January, Col 25):

"Tribunals and public inquires can be set up in a variety of ways. So far as ad hoc tribunals and inquires are concerned (for example, into major accidents) the Government already pays the administrative costs. So far as the costs of legal representation of parties to any inquiry are concerned, where the Government have a discretion they always take careful account of the recommendations on costs of the tribunal or inquiry concerned. In general, the Government accept the need to pay out of public funds the reasonable costs of any necessary party to the inquiry who would be prejudiced in seeking representation were he in any doubt about funds unless there are special circumstances."

5. Subject to any points that you (or others) may have, I very much hope that, if and when further ad hoc inquires or tribunals have to be set up by your department, you will draw these guidelines to the attention of the chairman and secretary of the tribunal concerned. The guidelines should not preclude asking other parties to contribute to the costs of those who would otherwise be prejudiced in seeking representation (as did Occidental in relation to the Piper Alpha inquiry). Any provision from public funds would, of course, be subject to the normal public expenditure considerations and supply procedures.

6. The guidelines set out above follow very closely those laid down by Sir John May at the Guildford and Woolwich inquiries preliminary hearing on 4 December 1989. He said:

"It is right that I should mention the question of costs. There are no statutory provisions governing this inquiry and I therefore have no power to order the payment of costs from public funds or by any parties. However, the Home Secretary and the Attorney General have indicated to me that if I recommend that a party's costs should be meet from public funds then this will be considered sympathetically by them. When I do recommend payment it will be on the standard basis . In the absence of the formal machinery of the court for taxing such costs the solicitors' bills will be taxed on an informal basis by the Treasury Solicitor's Department."

"It may be useful if I say now that I intend to make a recommendation in respect of the reasonable costs of any party whom I consider would be prejudiced in seeking representation now were he in any doubt about funds becoming available. For example, I shall certainly recommend that the costs of the defendants in both trials should be borne by public funds, although I shall in due course listen to argument on the mode of representation. I should also like to say that the costs of public bodies and trade unions and other staff association will not be met from public funds unless there are special circumstances."

7. These remarks, in turn, were consistent with those made by Lord Chief Justice Taylor at the beginning of the inquiry into the Hillsborough disaster (April 28, 1989). He said:

"It may be helpful if I say now that I intend to make a recommendation in respect of the reasonable taxed costs of any party who I consider would be prejudiced in seeking representation now were he in doubt as to funds becoming available. For example, I shall certainly recommend that the costs of the injured and bereaved being represented here should be borne out of public funds."

Lord Justice Taylor went on to say that the costs of the Football Supporters' Association would also be met out of public funds. By way of contrast, the insurers who were handling the interest of Sheffield Wednesday Football Club and the Football League were told that they would be considered at the end of the inquiry.

684

The same was said to apply to Sheffield City Council and what we described as other "substantial bodies", such as South Yorkshire police.

8. I hope this clarifies the position.

9. I am copying this letter to the Principal Finance Officers and the attached list. I hope they too, if they were involved in setting up an ad hoc tribunal or inquiry, will draw the guidelines to the chairman and secretary concerned.

Yours,

Mrs A F Chase

APPENDIX Z

Guide to the Summary Assessment of Costs

Introduction

1 The Practice Direction supplementing Parts 43 to 48 of the Civil Procedure Rules **Z–001**
deals with costs. Sections Sections 13 and 14 of the Practice Direction deal with the
general provisions relating to summary assessment. Rule 43.2 defines "costs" and
Rule 44.7 contains the court's power to make a summary assessment (Appendix
1).

2 The general rule is that the court should make a summary assessment of the
costs:

  (a) at the conclusion of the trial of a case which has been dealt with on the fast
      track, in which case the order will deal with the costs of the whole claim;
      and
  (b) at the conclusion of any other hearing which has lasted not more than one
      day, in which case the order will deal with the costs of the application or
      matter to which the hearing related. If this hearing disposes of the claim,
      the order may deal with the costs of the whole claim.

3 If there is a conditional fee agreement or other funding arrangement, Rule 44.3A
(Appendix 1) prevents the court from making a summary assessment of an
additional liability before the conclusion of the proceedings or the part of the
proceedings to which the funding arrangement relates. In such a case, the court
should nonetheless make a summary assessment of the base costs of the hearing or
application unless there is good reason not to do so. Where the court makes a
summary assessment of the base costs, all statements of costs and estimates put
before the Judge will be retained on the court file and the Judge carrying out a final
assessment must be supplied with copies of all the costs orders previously made and,
if required, be shown all the previous costs statements and estimates.

4 The court should not make a summary assessment of the costs of a receiving
party who is an assisted person or LSC funded client. The court may make a
summary assessment of costs payable by an assisted person or by a LSC funded
client. Such an assessment is not by itself a determination of that person's liability to
pay those costs (as to which see Rule 44.17 (Appendix 1) and paragraphs 20.1 to
22.33 of the Costs Practice Direction.

5 The court must not make a summary assessment of the costs of a receiving party
who is a child or patient within Part 21 unless the solicitor acting for the child or
patient has waived the right to further costs. The court may make a summary
assessment of costs payable by a child or patient.

6 The court awarding costs cannot make an order for the summary assessment to
be carried out by a costs officer. If summary assessment of costs is appropriate but
the court awarding costs is unable to carry out the assessment on the day it must give
directions as to a further hearing before the same Judge or order detailed assessment.

The Approach to Costs

7 General approach to summary and detailed assessment should be the same. For the
summary assessment to be accurate the Judge must be informed about all previous
summary assessments carried out in the case. This is particularly important where
the Judge is assessing all the costs at the conclusion of a case.

8 The court should not be seen to be endorsing disproportionate and unreasonable costs. Accordingly:

(a) When the amount of the costs to be paid has been agreed the court should make this clear by saying that the order is by consent.
(b) If the Judge is to make an order which is not by consent, he will, so far as possible, ensure that the final figure is not disproportionate and/or unreasonable having regard to Part 1 of the CPR. He will retain this responsibility notwithstanding the absence of challenge to individual items in the make-up of the figure sought.

9 Where a case is simple and straightforward it is obviously easier to decide whether the final figure is disproportionate than where the case is more complex. For this reason, it is impossible to ignore the work on the case, which has had to be done.

10 The fact that the paying party is not disputing the amount of costs can be taken as some indication that the amount is proportionate and reasonable. The Judge therefore will intervene only if satisfied that the costs are so disproportionate that it is right to do so.

11 The court can allow a sum which it considers to be proportionate as a payment on account whilst at the same time ordering detailed assessment.

The Basis of Assessment

The Standard Basis

Z–002   12 Rule 44.4(1) and (2) (Appendix 1) provide that where the court assesses the amount of costs on the standard basis it will not allow costs which have been unreasonably incurred or are unreasonable in amount and will only allow costs which are proportionate to the matters in issue. The court will resolve in favour of the paying party any doubt which it may have as to whether the costs were reasonably incurred or were reasonable and proportionate in amount.

The Indemnity Basis

Z–003   13 Rule 44.4(1) and (3) (Appendix 1) provide that where the court assesses the amount of costs on the indemnity basis it will not allow costs which have been unreasonably incurred or are unreasonable in amount and it will resolve in favour of the receiving party any doubt which it may have as to whether costs were reasonably incurred or were reasonable in amount. The test of proportionality is not mentioned in the definition of the indemnity basis.

Proportionality

Z–004   14 "Proportionality" is not defined in the rules or the Practice Direction. Section 11 of the Costs Practice Direction indicates, however, that in applying the test of proportionality the court will have regard to rule 1.1(2)(c) by, so far as practicable, dealing with the case in ways which are proportionate:

   (i) to the amount of money involved;
  (ii) to the importance of the case;
 (iii) to the complexity of the issues; and

     i. to the financial position of each party.

15 Paragraphs 11.1 to 11.3 of the Practice Direction give the following warnings as to the test of proportionality.

(i) The relationship between the total costs incurred and the financial value of the claim may not be a reliable guide. A fixed percentage cannot be applied in all cases to the value of the claim in order to ascertain whether or not the costs are proportionate.

(ii) In any proceedings, there will be costs which will inevitably be incurred and which are necessary for the successful conduct of the case. Solicitors are not required to conduct litigation at rates which are uneconomic. Thus in a modest claim the proportion of costs is likely to be higher than in a large claim and may even equal or possibly exceed the amount in dispute.

(iii) Where a trial takes place the time taken by the court in dealing with the particular issue may not be an accurate guide to the amount of time properly spent by the legal or other representatives in preparation for the trial of that issue.

Summary Assessment where Costs Claimed Include an Addittional Liability

16 Rule 44.3A (Appendix 1) deals with costs orders relating to funding arrangements. An order for payment of "costs" includes an additional liability incurred under a funding arrangement. Where the court carries out a summary assessment of base costs before the conclusion of proceedings it is helpful if the order identifies separately the amount allowed in respect of: solicitors charges; counsel's fees; other disbursements; and any value added tax. If this is not done, the court which later makes an assessment of an additional liability, will have to apportion the base costs previously assessed.

17 Rule 44.3B (Appendix 1) sets out the limits on recovery under funding arrangements. The court will consider the amount of any additional liability separately from the base costs and when considering the factors to be taken into account under rule 44.5 in assessing an additional liability the court will have regard to the facts and circumstances as they reasonably appeared to the solicitor or counsel when the funding arrangement was entered into and at the time of any variation of the arrangement.

Z–005

Orders Made Before The Conclusion Of Proceedings

18 Where an order for costs is made before the conclusion of the proceedings and a legal representative for the receiving party has entered into a conditional fee agreement the court may summarily assess the base costs. An order for payment of those costs will not be made unless the court is satisfied that the receiving party is at the time liable to pay to his legal representative an amount equal to or greater than the costs claimed. If the court is not so satisfied it may direct that any costs, for which the receiving party may not in the final event be liable, be paid into court to await the outcome of the case or shall not be enforceable until further order, or the court may postpone the receiving party's right to receive payment in some other way.

Z–006

Orders Made At The Conclusion Of Proceedings

19 Where the court makes a summary assessment of an additional liability at the conclusion of the proceedings, that assessment must relate to the whole of the proceedings; this will include any additional liability relating to base costs allowed by the court when making a summary assessment on a previous application or hearing.

Z–007

Factors to be taken into Account in Deciding the amount of Costs

Z–008   20 Rule 44.5 (Appendix 1) sets out the factors to be taken into account. Those factors include: the conduct of all the parties, including in particular, conduct before as well as during the proceedings and the efforts made, if any, before and during the proceedings in order to try to resolve the dispute.

21 In deciding whether the costs claimed are reasonable and (on the standard basis) proportionate, the court will consider the amount of any additional liability separately from the base costs.

22 The Judge, before concluding a summary assessment should step back and consider the proportionality of the costs he has in mind to allow. If previous orders for summarily assessed costs have been made the Judge should, subject to paragraph 23, consider the proportionality of the total costs of the proceedings.

23 In arriving at a final figure the Judge should not reduce the costs of the receiving party on account of the costs awarded to that party under a previous summary assessment. To do so would impugn the decision of the earlier Judge. Where however the amount of costs previously ordered to be paid has been agreed by the parties with no judicial assessment there is nothing to prevent the court taking these figures into account when considering proportionality.

Conditional Fee Agreements With A Success Fee

24 The factors to be taken into account when deciding whether a percentage increase is reasonable may include:

   (a) the risk that the circumstance in which the costs, fees or expenses would be payable might or might not occur;

       a. the legal representative's liability for any disbursements;

   (c) what other methods of financing the costs were available to the receiving party.

The court has the power to allow different percentages for different items of costs or for different periods during which costs were incurred. The court should have regard to the facts and circumstances as they reasonably appeared to the solicitor or counsel when the funding arrangement was entered into, and at the time of any variation of the agreement.

25 A percentage increase should not be reduced simply on the ground that, when added to base costs which are reasonable and (where relevant) proportionate, the total appears disproportionate.

Insurance Premiums

Z–009   26 Relevant factors to be taken into account when deciding whether the cost of insurance cover is reasonable include:

   (a) where the insurance cover is not purchased in support of a conditional fee agreement with a success fee, how its cost compares with the likely cost of funding the case with a conditional fee agreement with a success fee and supporting insurance cover;
   (b) the level and extent of the cover provided;
   (c) the availability of any pre-existing insurance cover;
   (d) whether any part of the premium would be rebated in the event of early settlement;

(e) the amount of commission payable to the receiving party or his legal representatives or other agents.

Membership Organisation—Additional Amount

27 When considering a provision made by a membership organisation the court should not allow a provision which exceeds the likely cost to the receiving party of the premium of an insurance policy against the risk of incurring a liability to pay the costs of other parties to the proceedings. In those circumstances the court will have regard to the factors set out in paragraph 26 above in addition to the factors set out in rule 44.5 (Appendix 1).

Z–010

PROCEDURE FOLLOWING SUMMARY ASSESSMENT WHERE A LEGAL REPRESENTATIVE WISHES TO RECOVER FROM HIS CLIENT AN AGREED PERCENTAGE INCREASE WHICH HAS BEEN DISALLOWED OR REDUCED ON ASSESSMENT

28 A court which has made a summary assessment which disallows or reduces a legal representative's percentage increase may then and there decide the issue whether the disallowed amount should continue to be payable. The court may do this if:

Z–011

(a) the receiving party and all parties to the relevant agreement consent to the court doing so;

(b) the receiving party (or, if corporate, a duly authorised officer) is present in court; and

(c) the court is satisfied that the issue can be fairly decided then and there.

29 In any other case the court will give directions to enable an application to be made by the legal representative for the disallowed amount to be payable by his client, including if appropriate a direction that the application will be determined by a Costs Judge or District Judge of the court dealing with the case.

General Principles to be applied in Summary Assessment

The Indemnity Principle

[Note: The Government's conclusions following consultation on: Collective Conditional Fees (paras 29ff), states that rules of court should provide that the indemnity principle will not apply when assessing costs. Until those rules are in force the following three paragraphs apply.]

Z–012

30 A party in whose favour an order for costs has been made may not recover more than he is liable to pay his own solicitors. See *Harold v Smith* [1865] H&N 381, 385; and *Gundry v Sainsbury* [1910] 1 KB 645 CA.

31 The statement of costs put before the court for summary assessment must be signed by the party or its legal representative. That form contains the statement:

"The costs estimated above do not exceed the costs which the [party] is liable to pay in respect of the work which this estimate covers".

32 Following the decision of Lord Justice Henry in *Bailey v IBC Vehicles Ltd.* [1998] 3 All ER 570 CA, the signature of a statement of costs (or a bill for detailed assessment) by a solicitor is, in normal circumstances, sufficient to enable the court

to be satisfied that the indemnity principle has not been breached. A solicitor is an officer of the court and as Henry LJ stated:

> "In so signing he certifies that the contents of the bill are correct. That signature is no empty formality. The bill specifies the hourly rates applied . . . If an agreement between the receiving solicitor and his client . . . restricted (say) the hourly rate payable by the client that hourly rate is the most that can be claimed or recovered on [assessment] . . . The signature of the bill of costs . . . is effectively the certificate of an officer of the court that the receiving party's solicitors are not seeking to recover in relation to any item more than they have agreed to charge their client . . . ".

Deferring Payment of Costs

Z–013   33 As a general rule a paying party should be ordered to pay the amount of any summarily assessed costs within 14 days. Before making such an order the court should consider whether an order for payment of the costs might bring the action to an end and whether this would be just in all the circumstances.

Litigants in Person

Z–014   34 Where the receiving party is a litigant in person rule 48.6 (Appendix 1) governs the way in which the question of costs should be dealt with. It is necessary to decide whether or not the litigant has suffered any financial loss. If he has, he is entitled to a reasonable sum in respect of that loss. If the litigant in person has not suffered any financial loss, he is to be allowed in respect of the time reasonably spent not more than £9.25 per hour.

35 In all cases there is an absolute cap on the amount recoverable by a litigant in person, namely the reasonable costs of disbursements plus two thirds of the amount which would have been allowed if the litigant in person had been legally represented. (48.6(2)). The litigant in person is entitled to recover in addition: payments reasonably made for legal services relating to the conduct of the proceedings; and the costs of obtaining expert assistance in connection with assessing the claim for costs. This does mean that a litigant in person may be able to claim both the cost of obtaining legal advice and services as well as the cost of undertaking the litigation in person. Those qualified to give expert assistance in connection with assessing the claim for costs are: a barrister, a solicitor, Fellow of the Institute of Legal Executives, Fellow of the Association of Law Costs Draftsmen, a law costs draftsman who is a member of the Academy of Experts and a law costs draftsman who is a member of the Expert Witness Institute.

36 Although the definition of litigant in person includes a solicitor, a solicitor who instead of acting for himself is represented in the proceedings by his firm, or by himself in his firm name, is not, for the purpose of the Civil Procedure Rules, a litigant in person (see Section 52 of the Costs Practice Direction).

Solicitors Hourly Rates

Z–015   37 In the past solicitors have sought to recover their charges on what is known as the A plus B basis, namely an hourly expense rate (A) and an uplift for care and conduct (B). The CPR and Costs Practice Direction discourage the use of this method of calculating charges and solicitors are therefore urged to claim costs at a single charging rate, which will normally be the rate which they have agreed to charge their client. If the rates agreed or claimed are unreasonable the paying party will not be required to pay them.

Guideline Figures

38 Guideline figures for solicitors' charges are published in Appendix 2 to this **Z–016**
Guide, which also contains some explanatory notes. The guideline rates are not scale
figures they are broad approximations only. In any particular area the Designated
Civil Judge may, after consultation between District Judges and local Law Societies,
supply more up to date guidelines for rates in that area. Costs and fees exceeding the
guidelines may well be justified in an appropriate case and that is a matter for the
exercise of discretion by the court.

39 The guideline figures are not intended to replace figures used by those with
accurate local knowledge. They are intended to provide a starting point for those
faced with summary assessment who do not have that local knowledge.

Solicitor Advocates

40 Remuneration of solicitor advocates is based on the normal principles for **Z–017**
remuneration of solicitors. It is not therefore appropriate to seek a brief fee and
refreshers as if the advocate were a member of the Bar. If the cost of using a solicitor
advocate is more than the cost of instructing counsel, the higher cost is unlikely to
be recovered. The figures properly recoverable by solicitor advocates should reflect
the amount of preparation undertaken, the time spent in court and the weight and
gravity of the case.

41 Where the solicitor advocate is also the solicitor who does the preparation
work, the solicitor is entitled to charge normal solicitors' rates for that preparation,
but once the solicitor advocate starts preparation for the hearing itself the fees
recoverable should not exceed those which would be recoverable in respect of
counsel.

42 It is clearly wrong for the fees of a solicitor acting as a junior counsel to exceed
the fee appropriate for the leading counsel.

Counsel' Fees

43 A proper measure for counsels' fees is to estimate what fee a hypothetical counsel, **Z–018**
capable of conducting the case effectively, but unable or unwilling to insist on the
higher fees sometimes demanded by counsel of pre-eminent reputation, would be
content to take on the brief: but there is no precise standard of measurement and the
judge must, using his or her knowledge and experience, determine the proper figure.
(*Per* Pennycuick J in *Simpsons Motor Sales (London) Ltd. v Hendon Borough
Council* [1965] 1 WLR 112.)

Guideline Figures

44 Appendix 2 contains a table of counsels' fees relating to proceedings in run of the **Z–019**
mill cases in the Queen's Bench and Chancery Divisions and in the Administrative
Court. These figures are not recommended rates but it is hoped that Judges may find
the figures of some help when they are called upon to assess counsels' fees. It has not
been possible to publish more specific guideline figures because of lack of sufficient
data.

45 The figures contained in the table in Appendix 2 are based upon statistical data
from the SCCO and figures supplied by the Bar and in broad terms the figures are
averages based on that data. The SCCO data is published on the SCCO page of the
Court Service website.

The time spent by Solicitors and Counsel

Z–020 46 There can be no guidance as to whether the time claimed has been reasonably spent, and it is for the Judge in each case to consider the work properly undertaken by Solicitors and Counsel and to arrive at a figure which is in all circumstances reasonable.

A Model Form of Statement of Costs

47 A model form of Statement of Costs is to be found in Appendix 3.

Guide to the Summary Assessment of Costs in the Court of Appeal

Z–021 48. The Practice Direction supplementing CPR Part 52 identifies five types of hearing at which costs are likely to be assessed by way of summary assessment and states that parties attending any of those hearings should be prepared to deal with the summary assessment. The Costs Practice Direction (Section 13 paragraph 13.5) places a duty on the parties and their legal representatives to file and serve a statement of any costs they intend to claim in respect of such hearings.

49. In this Guide the term "counsel" includes a solicitor-advocate who is instructed by another solicitor.

(1) CONTESTED DIRECTIONS HEARINGS (2) APPLICATIONS FOR PERMISSION TO APPEAL AT WHICH THE RESPONDENT IS PRESENT AND (4) APPEALS FROM CASE MANAGEMENT DECISIONS

50. The guidance given below in relation to contested directions hearings, applications for permission to appeal at which the respondent is present and appeals from case management decisions relates to hearings which, although important, are not difficult or complex and are not of general public importance and are listed either for a hearing not exceeding one hour or for a hearing not exceeding one half day.

51. If these hearings are attended by solicitor and counsel the number of hours which it is reasonable to presume that the solicitor will undertake (in respect of preparation, attendance, travel in Central London and waiting) is 4 hours for a one hour appointment and 7.5 hours for a half day appointment. It s reasonable to presume that counsel who has between 5 and 10 years' experience merits a fee of approximately £500 (exclusive of VAT) for a one hour appointment and merits a fee of approximately £800 (exclusive of VAT) for a half day appointment.

52. If these hearings were attended by a solicitor without counsel it is reasonable to presume that the total number of hours the solicitor will spend (in respect of preparation, attendance, travel in Central London and waiting) is 5 hours for a one hour appointment and 10 hours for a half day appointment.

53. If these hearings are attended by a litigant in person it is reasonable to presume that the total number of hours the litigant in person will spend (in respect of preparation, attendance and waiting) is 9 hours for a one hour appointment and 14 hours for a half day appointment. In each case a further allowance should be made for time and expense in travelling to the appointment.

(3) DISMISSAL LIST HEARINGS AT WHICH THE RESPONDENT IS PRESENT

54. The guidance given below in relation to dismissal list hearings in the Court of Appeal at which the respondent is present, relates to cases which are listed for less than one hour and are of significantly less weight than the contested directions

hearings, applications for permission to appeal and appeals from case management decisions described above.

55. If the hearing is attended by solicitor and counsel (for the appellant or the respondent), it is reasonable to presume that the total number of hours to allow the solicitor (in respect of preparation, attendance, travel in Central London and waiting) is 2 hours, and it is reasonable to presume that counsel who has between 5 and 10 years' experience merits a fee of approximately £350 (exclusive of VAT).

56. If an appeal is dismissed and costs are awarded to the respondent, it will probably be appropriate to allow further costs in respect of work previously done in responding to the appeal. Consideration should be given to whether it is in fact appropriate to carry out a summary assessment, depending on the amount of work done by the respondent.

57. Subject to paragraph 56 if the hearing is attended by a solicitor without counsel it is reasonable to presume that the total number of hours to allow the solicitor (in respect of preparation, attendance, travel in Central London and waiting) is 3 hours.

58. Subject to paragraph 56, if the hearing is attended by a litigant in person it is reasonable to presume that the total number of hours to allow the litigant in person (in respect of preparation, attendance and waiting) is 6 hours with a further allowance for time and expense in travelling to the appointment.

(5) APPEALS LISTED FOR ONE DAY OR LESS

59. Appeals listed for one day or less vary enormously as to weight, complexity and importance. Thus, it is not at present possible to give guidance as to the number of hours reasonably spent by solicitors (in respect of preparation, attendances, travel and waiting) in such appeals. However, after research and consultation, it may be possible in future to give such guidance in relation to particular types of general and specialist appeals. Pending such research and consultation, the only guidance which can be given is as follows.   **Z–022**

(1) It may not be appropriate to carry out a summary assessment if a case lasts more than half a day or involves leading counsel since in those circumstances the case is likely to be complex and weighty. It will often be unwise for the court summarily to assess costs in a matter which is not simple and straightforward, unless the difference between the parties is comparatively small, or unless the correct allowance appears clear.

(2) The reasonable fees of counsel are likely to exceed the reasonable fees of the solicitor.

(3) The fact that the same counsel appeared in the lower court does not greatly reduce the reasonable fee unless, for example, the lower court dealt with a great many more issues than are raised on the appeal. It is reasonable for counsel to spend as much time preparing issues for the Court of Appeal hearing as he spent preparing those issues for the lower court hearing.

(4) If the case merits leading counsel it may merit also the instruction of a junior to assist him. The junior's fees should be allowed at one half of the leader's fees unless:

    a. the junior is a senior junior and the case merited both a leader and a senior junior.

    b. The junior took a responsibility which was equal to or larger than that taken by the leader.

    a. The junior undertook work not covered by the brief.

(5) In many cases the largest element in the solicitors' reasonable fees for work in the Court of Appeal concerns instructing counsel and preparing the appeal bundles. Time spent by the solicitor in the development of legal submissions will only be allowed where it does not duplicate work done by counsel and is claimed at a rate the same or lower than the rate counsel would have claimed.

(6) Although the solicitor may have spent many hours with the client, the client should have been warned that little of this time is recoverable against a losing party. Reasonable time spent receiving instructions and reporting events should not greatly exceed the time spent on attending the opponents.

(7) Given that the case will be presented by a barrister or a solicitor advocate there is usually no reason for any other solicitor to spend many hours perusing papers. A large claim for such perusal probably indicates that a new fee earner was reading in. Reading in fees are not normally recoverable from an opponent.

(8) Although it is usually reasonable to have a senior fee earner sitting with counsel in the Court of Appeal, it is not usually reasonable to have two fee earners. The second fee earner may be there for training purposes only.

(9) In most appeals it will be appropriate to make an allowance for copy documents. The allowance for copying which is included in the solicitor's hourly rates will have already been used up or exceeded in the lower court. An hourly rate charge is appropriate for selecting and collating documents and dictating the indices. If the paperwork is voluminous much of this should be delegated to a trainee. Note that:

a. for the copying itself, a fair allowance is 10p per page, i.e. £100 per 1,000 sheets. This includes an allowance for checking the accuracy of the copying.

b. Time spent standing at the photocopier and time spent taking the papers to a local photocopy shop is not recoverable. Such work is not fee earner work; it is secretarial.

(10) It must be borne in mind that skeleton arguments will have been lodged at an early stage, and, in respect of floating appeals, the case may have come into and out of the list. In those circumstances it may be necessary to change counsel which would inevitably increase the costs. New counsel may decide to submit a different skeleton argument. Where this has occurred, detailed assessment is to be preferred.

Solicitors Charges

Z–023 60. Although many appointments in the Court of Appeal merit the attendance of a senior fee earner familiar with the case, the most minor appointments may not. For example, on an application in the dismissal list in a case tried in Newcastle, if counsel who was briefed for the trial attends it may be unreasonable for a solicitor familiar with the case to travel from Newcastle to attend also. In order to arrive at a notional figure to represent the instruction of and costs of an agent, it may be appropriate to disallow most of the travel time and travelling expenses claimed by the solicitor.

61. The Court of Appeal has stated that it is the duty of litigators (particularly unions and insurers) to keep down the cost of litigation. This means that if they instruct London solicitors who charge London rates for a case which has no obvious connection with London and which does not require expertise only to be found there, they will, even if successful, recover less than the solicitors have charged (see *Wraith v Sheffield Forgemasters Ltd* [1998] 1 WLR 132 CA).

62. In relation to the first four types of hearing appropriate for summary assessment in the Court of Appeal, some guidance is given above suggesting the

number of hours which may be reasonable for the solicitor to spend. That guidance should be used as a starting point only. The court should also have regard to the number of hours actually claimed.

Counsels Fees in the Court of Appeal

63. Counsel's fees depend upon the seniority of counsel which it was reasonable to instruct and the market price for the item of work in question. It is not appropriate to specify an hourly rate for counsel and to remunerate them at a multiple of that rate according to the number of hours reasonably spent. Such an approach would reward the indolent and penalise the expeditious.

64. In previous paragraphs (paragraphs 51 and 55), figures were suggested for brief fees for counsel who has between 5 and 10 years' experience. For less experienced counsel it may be appropriate to reduce these figures; for more experienced counsel it may be appropriate to increase these figures. The guideline figures are a starting point only and the Court has the discretion to allow fees appropriate to the particular circumstances of the appeal.

Z–024

Costs Awarded to Litigants in Person

65. The starting point for most litigants in person is £9.25 per hour reasonably spent. The number of hours reasonably spent by a litigant in person will almost invariably exceed the number of hours which would have been reasonably spent by a solicitor.

66. It is open to a litigant in person to prove a financial loss greater than the starting point amount. That loss may be in respect of a period greater than the time reasonably spent by the litigant. For example, attendance at a one hour hearing may necessitate the litigant taking two days unpaid leave from his employment.

67. In all cases there is an absolute cap on the amount recoverable by a litigant in person, namely the reasonable costs of disbursements plus two thirds of the amount which would have been allowed if the litigant in person had been legally represented (rule 48.6(2)).

Z–025

Conditional Fee Agreements with Success Fees

68. Although not common for appellants to enter into such agreements, it is common for respondents (the successful party at first instance) whose claim or defence was conducted under a conditional fee agreement: such agreements usually also cover appeals brought by the opponent.

69. Attention is drawn to paragraph 3 of this Guide dealing with summary assessment of an additional liability at the conclusion of proceedings.

70. Paragraphs 24 and 25 set out the factors to be taken into account when deciding whether a percentage increase is reasonable.

Z–026

P. T. HURST

Senior Costs Judge
to Summary Assessment of Costs
19 January 2001

Guide to the Summary Assessment of Costs

APPENDIX 2

Guideline Rates for Summary Assessment

January 2003

The following figures replace the figures set out at pages 39 to 43 of the Guide (2002 Edition)

BAND ONE Grade *	A	B	C	D
GUIDELINE RATES	175	155	130	95
Aldershot, Farnham, Bournemouth (including Poole) Birmingham Inner Cambridge City Centre Canterbury, Maidstone, Medway & Tunbridge Wells Cardiff (Inner) Kingston/Guildford/Reigate/Epsom Leeds Inner (within 1 kilometer radius of the City Art Gallery) Lewes Liverpool, Birkenhead Manchester Central Newcastle—City Centre (within a 2 mile radius of St Nicholas Cathedral) Norwich Nottingham City Southampton, Portsmouth Swindon, Basingstoke				

BAND TWO Grade *	A	B	C	D
GUIDELINE RATES	**165**	**145**	**120**	**90**
Bath, Cheltenham and Gloucester Bristol, Bury Chelmsford North, Cambridge County, Peterborough, Bury St E, Norfolk, Lowestoft Chelmsford South Hampshire, Dorset, Wiltshire, Isle of Wight Hull (City) Leeds Outer, Wakefield & Pontefract Leigh Luton, Bedford, St Albans, Hitchin, Hertford Manchester Outer/ Oldham/Bolton/Tameside Oxford (Inner/Outer), Reading, Slough Milton Keynes, Aylesbury Sheffield and South Yorkshire Southport St Helens Stockport/Altrincham/Salford Swansea, Newport, Cardiff (Outer) Watford Wigan York, Harrogate				

BAND THREE Grade *	A	B	C	D
GUIDELINE RATES	150	135	115	85
Birmingham Outer Bradford (Dewsbury, Halifax, Huddersfield, Keighley & Skipton) Chester & North Wales Coventry, Rugby, Nuneaton, Stratford and Warwick Cumbria Devon, Cornwall, Exeter, Taunton & Yeovil Grimsby Hull Outer Kidderminster Lincoln Newcastle (other than City Centre) Northampton & Leicester Nottingham & Derbyshire Plymouth Preston, Lancaster, Blackpool, Chorley Accrington, Burnley, Blackburn, Rawenstall & Nelson Scarborough & Ripon Stafford, Stoke, Tamworth Teesside Trowbridge Weston Wolverhampton, Walsall, Dudley & Stourbridge Worcester, Hereford, Evesham and Redditch Shrewsbury, Telford, Ludlow, Oswestry South & West Wales				

LONDON BANDS

Grade *	A	B	C	D
City of London **	342	247	189	116
Central London	263	200	163	105
Outer London (including Bromley, Croydon, Dartford, Gravesend and Uxbridge)	189–221	142–189	137	100

* There are four grades of fee earner:

A. Solicitors with over 8 years post qualification experience including at least 8 years litigation experience.

B. Solicitors and legal executives with over 4 years post qualification experience including at least 4 years litigation experience.

C. Other solicitors and legal executives and fee earners of equivalent experience.

D. Trainee Solicitors, para legals and fee earners of equivalent experience.

Note: "legal executive" means a Fellow of the Institute of Legal Executives.

** Although a guideline figure is given for the top grade of fee earner in the City of London, it is recognised that in certain complex, major litigation the appropriate rate may exceed the guideline by a significant margin.

INDEX